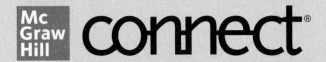

You're in the driver's seat.

Want to build your own course? No problem. Prefer to use our turnkey, prebuilt course? Easy. Want to make changes throughout the semester? Sure. And you'll save time with Connect's auto-grading too.

65%
Less Time Grading

Laptop: McGraw-Hill Education

They'll thank you for it.

Adaptive study resources like SmartBook® help your students be better prepared in less time. You can transform your class time from dull definitions to dynamic debates. Hear from your peers about the benefits of Connect at **www.mheducation.com/highered/connect**

Make it simple, make it affordable.

Connect makes it easy with seamless integration using any of the major Learning Management Systems—Blackboard®, Canvas, and D2L, among others—to let you organize your course in one convenient location. Give your students access to digital materials at a discount with our inclusive access program. Ask your McGraw-Hill representative for more information.

Padlock: Jobalou/Getty Images

Solutions for your challenges.

A product isn't a solution. Real solutions are affordable, reliable, and come with training and ongoing support when you need it and how you want it. Our Customer Experience Group can also help you troubleshoot tech problems—although Connect's 99% uptime means you might not need to call them. See for yourself at **status. mheducation.com**

Checkmark: Jobalou/Getty Images

FOR STUDENTS

Effective, efficient studying.

Connect helps you be more productive with your study time and get better grades using tools like SmartBook, which highlights key concepts and creates a personalized study plan. Connect sets you up for success, so you walk into class with confidence and walk out with better grades.

Study anytime, anywhere.

Download the free ReadAnywhere app and access your online eBook when it's convenient, even if you're offline. And since the app automatically syncs with your eBook in Connect, all of your notes are available every time you open it. Find out more at www.mheducation.com/readanywhere

> *"I really liked this app—it made it easy to study when you don't have your text-book in front of you."*
>
> - Jordan Cunningham, Eastern Washington University

Calendar: owattaphotos/Getty Images

No surprises.

The Connect Calendar and Reports tools keep you on track with the work you need to get done and your assignment scores. Life gets busy; Connect tools help you keep learning through it all.

Learning for everyone.

McGraw-Hill works directly with Accessibility Services Departments and faculty to meet the learning needs of all students. Please contact your Accessibility Services office and ask them to email accessibility@mheducation.com, or visit **www.mheducation.com/about/accessibility** for more information.

INTERNATIONAL BUSINESS

SECOND EDITION

J. Michael Geringer
OHIO UNIVERSITY

Jeanne M. McNett
NORTHEASTERN UNIVERSITY

Donald A. Ball

McGraw Hill

INTERNATIONAL BUSINESS, SECOND EDITION

Published by McGraw-Hill Education, 2 Penn Plaza, New York, NY 10121. Copyright ©2020 by McGraw-Hill Education. All rights reserved. Printed in the United States of America. Previous edition ©2016. No part of this publication may be reproduced or distributed in any form or by any means, or stored in a database or retrieval system, without the prior written consent of McGraw-Hill Education, including, but not limited to, in any network or other electronic storage or transmission, or broadcast for distance learning.

Some ancillaries, including electronic and print components, may not be available to customers outside the United States.

This book is printed on acid-free paper.

1 2 3 4 5 6 7 8 9 LWI 24 23 22 21 20 19

ISBN 978-1-259-68522-4 (bound edition)
MHID 1-259-68522-5 (bound edition)
ISBN 978-1-259-85273-2 (loose-leaf edition)
MHID 1-259-85273-3 (loose-leaf edition)

Portfolio Manager: *Peter Jurmu*
Product Developer: *Haley Burmeister*
Executive Marketing Manager: *Nicole Young*
Content Project Managers: *Melissa Leick, Bruce Gin, Karen Jozefowicz*
Buyer: *Sandy Ludovissy*
Design: *Matt Diamond*
Content Licensing Specialist: *Abbey Jones*
Cover Image: *©Rost9/Shutterstock*
Compositor: *Aptara®, Inc*

All credits appearing on page or at the end of the book are considered to be an extension of the copyright page.

Library of Congress Cataloging-in-Publication Data

Names: Geringer, J. Michael (John Michael), author. | McNett, Jeanne M.,
  1946- author.
Title: International business / J. Michael Geringer, Ohio University, Jeanne
  M. McNett, Northeastern University.

Description: Second edition. | New York, NY : McGraw-Hill Education, [2020]
Identifiers: LCCN 2019017083| ISBN 9781259685224 (hard cover : alk. paper) |

  ISBN 1259685225 (hard cover : alk. paper)
Subjects: LCSH: International business enterprises. | International trade. |

  International finance. | International economic relations.
Classification: LCC HD2755.5 .G47 2020 | DDC 658/.049–dc23 LC record
available at https://lccn.loc.gov/2019017083

The Internet addresses listed in the text were accurate at the time of publication. The inclusion of a website does not indicate an endorsement by the authors or McGraw-Hill Education, and McGraw-Hill Education does not guarantee the accuracy of the information presented at these sites.

BRIEF CONTENTS

DEDICATION

Mike dedicates this book to his parents, Raymond and JoAnn, who have provided continued support and encouragement for his writing and other life activities.

Jeanne dedicates this book to her best friends, Nick Athanassiou and Raven McCrory, her finance professor, Dr. N. D. Qui, and her ION research buddies.

ABOUT THE AUTHORS

J. Michael Geringer

J. Michael Geringer is the O'Bleness Professor of International Strategy at Ohio University. He earned a BS in business at Indiana University and MBA and Ph.D. degrees at the University of Washington. He has authored or edited over 30 books and monographs, more than 140 published papers, and more than 40 case studies; he serves on the editorial boards of several leading international academic journals including editor-in-chief or associate editor for four journals; he served as the Saastamoinen Foundation chair at the Helsinki School of Economics in Finland; he was the founding chair of the Strategic Alliances Committee of the Licensing Executives Society; he served as the chair of both the International Business and the Strategy and Policy divisions of the Administrative Sciences Association of Canada; and he is past chair of the Academy of Management's International Management division. His research has appeared in *Strategic Management Journal, Academy of Management Journal, Journal of International Management, Columbia Journal of World Business, Management International Review, Journal of Management Studies, Human Resource Management Journal, Long Range Planning, Organisation Studies, Thunderbird International Business Review,* and *Journal of Applied Psychology,* among others. He has received 11 "best paper" awards for his research, including the Decade Award for most influential article from the *Journal of International Business Studies.* In addition to spending many years living abroad, he has traveled and worked in dozens of nations worldwide. His teaching performance has earned numerous awards in the United States, Canada, Asia, Africa, Australia, and Europe, including the University Distinguished Teacher Award. In addition to many service activities with various social and nongovernmental organizations, Geringer is active in consulting and executive development for multinational corporations and executives from six continents.

Jeanne M. McNett

Jeanne M. McNett is a researcher at Northeastern University in the D'Amore-McKim College of Business and Professor of Management, Emerita, at Assumption College. Dr. McNett also has taught at Morris College and the University of Maryland in their Asian and European divisions. She earned her Ph.D. at the University of Massachusetts, Amherst, and her MBA at the Cass School of Business, City University, London, United Kingdom. She has had expatriate assignments in Germany, the United Kingdom, Saudi Arabia, Japan, and Korea. Her interests include the role of culture in international business and the pedagogy of international management. Her publications include the *Blackwell Encyclopedia of Management, International Management,* second and third editions (Blackwell, 2006; Wiley, 2015); *The Blackwell Handbook of Global Management* (Blackwell, 2004); and *A Primer on Sustainability* (Business Expert Press, 2014). Her teaching, research, and presentations have received awards, including the Roethlisberger Best Paper of the Year Award from the *Journal of Management Education* and the Alpha Phi Alpha Teacher of the Year Award. She is involved in community sailing on Cape Cod and in Open University Wellfleet, a community education effort.

Donald A. Ball

Donald A. Ball, a consultant to multinational corporations, was a professor of marketing and international business for several years after leaving industry. He has a degree in mechanical engineering from Ohio State and a doctorate in business administration from the University of Florida. Ball has published articles in the *Journal of International Business Studies* and other publications. Before obtaining his doctorate, he spent 15 years in various marketing and production management positions in Mexico, South America, and Europe.

Welcome to *International Business*. We are enthusiastic about the field of international business and the interesting challenges and opportunities it provides. In preparing *International Business* for you, our goal is to create the most accessible and personal learning program, so that our readers can share in the excitement we find in this field. Whether you are an undergraduate or are in an MBA program, an international business course is a necessary venue for helping you explore and understand the complexities that face us in today's ever more global business world. Our hope is that our content will answer questions about business in different cultures, the impact of geography, why products are the same (or different) across cultures, why people have different practices, the continued growth and effect of the Internet on international business, how you can succeed in this global world, and many, many more questions. The field of international business is exciting and dynamic, so there are always new questions and sometimes there are new answers to old questions.

Each of the 15 modules provides you with a condensed presentation of international business topics. Within each module, contemporary, student-focused examples offer you an immediate appreciation of the critical importance of the concept under discussion. Alongside more traditional developed-country applications throughout the text, we also integrate extensive examples that apply to emerging-market contexts, and that highlight key changes occurring in the global economy. All applications are current, relevant, readable, and challenging. Together they provide you with a truly global view of business. Eye-catching photos, maps, and figures, plus exclusive features like *Get That Job! From Backpack to Briefcase* vignettes and *Culture Facts* cultural highlights, reinforce the appeal and readability of the material, personalize the content, and enhance your enjoyment and your learning. Looking for an even more personal experience, and an efficient and effective way to study? Ask your instructor how you can access this content via Smart-Book® or visit www.learnsmartadvantage.com.

We wish you an exciting journey of discovery within the field of international business, both in your academic training and in your personal and professional careers!

Sincerely,

Mike   *Jeanne*   *Don*

geringer@ohio.edu   J.mcnett@northeastern.edu

International Business was developed to make international business more accessible and the teaching and learning experience more personal in order to allow all students to become informed global citizens with a global mind-set.

FLEXIBLE LEARNING EXPERIENCE ACCESSIBLE TO ALL

- This new learning program presents the essential content in **15 compact modules** that are carefully written with today's student reader in mind.
- The chapters are designed from the ground up to speak to your students by introducing them to international business concepts unfolding in the world around them. **Contemporary examples** explore the decisions of businesses from around the world, such as YouTube, Twitter, Walmart, Xiaomi, eBay, Nestlé, Mondelez, Starbucks, Zara, Nissan, Mattel, Apple, McDonald's, Cognizant, Kiva, Chobani, and Google. Specific student-relevant features of every chapter include an introductory example that focuses on the chapter's main ideas with a narrative to which students can relate.
- In-text *Global Debate* material, eye-catching photos, maps, and figures reinforce the appeal, build geography skills, and increase accessibility and readability.

PERSONAL LEARNING EXPERIENCE

- To provide a more personal connection with the student reader, the authors connect the content to **culture** wherever appropriate in the narrative, and include additional fun *Culture Facts* cultural highlights to provide a stimulating set of examples to help intrigue and interest the students and make content more personally relevant.
- Exclusive *Get That Job! From Backpack to Briefcase* vignettes feature recent graduates succeeding in international roles within their organizations.
- The SmartBook® program provides students with an easy-to-use, effective, and efficient study experience. The adaptive learning platform paces and reinforces learning, and supports a flipped classroom pedagogy in which students learn the basic material outside of class and class time is dedicated to applications and problem solving.
- The authors have written the content in a unique, modular format allowing faculty to personalize their course according to specific requirements and course goals. Each module and the bonus modules have been written to stand on their own, a unique feature that provides additional flexibility to the instructor and enhances comprehension for students.

CURRENT AND RIGOROUS COVERAGE OF ESSENTIAL CONTENT

- The text's presentation of basic concepts includes the latest research and theory highlighted by engaging, student-centered applications. We believe rigor enriches learning, and when combined with the exceptional readability and relevance of our approach to the material, this rigor can motivate the learner to perform at a higher level. Rigor, readability, and relevance differentiate our book.
- The growing role of emerging markets, including the BRIC countries of Brazil, Russia, India, and China, is stressed in examples throughout the modules.

AUTHOR-CREATED RESOURCES FOR EVERY COURSE FORMAT

- Instructors adopting *International Business* will find it easy to deliver the course in a variety of formats, including large lecture, online, hybrid, and flipped classrooms. The author team has carefully developed instructor support materials as well as application exercises designed to involve students and bring them closer to the concepts covered.
- An **end-of-module mini-case** is provided to spark class discussion and apply concepts to the situation facing an international business or international manager.

International Business is organized into three sections to maximize its utility to instructors and students alike. The opening section, Module 1, defines the nature of international business and the three environments in which it is conducted, as well as the nature and continuing importance of international institutions and how they affect business. The second section, comprised of Modules 2 through 8, focuses on the uncontrollable forces at work in all business environments and discusses their inevitable impact on business practice. We devote the third and final section, Modules 9 through 15, to a discussion of how managers deal with all the forces affecting international business.

Module 1: The Challenging Context of International Business: Discusses the importance of international business and how it differs from domestic business. Describes the history of globalization and the internationalization of business and markets, including the driving forces encouraging firms to internationalize their operations. Compares key arguments in favor of and opposing the globalization of business.

Module 2: International Trade and Investment: Describes trends and traits of international trade and foreign direct investment. Introduces and distinguishes among the theories that explain why certain goods are traded internationally. Describes the growth of and explanations for foreign direct investment.

Module 3: Sociocultural Forces: Explores what culture is and its influence on business. The module looks at how cultures show themselves, provides frameworks for analyzing cultures, describes the global mind-set and a model for building strength from diverse cultures, and closes with advice for operating in other cultures.

Module 4: Sustainability and Natural Resources: Describes environmental sustainability in a business context, provides frameworks for sustainability, examines the characteristics of environmentally sustainable businesses, and then moves to a discussion of natural resources that includes geography and energy options.

Module 5: Political Forces That Affect Global Trade: Looks at government involvement in business, the importance of government stability to business, the role of country risk assessment, and the ways governments impede trade through tariffs and other trade barriers.

Module 6: Intellectual Property Rights and Other Legal Forces: Reviews legal systems and the rule of law, discusses legal concerns in international business, the ways intellectual property can be protected, and the international standardization of some laws. Examines specific national-level legal approaches in competition, trade, tort, ethics, and accounting.

Module 7: Economic and Socioeconomic Forces: Explains the purpose of economic analysis and discusses different categories of countries based on levels of national economic development. Explores human-needs development and global population trends involving urbanization, treatment of gender, ethnicity, and other sociocultural factors.

Module 8: The International Monetary System and Financial Forces: Describes the development of the international monetary system from the gold standard through today's floating currency exchange rate system and describes the process of exchange rate movement. Discusses the financial forces governments can exert and the significance of the balance of payments to international business decisions.

Module 9: International Competitive Strategy: Examines international competitive strategy and how companies use strategic planning to address international business opportunities and challenges. Discussion includes how companies develop competencies to give them competitive advantage in national, regional, and global markets.

Module 10: Organizational Design and Control: Explains why the design of organizations is important to international companies and the various dimensions managers must consider when designing their organizations. Explains why and how decision making is allocated across subsidiaries of an international company, both wholly owned and jointly owned.

Module 11: Global Leadership Issues and Practices: Covers issues associated with global leadership, including the importance of creating a global mind-set, what is different between global leadership and domestic leadership, and the competencies necessary for effective global leadership. Identifies approaches for selecting and developing effective global leaders, as well as the challenges of leading global teams and global change.

Module 12: International Markets: Assessment and Entry Modes: Provides approaches to market screening and environmental analysis. Describes some of the issues market researchers may encounter in foreign markets. Explains international market entry modes.

Module 13: Marketing Internationally: Looks at considerations associated with marketing products internationally and ways in which these considerations differ from domestic marketing activity.

Addresses issues including discussion of differences between the total product, the physical product, and the brand name; considerations in deciding which parts of the marketing mix to standardize, localize, or "glocalize"; and international pricing and distribution strategies.

Module 14: Managing Human Resources in an International Context: Examines worldwide labor conditions and the international human resource management approach, including recruitment, selection, training and development, expatriation, and compensation. Identifies some of the challenges and opportunities of an expatriate position, for the expat and for his or her family members. Describes compensation packages for expatriate executives.

Module 15: International Accounting and Financial Management: Outlines the major accounting issues related to operating in international currencies, explores the benefits of triple-bottom-line accounting, reviews capital structure choices, describes why ICs move funds. Reviews foreign exchange risks and their hedging. Looks at taxation as an international financial force.

In addition to the 15 core modules discussed above, *International Business* provides three additional bonus modules, to provide coverage of selected material that may be of particular value to students and instructors.

Bonus Module A: International Institutions from a Business Perspective: Describes why international institutions are important to business, including an introduction to institutional theory. Describes several significant international and regional institutions, including the UN, the IMF, the World Bank, and the OECD. Examines the major trading blocs as successful institutions and their levels of economic integration.

Bonus Module B: Export and Import Practices: Examines practices and procedures for engaging in exporting and importing, including sources of export counseling and support, key terms used in exporting and importing, sources of export financing, and export documentation.

Bonus Module C: Global Operations and Supply Chain Management: An overview of important operations issues in conducting international business, including the management of international supply chains, the relationship between design and supply chain management, alternatives for global sourcing arrangements, and key issues in decisions regarding global standardization of production processes and procedures.

- **Student-focused introductory example** focuses on the module's main ideas with a narrative to which students can relate and develop a global mind-set.

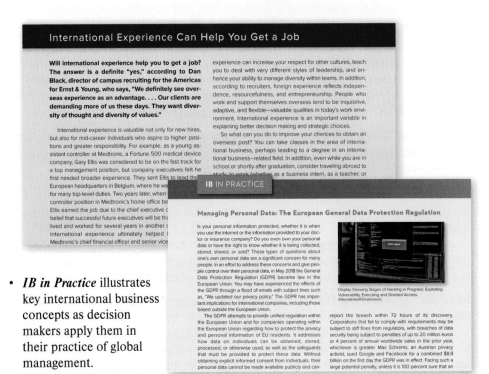

International Experience Can Help You Get a Job

Will international experience help you to get a job? The answer is a definite "yes," according to Dan Black, director of campus recruiting for the Americas for Ernst & Young, who says, "We definitely see overseas experience as an advantage. . . . Our clients are demanding more of us these days. They want diversity of thought and diversity of values."

International experience is valuable not only for new hires, but also for mid-career individuals who aspire to higher positions and greater responsibility. For example, as a young assistant controller at Medtronic, a Fortune 500 medical device company, Gary Ellis was considered to be on the fast track for a top management position, but company executives felt he first needed broader experience. They sent Ellis to lead the European headquarters in Belgium, where he wa[...] for many top-level duties. Two years later, when [...] controller position in Medtronic's home office be[...] Ellis earned the job due to the chief executive [...] belief that successful future executives will be th[...] lived and worked for several years in another c[...] international experience ultimately helped [...] Medtronic's chief financial officer and senior vice[...]

experience can increase your respect for other cultures, teach you to deal with very different styles of leadership, and enhance your ability to manage diversity within teams. In addition, according to recruiters, foreign experience reflects independence, resourcefulness, and entrepreneurship. People who work and support themselves overseas tend to be inquisitive, adaptive, and flexible—valuable qualities in today's work environment. International experience is an important variable in explaining better decision making and strategic choices.

So what can you do to improve your chances to obtain an overseas post? You can take classes in the area of international business, perhaps leading to a degree in an international business–related field. In addition, even while you are in school or shortly after graduation, consider traveling abroad to study, to work (whether as a business intern, as a teacher, or

IB IN PRACTICE

Managing Personal Data: The European General Data Protection Regulation

Is your personal information protected, whether it is when you use the Internet or the information provided to your doctor or insurance company? Do you even own your personal data or have the right to know whether it is being collected, stored, shared, or sold? These types of questions about one's own personal data are a significant concern for many people. In an effort to address these concerns and give people control over their personal data, in May 2018 the General Data Protection Regulation (GDPR) became law in the European Union. You may have experienced the effects of the GDPR through a flood of emails with subject lines such as, "We updated our privacy policy." The GDPR has important implications for international companies, including those based outside the European Union.

The GDPR attempts to provide unified regulation within the European Union and for companies operating within the European Union regarding how to protect the privacy and personal information of EU residents. It addresses how data on individuals can be obtained, stored, processed, or otherwise used, as well as the safeguards that must be provided to protect these data. Without obtaining explicit informed consent from individuals, their personal data cannot be made available publicly and can-

Display Showing Stages of Hacking in Progress: Exploiting Vulnerability, Executing and Granted Access.
©Gorodenkoff/Shutterstock.

report the breach within 72 hours of its discovery. Corporations that fail to comply with requirements may be subject to stiff fines from regulators, with breaches of data security being subject to penalties of up to 20 million euros or 4 percent of annual worldwide sales in the prior year, whichever is greater. Max Schrems, an Austrian privacy activist, sued Google and Facebook for a combined $8.8 billion on the first day the GDPR was in effect. Facing such a large potential penalty, unless it is 100 percent sure that an

- **IB in Practice** illustrates key international business concepts as decision makers apply them in their practice of global management.

GLOBAL DEBATE

LENDING TO THE POOR: Charitable Activity or For-Profit Business?

You might think it is foolish to lend money to the poor in a developing country. How will borrowers pay it back? But a tiny, or *microfinance*, loan to a new small-business owner or entrepreneur—a vegetable peddler, tailor, or candle maker— can make both [...] and good bu[...] Development org[...] the world are fina[...] the world's poore[...] many of whom a[...] their debts at ra[...] 100 percent.

Microloans give thousands of small ent[...] spurts of working capital when they need[...] establish credit, and let them borrow again [...] money helps them start or expand their bus[...] the local economy. The microcredit concep[...] by Muhammad Yunus, a U.S.-trained Bangla[...] through the Grameen Bank in Bangladesh[...] lished to administer his program, and [...] U.S. microcredit organization. Dr. Yunus w[...] Nobel Peace Prize in 2006 for his work figh[...]

Performance on microloan repayme[...]

investors. The move to private ownership that seeks a return on investment changes the microloan business model substantially, from *charity* to for-profit business. The charity model uses donated funds and funds from international financial institutions such as the World Bank and the European Bank for Reconstruction and Development, and it has relatively low interest rates. Compartamos now [...]

©Ute Grabowsky/Photothek/ Getty Images.

- **Global Debate** contrasts different perspectives on key international business issues, raises the pros and cons of ethical issues, and helps stimulate classroom discussion.

GET THAT JOB!   FROM BACKPACK TO BRIEFCASE

RYAN HULTZMAN IN DALIAN, CHINA: Challenge Yourself to Move beyond Your Comfort Zone

Courtesy of Ryan Hultzman.

I am a business major with a concentration in international management and a minor in psychology. At this point, my major career goal is to spend an extended period of time (over a year) working in another country. I know that this

it would be interesting to experience that kind of growth firsthand.

In China, I worked as an English teacher. I mostly taught children 2–10 years old, but I also taught one adult class for a month. I had only been accepted for this opportunity about a month before I was supposed to start, so my preparation was fairly rushed. I had no background in Mandarin, so I did what I could to learn some basic phrases before I left. I asked around and found a couple of people who had previously spent time working in China and I asked them about their experiences and whether they had any advice for me. I did a lot of research on the city I was going to be living in and tried to learn all I could about everyday life in China. Since I found this opportunity through AIESEC, my living arrangements and transportation from the airport were already established before I left, which was a huge benefit.

The most important thing I did to help myself adjust to the Chinese culture when I was abroad was make a few friends I could really trust. I ended up living in a couple of different places with some great American and Canadian friends that I made, but it was invaluable having a couple of Chinese friends on whom I could rely for help when I needed it. If I ever needed anything—from finding transportation to learning how to ask for a haircut—my friends were willing to provide their assistance.

Another big challenge for me was getting around in China without really knowing the language. Hand gestures can get you pretty far in most cases, but other things like being able to order food in a restaurant with menus that are written only in Chinese characters take some time. I had a

- **Get That Job! From Backpack to Briefcase** follows an actual student's transition from college to work in an international context, through such activities as study abroad, international internship and volunteer work, and early career decisions.

- **End-of-module mini-case** sparks class discussion and applies concepts to a situation facing international managers.

MINICASE

ARE YOU REALLY BUYING AMERICAN?

Consider the following scenario of a "typical" American family: The Osbornes, Jesse and Ann, live in the suburbs of Chicago. Jesse is a manager at Trader Joe's specialty grocery store chain. Ann is an advertising executive for Leo Burnett Worldwide.

Friskies, Hot Pockets, Stouffer's Lean Cuisine, Toll House, and Tidy Cat.
- Unilever, a British-Dutch multinational, makes Dove soap, Hellmann's, Q-tips, Lipton, Vaseline, and Ben & Jerry's.

- *Culture Facts* appear in the margin of each module, helping to build your interest as you read and to stimulate class discussion by illuminating cultural differences international managers face.

CULTURE FACTS @internationalbiz

@Switzerland Switzerland is landlocked, yet it won the America's Cup sailing competition in 2005. #landlocked #america'scup #sailing #2005

SOCIAL MEDIA

> **"WE HAVE** to SEND OUR BEST AND BRIGHTEST OVERSEAS AND MAKE SURE THEY HAVE THE TRAINING THAT WILL ALLOW THEM to BE THE GLOBAL LEADERS WHO WILL MAKE GE FLOURISH IN THE FUTURE."
>
> –*Jack Welch, former CEO of General Electric*[9]

- **Quotations** from notable thinkers highlight key points.

- **Key Terms** are highlighted and defined in the margin of the text.

...curs because of product differentiation, ...cts with the intention of influencing ...xported to the United States, and ...nsumers in these markets perceive a

product differentiation
Unique differences producer build into their products with the intent of positively influencing demand

...n international product life cycle (IPLC) ...eory addresses the role of innovation ...egins as a nation's export eventually ...ough a full life cycle. The initial stage

international product life cycle (IPLC)
A theory explaining why a product that begins as a nation's export eventually

- **Icons** in the margin highlight where each learning objective is addressed and call out related material in *McGraw-Hill Connect* to further enhance your comprehension and learning.

LO 2-1
Appreciate the magnitude of international trade and how it has grown.

- A **summary, key terms, critical thinking questions**, and a **globalEDGE research assignment** wrap up the module.

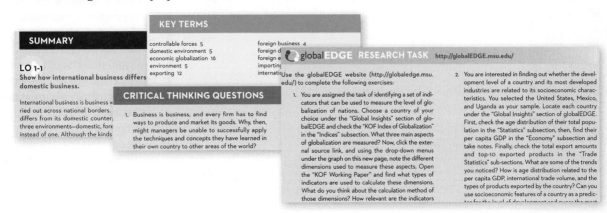

SUMMARY

LO 1-1
Show how international business differs domestic business.

International business is business ... ried out across national borders. ... differs from its domestic counter... three environments—domestic, fore... instead of one. Although the kinds ...

KEY TERMS

controllable forces 5
domestic environment 5
economic globalization 16
environment 5
exporting 12

foreign business 4
foreign d...
foreign e...
importing...
internati...

CRITICAL THINKING QUESTIONS

1. Business is business, and every firm has to find ways to produce and market its goods. Why, then, might managers be unable to successfully apply the techniques and concepts they have learned in their own country to other areas of the world?

global EDGE RESEARCH TASK http://globalEDGE.msu.edu/

Use the globalEDGE website (http://globaledge.msu.edu/) to complete the following exercises:

1. You are assigned the task of identifying a set of indicators that can be used to measure the level of globalization of nations. Choose a country of your choice under the "Global Insights" section of globalEDGE and check the "KOF Index of Globalization" in the "Indices" subsection. What three main aspects of globalization are measured? Now, click the external source link, and using the drop-down menus under the graph on this new page, note the different dimensions used to measure these aspects. Open the "KOF Working Paper" and find what types of indicators are used to calculate these dimensions. What do you think about the calculation method of those dimensions? How relevant are the indicators

2. You are interested in finding out whether the development level of a country and its most developed industries are related to its socioeconomic characteristics. You selected the United States, Mexico, and Uganda as your sample. Locate each country under the "Global Insights" section of globalEDGE. First, check the age distribution of their total population in the "Statistics" subsection, then, find their per capita GDP in the "Economy" subsection and take notes. Finally, check the total export amounts and top-10 exported products in the "Trade Statistics" sub-sections. What are some of the trends you noticed? How is age distribution related to the per capita GDP, international trade volume, and the types of products exported by the country? Can you use socioeconomic features of a country as a predic-

LEARN WITHOUT LIMITS

Today's learning extends beyond the classroom, beyond one format, beyond a singular style. That's why we deliver everything instructors and students need directly to your fingertips, integrating education seamlessly into your lives. We don't just improve results, we make the everyday a little smoother by providing intuitive technology that enables learning and simplifies life. *Connect* is the 2015 CODiE Award-winning digital teaching and learning tool that allows instructors to assign and assess course material. *Connect* makes digital teaching and learning personal, easy, and effective.

//CODiE//
2015 SIIA CODiE WINNER

Personal

- *Connect* makes teaching and learning personal for its users through adaptive technology, community and support programs, and by simply staying in touch with their needs.

Easy

- *Connect*'s intuitive interface and leading-edge technology eliminate barriers and create efficiencies for instructors and students.

Effective

- *Connect* is proven to improve performance across a range of outcomes and to increase faculty and student success.

Connect International Business includes:

- **SmartBook** SmartBook makes study time as productive and efficient as possible. It identifies and closes knowledge gaps through a continually adapting reading experience that provides personalized learning resources at the precise moment of need. This ensures that every minute spent with SmartBook is returned to the student as the most value-added minute possible. The result? More confidence, better grades, and greater success.

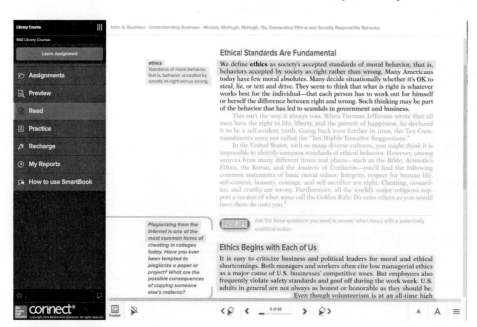

- **Interactive Applications** Each module of the text has interactive applications that allow students to practice real business situations, stimulate critical thinking, and reinforce key concepts. Students receive immediate feedback and can track their progress in their own report. Detailed results let instructors see at a glance how each student performs and easily track the progress of every student in their course.

- **Superior Instructor Resources** Because we understand how critically important it is for all resources to work together seamlessly to help instructors teach a better course, whether within a face-to-face, online, or flipped classroom delivery mode, the resource package includes these author-developed resources:
  - **Instructor Guide** The Instructor Guide includes an overview and summary of each module, teaching approaches and other teaching-related comments drawn from our experience with the material, lecture notes, suggestions for encouraging lively in-class discussions, and supplemental activities that will engage and challenge students. The Instructor Guide also contains suggestions for using the book effectively within online and flipped classroom environments.
  - **Instructor and Student PowerPoints** High-quality PowerPoint presentations for both instructor and student use accompany each of the modules of the book, enabling faculty to be more efficient and effective in preparing for their classes and providing useful content for face-to-face, hybrid, and online delivery. The student set of PowerPoints offers a review of the main module content to support student review and presentations.
  - **Test Bank** A rich test bank containing true-false, multiple-choice, and essay questions for each module will allow faculty to efficiently and effectively prepare assessment activities for their classes, including face-to-face, hybrid, and online delivery.
  - **Sample Syllabi and Personalized Syllabi** Template examples for customized course syllabi are provided. Beyond that, the authors are also available to work *directly with adopters* in creating personalized syllabi according to their desired course lengths, course concentrations, and pedagogical elements.
  - **International Business Video Library** Updated on a monthly basis, McGraw-Hill's International Business Video Library provides instructors with a library of video clips, curates the best of the web clips, and organizes them around the core international business topics. The site is updated on a monthly basis to ensure being current and relevant. For many of the cases McGraw-Hill provides teaching notes, critical thinking questions, and suggested answers.
  - **Updates** The author team will provide additional materials drawing on current business news, new scholarship, and new pedagogical trends that assist with course preparation. This will be a valuable free resource in the form of classroom activities, exercises, discussion topics, and video clips.
  - **Mobile Anywhere/Anytime** Students and instructors can now enjoy convenient anywhere/anytime access to *Connect* with a new mobile interface that's been designed for optimal use of tablet functionality. More than just a new way to access *Connect*, users can complete assignments, check progress, study and read material, with full use of SmartBook and Connect Insight—*Connect*'s new at-a-glance visual analytics dashboard.
  - **INSIGHT ENABLED** Connect Insight is *Connect*'s new one-of-a-kind visual analytics dashboard—available for instructors and students—that provides at-a-glance information regarding student performance, which is immediately actionable. By presenting assignment, assessment, and topical performance results together with a time metric that is easily visible for aggregate or individual results, Connect Insight gives the user the ability to take a just-in-time approach to teaching and learning, which was never before available. Connect Insight presents data that empowers students and helps instructors improve class performance in a way that is efficient and effective.

CREATE

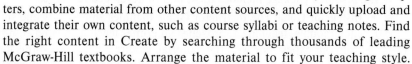

Instructors can now tailor their teaching resources to match the way they teach! With McGraw-Hill Create, **www.mcgrawhillcreate.com**, instructors can easily rearrange chapters, combine material from other content sources, and quickly upload and integrate their own content, such as course syllabi or teaching notes. Find the right content in Create by searching through thousands of leading McGraw-Hill textbooks. Arrange the material to fit your teaching style. Order a Create book and receive a complimentary print review copy in three to five business days or a complimentary electronic review copy via e-mail within one hour. Go to **www.mcgrawhillcreate.com** today and register.

TEGRITY: LECTURES 24/7

Tegrity in Connect is a tool that makes class time available 24/7 by automatically capturing every lecture. With a simple one-click start-and-stop process, you capture all computer screens and corresponding audio in a format that is easy to search, frame by frame. Students can replay any part of any class with easy-to-use, browser-based viewing on a PC, Mac, iPod, or other mobile device.

Educators know that the more students can see, hear, and experience class resources, the better they learn. In fact, studies prove it. Tegrity's unique search feature helps students efficiently find what they need, when they need it, across an entire semester of class recordings. Help turn your students' study time into learning moments immediately supported by your lecture. With Tegrity, you also increase intent listening and class participation by easing students' concerns about note-taking. Using Tegrity in Connect will make it more likely you will see students' faces, not the tops of their heads.

McGRAW-HILL CAMPUS™

McGraw-Hill Campus is a new one-stop teaching and learning experience available to users of any learning management system. This institutional service allows faculty and students to enjoy single sign-on (SSO) access to all McGraw-Hill Higher Education

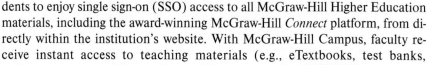

materials, including the award-winning McGraw-Hill *Connect* platform, from directly within the institution's website. With McGraw-Hill Campus, faculty receive instant access to teaching materials (e.g., eTextbooks, test banks, PowerPoint slides, animations, learning objectives, etc.), allowing them to browse, search, and use any instructor ancillary content in our vast library at no additional cost to instructor or students. In addition, students enjoy SSO access to a variety of free content (e.g., quizzes, flash cards, narrated presentations, etc.) and subscription-based products (e.g., McGraw-Hill *Connect*). With McGraw-Hill Campus enabled, faculty and students will never need to create another account to access McGraw-Hill products and services. Learn more at **www.mhcampus.com**.

ASSURANCE OF LEARNING READY

Many educational institutions today focus on the notion of *assurance of learning,* an important element of some accreditation standards. *International Business* is designed specifically to support instructors' assurance of learning initiatives with a simple yet powerful solution. Each test bank question for *International Business* maps to a specific chapter learning objective listed in the text. Instructors can use our test bank software, EZ Test, to easily query for learning objectives that directly relate to the learning outcomes for their course. Instructors can then use the reporting features of EZ Test to aggregate student results in similar fashion, making the collection and presentation of assurance of learning data simple and easy.

AACSB TAGGING

McGraw-Hill Education is a proud corporate member of AACSB International. Understanding the importance and value of AACSB accreditation, *International Business* recognizes the curricula guidelines detailed in the AACSB standards for business accreditation by connecting selected questions in the text and the test bank to the eight general knowledge and skill guidelines in the AACSB standards. The statements contained in *International Business* are provided only as a guide for the users of this product. The AACSB leaves content coverage and assessment within the purview of individual schools, the mission of the school, and the faculty. While the *International Business* teaching package makes no claim of any specific AACSB qualification or evaluation, we have within *International Business* labeled selected questions according to the eight general knowledge and skills areas.

McGRAW-HILL CUSTOMER EXPERIENCE GROUP CONTACT INFORMATION

At McGraw-Hill Education, we understand that getting the most from new technology can be challenging. That's why our services don't stop after you purchase our products. You can e-mail our Product Specialists 24 hours a day to get product training online. Or you can search our knowledge bank of Frequently Asked Questions on our support website. For Customer Support, call **800-331-5094** or visit **www.mhhe.com/support**. One of our Technical Support Analysts will be able to assist you in a timely fashion.

ACKNOWLEDGMENTS

Any effort to create a valuable new package of learning materials such as *International Business* involves the efforts not only of the authors and their invaluable editorial team, but also the insights, support, and encouragement of numerous other individuals and institutions. To the long list of individuals to whom we are indebted, we want to add Rachida Aissaoui, Ohio University; Nicholas Athanassiou, Northeastern University; Joseph R. Biggs, California Polytechnic State University–San Luis Obispo; Lorna Jean Edmonds, Ohio University; Paul Frantz, Long Beach State University; Colette Frayne, California Polytechnic State University–San Luis Obispo; Wendell McCulloch, Long Beach State University; Bill Pendergast, California Polytechnic State University–San Luis Obispo; Jere Ramsey, California Polytechnic State University–San Luis Obispo; Hugh Sherman, Ohio University; Mary Tucker, Ohio University; Ike Uzuegbunam, Ohio University; Ed Yost, Ohio University; and . . . we also wish to acknowledge Melinda Zuniga and Yana Saltaeva, who helped with research.

We would like to offer our special thanks to the outstanding editorial and production staff from McGraw-Hill Higher Education who worked so hard and so well to make this project succeed and stay on schedule, particularly Anke Weekes, Haley Burmeister, Nicole Young, Melissa M. Leick, Todd Schaefer, and Susan Gall. We feel honored to work with such a talented and professional team.

Many thanks go to the reviewers who provided their valuable feedback in the development of the first and second editions of this project.

Brad Ward, Kellogg Community College
Bruce D. Keillor, Youngstown State University
Chin-Chun Hsu, University of Nevada–Las Vegas
Constant Cheng, School of Management, George Mason University
Denny McCorkle, University of Northern Colorado
Eugene Lyle Seeley, Utah Valley University
Felix E. De Jesus, Monmouth University
Francis Sun, Woodbury School of Business at UVU and Goodman School of Business at Brock University
Hormoz Movassaghi, School of Business, Ithaca College
John Finley, Columbus State University
Linda C. Ueltschy, Dept. of Marketing, Florida Gulf Coast University, Fort Myers, Florida
Lisa Cherivtch, Oakton Community College
Lynn Wilson, DIBA, Saint Leo University
Mamoun Benmamoun, Saint Louis University
Mandeep Singh, Western Illinois University
Mark Fenton, University of Wisconsin–Stout
Michael Engber, Columbia College
Mitchell L Lautenslager, Fox Valley Technical College
Paul J. Myer, University of Maine Business School
Phillip Mixon, Troy University
Sam C. Okoroafo, University of Toledo
Stanford A. Westjohn, University of Toledo
Thomas Lynn Wilson, Saint Leo University
Yusufu Jinkiri, Belhaven University

CONTENTS

module 7
Economic and Socioeconomic Forces

module 8
The International Monetary System and Financial Forces

module 9
International Competitive Strategy

module 10
Organizational Design and Control

module 11
Global Leadership Issues and Practices

module 12
International Markets: Assessment and Entry Modes

module 13
Marketing Internationally

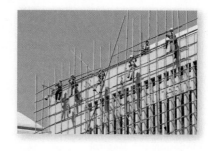

module 14
Managing Human Resources in an International Context

module 15
International Accounting and Financial Management

1 The Challenging Context of International Business

> **To tackle the challenges of globalization will require a serious commitment to making international knowledge and skills a policy priority.... Knowledge of the world is no longer a luxury, it is a necessity.**
>
> *—Nicholas Platt, President Emeritus of the Asia Society*[1]

©Rolf Bruderer/Blend Images.

LEARNING OBJECTIVES

After reading this module, you should be able to:

LO 1-1 **Show** how international business differs from domestic business.

LO 1-2 **Describe** the history and future of international business.

LO 1-3 **Discuss** the dramatic internationalization of business.

LO 1-4 **Identify** the kinds of drivers that are leading firms to internationalize their operations.

LO 1-5 **Compare** the key arguments for and against the globalization of business.

International Experience Can Help You Get a Job

Will international experience help you to get a job? The answer is a definite "yes," according to Dan Black, director of campus recruiting for the Americas for Ernst & Young, who says, "We definitely see overseas experience as an advantage. . . . Our clients are demanding more of us these days. They want diversity of thought and diversity of values."

International experience is valuable not only for new hires, but also for mid-career individuals who aspire to higher positions and greater responsibility. For example, as a young assistant controller at Medtronic, a Fortune 500 medical device company, Gary Ellis was considered to be on the fast track for a top management position, but company executives felt he first needed broader experience. They sent Ellis to lead their European headquarters in Belgium, where he was responsible for many top-level duties. Two years later, when the corporate controller position in Medtronic's home office became vacant, Ellis earned the job due to the chief executive officer's (CEO) belief that successful future executives will be those who have lived and worked for several years in another country. Ellis's international experience ultimately helped him become Medtronic's chief financial officer and senior vice president.

Although many companies want their top executives to have years of foreign experience, do CEOs recognize the value of international business education for all managers? Surveying CEOs of the 162 largest firms on *Fortune*'s list of the 500 largest U.S. corporations, we found that the CEOs strongly believed: (1) an international orientation should be an important part of college business education; (2) international business skills and knowledge were important not merely for promotion to senior executive positions but also for entry-level positions and across a broad array of functional as well as cross-functional areas; and (3) the importance indicated in the preceding points was magnified for companies that anticipated increasing importance of international activities in the next five years. For developing international skills, survey respondents believed that a number of courses in the international business curriculum are relevant to their companies. In addition to an Introduction to International Business course, the internationally oriented courses viewed as the most important for early career positions included topics related to: (1) international strategy and competitiveness, (2) international legal and political issues, (3) international negotiation, and (4) foreign language.

Did you note the reason for this emphasis on foreign experience for managers? It is increased involvement of the firm in international business. What about companies with no foreign operations of any kind? Do their managers need this global perspective? They do indeed, because it will help them not only to be alert for both sales and sourcing opportunities in foreign markets but also to be watchful for new foreign competitors preparing to invade their domestic market. International experience can increase your respect for other cultures, teach you to deal with very different styles of leadership, and enhance your ability to manage diversity within teams. In addition, according to recruiters, foreign experience reflects independence, resourcefulness, and entrepreneurship. People who work and support themselves overseas tend to be inquisitive, adaptive, and flexible—valuable qualities in today's work environment. International experience is an important variable in explaining better decision making and strategic choices.

So what can you do to improve your chances to obtain an overseas post? You can take classes in the area of international business, perhaps leading to a degree in an international business–related field. In addition, even while you are in school or shortly after graduation, consider traveling abroad to study, to work (whether as a business intern, as a teacher, or even in such positions as bartender or child care provider), or to volunteer in community development activities.

If you already have a job, you can enhance your opportunities for international experience by making your boss and the human resource management department aware of your interest and the fact that you have studied international business. Look for opportunities to remind them that you continue to be interested in a foreign assignment (your performance review is an ideal time to inform them). Try to meet people who work with the company's foreign subsidiaries as well as visitors from overseas. As evidence of your strong interest in foreign employment, take additional international business courses and study foreign languages. Make sure that people in your company know what you are doing.

Throughout this book you will find examples of ways to develop, apply, and promote your international skills and experience through features such as "Get That Job! From Backpack to Briefcase" vignettes that describe international experiences of current students and recent graduates. Hopefully, through effective application of these suggestions, you will build a successful foundation for your own international experiences!

Sources: "Gaining and Employment Edge—The Impact of Study Abroad," Institute of International Education, October 2017; "The Value of International Education to U.S. Business," Institute of International Education, July 4, 2018; Susan Adams, "How a Job Abroad Can Give Your Career a Big Boost," *Forbes*, November 04, 2010. www.forbes.com; Peder Greve, Torsten Biemann, and Winfried Ruigrok, "Foreign Executive Appointments: A Multilevel Examination," *Journal of World Business*, vol. 50, no. 4, October 2015, 674–686; Lisa Dragoni, In-Sue Oh, Paul E. Tesluk, Ozias Moore, Paul VanKatwyk, and Joy Hazucha, "Developing Leaders' Strategic Thinking Through Global Work Experience: The Moderating Role of Cultural Distance," *Journal of Applied Psychology*, vol. 99, March 02, 2014, 867–882; J. Michael Geringer, and W.R. Pendergast, "Firmly Rooting IB Research in the Soil of Relevance: Integration and Recommendations," *Thunderbird International Business Review*, vol. 54, no. 2, March/April 2012, 263–269; and J. Michael Geringer, and William R. Pendergast, "CEO Views on the Value of International Business Skills and Education," *The International Journal of Management and Business*, vol. 1, no. 1, January 2010, 1–29.

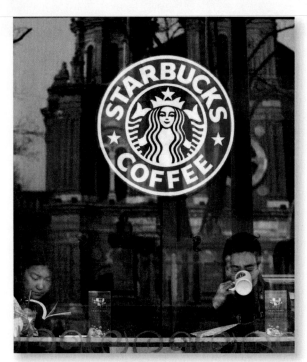

A Starbucks coffee store in Beijing, China. Company executives say China is the coffee chain's No. 1 growth market.
©Frederic J. Brown/AFP/Getty Images.

What about you? Are you involved in the global economy yet? Think back to how you began your own day. After you awoke to your Samsung smartphone's alarm and checked for messages, you may have switched on your bedside light from IKEA and turned on your Toshiba television for the news and weather while you showered. After drying your hair with a Conair dryer, maybe you slipped into some Lululemon athletic tights and Adidas running shoes, quickly swallowed some Dannon yogurt and a glass of Mott's apple juice, brushed your teeth with Close-Up toothpaste, and drove off to class in your Honda with its Firestone tires and a tank full of Shell gasoline. Meanwhile, on the other side of the world, a group of Nike-clad South Korean students may be turning off their Apple iPads after checking Facebook and debating whether they should stop for hamburgers and Cokes at McDonald's or coffee at Starbucks and then tweet their friends about where to join them. They toss their books and other materials into their JanSport backpacks and put on their North Face jackets and Oakley sunglasses as they head out the door.

What do you and the Korean students have in common? You are all consuming products made by foreign-owned companies. This is the result of international business.

All you have read so far points to one salient fact: all managers need to have a basic knowledge of international business to meet the challenge of global competition. Acquiring this knowledge consists, in part, of learning the special terminology of international business, an important part of every introductory course. To assist you in learning international business language, we've included a glossary at the end of the book and listed the most important terms at the end of each module. They also appear in bold print where they are first discussed in the text and with their definitions in the margin.

international business
Business that is carried out across national borders

foreign business
The operations of a company outside its home or domestic market

international company (IC)
A company with operations in multiple nations

What Is International Business and What Is Different about It?

Because international business is a relatively new discipline and is extremely dynamic, you will find that the definitions of a number of terms vary among users. To avoid confusion due to the range of different definitions of terms in international business, we will employ the following definitions, which are generally accepted by managers. **International business** is business that is carried out across national borders. This definition includes not only international trade and foreign manufacturing but also the growing service industry in areas such as transportation, tourism, advertising, consulting, construction, retailing, wholesaling, and mass communications. **Foreign business** denotes the operations of a company outside its home or domestic market; many refer to this as business conducted within a foreign country. This term sometimes is used interchangeably with "international business" by some writers, although that will not be our practice. An **international company (IC)** is a company with operations in multiple nations.

International business differs from domestic business in that a firm operating across borders must deal with the forces of three kinds of environments: domestic, foreign, and international. In contrast, a firm whose business activities are carried out within the borders of one country needs to be concerned essentially with only the domestic environment. However, no domestic firm is entirely free from foreign or international environmental forces because the possibility of having to face competition from foreign imports or from foreign competitors that set up operations in its own market is always present. Let us first examine these forces and then see how they operate in the three environments.

THE INFLUENCE OF EXTERNAL AND INTERNAL ENVIRONMENTAL FORCES

The term **environment** as used here means all the forces influencing the life and development of the firm. The forces themselves can be classified as external or internal. The external forces are commonly called **uncontrollable forces**, which are external forces management has no direct control over, although it can exert influence—such as lobbying for a change in a law or heavily promoting a new product that requires a change in a cultural attitude. External forces consist of the following:

1. *Competitive:* kinds and numbers of competitors, their locations, and their activities.
2. *Distributive:* national and international agencies that distribute goods and services.
3. *Economic:* variables (such as gross national income [GNI], unit labor cost, and personal consumption expenditure) that influence a firm's ability to do business.
4. *Socioeconomic:* characteristics and distribution of the human population.
5. *Financial:* variables such as interest rates, inflation rates, and taxation.
6. *Legal:* the many foreign and domestic laws governing how international firms must operate.
7. *Physical:* elements of nature such as topography, climate, and natural resources.
8. *Political:* elements of nations' political climates such as nationalism, forms of government, and international organizations.
9. *Sociocultural:* elements of culture (such as attitudes, beliefs, and opinions) important to international managers.
10. *Labor:* composition, skills, and attitudes of workers.
11. *Technological:* the technical skills and equipment that affect how resources are converted to products.

Management must adapt to changes in the uncontrollable environmental variables in order to enhance the prospects for their company's survival and success. The internal forces over which management does have some control and can manage in response to changes in uncontrollable forces, such as human resources, finance, production, and marketing, are called the **controllable forces**.

Consider how change in political forces—the expansion of the European Union (EU) by 10 nations in 2004, two more in 2007, and another in 2013, and the 2016 UK vote to leave the EU—affected all the controllable forces of firms worldwide that do business in or with the 28 EU member-nations. Suddenly these firms had to examine their business practices and change those affected by these membership changes. For example, some European concerns and foreign subsidiaries in the EU relocated parts of their existing operations or established new facilities within other nations in the Union, such as Poland, in order to exploit differences such as access to more abundant or lower-wage labor.[2] Other companies, such as HSBC and JPMorgan, relocated hundreds of jobs or even their European headquarters from the United Kingdom to avoid potential complications from the United Kingdom's departure from the EU.[3] This has included companies such as TRW and 3M, which have acquired or expanded their operations in Poland due to the low cost and high quality of the workforce available there, as well as Poland's proximity to major European markets such as Germany. Some U.S. and Asian companies set up or acquire facilities in one or more of the member-countries to supply this giant free trade area. By doing this, companies such as Google and Apple have helped avoid or reduce import duties on products coming from their home countries.[4]

THE DOMESTIC ENVIRONMENT

The **domestic environment** is all the uncontrollable forces originating in the home country that surround and influence the life and development of the firm. Obviously, these are the forces with which managers are most familiar. Being domestic forces, however, does not preclude

environment
All the forces influencing the life and development of the firm

uncontrollable forces
The external forces that management has no direct control over

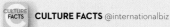

CULTURE FACTS @internationalbiz

The multinational aluminum company, Alcoa, encountered sociocultural challenges in Iceland when construction of an aluminum smelting plant experienced a six-month delay while an elf-monitoring "engineer" completed a government-required assessment of whether any of Iceland's elf-like "hidden people" lived beneath the construction site. #Alcoa #socioculturalchallenges #hiddenpeople

SOCIAL MEDIA

controllable forces
Internal forces that management administers to adapt to changes in the uncontrollable forces

domestic environment
All the uncontrollable forces originating in the home country that surround and influence the life and development of the firm

their affecting foreign operations. For example, if the home country is suffering from a shortage of foreign currency, the government may place restrictions on overseas investment to reduce its outflow. As a result, managers of multinationals find that they cannot expand overseas facilities as they would like to do. Similarly, a labor union may decide to call a strike at the domestic manufacturing operations of a company, causing disruption in the supply of parts to the company's assembly activities in another nation. In Spain, the October 2017 vote for independence by the prosperous Catalan region prompted a number of firms, including banks and construction companies, to consider relocating their businesses elsewhere in the country.[5]

THE FOREIGN ENVIRONMENT

foreign environment
All the uncontrollable forces originating outside the home country that surround and influence the firm

The foreign environment refers to all the uncontrollable forces originating outside the home country that surround and influence the firm. The forces in the foreign environment are the same as those in the domestic environment except they occur outside the firm's home country. However, they operate differently for several reasons, including those provided here.

Forces Have Different Values Even though the kinds of forces in the two environments are identical, their values often differ widely, and at times they are completely opposed to each other. A classic example of diametrically opposed political-force values and the bewilderment they create for multinational managers is the sanctions placed on Russia and selected Russian companies by the European Union, the United States, Canada, and other nations in response to Russia's actions in Ukraine in 2014, including the annexation of Crimea. The Russian government imposed retaliatory sanctions, including bans on the importation of food products from Europe. A number of salmon-farming companies in Norway suddenly lost access to the Russian market, their biggest export market, after Norway decided to participate in the anti-Russia sanctions. At the same time, fish farmers in the Faroe Islands, an autonomous part of Denmark, experienced a windfall from increased demand by Russia for their products.[6] Despite Denmark's participation in the Russian sanctions, the Faroe Islands exercised their autonomy and chose not to join their countrymen in imposing these sanctions, enabling them to capture record levels of export business.

Forces Can Be Difficult to Assess Another problem with foreign forces is they are frequently difficult to assess. This is especially true of legal and political forces. A highly nationalistic law may be passed to appease a section of the local population. To all outward appearances, the government may appear to be against foreign investment; yet pragmatic leaders may actually encourage it. A good example is Mexico, which in 1938 nationalized its oil industry and subsequently prohibited any foreign firms from participation in oil exploration and production in the country. However, despite Mexico's having one of the world's largest reserves of oil, production suffered continuing declines due to the government oil monopoly's lack of sufficient money or expertise to exploit promising new deposits from deepwater wells and shale rock formations. Governmental leaders in Mexico repeatedly and unsuccessfully attempted to reform legislation to allow access to foreign investment and technology, creating uncertainty for companies wanting to enter this promising market. The situation persisted until 2013, when Mexico finally passed an energy reform law that allowed foreign companies to invest in the country's energy sector.[7] Another good example is Greece. As part of the €86 billion bailout agreement in 2015 with its creditors, the Greek government committed to structural reforms intended to promote foreign investment into its country. However, corruption, bureaucracy, and legislative restrictions, along with uncertainty regarding political and economic stability, have continued to present extensive barriers to entry and investment by foreign firms.[8]

The Forces Are Interrelated As you study this text, it will be evident that the forces are often interrelated. This in itself is not a novelty, because the same situation confronts a domestic manager. On the foreign scene, however, the kinds of interaction that occur and the outcomes may differ. For instance, the combination of high-cost capital and an abundance of unskilled labor in many developing countries may lead to the use of a lower level of technology than would be employed in the more industrialized nations. In other words, given a choice between installing costly, specialized machinery needing fewer workers and installing less expensive, general-purpose machinery requiring a larger labor force, management will frequently choose the latter when faced with high interest rates and a large pool of available workers. Another example is the interaction between physical and sociocultural forces. Barriers to the free movement of a nation's people, such as mountain ranges and deserts, help maintain pockets of distinct cultures within a country, and this has an effect on decision making by international businesses.

THE INTERNATIONAL ENVIRONMENT

The international environment consists of the interactions between the domestic environmental forces and the foreign environmental forces, as well as interactions between the foreign environmental forces of two countries, such as when an affiliate in one country does business with customers in another. This agrees with our earlier definition of international business: business that involves the crossing of national borders.

> international environment
> Interaction between domestic and foreign environmental forces, as well as interactions between the foreign environmental forces of two countries

For example, employees at the headquarters of a multidomestic or global company work in the international environment if they work in any way with another nation, whereas those in a foreign subsidiary do not unless they too are engaged in international business through exporting or the management of other affiliates. In other words, a sales manager at the Chinese electronics firm Xiaomi does not work in the international environment if he or she sells cellular phones only in China. If Xiaomi's China operations export smartphones to another country such as India, then the sales manager is affected by forces of both China's domestic environment and India's foreign environment and thus is working in the international environment. International organizations whose actions affect the international environment are also properly part of it. These organizations include: (1) worldwide bodies (e.g., World Bank), (2) regional economic groupings of nations (North American Free Trade Agreement, European Union, Mercosur), and (3) organizations bound by industry agreements (Organization of Petroleum Exporting Countries, or OPEC).

Decision Making Is More Complex Those who work in the international environment find that decision making is more complex than it is in a purely domestic environment. Consider managers in a home office who must make decisions affecting subsidiaries in just 10 different countries (many ICs are in 20 or more countries). They not only must take into account the domestic forces but also must evaluate the influence of 10 foreign national environments. Instead of having to consider the effects of a single set of 10 forces, as do their domestic counterparts, they have to contend with 10 sets of 10 forces, both individually and collectively, because there may be some interaction.

For example, if management agrees to labor's demands at one foreign subsidiary, chances are it will have to offer a similar settlement at another subsidiary because of the tendency of unions to exchange information across borders. Furthermore, as we shall observe throughout this text, not only are there many sets of forces, but there are also extreme differences among them.

> **"WE HAVE to SEND OUR BEST AND BRIGHTEST OVERSEAS AND MAKE SURE THEY HAVE THE TRAINING THAT WILL ALLOW THEM to BE THE GLOBAL LEADERS WHO WILL MAKE GE FLOURISH in THE FUTURE."**
>
> *—Jack Welch, former CEO of General Electric*[9]

Self-Reference Criterion Another common cause of the added complexity of foreign environments is managers' unfamiliarity with other cultures. To make matters worse, some managers will ascribe to others their own preferences and reactions. Thus, a foreign production manager, facing a backlog of orders, may offer her workers extra pay for overtime. When they fail to show up, the manager is perplexed: "Back home they always want to earn more money." This manager has failed to understand that the foreign workers may prefer time off to more money. This unconscious reference to the manager's own cultural values, called the self-reference criterion, is probably the biggest cause of international business blunders. Successful managers are careful to examine a problem in terms of the local cultural traits as well as their own.

> self-reference criterion
> Unconscious reference to your own cultural values when judging behaviors of others in a new and different environment

A solid understanding of the business concepts and techniques employed in the United States and other advanced industrial nations is a requisite for success in international business. However, because transactions take place across national borders, three environments—domestic, foreign, and international—may be involved, instead of just one.

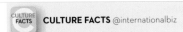

CULTURE FACTS @internationalbiz

People living in cultures in which unequal wealth and power are more acceptable, such as China, Russia, and India, are less likely to help people in need or donate to charitable causes than are people from nations with low scores on inequality acceptance, such as Canada, Australia, the United States, and Ireland. #unequalwealth #unequalpower #acceptable #nodonations

Thus, in international business, the international manager has three choices in deciding what to do with a concept or a technique employed in domestic operations: (1) transfer it intact, (2) adapt it to local conditions, or (3) not use it overseas. International managers who have discovered there are differences in the environmental forces are better prepared to decide which option to follow. To be sure, no one can be an expert on all these forces for all nations, but just knowing that differences may exist will cause people to "work with their antennas extended." In other words, when they enter international business, they will know they must look out for important variations in many of the forces they take for granted in the domestic environment.

The relationships among the forces in the three environments we have been discussing form the basis of our international business environments model as shown in Figure 1.1. The external or uncontrollable forces in both the domestic and the

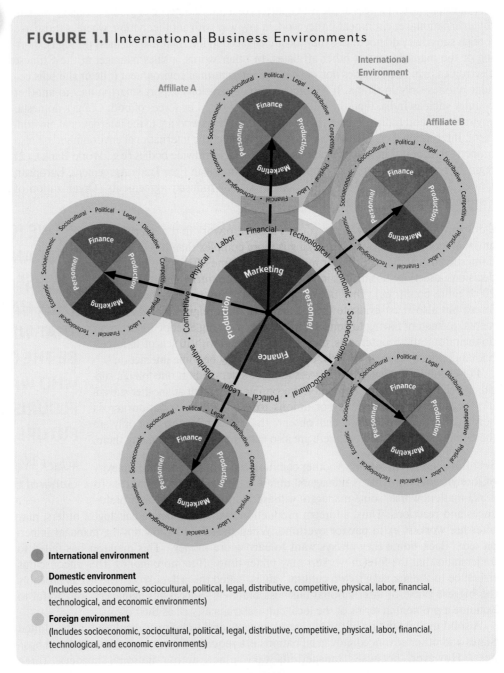

FIGURE 1.1 International Business Environments

● **International environment**

● **Domestic environment**
(Includes socioeconomic, sociocultural, political, legal, distributive, competitive, physical, labor, financial, technological, and economic environments)

● **Foreign environment**
(Includes socioeconomic, sociocultural, political, legal, distributive, competitive, physical, labor, financial, technological, and economic environments)

foreign environments surround the internal forces controlled by management. The domestic environment of the international firm's home country is surrounded by as many sets of foreign environments as there are countries in which the company does business. Solid lines connecting the internal forces at the home office to the internal forces in the foreign affiliates indicate the lines of control. The orange areas indicate the international environment in which employees in the headquarters of the international firm work. If, for example, the affiliate in foreign environment A exports to or manages the affiliate in foreign environment B, then its people are also working in the international environment, as shown by the orange section.

Is Internationalization of Business a New Trend, and Will It Continue?

LO 1-2
Describe the history and future of international business.

While international business as a discipline is relatively new, as a business practice it is not, so let's briefly explore the history of international business.

During the Hellenistic Age, before the Roman Empire was established, Phoenician and Greek merchants were sending representatives abroad to sell their goods. Subsequently, a vast expansion of agricultural and industrial production in China stimulated the emergence of an internationally integrated trading system stretching from Asia to the Mediterranean and Africa. The old saying that "all roads lead to Rome" might have instead been stated as "all roads lead to China" within the international trade system, as China was the world's leading manufacturing country for about 1,800 years, until it was replaced by Britain in about 1840.

The impact of the emerging international trading system was extensive. Politics, the arts, agriculture, industry, and other sectors of human life were profoundly influenced by the goods and ideas that came with trade. Public health was also affected. An interesting precursor to contemporary concerns about global health epidemics, such as the Zika virus and Ebola, was international trade's association with the spread of the plague, one of the worst natural disasters in history. Believed to have originated in Asia, the plague moved west with traders and soldiers, carried by fleas that lived on rodents on ships and caravans. Called the Black Death in Europe and repeated in waves from the mid-1300s through the 1600s, the plague ravaged cities, caused widespread hysteria, and killed one-quarter of China's people and one-third of the population of Europe.[10]

The rise of the Ottoman Empire before 1300, ultimately spanning Europe, North Africa, and the Middle East, profoundly influenced the emerging trade routes for people, goods, money, animals, and microorganisms that spanned from England to China, across the Mediterranean and northern Africa, and through Central Asia and the Indian Ocean region. The powerful central location of the Ottomans within this trading web had the effect of raising the cost of Asian trade for Europeans and thus drove a search for sea routes to Asia, including the expeditions that discovered the Americas.

In 1600, Great Britain's British East India Company, a newly formed trading firm, began to establish foreign branches throughout Asia, an action soon followed by many of the other European nations intent on exploiting trade opportunities for national advantage, including Portugal, the Netherlands, and France. In 1602, the Dutch East India Company was formed to carry out colonial activities in Asia and to open ocean trade routes to the East. The first company to issue stock, it is also frequently identified as the world's first multinational corporation.[11] By the end of the 1600s, ships commissioned by European trading companies regularly traveled to Asia via an interconnected Atlantic, Indian, and Pacific Ocean system of government-protected trade routes. Their goal was to acquire goods for sale or resale within various Asian markets and ultimately to return to Europe with valuable cargoes of cloth, spices, and other goods that would yield significant profits for investors. The 17th and 18th centuries have frequently been termed the "Age of Mercantilism" because the power of nations depended directly on the sponsorship and control of merchant capital, which expanded under the direct subsidization and protection of national governments.

A number of multinational companies existed in the late 1800s. One of the first U.S. companies to own foreign production facilities, have worldwide distribution networks, and market its products under global brands was Singer Sewing Machine. In 1868, Singer built a factory in Scotland and, by 1880, it had become a global organization with an outstanding international sales organization and several overseas manufacturing plants. Other firms, such as J&P Coats (United Kingdom) and Ford Motor Company, soon followed, and by 1914, at least 37 U.S. companies had production facilities in two or more overseas locations.[12] In contrast to today's situation, in the 1920s all cars sold in Japan were made in the United States by Ford and General Motors and sent to Japan in knocked-down kits to be assembled locally. European companies were also moving overseas. For example, pharmaceutical maker Friedrich Bayer purchased an interest in a New York plant in 1865, two years after setting up his plant in Germany. Then, because of high import duties in his overseas markets, he proceeded to establish plants in Russia (1876), France (1882), and Belgium (1908).[13]

As you have just read, multinational firms existed well before World War I, and the level of intracompany trade of multinationals in 1930, as a percentage of overall world trade, may have exceeded the proportion at the beginning of the 21st century.[14] Yet only in recent years have multinationals become the object of much discussion and investigation, especially concerning the increasing globalization of their operations. While most multinationals are based in the developed nations of the world, recently there has been a surge in the number arising in emerging economies.[15] Indeed, rapid urbanization of populations combined with industrialization in the emerging markets is quickly shifting the world's economic center of gravity from Europe and the Americas back to Asia, where it had been until the start of the industrial revolution in the 1800s. The rate at which this shift is occurring is unprecedented, as shown in Figure 1.2.

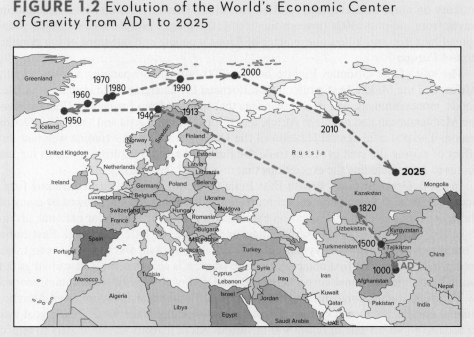

FIGURE 1.2 Evolution of the World's Economic Center of Gravity from AD 1 to 2025

Source: "Urban World: Cities and the Rise of the Consuming Class," *McKinsey Global Institute*, June 2012.

The Growth of International Firms and International Business

The number and size of U.S. and foreign international firms have been increasing rapidly in recent years, as have the levels of foreign direct investment (FDI) and exporting.

EXPANDING NUMBER OF INTERNATIONAL COMPANIES

A **transnational corporation** is an enterprise made up of entities in more than one nation, operating under a decision making system that allows a common strategy and coherent policies. It is estimated there are more than 103,000 transnational corporations with nearly 900,000 foreign affiliates.[16] These transnationals collectively account for more than half of world trade and 10 percent of world gross domestic product.[17] The 100 largest nonfinancial transnationals alone account for $4.5 trillion in assets and $8.0 trillion in annual sales and have 16.6 million employees.[18] While the vast majority of transnationals are privately owned, government ownership also represents an important element among the world's international companies. There is a minimum of 650 state-owned transnationals, from both developing and developed countries, with more than 8,500 foreign affiliates and assets exceeding $2 trillion.[19] Although less than 1 percent of all transnational corporations, these state-owned firms account for more than 10 percent of the world's foreign direct investment.

As a result of this expansion, the subsidiaries of foreign companies have become increasingly important in the industrial and economic life of many nations, both developed and developing. This situation is in sharp contrast to the one that existed when dominant economic interests were in the hands of local citizens. The expanding importance of foreign-owned firms in local economies came to be viewed by a number of governments as a threat to their autonomy. However, there has been a marked liberalization of government policies and attitudes toward foreign investment in both developed and developing nations in recent years.[20] Many government leaders know that local firms must obtain modern commercial technology in the form of direct investment, purchase of capital goods, and the right to use the international company's expertise if they are to be competitive in world markets.

Despite this change in attitude, there are still critics of large global firms who cite such statistics as the following to "prove" that host governments are powerless before them: In 2016, only 24 nations had gross national incomes (GNIs) greater than the total annual sales of Walmart Stores, the company with the greatest level of sales in the world.[21] However, a nation's GNI and a company's sales are not directly comparable because GNI is a measure of value added, not sales. If a nation's total sales were computed, the result would be far greater than its GNI because there would be triple and quadruple counting.

For example, suppose a steel manufacturer sells steel wire to a tire company, which uses it to build tires. Then the tire company sells the tires to automakers, which mount them on their automobiles, which they in turn sell to the public. Sales of the wire would be counted three times. However, in calculating GNI, governments merely sum the values added in each transaction, which is the difference between the sales of the company and the costs of materials bought outside the company. If company sales were measured by value added, Walmart's 2018 revenues of $496 billion would have been $15.1 billion on a value-added basis.[22] While Walmart's sales are about the same as Poland's GNI, when both the economy and the company are measured by the value added, Poland's economy is about 32 times the size of Walmart.

A firm's size may at times give it bargaining power, as in the case of a government that wants a firm to set up a subsidiary because of the employment it will offer and the purchases it will make from other firms in that country, in exchange for allowing the company to have access to the host nation and its market. Yet, regardless of the parent firm's size, each subsidiary is a local company that must comply with the laws in the country in which it is located. If it does not, it can be subject to legal action or even government seizure.

FOREIGN DIRECT INVESTMENT AND EXPORTING ARE GROWING RAPIDLY

foreign direct investment (FDI)
Direct investments in equipment, structures, and organizations in a foreign country at a level sufficient to obtain significant management control; does not include mere foreign investment in stock markets

exporting
The transportation of any domestic good or service to a destination outside a country or region

importing
The transportation of any good or service into a country or region, from a foreign origination point

One variable commonly used to measure where and how fast internationalization is taking place is total foreign direct investment. **Foreign direct investment (FDI)** refers to direct investments in equipment, structures, and organizations in a foreign country at a level sufficient to obtain significant management control. It does not include mere foreign investment in stock markets. The total level of outward FDI worldwide was $30.8 trillion at the beginning of 2018, which was nearly 14 times larger than what it was in 1990.[23]

Of course, a substantial amount of international business is exporting rather than FDI. **Exporting** is the transportation of any domestic good or service to a destination outside a country or region. It is the opposite of **importing**, which is the transportation of any good or service into a country or region, from a foreign origination point. Merchandise exports have grown faster than world output in nearly each of the past 60 years. World merchandise exports grew from $2.0 trillion in 1980 to $3.5 trillion in 1990, $6.5 trillion in 2000, $15.3 trillion in 2010, and $17.7 trillion in 2017. This means that exports in 2017 were 9 times larger than they were in 1980 and nearly 3 times larger than they were in 2000.[24] The level of service exports worldwide grew even more during this time, from $396 billion in 1980 to $831 billion in 1990, $1.5 trillion in 2000, $3.9 trillion in 2010, and $5.3 trillion in 2017. This means that services exports in 2017 were more than 13 times larger than they were in 1980.[25] Figure 1.3 shows the growth in outward FDI and in services and merchandise exports from 1990 to 2017.[26]

FIGURE 1.3 World Merchandise Exports, Commercial Services Exports, and Outward Foreign Direct Investment, 1990–2017 (US$ millions)

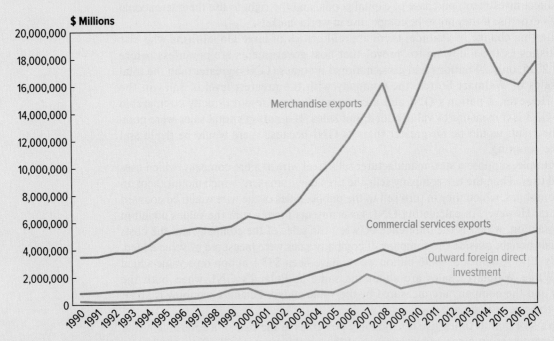

Sources: "Annex Table 2: FDI Outflows, by Region and Economy, 1990–2017," *UNCTAD*, Jun 06, 2018.; "Merchandise: Total Trade and Share, Annual, 1948–2017," *UNCTADSTAT*, July 4, 2018; "Services (BPM5): Exports and Imports of Total Services, Value, Shares and Growth, Annual, 1980–2013," *UNCTADSTAT*, July 4, 2018; and "Services (BPM6): Exports and Imports of Total Services, Value, Shares, and Growth, Annual, 2005–2017", *UNCTADSTAT*, July 4, 2018.

What Is Driving the Internationalization of Business?

LO 1-4
Identify the kinds of drivers that are leading firms to internationalize their operations.

Five major kinds of drivers, all based on change, are leading firms to internationalize their operations: (1) political, (2) technological, (3) market, (4) cost, and (5) competitive.

POLITICAL DRIVERS

There is a trend toward the unification and socialization of the global community. Preferential trading arrangements that group several nations into a single market, such as the North American Free Trade Agreement (NAFTA) and the EU, have presented firms with significant marketing opportunities. Many firms have moved swiftly to gain access to the combined markets of these trading partners, by either exporting to or producing in the area.

Two other aspects of this trend are contributing to the globalization of business operations: (1) the progressive reduction of barriers to trade and foreign investment by most governments, which is hastening the opening of new markets by international firms that are both exporting to them and building production facilities in them; and (2) the privatization of much of the industry in formerly communist nations and the opening of their economies to global competition.

Even with governmental actions to open their economies to international business, concerns about shielding markets from potential protectionism by host country markets may still remain a motive for a company to increase the level of its international business activity. For example, when a government sees that local industry is threatened by imports, it may erect import barriers to stop or reduce these imports. Even threats to do this can be sufficient to induce the exporter to invest in production facilities in the importing country.

 CULTURE FACTS @internationalbiz

In Scandinavian countries, low rankings on the masculinity scale versus the United States reflect greater emphasis on values of caring for others and quality of life. In these countries, the proportion of children who live in poverty in single-mother families is 11 percent; the comparable figure for the United States is 55 percent.
#scandinaviancountries #caring
#qualityoflife

 SOCIAL MEDIA

TECHNOLOGICAL DRIVERS

Advances in computers and communications technology are permitting an increased flow of ideas and information across borders, enabling customers to learn about foreign goods. Cable and satellite TV systems in Europe and Asia, for example, allow an advertiser to reach numerous countries simultaneously, thus creating regional and sometimes global demand. Global communications networks enable manufacturing workers to coordinate production and design functions worldwide so that plants in many parts of the world may be working on the same product.

The Internet and network computing enable small companies to compete globally because they make possible the rapid flow of information regardless of the physical location of the buyer and seller. Internet videoconferencing allows sellers to demonstrate their products to prospective buyers all over the world without the need to travel. It also permits international companies to hold corporate meetings among managers from headquarters and overseas subsidiaries without expensive, time-consuming travel. In addition, communicating via e-mail is faster and more reliable than using postal mail. In addition, the Internet has given home office managers greater confidence in their ability to direct overseas operations from afar.

Advances in computer-based communications are allowing virtual integration, which permits firms to become more physically fragmented as they search the world for lower-cost inputs. For example, practical, relatively inexpensive international communication enables large insurance, banking, software, and other firms to "body shop," that is, transmit computer-oriented tasks worldwide to a cheap but skilled labor force. The clients of numerous Indian software companies are based in the United States. A decade ago, software teams were required to fly back and forth between the two countries. Now, at the end of the day, customers in the United States e-mail their problems to India. The Indians then work on developing solutions and deliver these back to the United States early the next day. For their work, Indian software engineers often receive only 15 to 20 percent as much pay as do their U.S. counterparts.

MARKET DRIVERS

As companies internationalize, they also become global customers. Frequently, a firm will go abroad to protect its home market. Service companies (for example, in accounting, advertising, marketing research, banking, law) will establish foreign operations in markets where their principal accounts are located to prevent competitors from gaining access to those accounts. They know that once a competitor has been able to demonstrate to top management what it can do by serving a foreign subsidiary, it may be able to take over the entire account. Similarly, suppliers to original equipment manufacturers (for example, battery manufacturers supplying automobile producers) often follow their large customers. These suppliers have an added advantage because they are moving into new markets with a guaranteed customer base.

Managers are always under pressure to increase the sales and profits of their firms, and when they face a mature, saturated market at home, they begin to search for new markets outside the home country. They find that (1) markets with a rising gross domestic product (GDP) per capita and population growth appear to be viable candidates for their operations and (2) the economies of some nations where they are not doing business are growing at a considerably faster rate than is the economy of their own market. Indeed, the United States has only about 5 percent of the world's population, so the vast proportion of most U.S. companies' potential customers are located elsewhere.

COST DRIVERS

Going abroad, whether by exporting or by producing overseas, can frequently lower the cost of goods sold. Increasing total sales by exporting not only will reduce research and development (R&D) costs per unit but also will make other economies of scale possible. One means of achieving them is to globalize product lines to reduce development, production, and inventory costs. Management can also move production or other parts of the company's value chain to countries where costs are lower. For example, low electricity prices in Iceland due to extensive geothermal power has helped attract energy-intensive aluminum smelting facilities, which consume about 75 percent of the electricity produced in that country.[27]

Another factor that can positively affect the cost of goods sold is the inducements—such as reduced taxes or subsidies for R&D—that some governments offer to attract new investment. Many nations, especially developing countries, offer export processing zones in which firms, mostly foreign manufacturers, enjoy almost complete absence of taxation and regulation of materials brought into the zones for processing and subsequent re-export. Dramatic reductions in the cost of generating and transmitting information due to innovations in computing and telecommunications, as well as the decline in transportation costs, have facilitated this trend toward relocating activities worldwide.

Citgo Petroleum Corporation, although based in the United States, is majority owned by Venezuela's state-owned PDVSA.
Source: Library of Congress [LC-DIG-mrg-05333].

COMPETITIVE DRIVERS

Competition continues to increase in intensity. New firms, many from newly industrialized and developing countries, have entered world markets in automobiles, computers, and electronics, for example. Another competitive driving force for globalization is the fact that companies are defending their home markets from competitors by entering the competitors' home markets to distract them. Many firms that would not have entered a single country because it lacked sufficient market size have established plants in the comparatively larger trading groups (for example, EU, Association of Southeast Asian Nations [ASEAN], Mercosur). It is one thing to be shut out of Belgium, but it is another to be excluded from all of Europe.

Adapting Listerine to Meet the Different Requirements of International Markets

Listerine is a 140-year-old brand of antiseptic mouthwash sold by the consumer products company Johnson & Johnson. Although it is the dominant player in the United States's $1.5 billion market for mouthwash, that market has begun to mature with total penetration of about two-thirds of all American consumers, and company managers sought new growth opportunities in markets abroad, particularly in developing and emerging markets. For example, the market research firm Nielsen projects that the size of the middle class in the Middle East and Africa will double by 2030. Expanding populations, rising levels of disposable income, increasing standards of living, and heightened awareness of oral hygiene in emerging markets are among the factors that may produce higher levels of demand for products like Listerine.

While the middle class is expanding in regions such as Asia, the Middle East, Africa, and Latin America, exploiting the potential of these markets can prove to be a challenge. Johnson & Johnson's product development teams have responded by developing such product line extensions as Green Tea Listerine, which is targeted for Asian markets, and Listerine Zero, which is alcohol-free and appropriate for Muslim communities where spirits are forbidden.

In addition to developing products that meet local requirements, growing the sales of Listerine internationally will require modifications to other parts of Johnson & Johnson's business model. For example, trying to reach consumers across India will require fine-tuning the distribution model to ensure coverage in a country where many still live in small, rural villages with limited infrastructure and small mom-and-pop-style retailers. The company has been distributing single-use samples to help introduce the product to consumers. Advertising and promotion practices may also require adjustments, as local norms may frown on imagery such as men and women kissing or suggestions of intimacy and affection among unmarried people.

Critical Thinking Questions

1. What challenges might arise as the managers of consumer products such as Listerine attempt to respond to the many differences of consumers from a variety of nations and regions of the world?

2. How might these various challenges affect the different activities of a company, such as manufacturing, marketing, sales, and logistics?

Sources: Rachel Abrams, "Adapting Listerine to a Global Market," *New York Times*, September 12, 2014; "Why Colgate Can Grow Its Emerging Markets Sales Despite Stiff Competition," *Trefis*, March 15, 2013, https://www.trefis.com; and "Still Fresh?," *The Economist*, February 1, 2007, https://www.economist.com.

Companies may also be driven to internationalize their operations in order to guarantee the supply of key raw materials. Few developed nations possess sufficient domestic supplies of raw materials. Japan and Europe are almost totally dependent on foreign sources for many important materials, and even the United States depends on imports for more than half of its consumption of aluminum, chromium, manganese, nickel, tin, and zinc. To ensure a continuous supply and maintain their competitiveness, manufacturers in the industrialized countries are being forced to invest, primarily in the developing nations where most new deposits are being discovered.

A company might also invest in downstream markets as a way of protecting its existing international business. For example, a number of OPEC nations have invested in refining and marketing outlets, such as filling stations and heating-oil distributors, to guarantee a market for their crude oil at more favorable prices. A major foreign investor in the United States is the oil company Petróleos de Venezuela, which first invested in Citgo in 1986 and assumed full ownership in 1990.

The result of this rush to globalization has been explosive growth in international business. Many of the issues associated with globalization are highly complex, and there is no single measure of globalization or of integration within the world economy. Each element of global integration can have different effects. Following are some of the arguments for and against the globalization process and its outcomes.

What Are the Arguments for and against the Globalization of Business?

Although globalization is discussed everywhere—television shows, Internet chat rooms, political demonstrations, parliaments, management boardrooms, and labor union meetings—so far it has no widely accepted definition. In fact, its definition continues to broaden. Now, for example, social scientists discuss the political, social, environmental, historical, geographic, and even cultural implications of globalization.[28] Some also speak of technological globalization, political globalization, and the like.

economic globalization
The tendency toward an international integration and interdependency of goods, technology, information, labor and capital, or the process of making this integration happen

The most common definition and the one used in international business is that of economic globalization—the tendency toward an international integration and interdependency of goods, technology, information, labor, and capital, or the process of making this integration happen. The term "globalization" was first coined by Theodore Levitt in a *Harvard Business Review* article in which he maintained that new technologies had "proletarianized" communication, transport, and travel, creating worldwide markets for standardized consumer products at lower prices. He maintained that the future belonged to global corporations that did not cater to local differences in taste but, instead, adopted strategies that operated "as if the entire world (or major regions of it) were a single entity; [such an organization] sells the same things in the same way everywhere."[29]

The merits of globalization have been the subject of many heated debates in recent years. There have been extensive public protests about globalization and the liberalization of international trade at World Trade Organization (WTO) meetings and at other gatherings of international organizations and leaders. The debate is, in many respects, waged by diametrically opposed groups with extremely different views regarding the consequences of globalization. Sifting through the propaganda and hyperbole spouted by both sides is a challenge. However, it is important to recognize the various perspectives on globalization, as their arguments can generate appeal (or rejection) both intellectually and emotionally. The contributions of free trade and globalization to dramatic reductions in worldwide poverty are contrasted with anecdotal stories of people losing their livelihoods under the growing power of multinationals. Likewise, increases in service sector employment are contrasted against losses in high-paying manufacturing jobs.

CONCERNS WITH GLOBALIZATION

Those expressing concern with globalization have come from a range of sectors of society, and they express a correspondingly diverse set of concerns.[30] Some fundamentally oppose the very process and outcomes of globalization on ideological grounds,[31] while others may merely be concerned about finding ways to better manage globalization processes and the resulting outcomes. Some of the opponents' concerns may be viewed as naïve or clearly inconsistent with the preponderance of evidence. Other challenges to globalization may have theoretic merit or other supporting evidence and certainly may be worthy of discussion and the fostering of substantive change.

Although perspectives on the globalization debate may in many respects depend on one's values and ideology, thus further compounding efforts to reach a mutually agreed upon resolution, let us first ask this question: What are some of the primary concerns of the opponents of globalization? While many of the anti-globalizers concede that globalization "increases the size of the pie," they also claim that it has been accompanied by a broad array of injurious social implications. Among their

Demonstrators at a World Trade Organization meeting.
©Agung Kuncahya B./Xinhua News Agency/Newscom.

concerns, let us briefly examine three primary ones here: (1) that globalization has produced uneven results across nations and people, (2) that globalization has had deleterious effects on labor and labor standards, and (3) that globalization has contributed to a decline in environmental and health conditions.

Uneven Results across Nations and People In stark contrast to the positive picture presented by supporters of globalization, opponents describe the painful impact of foreign investment and trade liberalization on the people of the world. Far from causing everyone to be a winner, they say the promise of export-led growth has failed to materialize in several places. For example, most of Latin America has failed to replicate Asia's success despite efforts to liberalize, privatize, and deregulate its economies, with results ranging from disappointment in Mexico to catastrophe in Argentina. Similarly, efforts in sub-Saharan Africa have produced only limited benefits, and the number of people there who are living in extreme poverty rose 43 percent between 1990 and 2013, from 290 million to 389 million people.[32] According to the World Bank, China experienced a nearly 50 percent increase between 1981 and 2012 in the Gini coefficient, indicating a significantly higher level of economic inequality during this period of rapid internationalization of the Chinese economy.[33] Open world markets, it seems, may offer the possibility of economic development—but the recipe is neither easy in its implementation nor universal in its outcomes.

Many opponents of globalization have claimed that there is a huge gap between the world's rich and poor and that globalization has caused that gap to increase. The gap between rich and poor is unquestionable, but the evidence is perhaps unclear regarding the charge that globalization has been the cause of this inequality. Although Martin Wolf's analysis shows that income inequality has not risen in most developing countries that have integrated with the world economy, it does show that inequality has increased in some places, most notably in China. Inequality has risen in some high-income countries as well, but he attributes that more to the nature of technological change than to globalization. When income data are adjusted to reflect relative purchasing power, the inequality in income between poor and rich nations diminishes. Wolf also notes that while globalization of trade and investment is an enabler to improved income and living standards, the results may vary if obstacles exist such as poor governance or excessive borrowing.[34]

Deleterious Effects on Labor and Labor Standards The impact of globalization on labor standards has become an oft-mentioned concern of workers in the United States, Europe, and elsewhere. With trade liberalization through the WTO and increased mobility of capital, measures to keep a country's industries within its borders have been reduced, and companies have an easier time divesting their interests in one country and moving to another. Workers fear they lack the skills and resources to compete in an increasingly competitive global marketplace and will experience lower wages and benefits, fewer job opportunities, and higher risk of unemployment as a result.

Workers in developed countries frequently voice concerns that their jobs will migrate to developing nations where there are lower standards, and thus lower costs, leading to the infamous "race to the bottom," in which developed nations with more rigorous labor standards become disadvantaged. Indeed, the Labor Secretariat for NAFTA commissioned a report that found more than half of firms surveyed used threats to close U.S. operations as a tool to fight union-organizing efforts. After NAFTA's inception and the subsequent reduction in trade and investment barriers, these threats became more plausible. As reported by Public Citizen, during the first 20 years of NAFTA, in addition to over 845,000 workers in the United States losing their jobs due to imports from Mexico or Canada or relocation of facilities to those nations, the agreement also helped push down wages and increase income inequality in the United States.[36]

> **❝ WE'RE NOT** against **TRADE, WE'RE JUST** against **TRADE THAT KEEPS COSTING US JOBS. ❞**
>
> *—Leo Gerard, international president of the United Steelworkers Union*[35]

Is the "Bottom of the Pyramid" a Market Worth Serving?

The term "Bottom of the Pyramid," popularized by the late Professor C. K. Prahalad, refers to approximately 3 billion of the world's poorest inhabitants who survive on less than $2 per day. For people at this level of poverty, basic survival needs are just barely met.

Traditionally, it was common practice by businesses, donors, and governments to view these poor as victims. However, Prahalad suggested that they should instead be viewed as a tremendous potential market for the products of multinational companies. He suggested that the world's poorest inhabitants represented substantial untapped purchasing power. If served in ways appropriate to their needs, not only would the poor represent a huge market, but they could also receive tremendous benefit, and poverty could be reduced significantly. In addition, the ability of members of this population to achieve their full potential could be greatly enhanced.

Examples of companies that have been promoted as highlighting the potential of serving the bottom of the pyramid include microcredit companies (those who lend small amounts of money—as little as $5 or $10—to people with few or no assets); consumer products companies such as India's Hindustan Unilever (which offers single-use packets of shampoo that works effectively in unheated water); and retailers such as Brazil's Casas Bahia, which offer credit to people who otherwise would not qualify in order for them to purchase basic appliances and similar goods.

Others have questioned whether a focus on the bottom of the pyramid truly represented an attractive business opportunity. Prahalad's colleague at the University of Michigan, Professor Aneel Karnani, argued that profit opportunities associated with such a focus were modest at best, especially for large companies that required economies of scale. While the aggregate level of consumption might be substantial in dollar terms, 3 billion people times an average of perhaps $1.50 per day yields a total annual market of over $1.6 trillion, which is just a bit over 10 percent of the size of the U.S. economy alone. The costs of serving such a culturally disparate and geographically dispersed population of poor, a large portion who live in rural areas with limited infrastructure, will be quite substantial. Individual transactions will be of very small size and the customers highly price-sensitive. After accounting for costs of food, shelter, clothing, and fuel, they have limited room for nonessential items.

Beyond market attractiveness, some have questioned the proposal that multinationals serve the base of the pyramid market. For example, concerns have been raised about the ethical appropriateness of a profit-oriented focus on serving the most impoverished of the world's inhabitants, particularly with products such as tobacco, alcohol, or makeup.

Critical Thinking Questions

1. Do you think the bottom of the pyramid represents an attractive and appropriate market for multinational corporations? Why or why not? For which products or services might this market be most appropriate?

2. If customers at the base of the pyramid could be convinced to allocate some of their meager income to products such as cigarettes, alcoholic beverages, or cosmetics, would it be socially responsible for multinationals to pursue such opportunities? Why or why not?

Sources: Jason Haber, "Why the Bottom of the Consumer Pyramid Should Be Your New Target Market," *Entrepreneur*, May 26, 2016; Subinay Bedi, "A Foundational Criticism of the Base of the Pyramid Model," October 15, 2012; C. K. Prahalad, *The Fortune at the Bottom of the Pyramid: Eradicating Poverty Through Profits*. Upper Saddle River, NJ: Wharton School Publishing, August 25, 2004; Aneel G. Karnani, "The Mirage of Marketing to the Bottom of the Pyramid: How the Private Sector Can Help Alleviate Poverty," *California Management Review*, vol. 49, no. 4, July 01, 2007, 90–111; and Kirk Davidson, "Ethical Concerns at the Bottom of the Pyramid: Where CSR Meets BOP," *Journal of International Business Ethics*, vol. 2, no. 1, 2009, 22–32.

The concern can run both ways, however. Although labor standards in developing countries are usually lower than in industrialized countries, they are rising—and evidence shows that multinationals investing in host nations pay higher wages, create new jobs at a faster rate, and spend more on R&D than do local firms.[37] Developing countries may also view the imposition of more demanding labor standards within their borders as a barrier to free trade. They may feel that lower-cost labor constitutes their competitive advantage and that if they are forced to implement more stringent labor standards, then companies may no longer have an incentive to set up operations in their countries, damaging their prospects for improved economic development.

As Gary Burtless, Robert Z. Lawrence, Robert E. Litan, and Robert J. Shapiro, the authors of *Globaphobia*, ask, "Is it humane for the United States to refuse to trade with these countries because their labor standards are not as high as we would prefer? The consequence of taking this position is that many Third World workers will have no jobs at all, or must take jobs that pay even lower wages and have even worse working conditions than those currently available in the export-oriented sector."[38] For example, Mexico's agricultural sector, which represented a major portion of that country's employment, was estimated to have lost 2 million jobs after NAFTA was implemented, which contributed to many of them crossing the border into the United States in search of employment and better pay.[39]

A Decline in Environmental and Health Conditions Regarding concerns of anti-globalization forces that globalization contributes to declining environmental standards, former president Ernesto Zedillo of Mexico stated, "Economic integration tends to favor, not worsen, the environment. Since trade favors economic growth, it brings about at least part of the necessary means to preserve the environment. The better off people are, the more they demand a clean environment. Furthermore, it is not uncommon that employment opportunities in export activities encourage people to give up highly polluting marginal occupations."[40]

Yet a difficulty caused by NAFTA and the maquiladora program that began before NAFTA is the substantial increases in ground, water, and air pollution along the Mexico–U.S. border. Damage to the environment has been caused by the many new production facilities and the movement of thousands of Mexicans to that area to work in them. In addition, some health and environmental issues extend beyond the scope of trade agreements. Some of NAFTA's rules on trade in services may cause governments to weaken environmental standards for sometimes hazardous industries like logging, trucking, water supply, and real estate development.

For example, to comply with NAFTA's rules on trade in services, U.S. clean air standards were waived in order to allow trucks based in Mexico to haul freight on U.S. highways. Globalization opponents argue that this could increase air pollution and associated health concerns in border states, as the aging Mexican truck fleet pollutes more than similar U.S. trucks and these vehicles do not use the cleaner fuels required in the United States. Protesters have also claimed that, under liberalized rules regarding the globalization of trade and investment, businesses have an incentive to move their highly polluting activities to nations that have the least rigorous environmental regulations or a lower risk of liability associated with operations that can create environmental or health-related problems. On the other hand, the economic growth fostered by globalization can help generate and distribute additional resources for protecting the environment, and improved trade and investment can enhance the exchange of more environmentally friendly technologies and best practices, particularly within developing nations.

ARGUMENTS SUPPORTING GLOBALIZATION

Some argue that globalization and related developments have produced positive contributions for the world and its inhabitants.[41] This section of our discussion addresses some of the more prominent arguments in this regard.

Free Trade Enhances Socioeconomic Development The proposition that free trade is the best strategy for advancing the world's economic development is one of the few on which the majority of economists agree, not only because it is theoretically compelling, but also because it has been demonstrated in practice.

Data have shown a clear and definitive link between liberalization of trade and economic growth.[42] On a wide range of measures—poverty, education, health, and life expectancy—more people have become better off at a faster pace in the past 60 years than at any other time in history. Evidence is strong regarding the dramatic decline in both the proportion and the absolute number of destitute people. The world development indicators from the World Bank show that the number of people in extreme poverty declined from 35 percent of the world's population in 1990 to only 10.7 percent in 2013, meaning almost 1.1 billion fewer people worldwide were living in extreme poverty.[43] Even in economically advanced countries, studies suggest that

❝EXPANDING TRADE by A GROWING BODY of EVIDENCE SHOWS THAT COUNTRIES THAT ARE MORE OPEN to TRADE GROW FASTER over THE LONG RUN than THOSE THAT REMAIN CLOSED. AND GROWTH DIRECTLY BENEFITS THE WORLD'S POOR.❞

—Horst Kohler, managing director of the International Monetary Fund, and James Wolfensohn, president of the World Bank[46]

the majority of benefits from international trade go to the lower income segments of the population.[44] Overall, the annual benefits of international trade to improved living standards in the United States since World War II has been estimated at $2.1 trillion, meaning that more than one-tenth of what the country produces and consumes is the result of international trade.[45]

Life expectancy in the developing world has nearly doubled since World War II, and infant mortality has decreased in all developing regions of the world. The proportion of children in the labor force has fallen by approximately two-thirds since 1960.[47] Global literacy grew from 52 percent in 1950 to over 86 percent in 2016, and on average the more globally integrated countries spend more on public education, especially in developing countries.[48] In addition, citizens from more globally integrated countries have greater levels of civil liberties and political rights. Within a generation's time, there has been an enormous improvement in the human condition, and every one of the development success stories is based on export-led growth facilitated by the liberalization of trade.

Of course, countries can reject globalization, and some have, including Myanmar, the Democratic Republic of Congo, Sierra Leone, Rwanda, Madagascar, Guinea-Bissau, Algeria, the Republic of Congo, and Burundi. They are among the most impoverished countries in the world. As an article in the *Financial Times* puts it, "They are victims of their refusal to globalize."[49]

Free Trade Promotes More and Better Jobs Expanded trade is also linked with the creation of more and better jobs. Between 1992 and 2018—a period of immense technological change and growth in trade—around 40 million more nonfarm jobs were created than were destroyed in the United States, an increase of nearly 40 percent.[50] It is true that when a country opens to trade, just as when new technologies are developed, some of its sectors may not be competitive. Companies may go out of business, and some jobs will be lost. The general consensus is that more jobs are lost due to technological developments than to the impact of globalization. A recent study estimates that jobs lost in the United States due to imports represented only about 10 percent of overall job displacement, an average of about 312,000 per year from 2001 to 2016, a relatively modest amount in an economy adding about 200,000 jobs per month in recent years.[51] Many of these lost jobs involved standardized, low value adding, repetitive activities. But trade also creates new jobs, and these tend to be better than the ones that were lost, many of them in higher value adding, service-based activities such as design, engineering, finance, and health care. Indeed, between 2001 and 2016, exports alone created over 156,000 jobs per year or about half of the jobs lost to imports.[52] Overall, the benefits from increased international trade have exceeded the costs from lost wages and unemployment by a 50-to-1 ratio since World War II and by a 5-to-1 ratio since 2003.[53] Additional jobs have been created by foreign investment linked to globalization of markets and trade, with many of these new jobs being well-compensated. Indeed, wage rates in U.S.-based subsidiaries of foreign multinationals are about 30 percent above the national average.[54] The key is not to block change but, instead, to manage the costs of trade adjustment and to support the transition of workers to more competitive and higher value-creating employment.

"I think we need to defend, explain and market globalization," said Carlos Ghosn, the Brazilian-Lebanese-French former Chairman and CEO of French automaker Renault SA and also former Chairman of both Nissan Motor and Mitsubishi Motors of Japan. "We assume that the benefits are so obvious that everyone will understand this, but we have been wrong in many cases."[55] What about you? Do you think that economic globalization tends to be a process that creates more benefits than harm and should be encouraged? Or do you think that efforts should be undertaken to limit or even reverse the economic globalization process? Why? Admittedly, this is a complicated issue. Our hope is that by learning about international business, including through books such as this one, you can better understand the complex and interrelated phenomenon of globalization.

RYAN HULTZMAN IN DALIAN, CHINA: Challenge Yourself to Move beyond Your Comfort Zone

Courtesy of Ryan Hultzman.

I am a business major with a concentration in international management and a minor in psychology. At this point, my major career goal is to spend an extended period of time (over a year) working in another country. I know that this probably won't happen right away, but it is something that I will surely work toward. I have always been interested in traveling and learning about different cultures, and international business seemed like a great starting point to be able to eventually work with people from different parts of the world.

I worked in Dalian, China, for five months during the summer and fall of my senior year. I worked with AIESEC (an acronym for the Association Internationale des Étudiants en Sciences Économiques et Commerciales and the world's largest student-led organization) to get an international internship because I couldn't afford to study abroad. I chose to go to China because I wanted to challenge myself. The culture is extremely different from what I grew up with in the United States, and I wanted to live somewhere that would seriously challenge how I viewed the world. China has also been developing very rapidly, so I thought

it would be interesting to experience that kind of growth firsthand.

In China, I worked as an English teacher. I mostly taught children 2–10 years old, but I also taught one adult class for a month. I had only been accepted for this opportunity about a month before I was supposed to start, so my preparation was fairly rushed. I had no background in Mandarin, so I did what I could to learn some basic phrases before I left. I asked around and found a couple of people who had previously spent time working in China and I asked them about their experiences and whether they had any advice for me. I did a lot of research on the city I was going to be living in and tried to learn all I could about everyday life in China. Since I found this opportunity through AIESEC, my living arrangements and transportation from the airport were already established before I left, which was a huge benefit.

The most important thing I did to help myself adjust to the Chinese culture when I was abroad was make a few friends I could really trust. I ended up living in a couple of different places with some great American and Canadian friends that I made, but it was invaluable having a couple of Chinese friends on whom I could rely for help when I needed it. If I ever needed anything—from finding transportation to learning how to ask for a haircut—my friends were willing to provide their assistance.

Another big challenge for me was getting around in China without really knowing the language. Hand gestures can get you pretty far in most cases, but other things like being able to order food in a restaurant with menus that are written only in Chinese characters take some time. I had a Chinese tutor for the first two months, but once I left my first job I couldn't afford tutoring anymore, so I had to become very proactive in learning the necessities. I asked my bilingual friends a lot of questions and made flash cards so I could successfully navigate around the city on my own.

My greatest enjoyment from my time abroad was probably when one of my youngest classes started calling me "gēge lǎoshī" (in Mandarin, lǎoshī means "teacher" and gēge means "older brother"). Initially, the students referred to me as the "foreign teacher," but once they started calling me brother, I couldn't help but feel like my assimilation was complete.

I think my greatest learning points from my international experience have to be the things I learned about myself. I felt like I grew more as a person in the five months I spent in China than at any other time in my life. I have always seen myself as a very independent person, but my time abroad allowed me to prove it. I learned how to put my views and beliefs on hold in order to truly understand where people from different backgrounds are coming from.

As far as recommendations for success abroad, the most important thing is to keep an open mind. People view and value things very differently around the world, and unless you can understand and appreciate their perspective, you won't be successful working with people from other cultures. Also, don't be afraid to step out of your comfort zone when you're abroad. Most of the best stories that I have from my time in China have to do with situations that I wouldn't normally put myself in back home, and that is what made my time abroad so great.

Source: Ryan Hultzman

SUMMARY

LO 1-1
Show how international business differs from domestic business.

International business is business whose activities are carried out across national borders. International business differs from its domestic counterpart in that it involves three environments—domestic, foreign, and international—instead of one. Although the kinds of forces are the same in the domestic and foreign environments, their values often differ, and changes in the values of foreign forces are at times more difficult to assess. The international environment is defined as the interactions (1) between the domestic environmental forces and the foreign environmental forces and (2) between the foreign environmental forces of two countries when an affiliate in one country does business with customers in another.

LO 1-2
Describe the history and future of international business.

International business has a long and important history, extending thousands of years into the past. Politics, the arts, agriculture, industry, public health, and other sectors of human life have been profoundly influenced by the goods and ideas that have come with international trade. Rapid urbanization of populations combined with industrialization in the emerging markets is quickly shifting the world's economic center of gravity from Europe and the Americas back to Asia.

LO 1-3
Discuss the dramatic internationalization of business.

Global competition is mounting as the number of international companies expands rapidly. The huge increase in import penetration, plus the massive amounts of overseas investment, means that firms of all sizes face competitors from everywhere in the world. This increasing internationalization of business is requiring managers to have a global business perspective gained through experience, education, or both.

LO 1-4
Identify the kinds of drivers that are leading firms to internationalize their operations.

The five major kinds of drivers, all based on change, that are leading international firms to globalize their operations are as follows, with an example for each kind: (1) political—preferential trading agreements, (2) technological—advances in communications technology, (3) market—global firms become global customers, (4) cost—globalization of product lines and production helps reduce costs by achieving economies of scale, and (5) competitive—firms are defending their home markets from foreign competitors by entering the foreign competitors' markets.

LO 1-5
Compare the key arguments for and against the globalization of business.

Economic globalization refers to the tendency toward an international integration and interdependency of goods, technology, information, labor, and capital, or the process of making this integration happen. The merits of globalization have been the subject of many heated debates in recent years. Key concerns with the globalization of business include: (1) globalization has produced uneven results across nations and people; (2) globalization has had deleterious effects on labor and labor standards; and (3) globalization has contributed to a decline in environmental and health conditions. Key arguments in support of the globalization of business include: (1) free trade enhances socioeconomic development and (2) free trade promotes more and better jobs.

KEY TERMS

controllable forces 5
domestic environment 5
economic globalization 16
environment 5
exporting 12

foreign business 4
foreign direct investment (FDI) 12
foreign environment 6
importing 12
international business 4

international company (IC) 4
international environment 7
self-reference criterion 7
transnational corporation 11
uncontrollable forces 5

CRITICAL THINKING QUESTIONS

1. Business is business, and every firm has to find ways to produce and market its goods. Why, then, might managers be unable to successfully apply the techniques and concepts they have learned in their own country to other areas of the world?

2. Give examples to show how an international business manager might manipulate one of the controllable forces in answer to a change in the uncontrollable forces.

3. Although forces in the foreign environment are the same as those in the domestic environment, they operate differently. Why is this so?

4. Why, in your opinion, do the authors regard the use of the self-reference criterion as "probably the biggest cause of international business blunders"? Can you think of an example?

5. Discuss some possible conflicts between host governments and foreign-owned companies.

6. "A nation whose GNI is smaller than the sales volume of a global firm is in no position to enforce its wishes on the local subsidiary of that firm." Is this statement true or false? Please explain your rationale.

7. What examples of globalization can you identify within your community? How would you classify each of these examples (as international investment, international trade, other)?

8. Why is there opposition to globalization of trade and integration of the world's economy? Is there a way the debate can move beyond a simplistic argument for or against globalization and toward how best to strengthen the working of the global economy in order to enhance the welfare of the world and its inhabitants? What might this require?

9. You have decided to take a job in your hometown after graduation. Why should you study international business?

globalEDGE RESEARCH TASK　　http://globalEDGE.msu.edu/

Use the globalEDGE website (http://globaledge.msu.edu/) to complete the following exercises:

1. You are assigned the task of identifying a set of indicators that can be used to measure the level of globalization of nations. Choose a country of your choice under the "Global Insights" section of globalEDGE and check the "KOF Index of Globalization" in the "Indices" subsection. What three main aspects of globalization are measured? Now, click the external source link, and using the drop-down menus under the graph on this new page, note the different dimensions used to measure these aspects. Open the "KOF Working Paper" and find what types of indicators are used to calculate these dimensions. What do you think about the calculation method of those dimensions? How relevant are the indicators used? What other dimensions and indicators can be used to measure globalization?

2. You are interested in finding out whether the development level of a country and its most developed industries are related to its socioeconomic characteristics. You selected the United States, Mexico, and Uganda as your sample. Locate each country under the "Global Insights" section of globalEDGE. First, check the age distribution of their total population in the "Statistics" subsection, then, find their per capita GDP in the "Economy" subsection and take notes. Finally, check the total export amounts and top-10 exported products in the "Trade Statistics" sub-sections. What are some of the trends you noticed? How is age distribution related to the per capita GDP, international trade volume, and the types of products exported by the country? Can you use socioeconomic features of a country as a predictor for the level of development and guess the most developed industries in the country? How?

MINICASE

ARE YOU REALLY BUYING AMERICAN?

Consider the following scenario of a "typical" American family: The Osbornes, Jesse and Ann, live in the suburbs of Chicago. Jesse is a manager at Trader Joe's specialty grocery store chain. Ann is an advertising executive for Leo Burnett Worldwide.

Ann listens to the new Adam Lambert CD on her Alpine car stereo in her Jeep Cherokee while driving home from work, stopping for gas at the Shell station. At the grocery store, she fills her cart with a variety of items, including Ragu spaghetti sauce, Hellmann's mayonnaise, Carnation Instant Breakfast drink, CoffeeMate nondairy coffee creamer, Chicken-of-the-Sea canned tuna, Lipton tea, Dannon yogurt, several packages of Stouffer's Lean Cuisine frozen dinners, and some Hot Pockets. For a treat, she picks up some Ben & Jerry's ice cream, Toll House cookies, a Butterfinger candy bar, and some Tic Tacs. She also grabs some cans of Alpo for their dog, Sassy, and a box of Friskies and a bag of Tidy Cat cat litter for their cat, Lily. She goes down the toiletries aisle for some Dove soap, Aquafresh toothpaste, Q-tips cotton swabs, Tums, Vaseline lip gloss, and Jergen's moisturizing lotion. Before finishing, she calls Jesse on her Samsung smartphone to see whether there is anything else he needs. He asks her to pick up a case of Arrowhead water for use after his lunchtime workouts at the gym. She also stops at the bookstore and picks up the new Danielle Steele book published by Random House, signing the credit card slip with her Bic pen.

After leaving his office, Jesse stops at the BP gas station to fill his gas tank and checks the air pressure in his Firestone tires. He heads to the liquor store for a case of Budweiser beer and a bottle of Wild Turkey bourbon, then walks next door to the sporting goods store to pick up some Wilson racquetballs.

Ann's favorite TV show, *Jeopardy,* is just starting as Jesse comes in the door, so she pours herself a glass of Beringer wine from Napa Valley and turns on their Philips ultra high-definition television while Jesse prepares dinner and downloads the latest *Spiderman* installment onto his Lenovo computer.

While this may sound like a very typical evening for many Americans, foreign-owned firms produced nearly every item the Osbornes purchased or consumed:

- Trader Joe's is owned by a family trust set up by German businessman Theo Albrecht.
- Leo Burnett Worldwide is owned by Publicis of France.
- Sony Music of Japan produces and distributes Adam Lambert's CDs.
- Japan's Alps Electric produces Alpine car stereos.
- Jeeps are a brand of vehicles made by Chrysler, which is owned by Italy's Fiat.
- The British-Dutch company Royal Dutch Shell owns Shell.
- Nestlé of Switzerland produces Alpo, Arrowhead, Butterfinger, Carnation Instant Breakfast, CoffeeMate,

Friskies, Hot Pockets, Stouffer's Lean Cuisine, Toll House, and Tidy Cat.
- Unilever, a British-Dutch multinational, makes Dove soap, Hellmann's, Q-tips, Lipton, Vaseline, and Ben & Jerry's.
- Mizkan Group, a Japanese company, produces Ragu.
- Groupe Danone of France produces Dannon yogurt.
- Chicken-of-the-Sea tuna is made by Chicken of the Sea International, which is based in Thailand.
- Tums and Aquafresh are produced by GlaxoSmithKline of the United Kingdom.
- Ferrero SpA of Italy produces Tic Tacs.
- Japan's Kao owns Jergen's.
- Samsung smartphones are made by South Korea's Samsung.
- Bertelsmann AG of Germany owns 75 percent of Penguin Random House, and Pearson plc of the United Kingdom owns the remaining 25 percent.
- Société Bic of France produces Bic pens.
- Japan's Bridgestone Corporation owns Firestone.
- BP of the United Kingdom owns BP gas stations.
- Columbia Pictures, owned by Sony of Japan, released the *Spiderman* movies; Sony Pictures Television distributes *Jeopardy.*
- AB InBev of Belgium produces Budweiser.
- Davide Campari of Italy owns the Wild Turkey brand.
- Amer Sports of Finland owns Wilson Sporting Goods.
- Beringer Winery of Napa, California, is owned by Australia's Treasury Wine Estates.
- Philips televisions are sold by Philips of the Netherlands.
- Lenovo computers are produced by Lenovo of China.

This simple example reflects the impact of extensive foreign investments in the United States, especially in recent years. Even some of the best-known "American" products and brands are now produced by foreign firms.

Investments have also flowed outward from the United States. U.S. companies such as Coca-Cola, Starbucks, McDonald's, the Gap, Microsoft, and Levi's are found in Japan, South Korea, China, Australia, Singapore, and nearly every European nation. U.S. companies have also purchased a range of foreign companies and brands.

Critical Thinking Questions

1. Should it matter to consumers whether the companies that make their products are based in the consumers' home country or not? Explain your rationale.

2. Why has there been almost no negative backlash among Americans to the flood of foreign investment into their country?

Sources: From company websites (July 4, 2018).

NOTES

1. Nicholas Platt, President Emeritus of the Asia Society.

2. For example, see Marek Strzelecki, and Konrad Krasuski, "JPMorgan to hire 'thousands' for operations hub in Poland," *Bloomberg,* September 22, 2017, http://www.bloomberg.com, accessed August 17, 2018; and Dorota Bartyzel, and Konrad Krasuski, "Brexit Flight to Shift 30,000 Jobs to Poland, Minister Says," *Bloomberg,* January 23, 2017, http://www.bloomberg.com, accessed August 17, 2018.

3. For example, see "Companies Moving HQs and Jobs from London since Brexit Vote," *Associated Press,* August 17, 2018, https://www.independent.ie, accessed August 17, 2018; and Suzi Ring, "Brexit Deal Too Late to Stop Some EU Firms from Moving Business," *Bloomberg,* March 19, 2018, http://www.bloomberg.com, accessed August 17, 2018.

4. David Cay Johnston, "How Google and Apple Make Their Taxes Disappear," *Newsweek,* http://www.newsweek.com, accessed July 04, 2018.

5. Michael Stothard, "Catalan Business Exodus Signals Deep Corporate Concerns," *Financial Times,* https://www.ft.com, accessed July 04, 2018.

6. Leonid Bershidsky, "Russia Sanctions' Big Winners Smell Like Fish," *Bloomberg,* https://www.bloomberg.com, accessed July 04, 2018.

7. Stratfor, "Mexico Moves to Open Its Energy Sector," *Stratfor. com,* January 04, 2015.

8. U.S. Department of Commerce, International Trade Administration, Greece Country Commercial Guide, "Greece-1-Openness to and Restrictions upon Foreign Investment," https://www.export.gov, accessed July 04, 2018; U.S. Department of State, Bureau of Economic and Business Affairs, 2017 Investment Climate Statements—Greece, June 29, 2017, https://www.state.gov, accessed July 04, 2018.

9. Jack Welch, former CEO of General Electric.

10. "Black Death," https://www.history.com, accessed June 22, 2018; Encyclopedia Britannica, "Black Death," https://www.britannica.com, accessed June 22, 2018; and Robbie Robertson, "Globalization Is Not Made in the West," http://www.globalpolicy.org, accessed June 22, 2018.

11. "A Quick Guide to the World History of Globalization," http://www.sas.upenn.edu, accessed July 04, 2018; "Dutch East India Company," http://en.wikipedia.org, accessed July 04, 2018; BBC News, "Globalization: What on Earth Is It About?" http://news.bbc.co.uk, accessed July 04, 2018; and "The Growth of Global Industry," *The Wheel Extended,* vol. 4, 1989, 11.

12. Bruce Kogut, "Multinational Corporations," 2001, https://www.gsb.columbia.edu/faculty/bkogut/files/Chapter_in_smelser-Baltes_2001.pdf, July 04, 2018; and "Multinationals Come into Their Own," *Financial Times,* December 06, 1999, 16.

13. Bayer, "This Is Bayer: History: Overview," http://www.bayer.com, accessed July 04, 2018.

14. Alfred D. Chandler Jr., and Bruce Mazlish, eds., *Leviathans: Multinational Corporations and the New Global History,* New York: Cambridge University Press, 2005, 66, 88–89.

15. McKinsey Global Institute, *Urban World: Cities and the Rise of the Consuming Class,* June 2012, http://www.mckinsey.com/insights, accessed July 04, 2018.

16. Malgorzata Jaworek, and Marcin Kuzel, "Transnational Corporations in the World Economy: Formation, Development and Present Position," *Copernican Journal of Finance & Accounting,* vol. 4, no. 1, 2015, 55–70, http://apcz.umk.pl, accessed July 04, 2018.

17. M. Kordos, and S. Vojtovic, "Transnational Corporations in The Global World Economic Environment," *Procedia–Social and Behavioral Sciences,* vol. 230, 2016, 150–58.

18. UN Conference on Trade and Development, Table 1.7: Internationalization Statistics of the 100 "argest Non-financial MNEs, Worldwide and from Developing and Transition Economies," *World Investment Report 2018,* Geneva: United Nations, 2018, 29.

19. Alvaro Cuervo-Cazurra, Andrew Inkpen, Aldo Musacchio, and Kannan Ramaswamyi, "Governments as Owners: State-owned Multinational Companies," *Journal of International Business Studies,* vol. 45, no. 8, 2014, 919–42, https://link.springer.com/article/10.1057/jibs.2014.43; UN Conference on Trade and Development, *World Investment Report 2014,* Geneva: United Nations, 2014.

20. UN Conference on Trade and Development, *World Investment Report 2014,* Geneva: United Nations, 2014.

21. The World Bank, "GNI, Atlas Method (current US$)," https://data.worldbank.org, accessed July 04, 2018.

22. Calculation based on information found in *Walmart 2018 Annual Report,* http://s2.q4cdn.com/056532643/files/doc_financials/2018/annual/WMT-2018_Annual-Report.pdf, where value added is based on net operating profit before tax.

23. UN Conference on Trade and Development, "Annex Table 4: FDI Outward Stock, by Region and Economy, 1990–2017," *World Investment Report 2018,* http://unctad.org, accessed July 04, 2018.

24. UN Conference on Trade and Development, "Merchandise: Total trade and share, annual, 1948–2017," http://unctadstat.unctad.org, accessed July 04, 2018.

25. UN Conference on Trade and Development, "Services (BPM5): Exports and Imports of Total Services, Value, Shares and Growth, Annual, 1980–2013," http://unctadstat.unctad.org, accessed July 4, 2018; UN Conference on Trade and Development, "Services (BPM6): Exports and imports of Total Services, Value, Shares, and Growth, Annual, 2005–2017," http://unctadstat.unctad.org, accessed July 04, 2018.

26. Trends regarding FDI and exporting, along with theories that help explain the level and location of exports and FDI, are discussed in Module 2.

27. Askja Energy, "The largest consumers of electricity in Iceland," January 07, 2018, http://www.askjaenergy.com, accessed August 17, 2018.

28. World Health Organization, "Globalization," http://www.who.int, accessed July 04, 2018; British Broadcasting Corporation, "Negative Impacts of Globalisation," http://www.bbc.co.uk, accessed July 04, 2018; Fred W. Riggs, "Globalization Is a Fuzzy Term But It May Convey Special Meanings," The Theme of the IPSA World Congress 2000, July 1999, http://www2.hawaii.edu/~fredr/ipsaglo.htm, May 28, 2011; Abderrahman Hassi, and Giovanna Storti, "Globalization and Culture: The Three H Scenarios," *Intechopen,* http://www.intechopen.com, accessed July 04, 2018.

29. Theodore Levitt, "The Globalization of Markets," *Harvard Business Review,* vol. 61, no. 3, 1983, 92–93.

30. For more information on the issue of globalization, please see sources such as Gary Burtless, Robert Z. Lawrence, Robert E. Litan, and Robert J. Shapiro, *Globaphobia: Confronting Fears about Open Trade*, Washington, DC: Brookings Institution Press, 1998; Gary J. Wells, *The Issue of Globalization—An Overview*, Washington, DC: Congressional Research Service, 2001, https://digitalcommons.ilr. cornell.edu, accessed July 04, 2018; Alan Tonelson, *The Race to the Bottom: Why a Worldwide Worker Surplus and Uncontrolled Free Trade Are Sinking American Living Standards*, Boulder, CO: Westview Press, 2002; International Monetary Fund, "Globalization: A Brief Overview," https://www.imf.org, accessed July 04, 2018; Pat Choate, *Dangerous Business: The Risks of Globalization for America*, New York: Knopf, 2008; Daniel Griswold, "The Blessings and Challenges of Globalization," Cato Institute, http://www.cato.org, accessed July 04, 2018; John Audley, Sandra Polaski, Demetrios G. Papademetriou, and Scott Vaughan, *NAFTA's Promise and Reality: Lessons from Mexico for the Hemisphere*, Washington, DC: Carnegie Endowment for International Peace, 2003.

31. "Trade Liberalisation Statistics," gatt.org, http://www.gatt.org/ trastat_e.html, February 01, 2015.

32. World Bank, "Poverty–Overview," http://www.worldbank.org, accessed July 04, 2018; United Nations, *The Millennium Development Goals Report 2014*, http://www.un.org, accessed July 04, 2018.

33. Greg Autry, "Is the Global Trade System Broken?" *The Economist*, https://debates.economist.com, May 07, 2018.

34. Martin Wolf, *Why Globalization Works*, New Haven, CT: Yale University Press, 2004.

35. As quoted in Kate Ackley, "Trade Policy Hardly on Labor's Fast Track," September 25, 2013, https://www.rollcall.com, accessed August 17, 2018.

36. Public Citizen, *NAFTA's 20-Year Legacy and the Fate of the Trans-Pacific Partnership*, Washington, DC: Public Citizen's Global Trade Watch, 2014.

37. Ajai Gaur, and Ram Mudambi, "Four Fallacies about Trade and Globalization," *YaleGlobal Online Magazine*, https://yaleglobal.yale. edu, accessed July 04, 2018.

38. Burless et al., *Globaphobia*.

39. Laura Carlsen, "Under NAFTA, Mexico Suffered, and the United States Felt Its Pain," *New York Times*, November 24, 2013, http://www.nytimes.com, accessed August 17, 2018.

40. Ernesto Zedillo, "Can We Take Open Markets for Granted?" Plenary Session of World Economic Forum Davos, Switzerland,

January 28, 2000, http://zedillo.presidencia.gob.mx, accessed July 04, 2018.

41. International Chamber of Commerce, "ICC Brief on Globalization," July 04, 2003, https://www.osce.org/secretariat/42286? download=true, accessed July 04, 2018; Paul Krugman, "The Good News," *New York Times*, November 28, 2003, p. A31, http://www. nytimes.com/2003/11/28/opinion/the-good-news.html, accessed July 04, 2018; Horst Kohler and James Wolfensohn, "We Can Trade Up to a Better World," *Financial Times*, December 12, 2003, https://www.imf. org/external/np/vc/2003/121003.htm, accessed July 04, 2018; and Wolf, *Why Globalization Works*.

42. World Trade Organization, "The Case for Open Trade," http:// www.wto.org, accessed July 04, 2018.

43. World Bank, "Poverty–Overview."

44. Sarah Green Carmichael, and Pankaj Ghemawat, "Globalization: Myth and Reality," *Harvard Business Review*, https:// hbr.org, accessed February 24, 2017.

45. Gary Clyde Hufbauer, and Zhiyao Lu, *The Payoff to America from Globalization: A Fresh Look with a Focus on Costs to Workers*, Washington, DC: Peterson Institute for International Economics, 2017, https://pie.com, accessed July 04, 2018.

46. Kohler and Wolfensohn, "We Can Trade Up to a Better World."

47. United Nations, "Child Labour," http://www.un.org, accessed July 04, 2018; World Bank, *Facts and Figures on Child Labour*, 1999, http:// info.worldbank.org/etools/docs/library/237384/toolkitfr/pdf/facts.pdf, accessed February 01, 2015; UNICEF, "Child Labor," http://data.unicef. org/child-protection/child-labour, accessed February 01, 2015.

48. World Bank, "Literacy Rate, Adult Total (% of People Ages 15 and Above)," https://data.worldbank.org, accessed July 04, 2018.

49. Kohler and Wolfensohn, "We Can Trade Up to a Better World."

50. U.S. Bureau of Labor Statistics, "Charting the Labor Market: Data from the Current Population Survey (CPS)," June 01, 2018, https://www.bls.gov.

51. Hufbauer, and Lu, *The Payoff to America from Globalization*.

52. Ibid.

53. Ibid.

54. Gaur, and Mudambi, "Four Fallacies about Trade and Globalization."

55. Sean McLain, "Carlos Ghosn: Politicians need to be better at defending globalization," *Wall Street Journal*, https://www.wsj.com, accessed July 04, 2018.

2 International Trade and Investment

> **If you care about global poverty and, for that matter, about equality, your aim should be to raise the growth rates of poor countries. Successful countries have all exploited global market opportunities, predominantly international trade and, to a more variable extent, foreign direct investment, to accelerate their growth.**
>
> *—Martin Wolf, chief economics commentator, Financial Times*[1]

©Will Austin/Spaces Images/Blend Images.

LEARNING OBJECTIVES

After reading this module, you should be able to:

LO 2-1 **Describe** the magnitude of international trade and how it has grown.

LO 2-2 **Identify** who participates in trade.

LO 2-3 **Distinguish** among the theories that explain why certain goods are traded internationally.

LO 2-4 **Describe** the size, growth, and direction of foreign direct investment.

LO 2-5 **Explain** several of the theories of foreign direct investment.

Firms Invest Overseas, but They Also Export

Global competition, liberalized trade policies of foreign governments, and advances in technology were major reasons that foreign direct investment (FDI) from the United States to the rest of the world was nearly $1.5 trillion from 2013 to 2017. This volume of FDI represented an annual average investment more than double the U.S. average from 1995 to 2005. Because FDI generally is used to set up or acquire assets for producing goods and services abroad, we might expect that as FDI increases, U.S. exports would decline. Have they?

Apparently not. Although some flows of exported goods and services from the United States to foreign markets have been replaced by production from these investments abroad, the overall level of U.S. exports of goods and services was over $2.3 trillion in 2017, about triple the level in 1995, as shown in Figure 2.1. Over half the total exports were made by the 250 largest exporters, many of whom sell to 100 countries or more. Their competitiveness would be seriously damaged without sales and profit generated from foreign operations; some might be unable to remain in business. Yet, even large

multinationals with numerous production facilities overseas often find that having a factory in every market is not feasible due to the large amount of foreign investment required. In addition, many markets are too small to support local manufacturing; they must be served by exports.

Although supplying overseas markets is essential to most major U.S. corporations, smaller firms also conduct activities abroad. Small and medium-sized enterprises (SMEs) are companies with fewer than 500 employees, and they account for nearly 98 percent of all U.S. exporters and about one-third of U.S. exports' total value. Canada and Mexico, the two countries that share a border with the United States and are its partners in the North American Free Trade Agreement (NAFTA), were the most frequent export markets for SMEs, followed by China, Japan, Germany, and the United Kingdom. Unlike large multinationals, more than half of all SME exporters operate from a single location in the United States. Because they lack offshore subsidiaries that can circumvent trade barriers and improve access to foreign markets, these SMEs are more dependent than large multinational companies on government initiatives intended to open foreign markets to trade. Because of the potential impact on growth and

FIGURE 2.1 U.S. Exports of Goods and Services in Billions of Dollars, 1990–2017

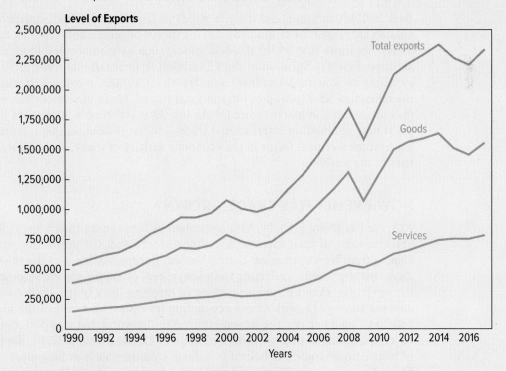

Sources: "U.S. Trade in Goods and Services—Balance of Payments (BOP) Basis," *U.S. Census Bureau, Foreign Trade Division,* June 6, 2018; "Goods Exports (BOP, current US$)," *The World Bank Group,* 2018; "Service Exports (BOP, current US$)," *The World Bank Group,* 2018; and "Exports of Goods and Services (BOP, current US$)," *The World Bank Group,* 2018.

profit, it is important for businesspeople to understand why and how to engage in international trade and foreign investment.

Much of the food we eat, the clothes we wear, the vehicles we drive, and the electronic goods we use are produced in other countries. Many of our jobs are dependent on exports, imports, or foreign investment. In this module, we examine (1) *international trade*, which includes exports and imports, and (2) *foreign direct investment*, which international companies make to establish and expand their overseas operations.

Sources: "Annex Table 02—FDI Outflows, by Region and Economy, 1990–2017," United Nations Conference on Trade and Development, 2018; "The FDI Report 2018: Global Greenfield Investment Trends," *Financial Times*, 2018; and "Profile of U.S. Importing and Exporting Companies, 2015–2016," *U.S. Census Bureau, Department of Commerce*, April 5, 2018.

LO 2-1
Describe the magnitude of international trade and how it has grown.

International Trade

In this section, we discuss who trades with whom and who are the largest importers and exporters in the world. We'll find out what the trend toward regionalization of international trade is about, including where it's happening and why. We'll see why knowledge of a nation's major trading partners is important for managers, and finally, we'll examine some leading theories that help explain why international trade occurs and how participants benefit from it.

VOLUME OF INTERNATIONAL TRADE

Back in 1990, international trade in goods and services reached a milestone when its volume surpassed $4 trillion. By 2017, exports of goods and services had grown to almost six times that level.[3] Physical goods, such as automobiles, food, and clothing, accounted for $17.5 trillion of the $23 trillion in international trade in 2017. Services, including such activities as insurance, travel, consulting, movies, and music, made up the remaining $5.4 trillion of international trade.[4] Trade in services has been growing faster than trade in merchandise for the last 20 years. Nearly 60 percent of global output is now destined for international trade—another indication that international trade has become a critical factor in the economic activity of many, if not most, of the countries of the world.[5]

HOW EVENLY HAS TRADE GROWN?

As trade has grown globally, have some nations fared better than others? Although the absolute value of their merchandise exports increased, the proportion of world trade coming from North America, Latin America, Europe, Africa, and the Middle East has *decreased* since 1983, reflecting the greater level of export growth in other regions of the world. For example, the proportion of merchandise exports from Asia has almost doubled since 1983, with China accounting for over 83 percent of the increase.[6] Not only has China become the largest exporter in the world, but also 500 million Chinese have been lifted out of poverty by their country's trade-driven policies. Rapid expansion of international trade has helped transform countries such as Singapore, Taiwan, and South Korea from conditions of Third World poverty in the 1950s to developed-country standards of living. Although the European Union has only modestly decreased its proportion of world trade, that result is largely attributable to the European Union's expansion to 28 member-countries.

What about service exports? Many services, such as travel and tourism, banking and insurance services, education and training, entertainment (such as videogames and movies), and architectural and engineering services, are sold to customers in other countries and make up a growing part of international business. All regions and essentially all the primary-world nations experienced an absolute increase in the dollar volume of their services exports, although the proportion of world exports of commercial services from Latin America, the European Union, Africa, and the Middle East has declined since 1980. However, the United States' proportion has risen by approximately one-third since 1980, and Asia's proportion has grown at an even greater rate, with China accounting for the largest part of that growth.[7]

Rapid expansion of world exports since 1980 demonstrates that the opportunity to increase sales by exporting is a viable growth strategy and one that can benefit exporting nations by creating jobs for their citizens. At the same time, however, the growth of exports from individual nations should be a warning to managers that they must be prepared to meet increased competition from these exports in their own domestic markets.

WHICH NATIONS ACCOUNT FOR THE MOST EXPORTS AND IMPORTS?

Table 2.1 presents the world's 10 largest nations in terms of exports and imports of merchandise and services. As you can see, they are generally developed countries, although China ranks in the top 5 on each list and India in the top 10 for both imports and exports of services. These 10 largest exporters and importers collectively account for over half the world's exports and imports, which highlights the fact that international trade continues to be unevenly distributed across countries and regions of the world.

> **"THE GLOBAL ECONOMY HAS BEEN TRANSFORMED** by **ADVANCES in INFORMATION AND COMMUNICATION TECHNOLOGY, MAKING IT POSSIBLE for COMPANIES** to **SHIFT PRODUCTION RAPIDLY** around **THE WORLD in SEARCH for LOWER WAGES AND NOVEL MARKETS. "**
>
> —Elisha Woyo, researcher, Zimbabwe[8]

TABLE 2.1 10 Leading Exporters and Importers in World Merchandise and Commercial Services, 2016 ($ billions)

Merchandise Exporters			Merchandise Importers			Service Exporters			Service Importers		
Rank	Nation	Value	Rank	Nation	Value	Rank	Nation	Value	Rank	Nation	Value
1	China	$2098	1	United States	$2251	1	United States	$733	1	United States	$482
2	United States	1455	2	China	1587	2	United Kingdom	324	2	China	450
3	Germany	1340	3	Germany	1055	3	Germany	268	3	Germany	311
4	Japan	645	4	United Kingdom	636	4	France	236	4	France	236
5	Netherlands	570	5	Japan	607	5	China	207	5	United Kingdom	195
6	France	501	6	France	573	6	Netherlands	177	6	Ireland	192
7	South Korea	495	7	Netherlands	503	7	Japan	169	7	Japan	183
8	Italy	462	8	Canada	417	8	India	161	8	Netherlands	169
9	United Kingdom	409	9	South Korea	406	9	Singapore	149	9	Singapore	155
10	Belgium	396	10	Italy	404	10	Ireland	146	10	India	133

Sources: Central Intelligence Agency, *The World Factbook*, https://www.cia.gov, accessed July 4, 2018; World Trade Organization, *World Statistical Review* 2017, https://www.wto.org, accessed July 4, 2018; and United Nations Conference on Trade and Development, "UNCTADSTAT," http://unctadstat.unctad.org, accessed July 4, 2018.

LO 2-2

Identify who participates in trade.

Direction of Trade

Where are all these merchandise exports going? You might think international trade consists mainly of manufactured goods exported by industrialized nations to developing nations in return for raw materials. This is only partially correct. A major portion of the exports from developing nations do go to developed countries, but this proportion has declined from 72 percent in 1970 to about 43 percent by 2015 as developing nations participate more extensively in trade with other developing nations.[9] About two-thirds of exports from developed economies go to other industrialized nations.

THE INCREASING REGIONALIZATION OF TRADE

World trade continues to be dominated by exchanges within—not between—geographic regions. For example, in 2017, approximately half the exports from North American nations went to other nations in North America. Most of Canada's exports go to the United States and nearly 20 percent of U.S. exports go to Canada, mainly as a result of NAFTA and other treaties between the two nations.[10] In 2017, U.S. exports to Mexico (the other NAFTA signatory) were approximately six times the level in 1991.[11] Similarly, a little more than half of Asian nations' exports went to other Asian nations, and over 70 percent of exports from European nations went to other European countries.[12]

This regionalization of trade is being reinforced by the development of expanded regional trade associations and agreements, such as the Association of Southeast Asian Nations (ASEAN, which includes Brunei, Cambodia, Indonesia, Laos, Malaysia, Myanmar, Philippines, Singapore, Thailand, and Vietnam); Mercosur in South America (composed of full members Argentina, Brazil, Paraguay, and Uruguay,[13] and associate members Bolivia, Chile, Peru, Columbia, Ecuador, and Suriname); and the 28-nation European Union.[14] Overall, the three largest regional trade agreements, the European Union, ASEAN, and NAFTA, accounted for 55 percent of total world exports and 58 percent of total world imports.[15] There are more than 260 regional trade agreements in operation worldwide, and the share of world trade they account for increased from 37 percent in 1980 to more than 70 percent by 2018.

At the same time, U.S. exporters have made major inroads in developing country markets, which, in turn, are selling more to the United States. This growth is due in part to developing countries' increasing ability to export manufactured goods. It also reflects the growing volume of trade among international companies' affiliates around the world, such as when a clothing manufacturer sends cloth manufactured in its Indian operations to its production facility in Bangladesh, where the cloth will be sewn into garments. The fact that members of trade groups are increasingly selling to one another will influence international companies' choices of locations for their plants and other operations.

MAJOR TRADING PARTNERS: THEIR RELEVANCE FOR MANAGERS

Suppose we want to consider looking for business opportunities abroad. Why should we know which countries are our own nation's major trade partners? Here are some of the advantages:

1. The business climate in these importing nations is already relatively favorable.
2. Export and import regulations are not insurmountable.
3. There should be no strong cultural objections at home to buying that nation's goods.
4. Satisfactory transportation facilities have already been established.
5. Import channel members (merchants, banks, and customs brokers) are experienced in handling import shipments from the exporter's area.
6. Currency from the foreign country is available to pay for the exports.
7. The government of a trading partner may be applying pressure on its importers to buy from countries that, like the United States, are good customers for that nation's exports.

These sorts of advantages promote the expansion of trade among countries that are major trading partners, and their presence may present a company with improved prospects for expanding its international trade activities.

MAJOR TRADING PARTNERS OF THE UNITED STATES

Figure 2.2 shows the major trading partners of the United States. The top 10 accounted for 66 percent of total U.S. exports and 70 percent of total U.S. imports in 2017.[16] The data suggest the United States generally follows the trend we identified earlier—developed nations trade with one another and members of regional trade agreements trade with one another. Mexico and Canada are major U.S. trading partners in great part because they are part of NAFTA. They also each share a common border with the United States, which means lower freight charges, shorter delivery times, and easier and less expensive contacts between buyers and sellers than would otherwise be the case.

Of the top 15 nations from which the United States imports, seven (Canada, Mexico, Japan, Germany, United Kingdom, Italy, and France) have consistently remained on the list over the past 45 years, although their rankings have changed over time. Besides the long-term trade partner, Japan, nations from Asia have become increasingly important trade partners in recent years. China, South Korea, India, Vietnam, Taiwan, and Malaysia supply the United States with huge quantities of electronic products and components as well as a variety of largely labor-intensive manufactured goods, many of which are produced by affiliates of U.S.-based international companies. Apple, Nike, Walmart, and VF Corporation (an apparel manufacturer whose brands include The North Face, Vans, Wrangler, and JanSport) are among the many multinationals that source extensively from affiliates and supplier companies based in China. Between 1991 and 2017, China rose from sixth to first place in exports to the United States, and to third place as an importer of U.S. goods. Although, note

FIGURE 2.2 Major Trading Partners of the United States, Goods Only, 2017 ($ billions; % of total trade)

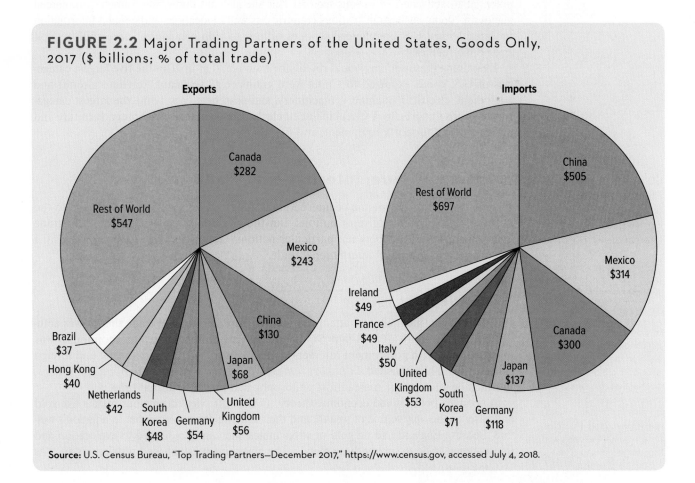

Exports

- Canada $282
- Mexico $243
- China $130
- Japan $68
- United Kingdom $56
- Germany $54
- South Korea $48
- Netherlands $42
- Hong Kong $40
- Brazil $37
- Rest of World $547

Imports

- China $505
- Mexico $314
- Canada $300
- Japan $137
- Germany $118
- South Korea $71
- United Kingdom $53
- Italy $50
- France $49
- Ireland $49
- Rest of World $697

Source: U.S. Census Bureau, "Top Trading Partners—December 2017," https://www.census.gov, accessed July 4, 2018.

trade deficit
The amount by which the value
of imports into a nation
exceeds the value of its
exports

that the $130 billion level of Chinese imports was only about one-quarter of the level of exports it sent to the United States, resulting in an annual difference of approximately one-third of a trillion dollars. This difference is a trade deficit—the amount by which the value of imports into the nation exceeds the value of its exports. Trade deficits can be the source of economic, political, and other concerns, as suggested by the Trump administration's recent efforts to renegotiate trade treaties, impose tariffs, or engage in other actions to reduce the deficit between the United States and many of its trading partners, including China.

Many Asian countries are both import and export partners of the United States because (1) their rising standards of living enable their residents to afford more imported products, and the countries' export earnings provide the monies necessary to pay for them; (2) they are purchasing large amounts of capital goods to further their industrial expansion; (3) they are importing raw materials and components that will be assembled into subassemblies or finished goods that will subsequently be exported, often to the United States; and (4) their governments, pressured by the U.S. government to lower their trade surplus—the amount by which the value of a nation's exports exceeds the value of its imports—have sent buying missions to the United States to look for products to import.

trade surplus
The amount by which the value
of a nation's exports exceeds
the value of its imports

What kinds of products do these countries import from the United States? The U.S. Census Bureau maintains a site with downloadable files of trade statistics. One entry, "About the Foreign Trade Programs and Products" (http://www.census.gov/foreign-trade/about/index.html), contains extensive links to statistics on exports and imports, as well as information about the exporter database of all U.S. exporters. Another entry, "Foreign Trade—Trade Highlights" (http://www.foreign-trade.com/highlights.htm), has links to data on top trading partners by year, country, industry, product, and state. There are also tables on the Commerce Department's export website (https://www.export.gov) that list imports and exports from a range of different industries. These tables present multiyear data on levels of imports and exports between the United States and the other countries, providing an idea of the size and potential attractiveness of various sectors. This site also has numerous country commercial guides for "doing business in" various countries, as well as locations and contact information for international U.S. commercial services offices, to help companies successfully exploit trade opportunities.

Examining these sources would reveal, for example, that in 2016 the five largest categories of U.S. goods exported to China were grains (e.g., soybeans), civilian aircraft and equipment, electrical machinery, machinery, and passenger cars, while the largest categories of goods imports from China included electrical machinery, machinery, furniture and bedding, toys and sports equipment, and footwear.[17]

Explaining Trade: International Trade Theories

LO 2-3
Distinguish among the
theories that explain why
certain goods are traded
internationally.

We have seen that the volume of international trade is large, growing, and critical to the economic performance of most nations. But the question remains: why does this trade occur, both overall and between particular nations? To answer, we will briefly examine several leading theories of international trade.

MERCANTILISM

A profoundly influential early attempt to develop an international trade theory was actually politically motivated. Adam Smith, a Scottish philosopher and economist, was incensed by British government intervention and control over both domestic and foreign trade. In 1776, he published *An Inquiry into the Nature and Causes of the Wealth of Nations*, in which he attacked the mercantilist philosophy that prevailed at that time.

mercantilism
An economic philosophy
based on the belief that (1) a
nation's wealth depends on
accumulated treasure, usually
precious metals such as gold
and silver; and (2) to increase
wealth, government policies
should promote exports and
discourage imports

A complex political and economic theory, mercantilism viewed precious metals like gold and silver as the only source of wealth, and their accumulation as essential to a nation's welfare. Because England had no gold or silver mines, mercantilists looked to exploration and international trade to supply these metals. The government established restrictions such as import duties to reduce imports and subsidies to exporters to increase exports. In addition to protecting jobs within the mercantilist nation, those acts created a trade surplus meant to generate increased holdings of gold and silver. Of course, mercantilism also generated benefits for certain economic groups, such as domestic merchants, artisans, and shippers, though at a cost to other groups such as consumers and emerging industrialists.

Although the mercantilist era ended in the late 1700s, its arguments live on. Many people see trade as a zero-sum activity, in which one party must lose in order for another to gain. We still use the term "favorable" trade balance to mean a nation exports more goods and services than it imports. In balance-of-payments accounting, an export that brings money to the country is called *positive*, but imports that cause monetary outflows are labeled *negative*.

Many of the world's managers see China as a present-day "fortress of mercantilism" that raises barriers to imported goods while giving its own exporters an unfair advantage. Despite impressive economic growth and burgeoning trade surpluses, Chinese authorities have limited the extent to which that country's currency, the yuan, can appreciate in value relative to the U.S. dollar. The Chinese authorities have improved the international cost-competitiveness of Chinese companies relative to those of other nations. One study argues that 40 percent of the price advantage of Chinese companies is due to the mercantilist policies of their central government, including an undervalued currency, export subsidies, and lax regulatory oversight.[18] Some international observers have also suggested that the United States has adopted a more mercantilist approach in recent years.[19]

THEORY OF ABSOLUTE ADVANTAGE

Adam Smith argued against mercantilism by claiming that market forces, not government controls, should determine the direction, volume, and composition of international trade. He advocated free, unregulated trade, in which each nation should specialize in making those goods it could produce most efficiently—goods for which it had an absolute advantage, either natural or acquired. **Absolute advantage** exists when a nation can produce more of a good or service than another country for the same or lower cost of inputs. Nations would then export some goods to pay for imports that have been produced more efficiently elsewhere. With his theory of absolute advantage, Smith showed that both nations gain from trade.

Absolute Advantage: An Example Assume a world of two countries and two products, with no transportation costs and **perfect competition**, a market situation in which there is a sufficiently large number of well-informed buyers and sellers of a homogeneous product such that no individual participant has enough power to determine the price of the product, resulting in a marketplace that is efficient in production and allocation of products. Suppose that in the United States and China (a) one unit of input (a combination of land, labor, and capital) can produce the quantities of soybeans and cloth listed in the following table; (b) each nation has two input units it can use to produce either soybeans or cloth; and (c) each country currently uses one unit of input to produce each product. If neither country imports nor exports, the quantities shown in the table are also those that are available for local consumption. The total output of the two nations is 4 tons of soybeans and 6 bolts of cloth.

absolute advantage
A nation's ability to produce more of a good or service than another country for the same or lower cost of inputs

perfect competition
A market situation in which there is a sufficiently large number of well-informed buyers and sellers of a homogeneous product, such that no individual participant has enough power to determine the price of the product, resulting in a marketplace that is efficient in production and allocation of products

Commodity	United States	China	Total Output
Tons of soybeans	3	1	4
Bolts of cloth	2	4	6

In the United States, 3 tons of soybeans or 2 bolts of cloth can be produced with 1 unit of input. Therefore, 3 tons of soybeans should have the same price as 2 bolts of cloth. In China, however, because only 1 ton of soybeans can be produced with the input unit that can produce 4 bolts of cloth, 1 ton of soybeans should cost as much as 4 bolts of cloth.

The United States has an absolute advantage in soybean production (3 to 1). China's absolute advantage is in cloth making (4 to 2). Will anyone anywhere give the Chinese cloth maker more than 1 ton of soybeans for 4 bolts of cloth? According to the example, all U.S. soybean producers should be willing to do so because they can get only 2 bolts of cloth for 3 tons of soybeans at home. Similarly, Chinese cloth makers, once they learn they can obtain more than 1 ton of soybeans for every 4 bolts of cloth in the United States, will be eager to trade Chinese cloth for U.S. soybeans.

Each Country Specializes Suppose each nation decides to use its resources to produce only the product in which it has an absolute advantage. The following table shows each nation's new output once it offshores production of goods from the country without absolute advantage to the country that has absolute advantage for each commodity, and then reallocates inputs for producing the good for which the country has absolute advantage. Note that with the same quantity of input units, the total output is now greater: 6 rather than 4 tons of soybeans, and 8 rather than 6 bolts of cloth.

Commodity	United States	China	Total Output
Tons of soybeans	6	0	6
Bolts of cloth	0	8	8

Terms of Trade (Ratio of International Prices) With specialization, the total production of both goods is greater, but to consume both products, the two countries must trade some of their surpluses. What are the limits within which they are willing to trade? Clearly, the Chinese cloth makers will trade some of their cloth for foreign soybeans if they can get more than the 1 ton they get for 4 bolts of cloth in China. Likewise, U.S. soybean growers will trade their soybeans for Chinese cloth if they get a bolt of cloth for less than the 1.5 tons of soybeans it costs them in the United States.

If the two nations take the midpoint of the two trading limits, so that each shares equally in the benefits of trade, they will agree to swap 1.33 bolts of cloth for 1 ton of soybeans. Both will gain from specialization because each now has the following quantities of each product:

Commodity	United States	China	Total Output
Tons of soybeans	3	3	6
Bolts of cloth	4	4	8

> **“NO COUNTRY HAS DEVELOPED SUCCESSFULLY IN MODERN TIMES WITHOUT HARNESSING ECONOMIC OPENNESS—TO INTERNATIONAL TRADE, INVESTMENT, AND THE MOVEMENT OF PEOPLE.”**
>
> —*Selina Jackson, Special Representative to the United Nations and World Trade Organization, World Bank Group*[20]

Gains from Specialization and Trade Because each nation specialized in producing the product at which it was more efficient and then traded its surplus for goods it could not produce as efficiently, both nations benefited. China gained 2 more tons of soybeans and the United States gained 2 more bolts of cloth.

Although Adam Smith's logic helped convince many governments to dismantle trade barriers and encourage increased international trade, it failed to calm concerns of those whose countries lacked an absolute advantage. What if one country has an absolute advantage in the production of both soybeans and cloth, and the other country is at an absolute disadvantage for both products? Will there still be a basis for trade?

THEORY OF COMPARATIVE ADVANTAGE

British economist David Ricardo demonstrated in 1817 that even though one nation held an absolute advantage over another in the production of each of two different goods, international trade could still be a positive-sum game in which both countries benefit. The only limitation to such benefit-creating trade is that the less efficient nation cannot be *equally* less efficient in the production of both goods.[21]

COMPARATIVE ADVANTAGE: Should Service Jobs Be Offshored to India?

SOCIAL MEDIA

CULTURE FACTS @internationalbiz
@CountryofIndia India has the world's second largest population of English-speaking people. #india #englishspeakers

Workers at a telemarketing facility in India. ©moodboard/Getty Images.

India has relatively few resources, but it does have a population of approximately 1.3 billion people, nearly half of whom are in the workforce. Therefore, it should have a comparative advantage in the production of goods or services that require large amounts of inexpensive labor and relatively little capital. However, India has an additional comparative advantage because about 350 million of its people are able to read English. About 125 million of those people understand spoken English and can communicate in English sentences with a high level of fluency, a figure expected to quadruple in the next decade. As Internet and cellular telephone communications continue to become less expensive, India is increasingly using its English-speaking pool of labor to export services—such as software engineering, telemarketing, reviews of credit or mortgage applications, preparation or review of legal documents, analysis of blood tests and other medical services, and claims processing—to foreign companies and their customers.

Fortune 500 companies such as Amazon, IBM, and American Express, as well as a range of more moderate-sized firms, have already sent millions of U.S. jobs abroad. During the decade after the start of the Great Recession in 2007, more than 2.4 million jobs were offshored from the United States, and India is well positioned to capture much of this business. Although the primary driver has been to reduce costs, access to internationally competitive capabilities has also been an important consideration in offshoring decisions. While many people think of low-skill jobs like telemarketing and call centers when they think of sending jobs to India, the sophistication and skill levels required for outsourcing jobs are rising rapidly, driven by the abundance of qualified and low-cost workers in India. For example, a typical Indian information technology (IT) engineer earns an annual salary of $6,500 and an experienced mid-career IT engineer earns $11,000—about one-tenth as much as their U.S. counterparts. The Indian IT industry accounts for about 65 percent of all outsourced jobs in IT worldwide, generating $126 billion in exports in 2017–2018 and a projected $300 billion in revenues by 2020. According to Noshir Kaka of the consulting firm McKinsey, "This industry can do for India what automobiles did for Japan and oil for Saudi Arabia."

Companies in financial services, accounting, and insurance have also been actively pursuing opportunities to

> **If we continue to offshore high-skilled professional jobs, the U.S. risks surrendering its leading role in innovation.**
>
> —John Steadman, president of the Institute of Electrical and Electronics Engineers[22]

move jobs to lower-cost foreign locations. More than 80 percent of global financial services companies have a facility abroad, and the range of services is broadening fast. There are more than 22,000 people employed by the Big 4 accounting firms in India. About 5 percent of U.S. audit work is currently offshored to India, along with preparation of an estimated 2 million U.S. individual and corporate tax returns annually. Documents obtained from taxpayers are scanned and shipped electronically to India, where forms are completed and sent back to the United States to be examined, approved, and signed by a U.S. accountant. While a U.S. tax preparer can cost more than $4,000 per month during the peak tax season, a comparable Indian worker might cost $200 to $400. There is no requirement that the taxpayer be informed the work is done abroad, and most accounting firms base their fees on a U.S. scale to boost profitability. Although sending service jobs abroad has generated concerns across a broad spectrum of society, widespread publicity may actually have speeded the trend by making more companies aware of the possible cost savings.

On the other hand, some have argued that sending jobs to lower-cost locations abroad will help strengthen

U.S. industry and the economy as a whole. Sending jobs abroad is not necessarily a zero-sum game, in which one foreign worker substitutes for one U.S. worker. From this perspective, when U.S. firms hire lower-cost labor abroad, they often must hire other workers at home to complement the increased level of foreign labor. Overseas expansion can also cause companies to modify their U.S. operations, focusing on more complex and higher-value-added activities rather than on the lower-skill positions that have been sent abroad. Shifting work to lower-cost locations abroad has the potential to lower prices in the United States, thus raising the purchasing power of U.S. consumers, enhancing consumer spending and economic activity, and in turn, creating more jobs. A study by the Center for Economic Performance at the London School of Economics reported that a 1 percent increase in the level of jobs sent to lower-cost foreign locations produced nearly a 2 percent increase in overall employment of workers in the United States. As the *Wall Street Journal* editorialized, "The world economy is a dynamic enterprise. Jobs created overseas generate jobs at home. Not just more jobs for Americans, but higher-skilled and better-paying ones."[23]

Critical Thinking Questions

1. Can a company gain advantages besides profit by offshoring? If so, what are they? If not, why not?
2. Does a company face ethical or legal considerations in deciding whether to offshore activities? Why or why not?
3. What might be the long-term implications of offshoring, from the perspective of the home country? The host country?

Sources: Zareer Masani, "English or Hinglish—Which Will India Choose?," *BBC News*, November 27, 2012; Rebecca Lake, "Outsourcing Statistics: 23 Facts And Trends," *CreditDonkey*, August 20, 2015; Brandon Gaille, "27 U.S. Outsourcing Statistics and Trends," *BrandonGaille*, May 27, 2017; "Mid-Career Software Engineer Salary (India)," *PayScale*, 2018; "Performance & Contribution towards Exports by IT-ITeS Industry," *Ministry of Electronics & Information Technology, Government of India*, 2018; Dena Aubin, and Sumeet Chatterjee, "Analysis: As More U.S. Audit Work Moves to India, Concerns Arise," *Reuters Business News*, October 17, 2012; "The World Factbook," *Central Intelligence Agency*, 2018; "IT & ITeS Industry in India," *India Brand Equity Foundation*, June 2018; "Offshoring Tax Returns Preparation to India," *Value Notes*, 2018; Linda Levine, Offshoring (or Offshore Outsourcing) and Job Loss Among U.S. Workers. Washington, DC: *Congressional Research Service*, December 17, 2012; and Suzy Khimm, "Offshoring Creates as Many U.S. Jobs as It Kills, Study Says," *The Washington Post*, July 12, 2012.

Comparative Advantage: An Example To illustrate how trade can benefit both parties, let us slightly change our first example so that China has an absolute advantage in producing *both* soybeans and cloth. Note that compared with China, the United States is less inefficient in producing soybeans (4 versus 5 tons produced from a single unit of input, or 80 percent as efficient as China) than in manufacturing cloth (2 versus 5 bolts of cloth from a single unit of input, or 40 percent as efficient). Therefore, the United States has a **comparative advantage** in producing soybeans.

comparative advantage
When one nation is less efficient than another nation in the production of each of two goods, the less efficient nation has a comparative advantage in the production of that good for which its absolute disadvantage is less

Commodity	United States	China	Total Output
Tons of soybeans	4	5	9
Bolts of cloth	2	5	7

Each Country Specializes If each country specializes in what it does best, its output will be as follows:

Commodity	United States	China	Total Output
Tons of soybeans	8	0	8
Bolts of cloth	0	10	10

Terms of Trade In this case, the terms of trade will be somewhere between the pre-trade price ratios of 1 ton of soybeans for 1 bolt of cloth that Chinese soybean growers must pay in China and the 1/2 bolt of cloth that U.S. cloth makers must pay for 1 ton of U.S. soybeans.

Let us assume the traders agree on an exchange rate of 3/4 bolt of cloth for 1 ton of soybeans. Both will gain from this exchange and specialization, as the following table shows:

Commodity	United States	China
Tons of soybeans	4	4
Bolts of cloth	3	7

This trade left China with 2 surplus bolts of cloth and 1 less ton of soybeans than it had before specializing. However, the Chinese cloth manufacturers should be able to trade 1 bolt of surplus cloth for at least 1 ton of soybeans elsewhere. Then the final result will be as follows:

Commodity	United States	China
Tons of soybeans	4	5+
Bolts of cloth	3	6

Gains from Specialization and Trade Gains from specialization and trade in this case are one additional bolt of cloth for each of the United States and China, and approximately 1 more ton of soybeans for China (the precise amount of additional soybeans will depend upon the final terms of trade that Chinese cloth makers achieve when trading elsewhere).

Comparative advantage serves as a basis for international trade even when one nation has an advantage over another in the production of each of the goods being traded. We have not mentioned money; however, a nation's comparative advantage can be affected by differences between the costs of production factors in that country's currency and their costs in other currencies. As we shall see in the next section, money can change the direction of trade.

HOW EXCHANGE RATES CAN CHANGE THE DIRECTION OF TRADE

Suppose the total cost of land, labor, and capital to produce the daily output of soybeans or cloth in our example of absolute advantage is $10,000 in the United States and 80,000 yuan in China. The cost per unit is as follows:

Commodity	Price per Unit	
	United States	**China**
Ton of soybeans	$10,000/3 = $3,333/ton	80,000 yuan/1 = 80,000 yuan/ton
Bolt of cloth	$10,000/2 = $5,000/bolt	80,000 yuan/4 = 20,000 yuan/bolt

To determine whether it is more advantageous to buy locally or to import, the traders need to know the prices in their own currencies. To convert from foreign to domestic currency, they use the *exchange rate*. The **exchange rate** is the price of one currency stated in terms of another. If the prevailing rate is $1 = 8 yuan, then 1 yuan must be worth $0.125.*

exchange rate
The price of one currency stated in terms of another

---

* If $1 = 8 yuan, to find the value of 1 yuan in dollars, divide both sides of the equation by 8. Then 1 yuan = 1/8 = $0.125.

©DAJ/Getty Images.

Using the exchange rate of $1 = 8$ yuan, the prices in the preceding example appear to the U.S. trader as follows:

	Price per Unit (dollars)	
Commodity	United States	China
Ton of soybeans	$3,333	$10,000
Bolt of cloth	$5,000	$ 2,500

U.S. soybean producers can earn $6,667 more per ton by exporting soybeans to China than they can by selling locally,[†] but can the Chinese cloth makers gain by exporting to the United States? To find out, they must convert dollars to Chinese yuan.

	Price per Unit (yuan)	
Commodity	United States	China
Ton of soybeans	26,664 yuan	80,000 yuan
Bolt of cloth	40,000 yuan	20,000 yuan

It appears that Chinese cloth makers will export cloth to the United States because they can sell at the higher price of 40,000 yuan per bolt. U.S. cloth makers, however, will need some very strong sales arguments to sell their products in the United States if they are to overcome the $2,500 price differential per bolt.

Soybeans to China and cloth to the United States will be the direction of trade as long as the exchange rate remains around $1 = 8$ yuan. But if the dollar strengthens to $1 = 24$ yuan (by "strengthening" we mean the dollar is worth more yuan than before), U.S. soybeans will cost as much in yuan as do Chinese soybeans, and importation of U.S. soybeans into China will cease. On the other hand, if the dollar weakens to $1 = 4$ yuan (meaning the dollar is worth fewer yuan than before), then 1 bolt of Chinese cloth will cost U.S. traders $5,000, and they will have little reason to import it to the United States. This example suggests that a nation can attempt to regain competitiveness in world markets through **currency devaluation**, which lowers the value of a nation's currency relative to other currencies and therefore effectively lowers the prices of its exports. (Note that in many but by no means all cases, this action can leave domestic prices largely unchanged.)

currency devaluation
A reduction in the value of a country's currency relative to other currencies

SOME NEWER EXPLANATIONS FOR THE DIRECTION OF TRADE

The international trade theories we have been discussing were essentially the only theoretical explanations of trade available to us until the second half of the 20th century. Since that time, however, several other possible explanations for international trade have been developed. Even though some aspects of the different theories may contradict elements of other theories, they all represent efforts to make sense of whether, why, when, and among whom international trade will occur. Let's look at those next.

resource endowment
The land, labor, capital, and related production factors a nation possesses

Differences in Resource Endowments Some countries have abundant **resource endowments**, or the land, labor, capital, and related production factors a nation possesses. For example, the United States has a large supply of fertile farmland, Chile has abundant supplies of copper, and Saudi Arabia has extensive amounts of crude oil.

[†] To calculate this figure, multiply the U.S. price of $3,333 per ton of soybeans by 8 yuan per dollar, yielding a price of 26,664 yuan per ton.

These differences naturally give countries different opportunity costs for producing goods and services. Nations are likely to export those products that are less expensive for them to produce and import those that are either unavailable at home or more cheaply produced in other nations. A theory developed by Eli Heckscher and Bertil Ohlin at the Stockholm School of Economics suggests that differences in resource endowments will make developed countries more likely to trade with developing countries whose resource endowments are likely to be very dissimilar than with other developed countries whose endowments are similar.[24] According to this theory, countries would export products requiring large amounts of their abundant production factors and import products requiring large amounts of their scarce production factors. This theory explains the international trade in many primary products, such as forest products, petroleum, and minerals. It can also help explain why the United States exports capital-intensive products such as aircraft while importing labor-intensive products such as jeans or athletic shoes.

Overlapping Demand In contrast to resource endowment–based theory, economist Stefan Linder proposed his theory of overlapping demand, which argues for the existence of similar preferences and demand for products and services among nations with similar levels of per capita income.[25] According to Linder, customers' tastes are strongly affected by their income levels, and therefore a nation's level of income per capita determines the kinds of goods its people will demand. For example, countries with high levels of average income may have substantial levels of demand for items such as large-display televisions, high-fashion branded clothing, jewelry, luxury automobiles, and gourmet foods and beverages. In contrast, countries with low average incomes may exhibit a greater demand for simpler and more basic items of food, clothing, and shelter. Because an entrepreneur will produce goods to meet the demands of consumers, the kinds of products manufactured will reflect the country's level of income per capita. Goods produced for domestic consumption will eventually be exported to countries that have similar levels of income, and therefore, demand.

The theory of overlapping demand suggests that international trade in manufactured goods will be greater between nations with similar levels of per capita income than between those with dissimilar levels of per capita income—the very situation we observed in our review of trade data earlier in this module. Even though two developed countries may have similar resource endowments, they still can have a large volume of trade in goods for which both countries have a demand.[26] For example, if a U.S. company such as Apple invents a sophisticated cell phone with advanced features for its home market, the best export opportunities for this phone will be in other high-income nations such as Japan and western European countries, rather than in lower-income nations such as sub-Saharan Africa.

Note that the theory of overlapping demand differs from the theory of comparative advantage in that it does not specify in which direction a given good will go. In fact, the intra-industry trade sparked by overlapping demand occurs because of product differentiation, the unique differences producers build into their products with the intention of influencing demand. In other words, whiskey from Europe is exported to the United States, and American whiskey is exported to Europe because consumers in these markets perceive a difference between the brands.

International Product Life Cycle The concept of an international product life cycle (IPLC) was developed by Raymond Vernon of Harvard. This theory addresses the role of innovation in trade patterns by explaining why a product that begins as a nation's export eventually becomes its import, thus viewing a product as going through a full life cycle. The initial stage of the cycle, innovation, borrows from the theory of overlapping demand in terms of the motivations and response of entrepreneurs to develop products that meet the rising demand in a particular market. The next three stages are illustrated in Figure 2.3 and described next. Let us apply the IPLC idea to the example of an innovation arising in the United States.

overlapping demand
The existence of similar preferences and demand for products and services among nations with similar levels of per capita income

product differentiation
Unique differences producers build into their products with the intent of positively influencing demand

international product life cycle (IPLC)
A theory explaining why a product that begins as a nation's export eventually becomes its import

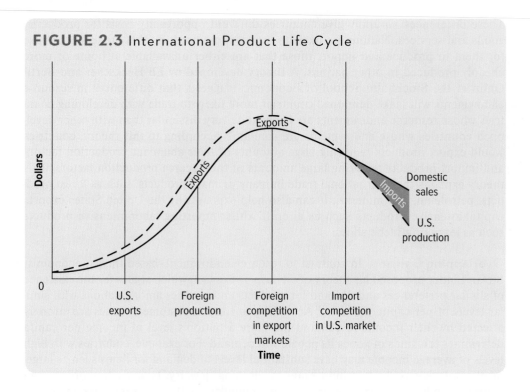

FIGURE 2.3 International Product Life Cycle

Stage 1. *U.S. innovates and exports:* Because the United States has the largest population of high-income consumers of any nation in the world, competition for their patronage is intense. Manufacturers constantly search for better ways to satisfy their customers' needs, maintaining large research and development laboratories and keeping in close contact both with the home market and with suppliers of the materials they need for product development, who are often local. For a while, U.S. firms will be the only manufacturers of a new product developed in the United States. As overseas customers learn about the product, they will have to buy it from U.S. firms. The export market develops over time, as the U.S. manufacturer ships products to these overseas customers.

Stage 2. *Foreign production begins:* Overseas consumers, especially in developed nations, are similar to U.S. customers in their need for and their ability to purchase the product. Export volume grows and may become large enough to support production abroad, especially in larger markets. The technology for producing the good has become fairly stable, and if the innovator is a multinational firm, it will often be sending new product information to subsidiaries, with complete details on how to produce it. Where there are no affiliates, foreign managers, as they learn of the product, will obtain licenses for producing the product from the innovating company (or, to capture the market opportunity, they may imitate or invent around the innovator's technology). Foreign production will begin, which also reduces the cost of transportation and local communication. The U.S. firm will still be exporting to those markets where there is no production, but its export growth will diminish as licensing and foreign direct investment substitute for exports as sources of supply to various international markets.

Stage 3. *Foreign competition appears in export markets:* As early foreign manufacturers gain experience in marketing and production, their costs will fall. Saturation of their local markets will cause them to look for buyers elsewhere. They may even be able to undersell the U.S. producers if they enjoy an advantage such as lower labor or raw material costs. In this stage, foreign firms are competing in U.S. export markets, and as a result, U.S. export sales will continue to decline. The innovating U.S. firms may have developed newer versions of the product and begun scaling back production of the original in order to begin focusing on innovations.

Stage 4. *Import competition appears in the United States:* If foreign producers attain sufficient economies of scale, they may be able to compete in quality with and underprice U.S. firms in the domestic market. From that point on, the U.S. market will be served exclusively (or nearly so) by imports. Televisions, footwear, and semiconductor chips are examples. The rise in imports puts increasing pressure on the innovating companies to achieve product innovation and improvement, which may initiate a new IPLC. The IPLC concept may even be repeated as less-developed countries (LDCs) with still lower labor costs obtain the technology and thus acquire a cost advantage over industrialized nations.

The international product life cycle theory may have its greatest usefulness in explaining trade and investment behavior when international firms introduce their new products in home markets first. For example, personal computers were initially introduced in the United States, and then exported to other countries. Over time, production moved to lower-cost locations such as Taiwan and China, and now almost all computers sold in the United States are imported from abroad.

However, as international competition and short product life cycles encourage more firms to introduce new products globally, this theory may be less applicable. Indeed, "born globals," a term sometimes applied to companies that internationalize their operations either at start-up or very early in their life cycle, may not internationalize their operations and products in the classic manner of the IPLC. Yet, although "born global" companies may engage in export activities from the very beginning of their existence, they often gradually increase their commitment to international markets—through exports or foreign production—in a manner consistent with the IPLC concept.[27]

Economies of Scale and the Experience Curve In the 1920s, economists began to consider that most industries benefit from economies of scale, which is the predictable decline in the average cost of producing each unit of output as a production facility gets larger and output increases. This occurs because larger and more efficient equipment can be employed, companies can obtain volume discounts on their larger-volume purchases, and fixed costs such as research and design and administrative overheads can be allocated over a larger quantity of output. Most manufacturing is subject to economies of scale, and mining and transportation industries also tend to benefit from increasing returns to scale. Production costs also drop because of the experience curve, which refers to the rising scale on which efficiency improves as a result of cumulative experience and learning. That is, as firms produce more, they learn ways to improve production efficiency, reducing production costs by a predictable amount.[28]

Economies of scale and the experience curve affect international trade because they can permit a nation's industries to become low-cost producers without having an abundance of the resources used as inputs, such as minerals or labor. Then, just as in the case of comparative advantage, nations specialize in the production of a few products and trade with others to supply the rest of their needs. International trade is promoted because a nation's companies may not be able to fully achieve the potential economies of scale by serving only the domestic market, even within countries as large as the United States. Consumers can benefit from higher quality and lower prices for products like semiconductors, computers, and commercial aircraft when Samsung, Apple, and Airbus can spread very high fixed costs over sales within foreign as well as home markets.

National Competitive Advantage from Regional Clusters British economist Alfred Marshall's seminal work on economic theory helps explain why, in many industries, firms tend to cluster together on a geographic basis.[30] He suggested three reasons: (1) the pooling of a common labor force means staffing requirements can be met quickly, even with unexpected fluctuations in demand; (2) specialized local suppliers can coordinate their operations and skills with the needs of the buyers; and (3) technological information can be readily shared, enhancing the rate of innovation. When all these reasons are present within a given nation, a domestic industry that exploits them can help achieve national competitiveness.

economies of scale
The predictable decline in the average cost of producing each unit of output as a production facility gets larger and output increases

experience curve
The rising scale on which efficiency improves as a result of cumulative experience and learning

> **"ARE THESE BENEFITS of FINANCIAL INFLOWS SUFFICIENT to OFFSET THE EVIDENT RISKS of ALLOWING MARKETS to FREELY ALLOCATE CAPITAL across THE BORDERS of DEVELOPING COUNTRIES? THE ANSWER WOULD APPEAR to BE A STRONG YES for FDI."**
>
> —*Barry P. Bosworth and Susan M. Collins, economists at the Brookings Institute*[29]

national competitiveness
A nation's relative ability to design, produce, distribute, or service products within an international trading context while earning increasing returns on its resources

National competitiveness is a nation's ability to design, produce, distribute, or service products within an international trading context while earning increasing returns on its resources.

Michael Porter, a management professor at Harvard, extended the work of Marshall.[31] His diamond model of national advantage claims that four kinds of variables will influence firms' ability to utilize their country's resources to gain a competitive advantage:

1. *Demand conditions:* The nature of domestic demand matters, rather than merely the size. If a firm's customers are sophisticated and demanding, the firm will strive to produce high-quality and innovative products and, in doing so, will obtain a global competitive advantage over companies located where domestic pressure is less.

2. *Factor conditions:* Porter distinguishes between basic factors (inherited factors, such as land, location, or natural resources) and advanced factors (those created from investments made by individuals, companies, or governments, such as a nation's transportation systems, or university research institutes). Lack of natural endowments has caused nations to invest in creating advanced factors, such as an educated workforce, deep-water ports, and advanced communications systems, to enable their industries to compete globally. Some Caribbean nations have upgraded their communications systems to attract banking and other service companies that have little dependence on the basic factors of production.

3. *Related and supporting industries:* Firms in an industry, with their suppliers, their suppliers' suppliers, and so forth, tend to form a cluster in a given location, providing a network of suppliers and subcontractors and a commercial infrastructure. For example, the San Francisco Bay Area in California has a range of related and supporting industries for the personal computer industry. These include the research, design, production, and service operations of semiconductor designers and manufacturers, technologically savvy venture capitalists, and intellectual property rights lawyers, as well as suppliers of scientific equipment, electronics telecommunications equipment, and software development, and a wide range of Internet-related companies.[32]

4. *Firm strategy, structure, and rivalry:* Porter says companies subject to heavy competition in their domestic markets are constantly striving to improve their efficiency and innovativeness, which makes them more competitive internationally. For decades, firms in oligopolistic industries have carefully watched their competitors' every move and even entered foreign markets just because their competitors had gone there. Japanese automakers such as Toyota, Honda, and Nissan have competed vigorously with one another for decades in their domestic marketplace, constantly pressuring one another to improve the quality and performance of their products or risk the loss of market share. This competition has enabled them to develop world-leading capabilities in auto design and manufacturing. As soon as one of these companies ventures into a new international market such as Europe, South America, or Southeast Asia, the competitors tend to be close behind hoping to avoid a decline in their relative international competitiveness.

In addition to these four variables, Porter claimed that competitiveness could be affected by government policies such as incentives, subsidies, temporary protection from foreign competitors, or infrastructure development, and by random events such as the location and timing of research breakthroughs or luck.

Porter argues that these factors are fundamentally interrelated, creating a "virtuous circle" of resource generation and application, as well as responsiveness in meeting the demands of customers, as depicted in Figure 2.4.

SUMMARY OF INTERNATIONAL TRADE THEORY

International trade theory shows that nations will attain a higher level of living by specializing in goods for which they possess a comparative advantage and importing those for which they have a comparative disadvantage. Generally, trade restrictions that stop this free flow of goods will harm a nation's welfare.

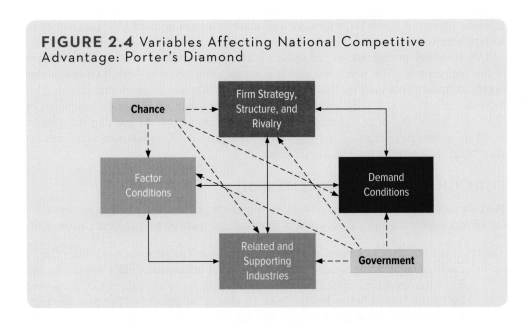

FIGURE 2.4 Variables Affecting National Competitive Advantage: Porter's Diamond

International trade exists because firms export. As you know, however, exporting is only one aspect of international business. Another—overseas production—requires foreign investment, the topic of the next section.

Foreign Investment

We can divide foreign investment into two components: **portfolio investment**, which is the purchase of stocks and bonds solely for the purpose of obtaining a return on the funds invested, and **direct investment**, by which investors may influence the management of the firm in addition to receiving a return on their money. The distinction between these two components has begun to blur, particularly with the growing size and number of international mergers, acquisitions, and alliances in recent years. For example, investments by a foreign investor in the stock of a domestic company generally are treated as direct investment when the investor's equity participation ratio is 10 percent or more.

In contrast, deals that do not result in the foreign investor's obtaining at least 10 percent of the shareholdings are classified as portfolio investments. With the increasing pace of business globalization, it is not uncommon for companies to form strategic relationships with firms from other nations in order to pool resources (such as manufacturing, marketing, technology, and other know-how), while still keeping their equity participation below 10 percent. Financing from foreign venture capitalists also tends to be treated as a portfolio investment, although these investors frequently become actively involved in the target company's business operations, with the goal of ultimately realizing substantial capital gains when the target company goes public.

PORTFOLIO INVESTMENT

Although portfolio investors are not directly concerned with the control of a firm, they invest immense amounts in stocks and bonds from other countries. For example, data from the Department of Commerce show that persons residing outside the United States had portfolio investments totaling $19.5 trillion at the beginning of 2018, including U.S. stocks and investment fund shares valued at $8 trillion.[33] This portfolio investment value was about five times the amount achieved at the beginning of 2000. This very substantial

LO 2-4
Describe the size, growth, and direction of foreign direct investment.

portfolio investment
The purchase of stocks and bonds to obtain a return on the funds invested

direct investment
The purchase of sufficient stock in a firm to obtain significant management control

increase is related to the large number and scale of acquisitions of U.S. companies by foreign companies.

U.S. investors, in contrast, owned foreign portfolio investments valued at $12.5 trillion at the beginning of 2018, which was nearly five times more than in 2000.[34] Of the foreign portfolio investments held by U.S. investors, $9.1 trillion was in corporate stocks. This increase reflects net U.S. purchases of foreign stocks, acquisitions of foreign companies by U.S. companies, and price appreciation in many foreign stocks. As you can see, foreign portfolio investment is sizable and will continue to grow as more international firms list their bonds and equities on foreign exchanges.

FOREIGN DIRECT INVESTMENT (FDI)

Next we look at direct investment abroad, including the volume, level, and direction of foreign direct investment and the influence of international trade on foreign direct investment.

The Outstanding Stock of Foreign Direct Investment The *book value*—or the value of the total outstanding stock—of all foreign direct investment (FDI) worldwide was $30.8 trillion at the beginning of 2018.[35] Although the proportion of FDI accounted for by the United States has declined by almost 30 percent in the past 20 years, U.S. individuals and corporations still had $7.8 trillion invested abroad in 2018. This total was more than four times the FDI of the next-largest investor, Hong Kong.[36] During the past two decades, the proportion of FDI accounted for by the European Union has increased, although a portion of that increase was due to the inclusion of additional member-countries in the EU calculations. Reflecting their continued economic expansion, developing countries have dramatically increased their share of FDI stock, from 1 percent in 1980 to over 22 percent at the beginning of 2018. Figure 2.5 highlights the rate of growth of FDI stock for selected nations and regions, particularly the M-BRIC emerging market economies, that is, Mexico, Brazil, Russia, India, and China.

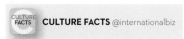

Annual Outflows of FDI Annual FDI outflow—the amount invested each year into other nations—often fluctuates substantially, due to factors such as the level of economic growth within and across nations and regions of the world. For example, FDI outflows hit a historical high in 2000—$1.16 trillion, more than 3.25 times the level in 1995.[38] However, the slowdown that began to hit most of the world's economies in late 2000 resulted in a subsequent decline in the overall level of annual FDI flows. By 2002, the total had declined to under $498 billion. Outflows subsequently increased, reaching $2.17 trillion in 2007 before declining again during the economic downturn that began late that year, bottoming out at $1.26 trillion in 2014. FDI outflows increased again thereafter, averaging over $1.5 trillion per year from 2015 through 2017.

The overall volume of outward FDI from developing nations in 2017, $381 billion, was 29 times the level in 1990, and the proportion of worldwide outward FDI that came from developing nations increased from 5 percent in 1990 to 27 percent in 2017.[39] Despite this increase, the vast proportion of outward FDI, about two-thirds, still originates from the developed countries. Despite a decline in their overall proportion, the United States and the European Union combined have continued to account for one-third to just over one-half of worldwide FDI in recent years. The United States was the leading single national source of FDI outflows through most of the period from 1990 to 2017, with an average of over 20 percent of total FDI outflows for 2013–2017. U.S. FDI outflows of $1.5 trillion from 2015 through 2017 were more than the combined outflows of the next three largest sources of FDI: Japan, China, and the Netherlands. The European Union's proportion of outward FDI grew from an average of around 47 percent in 1985–1997 to a peak of 69 percent by 2005, before subsequently declining to an average of 32 percent from 2013 to 2017.[40]

❝FOREIGN INVESTMENT ADDS A SENSE of COMPETITION; WE SHOULD SEE THIS as A WAKE-UP CALL to MODERNIZE AND UPGRADE. COMPANIES THAT DO NOT WILL UNDOUBTEDLY DIE.❞

—Ratan Tata, chair of Tata Group, India[41]

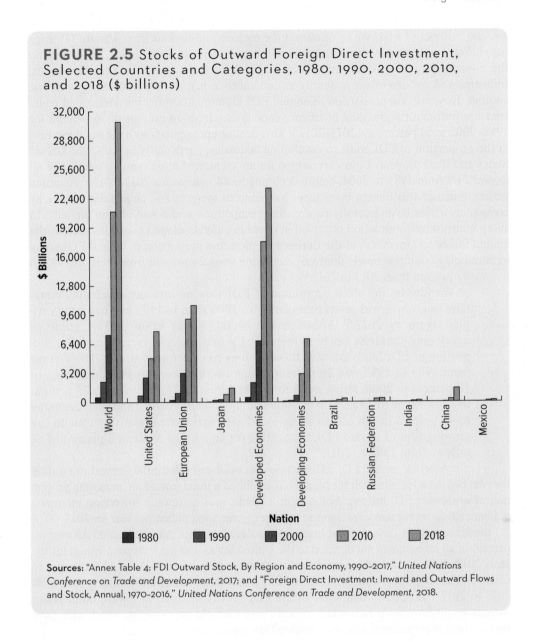

FIGURE 2.5 Stocks of Outward Foreign Direct Investment, Selected Countries and Categories, 1980, 1990, 2000, 2010, and 2018 ($ billions)

Legend: ■ 1980   ■ 1990   ■ 2000   ■ 2010   ■ 2018

Sources: "Annex Table 4: FDI Outward Stock, By Region and Economy, 1990–2017," *United Nations Conference on Trade and Development*, 2017; and "Foreign Direct Investment: Inward and Outward Flows and Stock, Annual, 1970–2016," *United Nations Conference on Trade and Development*, 2018.

Much of the world's outward FDI has been associated with mergers and acquisitions. Historically, approximately two-thirds of the value of corporate investments made in the United States from abroad have been spent to acquire existing companies rather than to establish new ones. (Similarly, the majority of U.S. investments into foreign markets have been utilized to acquire existing companies.) A number of reasons can be cited for this result: (1) corporate restructuring in the United States caused management to offer for sale those businesses or other assets that either did not meet their profit standards or were considered unrelated to the company's main business; (2) foreign companies wanted to gain rapid access to U.S. advanced technology, especially in computers and communications; (3) management of foreign firms felt that entry into the large and prosperous U.S. market could be more successful if they acquired known brand names rather than spending the time and money to promote new, unknown brands; and (4) increased international competitive pressures, including the pursuit of improved economies of scale, have led to restructuring and consolidation in many industries, and the acquisition of companies in major markets such as the United States has been a by-product of these industrial trends.

Annual Inflows of FDI   We've discussed the nations and regions from which FDI originated. You may ask, in which countries are these investments being made, and where do the investments come from? Analysis of FDI inflows helps us answer these questions. Industrialized nations invest primarily in one another, just as they trade more with one another. However, the proportion of annual FDI investments going into developed countries has declined significantly in recent years, falling from an average of 76 percent for 1998–2002 to 54 percent for 2013–2017.[42] This decline corresponds with the rapid increase in the proportion of FDI going to developing countries, particularly in Asia. The United States and the European Union accounted for an average of more than 60 percent of all inward FDI from 1985 to 2004, before declining to 44 percent for 2013–2017.[43] As noted earlier, much of this inward investment has gone to mergers and acquisitions made by companies whose businesses are confronting competition and consolidation globally. In sharp contrast to the situation observed in economically developed countries such as the United States and members of the European Union, the proportion of inward FDI going to developing countries nearly doubled, increasing from 24 percent from 1990 to 1992 to 43 percent from 2013 to 2017.[44]

Worldwide, the absolute volume of FDI flowing into the developing countries as a whole was seven times larger in 2000 than in 1990 and had nearly tripled again by 2017.[45] Although the overall dollar value of FDI going to developing countries has been increasing substantially in recent years, the proportion of FDI funds going to these nations has fluctuated widely. The average from 1985 to 1995 was 28 percent, rising to 38 percent in 1996, declining to 18 percent in 2000, rising again to 40 percent in 2004, declining to 27 percent in 2007, rising to 43 percent in 2009 and 54 percent in 2013, and then declining to 47 percent in 2017. African nations have participated relatively little in the growing flow of inward FDI, accounting for an average of about 3 percent of all inflows from 1985 to 2017.[46]

In Latin America, annual FDI inflows have also exhibited substantial fluctuations during the past two decades, although the region has exhibited a trend toward an increasing proportion of worldwide FDI inflows. For Asia as a whole, total inflows to the region increased dramatically in recent years, reaching an average of over $468 billion per year for 2013–2017, 3.7 times the average inward investments from a decade earlier. Asia accounted for over 60 percent of all investments not directed to the United States and the European Union for the years 2013–2017. A particularly important trend is the proportion of Asian FDI directed to China and its territories, which represented 54 percent of the total FDI flowing to Asia from 2013 to 2017.[47] It appears that some of the FDI previously directed toward other Asian nations might have been redirected toward these Chinese investments, which may have slowed these other nations' ability to develop their own economies.

Level and Direction of FDI   Even though it is impossible to make an accurate determination of the present value of foreign investments, we can get an idea of the rates and amounts of such investments and of the places in which they are being made. This is the kind of information that interests managers and government leaders and is analogous to what we seek in the analysis of international trade. If a nation is continuing to receive appreciable amounts of foreign investments, its investment climate must be favorable. This means the political forces of the foreign environment are relatively attractive and the opportunity to earn a profit is greater there than elsewhere. Other reasons for investing exist, to be sure; however, if the aforementioned factors are absent, foreign investment is not likely to occur.

DOES TRADE LEAD TO FDI?

Historically, foreign direct investment has followed foreign trade. One reason is that engaging in foreign trade is typically less costly and less risky than making a direct investment into foreign markets. Also, management can expand the business in small

Are Trade Deficits Good or Bad for a Country?

Arguing that trade balances are akin to a scorecard on international competitiveness, President Donald Trump suggests that the existence of trade deficits indicates the United States is losing in trade and is a major problem that needs fixing. The director of the president's National Trade Council, Peter Navarro, suggests the existence of trade deficits poses a danger to national security. In light of these stated concerns, are trade deficits necessarily bad for a country?

Most economists do not consider trade deficits to be inherently bad or good. At its simplest, a trade deficit indicates that a country is purchasing more products or services from other countries than it sells to those countries. What happens in such a situation? There would have to be a corresponding flow of capital to make up the difference in trade, such as investments in stocks, bonds, currency, or companies. Essentially, the deficit in trade would have to be "paid for" by a surplus of inflows of foreign investment.

Trade balances are affected by a variety of macroeconomic factors, including the relative strength of countries' currencies, their rates of saving and investment, their relative rates of growth, and tax policies. For example, the 2007–2008 financial crisis caused domestic consumption in the United States to falter, which resulted in a dramatic narrowing of America's trade deficit. Alternatively, a strengthening national currency can cause foreign-made products—for example, cars, food, or clothing—to be more affordable relative to domestically produced products. An increase in consumption of cheaper foreign-made products might help raise the standard of living in a country, giving its citizens access to a broader range of more competitively priced goods and services. Yet, these foreign-made goods might contribute to a loss of jobs in domestic industries impacted by growing imports, although such an outcome is not guaranteed.

Whether a trade deficit creates more or fewer jobs depends on what the country with the deficit does with the inflows of capital. Is the money being invested in activities with long-lasting economic returns, such as better roads and ports, new factories and machinery, improved worker education, and so forth? Is it helping to reduce the cost of debt, allowing money to be redirected to other value-creating activities? Or does the money fuel unsustainable bubbles in housing or financial markets, high levels of consumer spending fueled by access to low-cost debt, or excessive public expenditures?

So the mere existence of a trade deficit and its corresponding capital inflows, without insight into a country's priorities and how the monetary inflows are being put to use, does not provide much insight into whether such deficits are good or bad for a country.

Critical Thinking Questions

1. Why might a country be concerned about the level of its trade deficit?

2. What actions should a country encourage or discourage in order to minimize potential concerns about a trade deficit?

Sources: Neil Irwin, "What Is the Trade Deficit?," *The New York Times Company*, June 9, 2018; Kevin D. Williamson, "Understanding Trade Deficits," *National Review*, July 29, 2018; and Nick Timiraos, "Trump Advisor Peter Navarro: Trade Deficits Endanger U.S. National Security," *The Wall Street Journal*, March 6, 2017.

increments rather than making the considerably greater investments and finding the larger markets that a foreign production facility requires. Typically, a firm uses domestic or foreign agents to export. As the export business increases, the firm sets up an export department and perhaps hires sales representatives to live in overseas markets. It might even establish a sales company to import and sell the company's products in a foreign country.

Meanwhile, managers will watch the total market size closely, because they know their competitors are doing the same. Generally, because the local market is likely not large enough to support local production by all the firms exporting to it, the question is who will begin manufacturing there first. Experienced managers know that governments often limit the number of local firms making a given product so those that do set up local operations will be assured of a profitable and continuing business. Their success is especially important to developing countries dependent on foreign invest-ment to provide jobs and tax revenue.

This sort of linear path to market expansion is one that many international firms have taken and many still take today. However, the new business environment, with fewer gov-ernment barriers to trade, increased competition from globalizing firms, and new produc-tion and communications technology, is causing many international firms to locate production close to available resources in order to improve efficiency. They then attempt to integrate the entire production process, from raw materials until finished goods, on either a regional or a global basis in order to gain further improvements in international competitiveness and performance. As a result, the decision about where to locate may be either an FDI or a trade decision, depending on which is expected to produce the greatest improvement in the firm's competitiveness, which illustrates just how closely FDI and trade are interlinked.

LO 2-5
Explain several of the theories of foreign direct investment.

Explaining FDI: Theories of International Investment

This section examines several leading theories that attempt to explain why firms choose to invest in foreign markets rather than use alternatives such as licensing or exporting. FDI includes both ownership and control of real or physical assets such as plants and other facilities. It does not include other types of international investment such as portfolios of stocks, bonds, or other forms of debt. FDI can take place through **greenfield investment**, the establishment of new facilities from the ground up, or **cross-border acquisition**, the purchase of an existing business in another nation. We usually assume that strategic motives are the driving force for decisions to invest abroad, such as the desire to find new markets, access raw materials, achieve production efficien-cies, gain access to new technologies or managerial expertise, enhance political safety of the firm's operations, or respond to competitive or other pressures in the external environment.[48] To be successful with their foreign investment activities, firms must possess advantages not available to local firms in order to overcome liabilities associ-ated with being a foreigner—such as lack of knowledge about local market conditions, increased costs of operating at a distance, or differences in culture, language, laws and regulations, or institutions. FDI theories attempt to explain how these advantages might be developed and exploited.

greenfield investment
The establishment of new facil-ities from the ground up

cross-border acquisition
The purchase of an existing business in another nation

MONOPOLISTIC ADVANTAGE THEORY

monopolistic advantage theory
Theory that foreign direct investment is made by firms in industries with relatively few competitors, due to their pos-session of technical and other advantages over indigenous firms

The modern **monopolistic advantage theory** suggests that FDI is made by firms in industries with relatively few competitors, due to their possession of technical and other advantages over indigenous firms. This theory stems from research showing that FDI occurs largely in industries in which there are only a small number of competitors (such as pharmaceuticals or locomotives) rather than in those with a large number of vigorously competing firms. To limit the number of competitors, firms in these industries must possess advantages that are difficult for other firms, including local companies, to replicate or otherwise overcome. Smartphones (Apple, Samsung), magnetic resonance imaging machines (General Electric, Philips, and Toshiba), and commercial aircraft manufacturing (Boeing, Airbus) are examples of such industries. According to the monopolistic advantage theory, the advantages must be the result of economies of scale, superior technology, or superior knowledge in marketing, manage-ment, or finance. These advantages outweigh the liabilities associated with being a foreign firm and raise barriers to entry. By limiting the potential for local competitors to successfully emerge, the multinational enterprise is able to operate more profitably in foreign markets than can local competitors.[49]

STRATEGIC BEHAVIOR THEORY

Researchers have tried to explain how FDI occurs within an oligopolistic industry, which has a limited number of competing firms, such as the U.S. mobile phone market in which four firms (Verizon, AT&T, T-Mobile, and Sprint) controlled over 98 percent of the market in 2018.[50] In an oligopolistic situation, the actions of one firm can strongly affect the performance of others in that industry. For example, if a multinational automobile manufacturing company were the first to invest in an emerging economy, this firm might have a greater chance of dominating the emerging economy's market than competitors who fail to invest in that nation. The competitor moving first to make an investment might be able to leverage its competitive edge to gain advantage in other nations as well. Because the actions of each competitor affect the others in the industry, this interdependence increases the likelihood that firms will imitate the investment timing and location of their competitors as they expand internationally. The strategic behavior theory suggests that strategic rivalry between firms in an oligopolistic industry will result in firms closely following and imitating each other's international investments in order to keep one competitor from gaining an advantage.[51]

INTERNALIZATION THEORY

The internalization theory argues that to obtain a higher return on its investment, a firm will transfer its superior knowledge to a foreign subsidiary that it controls, rather than sell it in the open market. Internalization theory begins with the assumption that a firm may have knowledge superior to that of its competitors, such as knowledge that results from successful research and development efforts. However, due to high transaction costs, the firm may obtain a better price by using the knowledge itself than by selling it on the open market. By investing in foreign subsidiaries for activities such as supply, production, or distribution, rather than licensing the rights to these activities to others, the company is able to send the knowledge across borders while still keeping control of the knowledge within the firm. For example, both Samsung and Intel have invested heavily into developing world-leading knowledge in the production of memory chips and semiconductors, respectively, and they have traditionally protected this knowledge through investing in their own network of manufacturing facilities. The expected result, according to internalization theory, is the firm's ability to realize a superior return on the investment made to produce this knowledge, particularly as the knowledge is embodied in various products or services that are sold to customers.[52]

DYNAMIC CAPABILITIES THEORY

The dynamic capability theory suggests that for a firm to successfully invest overseas, it must have not only ownership of unique knowledge or resources, but also the ability to dynamically create, sustain, and exploit these capabilities over time. This perspective argues that ownership of specific knowledge or resources is necessary, but not sufficient, for achieving success in international FDI. The firm must also be able to effectively create, sustain, and exploit dynamic capabilities for superior quality- or quantity-based deployment, and these capabilities must be transferable to international environments in order to produce competitive advantage. Companies such as IBM or Microsoft typically develop centers of excellence in order to develop distinctive competencies that will be subsequently applied to their investments within the host countries.

ECLECTIC THEORY OF INTERNATIONAL PRODUCTION

The eclectic theory of international production, which combines elements of some of the theories we have already discussed, is currently the most widely cited and accepted theory of FDI. Developed by British economist John H. Dunning, it proposes an overall

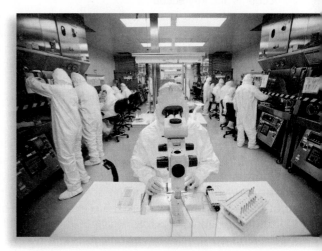

Workers in a clean lab at a production facility.
©Roger Tully/Getty Images.

oligopolistic industry
An industry with a limited number of competing firms

strategic behavior theory
Theory suggesting that strategic rivalry between firms in an oligopolistic industry will result in firms closely following and imitating each other's international investments in order to keep a competitor from gaining an advantage

internalization theory
Theory that to obtain a higher return on its investment, a firm will transfer its superior knowledge to a foreign subsidiary that it controls, rather than sell it in the open market

dynamic capability theory
Theory that for a firm to successfully invest overseas, it must have not only ownership of unique knowledge or resources, but also the ability to dynamically create, sustain, and exploit these capabilities over time

eclectic theory of international production
Theory proposing that for a firm to invest in facilities overseas, it must have three kinds of advantages: ownership specific, location specific, and internalization

MARK HAUPT: A Central California-Based International Career

Mark Haupt built an international career he could have at home. Courtesy of Mark Haupt.

Mark Haupt graduated with a business degree, concentrating in international business. He loved the West Coast, where he went to university, and wanted to continue living there, so he put together a career that is both international and allows him to work near home. Here's his story:

I think my interest in international business started when I was little. My father had a job with IBM and he was constantly traveling domestically and internationally. I'm also a big soccer fan and soccer is such a global sport that you start learning more and more about different countries, cities, cultures, etc. . . . and that has always been fascinating to me. I grew up with a lot of different ethnicities and cultures around and it's the differences—and sometimes similarities—that make things interesting to me.

After graduation, I wanted to remain in the Central Coast region of California, near the ocean, but also have international business opportunities. Despite the rural nature of this area, I was able to find a position with a local sporting goods company. I am in charge of our specialty/sporting goods division and my title is Specialty Sales Manager. I manage a network of sales representatives, domestic and international, as well as select independent accounts and key accounts.

In less than two years with the company, I have worked with customers in over 30 nations, including Mexico, Colombia, Brazil, Chile, Venezuela, Ireland, England, Germany, Italy, France, the Benelux Region, Scandinavia, Romania, Latvia, Belarus, China, Japan, South Africa, Egypt, and Russia. Most of these customers are distributors who work with my company's products as well as those of other firms.

To prepare for travel, I always like to research the country I am visiting. I start by finding out a little about that country's sport of choice. For me, that's always an easy conversation starter and something that almost everyone has an opinion on. Then I like to find out about popular venues, sights, etc. Finally, I find out what to do or not to do. I research online and talk to people who have already visited the country. I pack light because I never seem to need much besides a few business outfits and some casual clothes. English has been the accepted business language for all my travels, but I like to learn at least a few words of the local language. That shows that I am interested in the country, and people seem to appreciate that. I don't have any routines for when I return from travel. I always seem to take way too long to unpack to the point where I run out of clothes. I am working on that.

To adjust to being away, I always make sure I'm exhausted before I get on the plane. I sleep amazingly well on planes, probably because I have been flying ever since I was little. Usually, I wake up completely refreshed when I arrive.

To make my U.S. location convenient for my international counterparts, I have kept some odd hours. I rely on e-mail, but that usually creates a one-day delay and sometimes doesn't deliver the message effectively. If I use phone or video chat, I try to make the hours work for my customers, which isn't always easy. That's all part of the job.

My biggest challenge has been working on a special order from one of my customers in Asia. Our factory is located in Taiwan, and I have encountered endless complications with molds, materials, packaging, etc. It's easy enough to say you can make a special product and give pricing. It is much more complicated once this actually comes to fruition. For big special orders, it's important that you get everything right. Errors that you might not think about can ruin a project and, potentially, a business relationship.

My greatest learning point from my international experience is that I have learned to assume nothing. I have become so incredibly detailed in everything I do because I can never assume that a client understands something exactly the way I do, especially when English isn't their native language. It is much easier to go over something twice in the beginning rather than look back and try to correct a misunderstanding.

My advice for others who are interested in going abroad or working with others who are abroad is: if you have the chance, learn any language you can. This is an invaluable asset. Spend some time learning about the countries you are doing business with, and be extremely inquisitive. Do not act as if you already know everything. It's good to be knowledgeable and worldly, but people love talking about their country and culture and love it when you ask questions and are curious about their lifestyles. Be curious, but not ignorant. Make sure you don't ask anything that might bring up a sore subject.

Source: Courtesy of Mark Haupt.

framework for explaining why firms choose to engage in FDI rather than serve foreign markets through alternatives such as exporting, licensing, management contracts, joint ventures, or strategic alliances.[53] Dunning proposed that for a firm to invest in facilities overseas, it must have three kinds of advantages: ownership-specific, location-specific, and internalization:

1. *Ownership-specific advantage:* This is the extent to which a firm has or can develop a firm-specific advantage through ownership of tangible and intangible assets that are not available to other firms and that can be transferred abroad. The three basic types of tangible or intangible ownership-specific advantages are knowledge or technology, economies of scale or scope, and monopolistic advantages like unique access to critical inputs or outputs. The advantage generates lower costs or higher revenues that will offset the added costs of operating at a distance within a foreign location.

2. *Location-specific advantage:* A foreign market must have specific economic, social, or political characteristics, like market size, tariff or non-tariff barriers, or transport costs that will permit the firm to profitably exploit its firm-specific advantages by locating to that market rather than exporting to it.

3. *Internalization advantage:* Firms have various alternatives to entering foreign markets, ranging from making arm's-length market transactions to operating wholly owned subsidiaries. It is in the firm's best interests to exploit its ownership-specific advantages through internalization options, which mean retaining ownership and control, where either the market does not exist or it functions inefficiently, making the transaction costs of market-based (arm's-length) options too high.

The eclectic theory is sometimes referred to as the "OLI model", using the initials of the three advantages.

Most of the theories we've looked at have one assumption in common that is supported by evidence—most direct foreign investment is made by large, research-intensive firms in oligopolistic industries. The theories also offer various reasons companies find it *profitable* to invest overseas. However, all motives for FDI are linked in some way to the desire to increase or protect not only profits but also *sales* and *markets*.

SUMMARY

LO 2-1
Describe the magnitude of international trade and how it has grown.

The volume of international trade in goods and services measured in current dollars was $23 trillion in 2017, including merchandise exports of $17.5 trillion. Services exports were only $5.4 trillion, but their rate of growth has been faster than that of merchandise exports. The 10 largest exporting and importing countries account for over half the world's exports and imports, highlighting the fact that international trade continues to be unevenly distributed across countries and regions of the world. Nearly 60 percent of global output is now destined for international trade, another indication of the extent to which international trade has become a critical factor in the economic activity of many, if not most, of the countries of the world.

LO 2-2
Identify who participates in trade.

Developed countries tend to trade with developed countries and they account for a majority of the exports worldwide. More than half of the exports from developing countries also go to developed countries, although this proportion has been declining. The rise of regional trade agreements, as well as other factors, is transforming the volume and direction of world trade in merchandise and services. More than 70 percent of world trade now occurs between members of regional trade agreements.

LO 2-3
Distinguish among the theories that explain why certain goods are traded internationally.

The resource endowments theory proposes that a nation tends to export products requiring a large amount of a resource that is relatively abundant in that nation. In contrast, the theory of overlapping demand suggests that international trade in manufactured goods will be greater between nations with similar levels of per capita income. The international product life cycle theory states that many products first produced in the United States or other developed countries are eventually produced in less developed nations and become imports to the very countries in which their production began. Porter helped explain how nations can achieve competitive advantage through the emergence of regional clusters, claiming that four classes of variables are critical in this regard: demand conditions; factor conditions; related and supporting industries; and firm strategy, structure, and rivalry. Competitiveness can also be affected by government and by chance.

LO 2-4
Describe the size, growth, and direction of foreign direct investment.

The book value of FDI was $30.8 trillion at the beginning of 2018. Although the United States is the largest source of this FDI, the proportion of global foreign direct investment accounted for by the United States has been declining, while the proportion accounted for by the European Union has risen. The proportion of FDI originating from the developing nations has also been increasing. On an annual basis, more than 75 percent of the outstanding stock of FDI at the beginning of 2018 came from developed countries. In terms of destination for outward FDI, an average of nearly half of annual FDI investments have been going into developed countries in recent years, a substantial decline from historical averages, with a majority of this investment occurring in the form of acquisitions of existing companies. The direction of FDI follows the direction of foreign trade; that is, developed nations invest in one another just as they trade with one another.

LO 2-5
Explain several of the theories of foreign direct investment.

To be successful with their foreign investment activities, firms must possess advantages not available to local firms in order to overcome liabilities associated with being a foreigner, and FDI theories attempt to explain how these advantages might be developed and exploited. Monopolistic advantage theory suggests that advantages due to economies of scale, superior technology, or superior knowledge in marketing, management, or finance enable the multinational enterprise to operate more profitably in foreign markets than can local competitors. Strategic behavior theory suggests that strategic rivalry between firms in oligopolistic industries will result in imitation by the firms of one another's international investments in order to prevent competitors from gaining an advantage. Internalization theory states that firms will seek to invest in foreign subsidiaries, rather than license their superior knowledge, to receive a better return on the investment used to develop that knowledge. The dynamic capabilities theory suggests that firms must have not only ownership of specific knowledge or resources but also the ability to dynamically create and exploit capabilities in order to achieve success in FDI. The eclectic theory explains an IC's choice of its overseas production facilities. The firm must have location and ownership advantages to invest in a foreign plant. It will invest where it is most profitable to internalize its monopolistic advantage.

KEY TERMS

absolute advantage 35
comparative advantage 38
cross-border acquisition 50
currency devaluation 40
direct investment 45
dynamic capability theory 51
eclectic theory of international
    production 51
economies of scale 43

exchange rate 39
experience curve 43
greenfield investment 50
internalization theory 51
international product life cycle
    (IPLC) 41
mercantilism 34
monopolistic advantage theory 50
national competitiveness 44

oligopolistic industry 51
overlapping demand 41
perfect competition 35
portfolio investment 45
product differentiation 41
resource endowment 40
strategic behavior theory 51
trade deficit 34
trade surplus 34

CRITICAL THINKING QUESTIONS

1. Discuss and explain how international trade in merchandise and services has changed over the past two decades and what the major trends are. What future trends can you speculate about? How might this information be of value to a manager?

2. Where do merchandise exports come from, and where do they typically go? How and why has this been changing over time, and do you think these trends are likely to continue? Why or why not? Why might this information be valuable to a marketing analyst?

3. Describe mercantilism and explain why some call it a poor approach to promoting economic development and prosperity. Given the criticisms, why do some countries continue to rely on practices based on mercantilism?

4. Explain Adam Smith's theory of absolute advantage. What are the potential limitations of this theory for helping policy makers when making decisions related to international trade? How does Ricardo's theory of comparative advantage differ from the theory of absolute advantage?

5. "Sending service jobs to low-cost nations, such as India, is good for America." What are the arguments in support of such an assertion? Under what circumstances might such an assertion be viewed as false?

6. Name some products that you believe have passed through the four stages of the international product life cycle. Try to identify industries or products for which the international product life cycle still helps explain international trade and investment. Can you identify industries or products for which this concept does not apply?

7. Use Porter's diamond model of national advantage to explain why an emerging market such as Indonesia would be expected to experience great difficulty in achieving global competitiveness in a new industry sector such as smartphones or hybrid electric-gasoline automobile engines.

8. What are the possible explanations for the observed decline in the proportion of FDI accounted for by the United States and Japan? What are the implications of such a decline? Do you expect that this decline will continue in the future? Why or why not?

9. How has the level and direction of FDI changed over the past two to three decades, both overall and in terms of annual outflows and inflows? What might explain why these changes have occurred? Why would this information be of relevance to managers?

10. According to theories presented in this module, why might companies engage in foreign direct investment rather than international trade?

globalEDGE RESEARCH TASK   http://globalEDGE.msu.edu/

Use the globalEDGE website (http://globaledge.msu.edu/) to complete the following exercises:

1. You work for a high-tech company that plans to invest in new countries for manufacturing and licensing to supply finished products in different global regions efficiently. Review all the indices listed in the "Indices" page of a country in the "Global Insights" section of globalEDGE and pick the three most important indices that would guide your company selecting the best countries to invest in. Be ready to discuss your selection with the top management and explain to them why you believe those three are the most important indices for your company.

2. Your company, which is in the cosmetics industry, is interested in finding the market potential of Australia, Czech Republic, India, and Japan for international expansion. Your manager suggested using the population and per capita GDP for assessment, but you believe current imports of cosmetics in those countries would be a good indicator too. Locate each country under the "Global Insights" section of globalEDGE to find population, per capita GDP, and imports values of cosmetics using the menu items on the left and prepare a table for comparison. Which two of these indicators seem to be a better option and which one seems to be more important? Can you think of any other indicators? Prepare to discuss with your manager.

MINICASE

BRAZIL: A GLOBAL COMPETITOR IN INFORMATION TECHNOLOGY OUTSOURCING?

As the world becomes increasingly dependent on information technology (IT) products and services, the global IT outsourcing industry has expanded rapidly. Driven by global competitive pressures to reduce costs and focus on core competencies, corporations of all sizes have chosen to outsource and offshore many of their IT services. Worldwide, India has established a strong leadership position in the IT offshoring market, accounting for the largest share among countries. However, challenges have begun to emerge for India's IT sector, including increasing labor costs, inadequate physical infrastructure, and a daunting government bureaucracy, among other factors.

Although many people would associate the country with soccer or samba, Brazil has emerged as a global competitor in a range of sophisticated technology sectors. Now, Brazil has launched an active campaign to build a strong international competitive position in the IT offshoring business, viewing it as a source of skilled jobs and a basis for improving overall economic development.

Brazil's IT outsourcing sector is small relative to India's, but strong growth is projected based on the country's strengths along several dimensions. As the ninth largest economy in the world, Brazil has a sophisticated telecommunications and network services infrastructure, one that has been rated higher than India or China on such key measures as network availability. Brazil has a tradition of strong engineering schools, capable of producing high-quality technical graduates. With over 2 million people employed in the overall information technology and computers sector, including over 400,000 people employed in IT services, the size of Brazil's domestic market for IT services is comparable to that of world-leading India, although a much smaller level of IT services is exported. Brazil has one of the world's most automated and sophisticated banking sectors and a dynamic domestic marketplace for IT software and support services. Brazilian wage rates average less than 20 percent of comparable hourly positions in the United States. Employee turnover is less than 13 percent, versus up to 40 percent for some Indian IT companies. Total operating costs, which include labor, infrastructure costs, corporate taxes, and incentives, are lower than competitors from most competing low-wage and moderate-to-high-wage nations. Brazil also boasts only a single time zone difference to the East Coast of the United States and four time zones for the U.S. West Coast and parts of Europe. This minimal time zone difference provides Brazil with an advantage compared to competitors in China or India in terms of ease of real-time access and coordination with clients and the offshore project support teams. Brazilian business practices, culture, and values are more Westernized than is common for nations such as India and China, which can facilitate shared understanding and effectiveness of working relationships with companies in the United States and western Europe. "When outsourcing, it is important to be able to have trust in your supplier, which often requires learning about and building a strong relationship with them. This becomes much trickier when your outsourcing partner has different cultural sensibilities and is on the other side of the world," says Antonio Gil, chair of the Brazilian Association of Software and Services Export Companies. Encouraged by strengths such as these, companies such as Accenture, Hewlett-Packard, Electronic Data Systems, Whirlpool, Gap Inc., and IBM have been expanding their offshoring activities in Brazil. Even competitors from India, such as Tata Consultancy Services, Infosys, and Wipro, have begun to aggressively expand into Brazil. Overall, the IT sector is expected to grow from 8.8 percent of Brazil's gross domestic product in 2013 to 10.7 percent by 2022, including nearly $4 billion in exports and 3 million people employed.

Despite the country's many strengths, Brazil also has some limitations. For example, underinvestment in electrical generation could make the country prone to the brownout and blackout problems that have plagued other emerging markets, including India. The Portuguese-speaking Brazilian population has also been characterized as being weak in terms of English language skills, and there is a shortage of international experience among Brazilian technical and managerial ranks, which could be problematic for multinationals hoping to set up operations there. Only about 13 percent of the population of 207 million people have a university degree, and Brazil also suffers from a somewhat cumbersome regulatory climate, including inflexible labor laws, as well as a currency that has been prone to fluctuations over the past several decades. Even with wage inflation in India and China, Brazil's labor costs remain about 30 percent higher. Brazil also has problems in terms of crime and social inequality, especially in big urban centers such as Rio de Janeiro and São Paulo.

Critical Thinking Questions

1. Use the theories of international trade and investment in this module to help explain Brazil's intentions and actions regarding the international information technology sector.

2. What recommendations would you give to the Brazilian government and its outsourcing industry in order to improve their prospects for success in building a strong international competitive position in the information technology outsourcing business?

Sources: "The World Factbook," *Central Intelligence Agency,* 2018; Angelica Mari, "Brazil ICT to Represent 10.7 Percent of GDP by 2022," *ZDNet,* May 13, 2015; "Brazil Real Average Monthly Income," *Trading Economics,* June 23, 2018; Dino Pieczynski, "Employee Turnover Slows in Brazil, Evan as the Tech Sector Remains an Economic Bright Spot," *Radford Articles,* June 2016; Todd Benson, "Brazil Aims to Be Outsourcing Giant," *The New York Times Company,* May 18, 2005; Marcio Silva, "Brazil as an Outsourcing Destination," *Sourcingmag,* February 1, 2006; Gina Ruiz, "Brazil Seeks Outsourcing Dominance," *Workforce,* November 30, 2007; Stephanie Overby, "Outsourcing: Brazil Blossoms as IT Services Hub," *CIO,* September 8, 2010; Antonio Regalado, "Soccer, Samba, and Outsourcing?" *The Wall Street Journal,* January 25, 2007; and Diana Farrell, Martha Laboissiere, and Bruno Pietracci, "Assessing Brazil's Offshoring Prospects," *The McKinsey Quarterly,* March 2007.

NOTES

1. Martin Wolf, chief economics commentator, Financial Times.

2. Penny Pritzker, "U.S. Secretary of Commerce Penny Pritzker Recognizes May as World Trade Month," *Department of Commerce*, May 02, 2014.

3. The World Bank, "Exports of Goods and Services (BoP, current US$)," https://data.worldbank.org, accessed July 04, 2018.

4. The World Bank, "Service Exports (BoP, current US$)," https://data.worldbank.org, accessed July 04, 2018.

5. The World Bank, "Trade (% of GDP)," https://data.worldbank.org, accessed July 04, 2018.

6. World Trade Organization, *World Statistical Review 2017*, https://www.wto.org, accessed July 04, 2018.

7. Ibid.

8. E. Woyo, "The Uneven Playing Field in International Trade in Developing Countries: A Critical Interjection and Review," *Applied Economics and Business Review*, vol. 1, no. 1, 2014, 18–20.

9. World Trade Organization, *World Trade Statistical Review 2016*, https://www.wto.org, accessed July 04, 2018; United Nations, "World Exports by Provenance and Destination (Table D)," *2016 International Trade Statistics Yearbook Volume II*, 2017, https://comtrade.un.org, accessed July 04, 2018; *Monthly Bulletin of Statistics*, July 2001, 266–71, July 2000, 258–61, June 1997, 255–62, June 1993, 266–71, New York: United Nations; and *Statistical Yearbook*, New York: United Nations, 1969, 376–83.

10. U.S Census Bureau, "Top Trading Partners," https://www.census.gov, accessed July 04, 2018.

11. Ibid.

12. World Trade Organization, *World Statistical Review 2017*, https://www.wto.org, accessed July 04, 2018; World Trade Organization, *World Trade Statistical Review 2016*, https://www.wto.org, accessed July 04, 2018; U.S. Census Bureau, "U.S. International Trade in Goods and Services," https://www.census.gov, accessed July 04, 2018; Industry Canada, "Trade Data Online," http://www.ic.gc.ca, accessed July 04, 2018; GlobalEDGE, "Mexico: Trade Statistics," http://globaledge.msu.edu, accessed July 04, 2018; International Trade Centre, "Trade Map—International Trade Statistics," https://www.trademap.org, accessed July 04, 2018.

13. Venezuela is a full member of Mercosur but was suspended December 01, 2016, and remains suspended at the time of this writing.

14. Although the European Union had 28 members as of the time of this writing, the United Kingdom was in negotiations to exit the union as part of the so-called Brexit vote undertaken in that country in 2016.

15. World Trade Organization, *World Trade Statistical Review 2016*, https://www.wto.org, accessed July 04, 2018.

16. U.S. Census Bureau, "Top Trading Partners—December 2017," https://www.census.gov, accessed July 04, 2018.

17. Office of the United States Trade Representative, "U.S.-China Trade Facts," https://ustr.gov, accessed July 04, 2018.

18. Peter Navarro, *Report of "The China Price Project,"* Irvine, CA: Merage School of Business, University of California, http://www.peternavarro.com, accessed June 23, 2018.

19. For example, see Salman Ahmed, and Alexander Bisk, "Trump's National Security Strategy: A New Brand of Mercantilism?" Carnegie Endowment for International Peace, http://carnegieendowment.org, accessed June 23, 2018; Catherine Rampell, "Trump's Trade Policy Is Stuck in the '80s—the 1680s," *Washington Post*, https://www.washingtonpost.com, accessed June 23, 2018; and "How Donald Trump Is Changing the Rules for American Business," *The Economist*, https://www.economist.com, accessed June 23, 2018.

20. Selina Jackson, "Growth and Development: Why Openness to Trade Is Necessary but Not Sufficient," Brookings Institution, November 23, 2015, https://www.brookings.edu, accessed August 17, 2018.

21. David Ricardo, "The Principles of Political Economy and Taxation," in *International Trade Theory: Hume to Ohlin*, ed. William R. Allen, New York: Random House, 1965, 62–67.

22. Steadman, John, "The Rise of India," *Bloomberg Businessweek*, December 08, 2003.

23. "Outsourcing 101," *The Wall Street Journal*, May 27, 2004.

24. Eli F. Heckscher, and Bertil Ohlin, *Heckscher-Ohlin Trade Theory*, trans., ed., and intro. Harry Flam and M. June Flanders, Cambridge, MA: MIT Press, 1991.

25. Staffan Burenstam Linder, *An Essay on Trade and Transformation*, Stockholm: Almqvist & Wicksell, 1961.

26. Ricardo, "The Principles of Political Economy and Taxation," 174–77.

27. Kimberly C. Gleason, Jeff Madura, and Joan Wiggenhorn, "Operating Characteristics, Risk, and Performance of Born-Global Firms," *International Journal of Managerial Finance*, vol. 2, no. 2, 2006, 96–120; N. Hashai, and T. Almor, "Gradually Internationalizing 'Born Global' Firms: An Oxymoron?" *International Business Review*, vol. 13, 2004, 465–83.

28. F. Robert Jacobs, and Richard B. Chase, *Operations and Supply Chain Management*, 15th ed., Burr Ridge, IL: McGraw-Hill Irwin, 2018.

29. Barry P. Collins, and Susan M. Collins, "Capital Flows to Developing Countries: Implications for Saving and Investment," 1999, *Brookings Papers on Economic Activity*, ed., George L. Perry, Washington, DC: Brookings Institute, 143–80.

30. Alfred Marshall, *Principles of Economics*, 8th ed., London: Macmillan, 1920.

31. Michael E. Porter, *The Competitive Advantage of Nations*, New York: Free Press, 1990.

32. For example, see Christophe Lecuyer, *Making Silicon Valley: Innovation and the Growth of High Tech, 1930–1970*, Cambridge, MA: MIT Press, 2005.

33. U.S. Department of Commerce, Bureau of Economic Analysis, "U.S. Net International Investment Position at the End of the Period, Expanded Detail," June 27, 2018, https://www.bea.gov, accessed July 04, 2018.

34. Ibid.

35. UN Conference on Trade and Development, "Annex Table 4: FDI Outward Stock, By Region and Economy, 1990–2017," *World Investment Report 2018*, http://unctad.org, accessed July 04, 2018.

36. Ibid.

37. Jordan I. Siegel, Amir N. Licht, and Shalom H. Schwartz, "Egalitarianism, Cultural Distance, and Foreign Direct Investment: A New Approach," *Organization Science*, vol. 24, no. 4, 2013, 1174–94.

38. UN Conference on Trade and Development, "FDI Outflows, By Region and Economy, 1990–2017," *World Investment Report 2018*, http://unctad.org, accessed July 04, 2018.

39. Ibid.

40. Ibid.

41. Christabelle Noronha, "In Step with the Nation," Tata Group, http://www.tata.com, accessed January 08, 2015.

42. UN Conference on Trade and Development, "FDI Inflows, By Region and Economy, 1990–2017," *World Investment Report 2018*, http://unctad.org, accessed July 04, 2018.

43. Ibid.

44. Ibid.

45. Ibid.

46. Ibid.

47. Ibid.

48. Vintila Denisia, "Foreign Direct Investment Theories: An Overview of the Main FDI Theories," *European Journal of Interdisciplinary Studies*, December 2010, pp. 104–10.

49. Stephen Hymer, *The International Operations of International Firms: A Study in Direct Investment*, Cambridge, MA: MIT Press, 1976.

50. Statista, "Wireless Subscriptions Market Share by Carrier in the U.S. from 1st Quarter 2011 to 1st Quarter 2018," https://www.statista.com, accessed June 23, 2018.

51. Frederick T. Knickerbocker, *Oligopolistic Reaction and Multinational Enterprise*, Boston: Harvard University Press, 1973;

Grazia Ietto-Gillies, *Transnational Corporations and International Production. Concepts, Theories and Effects*, Cheltenham: Edward Elgar, 2005; Witold J. Henisz, and Andrew Delios, "Uncertainty, Imitation, and Plant Location: Japanese Multinational Corporations, 1990–1996," *Administrative Science Quarterly*, vol. 46, 2001, 443–75; Mauro F. Guillen, "Structural Inertia, Imitation, and Foreign Expansion: South Korean Firms and Business Groups in China, 1987–1995," *Academy of Management Journal*, vol. 45, 2002, 509–25; Sabine Bockem, and Anja Tuschke, "A Tale of Two Theories: Foreign Direct Investment Decisions from the Perspectives of Economic and Institutional Theory," *Schmalenback Business Review* 62, 2010: 260–90.

52. Ibid.; P. J. Buckley, and M. Casson, *The Future of Multinational Enterprise*, New York: Macmillan, 1976; J. F. Hennart, *A Theory of Multinational Enterprise*, Ann Arbor: University of Michigan Press, 1983; B. Williams, "Positive Theories of Multinational Banking: Eclectic Theory Versus Internalization Theory," *Journal of Economic Surveys*, vol. 11, no. 2, 1997, 71–100; Denisia, "Foreign Direct Investment Theories: An Overview of the Main FDI Theories."

53. John H. Dunning, *International Production and the Multinational Enterprise*, London: George Allen & Unwin, 1981, 109–10; Buckley, and Casson, *The Future of Multinational Enterprise*; D. Teece, *The Multinational Corporation and the Resource Cost of International Technology Transfers*, Cambridge, MA: Ballinger, 1986; A. M. Rugman, *Inside the Multinationals: The Economics of International Markets*, New York: Columbia University Press, 1986.

3

Sociocultural Forces

> " The domestic companies that are likely to see incremental growth in the coming decades are those that . . . are developing the strategic skill set to master doing business across cultures. Cross-cultural core competence is at the crux of today's sustainable competitive advantage. "

—Denise Pirotti Hummel,
CEO of Universal Consensus[1]

Brueghel's Tower of Babel story (in the book of Genesis) explains how God scattered the prideful people who built such a magnificent tower, confounding their speech and separating them with different languages and cultures. ©DeAgostini/G. NIMATALLAH/ Getty Images.

LEARNING OBJECTIVES

After reading this module, you should be able to:

LO 3-1   **Describe** what culture is.

LO 3-2   **Identify** the ways culture affects all business activity.

LO 3-3   **Describe** how culture shows itself.

LO 3-4   **Describe** four frameworks for analyzing culture.

LO 3-5   **Describe** the global mind-set and the MBI model.

LO 3-6   **Discuss** cautions for using cultural frameworks in business.

Language and Culture: Lost in Translation?

New research in cognitive psychology has revealed a strong connection between language and thinking. "Of course," you might say, "we use language to think." And in fact, the idea that words shape our thinking is not new, though it was abandoned for a time. Today, thanks to cognitive psychologists such as Lera Boroditsky and her colleagues, it is receiving new attention and acceptance.

Boroditsky and her colleagues explore whether our understanding of the basic phenomena we experience, like time, space, and causal relationships, is related to language. "Each language has its own cognitive toolkit," says Boroditsky. For instance, in Pormpuraaw, a remote Australian Aboriginal community, directions are conceptualized in terms of north, south, east, and west. There is no left and right. Not surprisingly, the people of Pormpuraaw have well-developed spatial orientation, can tell which compass direction they are facing at any time, and have solid navigational skills. The Piraha, a Brazilian Amazon tribe, don't count with numbers; they use words like "few" and "many" and don't keep track of exact quantities. Then there are Japanese speakers, who use different words for counting based on the shape of the things they are counting. Russians have more words for shades of blue than English speakers and can discriminate among them more precisely. Do words shape people's experience in each of these examples?

Boroditsky points out that each of the world's more than 7,000 languages—many of which have not yet been studied—reflects the adaptability of our human intelligence, its "ability to invent and rearrange conceptions of the world to suit changing goals and environments." Each language presents a way of organizing the world and making meaning of it, a collection of knowledge that has developed over thousands of years within a given culture. So, as we begin to understand the process of language, from the Tower of Babel to the present, we also gain new insight into how we've become who we are.

We now know there is a relationship between thought and language, but the interesting question is, "Which way does it go?" Recent studies suggest that if we change language, we change the way we think, as well. Here's the fascinating part: the work of Boaz Keysar at the University of Chicago suggests that when we speak a foreign language, it "provides a distancing mechanism that moves people from the immediate intuitive system to a more deliberate mode of thinking," which is to say that speaking a foreign language increases our risk taking and judgment abilities because it reduces emotional input for the decisions. Hence the excitement and liberation we find when we persist in our study and gain fluency in another language. Here's to study abroad!

Sources: Lera Boroditsky, "How Language Shapes Thought: The Languages We Speak Affect Our Perceptions of the World," *Scientific American*, February 2011; William Harms, "Foreign Language Thoughts Boost Risk-Taking," *Futurity*, April 25, 2012; Lera Boroditsky, "How Language Shapes Thought," *The Long Now Foundation*, October 26, 2010; and Lera Boroditsky, "How Language Shapes Thought: The Languages We Speak Affect Our Perceptions of the World," *Scientific American*, vol. 304, no. 2, February 2011, 63–65.

Cultural differences are an interesting topic for study on their own, and in business, their study presents an opportunity to gain a strategic advantage. The first step in getting to this strategic advantage is to understand a basic concept: *our way* is not the *only way* or even the *best way*. This reality sounds simple, but it is often difficult for us to grasp and internalize when we most need to when we are interacting with people from other cultures. Mishandling or ignoring cultural differences can lead to many business problems, such as lost sales, the departure of competent employees, and low morale that contributes to low productivity. When we adjust to cultural differences, when they are harmonized or blended successfully, they can result in powerful, innovative business practices superior to those that one culture could produce by itself. The whole can be greater than its parts!

> **" To HAVE ANOTHER LANGUAGE IS to HAVE ANOTHER SOUL. "**
> —*Charlemagne*[2]

What Is Culture and Why Is It Important?

LO 3-1
Describe what culture is.

There are many definitions of *culture*, and we'll share several that we find useful. The definitional differences depend mostly on the scientists' approach to the field, their level of analysis, whether they are looking at whole populations as groups or the individuals within these groups. Most anthropologists, whose focus it is to study culture, view it as the *sum total of the beliefs, rules, techniques, institutions, and artifacts that characterize human populations.*[3] Culture also can be understood from the individual level as the "individual worldviews, social rules, and interpersonal dynamics characterizing a group of people set in a particular time and place."[4] We encourage you to think of culture in the way that seems the most useful to you, given a particular situation. Most anthropologists also agree that:

1. Culture is *learned;* we are not born with a culture.
2. The various aspects of culture are *interrelated.*
3. Culture is *shared, patterned, and mutually constructed through social interaction.*
4. Culture *defines the boundaries* of different groups.[5]

Society is composed of people living in their culture, often unaware of its influence on them. To understand a specific group, be it an organization or a society, an ethnic group or a social group, we need to understand its culture. Yet, we cannot directly observe it, so we have to learn about culture by observing how it manifests itself: in the character of the social world in which it exists. In this book, we examine how culture at the national level affects individual and group behavior. Managers also will want to pay attention to understanding organizational cultures and various local ethnic and regional subcultures. Our concern when we discuss culture here is with deep culture—the beliefs, attitudes, and values we have learned, often as children—as well as culture at the surface level where it shows itself most readily. For example, our beliefs about marriage are often evidenced in the rituals connected to a marriage ceremony, such as the sipping of sake, the bride's use of henna, the breaking of a glass, the wedding dress, and the tossing of the bride's bouquet. We might think of surface culture and deep culture as an iceberg. The surface culture is the small, 10 percent visible part above the water, and the deeper, unknown portions of culture, values, attitudes, and beliefs are below the water line. We look at the surface level when we consider how culture shows itself, later in this module.

When we work in cultures different from our own, we have to communicate across social, legal, language, and other borders that we may not understand. Yet members of most societies consider their culture superior to all others, a habit known as **ethnocentricity**. When outsiders attempt to introduce their home culture's approach in a business environment (for example, the "German way," the "Chinese way," or the "British way"), the stubborn resistance they are likely to meet is a sign of this ethnocentricity.

How do international business managers learn to live, work, and meet business goals in other cultures? Sometimes it's a challenge. The first step is to accept that other cultures are different, and the next step is to learn the characteristics of those cultures in order to adapt to them. The anthropologist E. T. Hall claims managers can do this in only two ways: (1) spend a lifetime in a culture, or (2) undergo an extensive training program that covers the main characteristics of a culture, including the language. Such an intensive study program is more elaborate than a briefing on a country's customs. It is a study of what culture is and does that builds an understanding of the ways in which culture has institutionalized human behavior.[6]

So what does this learning program include for international managers? First, there is factual knowledge about the other culture, which is relatively easy to obtain. Managers also need sensitivity training to the nuances of cultural differences, which requires effort to develop. Unfortunately, most newcomers to international business need to get off to a fast start and can rarely afford the time necessary for in-depth study of new cultures, despite Hall's suggestions. They can, however, take the important first step of realizing that there *are* other cultures, and they can anticipate that these cultures will tend to be ethnocentric. In this module, we look at some of the important areas of sociocultural difference that concern businesspeople, and at some of the cultural frameworks that are useful for learning what to anticipate in working across cultures. We hope that in your own work you will look for cultural differences and seek out opportunities to build your knowledge of other cultures.

ethnocentricity
The belief that your own culture is superior to other cultures

Culture Affects All Business Functions

LO 3-2
Identify the ways culture affects all business activity.

Everything we do is influenced by culture, a fact most of us realize about other cultures, but not always about our own. Here we look at ways national cultural differences can affect the functional areas of a business with an international presence, a good place to begin our focus on the role of culture in international business.

MARKETING

As you might imagine, the wide variation in cultural attitudes and values across markets requires that many firms develop a variety of marketing mixes to reach their consumers. To build effective marketing campaigns, the marketer has to understand the foreign market beyond its surface. The more she or he can understand how customers in the target market give meaning to events in their world and how they think their world should be, the better. For example, a marketing campaign for a luxury automobile might emphasize abundant details about technological and performance specifications in Germany, while the marketing approach for the same product in the United States might place more emphasis on visual and experiential elements.[7]

Companies have made many costly mistakes introducing products into foreign markets, especially in product design, advertising, and pricing. A U.S. company trying to sell a cranberry liqueur called Bogs in the United Kingdom, where *bog* is slang for outhouse, is one example. Another is selling the soap Irish Mist and the Rolls-Royce Silver Mist in Germany, where *mist* means dung/manure. A challenge for the Gerber brand of baby food and other products is that, in the French language, the word "gerber" means "vomit." Then there are misunderstandings of local values. Pepsodent tried to sell whitening toothpaste in Southeast Asia where people chew betel nut purposely to darken their teeth. In Japan, where kitchens often don't have ovens, international marketers tried to sell a cake mix. They did their research, but they asked merely whether the Japanese homemaker would serve the cake to her family, and the cake was already baked when being market tested.

It's difficult to remember that we don't know what we don't know—until the evidence is there. Through these errors, however, marketers learn the importance of understanding their markets and other cultures. Acquiring knowledge about a new culture is time-consuming and expensive, but probably less so than recovering from a major marketing disaster.

> **"CULTURE IS THE FOUNDATIONAL ARCHITECTURE of OUR MINDS—WE SEE ITS MANIFESTATIONS, but NOT THE TREMENDOUS WORK IT DOES HOLDING SOCIAL SYSTEMS TOGETHER AND HELPING US to SOLVE SHARED PROBLEMS. "**
>
> *—Nicholas Athanassiou, professor, Northeastern University*[8]

HUMAN RESOURCES

Cultural values play key roles in motivating and evaluating employees. In some cultures, individual effort is rewarded, while in others, group effort is more highly valued. Other values that come into play in human resource (HR) contexts relate to our attitudes toward social status. Is social status something we earn through achievements—what we do—or is it a result of our family's social position—who we are? U.S. employees, for example, expect to be promoted based on their accomplishments; they are often surprised to learn of the significant roles family background and schooling in the "right" institutions play in careers in Great Britain. In some cultures, policies regarding how employees are to be treated are expected to be applied consistently to everyone, while in other cultures the expectation may be that applicable policies may depend on the individual and the situation.

Different attitudes toward authority, another cultural variable, arise in HR contexts. Is the manager expected to be the *patron*, an authoritarian figure responsible for employees' welfare? Or the first among equals? Is the annual review understood as a way to credit the employee's work and help him or her grow, or a means of extracting higher labor output from the worker? The answers to these questions, which have critical relevance to HR practices, are more deeply embedded in cultural values than we are often aware.

Cultural Misunderstandings Enflame BP's Disaster

British Petroleum (BP) undertook significant effort to position itself as a "green" company and a leader in corporate social responsibility during the 1990s and early 2000s, an initiative that was rewarded with a No. 1 ranking in 2007 in *Fortune*'s annual ranking of globally responsible businesses. However, this accomplishment was quickly reversed when an explosion occurred on BP's Deepwater Horizon oil rig in the Gulf of Mexico on April 20, 2010. In addition to 11 people being killed and many others injured, oil gushed from the wellhead on the sea floor 41 miles off the Louisiana coast for months. It was the largest accidental oil spill ever recorded, with an estimated release of 210 million gallons of oil over the next three months. Despite a massive and well-organized clean-up initiative, the spill contaminated 68,000 square miles of ocean, an area about twice the size of Hungary or South Korea, and ruined over 1,070 miles of coastline. Images of an oil rig in flames, oil-soaked coastal birds struggling for their lives, and oil-coated beaches filled television screens and front pages of newspapers and magazines.

Although BP's reputation was tarnished by the enormous environmental damage the spill caused along the Gulf coast, the company made things far worse for itself, and for others, through cultural misunderstandings about people in the United States and how they respond to crises. First, BP's top U.S. executives were British, although the United States "accounts for about a quarter of BP's production, almost a third of its reserves and more than half its refining capacity and retail outlets." Tony Hayward, BP's chief executive at the time, was also British, as were the heads of media and BP's two main operating businesses in the United States. The most senior U.S. staff member, Managing Director for the Americas and Asia Bob Dudley, had held a series of overseas appointments at BP and did not have deep local ties. To the angry public, BP was easily seen as a solidly British company with little connection to the United States. Even its PR firm was British.

Then there were mistakes in defusing anger over the spill. Hayward apparently did not recognize the seriousness of the crisis, nor the intense level of public emotion he faced. On May 14, he told the U.S. public, "The Gulf of Mexico is a very big ocean. The amount of volume of oil and dispersant we are putting into it is tiny in relation to the total water volume." Four days later, he said, "I think the environmental impact of this disaster is likely to be very, very modest." On May 30, his apparent selfishness and lack of empathy regarding the massive environmental catastrophe in the Gulf was

The Deepwater Horizon oil spill seen by NASA's Terra satellite on May 24, 2010. Source: Michon Scott/NASA's Earth Observatory/NASA Goddard Space Flight Center.

reflected in his cavalier comment on the *Today* show saying, "There is no one who wants this thing over more than I do. You know, I'd like my life back." And on June 4, "I'm so far unscathed. . . . They've thrown some words at me. But I'm a Brit, so sticks and stones can break my bones but words never hurt me, or whatever the expression is." Hayward's matter-of-fact response greatly disappointed and then angered a public that needed and expected emotion, apology, and sympathy. His British accent only heightened the contrast between what the public wanted and what it received. People thought BP was not taking the disaster seriously. Yet, for many British individuals, such a public show of emotion would be deeply unsettling.

Bob Dudley expressed his emotions about the environmental catastrophe: "I just feel sad. I've been working in the oil and gas business my whole career. It provides a product that people need, it's energy, and all of us can't believe this has happened." But Dudley was not in charge; Hayward was, although three months after the crisis began, Hayward was replaced as BP's CEO. As a result of this cultural collision, BP is still struggling to overcome this disaster and rebuild its reputation almost a decade later.

Critical Thinking Questions

1. Do you think the U.S. public's response to the disaster would have been different had the company been more localized, for example, with a U.S. PR firm and U.S. executives?

2. Do you think BP should have had someone like Dudley in charge of the response from the beginning? Why or why not?
3. What role may our common use of English have played in BP's decisions to have CEO Hayward manage the public aspect of the recovery?

Sources: Telis Demos, "Accounting for Accountability: Fortune's Annual Ranking of Business Responsibility," *Fortune*, November 1, 2007; Jo Detavernier, "Deepwater Horizon: A Look Back at a First Rate PR Disaster," *Swyft*, July 9, 2018; Anne C. Mulkern, "BP's PR Blunders Mirror Exxon's, Appear Destined for Record Book," *The New York Times*, June 10, 2010; Jim Polson, "BP Oil Still Ashore One Year After End of Gulf Spill," *Bloomberg*, July 16, 2011; "BP's Cultural Failings," *Naomi Stanford*, June 9, 2010; and Ed Crooks, and Andrew Edgecliffe-Johnson, "Cultural failings leave BP engulfed," *Financial Times*, June 8, 2010.

PRODUCTION AND PROCUREMENT

Production managers have found that cultural values around attitudes toward change can seriously influence the acceptance of new production methods. Plant layout is also influenced by culture. Think of the assembly line, devised by minds socialized in a sequential, linear culture, in which the task receives primary focus, not the social relationship. Contrast that system with the Uddevalla approach found in some Volvo plants in Sweden in the 1980s, where small, autonomous teams working in a circle assembled an entire car in several hours.[9] Cultural norms and rules structure the way the firm acquires resources, as well. In much of Asia, for example, procurement often exists in a web of social relationships and friendships, whereas in the United States, transparency and price frequently drive the process. Personal relationships are so critical in Japan that if a foreigner turned down an offer to join a Japanese colleague for a "hashigo," or pub crawl, it might prevent a deal from being concluded successfully.[10] Due to changing labor and tariff laws and other conditions, supply contracts and other agreements with Brazilian companies frequently require flexibility in interpretation and enforcement, while detailed written agreements and rigorous enforcement of supply contracts are more common for companies from the United States.

ACCOUNTING AND FINANCE

A culture's accounting controls directly relate to its assumptions about people's basic nature. Are the controls tight throughout the organization, suggesting low levels of trust, or loose, suggesting the culture assumes people will act honestly even when they are not closely monitored? Are the controls administered by formal institutions in a command-and-control approach, gaining compliance through rules and sanctions, or do they rely instead on social norms, that is, customary rules of behavior?

International treasurers or comptrollers confront the strength of cultural forces when, armed with excellent balance sheets, they approach local banks in a foreign country only to find that the banks attach far more importance to who the treasurer is than to how strong the companies look on paper. In some cultures, financial statements are notoriously unreliable because local norms allow creative accounting in order to keep the tax collector away. In one classic example, a U.S. business executive in Italy filed Italian tax documents the way he had in New York, where he had spent most of his career, despite the advice of his local employees that tax payment in Italy is a negotiation. As a result, the firm paid much more than was required.

CULTURE FACTS @internationalbiz

@EuropeanUnion In the European Union, accounting is based on principles, from which processes are deduced; in the United States, accounting is based on a collection of rules. #principles #collectionofrules

PREFERRED LEADERSHIP STYLES

The way we think about the role and function of our leaders varies across cultures. Desired leadership traits vary by culture as well. Is the usual relationship between leader and followers hierarchical or lateral? Is the leadership model paternalistic? Heroic? Does the ideal leader come up through the ranks? Or is someone placed in the leadership position due to family or status? When communicating and addressing issues facing the company, does an ideal leader get straight to the point or instead use indirect language and metaphors? Should a leader be comfortable with publicly disagreeing with others during a discussion, or instead avoid confrontation and focus on harmony and "save face"?[11] As for purpose and function, does leadership integrate a group of people, or does it provide direction for a collection of individuals? In Japan, which tends toward a paternalistic understanding of leadership, the firm's director often is asked to vet a company member's prospective bride or groom. In the United States, leaders of successful companies often are seen as heroes.

In these descriptions, we have touched only the very tip of the cultural iceberg. That leaves more than 90 percent of culture below the surface, for you to discover and explore. How can you help yourself to better accomplish this? Direct experience is invaluable. Seek out subcultures in your community, spend vacations abroad, and think about undertaking foreign study. You also may want to consult the results of the Global Leadership and Organizational Behavior Effectiveness (GLOBE) Research Project, a study developed and led by the scholar Robert House that engages social scientists and management scholars from around the world in ongoing research in an effort to better understand how culture affects leadership.[12]

LO 3-3
Describe how culture shows itself.

aesthetics
A culture's sense of beauty and good taste

Tattoos add aesthetic appeal, or do they? ©Ryan McVay/Getty Images.

How Culture Shows Itself

Now that we have discussed what culture is and its importance to international business managers, we'll take a look at how a society's culture shows or manifests itself. It's quite simple, really: culture manifests in everything. We look briefly at aesthetics, religion, material culture, language and communication, and social organization. We then look at gift giving, because it is a complex, cultural area new international managers often face.

AESTHETICS

Aesthetics is the area of philosophy that deals with beauty, so a culture's aesthetics describes its sense of beauty and taste. The word's origin is the Greek *aisthētikos*, meaning perceptible by the senses. A culture's aesthetics is expressed in many areas, most directly and intentionally in art, drama, music, folklore, and dance. Art, including color and form, can convey a lot about culture to international managers because it contains symbolic meanings that are clues to values. Take the simple aspect of color. The color of mourning in the United States and Mexico is black, while it is black and white in East Asia, red in South Africa, and purple in Brazil and Thailand. You might want to consider those symbolic meanings in logo and packaging design. In the Islamic world, green is an optimistic and hopeful color, so an ad or package featuring green is inclined to evoke a positive response. Orange for Catholics in Northern Ireland is symbolic of the Protestant group Orange Order, perceived as hostile to Irish Catholics. So the slogan for the Orange telecommunications company (originally British, now French), "The future's bright. . . . The future's Orange" wasn't exactly what its marketers wanted to communicate.

Aesthetics applies to our ideas about our bodies and physical beauty, as well. Take, for instance, the view of an ideal weight, which differs markedly across cultures. Often in richer countries the affluent are thinner, while in poorer countries the indigent are thinner. In Japan, sumo athletes are intentionally obese, and in some areas of Nigeria, girls enter "fattening rooms" to bulk up. Tattoos represent another aspect of aesthetic value differences across cultures. In some cultures, they are seen as beauty-enhancing, while in others they are a desecration. The remains of one of the oldest preserved humans, Otzi the Iceman from about 3300 BCE, found in a glacier on the Austrian–Italian border, show that he was tattooed.[13] In an interesting meaning reversal, criminals in Japan were once tattooed by authorities as a way to identify and humiliate them. Today, the Yakuza, members of a Japanese crime syndicate, proudly tattoo themselves to establish their in-group identity.

Music and folklore also communicate a culture's aesthetics. A commercial that used a ballad in the United States might be better received in

Mexico if accompanied by a bolero, or in Brazil, a samba. A culture's folklore can disclose much about a society's way of life. Take, for example, the way Japanese accepted KFC's story of its rustic, agricultural origins to a background of "My Old Kentucky Home" and Colonel Sanders as one of their own venerated elders. Loy Weston, who established KFC in Japan, used the tune as background and placed large statues of the Southern gentleman colonel as a greeter outside every store. He claimed that luck was in play here, but that luck was based on his sensitivity to local folklore, which valued a romantic connection with an agricultural past and venerated male elders.

The incorrect use of folklore can sometimes cost the firm its share of the market. For example, associating a product with a cowboy, such as the Marlboro Man, would not be as effective in Chile or Argentina as in the United States, because in those countries the cowboy is a far less romantic figure; being a cowboy is just a job. Smirnoff's use of the famous Ernesto "Che" Guevara's image in an advertisement for spicy vodka in Cuba sparked controversy there because Guevara is a national hero and Cubans felt using his image to sell the product diminished him.[14] Procter and Gamble's Pampers introduction into Asia used images of the stork's arrival with the baby to signal product need, but most Asian cultures don't have babies brought by storks, so the images were confusing. In Japan, for example, babies are brought by large peaches. Folklore is powerful because it conveys a package of emotions and connotations, often efficiently, even with one image.

RELIGION

Along with its spiritual aspect, religion is an important component of culture and responsible for many attitudes and beliefs that influence human behavior. Knowledge of the basic tenets of the religions in your business markets will be useful as you build your understanding of these cultures. Each religion has its forms and traditions and expresses its beliefs through particular kinds of worship and prayer, rituals, dietary rules, and modes of dress.[15] Religion is also an area of personal belief in which ethnocentric tendencies can be quite strong.

The Islamic Dome of the Rock in the Temple Mount, Old City of Jerusalem. ©Medioimages/Photodisc/Getty Images.

TABLE 3.1 Followers of Five Major World Religions

Religion	Number of Followers (millions)	Cultural Tradition
Christianity	2,300	West Asian/Ambrahamic
Islam	1,800	West Asian/Ambrahamic
Hinduism	1,100	Indian
Buddhism	500	Indian
Judaism	10	West Asian/Ambrahamic

Sources: "The Center for the Study of Global Christianity," *Gordon-Conwell Theological Seminary*; Conrad Hackett, David Mcclendon, "Christians Remain World's Largest Religious Group, But They Are Declining in Europe," *Pew Research Center*, April 5, 2017; and "The World Factbook," *Central Intelligence Agency*, 2018.

Following is a brief description of the main beliefs or principles that define five of the major religions found in the world, along with Table 3.1, which shows the size of their following. Consider it simply a beginning for your further understanding of each.

Christianity Christianity has many denominations, and all of them share a belief that there is one God who is revealed through human history. Christians believe Jesus was God's son who came to earth as a man and lived in Israel, then called Palestine; he was killed about 30 CE by authorities of the Roman Empire but came back to life and ascended to heaven. Christians believe all who profess their faith in the resurrection of Jesus will be received into heaven after death.

Islam The religion of Islam, whose name comes from an Arabic word meaning "submitting," began in the 7th century CE and, like Christianity and Judaism, originated in the Middle East. Islam professes belief in one God, Allah. Muslims (those who practice Islam) focus on living their lives according to God's will, which is revealed through the Qur'an (the Scripture) and a long line of messengers. Mohammed is revered as the last and most important prophet of the Islamic religion and is believed to have received the words of the Qur'an directly from God in a series of visions.

Hinduism The oldest of the major world religions, Hinduism began in India around 2500 BCE. Hindus believe in one Supreme Reality, called Brahman, which takes many forms and names. They seek to be in harmony with Brahman by living an ethically good life through self-discipline, the sharing of wealth, and adherence to the teachings of the Scriptures (Vedas). Like Buddhists, they believe in reincarnation and hope to escape it to achieve union with God.

Buddhism Founded between the 6th and 4th centuries BCE in northeastern India, Buddhism is based on the teachings of Siddhartha Gautama, a royal prince who became known as the Buddha (Enlightened One). Buddhism encompasses several schools of thought established by different teachers over the centuries. In general, Buddhists believe earthly life, a continuous cycle of birth, death, and rebirth called reincarnation, is the cause of human suffering. When we finally escape this cycle to achieve a state of being called "nirvana," we become, like the Buddha, enlightened.

Judaism Begun about 1900 BCE in Israel, Judaism, then known as Canaan, shares with Christianity the belief that God acts in human history, especially in times of struggle and oppression. The Tanak, Judaism's Scripture, tells how the Jews were repeatedly conquered and enslaved by foreign powers but were freed by God's power acting through figures such as Abraham, Moses, and David. Jews believe God made a covenant or promise to protect them as long as they continue to believe in and worship the one God. See a map of the world's religions in Figure 3.1.

FIGURE 3.1 Map of the World's Religions

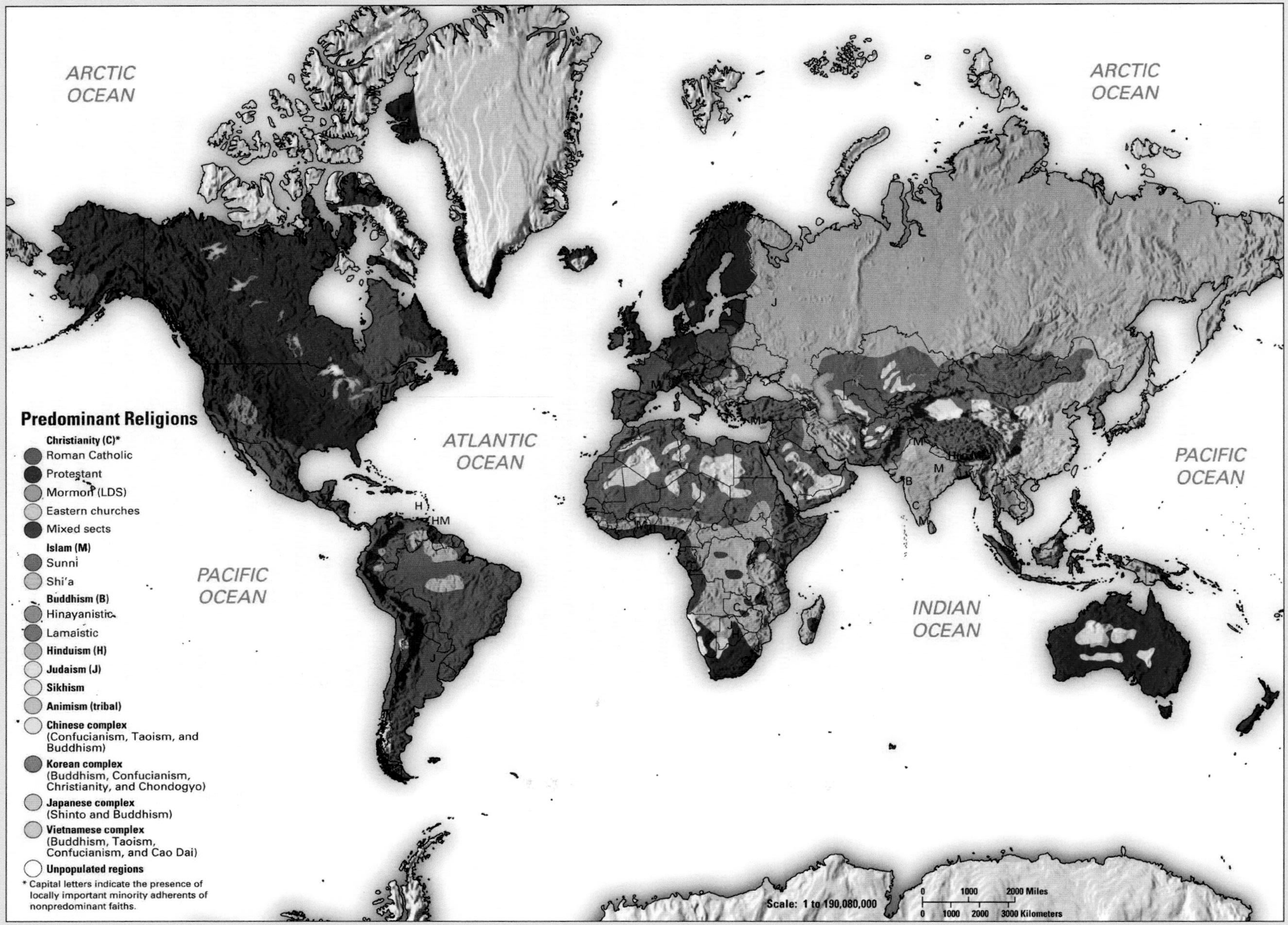

Predominant Religions

Christianity (C)*
- Roman Catholic
- Protestant
- Mormon (LDS)
- Eastern churches
- Mixed sects

Islam (M)
- Sunni
- Shi'a

Buddhism (B)
- Hinayanistic
- Lamaistic

Hinduism (H)

Judaism (J)

Sikhism

Animism (tribal)

Chinese complex (Confucianism, Taoism, and Buddhism)

Korean complex (Buddhism, Confucianism, Christianity, and Chondogyo)

Japanese complex (Shinto and Buddhism)

Vietnamese complex (Buddhism, Taoism, Confucianism, and Cao Dai)

Unpopulated regions

* Capital letters indicate the presence of locally important minority adherents of nonpredominant faiths.

ARCTIC OCEAN

ARCTIC OCEAN

PACIFIC OCEAN

PACIFIC OCEAN

ATLANTIC OCEAN

INDIAN OCEAN

Scale: 1 to 190,080,000

0   1000   2000 Miles

0   1000   2000   3000 Kilometers

MATERIAL CULTURE

material culture or artifacts
All human-made objects

Material culture or artifacts are all the human-made objects of a culture; people who study material culture are concerned with *how* people make things (technology) and *who* makes *what* and *why* (economics). Every culture prides itself on certain parts of its material culture. For example, in France, much of the material culture related to food, cooking, and eating has deep emotional meanings for members of the culture. Think of woodblock prints and pottery in Japan, worry beads and classical theater in Greece, artisan chocolates in Switzerland. Some awareness of these objects and the meanings they have can communicate your interest in the culture and help you understand more about it.

LANGUAGE

Probably the most obvious and distancing cultural distinction for newcomers to international business is language, spoken and unspoken. Language is an important key to a culture, and without understanding it, people find themselves locked out of all but a culture's perimeter. In fact, nothing equals the spoken language for distinguishing one culture or subculture from another. Even though many global businesspeople speak English, they often want to conduct business in their own language. Therefore, the foreign seller who speaks the local language has a competitive edge. Figure 3.2 shows a map of the major languages of the world.

Nonverbal communication, or the unspoken language, can often tell businesspeople something the spoken language does not if they can understand it. In cultures known as high context (HC) such as Middle Eastern and Asian cultures, meaning is conveyed through context rather than the words themselves. In these HC cultures, the unspoken language is used intensively to convey significant, intentional meaning. People in HC cultures often have developed an advanced ability to read unspoken language, such as body language and facial expressions. They can use contextual clues like eye contact, posture, and subtle facial expressions to communicate or receive meaning, perhaps without any special awareness that they are doing so.

Gestures vary from one region to another. Here is one simple example that persistently leads to misunderstandings: people from the United States and most Europeans understand the thumbs-up gesture to mean "all right," but in southern Italy and Greece, this gesture transmits a vulgar message. Similarly, making the "OK" sign with the thumb and the forefinger is friendly in the United States, but it means "you're worth nothing" in France and Belgium and is considered vulgar in Greece and Turkey.

Unspoken language also includes spatial relationships, including those where we work. In the United States, an office door that is closed suggests a request for privacy; the normal position of the door is open. Germans regularly keep their doors closed. Anthropologist Edward Hall suggests this does not mean the person behind the door wants no visitors, but only that he or she considers open doors sloppy and disorderly.[16] Office size and location can mean different things in different cultures, as well. In the United States, the higher the status of the executive, the larger and more secluded the office, but in the Arab world, the company president may be in a small, crowded office. In Japan, the senior person is likely to be closest to the center of the room, and the least valuable places on an office floor are by the windows. The French also locate important department heads in the center of activities, with their assistants going out from this center.

Conversational distance, the space between people in a conversation, also tends to vary across cultural borders. It tends to be much shorter in the Middle East than in Anglo cultures such as those of the United Kingdom, Australia, the United States, and Canada. It's not unusual to see two people with different expectations for conversational distance move, almost in a dance across a floor, as one tries to close the space and the other expands it. Neither may be aware of what is happening. Conversational distances vary by gender as well, and also by how well people know one another.

Then there are performance issues of spoken language. How does sequencing work? Does one person talk, and then another? Or does everyone chime in at the same time?

FIGURE 3.2 Major Languages of the World

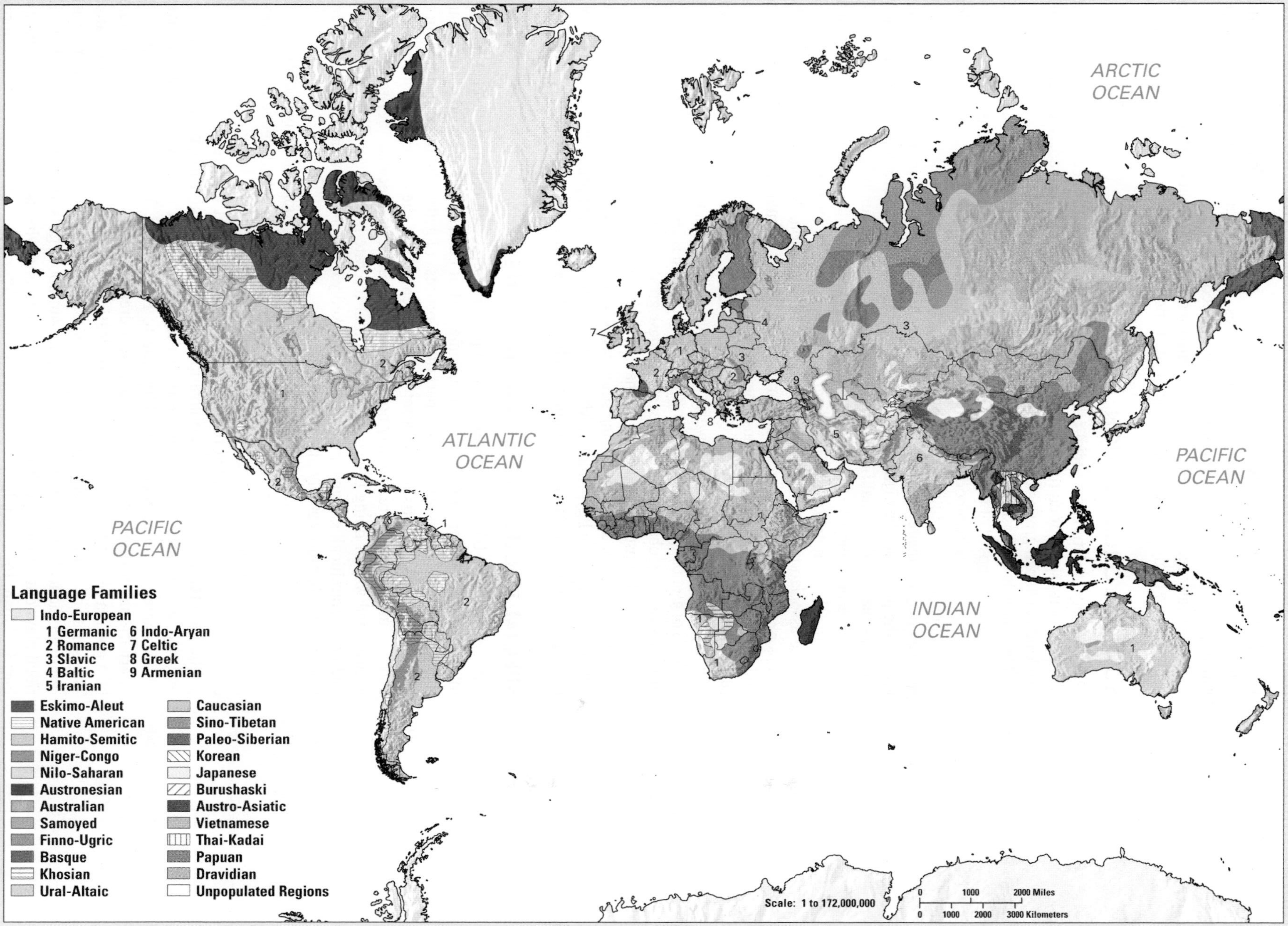

Language Families

Indo-European
1 Germanic 6 Indo-Aryan
2 Romance 7 Celtic
3 Slavic 8 Greek
4 Baltic 9 Armenian
5 Iranian

Eskimo-Aleut
Native American
Hamito-Semitic
Niger-Congo
Nilo-Saharan
Austronesian
Australian
Samoyed
Finno-Ugric
Basque
Khosian
Ural-Altaic

Caucasian
Sino-Tibetan
Paleo-Siberian
Korean
Japanese
Burushaski
Austro-Asiatic
Vietnamese
Thai-Kadai
Papuan
Dravidian
Unpopulated Regions

Scale: 1 to 172,000,000

0   1000   2000 Miles
0 1000 2000 3000 Kilometers

ARCTIC OCEAN

PACIFIC OCEAN

INDIAN OCEAN

ATLANTIC OCEAN

PACIFIC OCEAN

How do people interrupt one another, and how is that perceived? What are the unwritten rules of having a conversation? In some cultures, disagreement or argument is seen as a way of pulling people closer; in others, it pushes people away.

As you can see, there are many factors involved in trying to understand other cultures. Now you can begin to build your sense of the major language groups and their borders.

SOCIETAL ORGANIZATION

Every society structures its social relationships, and these patterned arrangements define an important aspect of culture: the way social groups are constructed. Sociologists define two kinds of social groups or institutions: *kinship* and *free association.*

The family is the basic unit of institutions based on kinship. Unlike the U.S. family, which is generally composed of parents and their children, families in many nations are extended to include all relatives by blood and marriage. This extended family can be a source of employees and business connections and also potential problems. The trust people place in their relatives may motivate them to buy from a supplier owned by their cousin's cousin, even though the price may be higher. Local HR managers may fill the best jobs with family members regardless of their qualifications. Although the extended family is large, each member's feeling of responsibility to the family is strong. The practice of favoring family members may violate the Western notion that nepotism should generally be avoided.

Free associations are the second class of social institution. Not based on kinship, these groups may be formed by age, gender, or common interest.[17] International managers need to understand these associations because they influence behavior at a fundamental level, and their rules and organization are likely to differ across cultures. Recently a new kind of free association has emerged on Facebook, Twitter, Instagram, WhatsApp, and other social networks in the form of groups with their own sets of unwritten cultural rules. Such organizations, in which messages can go global with one finger stroke, have greatly influenced the way business is conducted. Virtual consumer action groups have forced firms to change their products, the ways they promote them, and their pricing strategies. We also have seen social networks influence politics, specifically in Egypt and the Middle East during the Arab Spring uprisings of 2011. We can expect to see social networks continue to have a larger influence on firms.

SPECIAL FOCUS: GIFT GIVING IN BUSINESS

Gift giving in the business context is an important and often confusing aspect of every international manager's life. Everywhere, some sort of entertainment outside office hours that includes the exchange of gifts is part of the process of getting better acquainted. In all cultures, exchanging gifts follows a set of rules members of the culture have internalized and, in our native culture, we may not be aware of these rules because they represent our accustomed way of doing things. In cultures that tolerate high levels of social inequality and are hierarchical, gift-giving etiquette is markedly different from that in other cultures where power is more equally distributed.

Marcel Mauss, an anthropologist who studied the role of gifts in early societies, theorizes that gift giving operated within the society as a way to acknowledge interrelationships and obligations.[18] Mauss argued that in archaic societies, individual, family, and communal interests combined to make a social system that needed to acknowledge in public its interrelationships and obligations. A gift has a magic-like quality, he pointed out, because it carries with it more than the item itself; it carries some of the giver, which confers on the receiver an obligation to reciprocate. The ritual of gift giving in international business is important because it creates a social bond that requires you to be a giver, a receiver, and a holder of an obligation to the other person in the exchange. This series of roles and reciprocal obligations creates solidarity, which can lead to trust.

On a practical level, the first point to figure out about gifts in a new culture is how the ritual plays out. What constitutes an acceptable gift, and what is the public role of gift giving? In Japan, for example, people never give an unwrapped gift or visit a home empty-handed. A gift is presented with the comment that it is only a trifle, which implies that the

When in Rome, Should You "Do as the Romans Do" . . . and Feel Comfortable about It?

Overseas travel, whether for work or vacation, may force you to decide whether to follow local practices. Sometimes you have no choice—when in Britain, you drive on the left side of the road. Some local practices may seem liberating, but others may not make sense to you, and some may not seem morally right. The Japanese protect delicate tatami mats on their floors by removing their shoes. Do you conform? If you are a non-Muslim woman, do you wear a headscarf and long cloak when in a conservative Islamic country such as Saudi Arabia? Do you promote your manager's family members in Colombia?

Other customs may conflict with your home culture's moral or perhaps legal standards. If you are from a country or state where cannabis is illegal or reserved for medicinal use, do you visit the Grasshopper, a cannabis coffee shop, when you are in Amsterdam? At the business level, do you follow the corporate tax law as you would in your home country, or do you underreport and then negotiate, along with the locals, in Italy? Do you pay fixers or agents in cultures where this practice is widely followed? Such practices will violate most companies' ethical codes, and possibly legal statutes such as the U.S. Foreign Corrupt

Practices Act, which prohibits bribery and other influence-based activities. But what if your competitors localize their practices, leaving their moral judgment at home? Do you observe the Foreign Corrupt Practices Act in cultures where your competition readily pays bribes? Do you outsource your legal or moral issues to an agent, in order to distance yourself? In Saudi Arabia, do you avoid hiring women to sidestep the many gender issues you might encounter there? To what extent should you follow local practices and conform to local customs? Where are the lines? What do you think?

Critical Thinking Questions

1. Are all actions that conform to local customs morally defensible? Explain your reasoning.

2. If the competitive environment includes legally marginal activities, and you can distance yourself from those activities, should you follow them in order to compete successfully?

3. Recommend an approach to resolving ethical issues in the international business arena.

---

humble social position of the giver does not permit giving a gift in keeping with the high status of the recipient. The recipient, in turn, will not open the gift in front of the giver, in order to spare him or her any embarrassment. The intention of gift giving in Japan is to convey the giver's thoughtfulness and consideration for the receiver, who, over time, builds up trust and confidence in the giver.

Every country will have an etiquette and set of implicit rules around the giving of gifts: their timing, their value, how they are to be presented. Managers should become familiar with these rules.[19] Many organizations also have policies designed to separate gift giving from bribery or extortion, so managers will want to keep these guidelines in mind as well.

Culture Frameworks

LO 3-4
Describe four frameworks for analyzing culture.

International managers can quickly build a general sense of what to expect in a culture by using analytical frameworks developed by researchers. As we review several of these frameworks, remember two things: first, your own culture functions as an implicit reference point for comparison; and second, this is just the beginning, the very tip of the iceberg, of understanding the complexity of other cultures.

The studies of cultural values on which the frameworks are based include work by Hall,[20] Kluckhohn and Strodtbeck,[21] House,[22] Hofstede,[23] Schwartz,[24] and Trompenaars.[25] Here we look at four of these frameworks, those developed by Hall, Kluckhohn and Strodtbeck, Hofstede, and Trompenaars, so that you will have a sense of what conceptual tools are available to help you begin to understand other cultures. This rich material is an introduction to an area of multidiscipline research: international management, marketing, psychology, anthropology, and sociology. House's GLOBE Study, mentioned in our discussion of leadership across cultures, is an ambitious and interesting project that examines leadership patterns around the world using value and practice dimensions to measure culture. We hope you examine this study and its findings. In addition, Dr. Vas Taras has assembled a "Catalogue of Instruments for Measuring Culture," which has 145 entries (http://vtaras.com/wp-content/uploads/2015/11/Culture_Survey_Catalogue.pdf). As you can see, there is plenty to look at to investigate these ideas further.

HALL'S HIGH AND LOW CONTEXT

context
The relevant environment

Edward Hall, a U.S. anthropologist whose career included training people in the U.S. State Department, offers a great place to begin our selected framework review because his work is simple yet powerful. Hall classifies cultures based upon their communication styles and, specifically, on the role that context plays in the culture's communication patterns. Think of a communication's context as the total relevant environment beyond the words, including, for instance, the participants' body language, their places in the room, and the order in which they speak. In an HC culture, much communication is conveyed by context. HC cultures include Japan, China, many other Asian cultures, and Middle Eastern, Latin American, and African cultures. Here the participants have social ties that are long-standing and close, so they know to a great degree that the communication will be based on their shared experience and the communication signals they read from the situation. Communication tends to be implicit and indirect.

In LC cultures, the words contain most of the communication, and the context is relatively less significant. Anglo and northern cultures such as the United Kingdom and former British colonies—Canada, the United States, Australia—Germany, and the Scandinavian cultures are among the LC cultures. Relationships are of shorter duration with minimal shared history, so more of the communication has to be explicit for meaning to be conveyed. To get a feeling for the influence of context, think about your family, which will be relatively higher context than your relationships outside your family. See Figure 3.3 for a view of some of the HC–LC contrasts.

FIGURE 3.3 High- and Low-Context Attributes

High Context

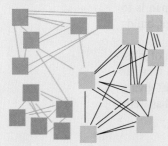

- Less verbally explicit communication; less written/formal information
- More internalized understandings of what is communicated
- Multiple cross-cutting ties and intersections with others
- Long-term relationships
- Strong boundaries—insider/outsider
- Knowledge is situational, relational
- Decisions and activities focus around personal face-to-face relationships, often around a central authority person

Low Context

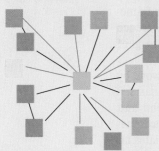

- Rule oriented, people play by external rules
- More knowledge is codified, public, external, and accessible
- Sequencing, separation—of time, of space, of activities, of relationships
- More interpersonal connections of shorter duration
- Knowledge is more often transferable
- Task-centered; decisions and activities focus around what needs to be done; division of responsibilities

FIGURE 3.4 Examples of High- and Low-Context Cultures and Occupations

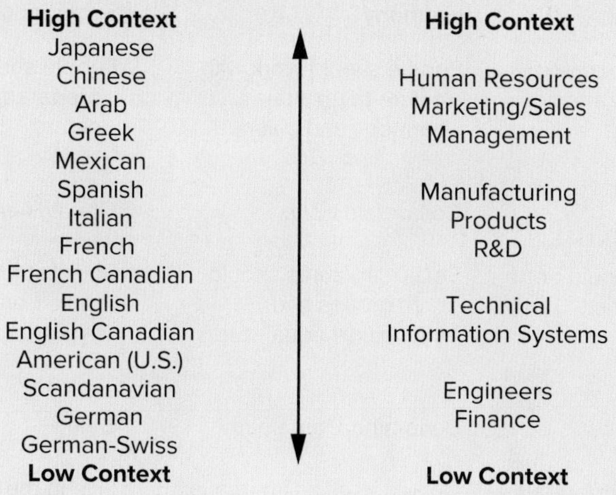

High Context	High Context
Japanese	
Chinese	Human Resources
Arab	Marketing/Sales
Greek	Management
Mexican	
Spanish	Manufacturing
Italian	Products
French	R&D
French Canadian	
English	Technical
English Canadian	Information Systems
American (U.S.)	
Scandanavian	Engineers
German	Finance
German-Swiss	
Low Context	**Low Context**

The explicit communicator in an LC culture is direct, unsubtle, and unambiguous: What you say is what you mean. There is relatively less subtlety. "Telling it like it is" is understood as a positive trait, whereas in HC cultures, such directness could be considered brash, rude, or embarrassingly unsubtle or naive. Figure 3.4 shows examples of HC and LC cultures and applies context to business areas, in order to help you build your sense of high and low context.

Hall's work also suggests that LC cultures tend to be monochronic, which means they characterize time as linear, tangible, and divisible into blocks, consistent with an economic understanding of time, that it is a scarce resource to be measured, saved, and spent.[26] A monochronic approach to time emphasizes planning and schedules. In contrast, HC cultures tend to be polychronic. That is, two or more activities are carried out within the same clock block; switching among activities can be both desirable and productive. We think of this as multitasking.[27]

monochronic
Having to do with linear time, sequential activities

polychronic
Having to do with simultaneous activities, multitasking

KLUCKHOHN AND STRODTBECK'S CULTURAL ORIENTATIONS FRAMEWORK

U.S. anthropologists Florence Kluckhohn and Fred Strodtbeck developed a classification system[28] for cultural values based on universal problems to which all cultures offer solutions. The five problems are:

1. What relationship should people have to nature? That is, how should they think about their activities with regard to nature?
2. What sorts of relationships should exist among individuals?
3. What are the preferred forms or modes of human activity?
4. What is the best way to think about time?
5. What is the basic nature of humans?

Kluckhohn and Strodtbeck's framework extends Hall's work, helping us further understand beliefs, and hence actions, in other cultures. These values are charted in Table 3.2, along with their categorization into high and low context, so that you can see how they might be useful together.

Relationship to nature describes the culture's understanding of how to live in the natural world. The values here range along a continuum from mastery to harmony

TABLE 3.2 Kluckhohn and Strodtbeck Values Orientation

Value Orientation	Modern/Low Context	Mixed	Traditional/High Context
Relationship to Nature	Mastery	Harmony	Subjugation
Beliefs in the society on the need or responsibility to control nature	People have a need and responsibility to attempt to control nature	People should work with nature to maintain harmony and balance	People should be prepared to submit to nature
Relationships among Individuals	Individualistic	Collateral/Group	Lineal/Hierarchy
Beliefs in the society about the legitimate form of social structure	The individual should be the basis of social structures	Social structures should give groups and individuals equal status	Social structure should be based on groups placed in hierarchy
Orientation for Human Activity	Doing	Becoming/Containing	Being
Beliefs in the society about appropriate human goals	Strive to accomplish goals	Develop self as integrated whole	Live in the present moment
Relationship with Time	Future	Present	Past
The extent to which past, present, and future influence people's decisions	Make decisions based on future prospects	Make decisions based on the present	Make decisions based on the past or traditions
Evaluation of Human Nature	Good	Neutral	Evil
Beliefs about the basic nature of humans	People are inherently good (Theory Y)		People are inherently evil (Theory X)

Source: Adapted from Hills, Michael D., "Kluckhohn and Strodtbeck's Values Orientation Theory," *Online Readings in Psychology and Culture*, vol. 4, no. 4, August 01, 2002.

and then to subjugation. In North America, for example, there is a predominant sense of mastery over nature, although with the rise of the environmental movement and awareness of climate change, a more harmonious orientation to nature may be growing. Think about the way humans in North America have modified the surface of the land to meet their needs: moving mountains, extending cities through landfills, and felling forests to harvest lumber and clear lands for pasture and development. A more harmonious relationship with nature may be found among American Indians and Buddhists, for example. A subjugated relationship would suggest that humans cannot change nature, that external forces such as fate and genetics determine the conditions of life.

The next value describes relationships among individuals. Should relationships stress the individual, as they tend to in LC cultures, should they give equal weight to the individual and groups, or should they focus on groups organized into hierarchies, as in HC cultures? In Asian cultures, the group is the main social structure, and hierarchy is often important. Think about the Japanese proverb, "The nail that sticks up gets hammered down."

Then come the values about human action. Are people meant to do things, to become, or to live in the present moment? *Doing* is a strong LC culture value, whereas being in the moment is valued in HC cultures. Action is a strong U.S. value, whereas in

France, a relatively HC culture, consideration of the action (theory) before doing is more the norm. Contrast both these approaches with the Buddhist goal to live in the present moment.

The fourth value that Kluckhohn and Strodtbeck's framework provides is the culture's understanding of time. LC cultures tend to focus on the future, whereas HC cultures tend to focus on the past and be more influenced by tradition, as in Asia. Contrast that with an understanding of time that focuses on the future or present, found in many LC cultures. The final value is the culture's belief about the basic nature of people. Are people inherently good, or do they need controls and structures to be protected from their inherent evil? Does the culture predominantly reflect Theory X (the assumption that people do not like work, require structure, and avoid risk) or Theory Y (the assumption that people naturally like to work, are creative, and seek responsibility)?

HOFSTEDE'S SIX DIMENSIONS

Geert Hofstede, a Dutch researcher and consultant trained in anthropology, initially developed his framework from surveys of global IBM employees in the late 1960s and later expanded and modified the framework. He is concerned primarily with work values, and he currently identifies six dimensions to help managers understand how national-level cultural differences affect organizations and management methods. His dimensions are empirically derived and have received significant attention from both managers (because they apply easily) and scholars (because they raise methodological issues). Some scholars have been critical of Hofstede's work, largely because of methodological survey issues: his analysis is done on the organizational level and then extrapolated to the national level; his data are dated; and his dimensions oversimplify the complexities of culture—six dimensions are not robust enough to describe a culture. While these are important issues, managers have found his work helpful. We look forward to continued refinement in this area of study.

There were originally four dimensions: individualism-collectivism, power distance, uncertainty avoidance, and masculinity-femininity. Recently, in collaboration with the anthropologist Michael Minkov, Hofstede added two dimensions, one that measures indulgence vs. restraint and another that measures pragmatic vs. normative behavior. You can see the latest version of his work on the Hofstede Center website.[29]

These dimensions support the assertion that management skills are culturally specific; that is, "a management technique or philosophy that is appropriate in one national culture is not necessarily appropriate in another."[30] They overlap and resemble Kluckhohn and Strodtbeck's values, which is not surprising since social organization is a major concern for all cultures. In fact, we should expect some redundancy among all the frameworks. Now to Hofstede's dimensions.

Individualism-Collectivism *The individualism-collectivism dimension* measures the degree to which people in the culture are integrated into groups.[31] People in highly *collectivistic* cultures belong to strong, cohesive in-groups that look after them in exchange for loyalty. In contrast, people in highly *individualistic* cultures are more loosely connected and look after themselves and their immediate family. The United States is highly individualistic; the culture rewards independence; the education system rewards outstanding individuals. This dimension plays out strongly in employee motivation and decision making. Countries with predominantly individualist cultures include the United States, Canada, the United Kingdom, Australia, the Netherlands, New Zealand, Sweden, France, and Germany. Collectivist cultures include Guatemala,

> **"With CULTURAL DIFFERENCES, FOCUSING on SIMILARITIES IS TEMPTING, BECAUSE IT IS EASY. WHAT WE NEED to DO IS BRIDGE DIFFERENCES to CREATE SHARED VALUES AND MOVE toward COLLABORATION."**
>
> *—Jeanne McNett, Northeastern University*[32]

Ecuador, Panama, Indonesia, Pakistan, Taiwan, China, Japan, and West and East African countries.

Power Distance *Power distance* is the extent to which members of a society expect power to be distributed unequally and accept that it is. Power distance is similar to inequality, but defined from below, not from above, and suggests that a society's level of inequality is endorsed by followers as well as by leaders. In large power distance societies, seniority, age, rank, and title are important. People will want direction, and formality is emphasized. In small power distance environments, a consultative style of leadership predominates, informality tends to be the norm, and there is or there is thought to be equal distance among people. For example, from season ticket holders of box seats at major sporting events to minimum-wage fast-food workers, just about everyone in the United States, a low power distance culture, self-identifies as middle class. Examples of large power distance cultures are Malaysia, Guatemala, Panama, Philippines, Arab countries, India, West African countries, and Singapore. Small power distance countries include Austria, Israel, Denmark, New Zealand, Republic of Ireland, Sweden, Norway, Canada, and Germany.

Uncertainty Avoidance *Uncertainty avoidance* describes a society's level of comfort with uncertainty. Hofstede points out that this dimension "ultimately refers to man's search for Truth" because it describes the extent to which a culture programs its members to feel either uncomfortable or comfortable in unstructured situations. Cultures that avoid uncertainty try to minimize the possibility of unstructured situations by "strict laws and rules, safety and security measures." Strong uncertainty avoidance cultures resist change, including career change and organizational change; they expect clear procedures and preserve the status quo. Weak uncertainty avoidance cultures see conflict as having positive aspects, expect innovation, encourage risk taking, and reward career change. Strong uncertainty avoidance cultures include Greece, Portugal, Guatemala, Uruguay, Japan, France, Spain, and South Korea. Examples of weak uncertainty avoidance cultures include Singapore, Jamaica, Denmark, Sweden, Hong Kong, United States, Canada, Norway, and Australia.

Masculinity-Femininity The *masculinity-femininity* dimension describes the distribution of roles between the sexes. Hofstede's data indicate that "women's roles across cultures differ less than do men's, and that men's values among countries vary considerably, from very assertive and competitive and maximally different from women's values on the one side, to modest and caring and similar to women's values on the other." The assertive pole is masculine, and the caring one feminine. "The women in feminine countries have the same modest, caring values as the men; in the masculine countries they are somewhat assertive and competitive, but not as much as the men, so that these countries show a gap between men's values and women's values."[33]

Notice that this dimension is about *the gap* between men's and women's roles in the culture. In a feminine culture, there is relatively less variation between male and female roles, which suggests that leadership and decision-making roles are equally open to men and women. Also in a feminine culture, quality of work life is important; people work in order to live, and environmental issues matter from a business perspective. In a masculine culture, male roles are more likely to be task-focused and female roles relationship-focused, achievements are emphasized, economic growth is central, people live in order to work, and business performance is the primary goal. Examples of masculine cultures include Japan, Austria, Venezuela, Italy, Mexico, and the Philippines. Feminine cultures include Sweden, Norway, the Netherlands, Denmark, Costa Rica, and Finland.

A word of caution is appropriate here. To think that feminine cultures are not concerned with production and business success is an error. Just think of all the globally successful Scandinavian firms: IKEA, Lego, Ericsson, H&M, Bang & Olufson, and Carlsberg head the list.

Indulgence vs. Restraint The dimension of *indulgence vs. restraint* is about happiness and describes a culture's tendency either to allow relatively free gratification of human desires or suppress human drives though strict social norms.[34] Indulgence tends to be strong in the Americas and western Europe, while restraint is strong in eastern Europe, Asia, and the Middle East. In indulgent cultures, people believe they have personal control over their lives; leisure is valued, as is freedom of speech; and people tend to be active in sports. There is relatively less effort invested in control and structure. In contrast, in restraining cultures, much more energy is dedicated to establishing order and structure and individuals are not "indulged." For example, in restraining cultures, the police-to-citizen ratio is higher than in indulging cultures.[35]

Pragmatic vs. Normative This dimension of *pragmatic vs. normative* is a measure of how people deal with the unexplainable in their lives. In normative societies, there is a strong desire to explain and to know the absolute truth. Concern for personal stability is high. There is respect for tradition, a low propensity to save, and a focus on quick results. In contrast, a pragmatic orientation suggests people who are not concerned with understanding so much because life as a complex process is a given. The challenge here is to live a virtuous life, and truth depends on context, time, and situation. There is a strong inclination to save and persevere. This is a modification of an earlier dimension called Confucian Dynamism.

Table 3.3 presents the scores for Hofstede's six dimensions for about one-third of the countries in his sample.

TROMPENAARS'S SEVEN DIMENSIONS

Dutch economist Fons Trompenaars's seven-dimension framework for understanding culture is derived from the social sciences, and his initial data are from 47 countries, later greatly expanded, in collaboration with the British management philosopher Charles Hampden-Turner. The first five dimensions address the culture's patterns for relationships among people, and the final two have to do with the way we understand time and nature.[36] Unlike Hofstede's dimensions, which describe values we cannot directly observe, many of Trompenaars's dimensions describe the behavior that results from an underlying cultural value. Let's look at what these seven dimensions are and how they work.

Universalism vs. Particularism (Rules vs. Relationships) The dimension of universalism vs. particularism addresses whether rules or relationships regulate behaviors. People in **universalist** cultures apply rules to all people at all times, without exception. People in **particularist** cultures consider the context before they apply the rule. Universalist cultures tend to be rule-based, while particularist cultures tend to be relationship-based. This dimension has wide applicability to our understanding of ethics in other cultures. The United States tends to be moderately rule-based, and U.S. adults tend to think everyone should follow the guidelines or rules, such as the Foreign Corrupt Practices Act. In other cultures, this judgment is situational—it all depends. It might depend on who is involved, on the specific circumstances of the event such as its location, or on other variables. You can see how cultural misunderstandings around ethics might arise between universalist and particularist cultures.

universalist
Condition in which concepts apply to all

particularist
Condition in which context determines what concepts apply

Individualism vs. Communitarianism The dimension of individualism vs. **communitarianism** has to do with whether people plan their actions with reference to individual benefits or group benefits. Notice its similarity to Hofstede's individualism-collectivism dimension and Kluckhohn and Strodtbeck's relationship value.

communitarianism
Belief that the group is the beneficiary of actions

Neutral vs. Affective (Unemotional vs. Emotional) How do members of a culture express emotions? People in neutral cultures tend to withhold emotional expression, while people in affective cultures are much more expressive. You can imagine that this dimension would come into play in communication patterns. Someone from an affective culture

neutral vs. affective
The withholding of emotion contrasted with its expression

TABLE 3.3 Selected Scores for Hofstede's Six Cultural Dimensions

Country	Power Distance	Uncertainty Avoidance	Individualism	Masculinity	Pragmatism	Indulgence/ Restraint
Mexico	81	82	30	69	24	97
Venezuela	81	76	12	73	16	100
Colombia	67	80	13	64	13	83
Peru	64	87	16	42	25	46
France	68	86	71	43	63	48
Chile	63	86	23	28	31	68
Portugal	63	104	27	31	28	33
China	80	30	20	66	87	24
Japan	54	92	46	95	88	42
United States	40	46	91	62	26	68
Australia	36	51	90	61	21	71
South Africa	49	49	65	63	34	63
New Zealand	22	49	79	58	33	75
Canada	39	48	80	52	36	68
United Kingdom	35	35	89	66	51	69
Ireland	28	35	70	68	24	65

Source: Geert Hofstede, "Country Comparison," *Hofstede Insights*, July 9, 2018.

might be seeking responses that would not be normal for another person from a neutral culture to give. For example, people from expressive Middle Eastern or Latin cultures may raise their voices during a discussion of an issue, which may cause colleagues from more neutral cultures such as Scandinavian or Asian to misperceive this behavior and interpret it as representing strong opposition to the issue being discussed.[37]

specific vs. diffuse
Life divided into public and private spheres contrasted with life undifferentiated

Specific vs. Diffuse The specific-diffuse dimension distinguishes among cultures based on their differentiation between private life and public or work life. In specific cultures such as the United States, people make distinctions between their work relationships and other relationships, so that work relationships do not carry over beyond work. In diffuse cultures such as those of East Asia, the work relationships carry over to other areas of life and influence them. Low-context cultures, to use Hall's terms, such as Germany, Canada, Australia, and the United States, tend to be specific, while high-context cultures, such as Japan and Mexico, tend to be diffuse. Table 3.4 lists more characteristics of this dimension.

achievement vs. ascription
What a person does contrasted with who a person is

Achievement vs. Ascription Ascription cultures consider a person's identity in terms of his or her family lineage, age, or other attributes. You are valued for who you are. Achievement cultures are meritocracies that reward what you do. In the United States, for example, achievement is a primary determinant of social status. This dimension may be especially helpful to keep in mind for staffing and interpersonal relationships.

TABLE 3.4 Characteristics of Specific and Diffuse Dimensions

Specific	Diffuse
Communication is direct, to the point, purposeful	Communication is indirect, seemingly "aimless"
Style is precise, blunt, definitive, transparent	Style is evasive, tactful, ambiguous, opaque
Principles and moral stands tend to be universal	Morality is situational (person and context)

Source: Adapted and modified from "Multicultural Impact: Specific vs. Diffuse," Stanford Chinese Institute of Engineers, https://web.stanford.edu/group/scie/Career/Wisdom/spec_dif.htm, accessed July 9, 2018.

Attitudes toward Time Trompenaars's time dimension has two aspects. The first identifies where the culture's primary focus is, whether it uses the past, the present, or the future as a lens to view the present. For example, in East Asia, traditional values are important, as are ancestors. History often plays an active role to help understand the present. In such past-focused cultures, change moves slowly. On the other hand, companies can take a long view. In contrast, present-focused cultures tend to neither plan nor dwell on the past. Now is what is important. There is a preference for short-term benefits and immediate results. Certain aspects of the U.S. economy, such as the culture of Wall Street and investors' expectations, clearly fit this present focus, as do attitudes in some African countries. Future-oriented cultures plan, anticipate, and see a better world evolving. Examples are Canada, some Latin American and European countries, and aspects of the U.S. culture.

CULTURE FACTS @internationalbiz

@London A U.S. manager encountered more difficulty than he expected when in the London office he placed a British manager with a working-class East End Cockney accent (think Michael Caine or Idris Elba) as head of a department, overseeing several members who spoke clipped and posh English like the Queen. #eastendcockney #poshenglish #queenrules

SOCIAL MEDIA

The second aspect of the time dimension describes whether actions are sequential (monochronic) or synchronous (polychronic). Linear actions follow one another. The controlling image of time is a river or stream. Scheduling is done in distinct units with no overlap. In polychronic cultures, many actions can occur at more or less the same time. For example, several meetings may take place at the same time, in the same space, overlapping one another. Middle Eastern cultures tend to be polychronic. In Saudi Arabia, the usual pattern of multiple, simultaneous meetings can be challenging for the untrained, non-native participant, who may feel insulted to not have the full attention of people in the meeting.

Attitudes toward the Environment Do we try to live in harmony with nature, or do we try to control it? Trompenaars's dimension of *internal vs. external direction* is similar to Kluckhohn and Strodtbeck's relationship to nature. In internal-direction cultures, people believe they control nature. In external-direction cultures, they believe the natural world controls them and they need to work with their environment. This dimension extends beyond the environment per se to the specific business context and is important for managers to consider. In external-direction cultures, where people tend to be responsive to external forces, a motivational approach that draws on self-directed leadership might be a costly misstep. Of course, training could change that. But a motivational approach that provides external resources such as rewards and regular feedback would be more in line with the cultural dimension of external direction. Another key issue is how people deal with obstacles—do they reconfigure them or adjust to them?

Figure 3.5 illustrates an application of Trompenaars's dimensions to China, Mexico, and the United States. Because they vary so greatly by subculture, the dimensions of time and environment are omitted.

FIGURE 3.5 Examples of Country Rankings on Trompenaars's Dimensions

China		
Dimension		
Universal --X -------------	Particularist
Individualist--X-------------------	Collectivist
Neutral --X------------------------	Affective
Specific ---X---------	Diffuse
Achievement--X ----	Ascription

Mexico		
Dimension		
Universal ---X-----------------------	Particularist
Individualist-------------------------X---	Collectivist
Neutral --X------	Affective
Specific -------------- X--	Diffuse
Achievement--X-----------------------	Ascription

United States		
Dimension		
Universal ------------ X--	Particularist
Individualist----------------X---	Collectivist
Neutral --X-------------------	Affective
Specific -------------------------------------X--	Diffuse
Achievement---------------X---	Ascription

LO 3-5
Describe the global mind-set and the MBI model.

When Does Culture Matter? The Global Mind-Set

As you accumulate experience in international management, you'll begin to recognize that culture matters all the time, but in different ways at different times. You'll come across many examples of failures because culture was ignored, and, interestingly enough, examples of brilliant successes because a manager successfully managed around culture.

Consider Magdi Batato's experience at Nestlé Malaysia.[38] Batato, a Swiss national, introduced work teams that were self-managed, known as semi-autonomous work teams, in Malaysia, despite the common assumption that due to cultural values (HC in Hall's terms, high-power distance and high collectivism in Hofstede's dimensions) they would not succeed. Yet his innovation was remarkably successful, and the teams increased production at Nestlé's manufacturing plants in Malaysia.

Batato's approach was to establish an organizational culture that was transparent, had open communication, and fostered high levels of trust. He established training and development programs for managers and built structures to support them and their teams. He created a fit between people and tasks. His subtle and nuanced understanding of culture helped him understand that his organization's structure could be modified, built on a careful engineering of the fit among people, task, and structure and drawing on a more subtle reading of Malaysian cultural traits. His team was able to create a competitive advantage for Nestlé's production in Malaysia.

The ability to build such a deep, almost tacit understanding of a culture is rare. One of the goals of international firms is to develop such global mind-sets in managers throughout their firms. A **global mind-set** includes an openness to diversity along with an ability to pull ideas together across boundaries created by that diversity.[39] This ability to synthesize across diversity requires a willingness to deal with complexity and can be enhanced through experiences in different cultures.

A useful tool for figuring out what matters when working across cultures is the Map-Bridge-Integrate model (MBI) developed by Martha Maznevski and Joe DiStefano.[40] MBI helps managers map cultural differences using a cultural framework and observations, then bridge them through communication, and finally integrate or manage them through participation, conflict resolution, and building on all ideas. MBI is linked with the global mind-set because it is a tool that helps us synthesize across diversity boundaries. Mapping requires identifying the cultural differences that exist in the group and understanding them. It brings the group to a shared understanding of how diverse members see the world. Bridging requires communicating across these differences that have been identified in mapping and building an awareness of shared values. The final step is to integrate, which requires managing the differences. This process values the differences among people and then creates value from these differences.

Going Forward: Cultural Paradoxes and a Caution

As your understanding of culture increases, you'll encounter **cultural paradoxes**, or contradictions between the culture's values you expect to see based on your use of the frameworks and your growing experience, and what you actually observe. Joyce Osland and Allan Bird have identified this phenomenon, and here are a few examples from their work. We review these paradoxes to help you anticipate how learning about cultures is a complex, intellectually challenging process, and that contradictions that may initially frustrate you are simply a part of moving forward. In fact, encountering them is a sign that you are making progress, that you are able to identify paradoxes and may be on your way to reconciling them.

The first example has to do with U.S. culture, described as individualistic according to many frameworks; yet the United States has the world's highest rate of charitable giving. The second example describes a phenomenon in Costa Rica. People in Costa Rica, a high-context culture, regularly prefer automated tellers to real tellers because the automated tellers are polite. The final example describes behavior in Japan and the United States. Japanese have low tolerance for ambiguity while U.S. managers have high tolerance for it (according to Hofstede). Yet U.S. contracts are very specific, while the Japanese introduce ambiguous clauses. These three examples remind us that we are working with complex systems and our understanding lags reality.

We close this section with a caution. Keep in mind that for all the frameworks we've described here, the score of each dimension represents a *mean value* for each country, its central tendency. In any culture, you'll find people who fit other points on the distribution curve rather than this mean value. The generalizations represented in the frameworks are at best sophisticated stereotypes[41] of the complex cultures we are trying to understand. They are useful as first guesses; as predictions, however, they can mislead because they ignore complexity and subtlety. Remember, too, that the researchers analyzed data at the national level, so the frameworks do not recognize the existence of subcultures within a specific region of a country.

global mind-set
Involves an openness to diversity along with an ability to synthesize across diversity

LO 3-6
Discuss cautions for using cultural frameworks in business.

cultural paradox
Contradictions in a culture's values

MALLORY WEDEKING: Attitude Is Everything!

Mallory Wedeking has studied and worked in Uganda and Rwanda. When asked to give advice to students studying international business on career development and breaking into the field, she had some helpful observations. Here are her comments:

My concentration in school is entrepreneurship and my career goals are to pursue a career in business in the context of international development. I became interested in international business when I first traveled, in Europe, after high school. Interacting with different cultures and lifestyles inspired my creativity and a desire to learn. I liked the added texture of doing business in an international context.

My most influential time abroad was the four months I studied in Uganda and Rwanda, where I was also able to do an internship through the nonprofit Food for the Hungry, working with a rural village to help foster economic development and financial responsibility. I was nervous about the transition. I had familiarized myself with the culture, but most of my cultural awareness I learned along the way. My valuable early lesson was that mistakes were unavoidable, and the attitude with which you deal with them is what matters. Learning another culture is a humbling experience.

My advice about working abroad is to realize that attitude is everything. Cultural miscommunications will happen no matter how much you prepare. Getting back up on my feet after a mistake, to keep moving forward, helped me learn. You need also to understand the phases of culture shock so you'll be able to identify where you are in order to deal with your feelings and emotions. There is a tendency at certain points of culture shock to retreat from the culture and surround yourself with only things familiar and comfortable. I experienced this feeling two months into my stay abroad, and retreated with other American students to watch American movies. I had to force myself to continue interacting with the Ugandan people.

Wedeking in East Africa. Courtesy of Mallory Wedeking.

Returning to the United States was a much more difficult cultural adjustment than arriving in East Africa. I had not expected that my home could feel overwhelming and unfamiliar. It took six months to completely feel comfortable again. I learned that the process cannot be rushed. You need to take time to absorb everything you learned while abroad.

I would highly recommend working internationally, beginning with volunteer work or an internship. The daily surprises keep things interesting and teach you invaluable qualities and skills. Even traveling for pleasure or studying abroad teaches you skills such as being adaptable, thinking and making decisions quickly, and developing advanced communication skills, all of which are extremely desirable to employers.

Source: Mallory Wedeking

RULES OF THUMB FOR MANAGERS DOING BUSINESS ACROSS CULTURES

Knowing your customer is just as important anywhere in the world as it is at home. Each culture has its logic, and within that logic are real, sensible reasons for the way they do things. The manager who can figure out the basic pattern of the culture will be increasingly effective interacting with foreign clients and colleagues. The following six rules of thumb can be helpful[42]:

1. *Be prepared:* Approach a foreign market having done your homework. A mentor is most desirable, complemented by lots of reading on social and business etiquette, history and folklore, current affairs (including relationships between the countries), the culture's values, geography, sources of pride (artists, musicians, sports), religion, political structure, and practical matters such as currency and hours of

business. Read local newspapers. A good site for international newspaper links is www.onlinenewspapers.com.

2. *Slow down:* In many countries, U.S. businesspeople are seen to be in a rush—in other words, unfriendly, arrogant, and untrustworthy. In other countries, the Japanese and Germans are considered somewhat time-obsessed.

3. *Establish trust:* Often, U.S.-style crisp business relationships will get you nowhere. Product quality, pricing, and clear contracts compete with the personal relationship and trust that are developed carefully and sincerely over time. The manager must establish himself or herself as simpatico, worthy of the business, and dependable in the long run.

4. *Understand the importance of language:* Obviously, translations must be done by a professional who speaks both languages fluently, who has a vocabulary sensitive to nuance and connotation, and who has a talent for the idioms and imagery of each culture. Having an interpreter is critical, even when one of the parties speaks the other's language.

5. *Respect the culture:* Manners are important. The traveling representative is a guest in the country and must respect the host's rules. As a Saudi Arabian official states in one of the Going International films, "Americans in foreign countries have a tendency to treat the natives as foreigners; they forget that actually it is they who are the foreigners."

6. *Understand the components of culture:* Any region's culture is a sort of iceberg with two components: surface culture (fads, styles, food) and deep culture (attitudes, beliefs, values). Less than 10 percent of culture is visible, so strangers must look below the surface.

SUMMARY

LO 3-1
Describe what culture is.

Culture is the *sum total of the beliefs, rules, techniques, institutions, and artifacts that characterize human populations.* In other words, culture consists of the "individual worldviews, social rules, and interpersonal dynamics characterizing a group of people set in a particular time and place." Most anthropologists agree that culture is *learned;* the various aspects of culture are *interrelated;* culture is *shared, patterned, and mutually constructed through social interaction;* and culture *defines the boundaries* of different groups.

LO 3-2
Identify the ways culture affects all business activity.

Culture affects everything we do, and, thus, national cultural differences affect the functional areas of international business. Wide variations in cultural attitudes and values across markets require that many firms develop a variety of marketing mixes to reach their consumers. HR motivation practices are culturally affected. Leadership is greatly influenced by culture, as well. What is leadership thought to be? Is it patriarchal and hierarchical? Is the leader one among equals? Production managers have found that cultural values around attitudes toward change can seriously influence the acceptance of new production methods. Is employee evaluation understood as a development aid or an adversarial process? A culture's accounting controls directly relate to its assumptions about people's basic nature. Are the controls tight throughout the organization, suggesting low levels of trust, or loose, suggesting the culture assumes people will act honestly even when they are not closely monitored? Every business action is influenced by national-level cultural values.

LO 3-3
Describe how culture shows itself.

Because culture is not directly observable; it is manifested in the sociocultural aspects of a society. Culture manifests in, for example, a society's aesthetics, religion, material culture, language, and social organization.

LO 3-4
Describe four frameworks for analyzing culture.

The four main frameworks we have reviewed are from Hall, Kluckhohn and Strodtbeck, Hofstede, and Trompenaars. Hall's framework differentiates on the issue of context, between HC and LC.

Kluckhohn and Strodtbeck's cultural orientations framework includes the relationship of people to nature, relationships among individuals, preferred forms of human activity, the relationship with time, and the relationship with human nature. The first two frameworks are theoretical, while the final two are based on data; they are empirical. Hofstede's framework is concerned primarily with work values. Its original four dimensions are individualism-collectivism, power distance, uncertainty avoidance, and masculinity-femininity. He later added two additional dimensions, pragmatic vs. normative and indulgence vs. restraint. Finally, Trompenaars's seven-dimension framework addresses the culture's patterns for relationships among people—actual behaviors—and time and nature. His dimensions are specific vs. diffuse, universalism vs. particularism (rules vs. relationships), individualism vs. communitarianism, neutral vs. affective (unemotional vs. emotional), achievement vs. ascription, attitudes toward time, and attitudes toward the environment.

LO 3-5
Describe the global mind-set and the MBI model.

Global mind-set describes a mind that is open to diversity and has an ability to synthesize across it. Such capabilities are needed in international management. They may well require a propensity to deal with complexity, yet they can be enhanced through experiences in different cultures. A useful tool for figuring out what matters when working across cultures is the Map-Bridge-Integrate model (MBI) because it helps to synthesize across the complexity.

LO 3-6
Discuss cautions for using cultural frameworks in business.

The frameworks are generalizations that are at best sophisticated stereotypes of the complex culture we are trying to understand. They are best used to establish likelihood; used to predict, they can be misleading because they ignore complexity and subtlety. This is an important caution. They are useful tools, especially when we recognize their limitations, for setting our expectations, but not for predicting them. Meanwhile, culture matters all the time, but in different ways at different times. In some situations, international managers have been successful with initiatives that are not in line with cultural values. Knowing when culture matters in a primary way is a result of experience combined with a global mind-set, which involves an openness to diversity along with an ability to synthesize across diversity.

KEY TERMS

achievement vs. ascription 80	ethnocentricity 62	particularist 79
aesthetics 66	global mind-set 83	polychronic 75
communitarianism 79	material culture or artifacts 70	specific vs. diffuse 80
context 74	monochronic 75	universalist 79
cultural paradox 83	neutral vs. affective 79	

CRITICAL THINKING QUESTIONS

1. Drawing on Hall's high and low contexts, describe some of the communication issues that might well arise when an Arab manager in a global company who has spent his career in the Middle East is sent on temporary assignment to Germany for a year to implement a process developed in one of the Middle Eastern production facilities.

2. Your company has a policy of no gift giving or accepting gifts. You are representing the company in negotiations in China for design of a multi-phased manufacturing facility. Discuss the role of gift giving you might expect in a culture such as China and how you plan to approach this issue.

3. You are a Mexican who has just accepted a short-term assignment in Ireland. What are some of the expectations you may have about Irish behavior, drawing on Hofstede's cultural dimensions?

4. If you had the choice of sending either a U.S. or Mexican businessperson to Japan for a three-year assignment, and both were equally qualified, why might sending the Mexican offer less risk on the culture side?

5. How could Trompenaars's universalism-particularism dimension be helpful in sorting out confusion over ethical behavior in a company's international division?

6. Give a short description of an example of Trompenaars's achievement-ascription dimension.

7. If you were advising a French colleague on her first work assignment in your home culture, and she asked you what aspects of the material culture she should pay attention to, what advice would you give her?

8. Choose a nationality of a foreign worker found in your home environment and suggest what culture-related difficulties such a worker might experience in your culture.

9. How do you evaluate your own global mind-set levels?

 globalEDGE RESEARCH TASK   http://globalEDGE.msu.edu/

Use the globalEDGE website (http://globaledge.msu.edu/) to complete the following exercises:

1. You work for a global wine producer, and you have recently been assigned to a new role in your company's subsidiary in Italy. To make the relocation and transition go smoothly both for yourself and your family, you are looking for information about life in Italy. Locate Italy under the "Global Insights" section of globalEDGE and review the "Kwintes-sential Language and Culture Specialists" in a new tab. Be ready to discuss the information on this page with your family members.

2. Your class agreed on learning about the business meeting etiquette and gift-giving practices of as many countries as possible. In order to achieve this, you agreed on dividing up the workload. Pick a country of your choice from the "Global Insights" section of globalEDGE and access to "Culture Crossing" through the "Culture" page. Note the basics of business meetings and gift giving of the country you picked and prepare a briefing to share with your friends in the classroom.

MINICASE

WHO WILL STAFF UP THE CHINA OPERATIONS?

Your international company headquartered in New Jersey is sending an expatriate to China for a three-year assignment to staff and run a new branch of its industrial products business. The main Chinese customers are using the products in their Middle Eastern and North African petroleum operations. You have extensive overseas experience and currently serve as VP, Human Resources. You chair the selection committee. There were 12 internal individuals interested in the position, and your committee has narrowed down the list to three final candidates, all of whom want this assignment. Here are the candidates:

Tom is a mid-level finance manager with stellar performance reviews. He has no foreign experience and would like to develop his career in this direction. He is single, has an MBA, and has been out of school for 20 years. His background is in finance at the undergraduate level, which he studied at Ohio State University, only 50 miles from his hometown. He is involved in the local Council on Foreign Relations and is an accomplished athlete.

Firdaus is a deputy VP of HR at corporate headquarters. Her family emigrated from Yemen to Chicago when she was in grade school, and she speaks, reads, and writes Arabic, both classical and the Yemeni dialect. She is married with two children. Her husband George is a professor of history and does not speak Arabic. Firdaus has a Ph.D. in engineering, joined the company on the operations side, and has made the midcareer transition to HR successfully. She finished her Ph.D. at the University of London in the United Kingdom before she began with the company and is now early in the middle of her professional career. Her performance reviews are stellar. She encountered an incident at headquarters several years ago when there was a discussion about her wearing a headscarf, but this was resolved without her changing her practice. She is well known and well liked throughout headquarters. Her husband is ready to take a leave of absence for three years to accompany her on the expat assignment.

Gunther is VP of the German-based division of the company. His functional background is accounting, and he is credited with the company's success within the European Union. He built the business from a small operation in Frankfurt to the EU sector leader in only seven years. He speaks German and English and is known for being well organized and formal in his approach. His work is timely, accurate, and detailed. Gunther's boss, the president of the international company, was a bit surprised that Gunther expressed interest in this position because the Chinese assignment is perceived as lower level to the position he holds now, although it would have an equivalent title on paper. Gunther has an undergraduate degree in

anthropology and took graduate-level accounting courses earlier in his career.

The company would like someone who could get the operation up and running, stay for three years, and then transfer the position to a local hire whom they would have developed for the responsibility.

Critical Thinking Questions

1. Drawing on the cultural dimensions that we have reviewed, along with your business knowledge, whom would you recommend for the position?
2. What would be your reasoning for this choice?
3. Whom would you suggest for a backup candidate, if the first selection declined the position?

NOTES

1. Denise Pirotti Hummel, "Understanding the Importance of Culture in Global Business," *Oracle*, May 2012, www.oracle.com.

2. Quote by Charlemagne.

3. I. Brady, and B. Isaac, *A Reader in Cultural Change*, vol. 1 Cambridge. MA: Schenkman Publishing, 1975, introduction, x.

4. Hy Mariampolski, *Ethnography for Marketers: A Guide to Consumer Immersion*, Thousand Oaks, CA: Sage, 2005, 123.

5. "What Is Culture?" Center for Advanced Research on Language Acquisition, University of Minnesota, http://www.carla.umn.edu, accessed July 09, 2018.

6. E. T. Hall, *Beyond Culture*, Garden City, NY: Doubleday, 1977, 54.

7. For example, see Florian Auckenthaler, "Marketing in the US vs. Marketing in Germany: Key Differences You Have to Know," https://www.designingit.com/blog, accessed July 09, 2018.

8. Nicholas Athanassiou, Professor, Northeastern University.

9. C. Berggren, *Alternatives to Lean Production: Work Organization in the Swedish Auto Industry*, Ithaca, NY: Cornell, 1992.

10. Supply Chain Resource Cooperative, "Cultural Effects on the Global Supply Chain," https://scm.ncsu.edu, accessed July 09, 2018.

11. For example, see Ginka Toegel, and Jean-Louis Barsoux, "3 Situations Where Cross-Cultural Communication Breaks Down," *Harvard Business Review*, https://hbr.org, accessed July 09, 2018; Erin Meyer, "When Culture Doesn't Translate," *Harvard Business Review*, https://hbr.org, accessed July 09, 2018; and John Hooker, "Cultural Differences in Business Communication," http://public.tepper.cmu.edu, accessed July 09, 2018.

12. Robert J. House et al., *Culture, Leadership and Organizations: The Globe Study of 62 Societies*, Thousand Oaks, CA: Sage, 2004.

13. South Tyrol Museum of Archeology, http://www.iceman.it/en, accessed July 09, 2018.

14. Anita Snow, "Ad Featuring 'Che' Guevara Sparks Furor," *The Monitor*, August 10, 2000, 8a.

15. K. M. Fisher, J. McNett, and P. Scherer, "Religion in the Workplace," in *Understanding and Managing Diversity*, 6th ed., ed. C. Harvey and J. Allard, Upper Saddle River, NJ: Prentice Hall, 2011.

16. E. T. Hall, *The Hidden Dimension*, Garden City, NY: Doubleday, 1969, 134–35.

17. M. J. Herskovits, *Man and His Works*, New York: Knopf, 1967, 303.

18. M. Mauss, *The Gift: Forms and Functions of Exchange in Archaic Societies*, London: Routledge, 1990. Original work published 1922.

19. Internet resources may be helpful, such as http://netique.com/giftsearch/international.html (July 9, 2018).

20. E. T. Hall, *The Silent Language*, New York: Doubleday, 1959; and *The Hidden Dimension, Beyond Culture*.

21. C. Kluckhohn, and K. Strodtbeck, *Variations in Value Orientations*, Westport, CT: Greenwood, 1961.

22. House et al., Culture, *Leadership and Organizations*, 2004.

23. Geert Hofstede, *Culture and Organizations: Software of the Mind*, London: McGraw-Hill, 1991.

24. S. H. Schwartz, "Universals in the Content and Structure of Values: Theory and Empirical Tests in 20 Countries," in *Advances in Experimental Social Psychology*, vol. 25, ed. M. Zanna, New York: Academic Press, 1992, 1–65.

25. Fons Trompenaars, *Riding the Waves of Culture*, Burr Ridge, IL: Irwin, 1993.

26. E. T. Hall, and Mildred Hall, *Hidden Differences: Doing Business with the Japanese*, Garden City, NY: Anchor Press/Doubleday, 1987.

27. Carol Kaufman-Scarborough, and Jay D. Lindquist, "Time Management and Polychronicity: Comparisons, Contrasts, and Insights for the Workplace," *Journal of Managerial Psychology*, 14, nos. 3-4, 1999, 288-312.

28. Kluckhohn, and Strodtbeck used the term "value orientation" to describe their work (*Variations in Value Orientations*, Evanston, IL: Peterson, 1961). Martha Maznevski uses their work in *International Management Behavior: Leading with a Global Mindset*, Chichester, UK: Wiley, 2009, by Henry Lane, Martha Maznevski et al.

29. You can explore the Hofstede dimensions at https://geerthofstede.com.

30. Geert Hofstede, "Cultural Dimensions in Management and Planning," *Asia Pacific Journal of Management,* January 1984, 81–84.

31. The source of the descriptions of the six dimensions of national culture is Hofstede's website, found at https://www.hofstede-insights.com. You can also find the raw scores for comparing countries against the six dimensions at https://www.hofstede-insights.com.

32. Jeanne McNett, Northeastern University.

33. Hofstede, Geert, "Dimensionalizing Cultures: The Hofstede Model in Context," *International Association for Cross-Cultural Psychology,* 1 June, 2009.

34. Geert Hofstede, G. J. Hofstede, and M. Minkov, *Cultures and Organizations: Software of the Mind,* 3rd ed. New York: McGraw-Hill, 2010.

35. Geert Hofstede, *Dimensionalizing Cultures: The Hofstede Model in Context* (online readings in *Psychology and Culture,* International Association for Cross-Cultural Psychology, 2011). See http://scholarworks.gvsu.edu, accessed July 09, 2018.

36. Fons Trompenaars, and Charles Hampden-Turner, *Riding the Waves of Culture,* New York: McGraw-Hill, 1997; John Bing, "The Use and Misuse of Questionnaires in Intercultural Training," ITAP International, http://www.itapintl.com, accessed July 09, 2018; David Thomas, *Essentials of International Management: A Cross-Cultural Perspective,* Thousand Oaks, CA: Sage, 2002; and Vas Tara et al., "Half a Century of Measuring Culture: Review of Approaches, Challenges, and Limitations Based on the Analysis of 121 Instruments for Quantifying Culture," *Journal of International Management,* vol. 15, 2009, 357–73.

37. Toegel and Barsoux, "3 Situations Where Cross-Cultural Communication Breaks Down."

38. Martha Maznevski and Tom Gleave, "Magdi Batato at Nestlé Malaysia (A): Introducing Team-Based Production," IMD-3-2199, 2011.

39. Nakiye Boyacigiller, "The Crucial Yet Illusive Global Mindset," in *The Blackwell Handbook of Global Management,* ed. H. A. Lane et al., Oxford: Blackwell Publishing, 2004.

40. Henry W. Lane et al., *International Management Behavior: Leading with a Global Mindset,* 6th ed., Chichester, UK: Wiley, 2009, Chapter 3, 65ff.

41. This observation is from conversation with Joyce Osland.

42. Lisa Hoecklin, *Managing Cultural Differences: Strategies for Competitive Advantage,* New York: Addison-Wesley Longman, 1995; and "How to Negotiate European Style," *Journal of European Business,* July–August 1993, 46.

4 Sustainability and Natural Resources

> **Pollution is nothing but the resources we are not harvesting. We allow them to disperse because we've been ignorant of their value.**
>
> —Buckminster Fuller, U.S. engineer, inventor, futurist (1895–1983)[1]

Consumption is a critical environmental issue. ©Chinaface/Getty Images.

LEARNING OBJECTIVES

After reading this module, you will be able to:

LO 4-1 **Describe** environmental sustainability and its potential influence on business.

LO 4-2 **Describe** frameworks for sustainability.

LO 4-3 **Summarize** ways to measure sustainability achievements.

LO 4-4 **Identify** the characteristics of environmentally sustainable business.

LO 4-5 **Describe** how the stakeholder model can help businesses achieve sustainability.

LO 4-6 **Describe** how geographic features of a country or region contribute to natural capital.

LO 4-7 **Outline** nonrenewable and renewable energy options available and their potential impacts on business.

In today's business environment, the concept of sustainability goes beyond doing what's right for the planet or complying with government regulations. For many global companies, sustainability has become an important component of their overall business model, with a direct impact on their bottom line. Savvy consumers have high expectations when it comes to buying products and services from companies that claim sustainability is an important part of their business practices.

Consider Whirlpool and its approach to energy-efficient appliances. More than 30 years ago, most consumers were just beginning to learn about environmental issues, including saving energy. Back then, a Pew research study listed energy efficiency low on the list of consumer priorities (no. 12) when it came to buying appliances. Today, energy efficiency ranks as the third most important factor after cost and performance when buying appliances, and companies are paying attention to such customer sentiment. For example, Whirlpool engineers recently partnered with the Green Kitchen Project in Europe to study energy consumption of Whirlpool ovens in an effort to reduce energy use by 20 percent, which would not only eliminate carbon dioxide emissions by 50 million tons in one year but would also make the cooking process more efficient.

Integrating sustainability as part of a company's corporate strategy makes sense from both a financial and operational standpoint. Estimates suggest that consumers worldwide who think about the environmental impact of their purchasing decisions make up a global market worth more than $500 billion. From an operational standpoint, managers need to understand how environmental factors such as climate change impact daily operations and then put plans in place to lessen potential exposure. For example, global supply chains are at risk for massive disruption when extreme weather occurs locally or halfway around the world. Recent statistics reported by the World Economic

Forum estimate weather disasters in 2016 caused more than $200 billion in losses worldwide. As globalization continues and companies expand operations into developing countries, the need to anticipate possible environmental issues and manage local resources (including water and infrastructure) becomes a corporate mandate.

Commitment to sustainable practices also has an impact on global trade and foreign investment. According to the 2018 Sustainable Trade Index commissioned by the Hinrich Foundation, trade is a key ingredient in economic development, but it cannot be pursued without companies—and countries—committing to environmental stewardship and developing social capital. Measuring both Asian and U.S. economies in terms of economic growth, environmental protection, and strengthened social capital, the Index results were mixed. However, several countries made significant progress in curbing air and water pollution, reducing inequality, raising labor standards, and increasing education levels. Such gains will not only help these nations improve their environment but also raise the social standards for their population, increase wealth, and attract more foreign investment.

The importance of sustainability as a competitive advantage cannot be underestimated. Increasing pressure from consumers, suppliers, shareholders, global investors, and others will continue to push companies and countries to make sustainability an integral part of their business agendas.

Sources: Andrew J. Hoffman, "The Next Phase of Business Sustainability," *Stanford Social Innovation Review*, vol. 16, no. 2, January 01, 2018, 34–39; "The Hinrich Foundation Sustainable Trade Index," *Hinrich Foundation*, 2018; Brian Dunch, and David Sapin, "Supply Chain Risk: How Prepared Is Your Supply Chain for the Inevitable Disruption Caused by Extreme Weather?," *PwC Bits & Bytes*, 2018; "A Turning Tide: Tracking Corporate Action on Water Security," *Carbon Disclosure Project*, November 2017; Valerio Marra, "Simulation Turns Up the Heat and Energy Efficiency at Whirlpool Corp.," *Appliance Design*, May 07, 2018; and Andrew J. Hoffman, "Getting Ahead of the Curve: Corporate Strategies That Address Climate Change," *Pew Center on Global Climate Change*, October 2006.

Sustainability in the Business Context

LO 4-1
Describe environmental sustainability and its potential influence on business.

The concept of environmental sustainability has a broad scope. It is about maintaining something—the environment, society, the economy, people within the economy, or the organization. Increasingly, when we use the term sustainability in a business context, we mean any of these applications.[2] The United Nations World Commission on Environment and Development, known as the Brundtland Commission, drafted a widely accepted definition of sustainable development: it "meets the needs of the present without compromising the ability of future generations to meet their needs."[3] This understanding of sustainability calls on businesses to develop new approaches to the way we "design, produce, distribute, and consume goods and services; the way we establish market prices for these goods and services; the way we provide and consume energy; the way we respect and regulate the environment; and the

environmental sustainability
State in which the demands placed upon the environment by people and commerce can be met without reducing the capacity of the environment to provide for future generations

SOCIAL MEDIA

way we ensure the health and well-being of all living creatures."[4] Sustainability, in fact, requires us to change the way we manage everything—government institutions, markets, business organizations, and our own individual behavior.

By its very nature, sustainability is a systems concept because it combines a group of interconnected elements that forms a complex whole. Whatever we are trying to sustain (a business, a way of life, the natural world) exists within a larger system, and if that larger system is not sustained, the subsystem is unlikely to survive. For example, are Florida's Everglades likely to be sustained if global temperature and precipitation patterns change significantly? Because of the characteristics of the system, sustainability is actually local and global at the same time; any specific location interacts with systems that are global. The phrase "Act locally, think globally" captures this multileveled sentiment and translates it into a guide for action.

More than 90 percent of CEOs view sustainability as important to the success of their companies, and 88 percent of students in business schools place priority on learning about environmental and social issues in business.[5] Because environmental sustainability requires the commitment of a business to operate without reducing the capacity of the environment to provide for future generations,[6] the environmentally sustainable firm has the challenge to think both about its competitive present and the needs of future generations. This is no easy feat since either option on its own could be consuming. Approaches to sustainability in the business context usually consider the ecological, social, and economic systems in which the business functions. In this section, we look at the characteristics of sustainability and sustainable business practices and then explore a stakeholder model that supports a company's adoption of sustainable approaches.

Nasa's blue marble composite image, released in 2012 and modeled on the original Apollo picture of Earth taken in 1972, helps us appreciate the need for sustainability. Source: NASA/NOAA/GSFC/Suomi NPP/VIIRS/ Norman Kuring/NASA.

In their early efforts at sustainability, firms examined their own operations and paid attention to the way they used resources. For example, they measured the amount of water saved and energy consumption reduced due to their conservation efforts. Then they began to examine their value chains, beginning with their direct suppliers and distributors. Today, they have enlarged their focus again to look at their entire supply chain, from raw materials extraction to manufacturing, distribution, use, and final disposal.[7] Rather than waiting for the market to create incentives for undertaking sustainable practices, companies instead are taking the lead in discarding outdated approaches that treat the environment as an unlimited source of materials and a dumping ground for waste.

Creating and implementing new, sustainable business models has been recognized as positive both for business and for the environment. Walmart realized as early as 2005 that it could compete on low price *and* build a sustainable business practice. Former CEO Scott Lee, who recognized early on that Walmart had to focus on the whole value chain, put it this way: "If we focused on just our own operations, we would have [addressed] 10 percent of our effect on the environment [and missed] 90 percent of the opportunity that's out there."[8] Consumers who consider environmental attributes in their purchase decisions are estimated to represent a worldwide market exceeding $500 billion, while 20 percent of all professionally managed investment assets in the United States, nearly $9 trillion, are from investors whose investment criteria include environmental, social, and governance factors.[9] Clearly, sustainability represents a large and growing area of interest and activity for businesses and their stakeholders.

Systems for Achieving Sustainability

LO 4-2
Describe frameworks for
sustainability.

We now look at several approaches that recently have been developed to help us think concretely about sustainability. Then we look at how to measure the impacts of our efforts to create sustainable enterprises.

LIFE CYCLE ASSESSMENT

Life cycle assessment (LCA) is an approach used to evaluate the environmental impact aspects of a product or service throughout its life cycle, sometimes called cradle-to-grave analysis. In the recent past, manufacturers handed over the product to the consumer at the factory gate, but no longer. Now manufacturers are concerned about the impact their product has on the environment. Using life cycle assessment, they examine the whole chain of activities that contributes to the production of their product, and to which their product contributes. This emerging "product stewardship" is a result of thinking informed by LCA and means companies are increasingly accepting responsibility for the extended impact of their activities.

life cycle assessment (LCA)
An evaluation of the environmental aspects of a product or service throughout its life cycle

In his work on sustainability in the business context, business educator Ronald Whitfield uses a pencil to illustrate the application of LCA. The pencil's environmental footprint consists of *all* the products of its manufacture, such as exhaust from the sawing and milling equipment, water used in the processing, emissions from the paint shop, and scrap wood, metal, and graphite. The manufacturer will analyze these components to discover cost-effective alternatives that are more ecologically efficient. In an extended analysis of the value chain, the manufacturer includes suppliers. Is the cedar being harvested in a sustainable way? What about the production of the pencil's stain, wax, paint, and eraser, and the transportation and distribution of these components? What happens to the pencil when it is no longer used? An LCA also often includes carbon dioxide emissions, ozone depletion, water use and release, toxic releases, and resource depletion.

Here's a simple yellow wooden pencil, but its LCA can be complex. ©Carson Ganci/DesignPics.

LCA helps us understand the cumulative impact of the products we purchase and can help a company focus on reducing its environmental footprint, its cost structure, and the potential dangers of carcinogens its inputs, processes, and waste might pose to employees, consumers, and the environment. Patagonia learned from an LCA that the production of one tee-shirt required more than 700 liters of water. In response, the company switched from industrially produced cotton to organic cotton, which uses far less water. Akzo Nobel, a chemical company, learned from a series of LCAs on packaging that steel drums are the best packaging for its chemicals, due to steel's high levels of recycling.[10] Coca-Cola and its bottling partners worldwide now replenish 100 percent of the water they use, 221 billion liters per year, through a global collaborative network of community and watershed projects.[11] The logistics company DHL plans to use clean transportation methods, including electric vehicles and bicycles, for 70 percent of its first- and last-mile services by 2025 and to achieve net-zero logistics-related emissions by 2050.[12] LCAs can help identify the "low-hanging fruit" for companies that want to improve their environmental performance. The actions they often suggest—such as retrofitting plants, installing energy-saving devices, and installing centralized controls for heating, lighting, and cooling systems—offer high returns on investment and short payback periods.

CRADLE-TO-CRADLE DESIGN

Some innovators have explored a totally new way to think about environmental issues, a cradle-to-cradle (C2C) design model. This approach suggests that products and services should be designed to completely close the production loop so that all resources needed to produce them are recycled and reused rather than discarded or left to pollute (see Figure 4.1). The model mimics nature, in which ecosystems recycle one agent's waste to

cradle-to-cradle (C2C) design model
A closed-loop design that recycles and reuses products

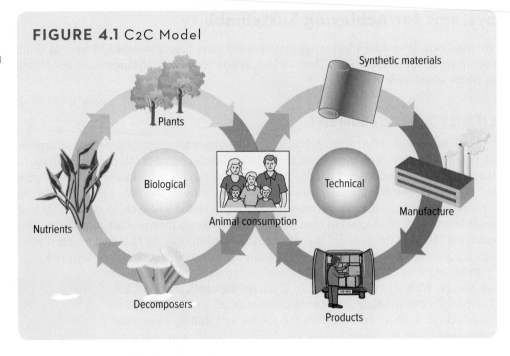

FIGURE 4.1 C2C Model

The concept of C2C is captured in the phrase "Waste = Food."

provide another's nutrition. In a forest ecosystem, for instance, trees use sunlight to power their manufacture of nutrients from carbon dioxide in the atmosphere. In the process, the trees produce oxygen that animals breathe. Their root systems filter water, and they provide seeds that not only ensure the birth of future generations but also provide food for other organisms. Fallen leaves turn into compost to sustain the trees and other living things. The system cycles all material and generates no toxic waste. The shorthand version of the C2C concept is the phrase "Waste = Food." (You might want to check out Rob van Hattum's documentary of the same name.[13])

Applied to products and services, C2C identifies two kinds of components, *technical nutrients* (which are inorganic, synthetic, and reusable) and *biological nutrients* (which are organic and decompose). The petroleum-based carpet manufacturers Interface, Desso, BASF, and Honeywell successfully apply C2C by taking used carpet from their customers and reusing it in a closed-loop process. Instead of being sent to landfills, Nylon 6, a synthetic ingredient of carpeting derived from oil and natural gas, is reprocessed into products of equal or greater value. Other companies, such as Patagonia, Trigema, and Eileen Fisher, take back their garments and recycle their basic material. Some critics feel the C2C model is impractical, but it presents us with a starting point as we develop new ways of thinking about sustainable making and selling.

Tools for Measuring Sustainability

LO 4-3
Summarize ways to measure sustainability achievements.

Once we have a way to think about sustainability and begin to practice it, we need a way to understand how successful our efforts are. We need to be able to measure and compare the impacts of our actions. Here we review a series of useful tools that can help us understand how we're doing in our sustainability efforts.[14]

These tools must meet a complex need: they must provide us with meaningful measures across different sectors, a common yardstick often referred to as the comparability test. There is a standardized platform that can provide comparable measurements, and it is used by several frameworks, including the Global Compact, the Global Reporting Initiative, the Carbon Disclosure Project, and carbon and water footprinting. The Dutch website International Portal for Sustainability Reporting (http://www.sustainability-reports.com) lists and explains these efforts.

UNITED NATIONS GLOBAL COMPACT

The United Nations Global Compact was begun in 2000 to address four areas: human rights, labor, the environment, and anti-corruption. Three of the compact's 10 principles address the environment. More than 9,600 corporations from 161 countries have signed on to the compact, including 40 percent of the 500 largest global companies. Participants in the Global Compact file an annual report using the compact's framework that needs to suggest a serious and committed engagement with sustainability. You can access the most recent Global Compact Report at https://www.unglobalcompact.org/library and check out the visual summary of corporate progress.

United Nations Global Compact
A voluntary reporting scheme for businesses that covers critical areas affecting the conduct of international business—human rights, labor, the environment, and anti-corruption efforts

GLOBAL REPORTING INITIATIVE

The Global Reporting Initiative (GRI) is a networked organization of stakeholders, mostly businesses, that have collaborated to develop a widely used sustainability reporting framework by the same name. The GRI guidelines provide businesses with information on measuring and reporting the environmental impacts of their operations, including how to report, what to report, what performance indicators to use, and how to apply them. Because the frameworks have been developed collaboratively among corporate members, they meet the needs of a broad range of users. You can explore GRI standards at https://www.globalreporting.org/standards.

Global Reporting Initiative (GRI)
Sustainability reporting framework developed among stakeholders

Carbon Disclosure Project (CDP)
Organization that provides reporting frameworks for greenhouse gas emissions and water use

CARBON DISCLOSURE PROJECT

The Carbon Disclosure Project (CDP) is a nonprofit organization that provides reporting frameworks for sustainable water use and the reduction of greenhouse gas emissions and advocates for their reduction. It has partnered with major corporations, as well as institutional investors, cities, states, and regions, to develop frameworks for reporting their progress in these areas, including the major standards for carbon emissions reporting. Like the UN's Kyoto Protocol, it is concerned about emissions reporting and their reduction, but unlike the Kyoto Protocol, which has nation-state members, the CDP has corporate members. Over 85 percent of the Fortune Global 500 corporations report their emissions to the CDP and use it to set targets for their environmental impact. The CDP has encouraged companies to monitor their supply chains, and, because corporations are accepting their stewardship responsibilities and requiring their suppliers to report emissions, CDP membership is fast becoming necessary for any firm doing business with many global companies. You can learn more about CDP and its activities at https://www.cdp.net.

 CULTURE FACTS @internationalbiz

Collectivist cultures tend to have higher levels of environmental sustainability, as do risk-avoidance (uncertainty avoidance) cultures.
#collectivistcultures
#environmentalsustainability
#riskavoidancecultures

 SOCIAL MEDIA

FOOTPRINTING

Two final sustainability measures are carbon and water footprints. A product's carbon footprint measures the volume of greenhouse gas emissions associated with it, usually throughout its life cycle. It is a complicated calculation that attempts to measure both direct consumption (as a result of product use) and indirect consumption (as a result of the manufacture of the product). Water footprints are even more complicated to calculate, in part because we use water locally but discharge it into a global system. Water's availability also varies greatly by location, so the costs of using it are not standardized. Yet measurements of water usage are growing steadily more common and water is also often segmented by source and type (blue water is fresh surface water, grey water is diluted with pollutants, and green water results from rainfall). As Patagonia found when it looked at water requirements for manufacturing tee-shirts, companies that pay attention to their water use can benefit from lower manufacturing costs.

Now that we have looked at ways to think about and measure sustainability, we can focus on the characteristics we can expect to find in sustainable businesses.

carbon footprint
A measure of the volume of greenhouse gas emissions caused by a product's manufacture and use

water footprint
A measure of the amount of water used in a product's manufacture and use

Characteristics of Environmentally Sustainable Business

Businesses that accept their responsibility for environmental sustainability have three characteristics in common. They recognize and accept that resources are limited; they develop ways to manage the interdependence of the systems in which they operate, and they recognize the need for equity in their supply chains.[15] Figure 4.2 illustrates these relationships among the ecological, social, and economic aspects of a business and their intersection at sustainability.

LIMITS AS PART OF THE SUSTAINABILITY CONTEXT

Limits address the reality that environmental resources are exhaustible. Water, soil, and air can be made toxic, and their use needs to be informed by awareness of that danger. To recognize the limits of the Earth's atmosphere to absorb emissions, and to incorporate this recognition into the way the business operates, is an ecologically responsible decision that supports sustainability. Many businesses are beginning to realize that taking the initiative to lead their sector in developing such sustainable operations can generate valuable competitive advantage.[16]

Extractive industries such as mining and oil offer ready examples of how recognizing limits can function in achieving sustainability. Freeport-McMoRan has recognized limits in its mining operations in Papua, Indonesia, where it pays special attention to ecological and social issues that arise among local tribes who live near its rural operations. The company provides education for tribal children and health care for local communities and is environmentally responsible in its approach to extraction—by its very nature a destructive action—with strict controls on water pollution and habitat destruction. In contrast, Shell Oil was responsible for two large oil spills in the Niger Delta, in the southeastern part of Nigeria populated by Ijaw and Ogoni peoples, causing extensive soil and water contamination. As a result, Shell paid about $80 million in compensation for these environmental disasters, although remediation efforts progressed slowly.[17] Since then, many additional oil

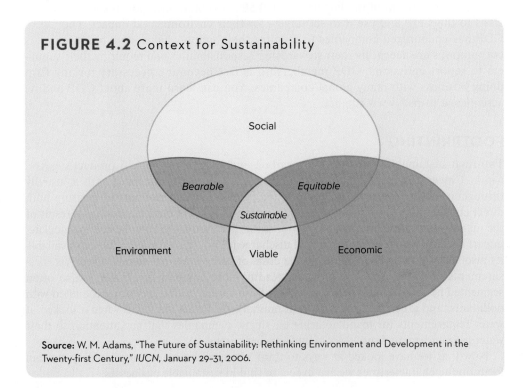

FIGURE 4.2 Context for Sustainability

Social

Bearable   Equitable

Sustainable

Environment   Viable   Economic

Source: W. M. Adams, "The Future of Sustainability: Rethinking Environment and Development in the Twenty-first Century," *IUCN*, January 29–31, 2006.

EUROPE LEADS THE WAY: Why the European Union Gets It on Environmental Issues

In the late 1960s, the United States led the world in environmental awareness, legislation, and responsibility. Congress established the Environmental Protection Agency (EPA) and passed the National Environmental Policy Act, the Clean Air Act, the Endangered Species Act, and the Clean Water Act. Yet today the European Union (EU) has far outpaced the United States in this area. Why? There is no simple explanation, but culture and demography contribute to the answer.

The United States was founded to protect individual citizens from a meddlesome, intrusive state. The United States is exceedingly individualistic, and business practices are thought of as acts of individual freedom. In Europe, communal values trump individualism, and business has quite a different purpose, one that includes obligations to society and higher levels of social responsibility. On demographics, Europeans also live in more densely populated cities than many in the United States, so environmental problems such as air and water pollution have a stronger, more directly observed impact. See Figure 4.3 for a map of Europe.

The European Union, therefore, applies the *precautionary principle* approach to environmentalism, which calls for regulation at the first sign of a possible danger rather than

FIGURE 4.3 European Market, Larger and Greener than the U.S. Market

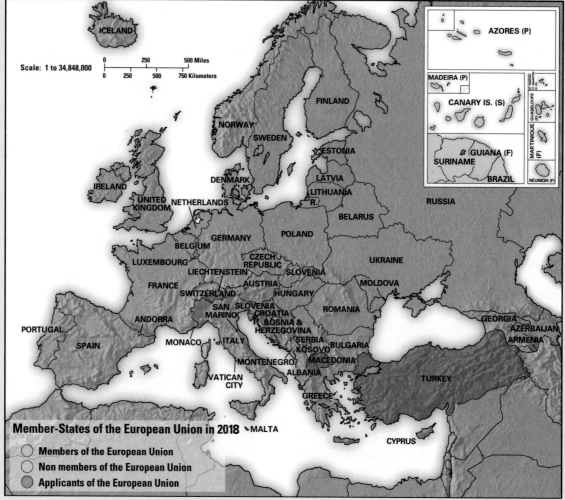

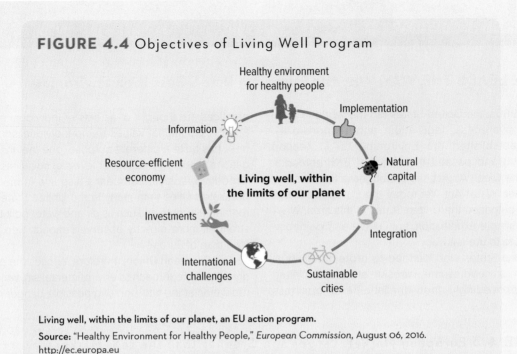

FIGURE 4.4 Objectives of Living Well Program

Healthy environment for healthy people

Implementation

Information

Natural capital

Resource-efficient economy

Living well, within the limits of our planet

Integration

Investments

Sustainable cities

International challenges

Living well, within the limits of our planet, an EU action program.

Source: "Healthy Environment for Healthy People," *European Commission*, August 06, 2016. http://ec.europa.eu

waiting for research to establish the facts. The precautionary principle puts the duty on industry to prove that its products are not dangerous. In contrast, the U.S. approach focuses on developing solutions for existing problems: "If it ain't broke, don't fix it." The EU's risk analysis and technology assessment (RATA) program, for example, is used to assess at various stages in the development process the potential environmental, human, and social risks associated with a new technology. Similarly, the EU's Registration, Evaluation and Authorization of Chemicals (REACH) regulation requires chemical companies to manage the risks from chemical substances, gather information about them that will ensure their safe handling and register it in a central database, and replace dangerous chemicals when alternatives have been identified. The purpose of these rules is to close the knowledge gap between the public and the industry.

In the United States, the Toxic Substances Control Act authorizes the EPA to regulate chemicals that pose an unreasonable risk to humans and the environment. The EPA has so far required testing of fewer than 200 of the 62,000 chemicals in use when the review began in 1979. It also requires a pre-manufacturing review of new chemicals that pose a hazard to humans. But in the United States, the government decides what to test, while in the European Union, industry must show the government that chemicals are safe and their risks managed before they can be manufactured or imported. In Europe, business has social responsibilities that in the United States are met by government regulation. See the outline of "Living well, within the limits of our planet, an EU action program," in Figure 4.4, or find out more about this program at http://ec.europa.eu/environment/newprg/index.htm. The European approach recognizes that business needs to be sustainable, while the U.S. approach looks to the government to act as a watchdog. Most Americans, if you ask them, are likely to say that the purpose of business relates directly to the bottom line, an understanding attributed to the economist Milton Friedman.

Critical Thinking Questions

1. Do you think Europe's approach to toxic substances could work in the United States? Why or why not?

2. Drawing on what you know about culture, do you think it helps to explain the EU's approach to environmental issues? Explain your reasoning.

Sources: "Science for Environment Policy: Putting Risk Analysis and Technology Assessment (RATA) into Practice to Support Technology Development," *European Commission*, May 24, 2018; "Living Well, Within the Limits of Our Planet," *European Commission*; "Reach," *European Commission*, 2018; "Environment," *European Union*, 2018; "Environment Action Programme to 2020," *European Commission*, 2018; "Toxic Substances Control Act of 1976," Wikipedia, 2018; and Milton Friedman, "The Social Responsibility of Business Is to Increase Its Profits," *The New York Times Magazine*, September 13, 1970.

spills have been reported. Shell has maintained very good relationships with the Nigerian government and, according to WikiLeaks, has placed key people in Nigerian government ministries.[18]

INTERDEPENDENCE AS PART OF THE SUSTAINABILITY CONTEXT

Interdependence describes the complex relationships that sustainable practices create among ecological, social, and economic systems, in which actions in one of these systems may affect the other two, often in ways that are not easily predicted. Consider, for example, the carbon emissions that occur as a result of transportation caused by a company's decision to outsource. Another impact is the social disruption that may be caused by locating manufacturing facilities in rural areas. Parents may take children from school to work in these plants, as Nike found. Traditional social patterns may be disrupted by women earning wages. The social consequences of fracking in rural areas of the United States—public health problems, increased traffic, social disturbances—have been largely unanticipated. What happens to waste from a small high-tech manufacturing plant in rural China that operates as a subcontractor to a manufacturer whose processes are open and transparent? How can we know about the social, environmental, and economic aspects of decision making? How can such complex processes be monitored effectively? Interdependence requires careful monitoring all along the value chain.

  CULTURE FACTS @internationalbiz

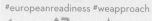

@Europe European culture is less individualistic than that of the United States, a difference reflected in European readiness to embrace partnerships between business and government—the "we approach"—and to pioneer the development of ecologically and sustainably "smart" cities. #lessindividualistic #europeanreadiness #weapproach

SOCIAL MEDIA

EQUITY IN DISTRIBUTION AS PART OF THE SUSTAINABILITY CONTEXT

Equity in distribution suggests that for system interdependence to work, there cannot be vast differences in the distribution of gains.[19] All stakeholders have to benefit to some degree from the value added by the business activities. Equity thus requires a business model that allocates the gains from businesses to a wide array of stakeholders. In addition to this ethical argument for equity, there is a commonsense one. In a globalizing world where information is increasingly more open, and we want increasing transparency, vast inequities may lead to social disruption and violence. This is an issue Shell might address in Nigeria.

One social and branding movement that has had a positive effect on integrating equity into the value chain is the Fair Trade movement. The Fair Trade label certifies that products are produced and marketed in ways that meet very modest claims to equity. Products must be grown and harvested to standards, working conditions and pay must meet certain criteria for safety and fairness, and sustainability along the supply chain must be monitored. When you buy Fair Trade products, your purchase supports the efforts of several loosely linked organizations to ensure reasonable work conditions, fair wages, and sustainable approaches.

Some businesses have pursued backward integration by establishing agricultural operations in order to control their supply chains and, in developing nations, to meet the need for increased efforts toward equity. As you might imagine, the interdependencies of sustainability require new ways of thinking. Yet when there is an effort to build equity, the interdependencies can work to the benefit of the firm and its stakeholders by some sharing of corporate gains.

No one ever said sustainability was simple or easy. Sustainable business models are complex; they involve more stakeholders and add specialized areas (waste reduction, sustainable technology, water conservation, to name a few) to the more traditional business model. We now look at the stakeholder model as a useful tool in the process of moving toward sustainability.

LO 4-5
Describe how the stakeholder model can help businesses achieve sustainability.

The Stakeholder Model for Sustainable Business

The traditional U.S. business model is economic and focuses on an input-process-output approach, where profitability is the goal, perpetual economic growth and unbridled consumption is encouraged, and nature's worth is measured primarily in terms of its potential for generating economic value.[20] This is not a universal understanding of business; the meaning people give to this process of value creation varies across cultures. Profit or the bottom-line understanding of the basic purpose of business is very strongly defended in the United States, where business is not assumed to have social obligations. It is a model whose overstatement—profitability at all costs, within legal limits—can be socially, economically, and environmentally dangerous. One difficulty in moving from the traditional model of doing business to a sustainable model, however, is that our thinking has been molded by the traditional approach, and for good reason: it has worked well. We also tend to resist change. Many people don't see yet that the traditional model is broken because we tend to focus on the economic benefits it has generated and ignore the ecological and social parts of the business context.[21] But sustainability is local and global simultaneously; it also requires a simultaneous focus inside the business and widely outside it. To help managers keep both the big picture context and the details of the business in their minds, the stakeholder model is useful.

stakeholder theory
An understanding of how business operates that takes into account all identifiable interest holders

Stakeholder theory was developed by the philosopher R. Edward Freeman,[22] and the model it offers differs substantially from the traditional economic business model. It calls for managers to identify and consider the network of tensions caused by the competing internal and external demands within which the business exists. The traditional economic model of business considers a far narrower scope of influences (employees, owners, and suppliers) that are driven by the single goal of creating profits. Stakeholder theory forces a business to address *underlying values and principles.* It "pushes managers to be clear about how they want to do business, what kind of relationships they want and need to create with their stakeholders to deliver on their purpose."[23] Stakeholder theory also gives all stakeholders a voice and suggests that the tensions among them can be balanced. Profit is then a *result* of value creation rather than the primary driver in the process, and business becomes a network of relationships in the larger social context and the responsibilities that develop from them. Freeman points out that many companies' operations are consistent with stakeholder theory, including Johnson & Johnson (J&J), eBay, Google, and Lincoln Electric.

To achieve the balance among competing tensions that characterize the stakeholder approach, a company needs to see itself in relation to its stakeholders and also in a societal context, as Figure 4.5 illustrates. Taking this view of itself leads the company to clearly identify its larger purpose, principles, and responsibilities through discussions both within the company and in its larger social context. The company then is able to identify limits for its operations, so that what it does is ecologically responsible and acceptable to its stakeholders; analyze and manage the various interdependencies among the ecological, social, and economic systems that form the context of the business; and address ways to achieve equity of distribution.

triple-bottom-line accounting (3BL)
An approach to accounting that measures the firm's social and environmental performance in addition to its economic performance

One way a company can measure its activities in this larger context and share the results of its social, environmental, and economic performance with its stakeholders is to use triple-bottom-line accounting (3BL). Note, though, that 3BL does not allow for comparisons across companies because the measurements, especially in the social and environmental areas, are not standardized. For an example of triple-bottom-line reporting, see Freeport-McMoRan's Sustainable Development Reports at https://www.fcx.com/sd. The company's public materials suggest it is using a stakeholder approach, increasing value, and contributing to the quality of life for many constituencies, including indigenous peoples,

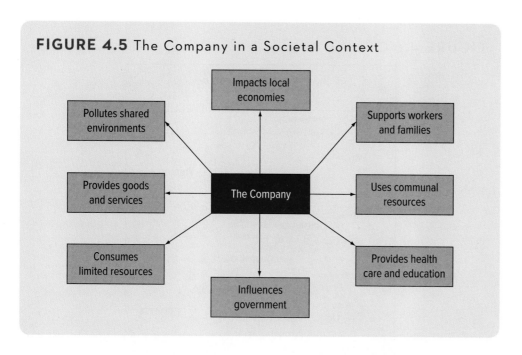

FIGURE 4.5 The Company in a Societal Context

Impacts local economies

Pollutes shared environments

Supports workers and families

Provides goods and services

The Company

Uses communal resources

Consumes limited resources

Provides health care and education

Influences government

while operating low-impact mining in one of the most socially and environmentally challenging sectors: extraction.

Companies that have been widely recognized for their stakeholder and sustainability efforts include L'Oreal, PG&E, Seventh Generation, Hasbro, Clif Bar, IKEA, J&J, Method, Apple, Timberland, Earthtec, Stonyfield Farm, United Air, Alaska Air, Starbucks, Interface & FLOR, P&G, and Patagonia. Note that this list includes large, global multinationals; small, privately held companies (Clif Bar), companies we might not expect (United Air and Alaska Air—remember, some of the metrics measure *improvement* of the carbon footprint); companies that use petroleum as a major ingredient of their products (Interface & FLOR); companies that specialize in e-sales (Abe's Market); fashion companies (Earthtec, Timberland); an electric utility (PG&E); and some of the traditional green leaders (Patagonia and Starbucks). Sustainability is moving forward across many sectors.

> **"THE WHOLE IDEA of COMPASSION IS BASED on A KEEN AWARENESS of THE INTERDEPENDENCE of ALL THESE LIVING BEINGS, WHICH ARE ALL PART of ONE ANOTHER, AND ALL INVOLVED in ONE ANOTHER."**
>
> *—Thomas Merton,*
> *U.S. Trappist monk, writer, and mystic*[24]

Geography: Describing Our Natural Capital

We now consider natural capital, the land, air, water, living organisms, and all of the formations of our ecosystem that provide us with the goods and services on which our survival depends. Natural capital is, in short, the basis for everything we do as humans.[25] We approach natural capital initially through the lens of geography, examining location, topography, and climate. We then look at natural resources.

LOCATION: POLITICAL AND TRADE RELATIONSHIPS

A country's location, its neighbors, and the location of its capital and major cities are part of its natural capital and explain many of its political and trade relationships. International managers should know how these contribute to the country's competitive advantage. It may seem obvious that we tend to trade with our neighbors, but let's look at how subtle such

LO 4-6
Describe how geographic features of a country or region contribute to natural capital.

natural capital
Natural resources such as air, land, and water that provide us with the goods and services on which our survival depends

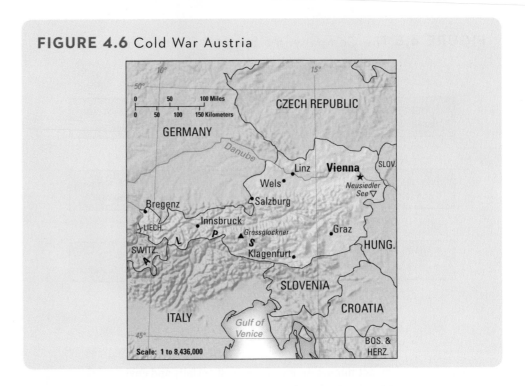

FIGURE 4.6 Cold War Austria

relationships can be. Singapore sits at the southern edge of Southeast Asia's Malay Peninsula. Historically it has been a critical replenishment port. To maintain its edge as a leading transshipment point between the Pacific and the Indian Ocean, oceans, Singapore developed state-of-the-art port facilities to exploit its geographic location. Another example is Austria. At the height of the Cold War's East–West face-off in the 1950s, its location enabled it to be a political bridge between the communist East and the noncommunist West (see Figure 4.6).

Austria's political neutrality also made it a good location for international firms that did business in the East. Because their country had led the Austro-Hungarian Empire until 1918, Austrians were completely familiar with the cultures and practices of those neighboring countries to which they had once been joined. Finally, Vienna, Austria's capital, was close to both Czechoslovakia (today's Czech Republic and Slovakia) and Hungary. Austria took advantage of its location to (1) increase trade with the East, (2) become the principal financial intermediary between East and West, and (3) strengthen its role as the regional headquarters for international businesses operating in Eastern Europe. Then, in 1991 when the collapse of the Soviet bloc (COMECON: Bulgaria, Czechoslovakia, East Germany, Hungary, Romania, Poland, the Soviet Union, Cuba, Mongolia, and Vietnam) forced Eastern European enterprises to reorient their trade toward the West, Austria's location and relationships allowed its entrepreneurs to capture an important share of the West's exports to the East.

In addition to being a major reason for trade between nations, geographic proximity also plays a role in the formation of trading groups. With proximity, knowledge of trade partners is likely, delivery faster, and freight and service costs lower. Two of the three major trading partners of the United States—Canada and Mexico—lie on its borders. Geographic proximity also shapes membership in trading groups such as the European Union, Mercosur (the Common Market of the South, consisting of Argentina, Brazil, Paraguay, Uruguay, and Venezuela, though the latter has been suspended since December 2016); ASEAN (the Association of Southeast Asian Nations); and NAFTA (the North American Free Trade Agreement). Proximity also helps explain why Japan has been one of China's largest sources of imports, along with South Korea and the United States.

TOPOGRAPHY

The features of the Earth's surface, such as mountains, plains, deserts, and bodies of water, contribute to differences in economies, cultures, politics, and social structures wherever they occur. These features can both hinder and aid physical distribution. They also may require that products be altered. For example, the effects of altitude require a change in baking instructions at heights above 3,000 feet. Internal combustion engines begin to lose power at 5,000 feet, which may require the manufacturer of gasoline-powered machinery to use larger engines. Because topography—the physical features of an area—contributes so powerfully to a nation's natural capital, we examine its major components: mountains, deserts, tropical rainforests, and bodies of water.

topography
The surface features of a region

Mountains Barriers such as mountains tend to separate neighbors and impede exchange and interaction, whereas plains and plateaus facilitate them unless climate makes exchange unlikely, as in the Sahara and Gobi deserts. Mountains that are massive and rugged, and that don't have to transect valleys, are significant barriers. Travel across the Himalayas is so difficult that transportation between India and China is by air or sea rather than over land, and the cultures and languages of the Indians to the south and the Chinese to the north are in high contrast to one another.

Another example of the influence of mountain barriers occurs in Afghanistan, where mountains dominate the landscape, running northeast to southwest through the center of the country, including the Hindukush area. More than 40 percent of Afghanistan sits at altitudes above 6,000 feet, and high passes cut through these mountains, creating a network for caravans. (In comparison, in the United States there are only two peaks east of the Mississippi River that reach 6,000 feet, Mt. Mitchell and Mt. Washington.) The 10 major ethnic groups and 33 languages spoken in Afghanistan offer further evidence of the ability of mountain ranges to separate populations.

In similar fashion, the Alps, Carpathians, Balkans, and Pyrenees have long separated the Mediterranean cultures of Europe from those of the North. These mountain ranges create regional markets, each with its own distinctive industries, climate, culture, dialect, and sometimes even language. In Spain, Catalonia and the Basque country have separate languages. In Switzerland, German, Swiss, Italian, and Romish regions, cultures, and

The Central Asian Hindu Kush runs from north central Pakistan through eastern and central Afghanistan.
©Ascent/PKS Media Inc./Stockbyte/Getty Images.

languages challenge firms that would like to standardize their products and marketing. In China, the government made Mandarin the official language in 1956, recognizing that language diversity was hindering the country's economic development. Yet there are at least 56 Chinese ethnic groups, each with its own language, and many separated by mountain ranges. In Colombia, the three major ranges of the Andes divide the country and separate people, as well.

Deserts and Tropical Forests Deserts and tropical forests also separate markets, increase the cost of transportation, and create population concentrations. More than one-third of the Earth's surface consists of arid and semiarid regions located either on the coasts of continents, where the winds blow away from the land, or in their interiors, where mountains or long distances cause the winds to lose their moisture before reaching these regions. Every continent has deserts and tropical forests, and every western coast between 20 and 30 degrees north or south of the Equator is dry. Only in latitudes where there is a major source of water, as in Egypt, is there a concentration of population.

In Figure 4.7, which depicts the distribution of the world's population, Australia well illustrates the relationship between water supply and population concentration. A continent the size of the continental United States but with just over 7 percent of the U.S. population, Australia has a coastline that is humid and fertile, while the huge center of the country is mainly desert, closely resembling the Sahara. Australia's population is concentrated along the coastal areas in and around the state capitals, which are also major seaports, and in the southeastern fifth of the nation, where more than half the population lives. Australia's topography creates one of the highest percentages of urban population in the world, at about 93 percent.

Tropical rainforests, at the other extreme, also are a barrier to economic development and human settlement, especially when they are combined with a harsh climate and poor soil, as in the Amazon basin, Southeast Asia, and the Congo. Except in parts of West Africa and Java, rainforests are thinly populated and economically underdeveloped.

The Canadian Shield, although neither desert nor rainforest, is a vast outcropping of bedrock thinly covered with soil that covers about half the country (1.7 million square miles),

The Green Wall of China, in Taipuisa, Inner Mongolia, planted to fend off the encroaching Gobi desert.
©Carl & Ann Purcell/Corbis/Getty Images.

FIGURE 4.7 World Population Map

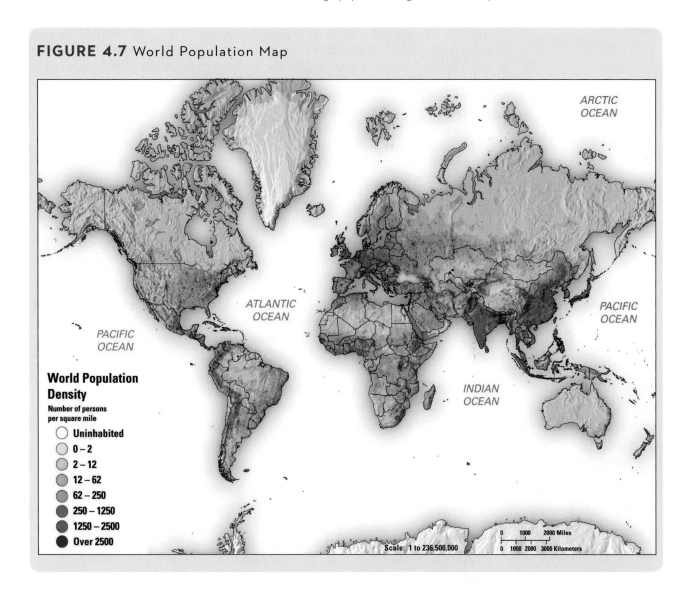

is mostly in permafrost, and does not support populations, although it is the source of minerals, diamonds, and ores.

International managers know that in more densely populated nations, marketing and distribution cost less because population centers are closer together, communication systems are more efficient, and more people are available for employment. Therefore, when they compare average population densities such as Canada's 3 inhabitants per square kilometer, Australia's 3, Brazil's 23, and the United States' 34 with the Netherlands' 495 or Japan's 351, they can avoid drawing the wrong conclusions. They know the populations of Canada, Australia, and Brazil are highly concentrated in relatively small areas because of deserts, tropical rainforests, and in Canada, the Shield. If you are interested in exploring population density further, helpful resources include The World Bank's population density tool,[26] Duncan Smith's World Population Density interactive map,[27] or Alasdair Rae's mapping of population density in Europe.[28]

Bodies of Water Unlike mountains, deserts, and tropical forests, bodies of water attract people and facilitate transportation. The world population map clearly shows that bodies of water have attracted more people than have areas remote from water. The world population map clearly shows that densely populated regions coincide with rivers, lakes, and seacoasts.

Water is necessary for life and critical for industry, yet it is invisible to most consumers when used in agriculture and manufacturing. Did you know that as many as 2,400 liters of water are used to produce one hamburger, while 11,000 liters can be consumed in the production of a pair of jeans?[29] Although water is an abundant natural resource, its distribution around the world is uneven. In general, the world's poor lack access to clean water. For example, in the slums of Dar es Salaam, Tanzania's largest city, 1,000 liters of water cost $8. The same amount of water in the wealthy areas of the same city costs $0.34, and in the United States $0.68, according to the London-based nonprofit group WaterAid, whose mission is to help poor communities establish clean water supplies.[30]

inland waterway
Waterway that provides access to interior regions

Inland waterways provide inexpensive access to interior markets. Before the construction of railways, water transport was the only economically practical carrier for bulk goods over long distances. Its use increased even after the building of railroads, and today, on every continent except Australia, which has no inland waterways, water transportation is significant, although diminished due to competition from air and road transport everywhere except in Europe. The Rhine waterway, mapped in Figure 4.8, has become the world's most important inland waterway system. It carries one-half of Switzerland's exports and nearly three-fourths of its imports. The Rhine-Main-Danube Canal, completed in 1992, creates access from the Netherlands and the North Sea through 15 countries to the Black Sea. From there, shipments can continue to Moscow over the interconnected system of the Volga and Don Rivers. Increasingly, firms have been turning to the Rhine

FIGURE 4.8 Map of the Rhine-Main-Danube Canal

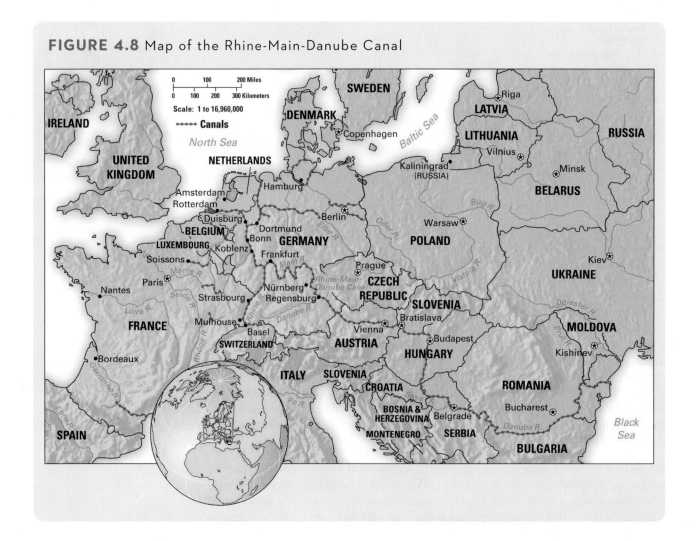

waterway as an environmentally friendly and more economical alternative to road or rail transportation.

Major inland waterways in South America include the Amazon and its tributaries, which offer about 36,000 miles of navigable waterways during the flood season, and the Paraná and Paraguay Rivers as a trade corridor being developed by the Mercosur governments of Argentina, Brazil, Paraguay, and Uruguay. In Asia, the major waterways are the Yangtze (China), the Ganges (India), and the Indus (Pakistan). Now that the massive Chinese Three Gorges hydroelectric dam project is finished, oceangoing vessels are able to travel to Chongqing, which has become an inland seaport 2,400 kilometers from the ocean. In the United States, two waterways are critical, the Great Lakes–St. Lawrence Seaway and the Mississippi River.

Historically, navigable waterways with connections to the ocean have been important because they permit low-cost transportation of goods and people from a country's coast to its interior. Today, they are the only means of access from the coasts of many developing nations. In Africa, where 14 of the world's 20 landlocked developing countries are located, access to the coast can be a major challenge. Landlocked nations must construct long, costly truck routes and extensive feeder networks for relatively low volumes of traffic. Furthermore, the governments that control the coastlines near landlocked countries are in positions to exert considerable political influence.

CULTURE FACTS @internationalbiz

@Switzerland Switzerland is landlocked, yet it won the America's Cup sailing competition in 2005. #landlocked #america'scup #sailing #2005

SOCIAL MEDIA

CLIMATE

Climate, the set of meteorological conditions of temperature, precipitation, and wind that prevail in a region, is important because it sets limits on what people can do. Where the climate is harsh, there are few human settlements, and where it is permissive, population density is higher. Similar climates occur in similar latitudes and continental positions, and the more an area is dominated by water, the more moderate its climate is.

For centuries, Northern writers have used climate differences to explain differences in human and economic development. This explanation, known as the *North-South divide*, suggests that the greatest economic and intellectual development has occurred in the temperate climates of northern Europe and the United States because less-temperate climates limit human energy and mental powers.[31] However, businesspeople must not be taken in by such ethnocentric reasoning. Given the advanced development of science, philosophy, and mathematics in China during the Song Dynasty and in Arabia during Europe's Middle Ages, we can see that other factors are at work.

Jared Diamond's Pulitzer Prize–winning *Guns, Germs, and Steel: The Fates of Human Societies* explores factors that contribute to differing levels of development.[32] Diamond argues that gaps in technology among human societies were caused by the development of early agricultural societies in places favored by climate and topographic features. These populations developed immunity to diseases that, along with other factors, allowed them to develop stable social groups. Such differences neither reflect nor lead to intellectual or moral superiority.

World Bank studies have shown that many of the factors responsible for underdevelopment in tropical nations are present because of the climate: continuous heat and the lack of winter cold means there are no constraints on the reproduction and growth of weeds, insects, viruses, birds, and parasites, and this results in destroyed crops, dead cattle, and people infected with debilitating diseases.[33] Techniques are becoming available to control pests and parasites, yet the impacts of climate change may reduce any advantage such control would bring to tropical Africa. Yet, thinking of climate as deterministic would be a mistake. It allows certain developments to occur, but it does not cause them.

Location, topography, and climate form the basic context for human activity, including business ventures. Try as the Swiss might to alter things, Switzerland is

climate
Meteorological conditions, including temperature, precipitation, and wind that prevail in a region

likely to continue to be a mountainous country with long, snowy winters on a heavily populated plain at the foot of the Alps. True, people may undertake massive modifications: the Netherlands, situated below the North Sea level, has protected itself from the sea through a system of dikes. Singapore has greatly increased its landmass by reclaiming land from the surrounding sea, as has Japan in Tokyo Harbor. Yet, for the most part, location and topography tend to be permanent facts, while climate, although not deterministic, may set limits for human activity that prove difficult to modify. In addition, climate on a global scale is being affected by the greenhouse gas emissions that accompany industrialization, resulting in warmer temperatures, melting ice at the polar caps, and rising sea levels. These climate changes may have passed the point where they can be reversed, and if so, they present further limitations to human activity.

We now move to another area of natural capital, natural resources. These sources of raw materials are, unlike location, topography, and climate, extractable and malleable. We consider the energy sources because they are natural resources critical to business, moving from the nonrenewable to the renewable.

LO 4-7
Outline nonrenewable and renewable energy options available and their potential impacts on business.

natural resources
Anything supplied by nature on which people depend

renewable energy
Energy that comes from sources that are naturally replenished, such as sunlight, wind, and water flow

Natural Resources

What are **natural resources**? For our purposes, they are anything supplied by nature on which people depend. Although all natural resources are important to business, those from which energy and the nonfuel minerals can be extracted have special importance, and it is those we consider here. They fall into two major categories: renewable and nonrenewable.

Among **renewable energy** sources, those that are naturally replenished are wind power, biomass fuels, solar photovoltaic power, concentrating solar thermal power, geothermal power, ocean energy, and hydropower. Figure 4.9 illustrates the evolution of the world's energy consumption by fuel from 1990 to 2040. Nonrenewable energy sources have dominated the market. We look at these first.

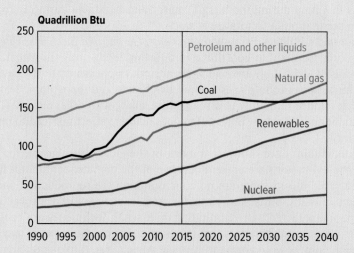

FIGURE 4.9 World Energy Consumption by Fuel Type, 1990–2040 (est.)

Source: "International Energy Outlook 2017," *U.S. Energy Information Administration*, September 14, 2017.

NONRENEWABLE ENERGY SOURCES

Nonrenewable energy is energy that comes from sources that cannot be replenished, the fossil fuels, including petroleum, coal, and natural gas. Nuclear energy is also nonrenewable, but on a quite different scale than the fossil fuels.

Petroleum Petroleum, or crude oil, has been a cheap source of energy and a raw material for plastics, fertilizers, and other industrial applications. We all realize the world will run out of oil, but exactly when is uncertain. So we look at discovery and production rates to help figure out how near we are to the end of our supply. Researchers are confident peak oil discovery occurred in the 1960s. Once we know peak oil production has been reached at the global level, forecasters anticipate the world's economies will enter a transition period in which there will be an increasing gap between what the market needs in petroleum products and what can be supplied at a reasonable price. Figure 4.10 illustrates this gap.

When will peak production occur? One group of oil industry professionals, the Association for the Study of Peak Oil and Gas, agrees we are probably in the peak period right now.[34] The group's critical question is: How much time do we have to make adjustments before the price of oil becomes prohibitive? The likely answer is that "Petroleum Man will be virtually extinct this Century,"[35] a prediction that gives us around 80 years. The U.S. Energy Information Administration projects that world energy consumption will continue to increase through mid-century, with dramatic increases in developing countries such as China and India as they continue to industrialize.[36] Oil and natural gas are projected to remain the world's dominant energy sources in this period.

Despite the best forecasts, estimates of the size of the world's oil reserves are uncertain for a number of reasons:

- New discoveries continue to be made with the aid of improved prospecting equipment.
- Above-ground issues such as political unrest, financial crises, and natural disasters impact territories available for exploration and production. Political unrest limits access to potential sites, and governments control access to their natural resources.

nonrenewable energy
Energy that comes from sources that cannot be replenished, such as the fossil fuels—petroleum, coal, and natural gas—and nuclear power

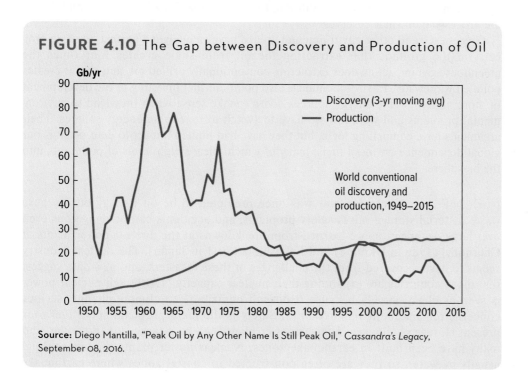

FIGURE 4.10 The Gap between Discovery and Production of Oil

World conventional oil discovery and production, 1949–2015

— Discovery (3-yr moving avg)
— Production

Source: Diego Mantilla, "Peak Oil by Any Other Name Is Still Peak Oil," *Cassandra's Legacy,* September 08, 2016.

- Improved techniques such as steam and hot-water injection, of which fracking is one, and oil recovery systems within layers of shale rock enable producers to put new areas into operation and increase output from existing ones. Such unconventional sources of petroleum include oil sands, oil-bearing shale, coal, and natural gas.
- Automated, less expensive equipment lowers drilling costs. For instance, wellheads located on the ocean floor can replace expensive offshore platforms once the technology has been developed to avoid leakage and spills. Automated equipment allows a company to profitably work smaller-sized discoveries that otherwise it would not touch. The remarkable innovation of horizontal drilling, different from the normal vertical direction, allows wells to combine vertical and horizontal approaches to pockets of oil with accuracy and increases the wells' contact area.[37]

shale
A fissile rock (capable of being split) composed of laminated layers of claylike, fine-grained sediment

Unconventional sources of oil include the world's major oil sands in Canada (Athabasca, in Alberta), Venezuela, and the Republic of Congo. The sands contain bitumen, a tarlike crude oil, and place Canada first in these reserves and second only to Saudi Arabia in overall proven reserves. Then there also is oil-bearing shale, a fine-grained sedimentary rock that yields 25 liters or more of liquid hydrocarbons per ton of rock when heated to 500°C. The largest known source of oil-bearing shale encompasses Utah, Colorado, and Wyoming in the United States. Oil shale has remained underdeveloped because of environmental problems in waste-rock disposal and the great quantities of water needed for processing. Recent technological advances have made these deposits accessible with minimal environmental impact, while increased oil prices have made the exploitation of shale oil economically feasible. These two petroleum sources—oil sands and oil-bearing shale—produce *synthetic oil*, that is, oil made from a chemical process. It is often called heavy oil because it does not flow easily. Heavy oil promises to shift the global balance of oil power. In addition to horizontal drilling, the technology called hydraulic fracturing can make shale oil and gas deposits available. Hydraulic fracturing, or fracking, is the cracking of rock by injecting a fluid under pressure. Both horizontal drilling and fracking have opened new reserves in the United States. In addition, Estonia, China, Brazil, Germany, and Russia are processing oil shale reserves.[38]

heavy oil
Oil that does not flow easily, presently sourced from oil sands and oil-bearing shale

Greenpeace and other environmental groups have campaigned against oil shale projects on the grounds that extracting the oil from shale creates four times the greenhouse-gas impact as does extracting conventionally drilled oil, and that it creates polluted wastewater. Environmentalists also point out that investing in the development of more nonrenewable energy sources doesn't make sense when they lead to environmental problems and we know we have to switch to renewable energy sources. Their arguments have compelling logic, but they have had limited impact to date. Such is our global dependence on fossil fuels, many of which release high levels of pollutants into the biosphere.

Nuclear Power Nuclear power was once predicted to be on its way out because waste material storage raises safety problems, and accidents can be dangerous even over large distances, as we learned from breakdowns at the nuclear power plants at Chernobyl (1986 in Ukraine) and Fukushima (2011 in Japan). The nuclear industry seems to have recovered from the challenges of these disasters, and new data suggest that many countries are expanding their nuclear capacity.[39] Although nuclear power is seen as clean, largely because it doesn't contribute to climate change, serious concerns remain about reliance on it. Safety is the main problem: spent fuel rods present storage challenges, nuclear power plants can be a target for terrorism, and many have been built in earthquake zones. Nuclear power plants require cooling, usually by water, so they are often constructed in coastal zones where earthquake risks are high.

FIGURE 4.11 Nuclear Reactors Around the World, 2016

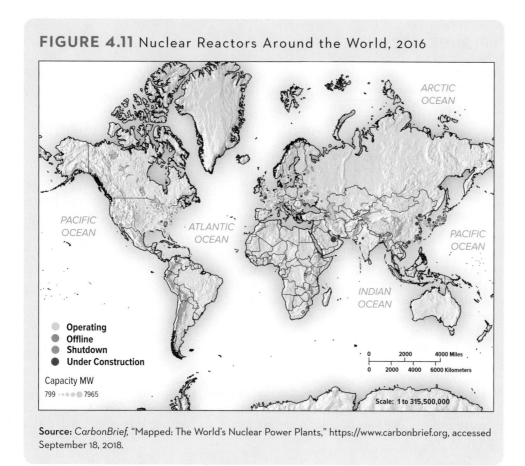

Source: *CarbonBrief*, "Mapped: The World's Nuclear Power Plants," https://www.carbonbrief.org, accessed September 18, 2018.

Figure 4.11 illustrates the global magnitude of nuclear power. The International Atomic Energy Agency lists 453 nuclear power plants in operation across 30 countries at the end of August 2018, with an additional 57 plants under construction.[40] The majority of new construction is occurring in China (15), India (7), Russia (6), South Korea (4), and the United Arab Emirates (4).[41] The U.S. Nuclear Energy Institute reports that more than eight nuclear power plant licenses are being actively pursued in the United States,[42] in addition to two plants under construction, although significant concern about safety remains. France also has turned to nuclear generation, producing 75 percent of its electricity by nuclear power and achieving one of the lowest rates of greenhouse gas emissions in the industrialized world. Its strong commitment to nuclear power has enabled France to go from being a net importer of electricity to being the world's largest exporter, generating over 3 billion euros per year in revenues.[43]

Coal Coal, much like nuclear power, has been projected to decline as an energy source, largely because it pollutes heavily. Demand for coal is currently projected to level out through approximately 2025 and then decline through 2040, largely due to growth in consumption of natural gas and renewable energy sources.[44] The United States leads the world in recoverable coal reserves,[45] with enough to last more than 200 years at projected rates of consumption, and now exports coal to China. The emissions released by burning coal are directly responsible for global warming, although clean-coal technologies are being developed that reduce the level of pollution released as part of the energy generation process. There is no question, though, that through their continued use of coal, China, India, and the United States are contributing greatly to the release of greenhouse gases.

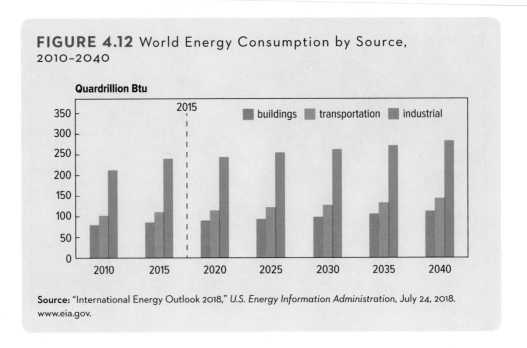

FIGURE 4.12 World Energy Consumption by Source, 2010–2040

Source: "International Energy Outlook 2018," *U.S. Energy Information Administration*, July 24, 2018. www.eia.gov.

Natural Gas Natural gas is the cleanest-burning among the fossil fuels, with greenhouse gas emissions significantly lower than those of oil or coal. As oil prices increase and new deposits of natural gas are found, its consumption is increasing as a substitute fuel.

RENEWABLE ENERGY SOURCES

Just about everyone in energy fields accepts the assertion that *at some time* an energy revolution that replaces nonrenewable energy sources such as fossil fuels with renewable energy sources is inevitable and data from the U.S. Energy Information Administration shows that such a change is underway. Figure 4.12 shows the world's energy consumption by source, from 2010 through projected 2040 usage.

This shift toward renewable energy sources will occur for one of two reasons: either the price of nonrenewable energy sources will become too high relative to the cost of developing sustainable renewable sources, or the nonrenewable sources themselves will become unavailable, due to either depletion or political risk. The commercial development of seven alternative energy sources is widely tracked by various organizations committed to their full commercialization: wind power, biomass fuels, solar photovoltaic power, concentrating solar thermal power, geothermal power, ocean energy, and hydropower. Other forms of alternative energy are under development or used in small applications, but these seven have commercial viability. None of them is available everywhere, but all appear to have applications under appropriate conditions.

In recent years, growth in the renewable energy sector has outpaced growth in the nonrenewable sector in both the European Union and the United States, and growth in the renewable energy markets in developing countries also has been rapid. In addition, although nonrenewable energy sources showed a decline in growth following the 2009 global financial crisis, renewables did not; their growth continued unabated. Presently over 164 countries have put in place renewable energy targets, nearly four times the 43 countries with such targets in 2005.[46] Now we take a look at each of the seven major renewable energy sources.

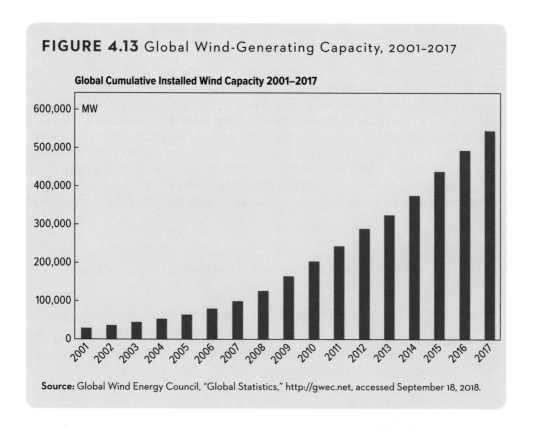

FIGURE 4.13 Global Wind-Generating Capacity, 2001–2017

Global Cumulative Installed Wind Capacity 2001–2017

Source: Global Wind Energy Council, "Global Statistics," http://gwec.net, accessed September 18, 2018.

Wind Power Both on land and offshore, wind power is now a mainstream electric energy source. As shown in Figure 4.13, global wind-generating capacity in 2017 was nearly 23 times the level of 2001. China represents 35 percent of the world's capacity and the United States 17 percent, while Germany (10 percent), India (6 percent), the UK (4 percent), and Canada (2 percent) trail behind.[47] Trends in wind power are toward offshore development and small-scale community projects, and projections for growth are strong.

Biomass **Biomass** is a category of renewable fuels derived from organic materials whose energy source is photosynthesis, through which plants transform the sun's energy into chemical energy. It is derived from agricultural, forestry, and municipal waste, and also from some crops grown expressly for fuel. You could think of biomass as a battery for storing the sun's solar energy. Biomass materials can be solid (straw, wood chips), liquid (vegetable oils and animal slurries), or gas (biogas) and are usually burned to generate power. A growing development within this sector is the co-firing of biomass fuels with coal, a process that reduces harmful emissions and can use existing coal power generating facilities.

Ethanol is a type of biomass fuel whose use rose dramatically as the cost of oil and concerns about carbon emissions increased. Corn, wheat, and sugarcane are its most popular sources. Brazil led the world in developing biomass fuel, and biomass heating has expanded as well, especially in China and Sweden. Over the past several years ethanol sales in the United States have dropped dramatically, in tandem with a reduction in fuel consumption explained by the recent financial crisis. The shale oil boom has also reduced U.S. consumers' motivation to use ethanol because shale oil brings the United States closer to its goal of independence from foreign fuel. In addition, environmentalists, who once thought ethanol part of the solution to our environmental problems, now see it as a

biomass
A category of fuels whose energy source is photosynthesis, through which plants transform the sun's energy into chemical energy

concern because corn, one major source of ethanol, has taken acreage away from food crops, especially in countries that need the food.[48]

Solar Photovoltaic Power   **Solar photovoltaic power (PV)** is power based on the voltage created when certain materials are exposed to light. The fastest-growing renewable power technology and the second-fastest overall power technology, outpaced only by natural gas, solar power is in use in over 120 countries.[49] Global solar-installed capacity increased between 2008 and 2016 by an astonishing 1,600 percent. Germany is the leader worldwide in solar PV generation, accounting for over 17 percent of global capacity, followed by China, Japan, Italy, and the United States. For the first time, over 100 gigawatts of solar PV power was to be added to global generating capacity in 2018, with that annual increment to capacity projected to be sustained at least through 2022.[50] Figure 4.14

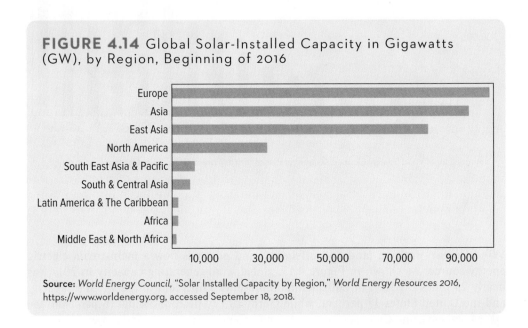

FIGURE 4.14 Global Solar-Installed Capacity in Gigawatts (GW), by Region, Beginning of 2016

Source: *World Energy Council,* "Solar Installed Capacity by Region," *World Energy Resources 2016,* https://www.worldenergy.org, accessed September 18, 2018.

Solar photovoltaic power can be useful for producing energy even in remote or relatively primitive areas.
©Michael Runkel/robertharding/Getty Images.

shows the total amount of installed capacity for solar power generation, by region, at the beginning of 2016.

Concentrating Solar Thermal Power Concentrating solar thermal power (CSP) uses mirrors or lenses to collect sunlight that heats water running in tubes behind the collector's surface. This heat then drives an engine, often a steam turbine, connected to an electrical power generator. CSP is categorized as a different type of power than solar PV because it relies on a different technology. Although commercial applications of CSP began in the United States in 1984, initial expansion of CSP was slower than for solar photovoltaic power. Since 2004, global CSP capacity expanded tenfold, with Spain and the United States emerging as leaders.[51] Recent CSP capacity expansion has particularly focused on developing countries and countries receiving high solar radiation.

concentrating solar thermal power (CSP)
A system using mirrors or lenses to collect sunlight for heating water that powers an electrical generator

Geothermal Power Geothermal power derives from the heat stored in the earth and may rely on many technologies. Heat can be drawn from hot water or steam reservoirs deep in the earth that are accessed by drilling, from geothermal reservoirs that create hot springs, and directly from the earth's close-to-the-surface temperature of 508–608°F. This heat can be used directly or to generate electricity. Although it represents only a small share of global energy production, in 2017, geothermal capacity increased by 4.3 percent worldwide.[52] The largest sources of geothermal power are the United States, with 28 percent of the world's capacity, followed by the Philippines, Indonesia, and New Zealand. Kenya generates over 40 percent of its power with geothermal and Iceland over 25 percent of its electricity. Seventy nations have projects underway in the rapidly expanding geothermal market.[53] Figure 4.15 illustrates the growth of geothermal-generating capacity since 2000.

geothermal power
Power from heat stored in the earth

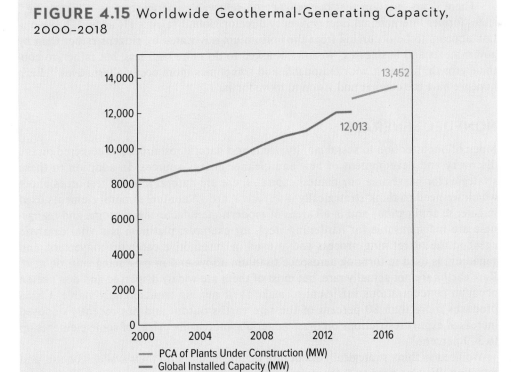

FIGURE 4.15 Worldwide Geothermal-Generating Capacity, 2000–2018

Source: *Geothermal Energy Association, "Current Use," http://geo-energy.org, accessed September 7, 2018.*

Ocean Energy The sun's heat on the water and the mechanical energy of the tides and waves are the two sources for ocean energy, the least mature of the renewable energy sources. Interest is building in wave, tidal, and ocean thermal energy conversion systems. France generates power from tidal forces at La Rance, with a barrage (dam) that began operating in 1966, and South Korea has a facility that began operation in 2011.[54] Smaller projects have been commissioned in Portugal, China, Russia, Denmark, Korea, Spain, the United States, and Canada.[55] The United Kingdom operates the only commercial-scale tidal turbine to generate electricity, at an installation in Scotland that was launched in 2016.[56] At least 70 companies have developed technologies for generating electricity from tidal power and more than 25 countries are engaged in some sort of ocean energy development research activity.

Hydropower Drawing on the energy of moving water to generate power, hydropower is the world's largest renewable source of electricity. China quadrupled its hydropower capacity since 2000, spurred by completion of the massive Three Gorges Dam project along with other installations that brought total installed capacity to over 341 gigawatts by the beginning of 2018. This figure represents nearly 20 percent of China's electrical-generation capacity.[57] In Africa, Ethiopia's massive Tekeze Dam, developed and built by the state-owned Chinese National Water Resources and Hydropower Engineering Corporation (Sinohydro), has begun operating, with additional projects going forward there, also designed and built by China.[58] In rural areas of Africa that lack electricity, small hydropower operations on local rivers are often used to replace diesel generators. Hydropower accounts for over 90 percent of electricity production in several African nations, including Ethiopia, Democratic Republic of Congo, Namibia, Sudan, Togo, and Zambia. Large increases in hydropower are expected elsewhere in the world, with major plants being finished in Brazil, China, India, Burma, and Ethiopia. Small-scale hydro applications are also expected to increase.[59]

"There is no question that our reliance on renewable energy sources is increasing," states former International Energy Agency director Nobuo Tanaka. He adds, "The revolution appears to be occurring from the bottom up, advocated by citizens rather than by governments and businesses. We are not asked to do more with less, but rather, to continue growth, fueling it with reasonable and sometimes more costly alternatives.[60] Let's hope we have the courage and vision to move forward."

NONFUEL MINERALS

Much of our attention to sustainability needs and natural resources has centered on the discovery and development of new and cleaner energy sources. In addition to these strategies for harvesting our natural capital, there are natural mineral resources about which we need to think strategically. **Rare earths** are 17 nonfuel mineral elements used in defense applications and in all areas of modern manufacturing. Chrome and manganese are indispensable for hardening steel, for example; platinum is a vital catalytic agent in the oil-refining process and is used in automotive catalytic converters; and vanadium is used in forming aerospace titanium alloys and in producing sulfuric acid. Rare earths are not actually rare, but most of them are widely dispersed and don't often occur in concentrations sufficient to make their mining commercially viable. China produces more than 80 percent of the rare earths output and has recently imposed increased export restrictions on these materials, increasing prices of some elements up to 300 percent.[61]

We need to think strategically about rare earths, focusing on their availability, use, and recycling. We also need to think strategically about how we use and develop the natural resources, both renewable and nonrenewable, that provide the energy that powers our world and makes our business efforts possible. They require our stewardship, including responsible planning and use.

rare earths
Seventeen elements used in defense and technology applications

Is the U.S. Exit from the Paris Climate Accord a Smart Move?

The Paris Accord is an agreement reached in December 2015 and signed by 195 countries to cut global greenhouse emissions in half. Scientific research had shown that continued increases in worldwide carbon emissions contribute to global warming and, left unchecked, could result in not merely a hotter planet but associated effects such as dramatic temperature fluctuations, disruption in historic rainfall patterns, rising sea levels, more powerful storms, droughts causing food shortages, and other extremes. The intention of the agreement was to collectively diminish emissions and increase utilization of alternative, noncarbon–emitting energy sources. Each nation was to establish goals for reducing carbon emissions to mitigate the extent of climate change. These outcomes were to be accomplished with assistance from larger, wealthier countries to smaller, less-developed ones.

Despite the beneficial intentions of the Accord, there is a disconnect between the goals and what is predicted to happen. According to *The New York Times*, scientists have estimated that the Accord will cut global greenhouse emissions by about half of what is actually needed to prevent catastrophic atmospheric temperature increases. While the Accord is set to limit global temperature rises to below 2 degrees Celsius, or 3.6 degrees Fahrenheit, some critics argue that the 2-degree goal is not enough to actually make a difference. Critics also note there was no specified penalty for nations that failed to meet their goals, causing some to question the likelihood of signatories' adherence to achieving set emission-reduction goals.

In addition, some critics from prosperous nations raised concern about the economic burden they would shoulder in order to assist poorer nations in achieving the desired emissions reductions. Over past decades, developed nations burned large quantities of fossil fuels as part of their efforts to develop economically and generate wealth. However, developing and emerging economies trying to follow a similar path to grow their economies are getting shamed for it, creating a problem of perceived inequality and unfairness among the member-nations of the Paris Accord agreement. As a result, the Accord called for more-developed nations to contribute $100 billion in annual aid to poorer nations by 2020, with that number expected to increase over time.

The United States, with less than 5 percent of the world's population, has produced nearly one-third of the excess carbon dioxide present in the Earth's atmosphere. This statistic led some proponents of the Paris Accord to suggest that full participation of the United States represented a moral imperative. Nevertheless, President Trump, who has characterized climate change as a hoax, suggested that participation in the Paris Accord could harm the U.S. economy and lead to a loss of jobs. Under the agreement, the United States pledged to reduce greenhouse gas emissions by 26 to 28 percent by 2025. Despite polls showing that a significant majority of Americans felt the United States should remain in the Paris Accord, President Trump announced in June 2017 that the country would exit the agreement. In pulling out, the United States joined Syria and Nicaragua as the only nations not participating in the Paris Accord. The departure of the United States from the agreement could encourage other nations to consider similar moves, threatening to reverse years of efforts to slow down or reduce the extent of climate change.

Ironically, the Trump administration recently acknowledged in a government report that it expects the Earth's temperature to increase by 7 degrees Fahrenheit by the end of the century. However, the administration believes the United States can do very little to mitigate this devastating rise in temperature, hence the decision to withdraw from the Paris Accord.

Critical Thinking Questions

1. How might the relationship between more-developed countries and less-developed countries be impacted by working toward a common goal but with vastly different requirements?
2. Would it have been worth the time to specify what is expected of each country and put in place ramifications if these goals are not accomplished or attempted?
3. How important are specific action steps to achieve a like-minded project?
4. Was it the correct decision by the United States to withdraw from the Paris Accord? Why or why not?

Sources: Juliet Eilperin, Brady Dennis, and Chris Mooney, "Trump Administration Sees a 7-Degree Rise in Global Temperatures by 2100," *The Washington Post*, September 28, 2018; Jonathan Ellis, "The Paris Climate Deal: What You Need to Know," *The New York Times*, June 01, 2017; Brian Resnick, "4 Things to Know About the Paris Climate Agreement," *Vox*, Jun 01, 2017; and "Paris Climate Agreement Q&A," *Center for Climate and Energy Solutions*, 2018.

JEREMY CAPDEVIELLE: Sustainability Work in Ecuador

Courtesy of Jeremy Capdevielle.

When I graduated in international business with an emphasis on entrepreneurship, I had no idea where my life would lead. The one thing I was certain of was that I would embark on a trip to explore foreign lands for six months or longer.

So I worked and saved for four months, enjoyed the beautiful beaches of Southern California, read and reflected to my heart's desire. After methodically pulling pieces together, I discovered a direction that offered potential, to work with and create organizations that are more conducive to people's happiness and personal well-being. South America sparked my interest, primarily because it seemed less explored, and I began to learn about its cultural and ecological landscapes. I booked a flight to Panama and soon after traveled to South America.

I sailed through the San Blas Islands from Panama to Cartagena, Colombia, where I lived with a family for two months in Cali. They introduced me to their warm and vibrant culture. I gained a further glimpse into the Cali lifestyle and the weekend life on the "fincas" (farms), learned to salsa (Cali is the "salsa capital of the world"), and independently taught English language courses. Cali is where I really experienced "culture shock." Some of it came from the different pace of culture and angles at which the world is viewed, but I think most of it came from my lack of Spanish-speaking skills. I'm grateful to those who worked with me to communicate and connect out of sheer interest for me as a person, but when groups gathered, alienated is the way I felt. My basic Spanish wasn't nearly enough to keep up, and the pace of conversation swept over me like a wave—leaving me with only tones, vibrations, and a feeling as to where the current of conversation was pulling.

When I left Cali, I headed south to the most ecologically diverse country in the world, Ecuador. What I expected to be a short trip through Ecuador en route to Peru evolved into a longer-term expedition and tremendous opportunity. Within days of arriving in Quito, I happened across the coordinator of a volunteer charity program and soon after, found myself volunteering, teaching English and assisting with community development projects in rural communities of Amazonian Ecuador.

The charity organization's approach strives to enhance education in order to help develop sustainable businesses and implement more efficient agricultural methods, all the while maintaining an awareness of the impacts each action has on the environment. Soon I moved into the role of coordinator of the Amazon Conservation and Community Development project. In the process, I've learned how important it can be to work ideas of progress and education around the ways of the community, rather than develop plans and attempt to mold the community to those.

Volunteering has offered me an incredible learning experience that I never would have had traveling from place to place without taking time to get involved at the local level. I constantly get new insights as I work with the local communities. I have learned that deadlines and appointments more often than not translate to best-case scenarios. And giving, especially within the community development sector, must be entered into with some caution, as it tends to lead to expectations.

My goal in writing this piece is to urge you to venture outside the road more commonly traveled. Yes, the pressure felt upon graduation can be frightening and overwhelming. Yet, this pressure alleviates as you develop a view of the world and its endless range of possibilities. It is not the only way, but openly exploring realms outside our own borders is one of the best ways to learn more about ourselves and the world in which we live. It can be a difficult and sometimes overwhelming task but try your best to be true to yourself. Challenge assumptions, observe the things that give you joy, and continually ask yourself—What do I love to do and how can I align this with a life that provides for what I need?

Source: Jeremy Capdevielle.

SUMMARY

LO 4-1
Describe environmental sustainability and its potential influence on business.

Sustainability is development that "meets the needs of the present without compromising the ability of future *generations* to meet their needs." This understanding calls on businesses to develop new approaches to the design, production, distribution, and consumption of goods and services; how we establish market prices for these goods and services; how we provide and consume energy; how we respect and regulate the environment; and how we ensure health and well-being for all. Sustainability requires changes to the way we manage everything: governmental institutions, markets, business organizations, and our own behavior.

LO 4-2
Describe frameworks for sustainability.

We examined two frameworks or ways to think about sustainability that are common at present in business, life cycle assessment and cradle-to-cradle design. Life cycle assessment is an evaluation of the environmental aspects of a product or service through its life cycle. Cradle-to-cradle design is a closed-loop design for products so that their components are recycled and reused.

LO 4-3
Summarize ways to measure sustainability achievements.

Tools for measuring the impact of efforts to build sustainable businesses have to provide a meaningful and comparable measure across different sectors that can serve as a common yardstick. The United Nations Global Compact maintains the largest database of corporate environmental sustainability reports, and the Global Reporting Initiative (GRI) is the most commonly used platform. The Carbon Disclosure Project and carbon and water footprinting are additional ways that are developing to measure sustainability.

LO 4-4
Identify the characteristics of an environmentally sustainable business.

Environmentally sustainable businesses have three characteristics in common. They recognize and accept that resources are limited; they develop ways to manage the interdependence of the systems in which they operate; and they recognize the need for equity in their supply chains.

LO 4-5
Describe how the stakeholder model can help businesses achieve sustainability.

Stakeholder theory forces a business to discuss its underlying values and principles with a broad array of stakeholders. The stakeholder model encourages managers to articulate clearly how they want to do business. What kind of relationships do they want and need to create with their stakeholders to achieve their purpose? This question leads to a public discussion about the responsibility of the business toward all its stakeholders.

LO 4-6
Describe how geographic features of a country or region contribute to natural capital.

Natural capital, the land, air, water, living organisms, and all formations of the Earth's biosphere, provides us with the ecosystem goods and services on which our survival depends. Geographic features like mountains separate people. They can divide nations into smaller regional markets that often have distinct cultures, languages, industries, and climates. Deserts and tropical forests also act as barriers to people, goods, and ideas. Bodies of water bring people together.

LO 4-7
Outline nonrenewable and renewable energy options available and their potential impacts on business.

Nonrenewable energy sources include petroleum, both from conventional sources and from nonconventional sources such as shale, oil sands, coal, and natural gas. Other nonrenewable sources are coal, nuclear power, and natural gas. Renewable energy sources include wind, biomass, solar (PV and CSP), geothermal, ocean, and hydropower. Each of these energy sources has a cost that impacts its use. As nonrenewable sources approach depletion, renewable sources will become more widely applied as their relative cost decreases. Businesses that explore renewable sources are establishing a competitive advantage in that they will be ahead of the inevitable transition.

KEY TERMS

biomass 113
Carbon Disclosure Project (CDP) 95
carbon footprint 95
climate 107
concentrating solar thermal power
   (CSP) 115
cradle-to-cradle (C2C) design
   model 93
environmental sustainability 91

geothermal power 115
Global Reporting Initiative (GRI) 95
heavy oil 110
inland waterway 106
life cycle assessment (LCA) 93
natural capital 101
natural resources 108
nonrenewable energy 109
rare earths 116

renewable energy 108
shale 110
solar photovoltaic power (PV) 114
stakeholder theory 100
topography 103
triple-bottom-line accounting
   (3BL) 100
United Nations Global Compact 95
water footprint 95

CRITICAL THINKING QUESTIONS

1. Comment on the assertion that the business of business is to generate profit and to pay attention to sustainability is to be taken off strategy by a passing fad.

2. Show through examples how the practice of sustainable business is both local and global.

3. Drawing on your own consumption patterns, describe the difference between cradle-to-grave and cradle-to-cradle design approaches.

4. Why is it challenging to measure how successful a business is practicing sustainability?

5. Explain how the stakeholder model applies to a specific sustainable business in your community or one you have learned about in the business press or a class discussion.

6. Of the 38 nations the United Nations identifies as the least developed in the world, 16 are landlocked. How might being landlocked slow a country's development? Remember that Switzerland is landlocked, yet it won the America's Cup sailing competition in 2005, as you think through this question.

7. Should we be investing in new technologies to access oil and other fossil fuels, or should all our efforts go toward facing the inevitable decline of fossil fuels? Explain your reasoning.

8. The safeguard and care of natural capital should be the responsibility of the government and not be left to private ownership. Agree or disagree with this assertion, explaining your position.

9. "Of course we'll have to transfer to renewable fuels sooner or later, but why should my company travel that route now? We don't need to be a first adopter or pay the first-mover price. There's plenty of oil left for us to stay the way we are for quite a while." Agree or disagree with this strategy, explaining your reasoning.

10. How does the stakeholder model help support the practice of sustainable business?

globalEDGE RESEARCH TASK   http://globalEDGE.msu.edu/

Use the globalEDGE website (http://globalEDGE.msu.edu/) to complete the following exercises:

1. You work for a company that is in the renewable energy industry and offers cost-efficient alternatives to nonrenewable energy sources such as oil and natural gas. Review the "Statistics" pages of the following European countries in the "Global Insights" section of globalEDGE in order to prepare an international expansion strategy to decide which of these countries your company should enter and in which order: Austria, Belgium, France, Germany, Italy, Norway, and the Netherlands. Get ready to discuss your findings with top management and answer questions such as which of the indicators on this page you used and what types of calculations you have made.

2. You will be visiting Japan on behalf of your company to make a presentation on your company's sustainability initiatives. You would like to be able to relate your initiatives to the audience, so you are researching some of the priorities for *sustainability in Japan*. Compile a list of the main priorities of Japanese companies from a Japan-specific sustainability resource you can find on globalEDGE.

MINICASE

THE BLUEGREEN ALLIANCE: A NEW WAY OF SUSTAINABILITY THINKING

BlueGreen Alliance consists of 13 of the largest unions and environmental organizations in the United States, in a partnership to build a cleaner and fairer economy.[62] This coalition of labor unions and environmental organizations demonstrates the way embracing sustainability helps us rethink our assumptions from the ground up.

Not traditionally collaborators, the United Steel Workers Union and the environmentalist group the Sierra Club launched an effort in 2006 to focus on environmental policy and expand the number and quality of jobs in the green economy. Both organizations saw that economic and environmental problems were linked, and that if they worked together, they could bring two very different visions to the solution process. The collaboration surprised many because environmentalists and unions had been opposed on many issues in the past, including oil drilling in the Alaska Arctic National Wildlife Refuge, the protection of specific species, and the opening of the Keystone XL pipeline, with unions often objecting to environmentalists' proposed solutions because unions thought they would cost jobs. Yet their collaboration found common ground and has been successful for several years, taking on many additional partners including the Communications Workers of America, the Natural Resources Defense Council, the Service Employees International Union, the National Wildlife Federation, and the Utility Workers Union of America.

The BlueGreen Alliance is currently working on a range of initiatives associated with three main issues: clean jobs, clean infrastructure, and fair trade. Its members lobby for legislative changes, educate themselves and other publics, and negotiate to include BlueGreen values in their contracts and other business relationships. For example, the Alliance's activities regarding jobs associated with climate change and the clean economy focus on educating businesses on reduced carbon emissions and the creation of green-collar jobs that come as a result of the move to clean energy. The BlueGreen Alliance conducts research in green job development and offers public education on its initiatives. The foundation also engages in various programs such as the Clean Economy Manufacturing Center, sponsorship of the Clean and Fair Economy Summit, providing databases for finding healthy, locally made, and energy efficient housing products, job development in transportation and energy sectors associated with movement toward cleaner and more efficient technologies, and the Chemical Hazard and Alternatives Toolbox (ChemHAT).

Critical Thinking Questions

1. Is the BlueGreen Alliance a partnership of convenience, or does it have the potential to build a new way of approaching sustainability, with limits, interdependence, and equity?

2. Unions may prefer protectionist measures to preserve jobs. Do you think this policy can fit a sustainable approach? Why or why not?

NOTES

1. Quote by Buckminster Fuller.

2. Phillip Sutton, "Sustainability, What Does It Mean?" *Green Innovations*, http://www.green-innovations.asn.au, accessed September 18, 2018.

3. G. H. Brundtland, United Nations World Commission on Environment and Development, Our Common Future: Report of the World Commission on Environment and Development, 1987, http://www.un-documents.net, accessed September 18, 2018.

4. Ronald Whitfield, and Jeanne McNett, *Sustainability: A Primer*, New York: Business Expert Press, 2014.

5. Andrew J. Hoffman, "The Next Phase of Business Sustainability," *Stanford Social Innovation Review*, Spring 2018, https://ssir.org, accessed September 18, 2018.

6. Paul Hawken, *The Ecology of Commerce*, New York: HarperCollins, 1994, 139.

7. Whitfield, and McNett, 10.

8. E. Plambeck, and L. Denend, *Wal-Mart's Sustainability Strategy* (Case No. OIT-71), Stanford, CA: Stanford Graduate School of Business, 2007.

9. Hoffman, "The Next Phase of Business Sustainability."

10. Anastasia Manuilova, 2003, Life Cycle Assessment of Industrial Packaging for Chemicals, Akzo Nobel.

11. The Coca-Cola Company, "Collaborating to Replenish the Water We Use," http://www.coca-colacompany.com, accessed September 18, 2018.

12. *Hinrich Foundation Sustainable Trade Index* 2018, http://hinrichfoundation.com, accessed September 18, 2018.

13 Whitfield and McNett point out this connection to Rob van Hattum's 2006 documentary film, "Waste = Food." See http://icarusfilms.com, accessed September 18, 2018.

14. This approach follows Whitfield and McNett's.

15. W. M. Adams, "The Future of Sustainability: Re-Thinking Environment and Development in the Twenty-First Century," Report of IUCN Renowned Thinkers Meeting, January 29-31, 2006, http://cmsdata.iucn.org, accessed September 18, 2018.

16. For example, see Andrew J. Hoffman, "The Next Phase of Business Sustainability," *Stanford Social Innovation Review*, Spring 2018, https://ssir.org.

17 Sarah Kent, "Pollution Worsens Around Shell Oil Spills in Nigeria," *The Wall Street Journal*, May 25, 2018, https://www.wsj.com, accessed September 18, 2018; and Ivana Sekularac, and Anthony Deutsch, "Dutch Court Says Shell Responsible for Nigeria Spills," *Reuters*, http://www.reuters.com, accessed September 18, 2018. Note that the court quashed other allegations.

18. David Smith, "WikiLeaks Cables: Shell's Grip on Nigerian State Revealed," *The Guardian,* http://www.guardian.co.uk, accessed September 18, 2018.

19. For example, see *Hinrich Foundation Sustainable Trade Index,* 2018, http://hinrichfoundation.com.

20. Hoffman, "The Next Phase of Business Sustainability."

21 For example, see *Hinrich Foundation Sustainable Trade Index,* 2018, http://hinrichfoundation.com.

22. R. Edward Freeman, *Strategic Management: A Stakeholder Approach,* Boston: Pitman, 1984.

23. R. Edward Freeman, Andrew C. Wicks, and Bidhan Pamar, "Stakeholder Theory and the Corporate Objective Revisited," *Organizational Science,* vol. 15, no. 3, May–June 2004, 364–69.

24. Quote by Thomas Merton.

25. Vivek Anand Voora, and Henry David Venema, "The Natural Capital Approach: A Concept Paper," International Institute for Sustainable Development, https://www.iisd.org, accessed September 18, 2018.

26. The World Bank, "Population Density (people per sq. km of land area)," https://data.worldbank.org, accessed September 18, 2018.

27. Duncan A Smith, "World Population Density," http://luminocity3d.org, accessed September 18, 2018.

28. Alasdair Rae, "Think Your Country Is Crowded? These Maps Reveal the Truth about Population Density across Europe," *The Conversation,* https://theconversation.com, accessed September 18, 2018.

29. Fiona Harvey, "Analysis: A Costly Thirst," Financial Times, April 4, 2008, 7. See https://nextbillion.net/news/making-the-case-for-fair-water-pricing, accessed September 18, 2018.

30. WaterAid is a nonprofit organization established in 1981 and based in London, United Kingdom. It works with local organizations in 37 African, Asian, Pacific, and Central American countries to help poor communities establish safe sanitation, clean water, and education on good hygiene. You can learn more about WaterAid and its activities at https://www.wateraid.org/us.

31. Rhoads Murphey, *The Scope of Geography,* London: Routledge, Kegan & Paul, 1982, 188–89.

32. Jared Diamond, *Guns, Germs, and Steel: The Fates of Human Societies,* New York: W. W. Norton, 1997.

33. Andrew M. Karmack, *The Tropics and Economic Development,* Washington, DC: World Bank, 1976, 5; Andrew Balls, the National Bureau of Economic Research, "Why Tropical Countries Are Underdeveloped," June 2001, http://www.nber.org/digest/jun01/jun01.pdf, accessed September 18, 2018; and Jeffrey D. Sachs, National Bureau of Economic Research, "Tropical Underdevelopment," February 2001, http://earth.columbia.edu/sitefiles/file/about/director/documents/nber8119.pdf, accessed September 18, 2018.

34. Association for the Study of Peak Oil and Gas, http://peak-oil.org, accessed September 18, 2018.

35. Ibid.

36. Energy Information Administration, "Annual Energy Outlook 2018," https://www.eia.gov, accessed September 18, 2018.

37. David Blackmon, "Horizontal Drilling: A Technological Marvel Ignored," Forbes, http://www.forbes.com, accessed September 18, 2018; PetroWiki, "Horizontal Wells," http://petrowiki.org, accessed September 18, 2018; and APPEA, "Horizontal Drilling Reduces Environmental Impacts, Increases Gas Production," https://www.appea.com, accessed September 18, 2018.

38. Osamu Tsukimori, "U.S. to Overtake Russia as Top Oil Producer by 2019 at Latest: IEA," Reuters Business News, https://www.reuters.com, accessed September 18, 2018.

39. "IAEA Releases Projections on Global Nuclear Power Capacity Through 2050," https://www.iaea.org, accessed September 18, 2018.

40. International Atomic Energy Agency, "Operational & Long-Term Shutdown Reactors," https://prisiaea.org, accessed September 18, 2018.

41. International Atomic Energy Agency, "Under Construction Reactors," https://pris.iaea.org, accessed September 18, 2018.

42. Nuclear Energy Institute, "Nuclear by the Numbers," https://www.nei.org, accessed September 18, 2018.

43. World Nuclear Association, "Nuclear Power in France," July 2018, http://www.world-nuclear.org, accessed September 18, 2018.

44. Energy Information Administration, "Annual Energy Outlook 2018," https://www.eia.gov, accessed September 18, 2018.

45. U.S. Energy Information Administration, "U.S. Coal Reserves," https://www.eia.gov, accessed September 18, 2018.

46. International Renewable Energy Agency, "Renewable Energy Targets," http://www.irena.org, accessed September 18, 2018.

47. Global Wind Energy Council, "Global Statistics," http://gwec.net, accessed September 18, 2018.

48. Gregory Meyer, "Against the Grain," *Financial Times,* U.S. edition, April 23, 2013, 5.

49. World Energy Council, *World Energy Resources* 2016, https://www.worldenergy.org, accessed September 18, 2018.

50. Mike Munsell, "Global Solar PV Installations to Surpass 104GW in 2018," *Green Tech Media,* https://www.greentechmedia.com, accessed September 18, 2018.

51. World Energy Council, *World Energy Resources, 2016.*

52. British Petroleum, "Geothermal Power," https://www.bp.com, accessed September 18, 2018.

53. Renewable Energy World, "Geothermal Energy," https://www.renewableenergyworld.com, accessed September 18, 2018; and Geothermal Energy Association, "Current Use," http://geo-energy.org, accessed September 18, 2018.

54. International Energy Agency, "Ocean Energy," https://www.iea.org, accessed September 18, 2018.

55. World Energy Council, *World Energy Resources: Marine Energy* 2016, https://www.worldenergy.org, accessed September 18, 2018.

56. Jamie Condliffe, "Scotland Waves Hello to the World's First Tidal Power Farm," *MIT Technology Review,* https://www.technologyreview.com, accessed September 18, 2018.

57. International Hydropower Association, "China," https://www.hydropower.org, accessed September 18, 2018.

58. "Hydropower Overload in China," http://www.loe.org, accessed September 18, 2018.

59. IEA Hydropower, http://www.ieahydro.org, accessed September 18, 2018.

60. IEA, http://iea.org/techno/etp/etp10/English.pdf, accessed February 12, 2014.

61. Arnold Tukker, "Rare Earth Elements Supply Restrictions: Market Failures, Not Scarcity, Hamper Their Current Use in High-Tech Applications," *Environmental Science & Technology,* 2014, vol. 48, no. 17, 9973–74; and U.S. Geologic Survey, "Rare Earths," https://minerals.usgs.gov, accessed September 18, 2018.

62. BlueGreen Alliance, https://www.bluegreenalliance.org, accessed September 18, 2018.

5 Political Forces That Affect Global Trade

In nearly every economic crisis, the root cause is political, not economic.

—Former prime minister
Lee Kuan Yew of Singapore[1]

©Luis Sandoval Mandujano/Getty Images.

LEARNING OBJECTIVES

After reading this module, you should be able to:

LO 5-1   **Describe** the goals of nationalizing and privatizing business.

LO 5-2   **Explain** government protection and stability and their importance to business.

LO 5-3   **Describe** the role of country risk assessment in international business.

LO 5-4   **Explain** the political motivations for government intervention in trade and the major types of government trade restrictions.

Linking Political and Economic Dimensions in International Trade: Venezuela's Ouster from Mercosur

Mercosur, or the Southern Common Market, is a South American political and economic bloc formed in 1991 by the Treaty of Asuncion. Mercosur's full members initially included Argentina, Brazil, Paraguay, and Uruguay, later adding Venezuela in 2012. The largest free trade and customs area in South America, members agreed to implement a common external tariff on certain imports from outside the bloc, eliminate customs duties for trade among the members, and adopt a common trade policy toward nonmember nations and blocs. Members had a vision of establishing a common market akin to the European Union, including agreements not only among the five member nations but also with associate member nations of Bolivia, Chile, Colombia, Ecuador, Guyana, Peru, and Suriname, along with other nations and international organizations. The bloc helped generate a number of benefits, including an increase in trade among its members from $4 billion in 1990 to more than $40 billion in 2000. By 2016, the five member nations had a combined gross domestic product of over $3 trillion.

In addition to promoting economic growth and stability, an aim of Mercosur was to help solidify democratic principles in the region, since each of the founding members had experienced dictatorships during the 1980s. The members created the Ushuaia Protocol on Democratic Commitment in 1998, which stated that "the full force of democratic institutions" was essential to integrating Mercosur members and that a member could be suspended if it evidenced a "rupture in democratic order."

In mid-2016, the presidents of Argentina, Brazil, and Paraguay met to discuss suspending Venezuela due to doubts about whether that country was meeting membership requirements. Declining oil prices had negatively impacted export revenues from the oil-rich nation, exacerbating Venezuela's economic mismanagement, food shortages, spiraling inflation, rapid currency devaluation, increasingly authoritarian government, and repression of human rights.

Although given a three-month period to correct the situation, Venezuela failed to meet Mercosur's rules regarding trade, politics, democracy, and human rights. On December 1, 2016, Venezuela was formally suspended from membership in Mercosur. The suspension was made indefinite in August 2017, with Brazil's foreign minister, Aloysio Nunes, stating, "We are saying: Stop with this! Enough with the deaths, enough with the repression. It is not possible to inflict such torture on the people."[2] Venezuela's suspension was to remain in place until the country achieved democratic order and stability. Matthew M. Taylor, an expert on South American political economy at American University, stated, "A reformist desire to deepen trade within the bloc, as well as genuine horror at Venezuela's descent into an economically dysfunctional dictatorship, have helped galvanize the four original members' willingness to slowly inch Venezuela out of the bloc."[3] In acting to suspend Venezuela's membership, Mercosur's member nations clearly linked access to economic benefits of international trade with corresponding behaviors on political and humanitarian levels.

Sources: Claire Felter, and Danielle Renwick, "Mercosur: South America's Fractious Trade Bloc," *Council on Foreign Relations*, September 10, 2018; "Venezuela Suspended from Mercosur Beginning December," *Yahoo*, November 22, 2016; Silvio Cascione, "Mercosur Suspends Venezuela, Urges Immediate Transition," *Reuters*, August 5, 2017; and "Protocolo de Ushuaia Sobre Compromiso Democrático en el Mercosur, La República de Bolivia y la República de Chile," *International Democracy Watch*, 2018.

The political climate of the country in which a business operates is as important as the country's topography, its natural resources, and its climate. Hospitable, stable governments can encourage business investment and growth, despite geographic or weather obstacles and a scarcity of natural resources. Switzerland is a landlocked nation with few natural resources, built at the base of massive mountains, yet it has remained politically neutral with a stable government and thus is prosperous.

The opposite is equally true, unfortunately. Some areas of the world that are relatively blessed with natural resources and manageable topography and weather have been little developed because of government instability. The Philippines and many African countries could realize great economic gains for their citizens once their governments are stable enough for the development of the institutions and infrastructure on which trade depends.

Occasionally, a country's government is hostile to investment in its territory by foreign companies, even though these companies might provide capital, technology, and training for development of the country's resources and people. The retention of local control of resources can be a powerful political argument, as we can see in India's control of foreign investment and Mexico's control of its oil resources. Both India and Mexico have recently loosened their controls somewhat.

Many of the political forces with which business must cope have ideological origins, including nationalism, protection of government-owned business, fear of terrorism, and unstable governments, among others. This influence runs in both directions: businesses can also greatly affect political forces. Some firms have budgets larger than the gross national income (GNI) of countries with which they negotiate. Although budgets and GNIs do not translate directly into power, companies with large budgets possess more assets and facilities with which to negotiate and often have implicit access to the political power of their home country. Because our goal here is to understand the political forces that can operate on and affect international business, however, we leave the interesting area of how business can influence politics for another study.

There is no question: international trade is heavily influenced by political forces. This module reviews the major ways in which those forces operate.

Governments and the Ownership of Business

LO 5-1
Describe the goals of nationalizing and privatizing business.

You might assume that governments own the factors of production only in countries with centralized economies and one-party communist or socialist orientations, such as North Korea, Cuba, Vietnam, and China, but nearly every country, regardless of political philosophy, has some government-owned businesses. From countries that follow more socialist philosophies, which advocate that major industries are owned and controlled by the government, to those that support the market-centered, privately owned business approach of free-trade capitalism, all have government involvement in business. In the United States, for example, the federal government owns a group of finance businesses, such as the Commodity Credit Corporation, the Export–Import Bank, and the Farm Credit Banks; infrastructure-related businesses, such as the St. Lawrence Seaway Development Corporation and the Tennessee Valley Authority; and service businesses, such as Federal Prison Industries, Gallaudet University, and the National Park Foundation.

NATIONALIZATION: WHY GOVERNMENTS GET INVOLVED

Governments decide to own businesses for many reasons. One fundamental motivation is the belief that governments can better ensure equal access to and control over basic services we consider public goods, such as education and health care than private owners could do. In addition, government ownership can protect against corruption, put social goals ahead of profit, and reliably provide vital services like national defense.

nationalization
The taking of private property by a government to make it public

When governments nationalize private firms, taking them from private to public ownership, some of the reasons are to extract more money from the firms, if the government suspects they are concealing profits; to increase profitability, if the government believes it can run the firms more efficiently and make more money; to follow an economic or political ideology; to save jobs by propping up dying industries; to control an earlier investment in a firm; and to enact political goals. Political goals were the motivation behind the Allies' nationalization of German-owned firms in Europe following World War II. During the financial crisis of 2008–2009, the U.S. government assumed a controlling interest in AIG and General Motors in order to steer them back toward health. These temporary actions were designed to meet the economic and political goals of saving jobs provided by the companies and supporting their recovery from the crisis.

Nationalization, sometimes called *expropriation*, occurs more frequently than most of us realize. Recent examples are not difficult to find and are spread remarkably widely across the liberal–conservative political spectrum. The Argentine government nationalized their country's railway network in 2015 to enhance transportation of goods and benefit areas outside the country's capital.[4] In 2012, the Bolivian government nationalized Transportadora de Electricidad (TDE), a Spanish company that owned 73 percent of the power lines in Bolivia, asserting that foreign owners were not investing sufficiently in Bolivia and were simply repatriating profits. The company's facilities were occupied by troops, while the Bolivian government assured the Spanish owners, Red Electrica, they would be compensated. Interestingly, the Spanish government has 20 percent ownership of Red Electrica.[5] In 2013, the Netherlands nationalized one of the largest financial institutions in the Netherlands, SNS Reaal, due to that company's troubled financial state and the significant threat it posed to the Dutch financial system's stability.[6] Venezuela, under the leadership of Hugo Chavez, nationalized most of its major industries and foreign-owned supermarkets, along with much of the agricultural production and processing industries.[7] In Iceland and Greece, responding to developments resulting from the global financial crisis of 2008–2009, governments nationalized banks to prevent their collapse.

During the Cuban revolution of the 1950s, the revolutionary Cuban government confiscated personal and business property without compensation. In Zimbabwe's land redistribution program led by President Mugabe, with a goal of changing the ethnic balance of land ownership in Zimbabwe, its later phase included forced confiscation of farms from white farmers for redistribution. In April 2014, the U.S. government seized a New York City skyscraper owned by an Iranian citizen as a part of continuing government sanctions against Iran. Proceeds from its sale are to be distributed to U.S. victims of attacks by Iranian-backed militants.[8]

PRIVATIZATION: WHY GOVERNMENTS SELL BUSINESSES

Governments sometimes *privatize* or sell their businesses, usually in order to see them run more efficiently, to reduce the government's size or the extent of its bureaucracy, or to raise money. Britain's prime minister Margaret Thatcher was a leader of Britain's most recent privatization movement. During her years in office (1979–1990), she decreased state-owned companies from a 10 percent share of Britain's GNP to 3.9 percent and sold more than 30 companies, raising some $65 billion. The UK government continues to privatize. It sold the Royal Mail in October 2013, in an IPO whose share price increased 50 percent over the initial offering.[9] Major owners are now its stockholders; it is a private company; and 22 percent of the stockholders are investment companies that invest government assets, known as sovereign wealth funds. You can buy shares of Royal Mail on the London Stock Exchange. The UK government also sold the military's helicopter search and rescue operation to a company in Houston, Texas.[10] The Government Pipeline and Storage System, which supplies UK military bases with aviation fuel, was sold in 2015 to Compania Logistica de Hidrocarburos of Spain.[11]

The motivation for UK privatizations, both under Thatcher and recently, was to raise money for the Treasury. Yet during the recent global financial crisis, the UK government took major stakes in Lloyds Bank and the Royal Bank of Scotland. The government planned to sell these companies back to the private sector once the financial crisis passed, with re-privatization of Lloyds bank completed in 2017 and re-privatization of the Royal Bank of Scotland initiated in 2018.[12]

Other countries have also been actively involved in privatization efforts. In Chile from 1975 to 1989, the government of dictator Augusto Pinochet overthrew Salvador Allende's socialist regime and sold its stakes in more than 160 Chilean corporations, 16 banks, and 3,600 agro-industrial plants, mines, and real estate operations. Germany and the Netherlands have sold their postal services to private investors. Greece engaged in many privatizations in the aftermath of the 2008–2009 financial crisis, including airports and telecom companies. In 2018, numerous nations were involved in plans for privatizing airports and other air transportation businesses and activities, including Bulgaria, France, Germany, Italy, Serbia, Spain, Saudi Arabia, India, Japan, Brazil, Chile, and Jamaica, among others.[13]

The United States concluded seven privatization deals totaling $53.1 billion between 2012 and the first half of 2013. Five of these transactions were offerings of AIG stock acquired during the 2008 rescue when the U.S. government raised money to save the

privatization
The selling of government-owned property to the private sector

company by acquiring its stock. China's privatization largely consists of share offerings in state-owned enterprises of which the government retains control.[14] Worldwide, we can expect privatization to continue, as governments make efforts to raise money, increase efficiency, and limit their involvements in businesses and business-like operations.

Recently, in arrangements similar to privatization, governments have contracted out to the private sector the provision of services they have provided in the past. For example, Thailand has at least one private company operating the passenger trains of its state-owned railroad. The U.S. federal government regularly contracts out military support functions such as cooking and laundry, even on the battlefront. Both U.S. federal and state-level prisons are run under contracts with privately owned firms. Some U.S. city and town public education boards have experimented with outsourcing the management of education to private firms, including for-profit companies.

Next, we look at government protection and stability, both important to the international manager because each affects the way the firm operates.

Government Stability and Protection

LO 5-2

Explain government protection and stability and their importance to business.

stability
Characteristic of a government that maintains itself in power and whose fiscal, monetary, and political policies are predictable and not subject to sudden, radical changes

instability
Characteristic of a government that cannot maintain itself in power or that makes sudden, unpredictable, or radical policy changes

Business prospers most when there is a stable government with policies that are permanent or that change only gradually. A government that has achieved stability has the ability to maintain itself in power and hold to predictable fiscal, monetary, and political policies that are not subject to sudden, radical changes. Instability, on the other hand, occurs when a government cannot maintain itself in power or makes sudden, unpredictable, or radical policy changes. When business thrives in stable environments, it does not suggest that business craves stasis; often businesses can profit from opportunities that accompany change. Besides, stasis is unlikely in our increasingly complex global environment. Yet the international manager wants to know the government will not make 180-degree policy shifts overnight. Political chaos and unpredicted change are not friends of most businesses.

How can a government protect its citizens when they are abroad? Governments maintain embassies in foreign capitals and consulates in larger cities to represent their interests and offer protection to their citizens who are abroad. For example, consular offices and embassies provide information about local political risks, they can help citizens contact family and friends for money transfers if needed, they monitor nationals imprisoned abroad, and in the case of abuse of citizens, they may file protests. In terms of actual protection, though, as the U.S. Department of State's International Travel website says, "Expectations of rescue by helicopters, the U.S. military, and U.S. government-provided transportation with armed escorts reflect a Hollywood script more than reality."[15]

STABILITY: ISSUES WITH LACK OF PEACE AND PREDICTABILITY

Business likes peace and predictability because they provide stability and safety for assets and people. Here we take a look at some of the challenges to peace and predictability businesses encounter. Unstable governments can present challenges to businesses that range from the inability to ensure peace to a pattern of unpredictable changes. In nations with warring clans, such as Somalia, the Congo, Afghanistan, and the Central African Republic, warring factions are a danger, and business managers actually might fear for the physical safety of their employees and business property.

In some countries, as they develop their business and trade institutions, the predictability of change may be an issue. China is a market with tremendous potential, and for many international companies, that potential is being realized. Greater China (which includes Hong Kong and Taiwan) accounts for around 20 percent of Apple's total sales, 65 percent of Qualcomm's, and 20 percent of Starbuck's.[16] Yet international firms have realized that the Chinese government, including state-owned media, can create difficult operating conditions for business through unpredictable government actions. Without predictability, the business cannot adjust. The resulting costs may be critical to the business. For example, laws may change with no warning, and regulatory agencies may find a company's products or actions of which they approved yesterday problematic today. These surprises to the companies may be because explicit government guidelines may be in the process of being developed, or may have wide latitude in their interpretation, or may be unexplainable.

Yum! Brands (which owns KFC) saw monthly sales drop 20 percent recently after the Shanghai Food and Drug Administration alleged the company used excessive amounts of antibiotics in its chicken and China's state television CCTV reported that the chickens were fed antiviral drugs and hormones to promote quicker growth.[17] The allegations were unsubstantiated by independent researchers, and the company agreed to cooperate with the government to fix any problems in its supply chains, which are fragmented with many small Chinese suppliers, some of which are government-owned businesses. That is, the chicken KFC gets from the local market is the same chicken found in the general market. The same observation holds for late summer 2014 charges made against a group of foreign fast-food companies, including McDonald's, KFC, Pizza Hut, and Papa John's, in a Chinese media undercover report of the use of meat after its expiration date.[18] Although Yum! has planned to vertically integrate and operate its own supplier businesses, land in China is difficult to acquire, as are operating licenses for foreign businesses.

In 2013, Apple made a public apology in China for poor customer service and unsatisfactory warranty on iPhones.[19] In 2018, Mercedes-Benz apologized to Chinese consumers for using an advertisement that quoted the Dalai Lama, the exiled Tibetan spiritual leader.[20] *The Wall Street Journal*'s "Heard on the Street" column observes that "given the state media's penchant for attacking big foreign brands and the government's desire to promote its own national champions, a strong Chinese growth story" works both ways for the international firm.[21] The U.S. State Department's 2013 Investment Climate Statement on China suggests that foreign companies in China face an uneven playing field and policies that protect state-owned and other domestic Chinese firms, and that foreign firms will "be subject to inconsistent regulations, growing labor costs, licensing and registration problems, shortages of qualified employees, insufficient intellectual property (IP) protections, and other forms of Chinese protectionism that have contributed to China's unpredictable and discriminatory business climate."[22]

CULTURE FACTS @internationalbiz

@China The saving of face in China is an important social process that may underlie public relations challenges that foreign businesses face there. Public actions understood to be disrespectful violate deep Chinese cultural values.
#socialprocess
#publicrelationschallenges
#disrespectfulactions #violation
#chineseculturalvalues

PROTECTION FROM UNFAIR COMPETITION

In addition to fostering a stable, predictable context for business, governments, whatever their ideology, have historically functioned to protect the economic activities of their citizens—including farming, mining, manufacturing, and the delivery of services—within their area of control. These activities require protection from unfair competition and also, more directly, from attacks and destruction or theft by robbers, revolutionaries, and terrorists, both foreign and domestic, in real time and space as well as online. Unfair international competition is minimized through national laws, negotiations between governments, and the efforts of institutions such as the World Trade Organization.

PROTECTION FROM TERRORISM, CYBERCRIME, AND OTHER THREATS

Four areas of increasing concern to governments as they try to protect the business activities of their citizens, and of concern to international managers because they are frequent targets of these activities, are terrorism, kidnapping, piracy, and cybercrime. We'll look at each and then address how businesspeople deal with them.

terrorism
Unlawful acts of violence
committed for a wide variety
of reasons

Terrorism Unlawful acts of violence committed to achieving a variety of objectives are known as **terrorism**. Terrorists may want to collect a ransom, overthrow a government, gain the release of imprisoned colleagues, exact revenge for real or imagined wrongs, and punish nonbelievers. Since at least the 1970s, their techniques have included airplane hijackings, suicide missions that may include vehicle attacks and the use of chemical and biological weapons, assassinations, kidnappings, and bombings. The U.S. State Department keeps a list of foreign terrorist organizations that includes Al Qaeda, the Irish Republican Army (IRA), Hamas, Hezbollah, Abu Nidal, other Islamic fundamentalist groups, the Basque Separatist Movement (ETA), and the Japanese Red Army. Terrorism introduces instability into a country, making it difficult for businesses to know what the political environment will be in the future, and some terrorist groups have developed a networked global presence. Terrorism may also present dangers to firm employees and their families.

A number of security organizations rank countries by their level of terrorism risk. Aon, for instance, posts an interactive map that ranks terrorism and political violence risk and reports incidents (https://www.riskmaps.aon.co.uk/mSite/terrorism_map). Figure 5.1 maps these risks for 2018. The risk analysis and mapping firm Verisk Maplecroft (https://www.maplecroft.com) releases a Terrorism Risk Index that currently rates 196 countries and territories for their relative level of risk.

Kidnapping Kidnapping for ransom is a weapon used by terrorists and other criminals that targets international managers as well as tourists. Although ransom payments are not

FIGURE 5.1 Terrorism and Political Violence Risk Map

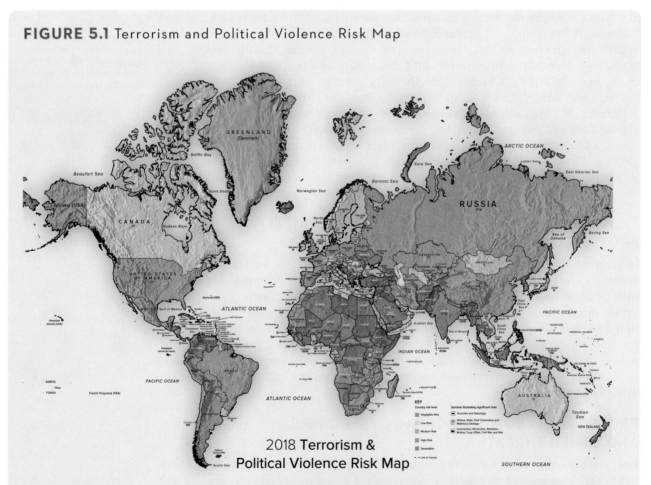

2018 Terrorism &
Political Violence Risk Map

Source: Aon, "2018 Terrorism & Political Risk Map," https://www.riskmaps.aon.co.uk/mSite/docs/trm_maps/Terrorism%20Risk%20Map%202018.pdf, accessed September 17, 2018.

publicized often, we know that many ransoms are paid and, as a result, kidnapees released. Yet there are no solid data on ransoms paid. An estimated 80 percent of kidnapping incidents do not get reported by governments and businesses, and in fact, they often deny having paid ransoms.[23]

Ransom requests are frequently for very large amounts and provide terrorists a source of operating funds. Worldwide, an estimated 16,000 or more ransom and kidnapping situations occur every year and kidnappers take home more than $1.5 billion.[24] Figure 5.2 shows the risk of kidnapping by nation. South America, North Africa, the Philippines, and the Middle East have the highest risks at present. While the level of reported kidnapping incidents has moderated a bit recently in nations such as Colombia and Mexico, continued economic crises and political volatility have facilitated high and increasing levels of risk in nations such as Venezuela, Yemen, Libya, and Afghanistan.[25]

Recent reporting suggests that Al Qaeda generated $120 million in 2015 through kidnap ransoms and that al-Qaeda in the Islamic Maghreb (AQIM) generated 90 percent of that organization's revenues from abductions in the African nations of Algeria, Mali, Mauritania, and Niger.[26] And those are just payments about which we know.

A new type of kidnapping, sometimes referred to as "express kidnapping," that seems relatively safer and quicker than the traditional approach, targets expatriates and other international business travelers. The victim is kidnapped, often near an airport or international hotel, and forced to withdraw money from cashpoints or ATMs before being released. This opportunistic crime requires much less planning and can be carried out in as little as 15 minutes, avoiding a drawn-out negotiation period. Its incidence is on

FIGURE 5.2 Global Kidnapping Risk Map 2017

**KIDNAPPING
SECURITY RATING**

- Severe
- High
- Moderate
- Low
- Minimal

Source: Red24, *Threat Forecast* 2017, p. 61, https://www.agcs.allianz.com, accessed September 17, 2018.

the rise in countries such as Ecuador, Mexico, Venezuela, Honduras, and Brazil. For example, between 2016 and 2017, there was a 44 percent increase in reported incidents in Rio de Janeiro, Brazil.[27] This type of kidnapping was largely a crime against locals, but the globalization of banking has provided kidnappers with accessible ATMs in many foreign capitals.

Kidnappers target businesspeople and hold them for ransom not because they are anti-business, but because they assume that businesses have deep pockets and will be willing to pay for the safe return of their employees. Despite their focus on business targets, kidnappers are increasingly targeting humanitarian and aid workers. The UN service that coordinates humanitarian affairs, IRIN, reports that kidnapping for ransom has grown to outnumber shootings of aid workers. The number of reported kidnappings of aid workers quadrupled each year between 2002 and 2014.[28] Unlike businesses, which tend to say nothing about their policies regarding the paying of a ransom, many humanitarian organizations, including Save the Children and Oxfam, make public their intention not to pay ransoms. Instead, they provide defensive training for their staff who are going to areas where hostage-taking is known to occur. The goal of this strategy is to reduce kidnappings of humanitarian aid workers.

Many governments claim not to pay ransoms as well. Everyone agrees that long-term, doing so is counterproductive because paying ransom rewards the kidnappers, reinforces their actions, and funds terrorism. Yet we know that victims of kidnapping for ransom do get released. Whether ransoms are paid, or third-party negotiators find other ways to meet the kidnappers' needs, is not public knowledge. What we do know is that payment of ransoms to terrorist organizations violates international law, and the debate over how to address kidnapping for ransom continues.

In 2017, the UN Security Council reaffirmed its commitment to reduce the payment of ransoms through the adoption of a resolution calling on governments to cooperate to reduce kidnapping incidents through exchange of information, coordinated financial tracing and seizing of ransom assets, and collaborated law enforcement to reduce the instability that leads to kidnapping.[29] This is a solid step forward, albeit on a long-term path, because the way to end kidnapping is to reduce the lawlessness that instability generates.

Piracy Piracy, which is a hijacking that includes kidnapping on the seas, has shown fluctuations in recent years but remains a significant source of concern. Table 5.1 shows the number of maritime piracy incidents that occurred during 2013–2017. While most of the incidents occurred in Africa and Asia, the number of incidents has spiked recently in Latin America and the Caribbean. In some regions, such as the ocean off Somalia and the Gulf of Aden in East Africa, and in the waters around Malaysia and Indonesia, there have been decreased incidents due to efforts including an increased number of international naval vessels patrolling the area; the defensive hardening of vessels with razor wire, electric fences, and high-pressure water hoses; the use of armed security teams; and police actions taken by governments in the region.[30] You can view active piracies on the International Chamber of Commerce Piracy Map at https://www.icc-ccs.org/piracy-reporting-centre/live-piracy-map. The Chamber's International Maritime Bureau maintains a 24-hour center that collects information from and provides information to ships, law enforcement agencies, and governments.[31]

cybercrime
Any illegal Internet-mediated activity that takes place in electronic networks

Piracy continues to be a major threat to governments and businesses around the world. ©Lawrence Manning/Corbis/Getty Images.

Cybercrime Cybercrime is any illegal Internet-mediated activity that takes place in electronic networks. Among the cybercrimes that most often target businesses are

TABLE 5.1 Maritime Piracy Incidents, 2013–2017

Number of Piracy Incidents	Africa	Asia	Latin America and the Caribbean	Rest of World	Total Incidents
2013	79	167	18	0	264
2014	55	183	5	2	245
2015	70	202	8	1	281
2016	122	101	27	1	251
2017	151	95	71	4	321

Sources: Oceans Beyond Piracy, *The State of Maritime Piracy 2017*, http://oceansbeyondpiracy.org/reports/sop, accessed September 17, 2018; and ICC International Maritime Bureau, *Piracy and Armed Robbery Against Ships*, http://www.allaboutshipping.co.uk, accessed September 17, 2018.

hacking, data espionage, and domain- or name-related offenses. International property theft may also use computer networks. Business-targeted cybercrime can cause harm to an entire organization with a few keystrokes; the goal tends to be economic gain, and any harm to individuals is incidental. Because cybercrime is borderless, no one government or legal system can control it; international cooperation is necessary, including harmonizing laws, improving investigation techniques and collaboration, and coordinating enforcement.

The 2017 U.S. State of Cybercrime survey, conducted by CSO, the U.S. Secret Service, and Carnegie Mellon University, reports that many organizational leaders have little idea what they are up against in fighting cybercrime and lack a clear understanding of how to develop strategies to protect their organizations.[32] In addition, many business leaders increase their organization's potential vulnerability to cybercrime by not monitoring both their IT supply chain and their traditional supply chain, and by expanding the boundaries of their organizations with technological innovations such as mobile devices and cloud storage without considering the impact such actions have on their cybersecurity.

Cybercrime exacts massive costs on businesses. The potential scale and scope of cyberattacks threaten to increase substantially, as shown by the recent Petya and NotPetya ransomware events that hijacked organizational computer systems in 2016 and 2017, respectively. The latter event infected computer systems in at least 65 countries.[33] The cybercrime threat is exacerbated by the increasing capabilities of cybercriminals, sometimes with the assistance of government-linked agencies and their hacking tools, and the vulnerabilities created by new technologies such as the Internet of things (IoT). The global cost of cybercrime is estimated at up to $600 billion per year, with the average cost of dealing with a single attack at $2.4 million.[34] Businesses in defense, financial services, and energy and utilities were frequent targets of cybercriminals. Denial-of-service attacks, which interrupt and suspend the services of an Internet host, and data theft were by far the most common forms of attack. Data breaches affect both business and consumer segments within and across nations. In 2018, the Aadhaar data breach was believed to have compromised personal information of 1.1 billion Indian citizens, while the Exactis data breach that same year breached the records of about 340 million individuals and businesses in the United States.[35] Verizon prepares a well-respected annual report on data breaches, identifying more than 53,000 incidents and 2,200 data breaches in 2017 alone.[36]

The cybercrime environment is a fluid one, populated by quick learners, so defenses have to be continuously upgraded and updated. It's not enough to build a firewall; the process is constant. The layers of defense include the host, the actual physical layer (buildings, servers), the human, the application, the data, and then the network. Each of these layers must be monitored all along the supply chain all the time. For instance, a security effort might include auditing, reviewing usage traffic, and testing for vulnerabilities at each of the layers, plus updating.

To reduce cybercrime, legal systems around the world have made the cost of being apprehended and convicted increasingly high. Within the organization, both technical and behavioral strategies contribute to reducing cybercrime. Technical defenses are increasingly sophisticated and include firewalls and other security measures, antivirus programs, monitoring, and testing, often provided by an external vendor. Behavioral countermeasures against cybercrime require an organizational culture in which all members know the vulnerable areas and how their own security behavior, including the use of password-protected sites and the frequent changing of passwords, can contribute to cyber safety. Mobile technology is currently the most vulnerable area for many organizations, and its users are the least aware of how their behavior, such as texting confidential or password-protected material, can contribute to the company's vulnerability to attack.

Country Risk Assessment and Countermeasures to Threats

LO 5-3
Describe the role of country risk assessment in international business.

The first step in managing risk, including political risk, is learning about the environment. Get to know local market players, including government officials, who may have access to useful information before it becomes public. The manager embedded in the local environment will have an informal information network that may be valuable in providing information about anticipated political risk.

country risk assessment (CRA) An assessment of a country's economic situation and politics to determine how much risk to employees, property, and investment exists for the firm doing business there

Country risk assessment (CRA) is an assessment of a country's economic situation and politics to determine how much risk to employees, property, and investment exists for the firm doing business there. Companies have done their own evaluations of these risks for many years, yet recently, because of the increasing complexity of the political environment, they are using specialized consulting and research firms to assess risk.

Country risks are often political, including wars, revolutions, and coups. The company's home country may be a factor: Does the host country bear a friendly attitude toward it or not? Do political issues arise that may lead to sanctions by the home country government? The risk American energy companies with operations in Russia face, given U.S. sanctions on Russia for its recent annexation of Ukraine's Crimea, is an example. Russia's countersanctions on food imports present political risk to American farmers, as well. Less dramatic but nevertheless important for businesses are elections of new governments that may be hostile to private business, and particularly to foreign-owned business. Economic and financial country risks can take the form of persistent balance-of-payments deficits, high inflation rates, and loans that are unpaid or in arrears. Labor conditions can also cause investors to pause. Labor productivity may be low, or labor unions may be militant. Laws may be changed that govern taxes, currency convertibility, tariffs, quotas, labor permits, and other areas that affect business. The chances for a fair trial in local courts also must be assessed. And there is the risk of terrorism. Can the company protect its people and property?

The types of information a firm will need to judge country risks vary according to the nature of its business and the length of time required for the investment, loan, or other involvement to yield a satisfactory return. The financing of exports usually offers the shortest period of risk exposure. One approach here is to have a variety of export contracts across a spectrum of countries or a list of backup buyers. In contrast to exports, when the overseas operation includes product assembly, mixing, manufacture,

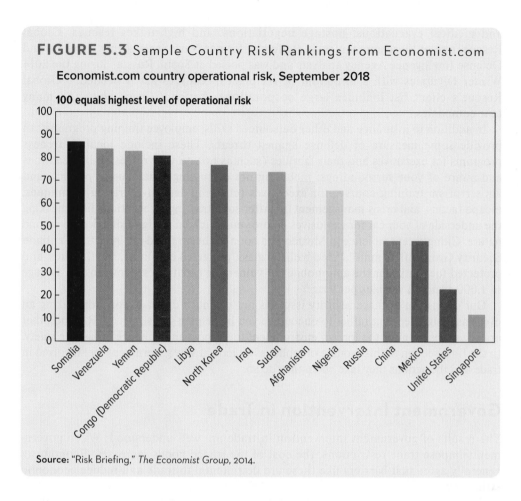

FIGURE 5.3 Sample Country Risk Rankings from Economist.com

Economist.com country operational risk, September 2018

100 equals highest level of operational risk

Source: "Risk Briefing," *The Economist Group*, 2014.

or extraction in the host country, long-term commitments are necessary, and these often bring problems that increase over the time of the investment and cannot be resolved. For example, extraction operations often result in conflicts with indigenous local populations whose lives are changed by the activities of the business. Most such investment opportunities require 5, 10, or more years to pay off. The longer the time horizon, the less reliable the risk analysis can be. On the selling side, Figure 5.3 shows sample data from a country risk ranking done by the Economist Intelligence Unit, which provides close to real-time data that can be drilled for additional information.

Businesses obtain information, then, from their internal sources, governments, and CRA firms to inform the decisions they make about foreign involvements. The next issue is how the firms and individual employees who face overseas threats protect themselves. The threats that target individuals are insurable, and many firms do insure against them. This insurance, called KRE (kidnap, ransom, and extortion), generates well over $500 million in premiums each year and covers the ransom, the fees of specialist negotiators, the salary of the hostage, and counseling for the victim and family. Insurers keep specialists around the globe, with language ability and many other skills, ready for active response. (See https://www.worldaware.com as an example.)

Real-time country-by-country risk analyses are available, as well, so that managers can have a realistic view of the possible dangers in their environment. Some businesses specialize in coping with crises once they occur, providing increased security and medical evacuations, hostage negotiations, and high-stakes rescues. Global Rescue, one of these companies, is staffed by former Navy Seals, Army Rangers, and Defense Intelligence Agency analysts and was poised at Sochi, Russia, during the 2014 Winter Olympics with a minimum of six planes, ready to act if needed.[37] Global Rescue's client list includes large corporations, *National Geographic,* and many tour companies.

In addition to insurance and other outsourced skills, employee training programs can provide some measure of defense against threats. These include local awareness programs for executives and their families (such as how to vary routes and be cautious and aware of your surroundings, including not discussing schedules in public), and antiterrorism training courses for executives (covering defensive driving techniques, escape tactics, and crisis management).[38] After such training, precautions like checking the underside of your car for explosives before you switch on the ignition become second nature. Citing recent violence in Mexico as a boon to the armored-car industry, Centigon Security Group offers multilayered ballistic glass, protected car floors, run-flat tires, and protected fuel tanks for the automobiles of vulnerable expatriates, providing an average of 1,000 armored vehicles per year.[39]

Our discussion of these security issues is not meant to dissuade you from taking an overseas assignment but rather to encourage you by helping you see that CRA and other organizations monitor the foreign environment to support and enhance expatriate safety. In the final section of this module on politics, we look at why governments get involved in trade and the actions they take when they do so.

Government Intervention in Trade

LO 5-4

Explain the political motivations for government intervention in trade and the major types of government trade restrictions.

The results of government intervention in trade are well understood. When governments impose trade restrictions, the cost of the traded goods increases. Economists generally agree that barriers like these are detrimental to trade and reduce economic efficiency.

Agricultural trade restrictions, for instance, exist in most countries as a result of political willingness to protect domestic farmers, especially small farmers. You might think agricultural protectionism matters only to developing economies, but that's not the case. As of 2018, agricultural tariffs averaged 62 percent worldwide, compared to 4 percent for manufactured goods.[40] U.S. agricultural tariffs are about 12 percent, while the EU's average 30 percent and Japan's 50 percent. Canada carved out an exception in the NAFTA negotiations, which generally eased trade, in order to impose a 241 percent tariff on milk exports above a stated quota, 270 percent on blended dairy powder, and up to a 314 percent tariff on certain other dairy products from the United States, much to the disappointment of Pennsylvania's and Vermont's dairy farmers and a point of contention during NAFTA renegotiation efforts in 2018.[41]

Although there is strong theoretical support for free trade's benefits, the World Trade Organization (WTO) is having difficulty successfully completing trade negotiations due to politically motivated agricultural tariff barriers. This situation is likely to continue in coming years, given the impacts of inflationary pressure, climate-related supply problems, and resource limitations on agriculture. You can check the latest summaries of WTO trade discussions at https://www.wto.org/english/news_e/news_e.htm. Every government has a trade office and an ambassador-level trade representative who makes an annual report to the government on trade issues the country faces. You can read the U.S. Trade Representative's annual report to Congress at https://ustr.gov.

 CULTURE FACTS @internationalbiz

@SilkRoad Cultures influence one another's long trade patterns. The musician Yo-Yo Ma has organized an effort to trade the diffusion of musical influence along the Silk Road, which connected the ancient empires of China and Rome. (See http:// www .silkroadproject.org.) #cultureinfluences #yoyoma #musicalinfluence #silkroad #china #rome

REASONS FOR RESTRICTING TRADE

Why do governments restrict trade? The main reasons are to promote the national defense, to impose sanctions on other countries, to protect domestic infant industries, to create or preserve domestic jobs, to ensure fair competition, and to retaliate for the trade restrictions or unfair practices of other governments. In some countries with a national trade or industrial policy, such as Japan, government intervention in trade can also reflect a government trade strategy. In many countries, trade has become a political issue for small groups of activists who seek to protect domestic business from foreign competition.

Provide for National Defense The national defense argument for trade restrictions suggests that certain industries need protection from imports because these industries are vital to security and must be kept operating, even though they are not competitive with foreign suppliers. Economists suggest that most of these arguments are weak and use a call to patriotism to gain emotional advantage. Direct government subsidies would be a better way to protect such industries and also would clearly indicate to taxpayers the cost of maintaining these companies in the name of national security. As one example, most U.S. ocean shipping companies receive government subsidies, without which they could not remain in business, given the competition they face from foreign firms with lower operating costs. But through these subsidies, the U.S. government has created a merchant marine ready in case of hostile actions by other countries.

Similar national defense arguments have been offered in support of bans on the export of advanced technologies. The reasoning goes that such bans prevent valuable technologies from being used to strengthen competitors, especially militarily. However, these bans reduce export revenues for the country's manufacturers by closing off potential foreign markets. They can also impede efforts to sustain international market share and fund continued innovation, which enables competitors from other nations to improve their competitiveness. In 2018, the Trump administration invoked national security as a basis for imposing tariffs on selected products such as steel, aluminum, automobiles, and auto parts.[42]

Impose Sanctions Some trade restrictions are imposed to inflict economic damage on other nations, as a way of punishing them or otherwise encouraging them to modify their behavior. A common approach is to pass legislation that prohibits trade with the offending nation or with specific citizens of that nation. U.S. trade policy in 2018 included active sanctions with a range of nations, including Cuba, Iran, North Korea, Somalia, Sudan, Libya, Venezuela, Russia, and Syria. In addition, the United States imposes partial sanctions against other nations or even specific people, such as former administration members of deposed Liberian leader Charles Taylor, who was convicted of war crimes.

Sanctions seldom achieve their goal of forcing change in the targeted country; they also tend to produce collateral economic damage in the nations applying them, in addition to the harm caused in the sanctioned nation.[43] Economic sanctions during the 1990s alone may have cost the United States some $15 to $23 billon annually in exports, in addition to losses resulting from restrictions on foreign direct investment, capital flows, tourism, and other sources of income or output.[44] These estimates do not include the many missed opportunities that accompany sanctions, as well. Punishment sanctions, much like those justified with the national defense argument, give the sanctioned markets to the acting country's international competitors. Some skeptics of punishment sanctions also ask how isolating nations helps influence their behavior.

Protect an Infant or Dying Industry Advocates for the protection of an infant industry claim that in the long run it will have a comparative advantage, but in the meantime these firms need protection from imports until they obtain the required investment capital, train the labor force, master production techniques, and achieve economies of scale. Without this protection, advocates argue, a firm will not be able to survive because lower-cost imports from more mature foreign competitors will underprice it in its local market.

Efforts to protect emerging industries are not limited to developing nations, of course. Until 2012, the United States levied a protective 54-cents-a-gallon import duty on foreign-produced ethanol, including imports from low-cost producer Brazil, in order to give "our infant industries a greater chance to grow." Although the United States has become the largest producer of ethanol in the world, protection of this industry has continued. The cost of direct and indirect subsidies to U.S. ethanol producers, including import tariffs, antidumping restrictions, and tax credits, is estimated at $3 to $10 billion annually.[45]

A related argument justifies the protection of a dying industry, one threatened by an onslaught of imports that endanger the survival of domestic companies and the jobs they provide. Under this argument, industries need time to make the necessary adjustments to move labor and capital out of the industry and into other sectors. Protecting the industry from imports can facilitate a smoother transition. This logic has been used to justify protection for textiles and footwear in the United States and Europe. Other aid, such as subsidies for relocating and assisting displaced workers, may also be part of the proposed solution.

Protect Domestic Jobs   Protectionists who use the "cheap foreign labor" argument usually compare low foreign wage rates to those paid in their home country. They conclude that foreign exporters can flood the home country's market with low-priced goods and eliminate jobs of home-country workers. Yet the cost-of-labor argument is a complex one.

The first problem with this argument is that wages don't account for all production costs, or even for all labor costs, so a comparison based on relative hourly wages alone would be misleading. Nor does the argument take into account relative productivity rates of workers in different countries. But because the argument is used so often and has such strong emotional appeal, let us look at wage differentials in auto plants in the United States and Mexico.

The average hourly labor cost for auto workers in Mexico has been estimated at $3.29, while the average in the United States is $23.83. These are both union-negotiated rates. Labor accounts for approximately 10 percent of an auto's cost. Meanwhile, the productivity rate, as measured by the international Organisation for Economic Co-operation and Development (OECD) in GDP per hour worked, is $20.50 in Mexico and $69.60 in the United States.[46] Productivity per worker is often much greater in more developed countries because of superior management, advanced technology that contributes to higher efficiency, and more capital per worker, which results in better equipment and work conditions. As the U.S.–Mexico comparison suggests, the labor-cost component of the goods being produced is not a function only of wage rates. The labor-cost component can be lower in one country, even though wages there are higher.

Ensure Fair Competition   Supporters of fair competition want an import duty that will bring the cost of imported goods up to the cost of domestically produced goods. This will eliminate any "unfair" advantage a foreign competitor might have because of superior technology, lower raw material costs, lower taxes, lower labor costs, or a combination of these factors. The intent is not to ban imports but only to equalize the import process to ensure "fair" competition. The level of such duties is likely to be set to protect the least efficient domestic producer, however, while more efficient domestic producers earn increased profits. Meanwhile, efficient foreign producers are penalized and their comparative advantage is eliminated. The impact on consumers might also be viewed as unfair because the import duty increases the price they pay.

Retaliate   Representatives of an industry whose exports have had import restrictions placed on them by another country may ask their government to retaliate with similar restrictions. An example of the way retaliation begins and can escalate is the ban by the

European Union on imports of hormone-treated beef from the United States. Because it considers the use of hormones in animal production a health hazard, the European Union closed its market to U.S. beef in 1988, shutting off 12 percent of total U.S. meat exports. U.S. beef producers complained that no scientific evidence supported the EU claim, and the United States promptly retaliated against the European Union by putting import duties on about $100 million worth of EU products, including boneless beef and pork, fruit juices, wine coolers, tomatoes, French cheese, and instant coffee.

The European Union then threatened to ban U.S. shipments of honey, canned soybeans, walnuts, and dried fruit worth $140 million. In response, the United States announced it would ban all European meat. If that had happened, about $500 million in U.S.–EU trade would have been affected.

In 2009, the two sides agreed that the United States would lift sanctions gradually, corresponding with a phased increase in the allowed importation into the European Union of hormone-free U.S. beef. In 2011, a year ahead of schedule, the United States ended retaliatory sanctions on EU goods. These threats and counterthreats, actions and counteractions continued until 2012 when a compromise was reached, with neither side winning.[47] The EU parliament voted to allow untaxed imports of hormone-free U.S. and Canadian beef in the spring of 2012, although the amount of beef allowed to be imported was limited by a quota.[48] The Europeans have continued to insist on a ban of hormone-treated beef.[49] During all these years, consumers did not have access to the sanctioned imports. By 2018, the Trump administration tried to link access to the EU market for U.S.-produced beef to trade negotiations for other products, including aluminum, steel, and autos.[50]

Two additional causes for retaliation in trade are dumping and subsidies. We can define **dumping** in three ways: it consists of selling a product abroad for less than the cost of production, less than the price in the home market, or less than the price to third-party countries. A manufacturer may dump products to sell excess production without disrupting prices in its domestic market, as a response to cyclical or seasonal factors (during an economic downturn or at the end of a fashion season, for example), or as a way to increase market share. A manufacturer may also lower its export price to force the importing nation's domestic producers out of business, expecting to raise prices once that objective has been accomplished. This is called *predatory dumping*.

The United States became the first country to prohibit the dumping of foreign goods into its own market in 1916. There is no U.S. law prohibiting U.S. firms from dumping their goods abroad, however. The area of dumping, its regulation, prosecution, and prevention, is now within the domain of the WTO, yet most governments retaliate when they perceive dumping to be harming local industry. For example, in 2018, the United States imposed punitive tariffs of 30 percent and more on Chinese solar panels and modules in retaliation for China's dumping of under-market-priced panels. China holds 60 percent of the solar panel market and is alleged to have forced several U.S. manufacturers out of the business with its under-market pricing.[51] In the European Union, anti-dumping tariffs against Chinese bicycle manufacturers have been in place since 1993 and, in 2018, European bike manufacturers requested a five-year extension of the 48.5 percent tariff in order to avoid damage to their industry.[52]

Social dumping occurs when producers have lower wage rates, lower social costs such as unemployment taxes and environmental regulations to support the general welfare, poor worker benefits, and poor working conditions, all of which undermine social support systems. And e*nvironmental dumping* occurs when an exporter can sell at lower costs due to the country's lax environmental standards.

Another cause of retaliation is **subsidies** a government makes to a domestic firm, either to encourage exports or to help protect the firm from imports. Subsidies can take the form of cash payments to the firm, government participation in ownership, low-cost loans to exporters and foreign buyers to encourage purchase, and preferential tax treatment. For example, as shown in Figure 5.4, OECD nations provide billions of dollars

dumping
Selling a product abroad for less than the cost of production, less than the price in the home market, or less than the price to third-party countries

subsidies
Financial contributions, provided directly or indirectly by a government, that confer a benefit, including grants, preferential tax treatment, and government assumption of normal business expenses

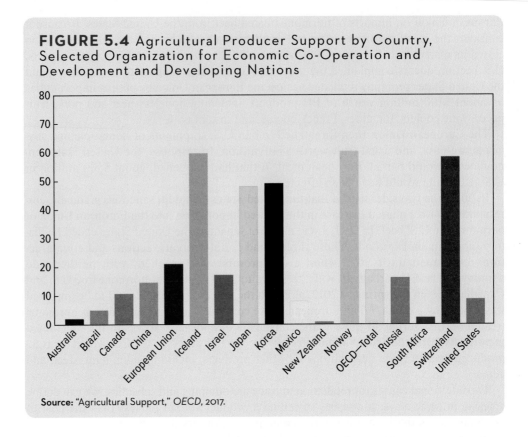

FIGURE 5.4 Agricultural Producer Support by Country, Selected Organization for Economic Co-Operation and Development and Developing Nations

Source: "Agricultural Support," *OECD*, 2017.

per year to their farmers in subsidy supports, estimated at a total of $228 billion in 2016.[53] Perhaps the greatest damage caused by this assistance in developed economies is its effect on the millions of farmers in the poorest nations. Most of the agricultural subsidies in developed countries go to a small percentage of recipients, usually large enterprises. The subsidies enable them to undersell unsubsidized, small farmers in developing economies on the world commodities markets. These agricultural subsidies are the current focus of the WTO, and talks about them have been making very slow progress. The Global Debate box provides a more detailed example of subsidies for sugar producers in the United States.

Competitors in importing nations frequently ask their governments to impose **countervailing duties** to offset the effects of a subsidy. In the United States, for example, when the U.S. International Trade Commission receives a petition from a U.S. firm claiming imports from a particular country are subsidized, it first determines whether a subsidy was actually given. If so, the Trade Commission imposes countervailing duties equal to the subsidy's amount. You can read the letters of complaint at https://www.usitc.gov/petitions_and_complaints.

We have established that governments have reasons to restrict trade, even if these restrictions do not add to the overall economic good. Now we look at the actual tariff and nontariff barriers governments use to impede trade.

TARIFF BARRIERS

Tariffs, or import duties, are taxes levied on imported goods primarily to raise their selling price to reduce competition for domestic producers. A few smaller nations also use them to raise revenue on both imports and exports. For example, exports of commodities such as coffee and copper are sometimes taxed in developing nations. However, the imposition of tariffs can result in harmful retaliation.

countervailing duties
Additional import taxes levied on imports that have benefited from export subsidies

tariffs
Taxes on imported goods for the purpose of raising their price to reduce competition for local producers or stimulate local production

SUGAR SUBSIDIES: Sweet for Producers but Sour for Food Manufacturers and Consumers?

The debate over sugar subsidies for farmers continues today.
©Rodrigo Torres/Glowimages.

The United States, Japan, and the European Union strongly protect their domestic sugar industries, though they all lack comparative advantage in sugar production. A World Bank report called sugar the "most policy-distorted of all commodities." Before the WTO forced changes in 2005, the EU's domestic sugar prices were triple world market prices.

U.S. sugar tariffs were first put in place in 1789. Currently, sugar imports are limited by quotas distributed among 40 nations, representing about 15 percent of the U.S. market. The U.S. Department of Agriculture also provides loans that guarantee domestic sugar farmers a minimum price, regardless of the market. The farmer repays the loan in either sugar or revenues from sugar sold at the market price. This policy encourages domestic overproduction, yet the U.S. price has recently averaged more than double the world price.

Protecting a small number of U.S. sugar growers in 18 states, who provide 146,000 U.S. jobs, costs U.S. consumers and businesses an estimated $4 billion annually. Free trade in sugar would eliminate fewer than 2,500 workers, meaning the cost of each protected job is more than $1.5 million a year. High sugar prices also create problems for sugar-using industries, such as soft drinks, candy, and confections. High domestic sugar prices cut into manufacturers' margins, prompting some to leave for Canada and Mexico, eliminating tens of thousands of jobs in the United States and increasing U.S. imports of sugar-containing products. The Life Saver candy brand moved its plant from Michigan to Montreal so it could acquire sugar on the world market, which as a U.S. company it could not import. High sugar prices have also encouraged manufacturers to increase use of high fructose corn syrup, a cheaper ingredient but one linked to increasing levels of obesity and diabetes.

Sugar accounts for less than 1 percent of U.S. agricultural sales, but an estimated 17 percent of all agricultural political contributions since 1990, totaling over $50 million in the past decade. "It's a very effective lobby," commented Claude Barfield of the American Enterprise Institute. "They've traditionally given a lot of money to both parties."

Change may yet occur. Congress continues to attempt reform, but the 2014 Farm Bill extended the protection of sugar until 2018. In 2017, the Trump administration reinstated duties and quotas against Mexico, which previously accounted for about half of all U.S. sugar imports. The Coalition for Sugar Reform, representing hundreds of food companies, responded to this action by stating, "U.S. sugar policy should empower America's food and beverage companies to create more jobs, not put hundreds of thousands of good-paying U.S. jobs at risk just to benefit one small interest group."[54] Indeed, two Iowa State University economists, John Beghin and Amani Elobeid, developed a model of a free sugar market which would result in a $2.9 to $3.5 billion annual increase in U.S. consumers' welfare, create 17,000 to 20,000 new jobs in food manufacturing and related areas, and dramatically reduce importation of sugar-containing products.

Free trade in sugar and trade in alignment with WTO principles sounds like a good idea whose time may be approaching. Encouraging lawmakers to act, the Coalition for Sugar Reform stated, "It's time for Congress to shoulder the responsibility of fixing this broken program." After all, 1789 was a long time ago.

Critical Thinking Questions

1. Should sugar continue to be a protected commodity? Why or why not?

2. Should the U.S. consumer continue to fund protection for U.S. sugar farmers? Why or why not?

Sources: "FY 2018 WTO Tariff-Rate Quota Allocations for Raw Cane Sugar, Refined and Specialty Sugar and Sugar-Containing Products," *United States Trade Representative*, 2018; James Bovard, "Why Americans Pay Triple the World Price for Sugar," *Foundation for Economic Education*, March 09, 2017; Caitlin Dewey, "Why Americans Pay More For Sugar," *The Washington Post*, June 8, 2017; Julie Wernau, and William Mauldin, "Wilbur Ross Sets Deadline in U.S.-Mexico Sugar Dispute," *The Wall Street Journal*, May 2, 2017; John C. Beghin, and Amani E. Elobeid, "The Impact of the U.S. Sugar Program Redux," *Food and Agricultural Policy Research Institute*, May 2013, 1–33; and Laura Collins, "The 2014 Farm Bill Subsidy Reforms Don't Go Far Enough," *American Action Forum*, February 7, 2014.

Trade as a Political Weapon: Sanctions for Russia's Annexation of Crimea

Crimea, Ukraine, and Russia.

The international response to Russia's occupation of Crimea in the spring of 2014 illustrates the use of trade sanctions that are politically motivated and serve as an alternative to a military response. The question these sanctions raise is, "Who pays their costs and bears their impacts?"

In spring of 2014, right after the Winter Olympics concluded in Sochi, Russia, Vladimir Putin, Russia's president, declared that Crimea, a peninsula jutting into the Black Sea and part of Ukraine with a large population of Russian speakers (in the 77 percent range), was now a part of Russia. This annexation occurred without negotiation. Russia declared it had redrawn an international border of an area that has been recognized as a part of Ukraine for 23 years since the collapse of the Soviet Union.

The declaration was celebrated by many people of Russian heritage in Crimea, but not all citizens of the area, some of whom hold Russian nationality, and certainly not all Ukrainians, welcome Russia's occupation of Crimea and the threat of occupation of additional parts of Ukraine. For those celebrating the annexation, Putin's act was heroic, a restoration of part of Russia's historic empire. For Ukraine, the United States, and the European Union, it was both an outrage and a surprise, and they refused to recognize Putin's actions, which challenge developing values in Europe that oppose territorial change by force.

The West's response was to try to stop any further Russian actions by invoking trade sanctions against Russia, targeting specific individuals close to President Putin, some of whom were in government, some of whom allegedly helped him manage his personal wealth, and some of whom were Ukrainian collaborators—and companies associated with these people. The United States imposed travel bans on specific individuals, froze assets of specific individuals and companies, and banned high-technology trade with Russia. These sanctions were somewhat stronger than those of the European Union, largely because Europe is more dependent on oil and gas from Russia than is the United States. Canada joined Western efforts to warn Russia that continued action in Eastern Ukraine will be costly for the Russian economy in general and for individual, targeted Russians in Putin's inner circle in particular.

As a political signaling tool, sanctions were the West's attempt to send the message that territorial grabs are unacceptable. The sanctions reduced trade between Russia and the West, affecting businesses in both, especially in the defense and energy-related sectors. Foreign direct investment (FDI) into Russia declined. Some Western businesses whose trade was affected by the sanctions felt the impact, along with their stockholders. Russian citizens paid as well because prices of imported goods that were still available increased. They also paid as their economy continued to decline. And the individuals targeted by the sanctions? Their assets were frozen, wherever the EU, U.S., and Canadian governments could reach them. The Russian economy experienced negative growth rates in 2015 and 2016, at least in part due to a global decline in oil prices. Russian credit ratings dropped to junk-bond status and FDI fled the country.

Yet, despite continued waves of sanctions against Russia, its economy and people seemed to adapt to this new reality. The economy began growing again in 2017, expanding over 1.5 percent in that year and continuing its recovery into 2018. "I would say that the actual effect of the sanctions on the GDP has been negligible; a high estimate is at half a percent and it's probably closer to zero,"[55] stated Andrey Movchan of the Carnegie Foundation. "Effectively, the sanctions have been one of the major reasons for the increase of support to the central government and the Kremlin in Russia."[56] Denis Volkov of the Russian polling firm Levada Center stated, "The main thing is this feeling, after the Crimea annexation, that Russia once again became a great power and can lead any foreign policy it likes, regardless of criticism or Western sanctions."[57] Putin's approval ratings, which were as low as 60 percent prior to the annexation, soared to over 90 percent. According to Movchan, rather than engaging in punitive sanctions, the West should emphasize "the advantages of the proper behavior of the country—giving them carrots rather than sticks."

> "Sanctions seem to lend themselves well to international governance. They seem more substantial than mere diplomatic protests, yet they are politically less problematic, and less costly, than military incursions."
>
> —Joy Gordon, author and professor, Fairfield University[58]

A classic example of the harm tariffs can cause is the Smoot-Hawley Tariff Act in the United States. In the late 1920s, declining economic fortunes led U.S. farmers and producers to lobby Congress for tariff protection. The resulting legislation increased tariffs for more than 20,000 items across a range of industries. The act passed on October 28, 1929, the day the stock market crashed, and President Herbert Hoover signed it over the objections of 34 foreign governments. A trade war followed that engaged most of the world's economies. World trade plummeted from $5.7 billion in 1929 to $1.9 billion in 1932, unemployment skyrocketed, and the world entered a decade-long economic depression to which Smoot-Hawley contributed.

There are three types of tariffs or import duties: ad valorem, specific, and compound. An **ad valorem duty** is stated as a percentage of the invoice value of the product. For example, the U.S. tariff schedule subjects flavoring extracts and fruit flavors not containing alcohol to a 6 percent ad valorem duty. Therefore, when a shipment of flavoring extract invoiced at $10,000 arrives in the United States, the importer is required to pay $600 ($0.06 \times $10,000$) to U.S. Customs before taking possession of the goods. A **specific duty** is a fixed sum of money charged for a specified physical unit of the product. A company importing dynamite in cartridges or sticks suitable for blasting pays $0.37 per pound, regardless of the shipment's invoice value. When flavoring extracts and fruit flavors contain more than 50 percent alcohol by weight, they are subject to a specific duty of $0.12 per pound plus a 3 percent ad valorem tax. Thus, on a $10,000 shipment weighing 5,000 pounds, the importer will pay a **compound duty** of $900 [($0.12 \times 5,000$ pounds) + ($0.03 \times $10,000$) = $600 + $300].

In an inflationary period, a specific duty soon loses its importance unless it is raised frequently, whereas the amount collected from an ad valorem duty increases as the invoice price rises. Sometimes, however, an exporter may charge prices so much lower than domestic prices that the ad valorem duty fails to close the gap. Some governments set *official prices* or use *variable levies* to correct this deficiency. An official price guarantees that a certain minimum import duty will be paid regardless of the actual invoice price. It also thwarts a fairly common arrangement that many importers in high-duty nations have with their foreign suppliers, whereby the seller issues a false low invoice price to reduce the amount of duty to be paid. The importer sends the seller the difference between the false invoice price and the true price separately.

ad valorem duty
An import duty levied as a percentage of the invoice value of imported goods

specific duty
A fixed sum levied on a physical unit of an imported good

compound duty
A combination of specific and ad valorem duties

> "[WHEN] . . . JAPANESE CASSETTE RECORDERS STARTED to INUNDATE THE FRENCH MARKET, . . . [THEY] RULED THAT ALL IMPORTED VCRS HAD to CLEAR CUSTOMS at A . . . CUSTOMS POST . . . [UP in THE MOUNTAINS], A LONG WAY from ANY BORDER [OR PORT]. . . . THE JAPANESE GOT THE POINT AND AGREED to LIMIT THEIR EXPORTS to FRANCE."
>
> —R. C. Longworth, reporter, Chicago Tribune, July 6, 1985[59]

variable levy
An import duty set at the difference between world market prices and local government-supported prices

nontariff barriers (NTBs)
All forms of discrimination against imports other than import duties

quotas
Numerical limits placed on specific classes of imports

A **variable levy** guarantees that the market price of the import will be the same as that of domestically produced goods; the European Union has used this levy for imported grains. Calculated daily, the duty level is set at the difference between world market prices and the support price for domestic producers.

Tariffs often are set to encourage local input. For example, the finished product ready for sale to the consumer may have a 70 percent import duty. However, if it is imported in bulk so that it must be packaged in the importing nation, the duty level may be only 30 percent to encourage some local production. These situations protect domestic jobs and can provoke foreign manufacturers of low-technology products, such as toiletries, to get behind a high-tariff wall with very modest investments.

Tariffs assessed at very low rates are sometimes referred to as *nuisance tariffs* because importers are still required to go through the frequently lengthy process of paying them, even though their low levels may no longer serve the original intention, such as protecting domestic producers.

NONTARIFF BARRIERS

Nontariff barriers (NTBs) are all forms of discrimination against imports other than the import duties we have been examining. As a result of WTO agreements, nations have reduced import duties, and nontariff barriers have thus gained greater importance and wider use. For example, government-required testing and certification have increased exponentially since the mid-1990s. NTBs can take many forms, including the quantitative and nonquantitative ones discussed next. They impose additional costs on producers and exporters, and thus on customers, and they discourage trade.

Quantitative Barriers   One type of quantitative nontariff barrier is the **quota**, which sets numerical limits for specific kinds of goods that a country will permit to be imported during a specified period. If the quota is *absolute*, once the specified amount has been imported, further importation for the rest of the period (usually a year) is prohibited. Quotas are generally *global*; that is, the total amount is fixed without regard to source. They may also be *allocated*, in which case the government of the importing nation assigns quantities to specific countries. The United States allocates quotas for specific tonnages of sugar to 40 nations, for example. In 2018, the quota ranged from a low of 7,258 metric tons of raw cane sugar allocated to each of 10 exporting nations, to a high of 185,335 metric tons for the Dominican Republic.[60] Some goods are subject to *tariff-rate quotas*, which permit a stipulated amount to enter duty-free or at a low rate, but when that amount is reached, a much higher duty is charged for additional quantities.

Some producers have used transshipping to evade allocated quotas. In such cases, the finished goods are first shipped to a country with either an unfilled or no quota, where the goods are labeled as products of that country, and then shipped to the quota-imposing nation. In other cases, goods are subjected to a small level of modification in the intermediate nation before the then-finished goods are re-exported to the quota-imposing nation. For example, in 2018, the United States suggested that millions of tons of Chinese steel were being re-routed through various Southeast Asian nations, including Vietnam, Thailand, and Malaysia, in order to avoid trade restrictions on imports of Chinese steel.[61] The EU's anti-fraud office initiated similar investigations of Chinese transshipping beginning in late 2016.[62]

Voluntary Export Restraints   For many years, nations have agreed not to impose quotas unilaterally on goods, except for agricultural products. Therefore, governments have negotiated **voluntary export restraints (VERs)**, or export quotas, with other countries. These are a different kind of quantitative trade barrier, offered by the exporting country rather than imposed by the importing one. The Japanese government established a VER to restrict the number of automobiles its manufacturers could export to the United

voluntary export restraints (VERs)
Export quotas imposed by the exporting nation

States annually, and the Canadian government agreed to a VER to limit the amount of Canadian lumber exported to the United States. Orderly marketing arrangements are VERs consisting of formal agreements between the governments of exporting and importing countries that stipulate the import or export quotas each nation will have for a good in order to restrict international competition and preserve some of the national market for local producers.

orderly marketing arrangements
Formal agreements between exporting and importing countries

Nonquantitative Nontariff Barriers Many international trade specialists claim that the most significant nontariff barriers today are the nonquantitative type. An example is the U.S. requirement that foods sold to the U.S. Department of Agriculture for use in school lunches be produced in the United States. The major producers of tuna fish are all foreign-owned—Chicken of the Sea by a Thai company, Bumble Bee by a UK company, and StarKist by a South Korean company. StarKist's products qualify for use in the school lunch program, however, because the company's operations are in a U.S. territory, American Samoa.[63] So StarKist provides jobs in Samoa and is an accidental beneficiary of this nonquantitative nontariff barrier to trade.

NTBs can be classified into three major groupings: direct government participation in trade, customs and other administrative procedures, and standards.

1. *Direct government participation in trade.* The most common form of direct government participation in trade is the subsidy. Besides protecting industries through subsidies, as we have seen earlier, nearly all governments subsidize agriculture. Government procurement policies are also trade barriers if they favor domestic producers and restrict purchases of imported goods by government agencies.

   Policies may also require that products purchased by government agencies have a stipulated minimum *local content.* Since the WTO Government Procurement Agreement went into effect, most nations have opened their government business to foreign bidders to comply with its requirements. However, the U.S. government still has policies in place that may substantially interfere with international trade. For example, the Buy American Act and buy-American provisions of other legislation contain measures that either prohibit public-sector organizations from purchasing from foreign suppliers or hinder such purchases through mechanisms such as requirements for local content or the provision of advantageous pricing terms for U.S. suppliers. The Department of Defense, the U.S. government's largest public procurement agency, excludes foreign suppliers from many contracts.

2. *Customs and other administrative procedures.* Customs (a general term for duties paid on imports) and administrative barriers cover a large variety of government policies and procedures that either discriminate against imports or favor exports. For example, in some nations, a product being imported may be subject to different rates of duty depending on the port of entry, and an arbitrary determination of the customs value. Because of this variability, customs charges often depend on negotiations between customs officials and managers, which may not only increase uncertainty into the process but also create an opportunity for corruption.

   Governments have also found ways to discriminate against the exportation of services. When serving international markets, airlines face a number of situations in which the national airline receives preferential treatment, such as in the provision of airport services, the allocation of airport counter locations, and the allowed number of landing slots. Other examples of discrimination are the Canadian government's tax deductions for local businesses that advertise on Canadian TV unless they use U.S. stations considered to be in the same market and Australia's requirement that television commercials shown there be shot in Australia.

3. *Standards.* Governmental and private standards to protect the health and safety of a nation's citizens are both certainly desirable, but exporting firms are plagued by many standards that are complex and discriminatory. For example, the European Parliament passed biotech food labeling requirements that impose mandatory traceability of genetically modified organisms (GMOs) and stringent labeling of foods that contain GMO ingredients. The requirements include labels stating, "This product is produced from GMO organisms" and place strict limits on mixing GMO and non-GMO ingredients in food exported to the European Union. The United States is one of the world's leading producers and exporters of GMO crops.

Since 2014, the OECD has offered a Services Trade Restrictiveness Index (STRI), with the ability to compare nations on their relative level of restrictiveness across a range of service sectors, such as accounting, legal, broadcasting, air transport, insurance, construction, and more. Current ratings on the STRI can be found at the OECD's interactive website, http://www.compareyourcountry.org/service-trade-restrictions. Overall, the number of technical barriers to trade has increased significantly in the past decade, as shown in Figure 5.5.

Trade restraints cost consumers everywhere tens of billions of dollars per year, while they benefit a small number of companies in the protected sectors of the economy. An increase of $1 in tariff revenues can result in an estimated decline of $2.16 in world exports and $0.73 in world income.[64] The Tax Foundation estimated that tariff increases enacted and proposed by the Trump administration in 2018 would yield $175 billion in tariff revenues but would decrease long-run GDP by 0.6 percent, cause GDP to decline by $151 billion, reduce wages by 0.4 percent, and eliminate approximately 470,000 full-time jobs.[65] A study of 25 product groups in protected industries showed that the average increased product cost paid by consumers due to protectionism was $516,208 for each job saved.[66] As OECD trade director Ken Ash says, with protectionism, ". . . nobody benefits. Everybody loses."[67] Protectionism hurts individual countries and consumers as well as the global economy.

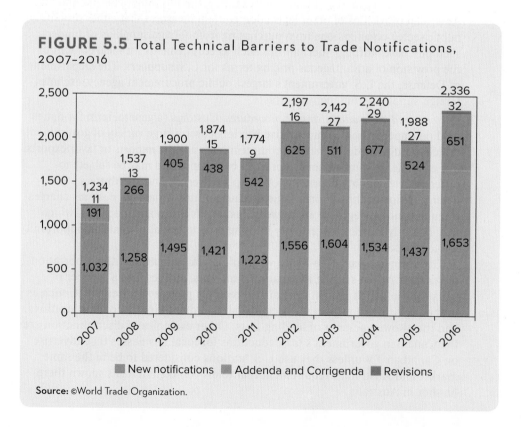

FIGURE 5.5 Total Technical Barriers to Trade Notifications, 2007–2016

Source: ©World Trade Organization.

FERNANDO VILLANUEVA: "There Is So Much Beauty in the World!"

Courtesy of Fernando Villanueva.

Fernando Villanueva, a recent graduate majoring in international business, financed most of his college education and has advice for others wanting to join him in international business.

When I was 16, I participated in The Experiment in International Living Program (School for International Training and World Learning, Vermont) and spent time in France. I lived with a French family and took language courses with people from all over the world. Ever since then, I knew international business was the right place for me.

A year after graduating, I worked in the Czech Republic, thanks to an AIESEC* traineeship with the Univerzita Pardubice. My responsibilities included research for business-related articles; coordinating and conducting presentations for professors in the European Union; coordinating student events; and editing and reviewing articles being considered for publication. I even was credited as a translator and editor of two published books. I also was able to travel all over Europe and to Turkey and Egypt. I met many interesting and amazing people, and I have continued to maintain good connections with many of them via e-mail and Skype.

Two of my biggest challenges while working abroad were the different ways of conducting business and the bureaucracy. One recommendation I can offer that I have learned from personal experience is to not assume business will be conducted in the same manner in each country. Telling people that they are doing a task wrong just because they are doing that task in a different way than it is done back home normally is not received well. Also, people do not like to hear what you believe is wrong about their country and what makes yours better. If you focus most of your energy on pointing out what is wrong, or what you hate, about the country you are visiting, you will lose the opportunity to see what is great about it. There is so much beauty in the world; allowing yourself to have the opportunity to see a small part of it is truly amazing.

Source: Fernando Villanueva.

*AIESEC is a student-run international nonprofit organization that provides leadership training and internship opportunities, https://www.aiesec.org.

SUMMARY

LO 5-1
Describe the goals of nationalizing and privatizing business.

Governments nationalize or take firms or organizations out of private and into government hands to extract more money from the firms; to increase profitability; to pursue an ideology; to preserve jobs; to save jobs by putting dying industries on life-support systems; to control a previous investment; or to enact political goals. Governments also sometimes privatize, meaning they sell government assets to private parties or contract with private firms to perform functions usually performed by governments. The primary motivations are to raise cash for the government and reduce its size.

LO 5-2
Explain government protection and stability and their importance to business.

Government stability is the government's ability to maintain itself in power and prevent sudden or radical changes in its fiscal, monetary, and political policies. Businesses flourish in environments where change is predictable and the government is stable. When conditions are unpredictable, business is challenged because it cannot make good decisions about which risks to take. Stability also creates an environment in which terrorism, kidnapping, piracy, and cybercrime are less likely.

LO 5-3
Describe the role of country risk assessment in international business.

Country risk assessment (CRA) is an evaluation that assesses a country's economic situation, policies, and politics to determine how much risk exists of losing an investment. Country risks are increasingly political in nature. Among them are wars, revolutions, and coups. Less dramatic, but nevertheless important for businesses, are government changes caused by the election of a new government that may be hostile to private business and particularly to foreign-owned business. Risks may also be economic or financial.

LO 5-4
Explain the political motivations for government intervention in trade and the major types of government trade restrictions.

The main reasons governments give for involvement in trade are national defense, sanctions, protection of domestic jobs or infant industries, fair competition, and retaliation for dumping or subsidies. They may impose import duties (tariff barriers); nontariff barriers, such as quotas, voluntary export restraints, and orderly marketing arrangements; and nonquantitative nontariff barriers, such as direct government participation in trade, complex customs procedures, and other administrative procedures and standards for health, safety, and product quality.

KEY TERMS

ad valorem duty 143
compound duty 143
countervailing duties 140
country risk assessment (CRA) 134
cybercrime 132
dumping 139
instability 128

nationalization 126
nontariff barriers (NTBs) 144
orderly marketing
    arrangements 145
privatization 127
quotas 144
specific duty 143

stability 128
subsidies 139
tariffs 140
terrorism 130
variable levy 144
voluntary export
    restraints (VERs) 144

CRITICAL THINKING QUESTIONS

1. Why might a government-owned firm have an unfair advantage over privately owned companies?

2. Why do countries that are committed to open markets and capitalism have publicly owned enterprises?

3. When they accept foreign assignments, how can expatriates prepare for risks associated with such an assignment?

4. If you were responsible for developing your company's international strategy, what role would country risk assessment play?

5. Why do U.S. consumers tolerate paying, at times, as much as twice the world sugar price for their sugar supply? How might an economist evaluate the U.S. sugar policy?

6. Why could transporting cheese as you drive across the border from the United States into Canada be risky behavior?

7. It seems that free, unrestricted international trade, in which each nation produces and exports products for which it has a comparative advantage, will enable everyone to have a higher level of living. Why, then, does every country have import restrictions?

8. A protectionist argument for the defense industries suggests that since we need them, we must protect them from import competition by placing restrictions on competitive imports. Is there an alternative to trade restrictions that might make more economic sense to consider in this case?

9. Governments assert that their safety standards for food imports are important to ensure that their citizens not be harmed by unsafe foods. Comment on how such a concern may be a nontariff barrier.

10. Almost all governments are on guard against dumping. Why would a government be opposed to its citizens or businesses being able to obtain products at lower costs?

11. A union leader in the auto industry argued, "Workers are paid $20 an hour in the United States but only $4 in Taiwan. Of course we can't compete. We need to protect our jobs from cheap foreign labor." What are some possible problems with this statement?

12. There are two general classifications of a nation's import duties: tariff and nontariff barriers. Which would be more difficult for a business in consumer products to factor into its export pricing?

globalEDGE **RESEARCH TASK**   http://globalEDGE.msu.edu/

Use the globalEDGE website (http://globaledge.msu .edu/) to complete the following exercises:

1. As the global supply chain manager of your company, you are interested in finding a new manufacturing location in South America and you would like to make a country risk assessment for the following countries: Argentina, Brazil, and Chile. Visit the "Risk" page of each country in the "Global Insights" section of globalEDGE and review the country risk rating, business climate rating, as well as the strengths and weaknesses of the countries. Get prepared to present your selection for your company's new manufacturing site to the top management and explain your reasoning with your findings.

2. The level of economic and political freedom of consumers in countries affects the business decisions of international companies. Visit the "Market Potential Index (MPI)" on globalEDGE and review rankings of countries for "Economic Freedom". How are big and developing economies of the world, such as China, India, Russia, and Mexico, rated? Check the bottom of the page to see what indicators are used to measure the economic freedom. Visit the websites of the data sources used for these indicators to prepare a brief summary of these resources and what they do.

MINICASE

CHOCOLATE: IS YOUR TREAT THE RESULT OF UNFAIR LABOR AND THE EXPLOITATION OF CHILD LABOR?

When you last indulged in a bar of rich chocolate, a cup of hot cocoa, a piece of chocolate cake, or a scoop of chocolate ice cream, did you know that you may have been consuming a product made in part by child slaves? The Côte d'Ivoire (Ivory Coast) produces about 60 percent of the world's cocoa, nearly twice as much cocoa as the second-largest producer, Ghana.

According to a 2016 study commissioned by Mondelez, a global confectionery, food, and beverage company, more than 500,000 children work in hazardous conditions in the cocoa-producing regions of Côte d'Ivoire. Although estimates vary, thousands of these child laborers are victims of human trafficking, with many working in conditions described as slavery-like and children reporting they were not free to leave their place of employment. Many had been brought into the cocoa-growing areas from distant regions including poverty-stricken countries such as Burkina Faso, Mali, and Togo, often after being kidnapped. Some were sold by their parents in expectation that the child's earnings would be sent home.

Although paid less than 60 percent of the rate of adult workers, children frequently worked for more than 12 hours per day, 6 days a week, and were regularly beaten. More than half applied pesticides to crops without the benefit of protective gear. Only 34 percent of the children working on cocoa farms went to school, which was about half the level for children who were not working on cocoa farms. The rate of school enrollment was even lower for girls. These child laborers

seemed to be trapped in a vicious cycle: forced into work due to kidnapping or economic circumstances faced by themselves and/or their families, they earned subsistence wages, and because most had not been to school and had minimal skills, their prospects for seeking other employment were limited.

Chocolate is one of the most heavily traded agricultural products in the world. The top 10 chocolate-consuming nations are the United States and countries in Western Europe. In usual practice, beans from different nations are mixed together during their export from West Africa and transported to processing plants in the importing nations. So essentially all the chocolate treats regularly enjoyed by hundreds of millions of consumers are likely to include cocoa from the Côte d'Ivoire. Efforts to raise awareness of the circumstances behind the production of chocolate, including exploitation of child labor in the production of cocoa, face great challenges. Meanwhile, the farms have become increasingly secretive and no longer allow visitors.

Some important cocoa-producing nations have worked with the International Labor Organization and the International Programme on the Elimination of Child Labour to establish national programs to eliminate child labor in their countries. However, evidence suggests that child labor continues to be a widespread problem in Côte d'Ivoire and Ghana. Industry representatives have complained that progress toward eliminating child labor in cocoa production has been hindered by traditional culture in the agriculturally based

Child labor of cocoa in Côte d'Ivoire. ©Tyler Hicks/Getty Images.

producing nations, compounded by civil war and other complications. Agreed deadlines for eradicating the most pernicious forms of child labor have been repeatedly pushed back.

In the absence of prompt and effective action by the chocolate and cocoa industry, a number of companies have begun producing Fair Trade–certified chocolate. By observing a strict set of guidelines associated with Fair Trade certification, these companies can guarantee that their chocolate products are ethically sourced. Farmers in developing countries are paid subsidies, ensuring that those certified as engaging in fair-trade practices will receive a price for their produce that will at least cover their costs of production. By providing a price floor, fair-trade practices protect third-world farmers from global fluctuations in commodity prices that result from trade practices. At the same time, Fair Trade certification requires that farmers engage in appropriate social, labor, and environmental practices, such as paying livable wages and not using child or slave labor. In addition to the cocoa program, Fair Trade certification programs have been implemented for a range of other products, such as coffee, tea, and crafts.

Already, more than 60 companies make Fair Trade chocolate products in the United States, including ClifBar, Cloud Nine, Newman's Own Organics, Scharffen Berger, and Sweet Earth Chocolates, but cocoa sold with the Fair Trade label accounts for less than 1 percent of the market.

Critical Thinking Questions

1. Should labor practices in another country be a relevant consideration in international trade? Why or why not?

2. With regard to trade in products such as cocoa, what options are available to governments, businesses, and consumers for dealing with practices such as child labor or slave labor in other countries? What are the implications associated with each of these options?

3. How would international trade theorists view the Fair Trade movement?

Sources: "The Chocolate Industry," *International Cocoa Organization*, February 08, 2018; Aarti Kapoor, "Children At the Heart: Assessment of Child Labour and Child Slavery in Cote d'Ivoire's Cocoa Sector and Recommendations to Mondelez International," *Mondelez International*, 2018; Portia Crowe, "Understanding the Roots of Ghana's Child Labor," *Inter Press Service*, July 18, 2012; Jennifer Doody, "The Dark Side of Chocolate," *Harvard Gazette*, March 22, 2013; "Cocoa: The Global Market," *LMC International*, October 2018; Brian O'Keefe, "Behind a Bittersweet Industry," *Fortune*, March 1, 2016; and Lidz-Ama Appiah, "Slave-Free Chocolate: A Not-So-Guilty Pleasure," *CNN*, June 07, 2017.

NOTES

1. Lee Kuan Yew, Former Prime Minister of Singapore.

2. Aloysio Nunes, Brazilian Foreign Minister.

3. Claire Felter, and Danielle Renwick, "Mercosur: South America's Fractious Trade Bloc," Council on Foreign Relations, September 10, 2018.

4. Telesur, "Argentina's Fernandez Signs Railway Nationalization Bill," https://www.telesurtv.net, accessed September 17, 2018.

5. Phillip Inman, "Bolivia Nationalizes Spanish-Owned Power Grid," *The Guardian*, https://www.theguardian.com, accessed September 17, 2018.

6. David Jolly and Jack Ewing, "Dutch Government Takes Control of SNS Reaal," *The New York Times*, https://dealbook.nytimes.com, accessed September 17, 2018.

7. Mariana Zuniga, and Nick Miroff, "Venezuela's Paradox: People Are Hungry, but Farmers Can't Feed Them," *Washington Post*, https://www.washingtonpost.com, accessed September 17, 2018.

8. "Iran Condemns US Seizure of Alavi Foundation Building," BBC News, https://www.bbc.com, September 17, 2018.

9. Richard Seymour, "A Short History of Privatization in the UK: 1979–2012," *The Guardian*, https://www.theguardian.com, accessed September 17, 2018.

10. Charles Forelle, "Thatcher's Privatizations Cast a Long Shadow," *The Wall Street Journal*, https://www.wsj.com, accessed September 17, 2018.

11. UK Ministry of Defence and Philip Dunne, "MOD Sells the Government Pipeline and Storage System for £82 Million," https://www.gov.uk, accessed September 17, 2018.

12. Chad Bray, "U.K. Government Sells Final Stake in Lloyds Banking Group," *The New York Times*, https://www.nytimes.com, accessed September 17, 2018; and Max Colchester, "U.K. Government Sells 7.7% Stake in RBS for $3.3 Billion," *The Wall Street Journal*, https://www.wsj.com, accessed June 5, 2018.

13. Robert W. Poole, Jr., *Annual Privatization Report: Air Transportation*, Reason Foundation, https://reason.org, accessed September 17, 2018.

14. Jane Cai, "Forget Privatisation, Xi Has Other Big Plans for Bloated State Firms," *South China Morning Post*, https://www.scmp.com, accessed September 17, 2018; and "Privatization in China: Capitalism Confined," *The Economist*, https://www.economist.com, accessed September 17, 2018.

15. U.S. Department of State, "U.S. Passports and International Travel," https://travel.state.gov, accessed September 17, 2018.

16. GCiS, China Strategic Research, "Importance of China to Western Multinationals," http://www.gcis.com.cn, accessed September 17, 2018; and Philip Van Doorn, "Apple, Nike and 18 Other U.S. Companies Have $158 Billion at Stake in China Trade War," *MarketWatch*, https://www.marketwatch.com, accessed September 17, 2018.

17. Sarah Halzack, "Would You Trust Chicken from a KFC In China? The Chinese Still Don't," *Washington Post*, https://www.washingtonpost.com, accessed September 17, 2018; "China Probes Safety of Yum Brands' KFC Chicken Products," *Reuters*, https://www.reuters.com, accessed September 17, 2018; and Julie Jargon, and Laurie Burkitt, "KFC's Crisis in China Tests Ingenuity of Man Who Built Brand," *The Wall Street Journal*, https://www.wsj.com, accessed September 17, 2018.

18. Rich Duprey, "China Is About to Roast McDonald's and KFC's Chicken," https://www.nasdaq.com, accessed September 17, 2018; Anthony Kuhn, "Fast-Food Scandal Revives China's Food Safety Anxieties," *National Public Radio*, https://www.npr.org, accessed September 17, 2018.

19. Katie Shonk, "Cultural Barriers and Conflict Negotiation Strategies: Apple's Apology in China," https://www.pon.harvard.edu, accessed September 17, 2018; and David Barboza, and Nick Wingfield, "Pressured by China, Apple Apologizes for Warranty Issues," *The New York Times*, https://www.nytimes.com, accessed September 17, 2018.

20. Amy B. Wang, "Bowing to Pressure from China, Mercedes-Benz Apologizes for Quoting the Dalai Lama in Ad," *Washington Post*, https://www.washingtonpost.com, February 06, 2018.

21. Tom Orlik, and Rolfe Winker, "Heard on the Street," *The Wall Street Journal*, https://www.wsj.com, accessed September 17, 2018.

22. U.S. Department of State, "Investment Climate Statement for 2018," https://www.state.gov, accessed September 17, 2018.

23. Christopher Mellon, Peter Bergen, and David Sterman, "To Pay Ransom or Not to Pay Ransom?: An Examination of Western Hostage Policies," https://www.newamerica.org, accessed September 17, 2018; and Cognizant, "Kidnap and Ransom Insurance: At an Inflection Point," https://www.cognizant.com, accessed September 17, 2018.

24. Cognizant, "Kidnap and Ransom Insurance: At an Inflection Point"; and National Consortium for the Study of Terrorism and Responses to Terrorism, *Annex of Statistical Information: Country Reports on Terrorism 2016*, https://www.state.gov, accessed September 17, 2018.

25. Red24, *Threat Forecast 2017*, https://www.agcs.allianz.com, accessed September 17, 2018.

26. Annelies Pauwels, "Competing for Ransom: AQIM vs. Daesh," European Union Institute for Security Studies, https://www.iss.europa.eu, accessed September 17, 2018; and Center for the Analysis of Terrorism, *ISIS Financing 2015*, https://cat-int.org, accessed September 17, 2018.

27. Jack Wallis, "Foreign Nationals Face Persistent Kidnap Threat in Rio de Janeiro," https://www.nyarisk.com, accessed September 17, 2018.

28. IRIN, "Aid Worker Kidnappings Rise, Fuelling Debate Over Ransom," http://www.irinnews.org, accessed September 17, 2018; and Malaka Gharib, "Kidnapping Is a Rising Concern for Aid Workers Around the World," *National Public Radio*, https://www.npr.org, accessed September 17, 2018.

29. United Nations, "Unanimously Adopting Resolution 2368 (2017), Security Council Reaffirms Its Resolve to Combat Terrorism," https://www.un.org, accessed September 17, 2018.

30. International Maritime Bureau, International Chamber of Commerce, https://www.icc-ccs.org/index.php, accessed September 17, 2018; Oceans Beyond Piracy, *The State of Maritime Piracy 2017*, http://oceansbeyondpiracy.org, accessed September 17, 2018.

31. International Chamber of Commerce, International Maritime Bureau, https://www.icc-ccs.org/index.php/piracy-reporting-centre, accessed September 17, 2018.

32. Michael Nadeau, "State of Cybercrime 2017: Security Events Decline, but Not the Impact," https://www.csoonline.com, accessed September 17, 2018.

33. Ms. Smith, "NotPetya Ransomware Hits Hospitals, While Shadow Brokers Touts Its July VIP Service," CSO, https://www.csoonline.com, accessed September 17, 2018.

34. Kevin Richards, Ryan LaSalle, and Floris van den Dool, *2017 Cost of Cyber Crime Study*, https://www.accenture.com, accessed September 17, 2018; and James Lewis, *Economic Impact of Cybercrime—No Slowing Down*, https://www.mcafee.com, accessed September 17, 2018.

35. David Bisson, "The 10 Biggest Data Breaches of 2018 . . . So Far," *Barkly*, https://blog.barkly.com, accessed September 17, 2018.

36. Verizon, "2018 Data Breach Investigations Report," http://www.verizonenterprise.com, accessed September 17, 2018.

37. Claire Martin, "At the Ready, at the Sochi Games," *The New York Times*, https://www.nytimes.com, accessed September 17, 2018.

38. S. A. Ast, *Managing Security Overseas: Protecting Employees and Assets in Volatile Regions*, New York: Taylor Francis, 2010.

39. Centigon Security Group, "Centigon in Figures," https://www.centigon.com, accessed September 2018.

40. World Trade Organization, *World Tariff Profiles 2017*, https://www.wto.org, accessed September 17, 2018.

41. Josh Wingrove, and Erik Hertzberg, "How Canada's Sacred Cows and 270% Tariffs Set Trump Off at G-7," *Bloomberg*, https://www.bloomberg.com, accessed September 17, 2018.

42. William Mauldin, Timothy Puko, and Kate O'Keeffe, "Trump Administration Looks Into New Tariffs on Imported Vehicles," *The Wall Street Journal*, https://www.wsj.com, accessed September 17, 2018; and Menzie Chinn, "What Is the National Security Rationale for Steel, Aluminum and Automobile Protection?" *Econofact*, https://econofact.org, accessed September 17, 2018.

43. Lance Davis, and Stanley Engerman, "History Lessons: Sanctions: Neither War nor Peace," *Journal of Economic Perspectives*, vol no. 17, no. 2, Spring 2003, 187, http://www.aeaweb.org.

44. Gary C. Hufbauer, "Economic Sanctions: America's Folly," in *Economic Casualties: How U.S. Foreign Policy Undermines Trade, Growth and Liberty*, eds. S. Singleton and D. T. Griswold, Washington, DC: Cato Institute, 1999, 90–99; and Hossein Askari, John Forrer, Jiawen Yang, and Tarek Hachem, "Measuring Vulnerability to U.S. Foreign Economic Sanctions," *Business Economics*, vol. 40, no. 2, April 2005, 41–55, https://link.springer.com.

45. Michael Helmar, Stanley R. Johnson, Robert J. Myers, Jarrett Whistance, and Harry Baumes, "The Economic Impacts of U.S. Tariffs for Ethanol and Biodiesel," United States Department of Agriculture, https://www.usda.gov, accessed September 17, 2018; Jillian Kay Melchior, "Trump's Support for Ethanol Is Bad for Taxpayers and Their Cars," *National Review*, https://www.nationalreview.com, accessed September 17, 2018; and Robert Rapier, "Addressing Misconceptions from Senator Grassley's Ethanol Editorial," *Forbes*, https://www.forbes.com, accessed September 17, 2018.

46. Wolf Richter, "Mexico's Wage Repression Scheme Creates a Nirvana for Global Automakers," *Business Insider*, https://www.businessinsider.com, accessed September 17, 2018; Mark Stevenson, "In Mexico, $2-per-hour Workers Make $40,000 SUVs," *The Detroit News*, https://www.detroitnews.com, accessed September 17, 2018; and OECD, "Level of GDP per Capita and Productivity," https://stats.oecd.org, accessed September 17, 2018.

47. "Win-Win Ending to the 'Hormone Beef Trade War,'" *European Parliament News*, http://www.europarl.europa.eu, accessed September 17, 2018.

48. Juliane von Reppert-Bismarck, "U.S. Lifts Sanctions in EU Beef Hormone Row," *Reuters*, https://www.reuters.com, accessed September 17, 2018; "Europe's Burden," *The Economist*, May 22, 1999, 84; and "Brie and Hormones," *The Economist*, January 7, 1989, 21–22.

49. Gilbert Reilhac, "Vote Ends EU-US Hormone-Treated Beef Row," *Reuters*, https://www.reuters.com, accessed September 17, 2018.

50. Wyatt Bechtel, "More U.S. Beef Could Be Destined for Europe," Drovers, https://www.drovers.com, accessed September 17, 2018; and Bill Tomson, "Perdue: US and EU Make Strides Toward Beef Deal," https://www.agri-pulse.com, accessed September 17, 2018.

51. Emma Foehringer Merchant, "Trump Tariffs on Chinese Solar and Battery Products to Have Minimal Impact," *GreenTechMedia*, https://www.greentechmedia.com, accessed September 17, 2018.

52. Reuters, "EU Looks into Extending Dumping Duties on Chinese Bicycles," *CNBC*, https://www.cnbc.com, accessed September 17, 2018.

53. OECD, "Agricultural Support," https://data.oecd.org, accessed September 17, 2018.

54. Dewey, Caitlin "Why Americans Pay More For Sugar," *the Washington Post*, June 08, 2017.

55. Movchan, Andrey, "Western Sanctions on Russia: Lots of Noise and Little Impact," *Deutsche Welle*, May 04, 2018.

56. Ibid.

57. Ibid.

58. Joy Gordon, "Economic Sanctions, Just War Doctrine, and the "Fearful Spectacle of the Civilian Dead," *CrossCurrents*, vol. 49, no. 3, 1999, 387–400.

59. R. C. Longworth, "Free Trade Still Mainly An Ideal," *Chicago Tribune*, July 05, 1985.

60. United States Trade Representative, "FY 2018 WTO Tariff-Rate Quota Allocations for Raw Cane Sugar, Refined and Specialty Sugar and Sugar-Containing Products," https://ustr.gov, accessed September 17, 2018.

61. Chuin-Wei Yap, Scott Patterson, and Bob Tita, "U.S. Accuses Chinese Firms of Rerouting Goods to Disguise Their Origin," *The Wall Street Journal*, https://www.wsj.com, September 17, 2018.

62. Maytaal Angel, "EU Investigates Tariff Avoidance by Chinese Steel Firms," *Reuters*, https://www.reuters.com, accessed September 17, 2018.

63. James R. Hagerty, "Now Packed with Drama: Cans of Tuna Fish," *The Wall Street Journal*, February 18, 2014, B1.

64. OECD, "Trade Policy and the Economic Crisis," 2010, http://www.oecd.org/trade/45293999.pdf, accessed September 17, 2018; and WTO, OECD, the World Bank, and ILO, "Seizing the Benefits of Trade for Employment and Growth," 2010, http://www.oecd.org, accessed September 17, 2018.

65. Erica York, and Kyle Pomerleau, "Tracking the Economic Impact of U.S. Tariffs and Retaliatory Actions," https://taxfoundation.org, accessed September 17, 2018.

66. *Mark J. Perry, "Yes, Protectionism Can Save Some US Jobs, But at What Cost? Empirical Evidence Suggests It's Very, Very Expensive," American Enterprise Institute*, http://www.aei.org, accessed September 17, 2018.

67. Ken Ash, director of the OECD Trade and Agriculture Directorate, http://www.youtube.com/user/oecden,?v=4tHpspY2_sU&lr=1, February 21, 2014.

6

Intellectual Property Rights and Other Legal Forces

> **Law is the essential foundation of stability and order both within societies and in international relations.**
>
> —J. William Fulbright[1]

©Qilai Shen/Bloomberg/Getty Images.

LEARNING OBJECTIVES

After reading this module, you should be able to:

LO 6-1 **Describe** the three types of legal systems.

LO 6-2 **Describe** the rule of law and its sources.

LO 6-3 **Discuss** the general legal concerns in global business.

LO 6-4 **Identify** methods to protect intellectual property.

LO 6-5 **Discuss** the standardization of laws among nations.

LO 6-6 **Describe** the impacts of the national-level legal forces in the areas of competition, trade, tort, ethics, and accounting.

Are the Drugs You Take Safe? The Worldwide Threat of Counterfeit Pharmaceuticals

You are feeling under the weather while traveling abroad, so you visit a doctor, fill your prescription at a local pharmacy, and swallow a pill with your bottled water. Soon you will be feeling better. Or will you? Is the medication you just took genuine or fake?

A special kind of challenge that confronts both developed and developing nations is the counterfeiting of pharmaceuticals. In addition to producing exact copies of branded prescription drugs, counterfeiters make products that contain the correct active ingredients but in the wrong proportions, products that do not contain any active ingredients, and products that contain toxic ingredients or other impurities. Counterfeit drugs represent an industry that is growing rapidly both in size and in its worldwide risk to public health. They range from fake antimalarial pills, counterfeit HIV/AIDS medications, and tainted birth control pills to contaminated or substandard medications for heart disease, weight loss, or erectile dysfunction. An estimated 1 million patients die each year from counterfeit pharmaceuticals, including an estimated 450,000 people who die of malaria and at least 72,000 children who die from pneumonia due to treatment involving substandard or falsified pharmaceuticals. With an estimated global value of $200 billion, sales are increasing at nearly double the rate of legitimate drugs.

The proportion of counterfeit drugs in circulation worldwide ranges from 1 percent in some developed countries to 30 percent in some developing nations. About one-third of all nations lack effective drug regulation agencies, meaning that tens of millions of people are exposed to potentially deadly drugs. About 95 percent of the 50,000 online pharmacies in operation fail to meet legal and industry standards designed to protect patients from this scourge, with 90 percent of drugs bought online originating from a different nation than claimed on the website. The U.S. Food and Drug Administration posts a warning list of recently uncovered counterfeit pharmaceuticals on its website (www.fda.gov), and it has repeatedly warned consumers about risks associated with fake popular prescription drugs sold by pharmacies in Mexican border towns or through online sources. "Counterfeiters can make more money than hard-drug traffickers, and they have less of a chance to go to prison," according to Interpol's coordinator of the Medical Products and Counterfeiting Crime unit, Aline Plançon. She reported that the profit margin for selling counterfeit Viagra, for example, is roughly 10 times that of selling heroin, while the legal consequences are much lower. For example, traffickers of hard drugs may face prison or death, yet those trafficking in counterfeit pharmaceuticals usually face charges under trademark, fraud, or similar laws.

Besides causing legitimate manufacturers to lose sales, fake drugs can bring tragedy to users when the drugs fail to perform as well as the original. In Mexico, officials confiscated 15,000 counterfeit burn remedies because many contained sawdust or dirt and caused raging infections, while hundreds of infants and others were killed in recent years in Bangladesh, Panama, Nigeria, Haiti, and India after using cough syrup containing diethylene glycol, a toxic chemical used for making antifreeze.

A range of public- and private-sector organizations have organized efforts to fight the global outbreak of counterfeit drugs. They include the Pharmaceutical Security Institute (which tracks pharmaceutical counterfeiting), the European Alliance for Access to Safe Medicines (which is working to exclude counterfeit and substandard medicines from supply chains), and the WHO-sponsored International Medical Products Anti-Counterfeiting Taskforce (IMPACT). Ongoing efforts have raised awareness of the nature and extent of the problem, pushed for appropriate legislation and enforcement efforts to locate and punish offenders, and identified innovative ways of ensuring the safety of pharmaceutical supply chains from raw material to consumer. Initiatives include the experimental use of blockchain technology as well as standards for mandatory "mass serialization." By providing each drug package with a unique identifier, such as a barcode or radio frequency identification code, tracking and tracing of products throughout the journey from manufacturing to wholesaling to retailing is enhanced. But protecting the health of consumers and the intellectual property rights of pharmaceutical makers and other companies remains an ongoing challenge worldwide.

Sources: Rae Ellen Bichel, "Fake Drugs are a Major Global Problem, WHO Reports," *National Public Radio*, November 29, 2017; Peter Behner, Marie-Lyn Hecht, and Fabian Wahl, "Fighting Counterfeit Pharmaceuticals: New Defenses for an Underestimated—and Growing—Menace," *Strategy&*, June 29, 2017; Tomasz Wieclawski, "Expert: Counterfeit Drugs Kill 1 Million People Each Year," *Science in Poland*, March 12, 2018; "Counterfeit Medicines," *Centers for Disease Control and Prevention*, October 23, 2017; and Natalie Southwick, "Counterfeit Drugs Kill 1 Mn People Annually: Interpol," *InSight Crime*, October 24, 2013.

In this module, we examine international law and international dispute settlement, including disputes dealing with intellectual property and other key company assets. Then we look at a variety of specific national-level laws that have had a large influence on international business. We begin, though, at a more basic level, with a review of the types of legal systems found around the world and some general legal concerns international businesses face.

Types of Legal Systems

LO 6-1
Describe the three types of legal systems.

The legal system of a country is the collection of governing principles, such as a written or oral constitution, and the legislation and regulations enacted by governing bodies established to provide for the welfare of the country. Legal systems follow one of three distinct approaches that are found in civil law, in common law, or in religious law. These approaches reflect the historic context of the legal system's development.

CIVIL LAW

The civil law approach is based on codification, that is, a systematic collection of laws designed to cover all areas of concern and, hence, is bureaucratic. The tradition of civil law was derived from ancient Roman law and has been influenced by codified religious law such as Islamic law and canon or Christian law. Today it is the most widespread system globally. Napoleonic law, drafted in post-revolutionary France in 1804, incorporated the values of the French Revolution, especially liberty and equality, into a civil code. It has influenced the approach to the law of Spain, Italy, the Benelux countries (Belgium, the Netherlands, and Luxembourg), the Latin American countries, and the former French colonies, including the U.S. state of Louisiana. The German civil law tradition, which is based on the application of general laws to individual cases, has influenced the development of law in Greece, Portugal, Turkey, Japan and, partially, in China. In civil law, the system tends to be less adversarial than that found in common law (see next section), since the role of the judge is to apply codified law rather than to interpret law, previous rulings, and tradition. Thus the court in a civil law environment is not a forum where two sides battle to demonstrate to a judge or jury who is right and who is wrong, as is the case with common law, where the judge is supposed to be impartial. The civil law approach is inquisitorial; that is, judges often actively question the prosecution, the defense, and their witnesses during proceedings and may challenge evidence in their efforts to track down the truth. The judge also issues the decision. Trial by jury is less frequent in civil law systems.

COMMON LAW

The common law approach relies on decisions made by judges in previous cases along with statutes and regulations made by legislatures. The relationship between judicial decisions and statutes can be complex because the results of earlier decisions (called precedents) are part of the process, and the law is always in process. In some areas, judges decide on the meaning and constitutionality of statutes. England follows the common law system, as do its former colonies including the Commonwealth nations: Canada (except Quebec), the United States (except Louisiana), Australia, Uganda, Hong Kong, and Singapore. Principles of common law systems include:

1. The rights of the individual exist alongside those of the state;
2. The trial is adversarial;
3. The defendant is presumed innocent until proven guilty;
4. Case law develops through judgments and precedents;
5. Case law co-exists with statute law and—in most cases—a constitution;
6. Crimes are punished and civil wrongs are rectified by compensation.[2]

Although common law systems tend to be more adversarial than civil law systems, they are also more flexible because the judge is charged with interpreting law, tradition,

Judges from Coté d'Ivoire, a former French colony, with a civil law system (left), and Malawi, a former British protectorate, with a common law system (right). ©Pascal Guyot/AFP/Getty Images (left), ©Amos Gumulira/AFP/Getty Images (right).

and custom in the light of the particular case being heard. The judge's ruling then serves to provide increased legal guidance in the form of a precedent that can be called upon in future cases.

RELIGIOUS LAW

In religious law, a religious document or source is the basis of the legal system. Religious law is followed in Iran, Saudi Arabia, Libya, and Morocco, among other countries. In Islam, Sharia law's fundamental documents are the Qur'an and Sunnah, while some rulings may be developed by jurists (legal experts) guided by religious documents, reasoning, and opinions from the religious community. One aspect of Sharia law relevant to international managers is the prohibition of charging interest. Instead, equity partnerships are used as a financing instrument, with the lender assuming a share in the operating risk.

Jewish Halakha is based on the Torah and Jewish tradition and informs the law of Israel. It also is used to settle disputes among members of the faith who voluntarily agree to be governed by it.

Legal systems are used in combination, as well. Israel, Thailand, and Pakistan are examples of countries that have combined systems. The CIA *World Factbook*'s Field Listing of Legal Systems is a source of descriptions of countries' legal systems and also indicates whether they accept the jurisdiction of the United Nations International Court of Justice (https://www.cia.gov/library/publications/the-world-factbook/fields/2100.html).

International Legal Forces

LO 6-2
Describe the rule of law and its sources.

Many issues related to intellectual property rights and other legal forces confront global companies wherever they operate, although seldom are their impacts as severe as those associated with the deadly counterfeit pharmaceuticals described in this module's opening vignette. Participants in international business should understand the breadth and depth of laws and legal issues in various jurisdictions worldwide, beginning with the type of legal system followed in the country. Anyone studying these legal forces soon realizes that their variety complicates the task of understanding the laws.

While businesses must be aware of laws in order to comply with them, they also expect those laws will assist them when necessary. Managers need to know whether the host country's government will be able to protect the foreign business with an adequate legal system that can enforce contracts and protect the basic rights of employees. In examining international legal forces, we must keep in mind that a stable government and an adequate court system are necessary to ensure a welcoming environment for foreign businesses.

> **"INSOFAR as INTERNATIONAL LAW IS OBSERVED, IT PROVIDES US with STABILITY AND ORDER AND with A MEANS of PREDICTING THE BEHAVIOR of THOSE with WHOM WE HAVE RECIPROCAL LEGAL OBLIGATIONS."**
>
> *—J. William Fulbright, U.S. politician and statesman diplomat*[4]

RULE OF LAW

International businesspeople need to determine that a country is governed by the rule of law, rather than by the rule of a political dictatorship or a powerful elite. When a country's legal system is based on the rule of law, foreign investment is encouraged because investors know their interests will be protected. Countries that follow the rule of law also tend to protect the human rights of local peoples, an increasing concern of global companies.

For example, while Shanghai has been attracting increased foreign investments since the global financial crisis in 2008, Hong Kong continues to offer advantages over Shanghai, largely because Hong Kong has a tradition of law adopted from British colonial days that has been tried and tested and is trusted by international businesses. Shanghai courts, on the other hand, have been perceived to favor Chinese litigants, a perception that has support from results across a range of jurisdictions in China.[3] This disparity in the two cities' legal systems has been reduced recently, and studies reveal that about 80 percent of the intellectual property cases brought to courts in China, including Shanghai, were decided in favor of the foreign party.[5] Yet perception lags reality in this case, and this lag favors Hong Kong.

The World Bank's "Doing Business" survey ranks Hong Kong third overall in the region to Singapore and Malaysia for protecting minority investors and fourth for contract enforcement. China ranks 17th for investor protection and second for contract enforcement, while among cities in China, Shanghai ranks fourth for contract enforcement.[6] A World Bank summary of governance indicators including the rule of law that scores nations on a 100-point scale gives China a 45 and Hong Kong a 94.[7] These rankings suggest that Hong Kong has advantages due to its more highly developed legal system. Figure 6.1 maps the rule of law globally.

FIGURE 6.1 Rule of Law Map, 2018

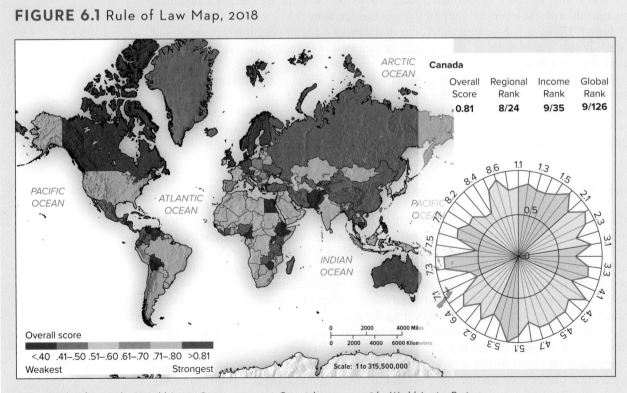

WHAT IS INTERNATIONAL LAW?

Each sovereign nation is responsible for creating and enforcing laws within its jurisdiction. Once laws cross international borders, the matter of enforcement is complicated by the necessity of agreement between nations. The same concepts that apply to domestic laws do not always apply to international law.

International law describes the set of rules nations have agreed to follow. Such rules help set the context for stable relationships among nations. We can divide international law into public international law and private international law. **Public international law** codifies the legal relationships between governments, including laws about diplomatic relations between sovereign nations and all matters involving their rights and obligations. In contrast, **private international law** includes laws governing the transactions between individuals and companies that cross international borders. A contract between businesses in two different countries falls under private international law, and public international law governs a dispute between two countries over trade subsidies.

SOURCES OF INTERNATIONAL LAW

International law comes from several sources, the most important of which are bilateral and multilateral **treaties** between nations. Treaties are agreements between countries and may also be called *conventions*, *covenants*, *compacts*, or *protocols*. These agreements often are reached as a result of the efforts of international organizations such as the United Nations and the World Trade Organization. The United Nations has sponsored many conferences that have led to multinational agreements on a range of matters, including postal delivery and use of driver's licenses in other countries. The United Nations International Court of Justice creates international law when it decides disputes brought before it by member-nations.

Another source of international law is customary international law, which consists of international rules derived from customs and usage over centuries. An example of customary international law is the prohibition against genocide (there is also a specific international statute against genocide); another is the immunity from prosecution of visiting foreign heads of state.

General Legal Concerns in Global Business

Three areas of the law are of special concern to international businesses because they affect business activities in the international setting and not in their domestic setting. These three areas are extraterritoriality, performance of contracts in an international setting, and litigation in an international setting.

EXTRATERRITORIALITY

What laws does the company have a duty or obligation to follow? At first thought, we might conclude that a nation's jurisdiction applies only within its geographic area. Many countries, though, including the United States and members of the European Union, attempt to enforce their laws outside their borders, not by force but through traditional, legal means. This process is referred to as the **extraterritorial application of laws**. For example, the U.S. government imposes taxes on U.S. citizens and U.S. permanent residents regardless of the source of income or the residence of the taxpayer. If a U.S. citizen is living in Madrid and receives all her income from Spanish sources, the United States will still expect her to comply with U.S. tax laws. Likewise, when U.S. companies operate in other countries with U.S.-based employees, these companies must comply with U.S. laws, including employment laws. Of course, they must also comply with the laws of the host country.

public international law
Law that governs relationships between governments

private international law
Law that governs relationships between individuals and companies that cross international borders

treaty
Agreement between countries, also known as convention, compact, and protocol

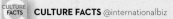

CULTURE FACTS @internationalbiz

Countries often use cultural differences as a reason for not living up to the conventions they sign, especially when it comes to ensuring the equal status of women. #culturaldifferences #conventions #equalstatus

LO 6-3
Discuss the general legal concerns in global business.

extraterritorial application of laws
A country's attempt to apply its laws to nonresidents and foreigners, and to activities that take place beyond its borders

Extraterritorial application of laws has been extended to many other areas in addition to tax and employment law, including antitrust and environmental laws. Also, the Alien Tort Statute allows non-U.S. nationals to file lawsuits in U.S. courts for alleged violations of international law, including human rights violations, even when the defendant has no ties to the United States and when the defendant is a corporation. Charles McArthur Emmanuel, the son of the former dictatorial ruler of Liberia, was convicted of torture and conspiracy to torture in a Department of Justice case, and victims were awarded over $22 million (*Kpadeh v. Emmanuel*, 2008). The U.S. Supreme Court ruled against the Nigerian claimants in *Kiobel v. Royal Dutch Petroleum*, which claimed the oil company aided the Nigerian government in the violation of human rights law in 2013. In 2018, the Supreme Court ruled that foreign corporations may not be defendants for lawsuits filed under the Alien Tort Statute.[8]

China and the United States engaged in a legal dispute about a U.S. court's extraterritorial imposition of a decision related to accounting and auditing. The U.S. judge suspended the China affiliates of the Big Four accounting firms from auditing U.S.-listed companies. The U.S. Securities and Exchange Commission (SEC) had requested auditing information from these accounting firms on specific Chinese companies trading in U.S. markets. The Chinese firms refused to hand over the documents to U.S. regulators, claiming that Chinese law considers such information a state secret. The long-running dispute was finally resolved with the four firms agreeing to pay $2 million in fines and, in the future, to follow procedures to provide audit documents on their Chinese clients to the SEC.[9]

PERFORMANCE OF CONTRACTS

Whenever businesses enter into agreements with other businesses, the possibility exists that there may be problems getting the other side to perform its obligations. No worldwide court has the power to enforce its decrees. The worldwide courts that do exist, such as the UN's International Court of Justice, rely on the voluntary compliance of the parties before them. Each nation in the world is sovereign and has its own rules for recognizing decrees and judgments from other nations.

When contracting parties are residents of a single country, the laws of that country govern contract performance and any disputes that arise between the parties. That country's courts have jurisdiction over the parties, and the courts' judgments are enforced in accordance with the country's procedures. When residents of two or more countries make a contract, those relatively easy solutions to dispute resolution are not available. Enforcing contracts that cross international borders is often complicated.

United Nations Solutions   Many countries, including the United States, have ratified the UN Convention on the International Sale of Goods (CISG) to solve jurisdictional problems related to contract performance. The CISG is a set of uniform legal rules that govern the formation of international sales contracts and the rights and obligations of the buyer and seller. It applies automatically to all contracts for the sale of goods between traders from different countries that have ratified it. This automatic application will take place unless the parties to the contract expressly exclude—or opt out of—the CISG.

Arbitration   Many people outside the United States dislike the U.S. court system. Likewise, many U.S. businesspeople dislike or fear litigation in other countries. Also, arbitration is, by agreement, binding, while one country's court decisions are difficult to enforce on a nonresident. For these reasons, international businesspeople often agree by stipulating in their contract that any disputes will be resolved by arbitration rather than by litigation. Arbitration is usually quicker, less expensive, and more private than litigation, and it is usually binding on all parties. At least 30 organizations now administer international arbitrations, the best known of which may be the

arbitration
A dispute resolution process agreed to by parties in lieu of going to court, in which one person or a body makes a binding decision

Managing Personal Data: The European General Data Protection Regulation

Is your personal information protected, whether it is when you use the Internet or the information provided to your doctor or insurance company? Do you even own your personal data or have the right to know whether it is being collected, stored, shared, or sold? These types of questions about one's own personal data are a significant concern for many people. In an effort to address these concerns and give people control over their personal data, in May 2018 the General Data Protection Regulation (GDPR) became law in the European Union. You may have experienced the effects of the GDPR through a flood of emails with subject lines such as, "We updated our privacy policy." The GDPR has important implications for international companies, including those based outside the European Union.

Display Showing Stages of Hacking in Progress: Exploiting Vulnerability, Executing and Granted Access.
©Gorodenkoff/Shutterstock.

The GDPR attempts to provide unified regulation within the European Union and for companies operating within the European Union regarding how to protect the privacy and personal information of EU residents. It addresses how data on individuals can be obtained, stored, processed, or otherwise used, as well as the safeguards that must be provided to protect these data. Without obtaining explicit informed consent from individuals, their personal data cannot be made available publicly and cannot be used in a manner that identifies them. This regulation applies to any enterprise established within the European Union or processing the personal data of any EU citizen, regardless of the location of the individual or the business. If your company has even a single user who is a citizen of or resides in the European Union, you must comply with the GDPR.

The GDPR will affect companies' operations in varying ways, depending on the size and operations of the company and how it stores and manages data. Indeed, the GDPR includes 99 different articles that address the different dimensions and implications regarding collecting, storing, processing, and sharing of personal information. As a result, the GDPR can impact various parts of an organization, from marketing through information systems and legal and compliance teams, in different ways. For example, if a company has a breach of its user data, as happened in 2018 when Under Armour's MyFitnessPal app had more than 150 million people's data compromised, the company must

report the breach within 72 hours of its discovery. Corporations that fail to comply with requirements may be subject to stiff fines from regulators, with breaches of data security being subject to penalties of up to 20 million euros or 4 percent of annual worldwide sales in the prior year, whichever is greater. Max Schrems, an Austrian privacy activist, sued Google and Facebook for a combined $8.8 billion on the first day the GDPR was in effect. Facing such a large potential penalty, unless it is 100 percent sure that an organization has no EU customers, it would be prudent to operate under the assumption that such customers do exist and proceed accordingly.

Critical Thinking Questions

1. What implications might the GDPR have even for small companies or nongovernmental organizations such as charities or churches that have a limited online presence and that are not based in the European Union?
2. Do you think that this extraterritorial application of EU laws to companies operating in other nations should be allowed? Why or why not?

Sources: Tiffany Robertson, "Top Five Concerns With GDPR Compliance," *Thompson Reuters*, March 05, 2018; "Special Briefing: Europe's New Privacy Regime," *OZY*, May 30, 2018; Tiku Nitasha, "Europe's New Privacy Law Will Change the Web, and More," *Wired*, March 19, 2018; Nick Ismail, "The Multinational Impact of GDPR," *Information Age*, December 18, 2017; and Almitra Karnik, "How Will GDPR Affect the Mobile Marketing World?," *Forbes*, May 9, 2018.

International Court of Arbitration of the International Chamber of Commerce in Paris. The Court has 176 members from 100 countries who arbitrate cases.[10] In addition, London and New York are centers of arbitration.

Some organizations specialize in the type of arbitration cases they will consider. For example, the World Intellectual Property Organization (WIPO) Arbitration and

Mediation Center handles technological, entertainment, and intellectual property disputes. For example, cybersquatting cases are a common dispute WIPO addresses. Cybersquatting involves such activities as entities registering a website under a well-known brand name or a nearly identical name, in order to either sell the website domain name or to mislead customers into believing they are using the brand name's website. In 2017, Victoria's Secret brought a case against Irish beautician Gillian Dowling, who had registered victoriassecret.ie as the domain name for her business, Gillian's Beauty Clinic. The Center ruled in favor of Victoria's Secret and the offending domain name was transferred to their control.[11] The International Centre for the Settlement of Investment Disputes specializes in investment disputes.

LITIGATION

litigation
Legal proceeding conducted to determine and enforce particular legal rights

Disputes in international trade are probably inevitable, and some of the time, arbitration and other resolution methods are not successful. In such cases, the parties settle their disagreements through litigation. Litigation, a legal proceeding conducted to determine and enforce particular legal rights, can be complicated and expensive. In addition to the trial itself, most lawsuits in the United States entail lengthy pretrial activities, including a process called *discovery*. Discovery is the means of finding facts relevant to the litigation, including facts known to the other side and documents in possession of the other side. Some discovery methods can seem quite intrusive because U.S. courts grant parties great latitude in obtaining information in the possession of the opposing side. In fact, discovery is one reason many people outside the United States dislike litigation in the United States.

Litigation of disputes that cross international borders can arise in both state and federal courts in the United States. Some countries freely allow U.S. litigators to obtain discovery, while others have restrictions. For example, if discovery is to occur in Switzerland, even in a case involving only U.S. parties, permission must be obtained from Swiss authorities. Failure to obtain permission may result in penalties, including possible criminal sanctions.

One of the major problems in cross-border litigation is the question of which jurisdiction's law should apply and where the litigation should occur. Each country (and each state in the United States) has elaborate laws for determining the answers to these questions. As in any other disputed matter, the final decision rests with the court that is being asked to hear the case. Occasionally, courts in two countries (or two states) will attempt to resolve the same dispute or will disagree over which judicial system should prevail.

Consider the resolution of the tragedy in Bhopal, India, in 1984, when poisonous gas used in the manufacture of pesticides was released at a plant, killing and harming thousands of Indians. The plant, an Indian subsidiary of Union Carbide (a U.S. company headquartered in New York at the time and now owned by Dow Chemical), was licensed by the Indian government, and 49.1 percent of it was owned by private Indian companies and banks. Subsidiaries are separate legal entities under the law in terms of taxes and liability. The Indian government declared itself the sole representative of the plaintiffs and filed a class action tort claim under U.S. law in federal court in New York. The New York judge refused to hear the case, ruling that it should be heard in India. The judge's reasoning suggested that the complaint was filed in the U.S. system to take advantage of U.S. tort law's generous damages, and that—because the victims, witnesses, and managers were all in India, because India did have established tort law it had applied in the past, and because Union Carbide India Limited was an Indian business—India was where the case belonged.[12]

In more routine business issues, such as a business contract dispute, the *choice-of-law* provisions in the contract specify which law will govern. For example, if there are a U.S. seller and an Australian buyer, the parties may agree that Australian law will govern any dispute. The choice defaults to the CISG rules if no other provisions have been made, a process that can be lengthy and complicated. For this reason, it is prudent to include both a choice-of-law clause and a choice-of-forum clause in contracts. A *choice-of-forum clause* in a contract specifies where the dispute will be settled. For example, the parties in the preceding example may agree to have the dispute decided in California in a process that begins with mediation and then moves, if required, to state courts in Los Angeles County, California.

Despite legal uncertainties of doing business in other countries, international business activities will continue to increase in the future, and it is likely that disputes will as well. For this reason, international businesspeople must be aware of the legal environment in which they find themselves. Legal systems vary significantly from country to country, and it is important to understand the differences. The assumptions we make on the basis of the U.S. or any other legal system may not apply in other countries.

CULTURE FACTS @internationalbiz

Unlike national-level law, international law cannot be enforced by any court or army. It is enforced by cultural values shared by people in most places in the world. Nations that violate international law may become isolated politically and commercially. #nationallevellaw #internationallaw #enforced #culturalvalues #violation #isolation

SOCIAL MEDIA

Intellectual Property Rights

LO 6-4
Identify methods to protect intellectual property.

Intellectual property (IP) is a creative work or invention that is protectable by patents, trademarks, trade names, copyrights, and trade secrets. Rights to intellectual property can be protected by patents, trademarks, trade names, copyrights, and trade secrets, depending on the jurisdiction. These terms, which we explore in the next sections, all describe safeguards to property rights.

Treaties, agreements, and conventions have helped nations standardize some aspects of intellectual property rights. The World Trade Organization's Trade-Related Aspects of Intellectual Property Rights (TRIPS) council works with the World Intellectual Property Organization (WIPO), a self-funding UN forum with 191 members, to develop an intellectual property (IP) system that operates for every nation's benefit.[13] WIPO has divisions related to each type of IP (brands and designs, global issues, development, innovation and technology, cultural and creative industries) and administrative and legal functions. It also mediates IP disagreements. WIPO and TRIPS also incorporate the earlier International Convention for the Protection of Industrial Property of 1883 (the Paris Union). Table 6.1 summarizes the major IP protection efforts.

intellectual property (IP)
A creative work or invention that is protectable by patents, trademarks, trade names, copyrights, and trade secrets

PATENTS

Every country has its own understanding of **patents**, government grants giving the inventor of a product or process the exclusive right to manufacture, exploit, use, and sell that invention or process. How governments protect IP can vary widely. In the European Union, for example, a patent is an understanding of rights between the inventor and the public.[14] In the United States, a patent is viewed more narrowly as a property right that "excludes others from making, using, offering for sale, or selling the invention"[15] and is divided into three types: utility, design, and plant. A utility patent is for an innovative, *useful* invention or process, and it gives the patent holder 20-year protection against use by others. A design patent is for an aesthetic, nonuseful creation, and it runs for 14 years. The plant patent is

patent
A government grant giving the inventor of a product or process the exclusive right to manufacture, exploit, use, and sell that invention or process

TABLE 6.1 The International Framework for IP Protection

Organization	Parent
World Intellectual Property Organization (WIPO)	UN
Trade-Related Aspects of Intellectual Property Rights (TRIPS)	WTO

CULTURE FACTS @internationalbiz

@China China, whose culture places high value on communal, shared property rights, decided to open a series of IP courts, beginning in 2014 in Guangdong and now operating in at least seven cities. #highvalue #IPcourts (*Ciang Li, Chuanshu Xu, and Hui Zhang, "China's Specialized IP Courts," Kluwer Patent Blog, http:// patentblog.kluweriplaw.com, accessed October 12, 2018*)

" THE MOST INNOVATIVE AND PROGRESSIVE SPACE WE'VE SEEN—THE INTERNET—HAS BEEN THE PLACE WHERE INTELLECTUAL PROPERTY HAS BEEN LEAST RESPECTED. "

—Lawrence Lessig, professor, Harvard Law School[19]

for innovations among growing things, such as mutants (genetically modified foods) and hybrids, and it runs for 20 years.[16] Other differences between U.S. and EU patent law include that the EU patent goes to the first person to register an invention, whereas, in the United States, the first inventor has the right to the patent. Also, the EU definition of novelty is much narrower than the U.S. definition. In the European Union, the innovation must be absolutely novel and not available to the public in any form.[17]

Patents are complex and can present the IP owner with massive challenges. In Europe, the European Patent Organization (EPO) has taken a major step toward the harmonization of patents, greatly reducing their complexity. Through EPO, an applicant for a patent need file only one application in English, French, or German to be granted patent protection in all 28 EU member-states. Before the EPO, an applicant had to file in each country in the language of that country. In addition to multiple countries, multiple companies are often party to the property rights patents confer, as in a joint-venture collaboration, which adds to the complexity of patent filings. For example, a U.S. patent for computer chips was issued to South Korea's LG Electronics Inc., which then licensed Intel Corp. to sell the chips. When Quanta, a Taiwanese manufacturer, used the chips it purchased legally from Intel, LG sued for royalties it asserted were due as a result of its property rights under the patent. The U.S. Supreme Court ruled, however, that patent rights become exhausted when the patented item is sold by another company under license.[18]

The Global Intellectual Property Center of the U.S. Chamber of Commerce has developed an IP index to measure different countries' momentum toward effective IP environment rights, one in which IP is safe from theft. Figure 6.2 shows the IP index for 2017–2018.

At the United Nations, smaller nations have been mounting attacks on the exclusivity and length of patent protection. They want to shorten the protection periods from the current 15 to 20 years down to 5 years or even 30 months. But multinational companies are resisting the changes. They point out that the only incentives they have to spend the huge amounts required to

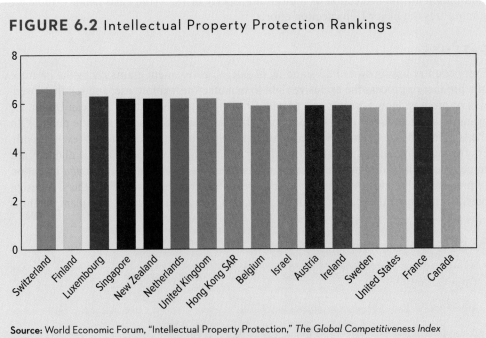

FIGURE 6.2 Intellectual Property Protection Rankings

Source: World Economic Forum, "Intellectual Property Protection," *The Global Competitiveness Index 2017-2018*, http://reports.weforum.org, accessed October 12, 2018.

develop new technology are periods of patent protection long enough to recoup their costs and make profits. The prescription drug industry is a case in point. It relies heavily on patents and other IP protection, whose failings are described in this module's opening story. Multinational pharmaceutical companies say they need years of patent protection to recoup expensive investments in the research and development of new drug treatments. Pfizer Inc. has a blockbuster drug in Lipitor, an anti-cholesterol medication. When Pfizer's patent ran out in June 2011, it negotiated an agreement with Indian generic-drug maker Ranbaxy Laboratories Ltd. to keep Ranbaxy's generic version off the U.S. market until May 2012. These types of extensions, called a "pay-for-delay deal," cost consumers and taxpayers in the United States alone an extra $3.5 billion per year.[20] In contrast, Indian generic drug maker Laurus Labs received preliminary approval from the U.S. Food and Drug Administration to offer anti-HIV drugs upon expiration of patents held by Gilead in late 2017 and early 2018.[21] Gilead was generating $600 million per year in U.S. sales from these drugs prior to patent expiration.

An added complexity of the patent environment is the spread of so-called patent trolls. These are lawyers and investors who buy patents mistakenly granted mostly to failed companies, and then try to cash in on them. In one case, a patent troll claimed that a patent bought for about $50,000 was infringed by Intel's microprocessors and threatened to sue Intel for $7 billion in damages. This is a fascinating sub-world populated not just by trolls but also by patent pirates, who steal IP rights by boldly using protected property. Patent thickets, multiple layers of property rights with different rights holders with whom a company must negotiate in order to make use of new IP, are another challenge.

TRADEMARKS

A **trademark** is a shape, color, design, phrase, abbreviation, or sound that stands for a company or its product and that is reserved for that company's sole use. For instance, the Apple logo, Starbucks' mermaid, Hello Kitty's kitten and heart, and the FedEx logo with its arrow are all protected trademarks. The trademark-protected Burberry plaid, known as the "Haymarket Check," is illustrated in Figure 6.3. China's State Administration for Industry and Commerce announced in late 2013 that it was canceling Burberry's trademark on the plaid on the basis of non-use for three years. Burberry, with 71 stores in China, appealed the decision, stating, "The Burberry Check remains a registered trademark exclusively owned by Burberry and no other parties can use the mark without Burberry's proper authorization."[22]

trademark
A shape, color, design, phrase, abbreviation, or sound used by merchants or manufacturers to designate and differentiate their products

FIGURE 6.3 The Distinctive Burberry Plaid Is Trademark-Protected

©Markos Dolopokos/Alamy Stock Photo.

Although blacksmiths who made swords in the Roman Empire may have been the first to use trademarks, the beer makers Löwenbräu and Stella Artois claim to have used them since the 14th century.[23] Much like patent protection, trademark protection varies from country to country, as does its duration, which may be from 10 to 20 years, with possible renewals.

Trademark protection in most of the world is covered by the Madrid Agreement of 1891. This agreement operates as a central filing system, with one application and one fee, but it does not standardize or harmonize actual trademark protection. It is administered by the World Intellectual Property Organization (WIPO), which issues an international registration that is then presented for acceptance in each location where the company seeks protection of its mark. The General Inter-American Convention for Trademark and Commercial Protection for the Western Hemisphere, an agreement of the Organization of American States, also acts to protect trademarks. In addition, bilateral agreements between nations may extend protection on the basis of friendship, commerce, and navigation treaties.

The European Union has standardized the rules on trademarks. The Office of Harmonization in the Internal Market (OHIM) is responsible for the recognition and protection of proprietary marks in all EU countries, including trademarks belonging to companies based in non-EU member-countries.

TRADE NAMES

trade name
A name used by a merchant or manufacturer to designate and differentiate its products

A **trade name** is the name used by merchants and manufacturers to designate and differentiate their products, and it is protected by WIPO and TRIPS. It is often different from the legal name of the business, and it may be the same as a brand name. Coca-Cola often refers to itself as Coca-Cola, its brand name, rather than as The Coca-Cola Company. KFC, Taco Bell, and Pizza Hut are trade names of Yum! Brands, Inc. A business may use a trade name for many reasons, including to focus the consumer on its product line, to distance itself from negative publicity, and to do business in multiple geographic or product areas with one legal corporation. Dove is a trade name of Unilever PLC/Unilever NV. (In Great Britain, PLC designates a public limited company, much like a corporation in the United States, and NV designates Naamloze Vennootschap, a Dutch term for the same form of business.) The Procter & Gamble Company uses the trade name P&G. It also uses the trade and brand name Fairy Liquid for its dishwashing soap in the United Kingdom and Australia, while the same or similar product sells in the United States with the trade and brand name Dawn. Businesses may have many trade names. Goods bearing illegal trade names, or false statements about their origin, are subject to seizure upon importation into countries that are members of WIPO or have signed the WTO's TRIPS agreement.

COPYRIGHTS

copyright
Exclusive legal rights of authors, composers, creators of software, playwrights, artists, and publishers to publish and dispose of their work

Copyrights, which are exclusive legal rights of authors, composers, software creators, playwrights, artists, and publishers to publish and dispose of their work, are protected under the Berne Convention of 1886, adhered to by 173 countries, the WIPO Copyright Treaty, and the TRIPS Agreement, to which all WTO members agree to abide (Figure 6.4). A copyright protects tangible property. So the idea itself is not afforded copyright protection; the idea has to be written, filmed, drawn, or somehow expressed. The Internet and its new forms of property and distribution (software, downloading, file sharing) offer new applications of copyright law. Court systems in both the United States and Europe have used copyright law to give intellectual property protection to computer software. Downloading or copying most copyrighted computer files, such as books and music, violates the property rights of the owners. The music-sharing site Napster was challenged by Metallica in a copyright lawsuit in 2000 and shut down by the United States Ninth Circuit Court of Appeals.

FIGURE 6.4 World Copyright Time Period

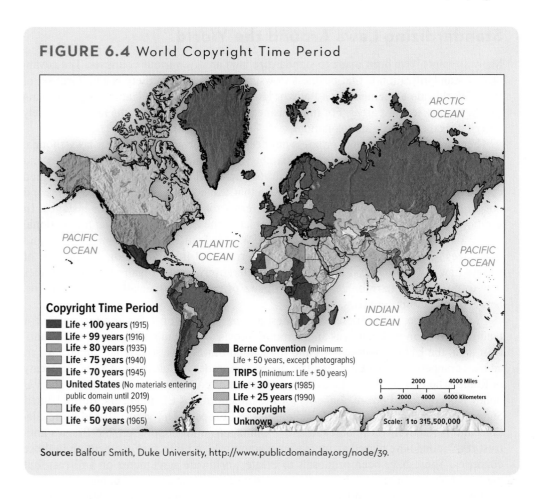

Copyright Time Period

- **Life + 100 years** (1915)
- **Life + 99 years** (1916)
- **Life + 80 years** (1935)
- **Life + 75 years** (1940)
- **Life + 70 years** (1945)
- **United States** (No materials entering public domain until 2019)
- **Life + 60 years** (1955)
- **Life + 50 years** (1965)
- **Berne Convention** (minimum: Life + 50 years, except photographs)
- **TRIPS** (minimum: Life + 50 years)
- **Life + 30 years** (1985)
- **Life + 25 years** (1990)
- **No copyright**
- **Unknown**

Scale: 1 to 315,500,000

Source: Balfour Smith, Duke University, http://www.publicdomainday.org/node/39.

TRADE SECRETS

A **trade secret** is any information not generally known to the public and that a business wishes to hold confidential. Trade secrets may include formulas, processes, patterns, designs, or other information or sets of information that could give a company an economic advantage over its competitors. Some countries permit production processes to be protected but not products. The company maintains the value of its trade secrets by not allowing them to be publicly known, and it must exercise reasonable efforts to ensure that they are not disclosed. While protection of trade secrets is not subject to expiration after a set period of time, there is no guarantee of secrecy if another party independently discovers the information. Trade secrets can be of great value, but each country deals with and protects them in its own fashion, so international companies must study and comply with the laws of each country where they may want to manufacture, create, or sell products while operating with trade secrets.

Trade secrets are the most common form of IP protection that international businesses pursue, rather than patents, trademarks, or copyrights.[24] Trade secrets have several advantages that appeal to managers: they do not require any registration process, nor do they require that the process or innovation be shared with the government. Protecting a trade secret is usually less costly than initiating a patent. Rather than hire lawyers and go through administrative processes with a foreign government, all you need to do is show you are making an effort to keep the confidential information secret. Nondisclosure agreements with employees and joint-venture partners and some control of the use of information in plants and offices are typical of this effort. There are disadvantages to trade secrets in comparison with patents, however. Once the secret is made public, anyone may use it. Others may discover it by inspecting and analyzing the product. And a trade secret may be legally discovered by another person and patented.[25]

trade secret
Any information that a business wants to hold confidential

Incoterms
Predefined commercial terms
established by the
International Chamber of
Commerce

Standardizing Laws Around the World

Many attempts have been made to standardize laws among various countries. The advantage of standardization is that business flows much better when there is a uniform set of rules. Worldwide agreement on a body of laws, known as harmonization, is progressing slowly, though, in most areas. For now, businesspeople must confront the reality of widely differing legal standards among nations.

There are some areas where progress has been made harmonizing various laws, though. The 11 **Incoterms** of the International Chamber of Commerce and its Uniform Rules and Practice on Documentary Credits are almost universally accepted. These predefined commercial terms create a common language that can be used to describe the duties and obligations of commerce. Table 6.2 lists the terms for water transport, for instance. In addition to the International Chamber of Commerce, the UN Commission on International Trade Law (UNCITRAL) works with the World Trade Organization (WTO) and specializes in commercial law reform. The International Institute for the Unification of Private Law (UNIDROIT) is an independent intergovernmental organization that studies how to modernize, harmonize, and coordinate private law, especially commercial law, between and among countries.

In the tax area, conventions, or treaties, among nations, on taxes and their payment tend to be similar, with patterns and common provisions found among them. In the antitrust area, the EU member-nations and the United States have somewhat similar laws to address competition. The European Union operates under Articles 81 and 82 of the Treaty of Rome. The U.S. approach focuses on protection of consumer welfare, whereas the EU policy has developed out of concerns for the integration of EU members. In the United States, enforcement is based on litigation; in the European Union, it is based on regulations and is relatively more bureaucratic.[26] China's Anti-Monopoly Act and Brazil's antitrust regulations have played an increasingly active role in protecting competition in those countries. There have been proposals to create worldwide agreements on antitrust, but present cooperation remains bilateral, that is, between countries. For example, agreements exist between the European Union and the United States, and the United States also has agreements with Canada, Germany, India, Japan, China, Israel, Brazil, Mexico, Chile, Australia, Peru, Colombia, South Korea, and Russia.[27]

As trade restrictions have dropped and the trade environment has become more liberalized thanks to the World Trade Organization, concerns have increased that competitive practices may function as barriers to trade. Yet every nation that has anticompetition legislation prefers its legislation to that of any other nation, so the inclination to harmonize across nations is low. Legal scholars predict that efforts made by the WTO will have to be long term and that, in the present, more informal agreements and bilateral agreements are likely to be more effective.[28]

TABLE 6.2 Examples of Incoterms

1. *FAS (free alongside ship—port of call).* The seller pays all the transportation and delivery expense up to the ship's side and clears the goods for export.

2. *CIF (cost, insurance, freight—foreign port).* The price includes the cost of the goods, insurance, and all transportation and miscellaneous charges to the named port of final destination.

3. *CFR (cost and freight—foreign port).* CFR is similar to CIF except that the buyer purchases the insurance, either because it can be obtained at a lower cost or because the buyer's government, to save foreign exchange, insists on use of a local insurance company.

Source: "Incoterms rules 2010," *International Chamber of Commerce,* 2010.

Fairly solid legal agreement exists in the area of international commercial arbitration, including enforcement of arbitration awards. If the disputed contract regulates investment from one country into another, the parties can submit it for arbitration by the International Center for Settlement of Investment Disputes at the World Bank. In addition, a number of other UN-related organizations and other worldwide associations have some harmonizing or standardizing effect on laws in their member-countries.

The UN Convention on the International Sale of Goods (CISG) provides some uniformity in international sales agreements for those parties who elect to use it. It has been signed by 89 states.[29] The UN Commission on International Trade Law (UNCITRAL) addresses accounting and bankruptcy standards and has made progress to standardize them worldwide with the Model Law on Cross-Border Insolvencies, which also served as the basis for Module 15 of the U.S. Bankruptcy Code, for example.

Standardization has made progress in areas other than the law, and hopefully, these successes set an example of the benefits of harmonization. The International Organization for Standardization (ISO), the International Telecommunications Union (ITU), and the International Electrotechnical Commission (IEC) are platforms that have successfully promoted harmonization. The IEC promotes standardization of measurement, materials, and equipment in almost every sphere of electrotechnology. The ISO recommends standards in other fields of technology. And the ITU provides global telecommunications standards. Most government and private purchasing agreements around the world demand products that meet IEC, ITU, and ISO specifications.

Some Specific National Legal Forces

Here we take a closer look at competition or antitrust law, laws that function as trade obstacles, tort and liability laws, and some miscellaneous laws, so that you'll be familiar with some of the complexities of working across national boundaries in the legal arena. The history of international business is filled with examples of companies whose managers decided they understood a foreign market well enough that they didn't need local legal help, only to encounter expensive learning experiences. For example, Disney's lack of local legal representation resulted in violations of local employment law and unenforceable construction contracts in Disneyland Paris.[30] Local counsel may be expensive, but not having local counsel is far more expensive. We begin with the way competition is treated legally, comparing the European Union and the United States.

LO 6-6
Describe the impacts of the national-level legal forces in the areas of competition, trade, tort, ethics, and accounting.

COMPETITION LAWS

Competition laws are intended to prevent inappropriately large concentrations of economic power, such as monopolies. Actions to enforce competition laws or antitrust laws usually are brought by government against business, but one business may also sue another. As suggested earlier, the EU and U.S. approaches to competition stem from different historic concerns, but the actual differences in their enforcement are narrowing. In both areas, competition laws are strictly enforced, in order to prevent price fixing, market sharing, and business monopolies. The U.S. Department of Justice is charged with enforcing U.S. antitrust laws, while in the European Union, the EU Commission is responsible for enforcing competition policy. The Commission also has the power to force EU member-governments to dismantle state monopolies that block progress toward an open, communitywide market. More than 120 countries now have antitrust laws.

A number of important differences in antitrust laws, regulations, and practices still exist between the United States and the European Union. One difference is the *per se* concept of U.S. law, under which certain activities, such as price fixing, are said to be illegal *"per se."* This means that they are illegal in and of themselves, even though no injury or damage results from them. The EU Treaty of Rome articles dealing with restrictive trade practices do not contain this per se illegality concept of U.S. antitrust law. The result is that a cartel that allows

competition laws
Another term for antitrust law, used by the European Union and other countries

antitrust laws
Laws that prevent inappropriately large concentrations of power and its abuse through price fixing, market sharing, and monopolies

consumers a fair share of the benefits is legally acceptable in the European Union, but not in the United States. Also, the European Union allows market dominance, unless it is misused to damage competitors or harm consumers. The per se concept illustrates the U.S. focus is on the potential impact of the business deal on the consumer, while the EU's focus is more on the industry's competitive structure and how businesses compete. So the United States looks to consumers first, while the European Union pays attention to rivals' objections. Both approaches result in benefit to the consumer.

In Japan, antitrust legislation was introduced by the United States during its occupation after World War II. This legislation, the Japanese Anti-Monopoly Law, was modeled on U.S. antitrust law and did not harmonize well with the existing cooperative *zaibatsu* (family-based financial and business conglomerates) the Japanese government had established. In fact, the Japanese approach to a rational development of the economy regarded antitrust measures as an impediment. However, with increasing foreign presence, Japanese companies have incorporated antitrust thinking into their strategies.

Because the Japanese culture so values cooperation, this is at times a challenge, especially when it comes to cartels, or companies such as Mitsubishi, which have interlocking business relationships through shareholding and a bank at the center.[31] Japan's Fair Trade Commission (FTC), whose responsibility is to enforce antitrust laws, is viewed as one of the weakest bodies in Japanese government, easily influenced by other powerful ministries such as finance and international trade and industry (MITI), which have vested interests in ensuring that Japan's traditional, collaborative ways of doing business prevail. Most of the FTC's targets are small, foreign, or weak; when it has investigated powerful industries such as domestic cars, car parts, and construction, it has punished them with "recommendations." The recommendations usually are accepted by the targeted company. If not, hearings follow, and then directives. However, Japanese courts lack the power to hold defendants in contempt for failure to comply with the FTC's cease and desist orders, because the FTC operates separately from the court system, unlike in the European Union and the United States.[32]

A major difference between U.S. and Japanese trust-busting is who initiates it. In the United States, 90 percent of the complaints are brought by private parties, while in Japan, a private antitrust action can be brought only if the FTC has investigated the case first. Because of Japan's limited discovery laws,[33] that is, laws requiring the sharing of evidence between the prosecution and the defense, the only way the FTC can obtain information about a firm is to raid it. As a result, the FTC won't make a move unless it is sure the laws are being broken. It is almost impossible to be sure of that without information. Yet, once it decides to raid, the FTC acts on its own authority; it does not require a warrant.

The U.S. government often attempts to enforce its antitrust laws extraterritorially. For example, a grand jury in Washington, DC, indicted three foreign-owned ocean shipping groups on charges of fixing prices without getting approval from the U.S. Federal Maritime Commission. The other governments, European and Japanese, protested bitterly, arguing (1) that shipping is international by definition, so the United States has no right to act unilaterally, and (2) that the alleged offenses were both legal and ethical practices outside the United States. The U.S. Supreme Court has repeatedly permitted overseas application of U.S. antitrust laws, although recent court decisions appear to have curtailed the potential of foreign plaintiffs to use U.S. courts in order to seek relief.[34] U.S. antitrust laws also provide for both civil and criminal penalties, and a U.S. federal court of appeals ruled that criminal antitrust laws apply to foreign companies even if the conspiracy took place outside the United States.

The EU Commission has increasingly sought enforcement of its competition policy abroad when there is an effect on commerce within the European Union. In 2017, the EU Commission issued a record $2.7 billion fine against Google for giving unfair preference to some of its own online services ahead of those of its competitors. "In Europe, companies must compete on the merits regardless if they are European or not," said the EU's antitrust chief, Margrethe Vestager. "What Google has done is illegal under E.U. antitrust rules."[35] In 2018, the European Union fined Google another record amount, this time $5.1 billion, for abuse of power in the mobile phone market.[36]

The Chinese Anti-Monopoly Act has recently received attention for slow, bureaucratic approval of international mergers and deal making that supports local businesses rather than reduces competition. Merger approvals are triggered by revenue thresholds within the approving countries. In 2018, despite receiving approvals from antitrust authorities in the United States and the European Union, chipmaker Qualcomm abandoned its $38 billion bid for rival chipmaker NXP of the Netherlands after the Chinese government's anti-monopoly authorities failed to grant approval for the deal.[37] China's approval was necessary because both companies conducted substantial amounts of business in China, and this approval was not received prior to the deadline for the merger. As a result of the termination, Qualcomm had to pay a $2 billion termination fee to NXP.

TRADE OBSTACLES

Trade obstacles are not only political and financial but legal as well. Every country has laws on these subjects. The stated purpose of a tariff is to raise revenue for the government, but it may serve the additional objective of keeping certain goods out of a country. Quotas limit the amount or source of imports.

There are many other forms of protection or obstacles to trade in national laws. Some are health or packaging requirements. Others deal with language, such as the mandatory use of French on labels and in advertising, manuals, warranties, and so forth, for goods sold in France, including websites hosted on servers that physically reside in France. When Vietnamese catfish imports flooded the U.S. market, lawyers for the U.S. catfish industry successfully argued that the Vietnamese product was not catfish but a different family of fish. After this failed to stop the imports, they reversed themselves and alleged that these catfish were being "dumped" on the U.S. market.[38] In many countries, U.S. and EU exports may encounter weak patent or trademark protection, high tariffs, quarantine periods, and a variety of other legal or regulatory obstacles. Table 6.3 provides a sampling of trade barriers.

TABLE 6.3 Examples of Tariffs and Other Trade Barriers, 2018

Product	Destination	Barrier
U.S. rice	Japan	Government-managed rice imports allocate U.S. rice almost exclusively to nonconsumer use (for industrial food processing or re-export as food aid) and without identifying it as U.S. rice
Beef, citrus, dairy		Tariffs: beef (38.5 percent), citrus (32 percent on oranges in winter months), and dairy (22.4 percent to 40 percent on various types of cheese)
New autos and motorcycles	India	Tariff: is 60 to 100 percent for imported vehicles
Lentils and chickpeas		Tariff: raised from 0 to 30 percent
Websites and website-based trade and commerce	China	Blocks market access for 12 of the top 30 global sites and up to 3,000 sites in total
Cloud computing services		Effectively prohibits use of leased lines and VPNs for cross-border provision of cloud computing services
Data storage and processing	Nigeria	Requires foreign businesses involved in international data storage and processing services to instead host and store within Nigeria all government data and data on Nigerian citizens
U.S. poultry and pork	Russia	Import prohibition

Source: Office of U.S. Trade Representative, *2018 National Trade Estimate Report on Foreign Trade Barriers*, httsp://www.ustr.gov, accessed October 12, 2018.

The United States has many options in dealing with trade obstacles abroad. It can impose retaliatory barriers on products from countries imposing barriers against U.S. goods. It sometimes uses tariffs and quotas. It also uses a form of quota called voluntary restraint agreements (VRAs) or voluntary export restraints (VERs). *Voluntary* is not quite accurate because these barriers are imposed by the U.S. government on the exporting countries. The inevitable result is higher costs to U.S. consumers because exporters send only the higher-priced top of their lines and importers charge more for scarcer products. The United States is not the only country that imposes VRAs and VERs on trading partners—far from it. Japan, Canada, EU countries, and many others require that countries exporting to them "voluntarily" limit the number or value of goods exported.

TORT LAW

tort
An injury inflicted on another person, either intentionally or negligently

Torts are injuries inflicted on another person, either intentionally or negligently. Tort cases in the United States may result in large monetary awards. Other countries restrict the amount of money that can be obtained in tort actions.

product liability
A standard that holds a company and its officers and directors liable and possibly subject to fines or imprisonment when their product causes death, injury, or damage

One important area of torts, especially in the international arena, is product liability. Product liability laws hold a company and its officers and directors liable and possibly subject to fines or imprisonment when its product causes injury, damage, or death. Such liability for faulty or dangerous products was a growth area for the U.S. legal profession beginning in the 1960s. Liability insurance premiums soared, and there were concerns that smaller, weaker manufacturing companies could not survive. In the 1980s, that boom spread to Europe and elsewhere. As foreign firms buy or build U.S. plants, they are being challenged by the same liability and insurance problems which U.S. companies have long faced.[39]

strict liability
A standard that holds the designer or manufacturer liable for damages caused by a product without the need for a plaintiff to prove negligence in the product's design or manufacture

Manufacturers of products are often held to a standard of strict liability, which makes the designer/manufacturer liable for damages caused by a product without the need for a plaintiff to prove negligence in the product's design or manufacture. There are several reasons to believe the impact of strict liability on product designers and manufacturers in Europe and Japan will not be as heavy or severe as it is in the United States. The European Union allows companies to use "state-of-the-art" or "developmental risks" defenses, which allow the designer/manufacturer to show that at the time of design or manufacture, the most modern, latest-known technology was used. EU countries also have the option to cap damages. In contrast, in the United States, product liability cases are heard by juries that can award plaintiffs actual damages plus punitive damages. As the name indicates, punitive damages have the purpose of punishing the defendant, and if the plaintiff has been seriously injured or the jury's sympathy can be otherwise aroused, it may award millions of dollars to "teach the defendant a lesson." Outside the United States, judges, not juries, hear product liability cases. Judges are less prone to emotional reactions than juries are, and even if the judge is sympathetic toward a plaintiff, punitive damages are not awarded by non-U.S. courts.

Punitive damage awards by U.S. courts have caused some foreign firms to keep their products out of the United States. For instance, Axminster Electronics, a British firm whose devices help prevent crib death by monitoring a baby's breathing, did not sell in the United States because it could not secure product liability insurance. Every drug company knows that if a person in the United States uses a drug and subsequently gets ill, there is a chance a jury somewhere in the country may impose liability on the manufacturer and order it to pay damages.

The Japanese law on product liability requires that the plaintiff prove design or manufacturing negligence, which is difficult with complex, high-tech devices. The plaintiffs' difficulties are increased by the fact that, as we've seen, discovery is limited in Japan.

In the United States, but not elsewhere, lawyers take many cases on a contingency-fee basis, whereby they charge the plaintiff no fee to begin representation and action in a product liability case. The lawyer is paid only when the defendant settles or loses in a trial, but then the fee is relatively large, running between one-third and one-half of the settlement or award. Another difference is that outside the United States, when the defendant wins a lawsuit, the plaintiff is often called upon to pay all the defendant's legal fees and other costs caused by the plaintiff's action.

The WTO and U.S. Dolphin-Safe Tuna Labeling: A Threat to National Sovereignty?

Dolphin-safe labeling can be used by sellers of canned tuna if they meet certain criteria in their fishing of tuna. In 2011, a World Trade Organization panel ruled that these long-standing "dolphin-safe" labeling requirements violated international trade rules by being more restrictive of trade than necessary for achieving dolphin-protection objectives. In this first case examining the compatibility of voluntary product labeling with the WTO agreement, acceptance of which is essentially the condition of membership, the finding against the United States could establish an important precedent for informational labeling efforts worldwide.

First, a bit of background on the case. In 1959, fishermen in the Pacific Ocean region stretching from Southern California to South America began using purse-seine fishing methods to harvest tuna. *Purse seining* sends out a mile or so wall of netting that encircles entire schools of fish, its bottom is pulled closed like a drawstring purse, and everything inside the net is pulled into the boat to be processed. Dolphins in this part of the Pacific tend to swim in schools above large schools of tuna, so fishing fleets seek out dolphins and encircle them with nets in order to capture the tuna that swim below.

While purse seining is successful in netting tuna, its consequences for dolphins can be catastrophic. Between 1959 and 1972, millions of dolphins were trapped in nets and drowned, and dolphin populations plummeted. In 1972, Congress passed the Marine Mammal Protection Act (MMPA), which prohibited the use by U.S. tuna fishermen of fishing methods that would cause dolphin deaths. In 1988, the MMPA was amended to ban tuna imports from nations whose fishing fleets caught tuna using purse-seine nets. In 1990, Congress passed the Dolphin Protection Consumer Information Act, creating the "dolphin-safe" label. Tuna caught with purse-seine nets could not be labeled dolphin-safe in the United States. These actions dramatically reduced dolphin deaths.

"Dolphin-safe" labeling is voluntary, and tuna harvested with purse-seine methods can be sold legally in the United States. The WTO ruled, though, that "dolphin-safe" was a technical regulation rather than a standard. The WTO asserted that anything impeding nonlabeled tuna's "marketing opportunities in the United States" represented a barrier to trade and that "dolphin-safe" labeling violated Article 2.2 of the WTO agreement, which prohibits technical regulations that are "more trade-restrictive than necessary to fulfill a legitimate objective." Therefore, the WTO ruled that the United States must discontinue the "dolphin-safe" labeling program or face WTO sanctions.

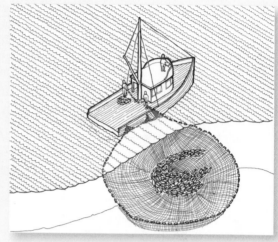

Source: Library of Congress [HAER AK,22-KAKE].

Source: C. Ortiz Rojas/NOAA's Fisheries Collection/NOAA.

©Scott J. Ferrell/CQ-Roll Call Group/Getty Images.

The United States appealed the WTO panel's ruling in 2012 and subsequently modified certain dolphin-safe labeling requirements to comply with WTO rulings and recommendations. Mexico challenged these changes as inadequate to eliminate the discrimination against their tuna fishing industry. In early 2017, the WTO authorized Mexico to impose $163 million annually in countermeasures against the United States, a decision that the United States appealed. In October 2017, the WTO ruled in favor of the United States and said that American regulations were consistent with international obligations and the conservation of dolphins.

In this instance, the WTO ultimately sided with the United States. However, in the event of a contrary ruling, ultimately there would be few options for the United States if the original WTO decision was upheld. This is because the United States agreed to the WTO treaty and, based on Article VI of the U.S. Constitution, this means that the WTO agreement "shall be the Supreme Law of the Land; and the Judges in every State shall be bound thereby."

Some see the WTO process on the tuna controversy as evidence that trade agreements can erode national policies enacted on the basis of public interest and welfare. Several observers have expressed concern that an adverse WTO ruling could create a precedent that could be extended to a range of other public policy issues, such as environmental protection of habitats, water, and air, or food chain safety.

Critical Thinking Questions

1. Do you think the WTO should be able to prohibit labeling that provides information of potential value to consumers? Why or why not?
2. Should the WTO ensure that the science behind local laws and regulations is sound and not a cover for protectionism? If so, how could it do so?
3. Some people have argued that member-nations give up national sovereignty rights by joining the WTO and allowing it to make decisions that are not in the best interest of a particular nation, especially since many WTO meetings are not open to the public. Do you agree with this interpretation and, if so, what could be done to address the situation?

Sources: Vicki Needham, "US Wins Trade Case over 'Dolphin Safe' Tuna Labeling," *The Hill*, October 26, 2017; "United States—Measures Concerning the Importation, Marketing and Sale of Tuna and Tuna Products," *World Trade Organization*, March 14, 2018; "Technical Information on Technical Barriers to Trade," *World Trade Organization*, 2018; "Tuna Purse Seining," *Food and Agriculture Organization of the United Nations*, 2018; "U.S. Constitution—Article 6," *Find Law*, 2018; Tom Miles and Krista Hughes, "WTO Rules Against U.S. Dolphin-Safe Canned Tuna Labels," *Scientific American*, 2018; and Loraine Mitchell, "Dolphin-Safe Tuna Labeling," *Economics of Food Labeling*, 2018.

MISCELLANEOUS LAWS

People working abroad must be alert to avoid falling afoul of local laws and police, army, or government officials. Legal penalties may be harsh. Some examples make the point.

- A British subject with a history of serious mental health problems was executed in China for carrying heroin into China, despite the efforts of the British government.[40]
- Saudi Arabia may strictly enforce sanctions against importing or drinking alcohol and wearing revealing clothing.
- Foreigners in Japan who walk out of their homes without their alien registration cards (*gaikakujin toroku*) can be arrested, as happened to one man while he was carrying out the garbage.
- An Australian writer was sentenced in Thailand to three years in jail for writing a novel that insulted the crown prince. Seven copies had been sold.[41]
- Caning as a punishment, sometimes conducted in public, is still used in various nations, including Malaysia, Singapore, Brunei, Saudi Arabia, and Sudan, among others. Offenses subject to caning include overstaying one's visa, being caught in bed with someone of the same gender, or being a woman found to be dressing "indecently."[42]

The law of the home country plays no role in a foreigner's arrest, so make an effort to know the local laws. In many majority Muslim nations, for example, alcohol is strictly forbidden. Violators may face a range of consequences, including being flogged, imprisoned, or deported.

We now look at two U.S. laws that influence the conduct of international business significantly, the Foreign Corrupt Practices Act and accounting law.

FOREIGN CORRUPT PRACTICES ACT

During the 1970s, revelations of questionable or dubious payments by U.S. companies to foreign officials rocked governments in the Netherlands and Japan. Congress considered corporate bribery bad business and unnecessary. In response to these corruption scandals, it passed the Foreign Corrupt Practices Act (FCPA). Key provisions of the act prohibit bribery of foreign officials and set requirements for transparency of accounting transactions. The FCPA makes it unlawful to bribe foreign government officials to obtain or retain business. Facilitating payments for routine government actions such as visa issuance, import approvals, and the processing of government papers are permissible under the FCPA, however.

There's no question that the intent of FCPA is positive. Yet, it does present U.S. businesses with some challenges. One is that there are a number of uncertainties about the terms used in the FCPA. According to the FCPA's drafters, for instance, the act does not outlaw *grease*, which refers to facilitating payments made solely to expedite nondiscretionary official actions like customs clearance. However, the law makes no clear distinction between supposedly legal grease payments and illegal bribes. The act is also very broad in defining what constitutes a foreign official, and the government's relevant criterion for a bribe is not the amount but rather the intent of the payment.

The accounting standards required by the FCPA have raised questions about how far management must go to learn whether any employees, subsidiaries, or agents may have violated the act. Even if management were unaware of an illegal payment, it could be in violation if it had reason to know or could be expected to know that some portion of a payment abroad might be used as a bribe.

The Department of Justice (DOJ) and the Securities and Exchange Commission (SEC) often pursue companies in situations that might encourage corruption, in a process called *sweeping*. When a company is reported to have engaged in corruption, DOJ and SEC will look closely at it and at other companies in the industry and related industries, and the travel and expense claims of their agents. The SEC even created a specialized FCPA unit in 2010 to enhance enforcement, particularly in cases of bribery.[43]

In 2018, Panasonic of Japan paid over $143 million in penalties due to its U.S. subsidiary offering a consulting position to an official of a state-owned airline to help in obtaining contracts with that airline.[44] Also in 2018, Dun & Bradstreet Corporation agreed to over $9 million in penalties to resolve improper payments made in violation of the FCPA by two subsidiaries in China.[45] Prioritization of enforcement efforts can be expected to produce a high level of FCPA prosecutions and fines in the future.[46]

When the FCPA was passed, critics believed it would harm U.S. companies' competitiveness abroad because it would demand of them a higher standard of behavior than was common in the competitive environment. Congress decided the potential economic damage to exports would be minimal and that the only companies hurt would be those whose sole means of competing was through the payment of bribes. The United States actively lobbied the international community to introduce similar legislation, which resulted in the OECD Convention on Bribery in 1997. The FCPA was amended in 1998 to incorporate antibribery conventions developed by the OECD.

You may wonder whether U.S. laws on bribery place U.S. businesses at a disadvantage in international competition. The FCPA, along with the OECD convention, EU legislation, UK legislation, and a UN initiative, has certainly brought a discussion of bribery and transparency out into the open. Such discussions were further stimulated by the Asian financial crisis of 1997, one of the apparent causes of which was a lack of transparency in financial dealings. Having an international reputation for transparency and integrity, and being perceived as "above board," have become increasingly important for global companies. With integrity, there is no invisible third party (the briber) in the transaction, the value of whose impact cannot be assessed. With an ethical approach, you know where your dollars are going and you can measure their impact. Unfortunately, we tend to be more aware of companies with unethical approaches, because their violations make them notable, but many ethical companies operate internationally, focused on keeping their

Foreign Corrupt Practices Act (FCPA)
U.S. law that prohibits payments to foreign government officials in order to receive special treatment

operations transparent and doing what is right. Companies from around the world recognized in 2018 for their ethical business approach by the Ethisphere Institute, a leader in setting the standards of ethical business practice, include Accenture, Allstate, Anthem, CBRE, Colgate-Palmolive, T-Mobile, Dell, GE, Intel, LinkedIn, Microsoft, Natura, Nokia, Radisson, Starbucks, Tata Steel, Volvo, and Wipro, among others.[47]

Among the most noteworthy of new agreements on bribery is the UN Convention against Corruption (UNCAC) and the United Kingdom Bribery Act. The UNCAC has been signed by 186 countries as well as the European Union, as of 2018.[48] It goes beyond bribery to address a broader range of corruption, such as general abuse of power and trading in official influence, as well as the recovery of assets from officials accused or convicted of engaging in corruption.

In 2011, the United Kingdom Bribery Act came into force, which includes penalties for corporate failure to prevent bribery. The person engaging in a bribe does not need to be British and the act of bribery does not need to have occurred in the United Kingdom. A corporation can be charged under this law as long as it engages in "a business or part of a business" in the United Kingdom, suggesting that this law applies extraterritorially.[49] In 2017, Kenya adopted legislation modeled after the U.K.'s Bribery Act and with severe penalties, to help counter endemic corruption in that nation.[50]

Finally, Transparency International's Corruption Perception Index is not formally connected to U.S. law, but it is published periodically and assesses the likelihood that firms from industrialized nations will engage in bribery abroad. It is developed through survey data obtained from government and corporate managers working internationally and focuses on countries rather than businesses. New Zealand received the first-place ranking in 2017, with Denmark second and Finland, Norway, and Switzerland tied for third. The Scandinavians set an example here! You can see all of the current rankings and raw scores at https://www.transparency.org/news/feature/corruption_perceptions_index_2017. Table 6.4 summarizes selected rankings of Transparency International's index. The fluctuation in the rankings suggests that businesses and national governments worldwide are placing more value on ethical business behavior and developing improved ways to monitor it, and changes in the political environment influence levels of transparency. One challenge of increasing ethical behavior is that, although we consider ethics at the national or business levels, ethical behavior actually occurs at the level of the individual manager, who in the international context often has a great deal of discretion. Training in the value of ethical, transparent approaches to doing business is critical.

ACCOUNTING LAW

Investor confidence in the integrity of financial reporting and corporate governance has been shaken by financial scandals worldwide. This crisis of confidence has substantially damaged the economic prospects of numerous companies, employees, retirees, customers, suppliers, and other stakeholders.

U.S. accounting practice is guided by the Securities and Exchange Commission (SEC) and the Financial Accounting Standards Board (FASB) and follows standards known as generally accepted accounting principles (GAAP), while most other countries, including those in the European Union, follow standards issued by the International Accounting Standards Board (IASB) known as the International Financial Reporting Standards (IFRS). These standards differ in many aspects, and a number of projects intended to create convergence between them were slated for completion in 2015, but this deadline has been moved back. For example, converged standards for revenue recognition were scheduled for calendar year-end 2018, and for 2019 for nonpublic companies following GAAP. About 90 nations have conformed fully to IFRS, while in the United States, full implementation is only permitted for private firms. Japan allows voluntary adoption of IFRS, but without a mandatory date for transition, and China has stated that convergence will occur, but at some future date.

As a response to corporate and accounting scandals in the early 2000s, including those implicating Tyco, Enron, and WorldCom, Congress passed the Sarbanes-Oxley Act (SOX) in 2002. This effort to increase ethical behavior requires higher standards

TABLE 6.4 Rankings on Corruption Perception Index for Selected Countries, 2002–2017

Country	2002	2006	2008	2013	2017
Singapore	9	12	9	5	6
Switzerland	2	1	3	7	3
Netherlands	6	8	3	8	8
Canada	5	5	1	9	8
Australia	1	3	8	9	13
Germany	9	7	5	12	12
United Kingdom	8	6	5	14	8
Belgium	6	9	1	15	16
Hong Kong	15	18	13	15	13
Japan	13	11	5	18	20
United States	13	9	9	19	16
France	12	15	9	22	23
Taiwan	19	26	14	36	29
Spain	11	13	12	40	42
Italy	17	20	17	43	54
South Korea	18	21	14	46	51
South Africa	n.a.	24	14	72	71
Brazil	n.a.	23	17	72	96
China	20	29	21	80	77
India	n.a.	30	19	94	81
Mexico	n.a.	17	20	106	135
Russia	21	28	22	127	135

Note: n.a. = data not reported.

Sources: "Corruption Perceptions Index 2017," *Transparency International*, February 21, 2018; "Corruption Perceptions Index 2008," *Transparency International*, September 22, 2008; "Corruption Perceptions Index 2006," *Transparency International*, November 6, 2006; and "Corruption Perceptions Index 2002," *Transparency International*, August 04, 2002.

for public company boards, their management, and their accounting firms that list in the United States, whether they are domestic or international. SOX holds corporate officers personally responsible for the accuracy of company filings. Studies show that although businesses continue to criticize SOX, primarily for its implementation costs, markets have benefited from the increased information available to potential investors. Legislators also exempted smaller companies, for whom the costs were especially burdensome.[51]

Rory Burdick: Career Launch in International

Rory Burdick's advice: "Take risks and prepare!"
Courtesy of Rory Burdick.

Rory Burdick graduated from California Polytechnic State University with a business major and economics minor, both with an international concentration. Here's a description of his transition into international work.

After completing my courses at Cal Poly, I joined a group of friends who were traveling to South Africa from East Asia. I went on to travel through London, Amsterdam, Berlin, and Prague. Then I returned to San Francisco to work in various technology start-ups. At this point for me, it was all about building experience and cash flow. I chose start-ups because they offered more interesting work sooner for a new hire.

One start-up that hired me initially for weekend work had a customer base that grew enough to require 24/7 customer support. Management decided to implement "follow-the-sun" coverage across the United States, Europe, India, and China. Because I would commit to a demanding 24-hour schedule, I got the assignment, my first international work experience, of managing the training of these offshore support groups. During this project, I learned how to address cultural, communication, and time zone issues, drawing on what I learned in international business classes and by trial and error.

I heard about an opportunity to interview for a position at Google, where I was known from my start-up training work. As a Google employee, I joined a small global team and traveled on assignment to Atlanta, New York, and Frankfurt. A director visiting my group in Mountain View mentioned he was looking for someone to take a position in Brazil. I expressed interest and arranged an interview with the hiring manager, which led to a six-month assignment in São Paulo that included a short assignment in Buenos Aires.

At Google, I worked hard to establish myself with local management as an ambitious self-starter who could be trusted with difficult projects where individual contributors would have minimal support from management. I was asked to travel to locations that were short-handed or needed project-specific burst labor. My travels enabled me to interact with employees from different locations around the world. This experience allowed me to make a case for a permanent assignment in Brazil.

Before I left for Brazil, I talked with people with experience in South America, Americans like me and Brazilians. These informational interviews helped me learn about the culture of Brazil, personal safety, cost of living, and what the city of São Paulo had to offer. All of them had insightful comments, but nothing would fully prepare me for my assignment.

My time in Brazil was the most challenging and most rewarding experience of my life. São Paulo has one of the most ethnically diverse populations in the world, and because of this, I blended in with everyone else. I inherited a project that was behind schedule and suffered from vendor, contractor, and internal customer issues. I had to find solutions quickly despite my language shortcomings— Spanish and a bit of Portuguese, while maintaining a positive relationship with our Brazilian business partners. I managed this by closely watching the cultural norms of those around me and maintaining a positive attitude with a quiet confidence. By demonstrating my desire to perform well and my interest in establishing positive relationships, I encouraged my Brazilian counterparts to work with me to find mutually beneficial solutions to our shared challenges.

Relocating to a foreign country for employment is exciting and overwhelming, an experience that is difficult for anyone to prepare for fully. While I would definitely recommend talking to people and reading about the culture and history of the country you will be visiting, even more important is learning the language and maintaining a positive attitude. My experience has been that people are curious about and outgoing toward visitors who show interest in learning about them. The abler you are to communicate with people, the more they will tell you about their culture, their country, and themselves. What I have learned in Brazil, interacting with people on a personal level, pales in comparison to everything I learned from my studies. Take the risk and prepare as you can and be excited about learning!

Source: Rory Burdick.

SUMMARY

LO 6-1
Describe the three types of legal systems.

The three types of legal systems are civil, common, and religious. Civil law is based on a collection of codes, and, hence, bureaucratic. The basis of common law (in the United States and the United Kingdom) is precedent and interpretation, and it tends to be complex and evolving. The basis of religious law is a religious text, such as the Qur'an and collected religious documents, as in Saudi Arabia.

LO 6-2
Describe the rule of law and its sources.

The rule of law exists when law rather than a political dictatorship or a powerful elite is the basis for a country's legal system. When a country's legal system is based on the rule of law, foreign investment is encouraged because investors know their interests will be protected. Countries that follow the rule of law tend to protect the human rights of local peoples, an increasing concern of global companies. Sources of law include the domestic laws of nations and international treaties developed through the efforts of organizations such as the United Nations and World Trade Organization (WTO). Some of the terms for these agreements are conventions, covenants, compacts, and protocols. There is also customary international law, such as the proscription on genocide.

LO 6-3
Discuss the general legal concerns in global business.

Three areas of the law of special concern to international business, because they affect activities in an international setting and not in a domestic setting, are extraterritoriality, performance of contracts, and litigation. A nation may attempt to apply its law extraterritorially, to citizens, nonresidents, and foreigners. Performance of contracts in an international setting becomes complex in the case of disputes because there is no ready resolution for them. International litigation, a legal proceeding conducted to determine and enforce particular legal rights, can be complicated and expensive. In addition to the trial itself, most lawsuits in the United States entail lengthy pretrial activities, including a process called *discovery*.

LO 6-4
Identify methods to protect intellectual property.

Rights to intellectual property can be protected by patents, trademarks, trade names, copyrights, and trade secrets, depending on the jurisdiction. A patent gives the inventor of a product or process the exclusive right to manufacture, exploit, use, and sell that invention or process. A trademark—a shape, color, design, phrase, abbreviation, or sound—can be used to designate and differentiate products. A trade name is a name used to designate and differentiate products. Finally, a trade secret is any information that a business wants to hold confidential. The UN's World Intellectual Property Organization (WIPO) was created to administer international property treaties, as was TRIPS, a WTO agency with a similar purpose.

LO 6-5
Discuss the standardization of laws among nations.

Attempts by nations to standardize their laws, especially those that affect trade, are underway, but they are progressing slowly. At present, there are widely differing legal standards among countries. There has been some progress, though, in specific areas. The Incoterms of the International Chamber of Commerce standardize commercial terminology; the UN Commission on Trade Law provides some agreement on bankruptcy and accounting standards; the UN Convention on the International Sale of Goods standardizes commercial procedures and duties, and the WTO has developed a set of standard trade practices. Tax treaties exist to harmonize tax laws. Competition law has evolved with differences, but also many similarities. There are also efforts to standardize private law, especially in the commercial area.

LO 6-6
Describe the impacts of the national-level legal forces in the areas of competition, trade, tort, ethics, and accounting.

National-level legal forces can have a significant impact on the practice of business. Competition laws are intended to prevent inappropriately large concentrations of economic power and impact business directly, especially in the areas of price fixing, market sharing, and business monopolies. Differences in these laws exist among countries. For example, the U.S. antitrust laws use the concept of *per se*: there is no need to show harm; the practice itself is illegal.

Trade obstacles often are the result of national laws such as tariffs, quotas, and health and packaging requirements. All of these laws function as barriers to trade.

Tort law in the United States, especially in the area of product liability, greatly concerns businesses due to the large jury-based awards tort actions can yield, based on the concept of strict liability.

The FCPA, along with the OECD convention, EU legislation, UK legislation, and a UN initiative, have brought a discussion of bribery and transparency out into the open.

This has had an impact on international business transparency.

Accounting practices also impact business practice. U.S. accounting practice is guided by the Securities and Exchange Commission (SEC) and the Financial Accounting Standards Board (FASB) and follows standards known as generally accepted accounting principles (GAAP), while most other countries, including those in the European Union, follow standards issued by the International Accounting Standards Board (IASB) known as the International Financial Reporting Standards (IFRS). These standards differ in many aspects, and a number of projects intended to create convergence between them were slated for completion several years ago, but this date has been moved forward.

KEY TERMS

antitrust laws 169
arbitration 160
competition laws 169
copyright 166
extraterritorial application of laws 159
Foreign Corrupt Practices Act
    (FCPA) 175

Incoterms 168
intellectual property (IP) 163
litigation 162
patent 163
private international law 159
product liability 172
public international law 159

strict liability 172
tort 172
trademark 165
trade name 166
trade secret 167
treaty 159

CRITICAL THINKING QUESTIONS

1. How might knowing a country's type of legal system (civil, common, religious) be helpful?

2. Does the concept of the rule of law (not the laws themselves) have the same meaning in different countries?

3. Since there is no international police or military force to back up international law, does it have any power? Why or why not?

4. What objections could other countries have to the extraterritorial application by one country of its laws in territories beyond its borders?

5. Would you consider plagiarism an intellectual property right violation? Explain your reasoning.

6. Does national culture influence the meaning of intellectual property? That is, in a culture where community is stressed, rather than the individual, would you expect intellectual property rights to

be defined differently than in a culture where individualism is strong?

7. You are a human resource manager for a U.S. company working in Saudi Arabia, with Saudi and American employees. All U.S. companies are required to follow U.S. Equal Employment Opportunity law. In Saudi Arabia, women usually do not work in public, and the genders do not mix in public. How would you explain to your Saudi employees that you have to follow U.S. law?

8. Why do understandings of appropriate limits to competition differ among nations?

9. Is product liability a legal concept that is standardized across nations?

10. Why would accounting law convergence across nations be a valuable achievement?

globalEDGE RESEARCH TASK   http://globalEDGE.msu.edu/

Use the globalEDGE website (http://globalEDGE.msu .edu/) to complete the following exercises:

1. Your company manufactures digital gauges for different industries and recently chose China as the next international market to enter. One of your friends who works at another company that already exports to China mentioned the "China Compulsory Certification (CCC Mark)" your company needs to acquire in order to export your products. Review the "Export Tutorials" section in the "Reference Desk" on globalEDGE and read about the CCC Mark on the external link provided. Prepare a summary for your management to explain what CCC Mark is about and what the application process is.

2. The Aerospace company you work for is trying to decide between Italy and Czech Republic (Czechia) as the new manufacturing location and you want to choose the locations that will provide the best protection for your company's intellectual property. Review the "Aerospace Industry Market Potential Index" on globalEDGE and visit the source used for the "intellectual property rights protection" measure. Compare the two countries on this new page and prepare a briefing about your decision and all the dimensions compared for these two countries. Anything that surprises you?

MINICASE

DETERMINING COUNTRY OF JURISDICTION FOR INTERNATIONAL BUSINESS DISPUTES

A California-based company is expanding quickly and has just made its first large export sale. All its sales and procurement contracts up to now have contained a clause providing that if any disputes arise under the contract, they will be settled under California law and that any litigation will be in California courts.

The new foreign customer, who is Italian, objects to these all-California solutions. She says she is buying and paying for a large volume of the products, so before finalizing the sales contract she wants the California company to compromise and allow Italian law and courts to govern and handle any disputes.

Critical Thinking Questions

1. You are the CEO of the California company, and you very much want this large export order. You are pleased with the service your law firm has provided, but you know it has no international experience. What are the various forms of dispute resolution available to your California company? What are the advantages and disadvantages of each for your company?

2. You must decide whether to use only California law for settling litigation or to allow the foreign customer's home nation as the venue for litigation. Would your decision be different if the customer were from China? From Russia? From the United Kingdom? Why or why not?

NOTES

1. Quote by United States Senator James William Fulbright.

2. "Chapter 63a: Legal Systems," *The News Manual*, http://www. thenewsmanual.net, accessed October 12, 2018.

3. William Weightman, "China's Progress on Intellectual Property Rights (Yes, Really)," *The Diplomat*, https://thediplomat.com, accessed October 12, 2018.

4. Quote by United States Senator James William Fulbright.

5. Dennis F. Berger, "IP Enforcement in China," posted at http:// www.eigerlaw.com, March 11, 2014; Erick Robinson, "Why You Should Protect and Enforce Your IP in China," *IPStars*, https://www.ipstars.

com, accessed October 12, 2018; Leighton Cassidy, Diana Sternfeld, and Heidi Hurdle, "Protection and Enforcement of IP Rights in China: Some Progress?" *Fieldfisher*, https://intellectualpropertyblog. com, accessed October 12, 2018; Kristina Sepetys, and Alan Cox, "Intellectual Property Rights Protection in China: Trends in Litigation and Economic Damages," *NERA Economic Consulting*, https://www. nera.com, accessed October 12, 2018.

6. World Bank, "Economy Rankings," *Doing Business: Measuring Business Regulations*, http://www.doingbusiness.org, accessed October 12, 2018.

7. World Bank, "Worldwide Governance Indicators," http://info.worldbank.org, accessed October 12, 2018.

8. For summaries of these and other opinions, see Supreme Court of the United States Blog, http://www.scotusblog.com, accessed October 12, 2018.

9. Kathy Chu, "China Criticizes Judge's Ruling Suspending Auditors," *The Wall Street Journal*, January 27, 2014, C3l; Raymond Doherty, "SEC Fines Big Four in China $2M," *Economia*, https://economia.icaew.com, accessed October 12, 2018; and Kara Scannell, "Big Four Auditors Face Crackdown on Global Operations," *Financial Times*, https://www.ft.com, accessed October 12, 2018.

10. International Chamber of Commerce, "Court Members," https://iccwbo.org, accessed October 12, 2018.

11. WIPO Arbitration and Mediation Center, "Victoria's Secret Stores Brand Management, Inc. v. Gillian Dowling, Gillian's Beauty Clinic, Case No. DIE2017-0002," http://www.wipo.int, accessed October 12, 2018.

12 M. Galanter, "Law's Elusive Promise: Learning from Bhopal," Module 9 in *Transnational Legal Processes: Globalization and Power Disparities*, ed. M. Likosy, Cambridge, UK: Cambridge University Press, 2002.

13. WIPO, "Member States," http://www.wipo.int, accessed October 12, 2018.

14. European Patent Office, "FAQ—Patent & IP Basics," https://www.epo.org, accessed October 12, 2018.

15. The U.S. Patent and Trademark Office, "General Information Concerning Patents," https://www.uspto.gov, accessed October 12, 2018.

16. Brian Farkas, "Types of Patents Available under U.S. Law," https://www.nolo.com, accessed October 12, 2018.

17. RSW Information for Intellectual Property Users, http://www.isarpatent.com, accessed August 15, 2014.

18. Michael Hurley, Paul Devinsky, and Justin Hill, "The Supreme Court Decides *Quanta v. LGE*/U.S. and European Perspectives," https://www.ipo.org, accessed October 12, 2018.

19. Quote by Lawrence Lessig.

20. Avery Johnson, "Pfizer Buys More Time for Lipitor," *The Wall Street Journal*, June 19, 2008, B1; L. Husten, "Atorvastatin Lifts Ranbaxy While Pfizer Abandons Its Lipitor Marketing Efforts," *Forbes*, https://www.forbes.com, accessed October 12, 2018; and Erin Fox, "How Pharma Companies Game the System to Keep Drugs Expensive," *Harvard Business Review*, https://hbr.org, accessed October 12, 2018.

21. "Laurus Labs Anti-Retro-Viral Copy Gets USFDA Tentative Nod," https://www.moneycontrol.com, accessed October 12, 2018; and Ari Altstedter, "This Company Is About to Flood the U.S. with Cheap HIV Drugs," *Bloomberg*, https://www.bloomberg.com, accessed October 12, 2018.

22. Laurie Burkitt, and Kathy Gordon, "Burberry Appeals China Ban on Its Trademark Pattern," *The Wall Street Journal*, https://www.wsj.com, accessed October 12, 2018; and Denise Roland, "Burberry's Trademark Check Under Threat in China," *The Telegraph*, https://www.telegraph.co.uk, accessed October 12, 2018.

23. Aaron Schwabach, *Intellectual Property: Reference Handbook*, Santa Barbara, CA: ABC Clio, 2007, 8.

24. James Pooley, "Trade Secrets: The Other IP Right," *WIPO Magazine*, http://www.wipo.int, accessed October 12, 2018.

25. WIPO, "Patents or Trade Secrets?" http://www.wipo.int, accessed October 12, 2018.

26. Eleanor Fox, "US and EU Competition Law: A Comparison," https://docplayer.net, accessed October 12, 2018.

27. U.S. Department of Justice, "Antitrust Cooperation Agreements," https://www.justice.gov, accessed October 12, 2018.

28. Anu Bradford, "International Antitrust Negotiations and the False Hope of the WTO," *Harvard International Law Journal*, vol. 48, no. 2, 2007, 383–439, http://www.harvardilj.org, accessed October 12, 2018.

29. United Nations Commission on International Trade Law, "Status United Nations Convention on Contracts for the International Sale of Goods (Vienna 1980)," http://www.uncitral.org, accessed October 12, 2018.

30. "Losing the Magic: How Euro Disney Became a Nightmare," https://www.independent.co.uk, accessed October 12, 2018.

31. Lee Youkyung, "Japan's Antitrust Watchdog Fines Samsung SDI, Ex-LG Affiliate for Price-Rigging," https://www.highbeam.com, accessed October 12, 2018.

32. James D. Fry, "Struggling to Teethe: Japan's Antitrust Enforcement Regime," *Law and Policy in International Business*, https://www.questia.com, accessed October 12, 2018; and Japan Fair Trade Commission, Legislation and Guidelines, "The Antimonopoly Act (AMA)," https://www.jftc.go.jp, accessed October 12, 2018.

33. Craig P. Wagnild, "Civil Law Discovery in Japan: A Comparison of Japanese and US Methods of Evidence Collection in Civil Litigation," *Asia-Pacific Law and Policy Journal*, vol. 3, no. 1, Winter 2002.

34. Molly S. Boast, and Hannah M. Pennington, "Extraterritorial Applications of U.S. Antitrust Laws: An Overview," http://www.abanet.org/antitrust/at-committees/at-ic/pdf/spring/05/boast.pdf, April 02, 2014, not an open site; John M. Connor, and Darren Bush, "How to Block Cartel and Price Fixing: Using Extraterritorial Application of the Antitrust Laws as a Deterrence Mechanism," *Penn State Law Review*, 112, no. 3, April 2008, 813–57, http://www.pennstatelawreview.org; and Leon B. Greenfield, and David Olsky, "From Bananas to Vitamins: The Evolving Doctrine of the Extraterritorial Application of US Antitrust Law," *The Licensing Journal*, March 2006, 7–12, https://www.wilmerhale.com.

35. Mark Scott, "Google Fined Record $2.7 Billion in E.U. Antitrust Ruling," *New York Times*, https://www.nytimes.com, accessed October 12, 2018.

36. Adam Satariano, and Jack Nicas, "E.U. Fines Google $5.1 Billion in Android Antitrust Case," *New York Times*, https://www.nytimes.com, accessed October 12, 2018.

37. Klint Finley, "China Blocks Qualcomm's Attempt to Buy Dutch Chipmaker," *Wired*, https://www.wired.com, accessed October 12, 2018.

38. Joseph Stiglitz, "The Secret Corporate Takeover of Trade Agreements," *The Guardian*, https://www.theguardian.com, accessed October 12, 2018; and Alan Beattie, "From a Trickle to a Flood—How Lawsuits Are Coming to Dictate the Terms of Trade," *Financial Times*, March 20, 2007, 11.

39. Harvey Kaplan, and Jon Strongman, "United States: Developments in U.S. Product Liability Law and the Issues Relevant to Foreign Manufacturers," January 5, 2010, http://www.mondaq.com, accessed April 02, 2014.

40. "Fury as China Executes British Drug Smuggler," *The Guardian*, https://www.theguardian.com, accessed October 12, 2018.

41. "Writer Jailed for Alleged Thai Monarchy Insult," *NBC News*, http://www.nbcnews.com, accessed October 12, 2018.

42. "The Countries That Cane Their Convicts," *BBC News*, https://www.bbc.com, accessed October 12, 2018; "Fact Sheet: Overstaying by More Than 90 Days Can Lead to Caning," *Transient Workers Count Too*, http://twc2.org.sg, accessed October 12, 2018; and Arno Maierbrugger, "Brunei Caning Astonishes Business World," *Investvine*, http://investvine.com, accessed October 12, 2018.

43. U.S. Securities and Exchange Commission, "SEC Names New Specialized Unit Chiefs and Head of New Office of Market Intelligence," https://www.sec.gov, accessed October 12, 2018.

44. U.S. Securities and Exchange Commission, "Panasonic Charged with FCPA and Accounting Fraud Violations," https://www.sec.gov, accessed October 12, 2018.

45. U.S. Securities and Exchange Commission, "SEC Charges Dun & Bradstreet with FCPA Violations," https://www.sec.gov, accessed October 12, 2018.

46. U.S. Securities and Exchange Commission, "SEC Enforcement Actions: FCPA Cases," https://www.sec.gov, accessed October 12, 2018.

47. "The 2018 World's Most Ethical Companies Honoree List," *Ethisphere*, http://www.worldsmostethicalcompanies.com, accessed October 12, 2018.

48. United Nations Office on Drugs and Crime, UN Convention Against Corruption, "Signature and Ratification Status," https://www.unodc.org, accessed October 12, 2018.

49. Business Anti-Corruption Portal, "Anti-Corruption Legislation: UK Bribery Act 2010," https://www.business-anti-corruption.com, accessed October 12, 2018; and United Kingdom, "Anti-Bribery Policy," https://www.gov.uk, accessed October 12, 2018.

50. Brian Ngugi, "How Israel, China Firms Bribe Kenyan Officials," *Daily Nation*, https://www.nation.co.ke, accessed October 12, 2018.

51. John Coates IV, and Suraj Srinivasan, "SOX Ten Years After: A Multidisciplinary Review," *Harvard Law and Economics Discussion Paper No. 758*, https://papers.ssrn, accessed October 12, 2018.

7 Economic and Socioeconomic Forces

> **China, India, and the United States will emerge as the world's three largest economies in 2050, with a total real U.S. dollar GDP of 70 percent more than the GDP of all the other G20 countries combined. In China and India alone, GDP is predicted to increase by nearly $60 trillion, the current size of the world economy.**
>
> —*Uri Dadush and Bennett Stancil, authors of "The World Order in 2050"*[1]

©Inti St Clair/Blend Images.

LEARNING OBJECTIVES

After reading this module, you should be able to:

LO 7-1   **Explain** the purpose of economic analyses.

LO 7-2   **Compare** different categories of countries, based on levels of national economic development.

LO 7-3   **Outline** the dimensions used to describe the economy and their indicators.

LO 7-4   **Discuss** the socioeconomic dimensions of economies and the indicators used to assess them.

Two Emerging Asian Superpowers: The China-versus-India Development Race

China and India, with the largest populations on the planet, are the emerging heavyweights competing with each other for wealth and influence in the Asia region and beyond. Which of them is likely to emerge as the winner in the development race?

Economically, China is currently in the lead in terms of wealth and economic development. China has a larger population (1.39 billion versus India's 1.34 billion); a larger economy (GDP at PPP levels of $23.2 trillion at the end of 2017 versus $9.5 trillion for India); a higher savings rate (46 percent versus 30 percent); a relatively better infrastructure; and a higher level of manufacturing productivity. Reflecting a desire for developing human capital, China boasts a larger number of top-500 ranked universities, a higher level of enrollment in higher education, and greater levels of spending on research and development. China attracted a stock of $1.5 trillion in foreign direct investment at the start of 2018; India drew one-quarter as much.

Some observers believe that India has advantages over the long run, however. Not only do more Indians speak English—125 to 200 million are completely fluent and perhaps 20 million speak it as their primary language—but many are watching *Friends* reruns at employer expense to speak without an accent. India may also have an edge due to its young population of current and future workers, with over 45 percent of the population being under 25 years old. In contrast, decades of a one-child policy for families means China's population is aging rapidly, with less than 30 percent of the population under 25. India's strength so far has been in services; China has been the manufacturing powerhouse, with 40 percent of GDP based in manufacturing, compared to India's 23 percent. China's average manufacturing labor cost per hour is over $5 and increasing at double-digit annual rates, versus less than $2 per hour in India. Both countries have become major destinations for the outsourcing of business activities from the United States and other Western nations.

Regardless of which is rich first, many observers feel that by mid-century, India and China will both have larger economies than the United States.

Sources: "Population, Total," *The World Bank Group*, September 20, 2018; Michael Heath, "Superpower India to Replace China as Growth Engine," *Bloomberg*, September 18, 2017; "The World Factbook," *Central Intelligence Agency*, September 20, 2018; Tadit Kundu, "What India Can Learn from China's Rise in Higher Education," *Livemint*, August 06, 2018; James Carbone, "Vietnam Becomes an Option for Low-Cost Electronics Manufacturing," *Source Today*, April 27, 2017; Mohit Bhalla, "Average cost of Factory Labour at less than $2 per hour Gives India Big Advantage of Wage Arbitrage," *The Economic Times*, April 03, 2018; and Bruce Einhorn, "India vs. China: The Battle for Global Manufacturing," *Bloomberg*, November 06, 2014.

When considering whether and where to conduct business, managers of international companies need to look at a host of variables. This module examines the critical economic and socioeconomic forces that shape business opportunities around the world. We begin by examining the purpose of conducting economic analyses and then look at how we categorize nations by their levels of economic development, and the economic and socioeconomic dimensions that are used along with their indicators.

International Economic Analyses

LO 7-1
Explain the purpose of economic analyses.

Economic forces are among the most significant uncontrollable forces in the external environment businesses face. How can managers and business analysts keep abreast of the latest developments and also plan for the future? For many years, firms have been assessing and forecasting economic conditions at the national and international levels. To do so, analysts use data published by governments and international organizations such as the World Bank and the International Monetary Fund (IMF). These data may not be as timely or as accurate as business analysts would like, but there is a large amount available.

Analysts do not work solely with government-published data. Private economic consultants—such as Data Resources Inc., Chase Econometric Associates, Business International, the Economist Intelligence Unit, and Wharton Economic Forecasting Associates—provide economic forecasts to which many multinationals subscribe (some

> ❝THE ANNUAL LABOUR of EVERY NATION IS THE FUND WHICH ORIGINALLY SUPPLIES IT with ALL THE NECESSARIES AND CONVENIENCES of LIFE WHICH IT ANNUALLY CONSUMES, AND WHICH CONSIST ALWAYS EITHER in THE IMMEDIATE PRODUCE of THAT LABOUR, OR in WHAT IS PURCHASED with THAT PRODUCE from OTHER NATIONS.❞

—Adam Smith, The Wealth of Nations[2]

foreign environment
All the uncontrollable forces originating outside the home country that surround and influence the firm.

offer industry forecasts as well). Other sources are industry associations that provide industry-specific forecasts to their members. In addition, economists and marketers use certain economic indicators that predict trends in their industry.

The purpose of economic analyses is to assess the overall outlook for the economy and the impact of economic changes on the firm. Figure 7.1 illustrates how a change in just one economic factor can affect all the major functions of the company.

Suppose an increase in employment is forecast in a particular market. It would cause most marketing managers to revise their sales forecasts upward, which in turn requires that production managers increase production. They might add an additional work shift, but if the plant is already operating 24 hours a day, new machinery will be needed. Either situation may require more workers and raw materials, which will result in extra workloads for human resource and purchasing managers. Should both the raw materials and labor markets be tight, the firm will probably have to pay higher-than-normal prices and wage rates. The financial manager may then have to negotiate with banks for a loan to enable the firm to handle the greater cash outflow until it receives additional revenue from increased sales. Note this cascade of effects occurs because of a forecast change in only one economic factor, an increase in employment. Actually, of course, at any point in time, many economic factors are involved, and their relationships are complex. An economic analysis isolates and assesses the impact of those factors believed to affect the firm's operations.

When a firm enters overseas markets, economic analyses become more complex because now managers must operate in two new environments: foreign and international. The **foreign environment** includes all the uncontrollable forces originating outside the home country that surround and influence the firm. There are many economies instead of one, and they can be very different. The **international environment** includes the interactions between domestic and foreign environmental

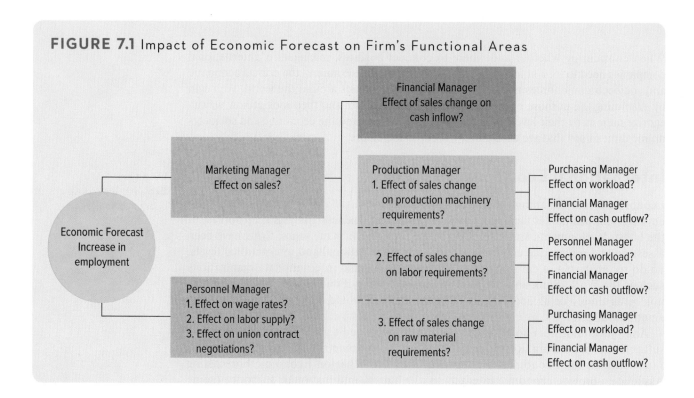

FIGURE 7.1 Impact of Economic Forecast on Firm's Functional Areas

forces, or between sets of foreign environmental forces when an affiliate in one country does business with customers in another. As you can see from this brief description, the decision to enter into overseas markets results in much greater complexity for the firm to manage.

Policies designed for economic conditions in one market may be unsuitable for conditions in another. For example, headquarters may require that its subsidiaries maintain the lowest inventories possible, and the chief financial officer may authorize only foreign currency-denominated loans, based on their favorable interest rates. For nations whose annual inflation rates are low (0 to 15 percent), these policies usually work well. But what about countries such as Zimbabwe, which saw inflation peak at an annual rate of 98 percent per day in November 2008?[3] Or Venezuela, which was battling an inflation rate approaching 1 million percent for 2018, according to the International Monetary Fund?[4] The least desirable scenario is for subsidiaries in these countries to have cash or foreign currency-denominated loans, so the policy for markets with high inflation rates will be just the reverse of what it is for countries with low inflation rates.

Besides monitoring foreign environments, analysts must stay informed about the actions taken by trading blocs and their members (European Union, Mercosur, the Association of Southeast Asian Nations) and international organizations (United Nations, International Monetary Fund, World Trade Organization). For example, in 2017, Mercosur suspended Venezuela as a member in that trade bloc. In 2017, President Trump announced that the United States would cease all participation in the Paris Agreement on climate change. In 2018, the United States imposed trade sanctions against its partners in the North American Free Trade Agreement (NAFTA), Mexico and Canada, and threatened to pull out of NAFTA altogether unless the agreement could be renegotiated to address U.S. concerns. Companies and their managers also closely follow the UN's progress in developing world pollution standards, health standards, and other actions that can seriously affect firms.[5]

International economic analyses should provide economic data on both actual and prospective markets. As part of the competitive forces assessment, many companies monitor the economic conditions of nations in which their major competitors are located because changing conditions may strengthen or weaken their competitors' ability to compete in world markets. The collection of data and the preparation of reports are usually the responsibility of the home office. However, foreign subsidiaries and field representatives are expected to contribute heavily to studies of their markets. Data from areas where the firm has no local representation can usually be less detailed and are generally available from national and international agencies.[6] Reports from central or international banks are especially good sources for economic information about single countries. Other possible sources are the chambers of commerce located in most of the world's capitals, the commercial officers in embassies, the United Nations, the World Bank, the International Monetary Fund (IMF), and the Organisation for Economic Co-operation and Development (OECD).

Levels of Economic Development

A nation's level of economic development affects all aspects of business conducted there, and international managers encounter markets with widely differing levels of development. One measure frequently used by economists and others is gross domestic product (GDP). Although it measures the overall economic output of a nation, GDP does not adequately account for flows of foreign income and investment into and out of a nation.[7] As a result, economists often choose to instead use gross national income (GNI) as a common basis for assessing economic development. GNI is the total value of all income generated by the residents of a nation, including both the domestic production of goods and services and income from abroad, as well as subtracting income paid to entities outside the nation. For example, the World Bank categorizes countries based

gross national income (GNI)
The total value of all income generated by the residents of a nation, including both the domestic production of goods and services and income from abroad

on their levels of GNI per person (usually referred to as GNI per capita), using the following figures for fiscal 2019:[8]

High-income economies: GNI per capita of $12,056 or more

Middle-income economies: GNI per capita of over $995 but less than $12,056, which can be further divided into:

Upper-middle-income economies: GNI per capita of $3,896 up to $12,055

Lower-middle-income economies: GNI per capita of $996 up to $3,895

Low-income economies: GNI per capita of $995 or less

Figure 7.2 shows the nations of the world, based on their per-capita GNI (in U.S. dollars) as categorized by the World Bank.

developing economies
A classification for the world's lower-income nations, which have less technically developed infrastructures and lower living standards

developed economies
A classification for high-income industrialized nations, which have high living standards and the most technically developed infrastructure

Another classification of economic development distinguishes between developed and developing economies, with low- and middle-income economies referred to as developing economies. There is no universally agreed-upon criterion to distinguish between developed and developing economies. Indeed, the United Nations Statistics Division states that they utilize terminology such as "developed" and "developing" only for statistical convenience and that these designations "do not necessarily express a judgment about the stage reached by a particular country or area in the development process."[9] However, developed economies are frequently characterized as those industrialized, or postindustrial, service-based nations that are economically advanced, with established infrastructures—roads, bridges, utilities, power supplies, communications, and other structural elements needed for the smooth operation of a society—and that have achieved high incomes per capita that support a high living standard, including material goods, access to health care, education, and other necessities. Countries the U.S. Central Intelligence Agency, the IMF, and other

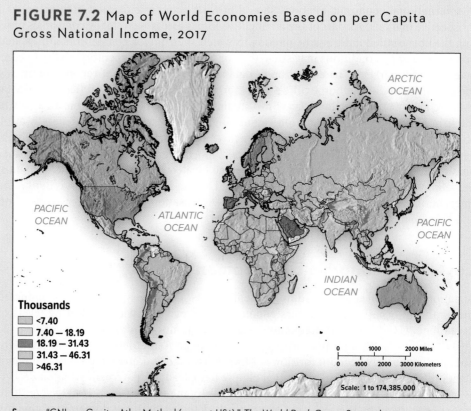

FIGURE 7.2 Map of World Economies Based on per Capita Gross National Income, 2017

Thousands
- <7.40
- 7.40 – 18.19
- 18.19 – 31.43
- 31.43 – 46.31
- >46.31

Scale: 1 to 174,385,000

Source: "GNI per Capita, Atlas Method (current US$)," *The World Bank Group*, September 20, 2018. Copyright ©2018 by The World Bank Group. All rights reserved. Used with permission.

TABLE 7.1 Characteristics of Developed and Developing Economies

Developed Economies	Developing Economies
Per capita gross national income of $12,056 or more (World Bank criterion).	Per capita gross national income of less than $12,056 (World Bank criterion).
A high material standard of living, high quality of life index, and a substantial middle class.	A moderate to low material standard of living and quality of life index, regional dualism reflecting a high productivity and incomes in some regions and little economic development in others, unequal distribution of income with a very small middle class.
Frequent application of the most advanced production techniques and equipment.	Technological dualism, meaning the presence of a mix of firms employing the latest technology and companies using very primitive methods.
A large base of productive capital, sophisticated financial markets and banking systems, and vigorous international trade in a range of sectors.	Low savings rates, inadequate banking facilities, and high dependence on a few products for export, generally agricultural products or minerals.
A very small share of total output coming from agriculture and a declining share for manufacturing.	A relatively unproductive agricultural sector that provides a living for most of the population.
Well-established governmental and legal systems.	Political instability and deficient governmental and legal systems.
Plentiful educational opportunities and low illiteracy.	High illiteracy rate and few educational facilities.
Relatively low levels of unemployment or underemployment.	Disguised unemployment or underemployment (two people do a job one person could do).
Adequate or high levels of nutrition and access to health care.	Widespread malnutrition and a wide range of health problems.
	Inhospitable topography, such as deserts, mountains, and tropical forests.

Sources: "World Bank Country and Lending Groups," *The World Bank Group*, September 20, 2018; "New Country Classifications by Income Level: 2018–2019," *The World Bank Group*, July 01, 2018; "The World Factbook," *Central Intelligence Agency*, September 20, 2018; Lynge Nielsen, "Classifications of Countries Based on Their Level of Development: How It Is Done and How It Could Be Done," *IMF Working Paper*, February 2011; and "LDC Identification Criteria & Indicators," *United Nations, Economic Analysis and Policy Division*, September 20, 2018.

organizations consider economically developed include the western European nations, Israel, Japan, Australia, New Zealand, Singapore, Taiwan, South Korea, Canada, and the United States. Most share the characteristics shown in the left-hand column of Table 7.1.

In contrast, the term "developing economy" identifies the world's lower-income nations, which are less technically developed. There is a much greater level of diversity among the many developing nations than among developed nations, yet most share the characteristics in the right-hand column of Table 7.1.

You can see from the table that the gap in living standards between the most advanced developed economies and those at the lower end of the developing economies is profound. Most of the world's inhabitants live in the middle-income countries between these two extremes. Many managers and international organizations have begun referring to these as **emerging market economies**, a subcategory of developing economies.

An emerging market is one with per-capita income in the low to middle range as measured by the World Bank. It is usually in a transition toward developed status, having embarked on programs of economic development and reform to open up and grow markets in order to emerge on the global scene. Rapid growth and related economic and trade opportunities often bring emerging markets an increase in both local and foreign investment. Employment then typically rises, labor and management skills improve, and technology and infrastructure grow stronger. Rising production increases gross domestic product

emerging market economies
Economies with per-capita incomes in the low to middle range that are in a transition toward developed status

and narrows the gap with developed economies. The process is challenging, though, and emerging economies can experience high levels of political and economic volatility. Among the most prominent emerging nations are China and India, which together are home to about 40 percent of the world's population and labor force and have a collective economic output that exceeds that of the United States or the European Union. Others include Brazil, Russia, India, Mexico, Turkey, Indonesia, Malaysia, and South Africa.

LO 7-3

Outline the dimensions used to describe the economy and their indicators.

Dimensions That Describe the Economy and Their Relevance for International Business

To estimate market potentials and provide input to the other functional areas of the firm, managers require data on the sizes and rates of change of a number of economic and socioeconomic factors. To be a potential market, an area must have sufficient people with the means to buy a firm's products. Socioeconomic data provide information about the number of people, and the economic dimensions tell us whether they have purchasing power. Among the more important economic indicators are gross domestic product, gross national income, economic growth rates, distribution of income, personal consumption expenditures, discretionary spending, unit labor costs, and the level of national debt.

MEASURING THE SIZE OF AN ECONOMY

When an international manager is considering where to do business, one of the first considerations is the size of the economy. We will now look at several ways in which the size of an economy is typically measured.

Gross National Income (GNI) As mentioned earlier, GNI is a measure of the total value of all income generated by the residents of a nation, including both the domestic production of goods and services and income generated from abroad, mainly through dividends and interest payments, minus similar payments made to other countries. For example, Germany's

CULTURE FACTS @internationalbiz

The more a country tends to avoid uncertainty and individualism in its values, the more likely it will value secrecy, and thus, the more likely its economic data are unreliable.
#secrecy #unreliabledata

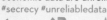

SOCIAL MEDIA

GNI includes the value of a Mercedes built in Germany, as well as the portion of a U.S.-assembled Mercedes made up of goods or services from Germany. If the German subsidiary assembling Mercedes autos in the United States makes a profit and then sends those profits back to the German headquarters, then Germany's GNI also includes these U.S.-derived profits.

Most international organizations prefer GNI to GDP for measuring the value produced in an economy because GDP measures only the market value of goods and services produced within a nation in a particular year. Country GNIs in 2017 ranged from $18.98 trillion for the United States to $56 million for the island nation Tuvalu.[10] What is the relevance of GNI for the international businessperson? Is India, with a 2017 GNI of $2.43 trillion, a more attractive market than Denmark, whose $319 billion GNI is about one-eighth the size?[11] To compare the purchasing power of nations, managers need to know among how many people the GNI is divided.

GNI per Capita Data on GNI per capita from the tables of the World Bank reveal that Denmark is far richer in purchasing power than India: GNI per capita in Denmark was $55,220 in 2017 versus $1,820 in India.[12] Although India's economic pie is nearly eight times larger than Denmark's, there are more than 233 times as many people to eat it.

What can we learn from GNI per capita? We can generally assume that the higher its value, the more advanced the economy. However, the rate of growth may be more important to marketers because a high growth rate indicates a fast-growing market—which is always desirable. Frequently, given the choice between investing in a nation with a low GNI per capita but a high growth rate and a nation with the conditions reversed, management will choose the former.

Although GNI per capita is widely used to compare the well-being of countries' citizens and to assess market or investment potential, managers must use it with caution. For example, to arrive at GNI, government economists must impute monetary values to various goods and services not sold in the marketplace, such as food grown for personal consumption. Moreover, many goods and services are bartered in both low-income nations (because people have little cash) and high-income countries (because people wish to reduce reported income to pay less income tax). Unrecorded transactions of this type are said to be part of the informal economy that we discuss later in this module.

Converting GNI to a Common Currency and Purchasing Power Parity Another problem with GNI estimates is that to compare them, we must convert them to a common currency—conventionally the U.S. dollar—by using an exchange rate. If the relative values of the two currencies, their market exchange rates, were to accurately reflect their consumer purchasing power in each nation, this simple conversion would be acceptable. However, that is not usually the case.[13] Often, in the developing economy, the consumer's market prices for goods are lower than in the developed markets. The United Nations International Comparison Program (ICP) has developed a method of comparing GNIs based on purchasing power parity rather than on the international demand for currency (market currency exchange rates). **Purchasing power parity (PPP)** is a means of adjusting the exchange rates for two currencies so the currencies have equivalent purchasing power. Here is how purchasing power parity rates are calculated.

purchasing power parity (PPP)
A means of adjusting the exchange rates for two currencies so the currencies have equivalent purchasing power

Suppose Thailand reports to the World Bank that its GNI per capita for last year is 170,766 baht per capita. The Bank must translate this value to U.S. dollars. If the current exchange rate is 31.8 baht = $1, then 170,766 baht is equivalent to $5,370 (170,766/31.8). How well does this measure Thailand's welfare? What can a Thai citizen purchase with the 170,766 baht compared with what a U.S. shopper can buy with the $53,670 per capita income of the United States? Suppose the following table reflects local prices in both countries for the same basket of goods:

Goods	Thailand (baht)	U.S. ($)
Soap (bar)	50	1.25
Rice (pound)	35	0.55
Shoes (pair)	905	70.00
Dress	780	85.00
Socks (pair)	95	3.25
Total	1,865 baht	$160.05

In Thailand, 1,865 baht buys what $160.05 buys in the United States. Therefore, comparing the purchasing power of the currencies, we find that 1,865 baht/$160.05 = 11.65 baht per $1. Using the exchange rate of 11.65 baht per dollar, Thailand's GNI/capita is now 170,766/11.65 = $14,658. At the official exchange rate of 31.8 baht/$1, Thailand's GNI is $5,370. Therefore, when using a purchasing power comparison, Thailand's GNI is 27 percent that of the United States (14,658/53,960) rather than the 10 percent (5,370/53,960) the official exchange rate might suggest. This difference is substantial when a marketer is considering whether the Thai people might be an attractive market for consumer goods.

Table 7.2 illustrates that comparisons based on PPP (second column of data) yield developed nation GNI per capita values that are considerably lower than those based on exchange rates and developing nation GNI considerably higher. That is, if we are using PPP, the gaps between the GNIs of developing and developed nations are smaller than with the generally published exchange-rate method of calculating GNI. These differences can be of great importance to businesspeople when deciding where to do business globally.

TABLE 7.2 GNI/Capita Based on UN ICP for Selected Countries

Country	GNI/Capita in US$ Converted at World Bank–Adjusted Exchange Rates	GNI/Capita in US$ Based on Purchasing Power Parity
Norway	$75,990	$ 63,530
Qatar	61,070	128,060
United States	58,270	60,200
Canada	42,870	45,750
United Kingdom	40,530	43,160
Japan	38,550	45,470
Saudi Arabia	20,080	54,770
Turkey	10,930	27,550
Malaysia	9,650	28,650
Russian Federation	9,232	24,893
China	8,690	16,760
Mexico	8,610	17,740
Ecuador	5,890	11,350
Iraq	4,770	17,010
Nigeria	2,080	5,680
India	1,820	7,060

Note: Data are for 2017.

Sources: "GNI Ranking, Atlas Method," *The World Bank Group*, September 20, 2018; "GNI per Capita Ranking, Atlas Method and PPP Based," *The World Bank Group*, September 20, 2018.

Atlas conversion factor
The arithmetic average of the current exchange rate and the exchange rates in the two preceding years, adjusted by the ratio of domestic inflation to the combined inflation rates of the euro zone, Japan, the United Kingdom, and the United States

underground economy
The part of a nation's income that, because of unreporting or underreporting, is not measured by official statistics

"ONE AGENCY with PARTICULAR INTEREST in THE SHADOW ECONOMY IS THE I.R.S., WHICH ESTIMATES—THE DIFFERENCE BETWEEN TAXES PAID AND TAXES OWED—IS about $345 BILLION."

—Freakonomics Radio podcast[14]

Modifying GNI with the Atlas Conversion Factor Dissatisfaction with both the PPP and conversions using official exchange rates caused the World Bank to adopt the Atlas methodology to derive per capita GNI estimates. The **Atlas conversion factor** was developed to reduce the impact of exchange rate fluctuations. It is the arithmetic average of the current exchange rate and the exchange rates in the two preceding years, adjusted by the ratio of domestic inflation to the combined inflation rates of the euro zone, Japan, the United Kingdom, and the United States. Incomes measured by the Atlas conversion factor are generally more stable over time, and changes in income rankings are more likely to be due to relative economic performance than to fluctuations in the exchange rate. As a result, managers evaluating international markets might find value in GNI estimates calculated using the Atlas conversion factor.

Accounting for the Underground or Informal Economy If a manager wants to analyze markets for their business potential, getting an accurate measurement of the overall size of an economy is an important consideration. But some part of the national income is *not* measured by official statistics because it is either under- or unreported. Included in this **underground economy** are undeclared production of goods and services that are legal (unreported income or assets) and illegal (drugs, pirated copies of

Using the Big Mac Index to Assess PPP

McDonald's in France. ©Bill Ryall/William Ryall.

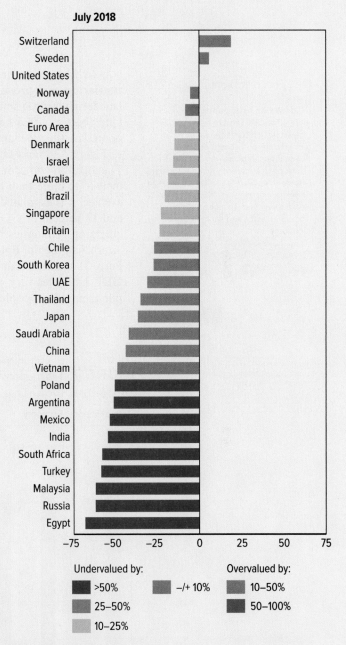

Source: "The Big Mac Index," *The Economist,* July 11, 2018.

The Economist, a British weekly magazine, presents a playful application of PPP theory in its "Big Mac Index," which substitutes a Big Mac for the basket of goods economists have traditionally used. The index calculates the exchange rate at which a Big Mac in other countries costs what it does in the United States.

The index begins by collecting data on the current price of Big Mac sandwiches at McDonald's restaurants around the world. By comparing these prices based on current exchange rates with the PPP-based price of a Big Mac, the index can indicate whether a particular currency is overvalued or undervalued. So, for example, in July 2018 in five cities in China, the Big Mac in U.S. dollars at the prevailing yuan–dollar exchange rate averaged $3.10, whereas in the United States a four-city average price was $5.51. In effect, the yuan is 44 percent below the implied PPP exchange rate. That's a pretty inexpensive burger.

The following figure shows the overvaluation and undervaluation of national currencies using the implied exchange rate, based on the market price of the Big Mac. The data are for July 2018. Switzerland's currency is about 19 percent overvalued, while Russia's is about 62 percent undervalued.

The Economist claims that in the long run, its Big Mac Index performs pretty well. Indeed, it has even resulted in a new term, "Burgernomics," based on data for McDonald's hamburgers. Of course, when assessing this index, we need to remember that the price of a Big Mac represents more than a basket of tradable goods, the situation PPP theory describes. For example, the service we receive with our Big Mac can't be traded, nor can McDonald's brand image. Nevertheless, the index is a helpful way to get a quick sense of relative currency values and where they may be heading. The latest version of the Big Mac Index might help you choose your next bargain vacation or spring break spot. The figure shows that Big Macs are considerably cheaper in India, South Africa, and Indonesia than in the United States. Meanwhile, in Switzerland and Sweden, the Big Mac is more costly. You can check the latest Big Mac Index and actual prices at https://www.economist.com/news/2018/07/11/the-big-mac-index.

copyrighted music or video, gambling, use of undocumented workers, human trafficking, and prostitution) along with their corresponding activities (money laundering by drug smugglers or terrorist organizations), and concealed income in kind (barter). As a general rule, the higher the level of taxation and the more oppressive the government red tape, the bigger the underground economy will be.[15]

Figure 7.3 shows estimates of underground economies within different nations. The underground economy in the United States increased from 4 percent of GDP in 1970 to more than 8 percent in 2003, then declined to 5.4 percent in 2017. On average, it is estimated that the underground economy accounted for between 16 and 17 percent of GDP in OECD countries and two to three times that level in emerging economies.[16] The underground economy in several nations, such as Azerbaijan, Benin, Bolivia, Gabon, Georgia, Guatemala, Haiti, Myanmar, Nigeria, Peru, Tanzania, Thailand, and Zimbabwe, is estimated to exceed 50 percent of GDP. Estimates vary widely because of the different methodologies used to compile them; also, people who have undeclared income are not likely to admit it. In

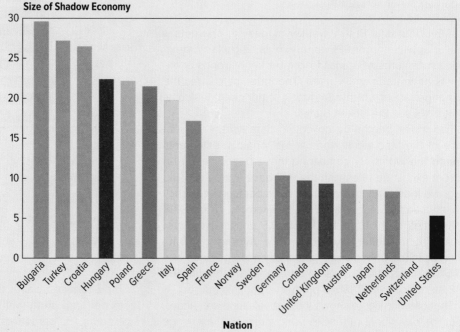

FIGURE 7.3 Shadow Economies as a Percentage of GDP in Selected Countries, 2017

Sources: Leandro Medina, and Friedrich Schneider, "Shadow Economies Around the World: What Did We Learn Over the Last 20 Years?" *International Monetary Fund*, January 24, 2018; and Niall McCarthy, "The Countries with the Largest Shadow Economies," *Forbes*, February 09, 2017.

addition to reducing the total taxes paid to the government, the underground economy can distort economic data, which managers must take into account when they use them for business decisions. Large underground economies can also create problems for public policy makers, as well as add complexity and uncertainty that can change managers' assessments of the attractiveness of specific international markets.

ECONOMIC GROWTH RATE

Data such as overall GNI or GNI per capita can provide a snapshot of the size of an economy, but they fail to inform a manager about whether and how fast an economy is growing, or perhaps even shrinking. As a result, most seasoned managers supplement their analyses by looking at economic growth rates as well as measures of an economy's absolute size.

The rationale for this approach is easy to understand. As shown in Table 7.3, emerging and developing economies grew two to three times faster in each of the years

TABLE 7.3 Economic Growth Rates of Various Countries and Categories of Nations (Growth Rates in Percentage Change, Year over Year)

	2012	2013	2014	2015	2016	2017	2018	2019
Developed Economies	**1.4**	**1.3**	**2.2**	**2.3**	**1.7**	**2.4**	**2.4**	**2.2**
United States	2.8	1.9	2.8	3.0	1.5	2.3	2.9	2.7
Euro area	−0.7	−0.4	1.0	1.4	1.8	2.4	2.2	1.9
Japan	1.4	1.7	1.7	1.0	1.0	1.7	1.0	0.9
Canada	1.7	1.7	2.2	2.4	1.4	3.0	2.1	2.0
Other developed economies	1.9	2.2	3.0	3.2	2.3	2.7	2.8	2.7
Emerging Market and Developing Economies	**4.9**	**4.7**	**5.1**	**5.4**	**4.4**	**4.7**	**4.9**	**5.1**
Central and eastern Europe	1.4	2.5	2.8	3.1	3.2	5.9	4.3	3.6
Commonwealth of Independent States	3.4	2.1	2.6	3.1	0.4	2.1	2.3	2.2
Russia	3.4	1.5	2.0	2.5	−0.2	1.5	1.7	1.5
Developing Asia	6.4	6.5	6.7	6.8	6.5	6.5	6.5	6.5
China	7.7	7.7	7.5	7.3	6.7	6.9	6.6	6.4
India	3.2	4.4	5.4	6.4	7.1	6.7	7.3	7.5
ASEAN-5 (Indonesia, Malaysia, Philippines, Thailand, Vietnam)	6.2	5.0	5.1	5.6	4.9	5.3	5.3	5.3
Latin America and the Caribbean	3.0	2.6	3.0	3.3	−0.6	1.3	1.6	2.6
Brazil	1.0	2.3	2.3	2.8	−3.5	1.0	1.8	2.5
Mexico	3.7	1.2	3.0	3.5	2.9	2.0	2.3	2.7
Middle East, North Africa, Afghanistan, and Pakistan	4.1	2.4	3.3	4.8	5.0	2.2	3.5	3.9
Sub-Saharan Africa	4.8	5.1	6.1	5.8	1.5	2.8	3.4	3.8

Note: Data for 2018 and 2019 were projections as of July 2018.

Sources: "Is the Tide Rising?" *International Monetary Fund,* January 2014; and "Less Even Expansion, Rising Trade Tensions," *International Monetary Fund,* July 2018.

2012–2017 than did developed economies, and forecasts suggested they would grow at more than double the rate in 2018 and 2019. Rapid and rising economic growth rates suggest consumer demand, which often indicates trade and foreign direct investment are likely to increase as well, suggesting an attractive market opportunity for international companies.

INCOME DISTRIBUTION

income distribution
A measure of how a nation's income is apportioned among its people

GINI index
A measure of the degree to which income within a country is distributed equally

Although differences in GNI per capita and economic growth rates do tell us something about the relative wealth of a nation's inhabitants, the information can be somewhat misleading because wealth is usually not evenly spread. Managers must refine these first crude estimates of purchasing power by incorporating data on how national income is actually distributed.

Data on **income distribution**, which indicates how a nation's income is apportioned among its people, are gathered by the World Bank from a number of sources and published yearly in the *World Development Indicators* (see Table 7.4). An additional measure of potential value for international companies is the **GINI index**, which measures the degree to which income within a country is distributed equally. A lower score indicates a more

TABLE 7.4 Percentage Share of Income or Consumption for Selected Segments of Selected Nations

Country	Lowest 20 Percent	20–40 Percent	40–60 Percent	60–80 Percent	Highest 20 Percent	Highest 10 Percent	GINI coefficient
Argentina (2017)	5	10	15	23	48	31	41.7
Bangladesh (2016)	9	12	16	21	41	27	32.4
Brazil (2015)	4	8	13	20	56	40	51.3
China (2016)	5	10	15	22	48	31	46.5
Ecuador (2017)	5	9	14	21	51	34	45.9
India (2011)	8	12	15	21	44	30	35.2
Mexico (2016)	6	10	14	20	50	35	43.4
Nigeria (2013)	5	10	14	22	49	33	48.8
Peru (2016)	5	10	15	22	49	33	43.8
Russian Federation (2015)	7	11	15	21	45	30	41.2
Rwanda (2013)	5	8	12	17	57	43	50.4
South Africa (2014)	3	5	8	17	68	51	63.0
Turkey (2016)	6	10	15	22	48	32	41.9
United States (2016)	5	10	15	23	47	31	41.5
Vietnam (2016)	7	12	16	22	42	27	35.3
Zambia (2015)	3	6	11	19	61	44	57.1

Note: Numbers in parentheses indicate the year of study for GINI data.

Sources: "World Development Indicators: Distribution of Income or Consumption," *The World Bank Group*, September 20, 2018; "GINI Index (World Bank estimate)," *The World Bank Group*, September 20, 2018; and "Distribution of Family Income—GINI Index," *The World Factbook*, September 20, 2018.

equal distribution. The range of GINI scores is wide: Iceland's is 29.2, the United States is 41.5, and South Africa's is 63.[17]

Despite the difficulties associated with income distribution studies, such as inconsistent measuring practices and wide variations in the representativeness of samples, the data provide useful insights for business:

1. They confirm the belief that, generally, income is more evenly distributed in the richer nations, although there are important variations among both developed and developing nations.

2. Comparisons over time demonstrate that income redistribution proceeds very slowly, so older data are still useful.

3. The same comparisons indicate that income inequality increases in the early stages of development and reverses in the later stages. The fact that the middle quintiles in some nations are growing at the expense of the top and bottom 20 percent signifies an increase in the number of middle-income families, which is especially significant to marketers.

Depending on the type of product and the total population, both relatively even and relatively uneven income distribution can suggest market opportunities. Although South Africa's GDP was $758 billion in PPP terms, over half the total income is received by only the top 10 percent of the population, indicating sizable numbers are potential customers for low-volume, high-priced luxury products. Given that the lowest-earning 60 percent receive only 16 percent of the national income, there also may be an attractive market for low-priced consumer goods requiring a high sales volume. This sort of simple calculation based on GNI, total population, and income distribution may be enough to indicate a particular country is or is not a good market; if the results look promising, the analyst will proceed to gather data on private consumption.

PRIVATE CONSUMPTION

One area of interest to marketers is the manner in which consumers allocate their **disposable income**—their after-tax personal income—between purchases of essential and nonessential goods. Manufacturers of household durables, for instance, will want to know the amounts spent in that category, whereas producers of nonessentials will be interested in the magnitude of **discretionary income**—disposable income less essential purchases and taxes—for this is the money available to be spent on their products. Fortunately, disposable incomes and the amounts spent on essential purchases are available from the *UN Statistical Yearbook*. More detailed expenditure patterns can be found in the *World Development Indicators* published by the World Bank. Some of these data are reproduced in Table 7.5, which shows private consumption expenditures for five high-income and five low-income economies, using PPP equivalents.

Because PPP-based consumer expenditures eliminate differences between prices, marketers use them to analyze how the composition of consumption changes with the level of development. For example, the percentages of household expenditures spent on food and beverages in developing nations are two to four times the percentages spent in industrialized nations. On the other hand, the percentages spent on (1) transport and communication, (2) consumer durables, (3) health care, and (4) other consumption by households of developed nations are twice those in developing nations. Note that percentage differences within a consumption category do not relate to consumption expenditures per capita; in spite of the allure of French haute couture, the percentage spent on clothing in France is one-fourth the level spent in Hong Kong.

International business managers know better than to underestimate the importance of small percentage differences among nations. They are aware that each percentage point is worth a large sum of money, especially in larger economies. To

disposable income
After-tax personal income

discretionary income
The amount of income left after paying taxes and making essential purchases

CULTURE FACTS @internationalbiz

@GulfCooperationCouncil A consumer preference for luxury goods and services in the Gulf Cooperation Council countries (Bahrain, Kuwait, Oman, Qatar, Saudi Arabia, and the United Arab Emirates) is reflected in their spending, on average, 260 percent more than other nations on airfares, 430 percent more on accommodation, and 558 percent more on dining. #livingthelife #luxury #luxurygoodsandservices

SOCIAL MEDIA

TABLE 7.5 Private Consumption Based on Purchasing Power Parity

Country	GNI/Capita Based on Exchange Rates, 2017	GNI/Capita Based on PPP, 2013	Household Consumption Expenditure % of GDP, 2017	Food and Non-Alcoholic Beverages	Clothing and Footwear	Education	Health Care	Transportation and Communication	Other Consumption
				Percentage of Household Consumption					
Australia	$51,360	$45,780	57	10	4	5	6	12	63
Canada	42,870	45,750	58	9	4	2	4	18	63
India	1,820	7,060	59	32	7	1	5	17	38
Germany	43,490	51,760	53	10	4	1	5	17	63
Japan	38,550	45,470	56	16	3	2	4	14	61
Kenya	1,440	3,250	80	47	3	3	2	11	34
Chile	13,610	23,150	62	18	6	4	7	16	49
Namibia	4,600	10,320	69	51	5	5	6	5	28
Laos	2,270	6,650	65	48	1	1	2	12	36
United States	58,270	60,200	69	6	3	2	22	12	55

Sources: "Households and NPISHs Final Consumption Expenditure (% of GDP)," *The World Bank Group*, September 20, 2018; "Gross National Income Per Capita 2017, Atlas Method and PPP Based," *The World Bank Group*, September 20, 2018; and "Final Consumption Expenditure of Households," *Organisation for Economic Co-operation and Development*, October 13, 2018.

appreciate how much, try multiplying the total per capita consumption expenditure by 1 percent of the population. If U.S. consumers had spent 1 percent more on clothing, for example, it would have amounted to $190 billion in additional sales for the clothing industry.

Other indicators that add to our knowledge of personal consumption measure (1) the ownership of goods and (2) the consumption of key materials. For example, commercial energy use per capita is related to the size of the modern sectors—*urban areas, industry*, and *motorized transport*. The World Bank has found that populations of high-income economies use nearly seven times as much commercial energy per capita as do people in developing economies, and the quantity and mix of energy constitute a rough indicator of a country's level of development. As Table 7.6 illustrates, industrialized nations generally have higher values for these indicators than do the developing nations.

UNIT LABOR COSTS

One factor that contributes to a favorable investment opportunity is lower **unit labor costs**, or total direct labor costs/units produced, than are currently available to the firm. Countries with low or slowly rising unit labor costs attract management's attention for two reasons. First, they suggest investment prospects for companies striving to lower production costs; second, they may become sources of new competition in world markets if other firms in the same industry are already located there or invest in production there.

Changes in wage rates may also cause a multinational firm to change its sources of supply. For example, Nike, which has no athletic footwear production in the United States, began using Japanese plants in 1964. When labor costs rose there in the mid-1970s, the company changed to factories in South Korea and Taiwan and later added Thailand. But as labor costs rose in those countries, Nike shifted most of its production to contracted factories in China. Then Nike became concerned as wage rates rose in China at a rate faster than productivity, with factory wages increasing by 64 percent between 2011 and 2016.[18] When adjusted for productivity, Chinese factory labor was only 4 percent less expensive than in the United States.[19] Nike has undertaken efforts to move production to other locations where wage rates can be at least 30 percent lower. The company has production in more than 700 factories in 44 countries, although much of its shoe production remains in low-cost Asian nations. For example, the proportion of Nike footwear produced in Vietnam increased by 50 percent between 2011 and 2017, to around 45 percent of the total.[20]

What are the reasons for the changes in labor costs? Three factors are responsible: compensation, productivity, and exchange rates. Hourly compensation tends to vary more widely than wages because of differences in fringe benefits. Unit labor costs will not rise in unison with compensation rates if gains in productivity outstrip increases in hourly compensation. In fact, if productivity increases fast enough, the unit costs of labor will decrease even though the firm is required to pay workers more.

Data reveal why international firms keep a close watch on labor compensation rates around the world. For example, in 1975, Sweden had the highest hourly rate, with the United States and Germany tied for fifth place, and Japan's average hourly rate was less than half the U.S. rate. However, by 1985, the U.S. rate was the world's highest, and U.S. managers were searching for overseas production sites. Yet, just 10 years later, the United States had fallen to 13th place in the hourly compensation cost ranking, and every European nation but the United Kingdom and Spain had higher costs. In 1995, Japan's labor compensation rate, less than half the U.S. rate in 1985, had jumped to 138 percent of it. In response, many Japanese firms moved significant production to other Asian countries with lower labor costs, such as Thailand, China, and Indonesia. (This movement abroad was also influenced by the retirement of many skilled machinists and other artisans in Japan, which made foreign labor more attractive.) Japan's

unit labor costs
Total direct labor costs divided by units produced

TABLE 7.6 Per Capita Ownership or Consumption of Key Goods and Services for Selected Countries

Region/Country	Mobile Cellular Subscribers per 100 Inhabitants, 2017	Electricity Consumption/ Capita (1,000 kWh), 2014	Internet Users per 100 Inhabitants, 2017
Europe			
Switzerland	133	7,520	94
Sweden	125	13,480	96
Italy	141	5,002	61
Middle East			
Israel	127	6,601	82
Kuwait	124	15,213	98
Saudi Arabia	122	9,444	80
Africa			
South Africa	162	4,198	54
Ghana	127	355	35
South Sudan	12	40	7
Ethiopia	60	70	15
Asia			
Japan	133	7,820	91
China	105	3,927	54
India	87	806	30
South America			
Chile	127	3,912	82
Brazil	113	2,601	61
Colombia	127	1,290	62
Eastern Europe			
Hungary	124	3,966	77
Russia	158	6,603	76
Kazakhstan	145	5,600	76
North America and Caribbean			
Cuba	40	1,434	43
United States	122	12,984	84
Trinidad and Tobago	148	7,134	73
Mexico	89	2,090	64

Sources: "Electric Power Consumption (kWh per capita)," *The World Bank Group*, September 20, 2018; "Mobile Cellular Subscriptions (per 100 people)," *The World Bank Group*, September 20, 2018; and "Individuals Using the Internet (% of Population)," *The World Bank Group*, September 20, 2018.

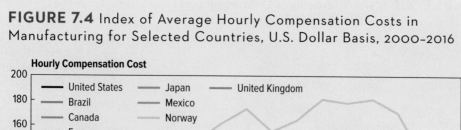

FIGURE 7.4 Index of Average Hourly Compensation Costs in Manufacturing for Selected Countries, U.S. Dollar Basis, 2000–2016

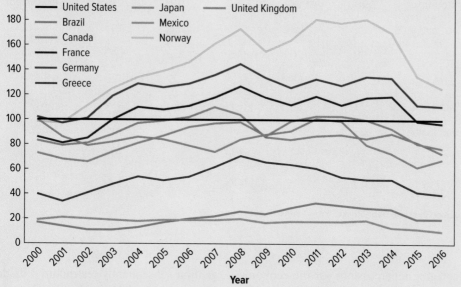

Note: Compensation costs include direct pay, social insurance expenditures, and labor-related taxes.

Sources: "Indexes of Hourly Compensation Costs in Manufacturing, U.S. Dollar Basis, 1996–2016," *U.S. Bureau of Labor Statistics*, September 20, 2018; "International Comparisons of Hourly Compensation Costs in Manufacturing, Summary Tables," *The Conference Board Inc.*, April 19, 2018; "International Comparisons of Hourly Compensation Costs in Manufacturing, 2012," *U.S. Bureau of Labor Statistics*, August 09, 2013.

labor costs later declined to below the average for OECD nations, in part due to the depreciation of the national currency relative to that of other developed countries. Figure 7.4 shows selected nations' hourly compensation costs for manufacturing during 2000–2016. The cost competitiveness of the United States improved relative to most of the other countries listed during the initial years after the global financial crisis of 2008–2009, which might suggest it became a more attractive location for investment, but an appreciating value of the U.S. dollar, decreasing unemployment levels, and other factors have more recently caused the relative U.S. cost competitiveness to experience a decline.

OTHER ECONOMIC DIMENSIONS

The large international debts of a number of middle- and low-income nations are causing multiple problems, not only for their governments but also for multinational firms. Look at the developing countries with some of the highest levels of debts to foreign lenders, shown in Table 7.7. Not only are the levels of debt substantial in absolute amount, but the overall level has been increasing rapidly. As the level of debt increases, more resources are redirected toward payment of interest rather than invested for productive uses. Concern about a country's ability to meet its debt obligations can also increase uncertainty about its future economic performance, hinder governmental investment and responsiveness to infrastructural and other pressures, and lower consumer confidence. For example, in 2002, Argentina's inability to repay its international loan obligations caused the country to default on its external debts, which produced violent street protests, a run on the banks, a 44 percent devaluation of its currency in less than three months, and a number of

TABLE 7.7 Major International Debtors among Developing Countries, Total External Stock of Debt ($ Billion)

Country	1980	1990	2000	2010	2016	2016 Debt as a Percentage of 1980 Debt
Argentina	27	63	150	126	191	707%
Brazil	72	120	243	352	543	754
China	5	55	146	735	1429	28,580
India	21	84	101	290	456	2,171
Indonesia	21	70	144	198	316	1,504
Mexico	58	105	153	246	423	729
Turkey	19	49	117	301	406	2,136

Source: "External Debt Stocks," *World Bank*, October 02, 2018.

damaging repercussions for the economy. Argentina subsequently restructured its debt load in 2005 and again in 2010 in an effort to overcome its debt problems, only to find itself in default again in 2014. Despite an infusion of capital after a new president took office at the end of 2015, public debt continued to rise, and Argentina had to once again seek financial assistance from the International Monetary Fund. The continued burden of debt and associated uncertainty has affected Argentina's economy in a variety of ways.

Is high indebtedness a problem for international bankers only, or should it concern multinational managements as well? Debt service difficulties become increasingly likely when the value of debt to exports reaches 200 to 250 percent and the debt service ratio—that is, debt service payments/export earnings—exceeds 20 to 25 percent. Let's examine the ramifications of these large foreign debts for an international firm.

A nation's available foreign currency, known as *foreign exchange*, needs to be available to businesses to pay for imports billed in foreign currency. If a major part of the foreign exchange cannot be used to import components for local products, then either local industries must manufacture the components or the companies that import them must stop production. Either alternative can cause the multinational to lose sales if it has been selling the parts made in one of its home country plants to its subsidiary. This is a common occurrence because the home plant usually has more **vertical integration** than its subsidiaries; that is, the home plant produces more of the inputs it needs for its own manufacturing processes. A scarcity of foreign exchange can also make it difficult for the subsidiary to import raw materials and spare parts for its production equipment. If headquarters wants its affiliate to continue production, it may have to lend required foreign exchange to the affiliate and wait for repayment. Some multinationals have closed their operations in a country, resorted to barter, or even begun to export their subsidiaries' products even though these actions have reduced exports or even local sales of their domestic plants.

Governments with high debt may impose price controls (which make it difficult for a subsidiary to earn a profit), cut government spending (which reduces company sales), and impose wage controls (which limit consumer purchasing power). The economic turmoil that follows can turn into a political crisis, as occurred in Greece after that nation passed an austerity plan to address the financial crisis of 2012.

Scarcity of foreign exchange can affect even firms that merely export to nations with high foreign debt because those governments will surely impose import restrictions in order to safeguard their foreign exchange so they can use it to service their debt. When Latin American debt

vertical integration
The production by a firm of inputs for its own manufacturing processes

What Is the Best Way to Measure a Nation's Development: Income or Quality of Life?

What is the best way to measure a nation's development? Should the primary focus be on the economic factors so important to international business? Or are there other ways to get a picture of development that includes the quality of life experienced by a nation's citizens? Until recently, we have relied on economic data such as GDP per capita, and then GNI per capita, to tell us about development, and many economists still do. Yet, often those figures do not capture what we actually want to know. We may be measuring the wrong things.

There are two basic approaches to assessing development, each with many variations. To date, the first and most frequently used approach is to focus on the economy, because that shows what a nation's people are producing, and thus what they are earning and able to consume. The second, evolving approach takes a closer look at people and the choices and options open to them for healthy, fulfilling lives.

In this module, we have followed and developed the basic arguments for using economic factors. The second approach, often called the human-needs approach, doesn't have nearly as strong a story. In 1990, the United Nations Development Program (UNDP) followed up on an earlier, people-centered approach introduced by the International Labour Organisation (ILO) in the 1970s that had been abandoned due to lack of

HDI Rank	Country	Life Expectancy at Birth (years), 2017	Expected Years of Schooling, 2017	GNI per Capita (PPP, US$), 2017
1	Norway	82.3	17.9	$68,012
2	Switzerland	83.5	16.2	57,625
3	Australia	83.1	22.9	43,560
4	Ireland	81.6	19.6	53,754
5	Germany	81.2	17.0	46,136
12	Canada	82.5	16.4	43,433
13	United States	79.5	16.5	54,941
182	Mali	58.5	7.7	1,953
183	Burkina Faso	60.8	8.5	1,650
184	Sierra Leone	52.2	9.8	1,240
185	Burundi	57.9	11.7	702
186	Chad	53.2	8.0	1,750
187	South Sudan	57.3	4.9	963
188	Central African Republic	52.9	7.2	663
189	Niger	60.4	5.4	906

Sources: "Human Development Report 2018," *United Nations Development Program*, September 20, 2018; Charles Kindleberger, and Bruce Herrick, *Economic Development*, New York, NY: McGraw-Hill, 1977, 1; Lee M. Stapleton, and Guy D. Garrod, "Keeping Things Simple: Why the Human Development Index Should Not Diverge from Its Equal Weights Assumption," *Social Indicators Research*, vol. 84, no. 2, November 2007, 179–88; Shyamal Chowdhury, and Lyn Squire, "Setting Weights for Aggregate Indices: An Application to the Commitment to Development Index and Human Development Index," *The Journal of Development Studies*, vol. 42, no. 5, 2006, 761–71; George Psacharopoulos, "Returns to Investment in Education: A Global Update," *World Development*, vol. 22, no. 9, September 1994, 1325–43; Jean-Philippe Cotis, "Economic Growth and Productivity," Government Economic Service, July 13 and 14, 2006; and William A. Allen, and Richhild Moessner, "The Liquidity Consequences of the Euro Area Sovereign Debt Crisis," *World Economics*, vol. 14, no. 1, January/March 2013, 103–26.

support in developed nations. This was during the Thatcher–Reagan years, a worldwide recession, and a concern that developing countries should repay their debts to international banks. The UNDP's answer to the question "What is human development?" suggested a human-needs approach that included the reduction of poverty, unemployment, and inequality in the distribution of income. The reduction of poverty also means less illiteracy, less malnutrition, less disease and early death, and a shift from agricultural to industrial production or service-based economic activity.

The UNDP's resulting Human Development Index (HDI) is based on three elements: (1) a long and healthy life, measured by life expectancy; (2) the ability to acquire knowledge, measured by adult literacy; and (3) access to resources needed for a decent standard of living, measured by GNI/capita, adjusted for differences in purchasing power. In the program's 2018 report, the source for the accompanying table, Norway is the most developed, and the 20 lowest-ranked countries are all located in Africa.

The HDI advocates an investment in people—human capital in economists' terminology—that recognizes that more than just capital accumulation is needed for growth, and that human development consists of more than economic achievements. Human achievements often accompany economic growth, but data also show that developed nations may do poorly on human-related indicators such as human rights, infant survival, and gender equity. For example, the United States ranks 45th in infant mortality rates, at 5.6 deaths per 1,000 live births, more than such countries as Serbia (5.1), Cuba (4.2), Poland (4.0), Belarus (2.9), Japan (2.0), Finland (1.9), and Slovenia (1.8).

Critical Thinking Questions

1. Which approach to measuring development do you think would be most useful for international managers to follow in assessing a potential market's level of development? Outline the reasons for your answer.

2. Do you agree or disagree with former U.S. Attorney General and presidential candidate Robert F. Kennedy's assertions that an approach to understanding development that relies on market data is not really what we need to know to understand our development as people (and markets)? Defend your answer.

3. If you were the manager of a subsidiary of an international company and you were asked by the host-country government to justify your proposed investment in a production plant based on human development needs, what arguments could you provide to help support your position?

Sources: Human Development Report 2018 Update (New York: United Nations Development Program), http://hdr.undp.org, accessed September 20, 2018; Charles Kindleberger, and Bruce Herrick, *Economic Development*, New York: McGraw-Hill, 1977, 1; Lee M. Stapleton, and Guy D. Garrod, "Keeping Things Simple: Why the Human Development Index Should Not Diverge from Its Equal Weights Assumption," *Social Indicators Research*, vol. 84, 2007, 179–88, https://link.springer.com, accessed September 20, 2018; Shyamal Chowdhury, and Lyn Squire, "Setting Weights for Aggregate Indices: An Application to the Commitment to Development Index and Human Development Index," *Journal of Development Studies*, vol. 42, no. 5, July 2006, 761–71, https://www.cgdev.org, accessed September 20, 2018; George Psacharopoulos, "Returns to Investment in Education: A Global Update," World Development, vol. 22, 1994, http://documents.worldbank.org, accessed September 20, 2018; Jean-Philippe Cotis, "Economic Growth and Productivity," July 13 and 14, 2006, http://www.oecd.org, accessed September 20, 2018; and William A. Allen, and Richhild Moessner, "The Liquidity Consequences of the Euro Area Sovereign Debt Crisis," *World Economics*, vol. 14, no. 1, January/March 2013, 103–26.

increased rapidly from 1981 to 1983, that region's share of U.S. exports dropped by one-third. To protect these export markets, U.S. firms had to extend long-term credit. Similarly, Cuba experienced a growing level of foreign commercial and public sector debt in the years after the global financial crisis of 2008–2009, exacerbated from 2016 onward as commodity prices declined, Venezuela's oil industry and overall economy began to collapse, and Hurricane Irma battered the island in 2017. Cuba's export earnings contracted by 24 percent between 2014 and 2016 alone, contributing to a shortage of foreign currency. In response, Cuba experienced a sharp decline in imports, along with escalating government budgetary deficits and reductions in electricity, fuel, and other supplies.[21] You can see why managers will expect to receive information about the status of foreign debt in nations where these debt levels are high.

LO 7-4

Discuss the socioeconomic dimensions of economies and the indicators used to assess them.

Socioeconomic Dimensions of the Economy and Their Relevance for International Business

To estimate the potential of a market and provide input to the other functional areas of the firm, managers require data on a number of socioeconomic factors in addition to the economic factors discussed above. For example, an area must have sufficient people with the means to buy the firm's products. Socioeconomic data provide information about the number of people, and the economic dimensions tell us whether they have purchasing power. We begin this section with an analysis of total population.

TOTAL POPULATION

Total population, the most general indicator of potential market size, is the first characteristic of the population that analysts examine. Population sizes vary immensely. Figure 7.5 identifies the 10 countries projected to have the largest populations in 2050, as well as their current population as of 2017, to help indicate both size and extent of growth in each.

The fact that many developed nations have fewer than 10 million inhabitants shows that population size alone is a poor indicator of economic strength and market potential. Only for a few low-priced products, such as soft drinks, cigarettes, and soap, might population size alone provide a basis for estimating consumption. For products not in this category, populations that are large or increasing rapidly may not signify an immediate enlargement of the market, but if incomes grow over time, eventually some part of the population will become customers. We can obtain insight into the speed at which this is occurring by comparing population and economic growth rates. Where GNI increases faster than the population, there is probably an expanding market, whereas the converse situation indicates possible market contraction and may even identify a country as a potential area of political unrest. This possibility is strengthened if an analysis of the educational system discloses an accumulation of technical and university graduates. These groups expect to be employed as and receive the wages of professionals, and when enough new jobs are not being created to absorb them, the government can be in serious trouble. Various nations already face this difficulty; Egypt is one example, Saudi Arabia another.

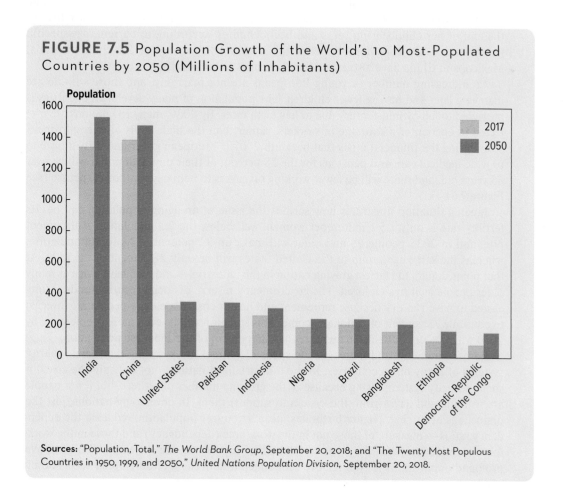

FIGURE 7.5 Population Growth of the World's 10 Most-Populated Countries by 2050 (Millions of Inhabitants)

Sources: "Population, Total," *The World Bank Group*, September 20, 2018; and "The Twenty Most Populous Countries in 1950, 1999, and 2050," *United Nations Population Division*, September 20, 2018.

AGE DISTRIBUTION

Because few products are purchased by everyone, marketers must identify the segments of the population more apt to buy their goods. For some firms, age is a salient determinant of market size, but the distribution of age groups within populations varies widely. Generally, because of their higher birthrates, developing countries have younger populations than do industrial countries.

The population of developing countries is more than three-quarters of the world's total population. Figure 7.5 shows that of the 10 nations predicted to have the largest populations by the year 2050, only one is a high-income country (the United States).

What does this mean for business managers? For developed nations, it brings increased demand for products bought by and for children, a smaller market for furniture and clothing, but an increased demand for medical care and related products, tourism, and financial services as the population ages. Firms confronting a decreasing demand for their products will have to look for sales increases in the developing economies, where the age distribution is reversed.

Many forces are responsible for reductions in birthrates. Governments are supporting family planning programs, to be sure, but there is ample evidence that improved levels of health and education along with an enhanced status for women, a more even distribution of income, and a greater degree of urbanization all act to reduce the traditional family size. In fact, experts have claimed for some time that the combined effects of a successful family planning program and the education of women beyond the primary level are extremely powerful in reducing family size.

The decrease in family size is welcomed by some countries in Africa and the Middle East, where fertility rates are as high as seven children per woman. But declining birthrates are causing concern in industrialized nations. The World Bank reports that in these countries the *fertility rates*—the number of children who will be born to a woman if she lives to the end of her childbearing years and bears children according to current, age-specific fertility rates—are considerably below the *replacement number* of 2.1 children. India, Mexico, and China have also experienced declines in their birthrates.

An increasing number of young Europeans are not marrying, and those who do are marrying later and having fewer children. The population of many developed countries is projected to fall by mid-century due to low birth rates. By 2030, many EU nations are projected to encounter a shortage of workers, rather than the high levels of unemployment seen during the financial crisis that began in 2008.[22] European governments will have to provide medical care and pensions for the 28 percent of their population that will be over 65 years old, and there will be fewer working taxpayers to help pay for those expenses (see Figure 7.6).

Japan's situation illustrates how serious the issue of an aging population can be. Its fertility rate is only 1.5 children per woman, well below the 2.1 population replacement rate, and in 2035 people 65 and older will make up 32 percent of its total population, whereas the same age group in the United States will be only 21 percent of the total. At that point, Japan, the fastest-graying nation in the industrial world, will have twice as many older people as it has children. The government's reserve of social security funds is forecasted to have run dry because retirement and health costs for elderly people are forecast to consume 73 percent of national income. This situation will be even more problematic by 2050 when older adults make up more than 36 percent of the Japanese population.

Early retirements and increased life spans of retirees are straining the social security systems of many other countries. In the industrialized nations, not only are the costs of social security systems rising because of the growing number of retirees, but fewer people are working and paying into the system to support them. In developing nations, just the opposite is occurring. Higher birthrates mean a younger population, reducing the dependency ratios—a measure of those not in the workforce (dependency) and those in the workforce (productive)—and the costs to workers of supporting the system, which can have profound implications for the relative economic attractiveness of developing versus developed nations.

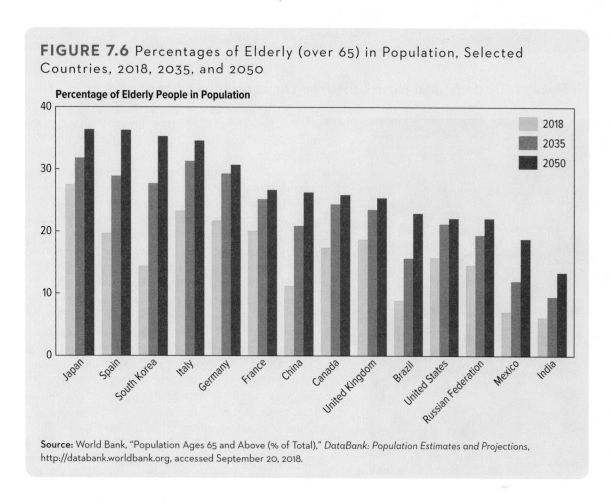

FIGURE 7.6 Percentages of Elderly (over 65) in Population, Selected Countries, 2018, 2035, and 2050

Source: World Bank, "Population Ages 65 and Above (% of Total)," *DataBank: Population Estimates and Projections,* http://databank.worldbank.org, accessed September 20, 2018.

POPULATION DENSITY AND DISTRIBUTION

Other aspects of population that concern business managers are **population density** and **population distribution**. Densely populated areas tend to make product distribution and communications simpler and less costly; thus you might expect Bangladesh, with 1,265 inhabitants per square kilometer of land area, to be an easier market to serve than Canada (4 inhabitants/square kilometer) or Brazil (25 inhabitants/square kilometer).[23] But we must know how these populations are distributed. While only 36 percent of Pakistan's population is urban, for instance, the percentages for Brazil and Canada are 86 and 81 percent, respectively.[24] The geographic features of these countries contribute heavily to their population concentrations.

Another factor, especially in developing countries, is that people worldwide are moving to cities in search of higher wages and more conveniences. As an indicator of the extent of this **rural-to-urban shift**, note that in 2008, for the first time, half the world's population was living in cities, and this proportion is projected to increase to 60 percent by 2030. As Table 7.8 indicates, the greatest urban shifts are occurring in low- and middle-income countries. The change is significant to marketers because city dwellers, being less self-sufficient than rural dwellers, must enter the market economy. Many will live in slums, raising a range of social, economic, and other challenges and opportunities.

OTHER SOCIOECONOMIC DIMENSIONS

Other socioeconomic dimensions can provide useful information to management. The increase in the number of working women, for example, is highly significant because it may result in larger family incomes, a greater market for convenience goods, and a need to alter promotional methods. Human resource managers are interested in this increase

population density
A measure of the number of inhabitants per area unit (inhabitants per square kilometer or square mile)

population distribution
A measure of how the inhabitants are distributed over a nation's area

rural-to-urban shift
The movement of a nation's population from rural areas to cities

Jason Jack Peters: Understand New Cultures through Immersion

Courtesy of Jack Peters.

As an undergrad, I majored in economics with a concentration in international business and a minor in Asian studies. While playing junior golf, I observed the cultural differences between the strong work ethic of the Korean players and the generally more relaxed style of the American players. That influenced my decision to spend my sophomore year studying at Yonsei University in Seoul, South Korea, where I took courses related to international business and Asian studies, including an intensive Korean language course. Living with international students opened my eyes to new cultures, foods, sports, and general views on life. During winter break I backpacked through Vietnam, Laos, Thailand, Cambodia, Singapore, and Indonesia and built on my understanding of many Asian cultures. Then I did a homestay program with a Korean family and learned that true learning comes from fully immersing oneself in other cultures. My host parents spoke only Korean, so my Korean improved tremendously compared to my peers in the dormitory.

Then I had an AIESEC internship in China after junior year, as an overseas management trainee at Mission Hills Golf Club, the world's largest golf club. Although I didn't speak Mandarin, I acquired it along the way, as basic translations were essential to performing well in my position. I take joy in surprising people with a greeting in their native tongue!

At the end of my senior year, I traveled to Florianópolis, Brazil, to study at Universidade Federal de Santa Catarina and completed my final two undergraduate courses. I spent my first month in Brazil studying Portuguese, living with a Brazilian host family. The language barrier was high in the beginning since I knew no Portuguese. However, my Spanish was useful in learning Portuguese. After the semester, I stayed in Brazil to travel. I lived in a favela in Rio de Janeiro, experienced the urban planning model city of Curitiba, and commuted by subway in São Paulo.

From my international experiences, I learned that the biggest challenge is yourself. Getting out of your comfort zone promotes learning. My recommendations for success abroad are to identify your goals prior to departure and formulate a plan to achieve them. Ask yourself, "Why am I going abroad?" If you'd like to learn about the host culture, immerse yourself within it and find ways to speak the host language. If your goals are business oriented, research the business culture of your hosts. Know the cultural nuances beforehand. Research as much about the host culture as possible: major cities, capital cities, population, demographic information, political information, the role of religion, the food, exercise opportunities. Finally, don't be afraid to make mistakes while speaking; it's going to happen, and that is the best way to improve. Stay positive and keep an open mind.

Source: Jason Jack Peters.

because it results in a larger labor supply but also brings changes in production processes, employee facilities, and human resource policies.

Data on a country's divorce rate will help alert the marketer to the formation of single-parent families and single-person households, whose product needs and buying habits differ in many respects from those of a two-parent family. In many countries, important ethnic groups require special consideration by both marketing and human resource managers.

TABLE 7.8 Rural-to-Urban Shift

	Percentage of Population in Urban Areas						
	1950	1970	1990	2010	2030	2050	Percentage Change, 1950–2050
World	30%	37%	43%	52%	60%	68%	127%
More developed regions	55	67	72	77	82	87	58
Less developed regions	18	25	35	46	57	66	267
Least developed countries	8	13	22	30	40	53	563

Note: Data for 2030 and 2050 are estimates.

Source: "World Urbanization Prospects: The 2018 Revision," *United Nations*, September 20, 2018.

SUMMARY

LO 7-1
Explain the purpose of economic analyses.

To keep abreast of the latest economic developments and also to plan for the future, firms regularly assess and forecast economic conditions at the local, state, and national levels. When they enter international operations, the economic analysis increases in complexity because managers are operating in two new environments: foreign and international. There are more economies to study, and these economies are frequently highly divergent.

LO 7-2
Compare different categories of countries, based on levels of national economic development.

Managers involved in international business encounter markets with far greater differences in levels of economic development than those in which they have been working in domestic business settings. A nation's level of economic development affects all aspects of business, and we commonly group them into categories based on their level of economic development, such as developed, developing, and emerging economies. Developing nations have certain common characteristics, including unequal distribution of income, technological and regional dualism, a large percentage of the population in agriculture, high population growth, high illiteracy rate, insufficient education, and low savings rates.

LO 7-3
Outline the dimensions used to describe the economy and their indicators.

The various functional areas of a firm require data on the size and rates of change of a number of economic and socioeconomic factors. Among the more important economic dimensions are GDP, GNI, economic growth rates, distribution of income, personal consumption expenditures, unit labor costs, and the level of national debt, as well as a range of other economic variables.

LO 7-4
Discuss the socioeconomic dimensions of economies and the indicators used to assess them.

To estimate market potential, managers require data on socioeconomic factors as well as economic factors. Among the more important socioeconomic dimensions of relevance to analysts are total population and rates of population growth, age distribution, population density, and population distribution.

KEY TERMS

Atlas conversion factor 192
developed economies 188
developing economies 188
discretionary income 197
disposable income 197
emerging market economies 189
foreign environment 186

GINI index 196
gross domestic product
    (GDP) 187
gross national income (GNI) 188
income distribution 196
international environment 187
population density 207

population distribution 207
purchasing power parity
    (PPP) 191
rural-to-urban shift 207
underground economy 192
unit labor costs 199
vertical integration 202

CRITICAL THINKING QUESTIONS

1. What impacts do economic forecasts have on a firm's functional areas? If management learns from the economic analysis of country A that wage rates are expected to increase by 10 percent next year, which functional areas of the firm will be concerned? Why will this be of concern to management?

2. When might a country's level of economic development mislead a marketer?

3. What might the differences between economically developing and developed nations mean to an international company considering entry into a foreign market?

4. Why should managers of international companies be concerned about purchasing power parity?

5. What is the value of using data on GNI per capita and population density when analyzing the attractiveness of an economy? What limitations or potential problems can arise when using these data in an analysis?

6. What social, political, and economic conditions might signal the existence of a large underground economy, and why should managers pay heed to such signals?

7. Why is income distribution important to marketers in international companies? What might be the attraction and concerns associated with relatively even distribution of income, and with highly uneven income distribution, and how might this assessment be impacted based on the level of the nation's economic development?

8. The staff economist of a large multinational with a Turkish subsidiary has given the firm's chief financial officer a report on Turkey's foreign debt situation, as shown in Table 7.7. What concerns might the chief financial officer have?

9. In developing economies, what factors are associated with reduced birthrates and what is the logic of these associations?

10. What implications might the rural-to-urban shift in developing countries have for international companies?

globalEDGE RESEARCH TASK   http://globalEDGE.msu.edu/

Use the globalEDGE website (http://globaledge.msu.edu/) to complete the following exercises:

1. You argue that economic indicators of a country can be used to estimate the development classification of that country. To collect evidence, visit the "by Classification" subsection under the "Global Insights" section of globalEDGE and review the averages of the economic indicators for the least developed, developing (emerging), and developed countries. How do the average values differ for different country classifications and do you see certain trends? Prepare to discuss the reasons for these trends for each indicator. (e.g., Why do the least developed countries have a

higher GDP growth rate than the developed countries?)

2. You are an aerospace parts manufacturer in the United States and you're searching for new international markets. Before you can start country due diligence, you would like to identify five prospect countries with the highest market potential for your industry. Utilizing the "Aerospace Market Potential Index" of globalEDGE, choose five prospect countries for further investigation. Did you use the overall score or the scores of any particular dimension/s to decide? Review the indicators (measures) used for each dimension and explain which of the dimensions are less/more relevant to your industry?

MINICASE

THE IMPACT OF DARAWAN'S DEVELOPMENT POLICY

Armando Suarez, CEO of Industrias Globales, and Pedro Garcia, the firm's director of international operations, are discussing a statement made today by the secretary of the treasury in the Republic of Darawan.

Suarez: Pedro, did you listen to the secretary's comments today about the proposed change in development strategy?

Garcia: Yes, I did, and I'm concerned. We have spent considerable time and money planning our entry into the Darawan market, and if the government proceeds with the new economic strategy, we've got to change our plant design, plan to produce different product lines, and completely change our marketing plans.

Suarez: This apparently is more serious than I thought. How can a change in their development strategy from one promoting replacement of foreign imports with products produced domestically to a strategy based on promotion of exports affect us?

Garcia: Hang on to your chair, Chief, and I'll explain each strategy and how the change will affect our entire start-up program in Darawan. Oh, and by the way, our Darawan competitors are going to have to make changes, too.

Critical Thinking Questions

Imagine you are Pedro Garcia.

1. Describe the two strategies for the CEO.

2. Explain how the change in Darawan's development strategy will affect the firm in many ways.

3. What changes in its entry plans will the firm have to make?

NOTES

1. Uri Dadush, and Bennett Stancil, "The World Order in 2050," *Carnegie Endowment for International Peace*, April 2010, 9.

2. Adam Smith, *An Inquiry into the Nature and Causes of the Wealth of Nations*, London, UK: A. and C. Black, 1859, 1.

3. Steve H. Hanke, and Alex K. F. Kwok, "On the Measurement of Zimbabwe's Hyperinflation," *Cato Journal*, vol. 29, no. 2, Spring–Summer 2009.

4. "The Half-Life of a Currency," *The Economist*, https://www.economist.com, accessed September 19, 2018.

5. Many of these factors also affect domestic firms, but multinational firms are generally more vulnerable and usually must act more quickly.

6. If management is interested in a country as a possible site for investment, it will require the same detailed information as it does for an area where the firm is already doing business.

7. "GDP and GNI," *OECD Observer*, December 2004–January 2005, http://oecdobserver.org, accessed October 2, 2018.

8. World Bank, "World Bank Country and Lending Groups," https://datahelpdesk.worldbank.org, accessed September 20, 2018. These categories are based on figures calculated using the Atlas method.

9. "Standard Country or Area Codes for Statistical Use," *United Nations Statistics Division*, March 31, 1996.

10. World Bank, "GNI, Atlas Method," https://data.worldbank.org, accessed September 20, 2018.

11. World Bank, "GNI per Capita Ranking, Atlas Method and PPP Based," https://datacatalog.worldbank.org, accessed September 20, 2018.

12. World Bank, "GNI per Capita Ranking, Atlas Method and PPP Based," https://datacatalog.worldbank.org, accessed September 20, 2018.

13. World Bank, "Backmatter," *World Development Indicators 2014*, Washington, DC: World Bank, 2014, http://documents.worldbank.org, accessed September 20, 2018); Tim Callen, "PPP versus the Market: Which Weight Matters?," *Finance and Development* vol. 44, no. 1, March 2007, http://www.imf.org/external/pubs/ft/fandd/2007/03/basics.htm, accessed January 21, 2015; and World Bank, "Structure of Consumption in PPP Terms," 2000 *World Development Indicators*, Washington, DC: World Bank, 2000, 224.

14. Stephen J. Dubner, "How Deep Is the Shadow Economy? A New Freakonomics Radio Podcast," *Freakonomics*, August 30, 2012.

15. Leandro Medina, and Friedrich Schneider, *Shadow Economies Around the World: What Did We Learn Over the Last 20 Years? International Monetary Fund Working Paper WP/18/17*, January 2018, https://www.imf.org, accessed September 20, 2018; Anoop Singh, Sonali Jain-Chandra, and Adil Mohommad, "Inclusive Growth, Institutions, and the Underground Economy," *IMF Working Paper WP/12/47*, February 2012, https://www.imf.org, accessed September 20, 2018; and Friedrich Schneider, Andreas Buehn, and Claudio E. Montenegro, "Shadow Economies All Over the World: New Estimates for 162 Countries from 1999 to 2007," *Policy Research Working Paper 5356*, Washington, DC: The World Bank, July 2010, http://documents.worldbank.org, accessed September 20, 2018.

16. Niall McCarthy, "The Countries with the Largest Shadow Economies," *Forbes*, https://www.forbes.com, accessed September 20, 2018; and Medina, and Schneider, *Shadow Economies Around the World: What Did We Learn Over the Last 20 Years?*

17. "GINI Index (World Bank estimate)," https://data.worldbank.org, accessed September 20, 2018.

18. "'Made in China' Isn't So Cheap Anymore, and That Could Spell Headache for Beijing," *CNBC*, https://www.cnbc.com, accessed September 20, 2018.

19. Brendan Menapace, "Nike, Adidas Starting to Move Away from China, and That Says a Lot," *Promo Marketing Magazine*, https://magazine.promomarketing.com, accessed September 20, 2018.

20. Marc Bain, "To See How Asia's Manufacturing Map Is Being Redrawn, Look at Nike and Adidas," *Quartz*, https://qz.com, accessed September 20, 2018.

21. Marc Frank, "Cash-Strapped Cuba Imposes New Restrictions on Imports," *Reuters*, https://www.reuters.com, accessed September 20, 2018; and Jose Luis Rodriguez, "Cuba and Its Economy: 2017–2018, a Preliminary Assessment," *Temas*, http://www.temas.cult.cu, accessed September 20, 2018.

22. U.S. Census Bureau, *International Data Base*, https://www.census.gov, accessed September 20, 2018; and United Nations Department of Economic and Social Affairs, *World Population Ageing, 1950–2050*, http://www.un.org, accessed September 20, 2018.

23. World Bank, "Population Density (People per Sq. Km of Land Area)," https://data.worldbank.org, accessed September 20, 2018.

24. World Bank, "Urban Population (% of Total)," 2018 Revision, https://data.worldbank.org, accessed September 20, 2018.

8

The International Monetary System and Financial Forces

> **The function of money is not to make money but to move goods. Money is only one part of our transportation system. It moves goods from man to man.**
>
> *—Attributed to Henry Ford in a speech at the Ford Motor Company*[1]

©Ralf Siemieniec/Shutterstock.

LEARNING OBJECTIVES

After reading this module, you should be able to:

LO 8-1 **Describe** the international monetary system's history.

LO 8-2 **Describe** today's floating currency exchange rate system, including the IMF currency arrangements.

LO 8-3 **Describe** the factors that influence exchange rate movement.

LO 8-4 **Discuss** financial forces governments can exert.

LO 8-5 **Explain** the significance of the balance of payments to international business decisions.

How International Terrorism Gets Funded

Terrorist operations are costly, and funding them requires the ability to launder money, disguise its sources, and move it unmonitored across international borders. Let's look at some ways security professionals think funds for terrorists are transferred across borders today and how governments have been responding to the nonbank financial institutions that serve terrorism.

A popular and informal funds-transfer method in Africa and the Middle East is *hawala* (an Arabic word for "transfer") or *hundi* (as referred to in India), which leaves few or no traces. In its legitimate use, foreign workers who want to send money home give the funds to their local hawala (the word describes both the process and the person who conducts it), with directions about who should receive it. The hawala then contacts his counterpart in the destination, and the designated recipient is told she can draw the funds. Brokers at both ends of the hawala transaction run balances that can be settled over time through cash or noncash transactions. They keep detailed records, but the sender receives no contract, receipt, or legal documentation; the transfer, communicated via phone, fax, or e-mail, is based on trust and honor. Hawalas, who may be part of the same extended family, make a small commission on the transaction, plus something on the exchange rate, although their rates often are better than those available at banks. The majority of hawala transactions are legal, and they serve an important function well, yet you can see how they would also meet the needs of terrorists.

In addition to hawalas and hundis, there are many other ways to transfer funds without a trail. One is to manipulate sales invoices so that excess value is transferred to the payee. An invoice for $200,000, if inflated 30 percent, transfers $60,000 without a traceable record of the cash transfer. Another area of concern involves the use of virtual currencies, such as Bitcoin. Largely unregulated and providing a high level of anonymity in the conduct of financial transactions, virtual currencies have the potential to be readily exploited by terrorist financiers seeking to move funds internationally while remaining undetected. There are also schemes to divert trade, to use charities, and to use Internet-based payments. Each of these approaches is complex and not easily traceable.

Every industrialized nation's treasury is monitoring money transactions that may support terrorism. There are also international coordination efforts. The Financial Action Task Force on Money Laundering (FATF), established by the G7 countries (France, Germany, Canada, Japan, Italy, the United Kingdom, and the United States), develops and promotes policies that make money laundering more difficult and riskier. This group works closely with the IMF, the World Bank, the United Nations, and national bodies such as the U.S. Department of the Treasury and that department's Terrorist Finance Tracking Program. FATF adopted a new operational plan for countering terrorist financing in February 2018, and FATF regularly reviews and reports on anti-laundering standards in specific countries and publishes the results. If the FATF report is critical, all governments are notified to advise their banks and other financial institutions to exercise appropriate due diligence and caution when transacting business in the listed countries. In October 2018, countries being monitored as high risk included the Democratic People's Republic of Korea, Ethiopia, Iran, Pakistan, Serbia, Sri Lanka, Syria, Trinidad and Tobago, Tunisia, and Yemen. The financial world is watching the listed countries closely, although some argue that these measures actually force the transfer of funds into methods and institutions that are less visible or transparent.

The FATF offers suggestions to help safeguard against terrorism: criminalize the financing of terrorism; freeze and confiscate terrorist assets; report suspicious transactions related to terrorism; track parallel or alternative remittance systems such as hawala; and monitor wire transfers, nonprofit organizations, and cash couriers. The U.S. Department of the Treasury lists countries, individuals, and networks subject to "311 actions," named after the section of the USA Patriot Act that provides the Treasury secretary with options to sanction specific organizations. You can see the updated 311 list at https://home.treasury.gov/policy-issues/terrorism-and-illicit-finance/311-actions.

Sources: "High-Risk and Other Monitored Jurisdictions," *FATF*, October 19, 2018; "Terrorist Finance Tracking Program (TFTP)," *U.S. Department of the Treasury*, August 21, 2018; "The IMF and the Fight Against Money Laundering and the Financing of Terrorism," *International Monetary Fund*, March 08, 2018; "FATF Actions Taken Under the 2016 Counter-Terrorist Financing Operational Plan," *FATF*, February 23, 2018; Nikos Passas, "Fighting Terror with Error: The Counter-Productive Regulation of Informal Value Transfers," *Crime, Law and Social Change*, vol. 45, no. 11, November 2006, 315–336.

The International Monetary System: A Brief History

LO 8-1

Describe the international monetary system's history.

The international monetary system consists of institutions, agreements, rules, and processes that allow for the payments, currency exchange, and cross-border movements of capital required for international transactions.[2] Because an understanding of the way these institutions and arrangements have evolved helps make your picture of current

gold standard
A monetary system that defines the value of a currency in terms of a fixed amount of gold

arrangements clearer, we begin with a brief history of the global monetary system. First, we look at the gold standard and a monetary system to support trade called the Bretton Woods system. Then we review the inherent conflict in having a national currency serve as a reserve currency and look at the evolution of the monetary system, leading up to the floating rate system.

THE GOLD STANDARD

Based on its scarcity and easily assessed level of purity, gold has been trusted since ancient times as a way for people to store, exchange, and measure value. From about AD 1200 to the present, the price of gold has generally been going up.[3] Until the last part of the 19th century, international traders used both gold bullion and coins.

However, as trade grew, carrying large amounts of gold became impractical: gold is heavy, it has transportation and storage costs, it does not earn interest, and it makes an obvious target for thieves. These drawbacks led to the development of a paper script as a proxy for the gold that was backed by governments with a pledge to exchange the script for gold at a fixed rate.

In 1717, Sir Isaac Newton, the great mathematician and master of the English mint, established the price of gold in terms of British currency at 3 pounds, 17 shillings, 10.5 pence per ounce, putting England on the **gold standard**. Until then, Britain had used the silver standard, as did China, Spain, and India.

Most trading or industrial countries followed England's move and adopted the gold standard. Each country set a certain number of units of its currency equal to an ounce of gold, and the ratios of these units of gold equivalence established the exchange rate between any two currencies on the gold standard. For example, if 5 British pounds were pegged at 1 ounce of gold and 10 French francs were pegged at 1 ounce, then the exchange rate was 2 French francs per British pound, or 0.5 pounds per franc.

Except during the Napoleonic Wars, England was willing to convert between gold and paper currency until 1914. During those two centuries, more than 90 percent of world trade was financed in London.[4] However, the cost of fighting World War I, which began in 1914, forced Britain to sell a substantial portion of its gold and suspend gold exchange. Other warring countries, including Germany, France, and Russia, suspended the exchange of paper money for gold and stopped exports of gold. Between World War I and World War II, which began in 1939, there was a short flirtation with the renewal of the gold standard, but it was not successfully reestablished.

Gold often serves as a way to store value during crises. ©Ayala_studio/iStock/Getty Images.

The simplicity of the gold standard was a large part of its appeal. Trade imbalances were corrected by a flow of gold in the direction of the surplus, and the money supply would rise or fall in direct relationship to the gold flows. Although the gold standard has not been the international monetary system for many years, it continues to have some ardent advocates—most economists not among them. The heart of supporters' argument is expressed in one word: *discipline.* Under the gold standard, a government cannot create money that is not backed by gold no matter how great the temptation to do so for political advantage.[5] Unfortunately, this discipline sacrifices a government's monetary flexibility. For example, on the gold standard, a government could not increase the money supply to ward off a recession. Such flexibility is necessary for a globalized monetary system, where quick adjustments to wide swings in a currency's value may be necessary. Economist Paul Krugman points out that this flexibility is the reason the 1987 stock market crash did not cause a depression similar to that of 1929.[6]

THE BRETTON WOODS SYSTEM

The 1944 discussions among 44 Allied nations at Bretton Woods, New Hampshire, to plan for post–World War II monetary arrangements reached a consensus that stable exchange rates were desirable, but that experience might dictate adjustments. Representatives at the conference also agreed that floating or fluctuating exchange rates had proved unsatisfactory. In establishing the International Monetary Fund (IMF), they also set up the new **Bretton Woods system**, also called the *gold exchange standard* and the *fixed-rate system.* This historic agreement served as the basis of the international monetary system from 1945 to 1971.

Bretton Woods set up **fixed exchange rates** among member nations' currencies, with **par value** based on gold and the U.S. dollar, which was valued at $35 per ounce of gold. Governments agreed that their central banks would keep their currencies tied to the value of the dollar, which was tied to gold. For example, the British pound's par value was US$2.40, the French franc's was US$0.18, and the German mark's was US$0.2732. There was an understanding that the U.S. government would redeem dollars for gold and that the dollar was the only currency to be redeemable for gold. This dollar-based gold exchange standard established the U.S. dollar as both a means of international payment and a reserve currency for governments to hold in their treasuries. **Reserves** are funds held by a nation's central bank or treasury and used to back its liabilities; they can include various hard currencies (Japanese yen, U.S. dollar, British pound sterling, EU euro) and gold. They are often called *central reserves.*

The Bretton Woods system supported substantial international trade growth during the 1950s and 1960s. Other countries changed their currency's value against the dollar and gold, but the U.S. dollar remained fixed at $35 per ounce of gold. This meant that the United States, in order to satisfy the growing demand of other countries for reserves (because countries would hold dollars as a proxy for gold), had to run a balance-of-payments deficit. This means the demand for and flow of dollars out of the United States was greater than the flow in. People outside the United States wanted to hold dollars because they operated as a proxy for gold. The external holdings far exceeded the inflow of dollars due to U.S. export sales and investments by foreigners in the United States. From 1958 through 1971, the United States ran up a cumulative deficit of $56 billion, which it financed partly by using its own gold reserves and partly by incurring liabilities to foreign central banks. As a result, U.S. gold reserves shrank from $24.8 billion to $12.2 billion,[7] and U.S. liabilities increased from $13.6 billion to $62.2 billion.[8] By 1971, the U.S. Treasury held only 22 cents worth of gold for each U.S. dollar held by foreign central banks.

An interesting paradox associated with reserve currencies was first pointed out by economist Robert Triffin. The reserve-currency nation's deficit, which is unavoidable, eventually inspires a lack of confidence in the reserve currency, which leads to a financial crisis. That is, the more of the reserve currency foreigners hold, the less confidence they have in the currency. This **Triffin paradox** is exactly what happened when, after trade deficits

Bretton Woods system
The international monetary system in place from 1945 to 1971, with par value based on gold and the U.S. dollar

fixed exchange rate
Exchange rate regime in which the currency's value is tied to the value of another currency or gold

par value
Stated value

reserves
Assets held by a nation's central bank, used to back up government liabilities

Triffin paradox
A problem in which a national currency that is also a reserve currency will eventually run a deficit, leading to lack of confidence in the reserve currency and a financial crisis

special drawing rights (SDR) An international reserve asset established by the IMF; the unit of account for the IMF and other international organizations

CULTURE FACTS @internationalbiz

@brettonwoods What is so extraordinary about Bretton Woods is that it was the first time in history that people from cultures all across the globe came together to set up a monetary system to support peaceful trade. #together #peacefultrade

occurred in the late 1960s, President Charles de Gaulle pushed the Bank of France to redeem its dollar holdings for gold. Eventually, in 1971, President Nixon suspended the dollar's convertibility into gold.

Finance ministers at Bretton Woods had foreseen the dangers of using one currency as a reserve currency and tried to make adjustments to avoid the impending crisis by creating an international reserve asset, **special drawing rights (SDR)**, which came into being in 1969. The SDR is a virtual currency with no tangible, physical presence; its value is based on a trade-weighted basket of five currencies: the euro, the Japanese yen, the British pound sterling, the Chinese renminbi, and the U.S. dollar. The IMF uses the SDR as its unit of account, as do its 189 members and 16 other international institutions. Yet today, the SDR has limited use as a reserve asset, and its ability to serve as a safety net should the international monetary system run into serious difficulty has yet to be tested. You can check the daily valuation of the SDR at https://www.imf.org/external/np/fin/data/rms_sdrv.aspx.

THE CENTRAL RESERVE/NATIONAL CURRENCY CONFLICT

Every member of the IMF keeps a *reserve account*, a bit like a savings account, with holdings the country can draw on when needed to finance trade or investments or to intervene in currency markets. The U.S. dollar has been the most used central reserve asset in the world since the end of World War II; at the end of June 2018, roughly 62 percent of the world's reserve assets were held in dollars and 20 percent in euros.[9] The dollars, held in the form of U.S. Treasury bonds, earn interest, so the more dollars held in a central reserve account, the better, from the holder's perspective. But the countries holding those U.S. dollars in their foreign reserve accounts don't want their central reserve asset to lose value, and therein lies a contradiction: at some point, holding large numbers of U.S. dollars (or any other product) causes them to lose value, per the Triffin paradox.

At the same time, the U.S. dollar is the national currency of the United States, whose government must deal with inflation, recession, interest rates, unemployment, and other internal problems. The U.S. government uses fiscal and monetary policies to meet these problems by manipulating tax rates, spending available revenue, growing or contracting the money supply, and controlling the rate of that growth or contraction.

It would be only accidental if the national interests of the United States coincided with the interests of the multitude of countries holding U.S. dollars in their central reserve asset accounts. For example, the United States might be slowing money supply growth and raising taxes to combat domestic inflation while the world needs more liquidity, in the form of U.S. dollars, to finance growth, trade, or investment. Or the United States might be stimulating its economy through faster money supply growth and lower taxes at a time when so many U.S. dollars are already outstanding that their value is dropping—not a happy state of affairs for countries holding U.S. dollars. It was a quirk of history that thrust the currency of the United States into this conflicting role. The IMF hoped a non-national asset, the SDR, would rescue the U.S. dollar and the world from this conflict when nations would begin to use the SDR as their main reserve. That has not yet happened.

LO 8-2
Describe today's floating currency exchange rate system, including the IMF currency arrangements.

The Floating Currency Exchange Rate System

In 1971, President Nixon announced that the United States would not exchange gold for the paper dollars held by foreign central banks, relieving the dollar of much of its role as a stabilizer for the international monetary system. The shock of Nixon's announcement led currency exchange markets to remain closed for several days, and when they reopened, they began to develop a new system for which few rules existed. Currencies were floating, their values based on market forces, and the stated US$ value of $35 per ounce of gold was now meaningless because the United States would no longer exchange any of its gold for dollars.

Two attempts were made to agree on durable new sets of fixed currency exchange rates, one in December 1971 and one in February 1973, resulting in the Smithsonian Agreements. Both times, however, banks, businesses, and individuals felt the central banks had pegged the rates incorrectly, and they were right each time. By March 1973, the major currencies were floating in the foreign exchange (FX) markets, with their value determined by supply and demand, and this system of floating exchange rates still prevails. The Jamaica Agreement that established the rules for the floating system was both worked out and accepted by IMF members after the fact, in 1976. It allows for flexible exchange rates among IMF members while condoning central bank operations in the money markets to smooth out volatile periods. It also demonetized gold, which was abandoned as a reserve currency. Such is our trust in gold's value, though, that many nations still use it as a reserve asset, including the United States and EU members.

floating exchange rates
Exchange rates determined by supply and demand that allow currency values to float against one another

Jamaica Agreement
The 1976 IMF agreement establishing flexible exchange rates among IMF members

CURRENT CURRENCY ARRANGEMENTS

The IMF now recognizes eight types of currency exchange arrangements, extended from an initial three. These eight strategies describe the way countries position their currencies in relationship to other currencies, and they vary in their degree of flexibility.[10]

- *Exchange arrangement with no separate legal tender:* One country adopts the currency of another, or a group of countries adopt a common currency. Examples of the first strategy are the adoption of the U.S. dollar in Ecuador, El Salvador, Marshall Islands, Micronesia, Palau, Panama, and Timor-Leste, while Andorra, Kosovo, San Marino, the Vatican, and Montenegro have adopted the euro. An example of the second arrangement, a common currency, is the euro, the shared currency in 19 EU member-countries.

- *Currency board arrangement:* A currency board arrangement commits the country's government to hold foreign reserves of a specific currency in an amount equal to its domestic currency supply and exchange the two at a fixed rate. Djibouti, Hong Kong SAR, Dominica, Grenada, St. Kitts and Nevis, St. Lucia, St. Vincent, and the Grenadines use the U.S. dollar. Bulgaria and Bosnia Herzegovina use the euro.

- *Conventional fixed-peg arrangement:* A fixed-peg or fixed-rate relationship allows a currency's exchange rates with one or a basket of currencies to fluctuate around a fixed rate within a narrow band of less than 1 percent. Aruba, The Bahamas, Bahrain, Barbados, Belize, Curaçao and Sint Maarten, Eritrea, Iraq, Jordan, Oman, Qatar, Saudi Arabia, Turkmenistan, and the United Arab Emirates are among the countries pegged to the dollar. Cabo Verde, Comoros, Denmark, São Tomé and Príncipe, Benin, Burkina Faso, Côte d'Ivoire, Guinea Bissau, Mali, Niger, Senegal, Togo, Cameroon, Central African Rep., Chad Rep. of Congo, Equatorial Guinea, and Gabon are pegged to the euro. Until 2018, Venezuela pegged its currency to the dollar, but then changed the peg to a new cryptocurrency, the petro, which is linked to movements in oil prices.

- *Stabilized arrangement: Pegged exchange rate within a horizontal band:* In a different peg arrangement, exchange rate fluctuations greater than 1 percent are allowed. Guyana, Lebanon, Maldives, and Trinidad and Tobago have this arrangement with the U.S. dollar. Macedonia has this arrangement with the euro.

- *Crawling peg:* In a crawling peg strategy, a currency is readjusted periodically at a fixed, preannounced rate or in response to changes in indicators. Honduras and Nicaragua both have this arrangement with the U.S. dollar.

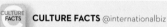

CULTURE FACTS @internationalbiz

Culture influences the way people think about and handle money. Even the notion of wealth itself is a cultural construct. In some cultures, such as some Native American cultures, people can acquire wealth through giving gifts, a distribution, rather than through acquisition. In some cultures, charging a borrower to use money—that is, financing without risk—is wrong, as in Islam's Sharia law. Is cost the critical issue in a transaction? Or is it risk? Do people tend to buy on price, as in North America? Or do they buy on relationship, as often occurs in most of Asia? #cultureinfluencesmoney #priceorrelationship

SOCIAL MEDIA

- *Crawling band:* A crawling band readjusts the country's currency to maintain fluctuation margins around a central rate. Only Tonga listed this arrangement, linked to a basket of currencies, but in times of crisis, it may be found useful. This arrangement is known as "a snake in the tunnel" in the London foreign exchange markets.

- *Managed floating:* In a managed float, the currency fluctuates, while the country's monetary authority actively intervenes on the exchange market without specifying or making public its goals and targets. Peru, Korea, Mexico, the Philippines, South Africa, Turkey, and India are among the many countries that follow this arrangement.

- *Free floating exchange rates:* Free floating exchange rates rely on the market. Governments may intervene, but to moderate the rate of change rather than to establish the currency's level. Countries following this approach are: Canada, the United Kingdom, the United States, Sweden, Japan, and the EU countries.

Table 8.1 shows the changes in currency arrangements from 2009 through 2017, using the original three IMF groups. The 2008 global financial crisis impacted exchange rate arrangements. Countries moved initially toward floating and then toward soft pegs, a term used to describe the peg, crawling peg, stabilized, and crawling band, or other arrangements.

The floating exchange rate system, both managed and free-floating, seems to be meeting its recent challenges, several of which—including a central bank liquidity crisis in the spring of 2008 and an ensuing global financial crisis—have been severe. In addition to the use of economic policy, coordination by the G7 countries (sometimes with Russia making a G8) has emerged as a key factor in the foreign exchange markets. In a recent coordinated intervention to stop the rise of the Japanese yen after the 2011 earthquake, central banks in Japan, Europe, and North America stabilized the strengthening yen, thereby stabilizing financial markets and avoiding a global crisis. This unusual intervention is discussed in the IB in Practice box.

TABLE 8.1 Three-Tiered Categorization of IMF Exchange Rate Arrangements with Percentage of Users

Exchange Rate Arrangement	2009	2013	2017
Hard Pegs	12.2	13.1	12.5
No separate legal tender	5.3	6.8	6.8
Currency board	6.9	6.3	5.7
Soft Pegs	34.6	42.9	42.2
Conventional peg	22.3	23.6	22.4
Stabilized arrangement	6.9	9.9	12.5
Crawling peg	2.7	1.0	1.6
Crawl-like arrangement	0.5	7.9	5.2
Pegged exchange rate within horizontal bands	2.1	0.5	0.5
Floating	42.0	34.0	39.5
Floating	24.5	18.3	19.8
Free floating	17.6	15.7	16.1
Residual			
Other managed relationship	11.2	9.9	9.4

Source: "Annual Report on Exchange Arrangements and Exchange Restrictions," *International Monetary Fund,* 2017. Copyright ©2017 by International Monetary Fund.

G7 Foreign Exchange Intervention

After a devastating earthquake and tsunami struck the east coast of Honshu, Japan, on March 11, 2011, the yen strengthened considerably. Before the quake, someone wanting to buy yen with dollars could do so at a rate of $1.00 buying ¥82.27. In the first week after the earthquake, however, that dollar would buy only ¥76.25. This change seems illogical at first because we would expect a country facing a disaster to have a weakening currency; that is, we could buy more yen per U.S. dollar. Japan's economy was severely damaged by the earthquake, tsunami, and nuclear disaster. In order to defend against a weakening currency, the Bank of Japan fed yen into the market to make sure they were available and that the market was liquid. This action should have weakened the yen, but instead, the yen's value against the dollar increased, an unexpected result that, because it was disorderly, threatened the stability of global economic markets.

The yen had strengthened on speculation by currency traders that Japanese global businesses would repatriate money to contribute to Japan's recovery, out of loyalty to their home country. Here's what happened next. The Bank of Japan, joined by European and North American central banks, all G7 members, intervened in the market and began selling more yen into it. The *Financial Times* reports that within hours, the yen's value had reversed course and begun to weaken. It moved quickly to above ¥80 to the dollar and continued to weaken.

This coordinated G7 currency intervention was the first in 10 years and was prompted by the disorderly trading pattern in the yen against the dollar, threatening financial stability far beyond Japan on a global level.

Critical Thinking Questions

1. With a natural disaster, why would we expect a country's currency to weaken?
2. Why were G7 members so quick to intervene?

Source: Graham Peter, "Action by G7 Marks Turning Point for Yen," *Financial Times*, March 23, 2011.

As G7 central banks have become more adept at influencing currency movements, the explosive growth in the volume of currencies being traded in the world's foreign exchange markets challenges their efforts. The U.S. dollar has been the main vehicle currency, present in about 88 percent of all currency transactions. From an annual volume of roughly $18 billion in 1979, foreign exchange transactions were in the range of $1,378 trillion in 2013.[11] Exchange volatility declined in recent years, due to calming of the markets as a result of record levels of liquidity provided by actions of central banks. However, fluctuations in the U.S. dollar and other developments in 2018 caused average daily trading volume to rise about 15 percent from a year earlier, reaching over $1.8 trillion in January 2018.[12] The developments illustrate that the market has increasing leverage to influence exchange rates. For example, if the foreign exchange market players believe the Japanese yen should increase in value against the US$ (strengthen against the U.S. dollar), sellers of the yen will increase its US$ price on the market, and the yen will strengthen in spite of any government market intervention. The floating exchange system seems to be able to respond to market movements with flexibility and relative order. Table 8.2 summarizes the history of the monetary system, from gold, through fixed, to floating.

Floating currencies can move against one another quickly and in large swings. Such changes have many causes, including political events, expectations, disasters and government economic policies that encourage trade imbalances and deficits. These currency fluctuations create major uncertainties that international managers must protect against, through a process called *hedging*, which is a way to manage risk.

There's one last development in the current monetary system that we should mention, the development of virtual currencies. This is a type of electronic money issued by

TABLE 8.2 Summary of the Monetary System

System	Gold	Bretton Woods Fixed Gold Exchange	Floating
Pros	Simple Widely trusted Mandated monetary discipline	Fixed rate Good for trade growth	Flexible (free/ managed float, peg) Responsive to market forces Good for huge volume
Cons	Impractical with large trade flows Costly to hold	Led to U.S. balance of payment deficit Led to U.S. government liabilities to foreign central banks Reduced U.S. gold reserves	Causes widely swinging currency values
Controlling Mechanism	Gold flows: price-specie-flow mechanism (Hume)	Government adjusted rates against dollar Dollar constant against gold	Market forces with some government intervention

its developers, which can be used for payment in some environments, but does not have any legal status—that is, not issued by and subject to control by a government. Among the most popular virtual currencies are Bitcoin, Ethereum XRP, Bitcoin Cash, and EOS.[13] Bitcoin can be used in exchanges with many local retailers and some larger ones, including Overstock and Expedia. You can locate local businesses that accept Bitcoin at https://www.coinmap.org. In the United States, the IRS treats Bitcoin as property rather than currency for tax purposes. If Bitcoin becomes more widely used, it may have the potential, much like the SDR, to operate as a trade currency, eliminating the risk of currency fluctuation.

THE BANK FOR INTERNATIONAL SETTLEMENTS

Bank for International Settlements (BIS) Institution for central bankers; operates to build cooperation in order to foster monetary and financial stability

The **Bank for International Settlements (BIS)** is an international organization of central banks that exists to build cooperation in order to foster monetary and financial stability. One way to understand how it functions is to think of it as the central bank for central bankers. It is the oldest international financial institution in the world, founded in 1930 to address war reparations imposed on Germany by the Treaty of Versailles. Today, the BIS has four main roles: it acts as a banker for central banks, a forum for international monetary cooperation, a center for research, and an agent or trustee for governments in various international financial arrangements. Central bankers of major industrial countries meet at least seven times a year at the BIS in Basel, Switzerland, to discuss the global financial system.

The BIS is known as the most discreet financial institution in the world, which may explain why it is often overlooked as an institution and even as a physical site. If you've ever spent time in Basel, Switzerland, you may have seen the round tower of the BIS just outside the main train station heading toward downtown. There is no sign identifying the building.

Financial Forces: Fluctuating Currency Values

LO 8-3
Describe the factors that influence exchange rate movement.

Having reviewed the basics of the international monetary system, we now are ready to focus on the financial forces, external to the firm and largely uncontrollable, that influence the context in which international managers make decisions. These forces include currency exchange rate fluctuation and exchange risk, currency exchange controls, taxation, inflation, and national-level balance-of-payments account balances. Although *uncontrollable* means that these financial forces originate outside the business and are beyond its influence, financial managers of a company are not helpless about them. When we consider financial management, we discuss ways to manage around these financial forces. We begin here with a focus on fluctuating currency values, examining foreign exchange, FX quotation, causes of exchange rate movement, and exchange rate forecasting.

FLUCTUATING CURRENCY VALUES

In a post–Bretton Woods monetary system, freely floating currencies fluctuate against each other. At times, central banks intervene in the foreign exchange markets by buying and selling large amounts of a currency in order to affect the supply and demand of that particular currency. The basis of this tactic is quite simple: as supply increases, price decreases, other things remaining constant, or *ceteris paribus*, as economists put it. These interventions are not announced, but we can infer them by looking at the market's movements, as discussed in the IB in Practice box example of the G7 intervention to weaken the Japanese yen after the 2011 earthquake.

For the most part, the major currencies—the U.S. dollar, the British pound sterling, the Japanese yen, and the euro—are allowed by their central banks to fluctuate freely against each other. Fluctuations can be quite large. For example, in January 1999, the euro's exchange rate was established at US$1.1667. In May 2000, the euro had sunk to US$0.8895, almost a 24 percent drop. Then the trend reversed and by June 2006 the euro was trading at US$1.2644, an increase of more than 42 percent. Two years later, in early June 2008, the euro was trading at US$1.5768. By May 2010 it was back to US$1.28, as a result of the challenges to the euro presented by problems in the Greek economy that revealed key flaws in the single-currency system. In March 2011, the euro was trading at US$1.4434, and in April 2014, it was at US$1.3833, before falling to US$1.0493 in March 2015 and rising again to US$1.2406 in February 2018. Figure 8.1 presents these same data, in terms of how many dollars the euro would buy. Clearly, there is significant movement in these currencies' values.

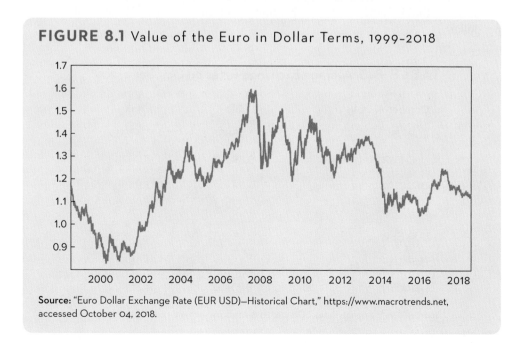

FIGURE 8.1 Value of the Euro in Dollar Terms, 1999–2018

Source: "Euro Dollar Exchange Rate (EUR USD)—Historical Chart," https://www.macrotrends.net, accessed October 04, 2018.

Currency fluctuations have considerable impact on financial transactions. They are among the factors that determine whether importing or manufacturing locally is more advantageous, for instance. Imagine you are operating with U.S. dollar earnings and you sign a purchase agreement for $100,000, payable in euros when you receive your purchase. At the time of signing, the cost of each euro was US$0.8895. Now, years later (we're exaggerating for the sake of our example), your purchase arrives but the price of each euro has risen to US$1.50. Your $100,000 purchase will now cost you $161,050 or $61,050 more in U.S. dollars than you anticipated at the time of purchase, a substantial difference.

We now look at why these currency fluctuations occur; that is, what forces determine exchange rates. We begin with a brief review of how exchange rates are determined and then move on to the interesting question of what causes them to fluctuate.

WHY FOREIGN CURRENCY EXCHANGE OCCURS

People often like to do business in their own currency because they don't like to assume the risks that can accompany currency exchange. Yet that's not always possible, because of customer needs or market competition. Foreign exchange quotations—the price of one currency expressed in terms of another—are reported in the world's currency exchange markets in terms of the U.S. dollar, and increasingly the euro and the local currency. Historically, the U.S. dollar has played a central role as a main central reserve asset of many countries, a vehicle currency, and an intervention currency. A **vehicle currency** is a currency that is used for international trade or investment. For example, the diamond market uses the U.S. dollar as a vehicle currency. An **intervention currency** is one that is used by central banks to intervene in the foreign currency exchange markets. Often the intervention involves buying up domestic currency to reduce its supply in the market, thereby strengthening it. As we saw in our discussion of the BIS, 88 percent of currency trades used the dollar as a vehicle currency.[14]

vehicle currency
A currency used as a vehicle for international trade or investment

intervention currency
A currency used by a country to intervene in the foreign currency exchange markets

EXCHANGE RATE QUOTATIONS AND THE FX MARKET

Table 8.3 is a partial listing of currency exchange rates on October 4, 2018. Prices are given for buying and selling. Assuming you are operating in dollars, you might want to look at how much of the foreign currency you can purchase per U.S. dollar or its reciprocal, how many U.S. dollars a unit of the other currency would buy. The **reciprocal currency** is a currency that is quoted as dollars per unit of currency instead of in units of currency per dollar.

reciprocal currency
In FX, using the dollar as the base currency, a currency that is quoted as dollars per unit of currency instead of in units of currency per dollar

TABLE 8.3 Average Exchange Rates on October 4, 2018

October 4, 2018	Bid	Ask
EUR/USD	1.15898	1.15912
USD/EUR	0.86272	0.86283
USD/JPY	113.94	113.95
USD/CAD	1.28177	1.28197
EUR/GBP	0.88867	0.88886
EUR/CHF	1.13646	1.13671
GBP/USD	1.30402	1.30422

Source: "Live Exchange Rates," *Oanda*, 2018. https://www.oanda.com.

The exchange rate for a purchase or trade for delivery within two business days is known as the spot rate. The spot rate for the euro on October 4, 2018, in dollar terms, was $1.16.[15] There is also a forward currency market that allows managers to lock in contracts to purchase currencies at known rates for delivery in the future. The forward rate is the exchange rate, the cost today, of a commitment to buy or sell an agreed amount of a currency at a fixed future date, usually 30, 60, 90, or 180 days from now. The forward rates can help you get a sense of where traders expect the currency's value to be headed. Most newspapers no longer quote forward rates, but you can check them online.

Now, let's look at the way the FX market actually operates. Most of the transactions are *over the counter (OTC)*, meaning that there is no actual trading floor; trades are done electronically. The market consists of banks and other large financial institutions such as pension funds and mutual funds. We've already mentioned buy and sell prices; they are known in the market as the bid and ask prices. The bid price is the highest-priced buy order currently in the market, while the ask price is the lowest-priced sell order currently in the market. The difference between the two, the *bid–ask spread*, provides a margin (the difference between the production or acquisition price and the selling price) for the bank or agency, which makes money both when they buy and when they sell in these trades. The rates listed on Internet sites are the interbank rates, the rates for customers buying large quantities, usually US$1 million or more. The rates charged to small customers are much less favorable to the customer.

As you can imagine, the FX markets are large, liquid, and quite competitive, with trading occurring 24 hours a day through international banks. The global average daily turnover for FX is $3 trillion to $5 trillion. FX markets are largely unregulated as well.[16] A *Wall Street Journal* writer described them as "a Wild West of global capitalism. . . . Unlike major stock and commodities markets, the foreign-exchange market, or FX, operates with virtually no government or regulatory oversight."[17]

In 2008, Congress and the president gave the U.S. Commodity Futures Trading Commission (CFTC) control over the contracts executed in the United States that financial managers use to protect their transactions from risks, called swap and future contracts, as a result of the financial crisis that began that year. The CFTC is now acting as a regulator in these FX markets and forming regulations. In this role, in February 2018, the CFTC issued an order settling charges against Deutsche Bank Securities Inc. (DBSI) for attempted manipulation of the U.S. Dollar International Swaps and Derivatives Fix, requiring DBSI to pay a $70 million civil monetary penalty.[18] The CFTC's website also warns potential investors of foreign exchange currency frauds they have uncovered, many of them online.

CAUSES OF EXCHANGE RATE MOVEMENT

Since 1973, the relative values of floating currencies and the ease of their convertibility have been set by market forces, influenced by factors such as supply and demand forecasts for the two currencies in question; inflation rates in the two countries; their relative productivity and unit labor cost; political developments such as unexpected election results; government fiscal, monetary, and currency exchange market actions; the two countries' balance-of-payments accounts; and basic psychology. Monetary and fiscal policies of the government such as decisions on taxation, interest rates, and trade policies, and other forces external to the business such as world events, all may play significant roles. Monetary policies control the amount of money in circulation, whether it is growing, and, if so, at what pace. Fiscal policies address the collecting and spending of money by the government.

While economists have not yet developed an accepted theory to explain exchange rate fluctuations, they have been able to identify several *parity relationships* among some of the factors that influence them. Parity relationships describe equivalencies, and two of these relationships, interest rate parity and purchasing power parity, are fundamental to our

spot rate
The exchange rate between two currencies for delivery within two business days

forward currency market
Trading market for currency contracts deliverable 30, 60, 90, or 180 days in the future

forward rate
The exchange rate between two currencies for delivery in the future, usually 30, 60, 90, or 180 days

bid price
Highest-priced buy order currently in the market

ask price
Lowest-priced sell order currently in the market

monetary policies
Government policies that control the amount of money in circulation and its growth rate

fiscal policies
Policies that address the collecting and spending of money by the government

law of one price
Concept that in an efficient market, like products will have like prices

arbitrage
The process of buying and selling simultaneously to make profit with no risk

Fisher effect
The relationship between real and nominal interest rates: The real interest rate will be the nominal interest rate minus the expected rate of inflation

international Fisher effect
Concept that the interest rate differentials for any two currencies will reflect the expected change in their exchange rates

purchasing power parity (PPP)
The amount of adjustment that must be made in the exchange rates for two currencies in order for them to have equivalent purchasing power

further consideration of exchange rates. They both rest on and are applications of the **law of one price**, which states that in an efficient market, like products will have like prices. If price differences exist, the process of **arbitrage**—simultaneous buying and selling to make a profit with no risk—will quickly close any gaps and the markets will be back at equilibrium.

When the law of one price is applied to interest rates, it suggests that interest rates vary to take account of differing anticipated levels of inflation. The economic explanation of this relationship, which results in *interest rate parity*, is known as the **Fisher effect**. It states that the real interest rate will be the nominal interest rate minus the expected rate of inflation. Where the real rate of interest (rr) is equal to the nominal interest rate (rn) minus the expected rate of inflation (I):

$$rr = (rn) - I$$

Thus, an increase in the expected inflation rate will lead to an increase in the interest rate. A decrease in the expected inflation rate will lead to a decrease in the interest rate. So, it makes sense that an investor would want to earn more in a high-inflation environment to compensate for the effect of inflation on the investment.

An interesting application of the concept of interest rate parity, the **international Fisher effect**, says that the interest rate differentials for any two currencies will reflect the expected change in their exchange rates.[19] For example, if the nominal interest rate in the United States is 5 percent per year and in the European Union it is 3 percent, we would expect the dollar to decrease against the euro by 2 percent over the year or the euro to strengthen against the dollar by that same amount.

A second important parity relationship is **purchasing power parity (PPP)**. PPP is the amount of adjustment that must be made in the exchange rates for two currencies in order for them to have equivalent purchasing power. We use it to show the number of units of a currency required to buy the same basket of goods and services in two markets with different currencies. PPP is an application of the law of one price to a basket of commodity goods, and it suggests that for a dollar to buy as much in the United Kingdom as in the United States, the cost of the goods in the United Kingdom should equal their U.S. cost times the exchange rate between the dollar and the pound. This relationship is expressed in the following equation, where P is the price of a basket of commodity goods:

$$£P(\$/£) = \$P$$

Another way to think about what PPP theory states is that currency exchange rates between two countries should equal the ratio of the price levels of their commodity baskets. This relationship is expressed in the following equation, where P is the price of a basket of commodity goods:

$$(\$/£) = \$P/£P$$

For example, if a basket of goods costs $1,500 in the United States and £1,000 in the United Kingdom, the PPP exchange rate will be $1.50/£. If, in the trading market, the actual spot exchange rate were $2/£, the pound would be overvalued by 33 percent, or, equivalently, the dollar undervalued by 25 percent.

The Economist, a British weekly magazine, presents an application of PPP theory in its "Big Mac index," substituting an omnipresent Big Mac for a basket of goods. The Big Mac PPP is the exchange rate that would have a Big Mac in other countries costing an amount equivalent to what it does in the United States. The Big Mac index suggests that in the long term, many of the developing countries' currencies are undervalued and the euro and many European currencies are overvalued. You can check the latest Big Mac index, and view a video explaining *The Economist*'s efforts to make economics as simple as it ought to be, by searching for the Big Mac Index at https://www.economist.com.

Fixed FX Rates, Perhaps Hooked to Gold, or Floating Rates, Hooked to Faith?

Most economists support the idea that floating exchange rates are beneficial for the world economy. A small minority of experts advocate a return to the gold standard and fixed exchange rates. Let's further consider this choice.

As we have seen, in the early 1970s, the U.S. government could not continue to guarantee that dollars floating around the world would be convertible to gold at the agreed rate. So it decoupled the dollar from gold, with the immediate effect that the world's currency exchange rates were not fixed anymore.

The economists Obstfeld and Rogoff argue that the main reason exchange rates could not stay fixed was the rapid evolution of world capital markets since the 1950s. Until the volume of trade grew, governments would buy or sell significant amounts of their currencies in the global markets in an effort to sustain their currency's supply and demand equilibrium. When the volume of global transactions started exceeding most countries' foreign exchange reserves, however, governments could no longer intervene effectively to sustain the value of their currency. At the same time, a speculative attack, that is, unexpected buying by previously inactive traders (a term first used in regard to FX trading by Krugman), on a specific currency by the market could cause a run on it that its government could not counter. With the advent of the Internet, in less than 15 years the amount of *daily* foreign exchange transactions increased from $1 trillion in 1994 to an estimated $2.05 trillion in the first week of February 2018. This growth in scale made government control of its currency's value difficult if not impossible. It also is difficult to imagine a day when the main currency regimes around the world would again be dominated by fixed-rate relationships.

Even if a central bank could support its currency effectively, the impact on the rest of the economy could be considerable. In an environment where currency A is becoming relatively stronger than currency B, the interest rates in country A are likely to be higher than those in country B. This increases the cost of doing business in country A relative to country B. It is the case that interest rate movements, exchange rate values, and inflationary pressures, all forces that influence the monetary picture, tend to be interlinked.

What are the key arguments for trying to fix exchange rates? First, floating rates increase the cost of trade for industries that ship products from one country to another because rates can change in the time lag between ordering and receiving. Whether the manufacturer or the buyer bears the risk, or both, there are ways to minimize foreign exchange risk related to timing, but they introduce a new cost to the transaction.

Second, exchange rate fluctuations of a floating rate system impede trade. They may lead to protectionist measures that can deprive a country's people of trade benefits. (Yet, we must note that a fixed exchange rate means the government is depriving itself of the ability to manage its own monetary policy.) In a floating system, there are also psychological factors at work in the market. A currency from which buyers are fleeing will weaken and the one they are moving into will strengthen. A strengthening currency has a negative impact on the country's ability to export because its goods become more expensive relative to others.

Finally, fixed-rate proponents say fixed exchange rates impose monetary discipline on a government, that is, a readiness to limit the money supply if necessary. This explanation implies, however, that a government can act in isolation from other governments, an impossible option today. It appears that we have gone from the thing we valued, gold as a currency, to a currency that operated as a proxy for gold, to currencies that float against one another in a largely free float, hinged not to gold but to our faith in the monetary system.

Critical Thinking Questions

1. If the SDR were used, would a viable fixed-rate regime be possible or not?
2. Given the inclusion of the SDR, outline the pro and con arguments for a fixed-rate regime.

Sources: Tommy Wilkes, "Forex Trading Up Sharply in 2018 as Volatility Returns," *Reuters*, February 15, 2018; M. Obstfeld, and K. Rogoff, "The Mirage of Fixed Exchange Rates," *Journal of Economic Perspectives*, vol. 9, no. 4, July 1995, 73–96; and P.B. Kenen, "Fixed versus Floating Exchange Rates," *Cato Journal*, vol. 20, no. 1, 2000, 109–13.

EXCHANGE RATE FORECASTING

Because exchange rate movements are so important to all aspects of international business—production, sourcing, marketing, and finance—many business decisions take the risk of exchange rate movement into consideration through forecasts. There are several approaches to forecasting, and three of the main ones are the efficient market approach, the fundamental approach, and technical analysis. We briefly examine each.

efficient market approach
Assumption that current
market prices fully reflect all
available relevant information

random walk hypothesis
Assumption that the unpredictability of factors suggests that
the best predictor of tomorrow's prices is today's prices

fundamental approach
Exchange rate prediction
based on econometric models
that attempt to capture the
variables and their correct
relationships

technical analysis
An approach that analyzes
data for trends and then
projects these trends forward

The **efficient market approach** assumes that current prices fully reflect all available relevant information. This assumption also suggests that forward exchange rates are the best possible predictor of future spot rates because they will have taken into account all the available information. For example, if interest rates are different between two countries, the forward rate will reflect this (per the international Fisher effect). The efficient market approach does not suggest the forward rate will predict the future spot rate with perfect accuracy, however. Rather, any divergence will be random. A forecasting theory related to the efficient market approach is the **random walk hypothesis**, which holds that because the factors that influence prices are unpredictable, stock market prices evolve much like a random walk, turning here and there without a controlling logic, so that the best predictor of tomorrow's prices is today's prices.[20] Burton Malkiel, an economics professor at Princeton, popularized this observation in his 1973 book, *A Random Walk Down Wall Street.*

The **fundamental approach** to exchange rate prediction looks at the underlying forces that help determine exchange rates and develops various econometric models to capture them and their correct relationships. The international finance scholars Cheol Eun and Bruce Resnick have surveyed the research on the various fundamental models and conclude that "the fundamental models failed to more accurately forecast exchange rates than either the forward rate model, which we have termed the efficient market model, or the random walk model."[21]

The third approach to exchange rate forecasting, **technical analysis**, looks at history and then, assuming that what was past will be future, projects these trends forward. Technical analysts think in terms of waves and trends. There is no theoretical underpinning to the technical approach, and while academic studies tend to dismiss it, it appears that traders often use it.

As for the performance of these forecasting approaches, research by Eun and Sabherwal concludes that the 10 commercial banks in their study could not outperform the random walk model.[22] Their findings also suggest that the forward exchange rate and the spot rate were both about equal in value for predicting future exchange rates. Neither the technical nor the fundamental approach appears to outperform the efficient market approach. Additional research suggests that combining forecasts generated by these and additional models may be helpful.

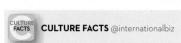

CULTURE FACTS @internationalbiz

Treasuries in collectivistic countries are willing to take more financial risk than those in individualistic countries because the collectivist in-groups that control the investments in these cultures, such as finance ministers and leaders of major companies, provide downside protection if the risks prove costly. #risktakers #downsideprotection

We have examined a major financial force that international managers have to address—foreign exchange fluctuations, their causes, and their prediction. We now look at some of the most significant additional financial forces, one that governments can exert, beginning with currency exchange controls, and then move on to taxation, inflation and interest rates, and balance-of-payments effects.

LO 8-4
Discuss financial forces
governments can exert.

Financial Forces Governments Can Exert

Governments can exert financial forces that affect companies, including currency exchange controls and taxation. Through their monetary policy, governments also influence inflation and interest rates. We examine these forces and their impacts on international managers.

CURRENCY EXCHANGE CONTROLS

A government has the power and authority to limit the amount of its currency that can be exchanged for another currency in any given transaction. Controls differ greatly from country to country and even within a country, depending on the type of transaction. Developed countries have few or no currency exchange controls, for instance, and many developing countries, such as Mexico, have reduced or eliminated them to encourage foreign investment. Currency exchange controls can change quickly and without much warning, so international business managers must keep informed.

Convertible currencies can be exchanged for other currencies without restrictions. Also known as hard currencies, these include the Japanese yen, the U.S. dollar, the British pound, and the euro. When a currency is *nonconvertible*, its value is arbitrarily fixed, typically at a rate higher than its value in the free market, and the government imposes exchange controls to limit or prohibit the legal use of its currency in international transactions. The government also requires that all purchases or sales of other currencies be made through a government agency. Limitations might also restrict the amount of domestic currency transferred into foreign currency. Such restrictions may influence a firm's ability to repatriate profits; that is, return profits to the home country. A black market inevitably springs up alongside such currency restrictions, but it is of little use to the international manager, who needs to abide by the laws.

Countries put limitations on the convertibility of their currency when they are concerned that their foreign reserves could be depleted. Foreign reserves are a source of currency for foreign debt service, import purchases, and other demands for foreign currency domestic banks might encounter. Ukraine, Argentina, Pakistan, and China are among the many countries that impose some sort of exchange controls. The Chinese renminbi (or yuan) is convertible in current accounts (accounts for day-to-day banking) but not yet in capital accounts (longer-term accounts), although China has made loosening of controls a goal so that the renminbi could become a hard currency, used for trade and as a part of foreign reserves.

When a government requires the firm to have permission to purchase foreign currency, exchange rates are often above the free-market rate. If the government doesn't grant permission or if the cost of foreign currency is too high, the international company may well consider the currency blocked and available for use only within

Foreign exchange in action. ©Mike Clarke/AFP/Getty Images.

the country. Such limitations on repatriation usually present international managers with the problem of finding suitable products and investments within the country or establishing other arrangements to move their stored value beyond the country's border, such as barter or swaps with other foreign firms needing local currency inside the country.

TAXATION

While taxation is a legal force, it is also a financial factor whose impact is significant. If a corporation can achieve a lower tax burden than its competitors have, it can lower prices to customers or generate higher revenue with which to pay higher wages and dividends. Governments around the world widely use three types of taxation to generate revenue: income tax, value-added tax (VAT), and withholding tax. The *income tax* is a direct tax on personal and corporate income. Figure 8.2 compares corporate taxation rates in G20 countries. Note that these are the statutory rates; the effective rates may be considerably lower, due to tax breaks that are a result of effective lobbying, tax planning strategies, and creative accounting. In 2017, Amazon reported profits of $5.6 billion in the United States and paid no federal income tax,[23] despite the 35 percent statutory U.S. corporate tax rate. Prior to the reduction of the top U.S. corporate tax rate from 35 percent to 20 percent in 2017, the Center on Budget and Policy Priorities, a nonpartisan research and policy institute, calculated that the average effective U.S. corporate tax rate on profits from new investments was 24 percent, while the average was in the 21 percent range for other G7 countries (Canada, France, Germany, Italy, Japan, and the United Kingdom).[24] Since 1980, the average statutory corporate tax rate worldwide has consistently declined, with the largest decrease occurring in the early 2000s.[25]

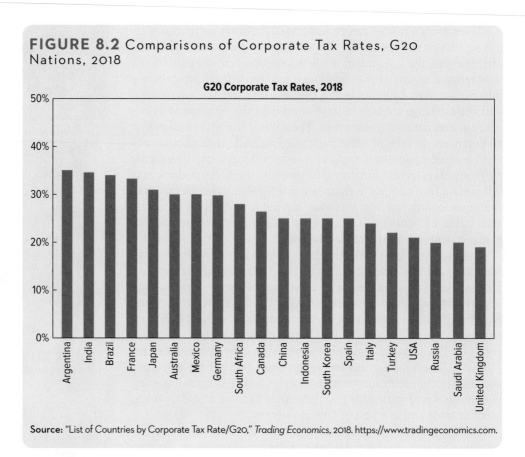

FIGURE 8.2 Comparisons of Corporate Tax Rates, G20 Nations, 2018

Source: "List of Countries by Corporate Tax Rate/G20," *Trading Economics*, 2018. https://www.tradingeconomics.com.

In addition to using tax benefits to decrease their effective tax rates, corporations also use two basic strategies to minimize their taxes, profit shifting and tax inversion. Profit shifting is moving profits to locations with lower tax rates, while tax inversion is buying a foreign company in a lower-taxed location and then using that company as the legal location for the corporation. In September 2014, the U.S. Treasury Department announced new regulations intended to reduce the attractiveness of this tax-avoidance technique, but analysts suggest that corporations will still find the inversion technique useful in reducing tax liability.[26] For example, in March 2018, Dana Inc. announced its intention to relocate its headquarters from Ohio to the United Kingdom, if its $6.1 billion takeover offer for the much smaller automobile axle business of GKN PLC was successful. Even with reduced tax rates and other benefits from the 2017 Tax Cuts and Jobs Act in the United States, Dana expected that this relocation would reduce the company's tax bill by about $600 million over several years.[27]

A *value-added tax (VAT)* is a tax charged on the value added to a good as it moves through production from raw materials to final purchaser. It is really a sales tax whose payment documentation from one stage to another becomes important for tax credits, because the seller collects the tax for the goods sold and then receives credits for VAT paid earlier in the production process. Countries that levy value-added taxes are permitted by World Trade Organization (WTO) rules to rebate the value-added taxes to exporters, an incentive that makes the exports less expensive and thus more competitive.

The third general tax category is the *withholding tax.* This is an indirect tax levied on passive income such as dividends, royalties, and interest that the corporation pays to non-residents, people, or companies in another tax jurisdiction. Countries establish bilateral tax treaties to categorize passive-income withholding rates. For example, on interest paid to residents of non-tax-treaty countries, the United States withholds 30 percent as withholding tax. So from UK residents, it withholds nothing, while from residents of Pakistan it withholds 30 percent.

International companies need to understand tax laws in each country in which they operate and how those tax laws relate to tax laws in other countries. This additional tax burden can create financial risk, but it can also be an opportunity for savings, given good tax planning.

INFLATION AND INTEREST RATES

Inflation is a sustained increase in prices. Some economists hold that it is caused by demand exceeding supply, while others view the cause to be an increase in the money supply. All, however, agree that in an inflationary economy, prices as a whole increase. Table 8.4 shows recent inflation levels in selected countries. Japan, the European Union, and the United States have had relatively good records in keeping inflation down in recent years. Historically, Latin American countries have had inflation troubles. However, these trends have been gradually reversed. Brazil experienced 3,118 percent inflation in 1990 and was able to decrease it to 5.9 percent in 2010. The overall highest rate recorded was found in Zimbabwe, where inflation reached 14.9 billion percent in July 2008. The IMF projected that Venezuela's inflation rate would hit 1 million percent in 2018.[28] Most inflation is measured by a *consumer price index (CPI)*, which captures the price changes over time for a basket of consumer goods. The world's average inflation rate for 2017 was 3.42 percent, calculated by the World Bank.

Inflation, a financial force external to a company, affects a firm in several major ways. First, the inflation rate determines the real cost of borrowing in capital markets. You'll

TABLE 8.4 Inflation Rates for Various Countries, Years 2015–2017

Country	2015 Rate	2016 Rate	2017 Rate
Argentina	26.58	40.07	34.3
Brazil	7.57	8.14	3.79
Chile	4.97	4.72	4.65
China	0.09	1.13	4.05
Egypt	9.93	6.24	22.93
France	1.18	0.18	0.99
Germany	2.01	1.32	1.53
Greece	−1.02	−0.95	0.67
India	2.07	3.46	2.99
Ireland	7.28	0.021	−0.30
Japan	2.14	0.27	−0.21
Norway	−2.82	−1.11	3.84
Russian Fed.	8.35	3.54	3.84
United Kingdom	0.45	1.97	1.96
United States	1.08	1.27	1.79
Venezuela	111.8	254.39	1,087.53
Zimbabwe	0.89	1.31	3.79

Source: "Inflation, GDP deflator (annual %)," *The World Bank*, 2018. Copyright ©2018 by The World Bank.

recall the Fisher effect from our discussion of exchange rates. When the firm operates in multiple countries, it has multiple currency exposures, and the complexity of dealing with inflation increases because inflation rates vary among countries. When management decides to raise capital, should they use equity or debt? In which capital markets? In what currency? These are critical questions, and inflation rates play a role in the answers.

Further, rising inflation rates encourage borrowing (debt) because loans can be repaid in the future with inflated, cheaper money. But high inflation rates also bring high-interest rates because banks have to offer more reward to draw in deposits. Then inflation may discourage lending because lenders may fear that, even with high-interest rates, the amount repaid plus interest will be worth less than the amount lent. Thus, you see how the relationship between inflation and interest rates can affect business decisions. And in our discussion of the international Fisher effect, we have seen the relationship between currency exchange rate trends and interest rates. So there is a relationship between inflation and currency exchange rates.

Inflated currencies tend to weaken. In inflated economies, instead of lending, the money holder may buy something that is expected to increase in value, thereby further fueling inflation. In Brazil, during a recent inflationary period, farmers hoarded their crops and then used them in barter for imported farming equipment and Mercedes cars.

Lenders have begun to use variable interest rates, which rise or fall with inflation, to shift financial risk to the borrower. This shift requires that the borrower be much more careful about borrowing. The original rate and any future changes are based on a reference interest rate, such as the U.S. prime rate (the rate of interest at which banks lend to their best customers) or the London Interbank Offer Rate (the bank-to-bank interest rate in London—LIBOR).

As Table 8.5 suggests, October 2018 interest rates in most developed countries varied across a small range, although rates are often higher in developing countries. This trend

TABLE 8.5 Sample Central Bank Interest Rates

Central Bank	Interest Rate as of October 2018
Bank of England	0.75
Bank of Japan	−0.1
European Central Bank	0
United States Federal Reserve	2.25
Swiss National Bank	−0.75
The Reserve Bank of Australia	1.5
Bank of Canada	1.5
Central Bank of Brazil	6.5
The People's Bank of China	4.35
Reserve Bank of India	6.5
Bank of Korea (South)	1.5
Bank of Mexico	7.75
Central Bank of the Republic of Turkey	24.00

Source: "Central Banks–Summary of Current Interest Rates," *Global-rates*, 2009–2018. Copyright ©2009–2018 by Global-rates.

may be explained by the integration of financial markets as they become more globalized. In the 13 countries shown, the average interest rate was 4.3 percent. The corresponding figure in 1993 was 6.9 percent and in 2014 it was 3.5 percent.

Finally, inflation rates cause the cost of the goods and services produced in a country to rise, and thus the goods and services become less competitive globally. Producers in the high-inflation country find export sales more difficult. Such conditions may lead to balance-of-payments deficits in the trade account, where a nation's international transactions are recorded, so under these conditions management must be alert to government policy changes that attempt to correct the deficits, such as more restrictive fiscal or monetary policies, currency controls, export incentives, and import obstacles. Because monitoring balance-of-payment accounts is important, we now take a look at the balance of payments.

Balance of Payments

The **balance of payments (BOP)** is a record of a country's transactions with the rest of the world. So it actually tracks the flows of capital in and out of the country. BOP data are of interest to international businesspeople for several reasons. First, a country's balance of payments reveals the demand for the country's currency. If a country is exporting more than it imports, there will be a high demand for its currency in other countries, so its customers can pay for the exported goods. This demand may well create pressure on the exporter's currency, in which case it might be expected to strengthen. Conversely, when a country imports more than it exports, its currency might be expected to weaken, or, if it is not a floating currency, to be devalued; that is, its value reduced by the government. Faced with such a trade deficit, as occurs when a country's citizens import more than they export, a government might lean toward restrictive monetary or fiscal policies. For example, it could introduce currency or trade controls. The BOP trend also helps managers predict what sort of changes in the economic environment might develop in the country. This prediction could affect their choice of strategic risks to take in a specific country. So international managers use BOP data when they build their anticipation about the future economic environment. Might currency controls be introduced? Might a devaluation be coming? Is the interest rate likely to move?

LO 8-5
Explain the significance of the balance of payments to international business decisions.

balance of payments (BOP)
Record of a country's transactions with the rest of the world

BOP ACCOUNTS

The BOP accounts are recorded in double-entry bookkeeping form. Each international transaction is an exchange of assets with a debit and a credit side. Payments *to* other countries, which are funds flowing out, are tracked as debits ($-$), while transactions that are payments *from* other countries, which are funds flowing in, are tracked as credits ($+$). The statement of a country's BOP is divided into several accounts and many subaccounts, as outlined in Figure 8.3.

DEFICITS AND SURPLUSES IN BOP ACCOUNTS

The BOP current account and capital account add up to the total account. A deficit in the current account is always accompanied by an equal surplus in the capital account and vice versa. Let's see how this works. If you purchase a case of French wine in the United States for $200, your payment, as it heads out of the United States and to the French winery, will be recorded as a debit in the U.S. current account. Once the winery receives your dollars, it has to do something with them. If the treasurer of the winery decides to deposit your payment in a dollar account at a U.S. bank, the amount will show up as a credit in the U.S. capital account. If the winery exchanges your dollar payment for euros, then the bank receiving the dollars will have to make a decision about how to spend or invest them. Sooner or later, these dollars will show up as a credit on the U.S. account.

FIGURE 8.3 Balance of Payments, Major Accounts

I. Current Account

Net changes in exports and imports of goods and services—tangibles and intangibles.

A. Goods or *merchandise account*—tangibles; net balance known as the *trade balance*.

B. *Services account*—intangibles.

C. *Unilateral transfers*—transfers with no reciprocity (gifts, aid, migrant worker earnings), to satisfy the needs of double-entry recording, entry made that treats the aid or gift as purchase of goodwill.

II. Capital Account

Net changes in a nation's international financial assets and liabilities; credit entry occurs when resident sells stock, bonds, or other financial assets to nonresident. Money flows to resident, while resident's long-term international liabilities (debit entry) increase.

A. *Direct investment*—located in one country and controlled by residents of another country.

B. *Portfolio investment*—long-term investments without control.

C. *Short-term capital flows*—such as currency exchange rate and interest rate hedging in the forward, futures, option, and swap markets; volatility and transaction privacy make this entry the least reliable measure.

III. Official Reserves Account

A. *Gold* imports and exports.

B. *Foreign exchange* (foreign currencies) held by government.

C. *Liabilities to* foreign central banks.

Contrary to commonly held belief, a current account deficit is not always a sign of bad economic conditions; it simply shows the country is importing capital. This is no more unnatural or dangerous than importing wine or cheese. A current account deficit is a response to conditions in the country. Among these could be excessive inflation, low productivity, or inadequate savings. In the case of the United States, a current account deficit could occur because investments in the United States are secure and profitable, so that many foreigners want to own them (foreign direct investment, an import of capital) and export their earnings (repatriation). If there is a problem, it is in the underlying conditions and not in the deficit per se.[29] Countries with relatively high price levels, high gross national products, high-interest rates, and strong exchange rates, as well as relatively low barriers to imports and attractive investment opportunities, are more likely to have current account deficits than are other countries.[30]

In recent years the United States has had a substantial deficit in its current account. Citizens of the United States are importing more goods than they are exporting, yet they are exporting more services than they are importing. There also is a surplus in the U.S. capital account. Those dollars that leave the United States to pay for imported goods come back into the United States in the form of foreign-owned investments in the country (for example, Treasury bills and investment property in New York City). So let's remember that a deficit or surplus in the current account cannot be explained or evaluated without simultaneously examining an equal surplus or deficit in the capital account. They need to be reviewed together.

At this point, the international monetary system is a work in progress, one that is evolving to support an expanding and increasingly complex global trading system. It is flexible, offers a way to store value, and does not have inordinate storage or transportation costs. We also believe in it. We have confidence that it will be able to transfer value accurately and swiftly among us all.

ANGELA SCHMITZ: Develop Experience by Traveling and Working Abroad

Angela Schmitz in Guatemala. Courtesy of Angela Schmitz.

"In the summer between my 2nd and 3rd year of college, I participated in an AIESEC exchange where I spent 8 weeks working for Acción Humana in Guatemala. My responsibilities included weekly graphic design tasks including website management and creating flyers and posters. I also was responsible for some minimal paperwork. Outside of the more business-like tasks I completed, I was given the opportunity to teach 4 English language classes. Each class held people of several different levels of English, so I had to basically teach 2 classes at once.

Some of my biggest challenges working in Guatemala were the atmosphere, cultural differences in professionalism, and the language barrier. I was thrown into an office that consisted of 3 desks in a small room with 2 computers and limited wi-fi and just 2 feet outside that office was my boss's home with 3 small children, his mother, and his cousin. It was interesting to be designing their website with a 7-month-old baby on my lap because his cousin asked me to help watch the baby. Outside the atmosphere, the cultural difference in professionalism was quite a gap. Guatemalans don't rely on time, like we do in the United States. Almost every time we set a meeting to begin at noon, it started at 4:00 pm. They were what I would call late by the standards in the U.S., but in their country they were exactly on time. Lastly, the language barrier was difficult. My level of Spanish was quite fluent on the comprehension side, but I struggled to be able to speak my opinions and respond. I was fortunate enough to have people on my team as well as my boss that spoke English.

Overall I gained skills in communication, project planning, and completing successful work in a very difficult environment. I attribute this experience to the success I've had in landing other internships and jobs in my career. This was an amazing first experience and I hope to have several more in my future."

Source: Angela Schmitz.

SUMMARY

LO 8-1
Describe the international monetary system's history.

The gold standard operated to support trade until 1914. Currencies were pegged to gold and adjustments were made by the exchange of gold. Next, followed a period of fixed rates under the Bretton Woods system, with the U.S. dollar exchangeable for gold. This pushed the United States into a persistent deficit and reduced gold in the U.S. reserves. The United States stopped the exchange of dollars for gold, and the dollar was allowed to float freely against other currencies on the open market. This began the period of floating exchange rates, which is where we are now. The IMF's Smithsonian Agreement worked out the rules and exchange regimes for the floating system, ranging from free floats to dirty floats to pegged currencies. Meanwhile, the World Bank established the SDR (special drawing rights) as a reserve currency.

LO 8-2
Describe today's floating currency exchange rate system, including the IMF currency arrangements.

Floating currency exchange rates are rates that are allowed to float against other currencies and are determined by market forces. The IMF now uses eight categories to describe the ways countries position their currencies in relationship to other currencies, characterized by their degree of flexibility. They are now separate legal tender, currency board arrangements, fixed peg, peg within a horizontal band, crawling peg, crawling band, managed float, and independent float.

LO 8-3
Describe the factors that influence exchange rate movement.

Since 1973, the relative values of floating currencies have been set by market forces, influenced by many factors. These factors include supply and demand forecasts for the two currencies; relative inflation in the two countries; relative productivity and unit labor cost changes; political developments, such as expected election results; expected government fiscal, monetary, and currency exchange market actions; balance-of-payments accounts; and a psychological aspect. What actually determines exchange rates is wide and potentially complex, such that economists have not yet developed an accepted theory to explain them. Economists have been able to determine several *parity relationships*—that is, relationships of equivalence—among some of the various factors in exchange rate movements. These include interest rate parity and purchasing power parity.

LO 8-4
Discuss financial forces governments can exert.

Governments can restrict the exchange of their currency for other currencies, set tax rates, and, through monetary policy, influence interest and inflation rates. Currency controls limit the number of foreign currency purchases or exchanges made inside the country and may limit the firm's ability to pay for imports and repatriate profits. Governments set currency exchange controls to reduce depletion of their foreign currency reserves.

Differences in taxation and inflation rates can influence the firm greatly, so they must be monitored and predicted constantly. Taxes increase the firm's costs, whether they are value-added taxes or income taxes. Inflation is a sustained price increase. It is measured by the consumer price index and accompanied by higher interest rates.

LO 8-5
Explain the significance of the balance of payments to international business decisions.

By monitoring balance of payments data, the firm can build a sense of a possible future. If a country is exporting more than it imports, there will be a high demand for its currency in other countries in order to pay for the exported goods. This demand might be expected, via supply and demand, to cause the currency to strengthen. Conversely, when a country imports more than it exports, the currency might be expected to weaken, either in the market or through government action. Faced with a trade deficit, a government might lean toward restrictive monetary or fiscal policies and introduce currency or trade controls. The BOP trend over time also helps managers predict what sort of changes in the economic environment might develop in the country and possibly affect their choice of strategic risks to take there.

KEY TERMS

CRITICAL THINKING QUESTIONS

1. Are people who argue today for a return to the gold system simply nostalgic or do they have a point? Please explain your logic.

2. Was the Bretton Woods system bound to fail? Why or why not?

3. You are on a business trip from Portugal to the United States for 90 days, and you have a per-diem expense account of 400 euros, no receipts required. This per diem is advanced to you before the trip (36,000 euros). You deposit the money into your checking account and use your Portuguese (euro) credit card to cover your costs while in the United States. After the first two weeks of your trip, the dollar weakens against the euro by 15 percent. What ethical dilemma might this currency fluctuation present for you? How will you handle it?

4. If all nations used the SDR, what might the impact be on business?

5. Your firm is generating considerable revenues in a country that suddenly imposes exchange controls prohibiting the purchase of foreign currency within the country and the export of currency. What are some of the issues you will want to discuss with your regional finance staff?

6. Your U.S. firm is about to sign a contract to supply services to a bank in Beijing, with an up-front payment agreement of 50 percent. Do you want this payment in U.S. dollars? Why or why not?

7. While the U.S. Federal Reserve has been increasing interest rates, the European Central Bank is holding interest rates steady. Could this policy difference have influenced the relative strength of the dollar against the euro? Why or why not?

8. Your Boston-based company earned 54 percent of its profits from Germany and France. Given your answer in question 7, are you happy today? Why or why not?

9. Your Munich-based company earns 64 percent of its revenues from high-precision auto component exports to the United States. You need to expand manufacturing capacity, and the U.S. market has great growth potential for your product. Your raw materials could be sourced in either location relatively easily and with no cost advantage in either. Given your answer to question 7, where would you be most likely to add capacity, in Germany or the United States? Why?

10. Why should managers regularly monitor the balance of payments of the countries in which their business operates?

globalEDGE RESEARCH TASK http://globalEDGE.msu.edu/

Use the globalEDGE website (http://globaledge.msu.edu/) to complete the following exercises:

1. Companies and individuals often try to use the differences in country tax rates, which creates a *financial secrecy* in certain countries, to their advantage. An estimated $21 to $32 trillion of private financial wealth is located, untaxed or lightly taxed, in tax havens around the world. Find a source on the country *indices* pages of globalEDGE that will help you understand how financial secrecy can be measured. Visit the external link to prepare a briefing about the top countries that offer the highest financial secrecy, how financial secrecy is defined, and what types of indicators are used to measure the level of financial secrecy.

2. Level of corruption is one of the most important criteria when considering investing in a new international market. Transparency International's *Corruption Perceptions Index* is a helpful tool to asses the corruption levels of countries and analyze regional trends. Review the "Corruption Perceptions Index" on globalEDGE and visit the external site. Check the heat map and be ready to discuss some of the regions where corruption seems to be a pervasive issue. Prepare a summary of the recommendations listed on the page to fight with corruption.

MINICASE

SDR EXCHANGE RISK

The Asian Development Bank (ADB), a multilateral development bank owned by its 67 members whose primary goal is poverty reduction, makes its loans in SDR. At the end of 2017, the ADB's loans, grants, and investments totaled $20.1 billion, in addition to $11.9 billion in co-financing from financing partners, including bilateral and multilateral agencies. The largest recipients of loans, including co-financing, at the end of 2017 were India, China, Pakistan, Bangladesh, Indonesia, and Vietnam. The ADB covers the exposure of its capital resources by selling into the forward market the currencies that make up the SDR basket. To learn more about the SDR basket, visit https://www.imf.org/external/np/fin/data/rms_sdrv.aspx.

Critical Thinking Questions

1. Why would ADB hold SDR instead of dollars or euros?
2. What are the currency amounts that make up the SDR?

Source: "Asian Development Bank, Annual Report 2017," *Asian Development Bank*, 2017.

NOTES

1. Quote by Henry Ford.

2. Cheol S. Eun, and Bruce G. Resnick, *International Financial Management*, 4th ed., Burr Ridge, IL: McGraw-Hill Irwin, 2007, 25.

3. Charles N. Henning, William Pigott, and Robert Haney Scott, *International Financial Management*, New York: McGraw-Hill, 1978, 149.

4. Albert C. Whitaker, *Foreign Exchange*, 2nd ed., New York: Appleton-Century-Crofts, 1933, 157; and Richard Cooper, "The Gold Standard: Historical Facts and Future Prospects," *Brookings Papers on Economic Activity* 1982, no. 1. The increases were gradual until the 1970s, when the price of gold spiked, largely as a result of the 1973 oil crisis.

5. Jacques Rueff, *La réforme du système monétaire international*, Paris: Plon, 1973.

6. Paul Krugman, "The Gold Bug Variations," http://www.pkarchive.org/cranks/goldbug.html, accessed October 04, 2018.

7. *Federal Reserve Bulletin*, September 1969 and January 1974.

8. *Federal Reserve Bulletin*, December 1971 and January 1974.

9. International Monetary Fund, "World Currency Composition of Official Foreign Exchange Reserves," http://data.imf.org, accessed October 04, 2018.

10. International Monetary Fund, *Annual Report on Exchange Arrangements and Exchange Restrictions*, 2017, https://www.imf.org, accessed October 04, 2018.

11. BIS, Triennial National Bank Survey, April 2013, https://www.bis.org/publ/rpfx13fx.pdf, accessed October 04, 2018, 16. (Daily average, 260 trading days per year.)

12. Tommy Wilkes, "Forex Trading Up Sharply in 2018 as Volatility Returns," *Reuters*, https://www.reuters.com, accessed October 04, 2018.

13. "Top 100 Cryptocurrencies by Market Capitalization," *Coin Market Cap*, October 04, 2018, https://coinmarketcap.com.

14. Michael B. Devereux, and Shouyong Shi, "Vehicle Currency," No. 10, Globalization and Monetary Policy Institute Working Paper from Federal Reserve Bank of Dallas, updated March 2011, Vehicle Currency, http://ideas.repec.org/p/fip/feddgw/10.html; and BIS, Triennial National Bank Survey, 6, April 08, 2014.

15. https://www.bloomberg.com/quote/EUR:CUR, accessed October 04, 2018.

16. Bank for International Settlements, "Triennial Central Bank Survey of Foreign Exchange and OTC Derivatives Markets in 2016," https://www.bis.org, accessed October 04, 2018; and Patrick Graham, "Daily FX Trade More Like $3 Trillion than 5—CLS," *Reuters*, https://www.reuters.com, accessed October 04, 2018.

17. "U.S. Probes Whether Big Banks Stifled Rival in Currency Trade," *The Wall Street Journal*, May 15, 2002, A1.

18. U.S. Commodity Futures Trading Commission, "CFTC Orders Deutsche Bank Securities Inc. to Pay $70 Million Penalty for Attempted Manipulation of U.S. Dollar ISDAFIX Benchmark Swap Rates," February 01, 2018, https://www.cftc.gov.

19. Eun, and Resnick, *International Financial Management*, 147–48. The technical explanations here are clearly described and well illustrated.

20. Ibid., 149.

21. Cheol Eun, and Bruce Resnick, *International Financial Management*, New York, NY: McGraw-Hill Companies, 2008, 151.

22. Cheol Eun, and Sanjiv Sabherwal, "Forecasting Exchange Rates: Do the Banks Know Better?" *Global Finance Journal*, 2002, 195–215; and Lillie Lam, Lawrence Fung, and Ip-wing Yu, "Comparing Forecast Performance of Exchange Rate Models," *Hong Kong Monetary Department*, 2008.

23. Michael Gardner, "Amazon Inc. Paid Zero in Federal Taxes in 2017, Gets $789 Million Windfall from New Tax Law," *Institute on Taxation and Economic Policy*, JustTaxesBlog, https://itep.org, accessed October 04, 2018.

24. Center on Budget and Policy Priorities, "Actual U.S. Corporate Tax Rates Are in Line with Comparable Countries," https://www.cbpp.org, accessed October 04, 2018.

25. Kari Jahnsen, and Kyle Pomerleau, "Corporate Income Tax Rates Around the World, 2017," *Tax Foundation*, https://taxfoundation.org, accessed October 04, 2018.

26. David Gelles, "New Rules Make Inversions Less Lucrative, Experts Say," *The New York Times*, https://dealbook.nytimes.com, accessed October 04, 2018.

27. Kyle Pomerleau, "Inversions Under the New Tax Law," *Tax Foundation*, March 13, 2018, https://taxfoundation.org.

28. Brian Ellsworth, "IMF Projects Venezuela Inflation Will Hit 1,000,000 Percent in 2018," *Reuters*, https://www.reuters.com, accessed October 04, 2018.

29. "The Case for Open Trade," World Trade Organization, https://www.wto.org, accessed October 04, 2018.

30. H. Kohler, and J. Wolfensohn, "We Can Trade Up to a Better Financial World," *Financial Times*, December 12, 2003.

9 International Competitive Strategy

> **"What business strategy is all about—what distinguishes it from all other kinds of business planning—is, in a word, competitive advantage. Without competitors there would be no need for strategy, for the sole purpose of strategic planning is to enable the company to gain, as effectively as possible, a sustainable edge over its competitors."**
>
> —*Kenichi Ohmae, McKinsey & Company consultant*[1]

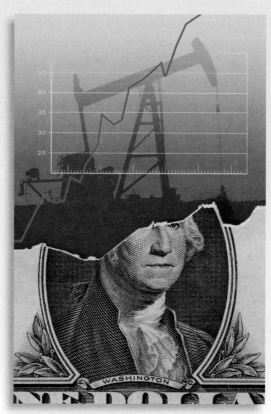

©Comstock Images/Getty Images.

LEARNING OBJECTIVES

After reading this module, you should be able to:

LO 9-1 **Explain** international strategy, competencies, and international competitive advantage.

LO 9-2 **Describe** the global strategic planning process and its components.

LO 9-3 **Describe** the features of a strategic plan.

LO 9-4 **Discuss** the time horizon, organizational level, and different methods of strategic planning.

LO 9-5 **Outline** new directions in strategic planning.

Netflix's Strategy for Global Dominance

Netflix, which provides streaming media services such as movies and television shows, has committed billions of dollars to an aggressive international expansion strategy to achieve global leadership in this rapidly growing industry. Founded in 1997 as a disruptive competitor to Blockbuster, the dominant player in the U.S. video rental industry at the time, Netflix offered convenient video rentals by mail rather than relying on standalone rental stores. In 2007, Netflix innovated further by shifting its business model away from mail-order rentals and toward Internet streaming and video-on-demand services. Soon, the company expanded into original content, including movies and television shows either licensed from others or developed in-house. The 2013 success of the political drama *House of Cards* reinforced Netflix's decision to provide original streaming content.

As the streaming business expanded, new competition arose in the United States from companies such as Amazon Video and Hulu LLC. Recognizing the U.S. market would soon become saturated and seeking to maintain its rapid growth, in 2010 Netflix announced a bold expansion strategy to extend its domestic leadership into foreign markets, with Canada as the first foreign location, followed by Latin America in 2011. This expansion would require substantial investments for Netflix to succeed.

To manage the risks of rapid international expansion, Netflix entered foreign markets with attractive, limited-time offers intended to minimize financial exposure and avoid the potential risk of introducing a full-service offering. These initial offerings allowed Netflix to identify potential cultural differences within and across regional markets, collect data on programming preferences, and enable effective responses to a diverse array of international regulatory environments. As a result, Netflix was able to create more effective, region-specific business models and content offerings. By the end of 2015, Netflix had established a presence in more than 60 countries, although the extent of its market penetration varied.

In January 2016, Netflix announced it would enter 130 additional countries, an acceleration of the pace and scope of their global expansion strategy. Netflix would now be available nearly worldwide, with the exception of nations under sanctions by the U.S. government, such as Syria and North Korea. Netflix's expansion plans excluded China, due to the extensive regulatory constraints imposed on China's entertainment and media industries.

Although Netflix's expansion plans involved operations in more than 190 nations, its streaming services would only be offered in 20 languages and, due to contractual and regulatory constraints, the content offered in foreign markets was much more limited than what was available in the United States. To help overcome these limitations, Netflix pursued partnerships to provide localized content, an expensive but necessary alternative in order to quickly capture local market share. In 2018, Netflix announced there would be an international focus in 80 of the 700 original shows the company was creating, the first time any media company had committed to such a large amount of internationally oriented content. The company also announced that more than two-thirds of new subscribers added in the third quarter of 2018 came from outside the United States, helping Netflix realize year-over-year growth in revenues of more than 48 percent and record profits. Netflix's globalization strategy seems to be moving forward successfully.

Sources: Michelle Castillo, "Netflix Surges After Crushing Earnings," *CNBC*, October 17, 2018, www.cnbc.com; Martin Armstrong, "Netflix's International Expansion Stays on Course," *Statista*, October 29, 2018, www.statista.com; Katie Kirk, "The Globalization of Netflix Builds Pressure," *Global Marketing Professor*, March 11, 2018, www.globalmarketingprofessor.com; Mark Scott, "In Global Expansion, Netflix Makes Friends with Carriers," *The New York Times*, February 26, 2018, www.nytimes.com; Therese Poletti, "Netflix Is Growing at a Stunning Rate—and So Is Its Profit," *MarketWatch*, April 21, 2018; and "International Expansion of Netflix," *Wikipedia*, October 29, 2018, www.en.wikipedia.org.

In this module, we focus on the business itself and the actions managers can take to help their companies compete more effectively in international markets. We discuss the concept of international strategy, the way companies use strategic planning, and the analysis of competitive forces to improve global competitiveness.

What Is International Strategy, and Why Is It Necessary?

International strategy is a plan that guides the way firms make fundamental choices about developing and deploying scarce resources internationally, including what products or services to offer, which markets to enter, and ways to compete.[2] It deals not with a single area such as marketing or production, but with all the functions and activities of a company and the

LO 9-1
Explain international strategy, competencies, and international competitive advantage.

interactions among them. To be effective, a company's international strategy needs to be consistent among all these functions, and among the company's products and regional units (internal consistency) as well as with the variety of demands in the international competitive environment (external consistency).

The purpose of having an international strategy is to enable a company to achieve and maintain a unique and valuable competitive position both within a nation and globally, generating higher rates of profit than its competitors—an ability that has been termed competitive advantage. To achieve a sustainable competitive advantage, the international company must either perform more compelling activities than its competitors or perform the same activities in superior ways, by developing skills or competencies that (1) create value for which customers are willing to pay; (2) are rare; (3) are difficult to imitate or substitute for; and (4) allow the company to exploit the competitive value of its valuable, rare, and difficult-to-imitate competencies.[3]

As you might imagine, managers of international companies attempting to develop a competitive advantage face a formidable challenge. Why? Because resources—time, talent, and money—are always scarce, and there are many ways to use them. Which nations should we enter? In which technologies should we invest? Which products or services should we develop and offer to customers? As managers, we are forced to choose what to do and what *not* to do, now and over time. Without adequate planning, we are more likely to make decisions that do not make good sense competitively, and the company's international competitiveness may be harmed.

To succeed in today's global marketplace, a company must be able to quickly identify and exploit opportunities wherever they occur, domestically or internationally. To meet these challenges, you must understand your company's mission, strengths, and weaknesses and be able to compare them accurately to those of your worldwide competitors. Strategic planning provides valuable tools that help managers accomplish this.

> ## 66 IF YOU FAIL to PLAN, YOU ARE PLANNING to FAIL. 99
>
> —*Benjamin Franklin*[4]

WHY PLAN GLOBALLY?

Strategic planning is the process by which an organization determines where it is going in the future, how it will get there, and how it will assess whether and to what extent it has achieved its goals. In response to increasingly complex environmental forces, many international firms have found it necessary to institute formal global strategic planning so top management can identify opportunities and threats from all over the world, formulate strategies to handle them, and stipulate how to finance and manage the implementation of these strategies.

Strategic plans help ensure that decision makers have a common understanding of the business, the strategy, the assumptions behind the strategy, the external business environment pressures, and their own direction. They also promote consistency of action among the firm's managers worldwide and encourage them to consider the ramifications of their actions in the firm's other geographic and functional areas. Strategic planning is also intended to increase the likelihood of strategic innovations, promoting the development, capture, and application of the new ideas needed to succeed in a challenging competitive environment.

Despite complaints about the challenges of effectively implementing planning efforts, especially within large and international companies, since 1993 Bain & Company's "Management Tools and Trends" survey has consistently reported that strategic planning is among the most commonly used management tool among global executives, and it is the tool with one of the highest reported levels of satisfaction.[5]

The Process of Global Strategic Planning

You should recognize that global strategic planning, the process by which an organization determines where it is going in the future, how it will get there, and how it will assess whether and to what extent it has achieved its goals, is a primary function of a company's managers. The ultimate manager of strategic planning and strategy making is the firm's chief executive officer. The process of strategic planning provides a formal structure in which managers address the following steps: (1) analyze the company's external environments; (2) analyze the company's internal environment; (3) define the company's business and mission; (4) set corporate objectives; (5) quantify goals; (6) formulate strategies; and (7) make tactical plans. We present these steps as a linear process, but there is considerable flexibility in the order in which firms complete them. Companies exist in contexts that are continually changing. As a result of this constant flux, the strategic planning process is iterative. During the analysis of the environments, for instance, committee members could skip to a later step to discuss the impact of a new development on a current corporate objective. For example, when the U.S. government imposed 10 percent tariffs on Chinese plastic shopping bags imported into the United States, the Vietnamese company An Phat, which manufactures plastic packaging, recognized that this ruling created an opportunity for it in the U.S. market.[6]

Committee members then go back to discuss the availability of assets needed to take advantage of the environmental change. If they conclude that the company had such a capability, the committee would try to formulate a new strategy for exploiting the opportunity that had arisen in the U.S. market. If a viable strategy was developed, the members would then establish the corporate objective that the strategy was designed to attain. "America has been a hard market to break into, and we saw we could make a push," said An Phat's deputy chief executive, Nguyen Le Hang. An Phat reviewed their projections and increased their U.S. sales forecast. This change led to other changes that cascaded throughout their operations, including manufacturing, sales, and marketing. Between July and October 2018, An Phat's sales to the United States more than doubled.[7]

The global planning process, illustrated in Figure 9.1, has the same basic format as the planning process for a purely domestic firm, and in fact, most activities of the two kinds of operations are similar. What makes the activities in a worldwide corporation more complex than those of a purely domestic firm is the wide range of potential variation in the uncontrollable forces external to the firm.

STEP 1: ANALYZE DOMESTIC, INTERNATIONAL, AND FOREIGN ENVIRONMENTS

Because a firm has little opportunity to control external forces, its managers must know not only how strong the forces currently are but also where they appear to be headed. An environmental scanning process is useful for a continuous gathering of information, but managers also need to develop and implement appropriate responses to any changes in key environmental

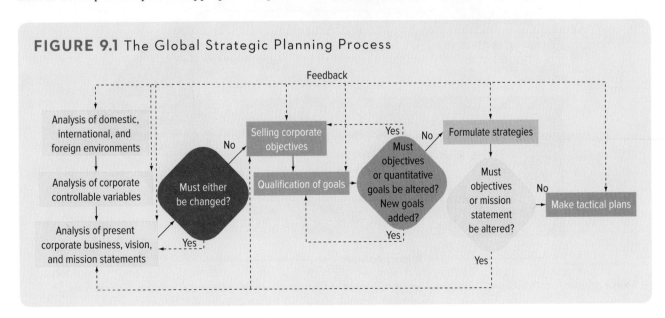

FIGURE 9.1 The Global Strategic Planning Process

forces such as competitors' actions and changes in government taxes and regulations. The consultants at McKinsey & Company found that, worldwide, most executives agree that environmental, social, and business trends such as the growth in consumer preference for natural products, the increased value stakeholders place on social responsibility, and the outsourcing of business activities that support key competitive strengths represent critical issues for company strategy and performance.[8] Despite this, relatively few companies appear to act on key international trends they observe. Why? Often they lack the skills and resources to decide whether, how, and when to act in order to deal effectively with these environmental forces.

STEP 2: ANALYZE CORPORATE CONTROLLABLE VARIABLES

An analysis of the forces controlled by the firm will also include a situational analysis and a forecast. The managers of the various functional areas will either personally submit reports on their units or provide input to a planning staff that will prepare a report for the strategic planning committee.

How can we undertake such a process? Often managers will analyze the firm's activities from the time raw materials enter the plant until the end product reaches the final user, conducting an analysis of the value chain. A value chain is a set of interlinked activities that adds value to the final product or service. A value chain analysis is an assessment conducted on the chain of interlinked activities of an organization or set of interconnected organizations, intended to determine where and to what extent value is added to the final product or service. As part of the analysis, managers must address three key questions about their business:

1. Who are the company's target customers?
2. What value does the company want to deliver to these customers?
3. How will this customer value be created?

Value chain analysis focuses primarily on the third question, and it refers to the set of value-creating activities in which the company is engaged, from sourcing basic raw materials or components to delivering the product or service to the final customer. A simplified value chain is shown in Figure 9.2.

value chain
A set of interlinked activities that adds value to the final product or service

value chain analysis
An assessment conducted on the chain of interlinked activities of an organization or set of interconnected organizations, intended to determine where and to what extent value is added to the final product or service

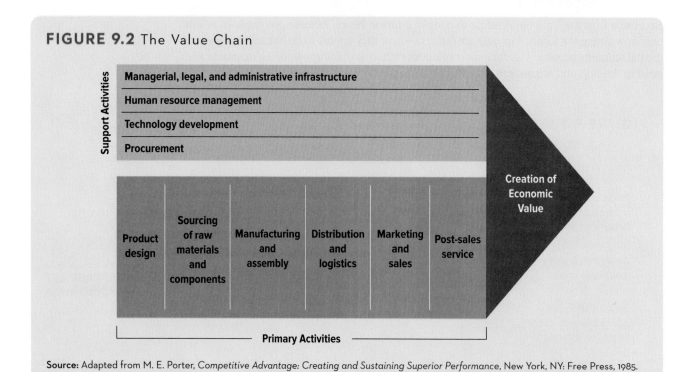

FIGURE 9.2 The Value Chain

Source: Adapted from M. E. Porter, *Competitive Advantage: Creating and Sustaining Superior Performance*, New York, NY: Free Press, 1985.

What is the goal of this analysis? It is to enable managers to identify the set of activities that make up the company's value chain, including those it will do itself and those it will outsource. Managers must also consider where to locate value chain activities—in the home nation, a lower-cost location abroad, or close to a customer abroad? They'll examine the links between the activities in the value chain. For example, does the link between sales and product development ensure that our customers' needs are effectively communicated and incorporated in new products? Are we working effectively with suppliers, partners, distributors, and customers at home and abroad? The outcome of the analysis is the identification and establishment of a superior set of well-integrated value chain activities and links between them, a system that will permit the organization to more effectively and efficiently develop, produce, market, and sell products and services to the target customers, thereby creating the basis for global competitive advantage.

Knowledge as a Controllable Corporate Resource In today's highly competitive, rapidly changing, and knowledge-intensive economy, companies have the potential to achieve competitive advantage by leveraging their organizational knowledge across national boundaries, a process known as **knowledge management**. Knowledge management refers to the practices that organizations and their managers use for identifying, creating, acquiring, developing, dispersing, and exploiting competitively valuable knowledge. The organizational knowledge base includes the capabilities of employees, individually and in teams, as well as the knowledge that gets built into the overall organization through its various structures, systems, and organizational routines.

To help accelerate the acquisition, development, and exploitation of competitively valuable knowledge, managers are developing ways to facilitate the flow of knowledge into and within their companies, to build knowledge databases, to transfer best practices within and across their international network of operations, and otherwise to create the foundation for a knowledge-based competitive advantage.

To effectively manage knowledge, companies must encourage individuals to work together on projects or somehow share their ideas. Much valuable knowledge is **tacit**, which means that it is known well by the individual but is difficult to express verbally or document in text or figures. As a result, systems are needed in order to convey this tacit knowledge to others, possibly by converting it into **explicit**, codified knowledge and then making this knowledge quickly and effectively accessible to other employees who need it. For example, cultural practices that affect business, such as relationships in the procurement process, are not a part of any manual, nor can they be described in a series of action steps. They are subtle norms that control behavior and that can best be learned through observation.

In addition, to effectively design and deliver products that meet customers' needs, companies need access to valuable knowledge possessed by their suppliers, customers, and other partner organizations as well. In some cases, managers even find it necessary to establish company facilities in other locations in order to gain access to this knowledge. For example, Nokia Siemens Networks and Ericsson, which are international leaders in telecommunications technology, both established offices in Silicon Valley. Their objective was to tap into the latest thinking of suppliers and customers located in that region, including Google, Apple, Intel, and a host of other companies, and then transfer this knowledge back to their respective headquarters in Europe.

Companies face an ongoing challenge to create mechanisms that reliably identify opportunities for developing and transferring knowledge and ensuring it is absorbed. They also must protect this proprietary knowledge from diffusion to competitors, so the company can maintain its competitiveness over time.

After the analysis of corporate controllable variables, the planning committee must answer questions such as the following: What are our strengths and weaknesses? What are our human

> ❝ **NONAKA COINED THE WORD 'ba' to DESCRIBE A MENTAL SPACE RATHER THAN A PHYSICAL ONE; IT IS SHARED CONTEXT, WHICH ALLOWS PEOPLE to WORK TOGETHER KNOWING THAT THEY ARE … SINGING from THE SAME SONG SHEET.** ❞
>
> —Thomas Stewart, editor of Harvard Business Review[9]

knowledge management
The practices that organizations and their managers use for identifying, creating, acquiring, developing, dispersing, and exploiting competitively valuable knowledge

tacit knowledge
Knowledge that an individual has but that is difficult to express clearly in words, pictures, or formulas and is therefore difficult to transmit to others

explicit knowledge
Knowledge that is easy to communicate to others via words, pictures, formulas, or other means

> **SETTLING for MUDDLING along RATHER THAN GOING for VICTORY with AN ALL-OUT, DIFFICULT STRATEGY MEANS THAT A COMPANY WILL INEVITABLY FAIL to MAKE THE TOUGH CHOICES AND THE SIGNIFICANT INVESTMENTS THAT WOULD MAKE WINNING EVEN A REMOTE POSSIBILITY.**
>
> —Alan Lafley and Roger Martin, Playing to Win: How Strategy Really Works[10]

mission statement
A broad statement that defines the organization's purpose and scope

vision statement
A description of the company's desired future position if it can acquire the necessary competencies and successfully implement its strategy

values statement
A clear, concise description of the fundamental values, beliefs, and priorities expected of the organization's members, reflecting how they are to behave with each other and with the company's customers, suppliers, and other members of the global community

and financial resources? Where are we with respect to our present objectives? Have we uncovered any facts that require us to delete goals, alter them, or add new ones? When it has completed this internal audit, the committee is ready to examine the company's mission, vision, and values statements.

STEP 3: DEFINE THE CORPORATE MISSION, VISION, AND VALUES STATEMENTS

The company's mission, vision, and values communicate to its stakeholders—employees, stockholders, governments, partners, suppliers, and customers—what the company is, where it is going, and the values that will guide the behavior of its members. The **mission statement** is a broad statement that defines the purpose of a company's existence, including its business, objectives, and approach for reaching those objectives. A **vision statement** is a description of the company's desired future position, of what it hopes to accomplish if it can acquire the necessary competencies and successfully implement its strategy. In contrast, a **values statement** is intended to be a clear, concise description of the fundamental values, beliefs, and priorities expected of the organization's members, reflecting how they are to behave with each other and with the company's customers, suppliers, and other members of the global community. A Booz Allen Hamilton/Aspen Institute survey of corporations in 30 countries revealed that 89 percent of these organizations had explicit, written statements of corporate values and that greater success in linking a corporation's values to its operations was related to superior financial results.[11]

What do these statements look like in practice? Google states its mission thus:

to organize the world's information and make it universally accessible and useful.[12]

As you can see, Google states its vision in very broad and general terms. In contrast, Amazon states its mission in a more specific manner, focusing explicitly on consumers, online shopping, and low pricing:

We seek to be Earth's most customer-centric company, where customers find and discover anything they might want to buy online, and endeavors [sic] *to offer its customers the lowest possible prices.*[13]

South Korean multinational Samsung's corporate mission is to

inspire the world with our innovative technologies, products and design that enrich people's lives and contribute to social prosperity by creating a new future.

The company has stated its Vision 2020 as "Inspire the World, Create the Future" and states:

The Vision 2020 is at the core of our commitment to create a better world full of richer digital experiences, through innovative technology and products. The goal of the vision is to become a beloved brand, an innovative company, and an admired company. For this, we dedicate our efforts to creativity and innovation, shared value with our partners, and our great people. We have delivered world best products and services through passion for innovation and optimal operation. We look forward to exploring new business areas such as healthcare and automotive electronics, and continue our journey through history of innovation. Samsung Electronics will welcome new challenges and opportunities with joy.[14]

The Mitsubishi Corporation (MC) of Japan states its group corporate vision this way:

The MC Group aims to deliver sustainable growth by adapting to changes in the business environment and fulfilling societal needs in due consideration of the United Nations' Sustainable Development Goals (SDGs). To achieve this aim, the MC Group shall rely on three core strengths, namely its collective capabilities to adopt a holistic view of industry, its foresight to identify new seeds of growth, and its execution skills to germinate them. Simultaneously generating economic value, environmental value and societal value through our businesses.[15]

Google's Values and Strategy versus Opportunity in China

Google, the leader in the Internet search engine business with over two-thirds of the market, has actively promoted its ethical values—including its unofficial motto "Don't be evil"—as a foundation for its business activity. To obtain permission for its 2006 entry into the rapidly growing Internet search market in China, Google agreed to modify its operating approach to meet Chinese requirements for censoring Internet searches, including those involving certain socially or politically sensitive topics. The company's decision reflected a belief that its participation might contribute to a gradual loosening of Beijing's restrictions on free speech. In an effort to raise awareness of censorship among Chinese Internet users, it included a disclosure statement on its site saying some search information had been removed.

By the end of 2009, Google had gained 36 percent of the Chinese market, second only to local company Baidu and far outdistancing rivals such as Microsoft and Yahoo. Google's Chinese revenues, estimated at $300 million in 2009 and projected at $600 million in 2010, were seen to have the potential to reach $5 billion to $6 billion by 2014.

Google Headquarters in China. ©Nelson Ching/Bloomberg/Getty Images.

However, after weighing the issues linked to this strategic decision, Google decided its reputation for ethical behavior was more valuable than potential returns from China's search engine market. In a highly publicized move, Google announced in 2010 that it would stop obeying censorship requirements on its Chinese site, instead, shutting the site down and moving its Chinese-language search activities to Hong Kong, a special administrative region of China with broader free speech protections than the mainland.

Google's high-profile exit was applauded by many. It positioned the company as a champion of free speech, restoring the reputation for ethical values and behavior that its censorship activities in China had tarnished. The move to Hong Kong was also expected to enhance customers' perceived trust in the company and its commitment to protecting their personal information. This was particularly important because Google's business model increasingly emphasizes cloud computing, in which individuals and businesses store data online instead of on their own computers and must implicitly trust that a company such as Google will protect these data.

However, Google's decision to exit the Chinese search engine market was not without detractors. Key competitors such as Microsoft did not choose to leave the Chinese market. Chinese Foreign Ministry spokesperson Qin Gang said, "The one whose reputation has been harmed isn't China, rather it is Google." The move threatened Google's ability to compete in the world's largest and fastest-growing Internet market, leaving the company exposed to the risk that the Chinese government could block access for users from the Chinese mainland. Google's exit also aided competitors that remained in China. Baidu's market share increased, reaching about 70 percent, while Google's share declined to under 3 percent.

In 2018, Google again stunned many people, including many of the company's employees, when it was revealed that the company had created a version of its search engine that would comply with China's censorship requirements. This development could enable Google to re-enter the massive Chinese market. When news of Google's secret development project was leaked, it unleashed a torrent of criticism. A letter signed by more than 1,400 Google employees protested the project, and several high-profile employees resigned in protest. Some U.S. policymakers accused Google of being evasive and suggested the company might face intense scrutiny over its management of user data and privacy. In response, the company commented, "Google is committed to free expression—supporting the free flow of ideas is core to our mission. Where we have developed our own content policies, we enforce them in a politically neutral way. Giving preference to the content of one political ideology over another would fundamentally conflict with our goal of providing services that work for everyone."

Critical Thinking Questions

1. What might have been the implications if Google had stayed in China's Internet search engine market in 2010? Would that have harmed Google's reputation and performance elsewhere in the world?

2. What could be the implication of Google's re-entering the Chinese search engine market? Will it hurt or hinder the company's ability to compete successfully in other parts of the world?

3. Overall, do you think Google made a good decision to leave China in 2010? Why or why not?

Sources: Brian Fung, "Google Really Is Trying to Build a Censored Chinese Search Engine, Its CEO Confirms," *Washington Post*, October 16, 2018, www.washingtonpost.com; Nitasha Tiku, "Google's CEO Says Tests of Censored Chinese Search Engine Turned Out Great," *Wired*, October 15, 2018, www.wired.com.; Nick Statt, "Leaked Google Research Shows Company Grappling with Censorship and Free Speech," *The Verge*, October 10, 2018, www.theverge.com.; "Search Engine Market Share China, Nov 2017–Nov 2018," *Statcounter Globalstats*, November, 2018, www.gs.statcounter.com; Tim Bradshaw, David Gelles, and Richard Waters, "Realism Lies behind Decision to Quit," *Financial Times*, March 24, 2010, 6, www.ft.com; Matthew Forney, and Arthur Kroeber, "Google's Business Reason for Leaving China: Of Reputation and Revenue," *The Wall Street Journal*, April 06, 2018, www.wsj.com; and Loretta Chao, "Google Braces for Fallout in China," *The Wall Street Journal*, March 24, 2010, B1, www.wsj.com.

The nonprofit microfinance organization, Kiva, states its vision this way:

We envision a world where all people hold the power to create opportunity for themselves and others.[16]

Qatar Petroleum's vision is

to become one of the best national oil companies in the world, with roots in Qatar and a strong international presence.[17]

The company lists six basic values to act as pillars for the company's culture and efforts to attain this vision, which are: (1) safety, (2) integrity, (3) respect, (4) excellence, (5) responsibility, and (6) collaboration.[18]

Once a company has defined its mission statement, management must then set corporate objectives.

STEP 4: SET CORPORATE OBJECTIVES

Objectives direct the firm's course of action, maintain it within the boundaries of the stated mission and vision, and ensure its continuing existence. For example, Intel states the following strategic objectives (termed "strategic imperatives" by the company): (1) defend and extend the core PC and server businesses; (2) expand into profitable, related adjacencies; (3) selectively disrupt markets and adapt Intel formula; and (4) continue to develop *Go Big* opportunities.[19] How does Intel know whether it achieves these objectives? How will the company assess whether it has been successful in attempting to "selectively disrupt markets," for example?

STEP 5: QUANTIFY THE OBJECTIVES

To develop a strategy for reaching its objectives, a company must quantify them. For example, Intel states a number of performance goals, including the following: for diversity ("Achieve full representation of women and underrepresented minorities at Intel in the U.S. by the end of 2018"); for supply chain responsibility ("Reach 90% compliance to each of our 12 environmental, labor, ethics, health and safety, and diversity and inclusion supplier expectations" and "Implement an enhanced green chemistry screening and selection process for 100% of new chemicals and gases by 2020"); and for environmental sustainability ("Achieve zero hazardous waste to landfill by 2020" and "Restore 100% of our global water use by 2025").[21]

> **"[WHEN CONSIDERING GLOBAL STRATEGIES,] WE MUST REMEMBER THAT DIFFERENCES between COUNTRIES ARE LARGER THAN GENERALLY ACKNOWLEDGED. . . . STRATEGIES THAT ASSUME COMPLETE GLOBAL INTEGRATION TEND to PLACE FAR TOO MUCH EMPHASIS on INTERNATIONAL STANDARDIZATION"**
>
> *—Pankaj Ghemawat, professor of global strategy, IESE Business School, Barcelona, Spain*[20]

But despite most top managers' preference for verifiable objectives, they frequently do have nonquantifiable or directional goals. Incidentally, objectives do tend to be more quantified as they progress down the organization to the operational level, because, for the most part, strategies at one level become the objectives for the succeeding level.

STEP 6: FORMULATE THE COMPETITIVE STRATEGIES

Competitive strategies are action plans to enable organizations to reach their objectives. Generally, participants in the strategic planning process will formulate alternate competitive strategies and corresponding plans of action that consider the directions the external environmental forces are taking, along with the company's strengths, weaknesses, opportunities, and threats.

competitive strategies Action plans to enable organizations to reach their objectives

When developing and assessing strategic alternatives, companies competing in international markets confront two opposing goals: to reduce costs and adapt to local markets. Firms must do what they can to lower per-unit costs so customers will not perceive their products or services as too expensive. This often results in pressure to locate some of the company's facilities where costs are low, as well as to develop products that are highly standardized across multiple nations.

Managers also must modify their products to meet the demands of the local markets in which they do business and the differences in distribution channels, governmental regulations, and cultural preferences they face. As you might imagine, such modifications can incur additional expense, which can cause the company's costs to rise.

These two opposing pressures suggest five different strategies for competing internationally: home replication, multidomestic, regional, global, and transnational. As suggested in Figure 9.3, the company's most appropriate strategy, overall and for various activities in the value chain, depends on the relative amount of pressure the company faces to adapt to local markets and achieve cost reductions.

Home Replication Strategy Companies pursuing a home replication strategy typically centralize product development functions in their home country. After they develop differentiated products in the home market, they often transfer them to foreign markets to capture additional value. To be successful, the company has to possess a valuable distinctive competency that local competitors lack in the foreign markets. The company's

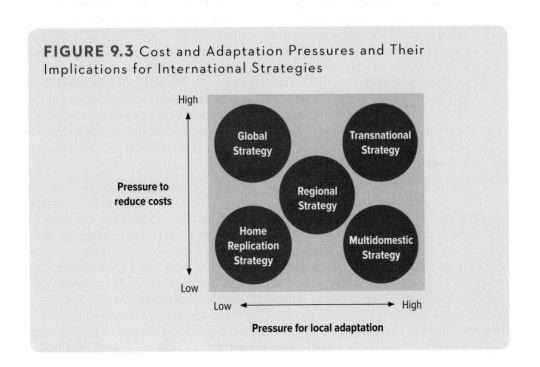

FIGURE 9.3 Cost and Adaptation Pressures and Their Implications for International Strategies

home-country headquarters usually maintains tight control over marketing and product strategy, and the primary responsibility of local subsidiaries is to leverage home-country capabilities. The extent of local customization of product offerings or marketing strategy tends to be limited. Once local demand and circumstances justify such an investment, the company may establish manufacturing and marketing functions in each major country in which it does business.

When might such a strategy be most appropriate? Generally, when the company faces relatively weak pressures for local responsiveness and cost reductions. When there are strong pressures for local responsiveness, however, companies pursuing a home replication strategy will be at a disadvantage compared with competitors that emphasize customization of the product offering and market strategy for local conditions. For example, Xiaomi introduced its first smartphone in mid-2011 and quickly gained a major share of its domestic Chinese market through a combination of good value, fashionable design, Chinese-based user interface, and a marketing approach well adapted to the fast-growing market.[22] The company sells almost exclusively through online channels, leveraging free press garnered from its status as a Chinese national hero and exploiting Chinese social networks such as Weibo and WeChat. The company has encountered challenges leveraging its strategy in international markets, where differences in market conditions, e-commerce, and consumer habits may limit the effectiveness of an approach honed for China. Companies pursuing a home replication strategy may also face high operating costs, due to duplication of manufacturing facilities across the markets they serve.

Multidomestic Strategy A multidomestic strategy is effective when the pressure to adapt products or services for local markets is strong. Decision making tends to be more decentralized, to allow the company to modify its products and respond quickly to changes in local competition and demand. Subsidiaries are expected to develop and exploit local market opportunities, which means knowledge and competencies should be developed at the subsidiary level. For its entry into India, Mattel did not rely solely on the same Barbie doll it markets in the United States. Instead, it also introduced an Indian Barbie, one modeled after a well-known Bollywood actress. By tailoring its products to specific markets, the company may not only increase its appeal but may also be able to charge higher prices.

Local adaptation of products usually will increase the company's cost structure, however. The company will have to invest in additional capabilities and acquire knowledge of

local culture, language, customer demographics, human resource practices, government regulations, and distribution systems. Adapting products too much to local tastes may also reduce the distinctiveness of a company's products. KFC's chicken outlets in China are highly popular because they are perceived to reflect U.S. values and standards, which might be lost if the company tried to adapt the stores and products to be more like other Chinese food outlets. The extent of local adaptation may also change over time, as when customer demands start to converge due to the emergence of global telecommunications, media, and travel, as well as reduced differences in income between nations. The cost and complexity of coordinating a range of different strategies and product offerings across national and regional markets can also be substantial.

Global Strategy A global strategy works when a company faces strong pressures for reducing costs and limited pressure to adapt products for local markets. Strategy and decision making are typically centralized at headquarters, and the company tends to offer standardized products and services. Overseas offices are expected to adopt the most efficient strategies found within the entire corporation. Value chain activities are often located in only one or a few geographic locations to assist the company in achieving cost reductions with economies of scale. International subsidiaries are expected to transmit information to headquarters and submit to centralized controls imposed by headquarters. Close coordination and integration of activities across products and markets are valued, as well as the development of efficient logistics and distribution capabilities. These strategies are common in industries such as semiconductors (Intel) and large commercial aircraft (Boeing).

A KFC restaurant in China. ©Michael Kemp/Alamy Stock Photo.

However, global strategies may leave the company with limited ability to adjust quickly and effectively to changes in customer needs across national or regional markets, increased transportation and tariff costs for exporting products from centralized production sites, and the risks of locating activities in a centralized location (which can, for example, cause the firm to confront risks from political changes or trade conflicts, exchange rate fluctuations, and similar factors).

Transnational Strategy A company that confronts simultaneous pressures for cost-effectiveness and local adaptation, and that can gain competitive advantage from responding to both, may adopt a transnational strategy. The company's assets and capabilities will be based where it is most beneficial for each specific activity, neither highly centralized as with a global strategy nor widely dispersed as with a multidomestic strategy. International subsidiaries are expected to contribute actively to the development of the company's capabilities, as well as to develop and share knowledge with company operations worldwide. Typically, "upstream" value chain activities, such as product development, raw materials sourcing, and manufacturing, will be more centralized, while the "downstream" activities, such as marketing, sales, and service, will be more decentralized, located closer to the customer.

Of course, as you might expect, achieving an optimal balance in locating activities is a challenge for management, as is maintaining this balance over time as the company faces changes in competition, customer needs, regulations, and other factors. Management must ensure that the comparative advantages of its locations are captured and internalized, rather than wasted due to limitations on its people, structures, and coordination and control systems.

Strategic decisions, as well as organizational structures and systems, are more complex given a transnational strategy. Caterpillar, for example, has tried to manufacture many of the standardized components of its construction and mining equipment in a few locations worldwide. At the same time, the company has set up assembly operations in each major market, sometimes accompanied by specialized local production capability, thereby promoting its ability to tailor products to local needs.

REGIONAL STRATEGIES FOR COMPETING GLOBALLY

Although many have argued that economic liberalization, declining transportation costs, and advances in telecommunications and computer technology have produced a "borderless" world in which a global strategy is not only appropriate but even essential for success, is that what we see in practice? Multinationals do represent a major force driving economic globalization; with nearly 70 percent of total sales and 65 percent of assets of the top 100 MNEs being international. Yet investigations of large multinationals in manufacturing and service sectors reveal that most generate the majority of their revenues within a single region rather than having broad and deep penetration of international markets as a whole. An average of about 80 percent of their worldwide revenues are generated within their home region in North America, the European Union, and Asia. These data suggest the world marketplace is triad-based rather than global in nature, at least for most companies and industries.[23]

Some researchers say this *semi-globalization* may be merely a stage in the evolution of international companies, and that increased globalization of sales and other value chain activities will occur over time as companies accumulate international experience and extend their reach. Firms may need to experiment and innovate with business models to accomplish this. There may also be a "threshold of internationalization" beyond which a multinational's performance declines, at least until the firm can develop competencies necessary for more globally dispersed operations. In fact, some findings suggest that if we look at value chain activities other than sales—including sourcing of labor, capital, production, and knowledge—we might find a less region-centric interpretation of multinationals' strategies.

Nevertheless, one result of this recent research is that it inspires us to think about applying international strategy on a region-by-region basis, rather than solely either globally or nation by nation. To the extent that a multinational's market position varies substantially across regions, its strategies may also need to vary by region to accommodate different competitive environments.

Standardization and Planning in Strategy Formulation While the preceding discussion addressed basic strategic alternatives at a business or corporate level, not all activities of an organization confront the same mix of globalization and localization pressures. For example, historically, companies have standardized more aspects of research and development and manufacturing than of marketing. Many top executives believe marketing strategies are best determined locally because of differences among the various foreign environments. Yet, many international companies want to achieve benefits from standardization too. They must look not only at current circumstances but also at how the situation may change in the future and the implications of these changes. This need to focus on the future helps explain companies' increasing use of scenarios in the planning process.

Standardization can be a key element for achieving consistent outcomes globally. ©Comstock/Getty Images.

scenarios
Multiple, plausible stories about the future

Using Scenarios in Strategy Formulation Because of the rapid pace of changes in the uncontrollable variables companies face, many managers have become dissatisfied with planning for a single set of events. Instead, they have turned to scenarios, which are multiple, plausible stories for probable futures. Scenarios integrate a variety of ideas about the future, including key certainties and uncertainties, and present these ideas in a useful and comprehensible manner. Managers can brainstorm various "what-if" scenarios, raising and challenging their assumptions and projected outcomes before committing to a specific course of action. Often, the what-if questions reveal weaknesses in current strategies. Scenarios should be developed in a manner consistent with company priorities and then be tied into strategic and operational decisions a company must make today and over time. Some subjects for scenarios are large and sudden changes in sales (up or down), sudden increases in the prices of raw materials, sudden tax increases, and a change in the political party in power.

Although the origins of scenario planning are unclear, the multinational company Royal Dutch Shell is widely recognized as a pioneer in popularizing the technique. Shell made scenario planning a staple of its strategic planning efforts almost 50 years ago when it was confronted with a severe and unexpected global oil shortage. In dealing with such uncertainty and change, traditional strategic planning approaches based on extrapolation of historical conditions are of limited value. Managers find it difficult to break away from their existing view of the world, one that results from a lifetime of training and experience. By presenting other ways of seeing the world, scenarios allow managers to envision alternatives that might lie outside their traditional frame of reference. This approach is particularly useful for international companies that face high levels of change and uncertainty because it allows managers to anticipate and prepare for opportunities and threats that cannot be fully predicted or controlled.[24]

In his classic book, *The Art of the Long View*, Peter Schwartz identifies the following seven steps to successful scenario planning:

1. Determine the area, scope, and timing of the decisions with the greatest relevance to or impact on your organization.
2. Research existing conditions and trends in a wide variety of areas (including those areas you might not typically consider).
3. Examine the drivers or key factors that will likely determine the outcome of the stories you are beginning to build.
4. Construct multiple stories of what could happen next.
5. Play out what the impact of each of these possible futures might be for your business or organization.
6. Examine your answers and look for those actions or decisions you'd make that were common to all two or three of the stories you built.
7. Monitor what does develop so as to trigger your early response system.[25]

What is the primary value of scenario planning efforts? It is not so much the strategic plans that are created but rather the transformation in strategic thinking that results from this activity.

Contingency Planning as Part of Strategy Formulation Contingency plans are plans for the best- or worst-case scenarios or for critical events that could have a severe impact on the firm. Many companies prepare contingency plans for worst- and best-case scenarios and for critical events as well.[26] Most producers of petroleum and hazardous chemicals have contingency plans, particularly in light of such ecological disasters as BP's 2010 oil spill in the Gulf of Mexico. Because of the important impact on profits of changes in the prices of jet fuel, contingency planning is a common strategic activity for domestic and international airlines. The threat of cyberattacks, such as the 2014 hacking of Sony Pictures or the 2017 hacking of Equifax, the giant credit reporting organization, could disrupt operations within companies as well as partner organizations.[27] The deadly terrorist attacks on the World Trade Center in New York and the Pentagon in Washington, DC, on September 11, 2001, as well as the Fukushima Daiichi nuclear tragedy that occurred in Japan after an earthquake and tsunami in March 2011, and Hurricane Sandy in October 2012, reminded many organizations of the importance of developing contingency plans to ensure the effective continuation of their operations in the event their headquarters or other key locations are attacked or otherwise incapacitated for a period of time.

contingency plans
Plans for the best- or worst-case scenarios or for critical events that could have a severe impact on the firm

The 2017 hacking of Equifax was an example of how cyberattacks can impact international businesses. ©Alex Milan Tracy/Sipa USA/Newscom.

Preparing International Strategies Requires Thinking about the Future

What do you think would happen if the price of petroleum or food skyrocketed (as both did during 2011, causing the stock prices of airlines like British Air and cruise companies like Carnival to plummet) or suddenly crashed (as petroleum prices did at the end of 2014)? What are the chances of a host government nationalizing key companies or an entire industry, as Argentina and Bolivia have recently done? What would be the implication of major environmental disasters, such as three hurricanes hitting the United States and the Caribbean in quick succession in 2017? What would happen if world credit markets dried up, as occurred in 2014 for Spain and Greece? How might global climate change affect economic development within and across different industries and regions of the world?

Because these types of changes can cause even the largest companies to suffer severe economic pressure or even bankruptcy, identifying and assessing changes in internal and environmental forces by building scenarios of possible futures is a key part of companies' strategic planning processes. The objective of scenario building is to force executives to question their assumptions about the environments in which the company operates and incorporate into their planning the uncertainties that might profoundly affect their strategic and operational performance around the world. Scenarios are intended to be plausible and challenging stories, but they are not forecasts based on the past. Rather, they are a means to force managers to realize that their assumptions based on past experience may no longer apply. Scenarios can help managers anticipate future challenges and make decisions to help their companies avoid or minimize potential problems.

Traditionally, strategic planners from a company's headquarters made the scenarios and presented them to line managers—a kind of "show and tell." Now managers are increasingly expected to develop their own scenarios for strategic decision making. How does the process operate? Typically working in teams of five to eight people, managers first identify the decision that must be made and then gather information by reading, observing, and talking with knowledgeable people. Next, the team identifies the driving forces and "critical uncertainties" in the decision and prioritizes them. Team members prepare three or four scenarios, each depicting a credible future rather than best-case, worst-case, and most likely situations. Then the team identifies the implications of each scenario and the leading indicators management must scan for, and they develop more robust and effective strategies. By anticipating the future and recognizing the warning signs of turbulence ahead, managers can both better understand what tomorrow may hold and make better-quality decisions to avoid crises that may come.

Critical Thinking Questions

1. How might the development of scenarios enhance an international company's performance?

2. What drawbacks could result if an international company decided to use scenarios as part of its international strategic planning?

Sources: Royal Dutch Shell, "Shell Scenarios, Modelling and Decision Making," *Shell Scenarios*, September 08, 2018, www.shell.com; Verity Julie, "Scenario Planning as a Strategy Technique," *European Business Journal*, vol. 15, no. 4, 2003, 185–95; Angela Wilkinson, and Roland Kupers, "Living in the Futures," *Harvard Business Review*, May, 2013, www.hbr.org; Muhammad Daim Amer, U. Tugrul, and Antonie Jetter, "A Review of Scenario Planning," *Futures*, vol. 46, November 2012, 23–40; and David Niles, "The Secret of Successful Scenario Planning," *Forbes*, August 03, 2009, www.forbes.com.

STEP 7: PREPARE TACTICAL PLANS

Because strategic plans are fairly broad, tactical (also called operational) plans are a requisite for spelling out in detail how the objectives will be reached. In other words, very specific, short-term means for achieving the goals are the objective of tactical planning. For instance, if the British subsidiary of a U.S. producer of prepared foods has a quantitative goal of a 20 percent increase in overall sales, its strategy might include selling 30 percent more to institutional users. The tactical plan could include such points as hiring three new specialized sales representatives, attending four trade shows, and advertising in two industry periodicals every other month next year. This is the kind of specificity found in the tactical plan.

Strategic Plan Features and Implementation Facilitators

What are the elements of a strategic plan, and who will implement them? This section will discuss the content and process details about strategic plans.

SALES FORECASTS AND BUDGETS

Two prominent features of the strategic plan are sales forecasts and budgets. The sales forecast, which is a prediction of future sales performance, not only provides managers with an estimate of the revenue to be received and the units to be sold but also serves as the basis for planning in the other functional areas. Without this information, managers cannot formulate production, financial, and procurement plans. Budgets are an itemized projection of revenues and expenses for a future time period. As is the case for sales forecasts, budgets are both a planning and a control technique. During planning, they coordinate all the functions within the firm and provide managers with a detailed statement of future operating results and the resources required to achieve those outcomes.

sales forecast
A prediction of future sales performance

budget
An itemized projection of revenues and expenses for a future time period

FACILITATION TOOLS FOR IMPLEMENTING STRATEGIC PLANS

Once the plan has been prepared, it must be implemented. Two of the most important facilitation tools for implementing plans are policies and procedures.

Policies Policies are broad guidelines issued by upper management for the purpose of assisting lower-level managers in handling recurring problems. Because policies are broad, they permit discretionary action and interpretation. A policy is intended to economize managerial time and promote consistency among the various operating units. For example, if a company's distribution policy states that sales will be made through wholesalers, marketing managers throughout the world know they should normally use wholesalers and avoid selling directly to retailers. Similarly, publicity regarding the widespread occurrence of bribery in various international markets has prompted numerous companies to issue policy statements condemning this practice. Managers have thus been put on notice that as a company policy they are not to offer bribes.

policies
Broad guidelines issued by upper management to assist lower-level managers in handling recurring issues or problems

Procedures Procedures are guides that specify the way certain tasks or activities will be carried out, thereby ensuring uniform action on the part of all corporate members. For instance, most international corporate headquarters issue procedures for their subsidiaries to follow in preparing annual reports and budgets. This assures corporate management that whether the budgets originate in Thailand, the United States, or Brazil, they will be prepared using the same format, which facilitates comparison.

procedures
Guides that specify ways of carrying out a particular task or activity

PERFORMANCE MEASURES

A key part of strategic planning is measuring performance in order to assess whether the strategy and its implementation are proceeding successfully or whether modifications need to be made. Companies consider at least three types of measures when assessing strategic performance: (1) measures of the company's success in obtaining and applying the required resources, such as financial, technological, and human resources; (2) measures of the effectiveness of the company's employees, within and across the firm's international network of operations, in performing their assigned jobs; and (3) measures of the company's progress toward achieving its mission, vision, and objectives and doing so in a manner consistent with the company's stated values.[28] A range of concepts and tools, including the balanced scorecard and triple-bottom-line accounting, have been promoted as alternatives for helping to measure strategic performance. For example, the balanced scorecard approach is based on an integration of strategic planning with a company's budgeting processes, and short-term results from the balanced scorecard can serve as a means of monitoring progress in achieving strategic objectives across four dimensions: financial, customer, internal, and learning and growth.

Kinds of Strategic Plans

Of course, strategic plans differ, and in many ways. Two important differentiators are the time horizon of the plan, and the level of the organization for which it is made.

TIME HORIZON

Although strategic plans may be classified as short, medium, or long term, there is little agreement about the definition of these periods. For some businesses, long-range planning may be for a five-year period. For others, such as manufacturers of commercial aircraft, this would be a medium-term plan; their long-term plans might cover 15 to 25 years or more. Short-range plans are usually for one to three years; however, even long-term plans are subject to annual or more frequent review as the situation requires. Furthermore, the time horizon will vary according to the age of the firm and the stability of its market. A new venture in a field such as social networking (WeChat or Instagram) or Internet television (Sling TV or Roku) is extremely difficult to plan for more than three years in advance, but a five- or six-year horizon may be sufficient for a mature company in a steady market.

CULTURE FACTS @internationalbiz

@panasonic Perhaps reflecting the long-term orientation characteristic of Japanese culture, the founder of Matsushita (now known as Panasonic) announced a 250-year plan for his company, consisting of ten 25-year periods. #longtermorientation #250yearplan

LEVEL IN THE ORGANIZATION

Each organizational level of the company will have its own plan. For example, if there are four organizational levels, as shown in Figure 9.4, there will be four plans, each more specific than the plan at the level above. In addition, the functional areas at each level will have their own plans and sometimes will be subject to the same hierarchy, depending mainly on how the company is organized.

METHODS OF PLANNING

How are strategic plans made? The three most common approaches are top-down, bottom-up, and iterative.

top-down planning
Planning process that begins at the highest level in the organization and continues downward

Top-Down Planning **Top-down planning** is a process that begins at the highest level in the organization and continues downward. In top-down planning, corporate headquarters develops and provides guidelines that include the definition of the business, the mission and vision statements, company objectives, financial assumptions, the content of the plan, and special issues. If there is an international division, its management may be told that this division is expected to contribute $350 million in profits, for example. The division, in turn, will break this total down among the affiliates under its control. The managing director in Germany will be informed that the German operation is expected to contribute $35 million; Brazil, $8 million; and so on. An advantage of top-down planning is that the home office, with its global perspective, should be able to formulate plans that ensure the optimal corporate-wide use of the firm's scarce resources. This approach may also promote creativity, because a corporate-wide perspective on market opportunities may yield insights not readily observable by managers within individual national markets.

Disadvantages of top-down planning are that it restricts initiative at the lower levels and shows some insensitivity to local conditions, particularly when a company's top management team exhibits ethnocentric tendencies. Furthermore, especially in an international company, there are so many interrelationships that consultation is necessary. Can top management, for example, decide to combine different manufacturing sites in an effort to enhance efficiency without obtaining the opinions of the local units as to its feasibility?

FIGURE 9.4 3M Strategic Planning Cycle

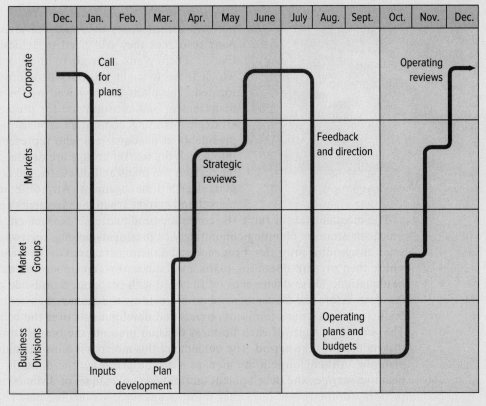

Source: Author discussions with executives from 3M.

Bottom-Up Planning Bottom-up planning operates in the opposite manner because it is a planning process that begins at the lowest level in the organization and continues upward. The lowest operating levels inform the top management about what they expect to do, and the total of these expectations becomes the firm's goals. The advantage of bottom-up planning is that the people responsible for attaining the goals are formulating them. Who knows better than the subsidiaries' directors what and how much the subsidiaries can sell in their respective geographic regions? Because the directors set the goals with no coercion from top management, they feel obligated to make good on their word. Their hands-on perspective may allow them to recognize potentially innovative opportunities to create and leverage value within their local markets, thus serving as a basis for improved performance or even strategic experimentation. However, bottom-up planning has a disadvantage: because each affiliate is free to some extent to pursue the goals it wishes to pursue, there is no guarantee that the sum total of all the affiliates' goals will coincide with those of headquarters. When discrepancies occur, top management must take extra steps to eliminate them.

bottom-up planning
Planning process that begins at the lowest level in the organization and continues upward

Iterative Planning Iterative planning consists of repetition of the bottom-up or top-down planning process until all differences have been reconciled. Iterative planning appears to be becoming more popular, especially in global companies that seek to have a single global plan while operating in many diverse foreign environments. Iterative planning combines aspects of both top-down and bottom-up planning. In 2017, for example, 3M generated over 60 percent of its $32 billion in sales from outside the United States, where it has operations in more than 70 nations and sales in more than 200.[29] Figure 9.4 illustrates how 3M's iterative planning process functions. Planning

iterative planning
Repetition of the bottom-up or top-down planning process until all differences have been reconciled

Business people in a meeting. ©Purestock/Getty Images.

starts in January with the operating managers of the company's five operating business groups, who analyze strengths and weaknesses and external forces, such as new technology and government regulatory changes; perform a competitor analysis; and identify the company resources they will need to achieve their objectives.[30] Their plans then go to the market group, in which three to eight business divisions are typically located. The plans are reviewed by the market group management and consolidated for presentation to the strategic planning committee, consisting of the vice presidents at headquarters who represent the markets into which the market groups are divided. The committee reviews the plans and discusses the results with the market group management. Any differences between market and market group managements are reconciled.

Two months later (in July), the corporate headquarters' management committee, to which the strategic planning committee vice presidents belong, reviews the plans and votes on spending priorities. Feedback and direction are given to the business divisions, which then prepare operating plans and budgets by December and submit them to headquarters. These documents are finalized with corporate worldwide plans. Then, a few days before the December operating reviews, the management committee holds brainstorming sessions to discuss trends and developments over the coming 15 years. The general manager of each business division presents the best picture possible for that industry for the period. The outcome of this meeting is a broad guide for strategic planning. Although operating managers do the planning, the director and staff of a planning services and development unit provide an analysis of 3M's 20 principal competitors worldwide and any other information the divisions require. They also try to identify opportunities and new products.

New Directions in Planning

LO 9-5

Outline new directions in strategic planning.

Strategic planning, particularly in the more traditional bureaucratic form still practiced in some corporations, has been described as a calendar-driven ritual, not an exploration of the company's potential. This traditional strategic planning approach commonly consists of a company's CEO and the head of planning getting together to devise a corporate plan, which is then handed to the operational staff for execution. This approach assumes the future will be similar to the present, even if there is evidence to the contrary.[31] Not surprisingly, the resulting strategic planning documents often fail to be implemented successfully.

Increasingly, the old process is being replaced by a *strategic management* approach, which combines strategic thinking, strategic planning, and strategic implementation, and which is increasingly recognized as a fundamental task of line management, rather than the job of specialized planners in staff positions. Although still susceptible to problems such as groupthink, this more contemporary approach attempts to incorporate changes in three areas: (1) who does the planning, (2) how it is done, and (3) the contents of the plan.

WHO DOES STRATEGIC PLANNING?

Although CEOs report that they would like to spend about one-third of their workday on strategy, strategic planning is no longer something only the company's most senior executives do.[32] Top management, at the urging of strategy consultants, is assigning strategic planning to teams of line and staff managers from different business, geographic, and functional areas, much as it has already done with process improvement and quality improvement. Frequently these teams include members ranging from junior staff members who have shown the ability to think creatively to experienced veterans who will "tell it like it is."

EDUARDO RANGEL: Growth in International Business through Experience

Courtesy of Eduardo Rangel.

Eduardo Rangel was born in the United States and spent his preschool years in Tijuana, Mexico, where his family lived while his father commuted to work in the United States. Here are some of his observations about how he got involved in international business:

Following a three-year stint in community college, I transferred to a state university to complete my studies. Although I took general courses to satisfy graduation requirements for a business degree, I directed most of my attention to the international business classes.

I was in search of an international position in business after graduation, rather than a job in the United States, in order to move outside my comfort zone. I joined a student club, AIESEC, which gave me the opportunity to apply for international internships. Asia was my first choice for working abroad, and I selected Beijing, China, for a nine-month internship during my senior year. China was among the most-discussed themes in my business classes, and by working in Beijing I figured I could learn about a new culture, beyond the popularized images presented in various mass market sources. My decision to go to China can best be described by Nike's slogan "Just Do It."

I arrived in Beijing three months before my internship in order to take an intense Mandarin course at a local university and travel around China. The point was to let the process of culture shock, that feeling of anxiety, loneliness, and confusion that people sometimes experience when living in another country, take its course. My friends struggled with the concept of accepting another country's values, and ultimately some of them even decided to leave China and head back home.

I remember a dismal week in Beijing when I disconnected myself from any interaction with friends and colleagues and stayed in my room waiting for some comforting advice. I called one of my professors, asking for help to regain the lost enthusiasm that existed when I first arrived in China. After I explained that I had been taking my time in China for granted by working long hours and ignoring invitations from friends to travel, she suggested I enjoy myself and return to feeling like a visitor again, continually learning about the local culture. So I followed her advice and it worked!

After returning to the United States from Beijing, I spent a semester completing my bachelor's degree. Then I returned to work for another two years in Beijing. The global recession served as a convenient excuse to stay longer in Beijing because I was earning a good income and living well there. Ultimately, although I returned to the States, my experience traveling to more than 10 countries and living in three of them has fueled my desire to continue learning about other cultures.

Here's what Eduardo mentioned as important things he learned from his work in China:

Patience Being productive in an international company does not necessarily equate to pushing ideas to your superiors or peers immediately after beginning your new position. Most companies in China are micromanaged and subordinates seldom approach their superiors about any dispute or concerns. Most foreigners mistakenly apply the same work habits from their home country to their host country. When they push their method onto their colleagues, the colleagues feel uncomfortable.

Theoretical vs. Experiential Learning Reading about the importance of a business card in China cannot replace the physical exchange during a meeting with a prospective Chinese client. The concept of *guanxi*, literally translating to "relationships," continues after the card exchange with dinners and constant communication. At times, the managers and I would have dinners with high-ranking officials in order to maintain an already established relationship. This is perceived as a way to solidify friendships by proving a client's worth. *Guanxi* is a term that I learned about in my international business courses, but I did not realize its importance until I was partaking in such behavior in my internship.

Knowing Your Objective Make a plan or outline of what you want to achieve from your trip, while also recognizing that there is always room to be flexible. I saw many foreigners stuck in China without any idea as to what their next objective would be. They stayed in China for work just because it was easy; it was all they knew to do. Being focused on your career goals is necessary in order to have an international career in business, rather than merely a business career in China.

Source: Eduardo Rangel

Another difference between the new and the old approaches: traditional planning is a company activity done in seclusion, while the new approach often includes interaction with such parties as important customers, distributors, suppliers, and alliance partners, in order to gain firsthand experience with the firm's markets. Other important stakeholders such as governments and activists (social, environmental, and political) are also relevant influences, if not necessarily direct participants, in this strategic planning process. Incorporating their perspectives can help a company creatively address the challenge of increasingly uncertain and changing international competitive environments.

HOW STRATEGIC PLANNING IS DONE

Top managers of many companies have come to realize there is no point in making new detailed five-year forecasts when international crises are exploding their earlier ones. Instead, they have moved toward less-structured formats and much shorter documents and accept that effective strategic planning encourages ideas to surface anywhere in the organization and at any time. We saw in Figure 9.1 that objectives and strategies are intertwined, as are tactics and strategy. If the planning team is unable to come up with suitable tactics to implement a strategy, it must alter the strategy. If strategies cannot be formulated to enable the firm to reach the objective, the objective must be changed.

CONTENTS OF THE PLAN

The contents of the plan are also different. Many top managers say they are much more concerned now with focusing on issues, strategies, and implementation and incorporating creative, forward-looking ideas essential to competitive success within an uncertain international environment. When firms often must place bigger bets on new technologies and other competitive capabilities, they cannot afford to direct large amounts of money in one direction only to discover years later that it was the wrong direction. Instead, they need an approach to strategic planning that effectively incorporates a long-term perspective to decision making and resource allocation decisions.

SUMMARY

LO 9-1
Explain international strategy, competencies, and international competitive advantage.

International strategy guides the way firms make fundamental choices about developing and deploying scarce resources internationally. The goal of international strategy is to create a competitive advantage that is sustainable over time. To do this, the international company should try to develop skills, or competencies, that are valuable, rare, and difficult to imitate and that the organization is able to exploit fully in order to build and sustain international competitive advantage.

LO 9-2
Describe the global strategic planning process and its components.

Global strategic planning provides a formal structure in which managers (1) analyze the company's external environment, (2) analyze the company's internal environment,

(3) define the company's business and mission, (4) set corporate objectives, (5) quantify goals, (6) formulate strategies, and (7) make tactical plans. Statements of the corporate mission, vision, and values communicate to the firm's stakeholders what the company is and where it is going, as well as the values to be upheld among the organization's members in their behaviors. A firm's objectives direct its course of action, and its strategies enable management to reach its objectives. Quantification of goals not only assists in highlighting priorities but can also serve as a basis for assessing progress toward achieving these goals. When developing and assessing strategic alternatives, companies competing in international markets confront two opposing needs: to reduce costs and to adapt to local markets. As a result, they have five different strategies for competing internationally: home replication, multidomestic, global, transnational, and regional. The most appropriate strategy, overall and for various activities in the value chain, depends on the relative strengths of the two needs (cost reduction and adaptation). Each has advantages and disadvantages.

LO 9-3
Describe the features of a strategic plan.

Two prominent features of the strategic plan are sales forecasts and budgets. The sales forecast provides managers with an estimate of the revenues and the units to be sold, and also serves as the basis for planning in the other functional areas. Without this information, managers cannot formulate plans for other activities such as production, finance, and procurement. Budgets, like sales forecasts, are both a planning and a control technique. On implementation, policies and procedures guide actions and performance measures provide feedback. One approach is the balanced scorecard, which is based on an integration of strategic planning with a company's budgeting processes. Short-term results from the balanced scorecard can serve as a means of monitoring progress in achieving strategic objectives across four dimensions: financial, customer, internal, and learning and growth.

LO 9-4
Discuss the time horizon, organizational level, and different methods of strategic planning.

Although strategic plans may be classified as short, medium, or long term, there is little agreement about the definition of these periods. Planning is done at all levels of the organization. Strategic planning can be a top-down, bottom-up, or iterative process. In top-down planning, corporate headquarters develops and provides guidelines that include the definition of the business, the mission and vision statements, company objectives, financial assumptions, the content of the plan, and special issues. Bottom-up planning is a process that begins at the lowest level in the organization and continues upward. Iterative planning, which is becoming more popular, especially in global companies that seek to have a single global plan while operating in many diverse foreign environments, combines aspects of both top-down and bottom-up planning.

LO 9-5
Outline new directions in strategic planning.

Increasingly, the old process is being replaced by a *strategic management* approach, which combines strategic thinking, strategic planning, and strategic implementation. Operating managers, rather than dedicated staff planners, now have assumed a primary role in planning. They use less structured formats and much shorter documents than in the past and are more concerned with issues, strategies, and implementation.

KEY TERMS

CRITICAL THINKING QUESTIONS

1. What is international strategy? Do you think it is useful for companies to take the time and effort to prepare international strategies if they are in rapidly changing competitive situations with high levels of uncertainty? Why or why not?

2. Why don't companies use the same strategic planning processes for their international business activities as for their domestic operations?

3. Suppose competitor analysis reveals that the U.S. subsidiary of your firm's German competitor is about to broaden its product mix in the U.S. market by introducing a new line against which your company has not previously had to compete in the home market. Your environmental analysis shows that the U.S. dollar is expected to weaken relative to the euro, making U.S. exports relatively less expensive in

Germany. Do you recommend a defensive strategy, or do you attack your competitor in its home market? How will you implement your strategy?

4. You are the CEO of the Mesozoic Petrochemical Company and have just finished studying next year's plans of your foreign subsidiaries. You are pleased that the African regional unit's plan is so optimistic because that subsidiary contributes heavily to your company's income. But OPEC is meeting next month to discuss whether its member countries should reduce production in order to raise the international price of petroleum. Should you ask your planning committee, which meets tomorrow, to construct some scenarios? If so, about what?

5. What are the main strengths and weaknesses of each of the competitive strategies: home replication, multidomestic, regional, global, and transnational? What challenges arise under each approach in terms of building and leveraging knowledge that can yield competitive advantage, and what can companies do to enhance the effectiveness of their knowledge management efforts under each approach?

6. If predictions are difficult to make accurately when there are high levels of uncertainty and change, why would scenario analyses have value? Aren't scenarios also likely to be inaccurate under such circumstances?

7. What strategic issues arise as a firm considers whether and how to transfer internationally the unique skills, and associated products, that result from the distinctive competencies it has developed in its home country?

8. Your firm has used bottom-up planning for years, but its subsidiaries' plans take different approaches to goals and assumptions—even their time frames are different. How can you, the CEO, get them to agree on these points and still solicit their individual input?

9. How can you apply the concepts of strategic planning to your own life, such as for getting a job or a better job? Which, if any, of the strategic planning approaches would not be applicable for you, and why?

globalEDGE RESEARCH TASK   http://globalEDGE.msu.edu/

Use the globalEDGE website (http://globalEDGE.msu .edu/) to complete the following exercises:

1. Your company plans to invest in China and you are leading a team that will create strategies for the company to mitigate risks in the country while doing business and guarantee future growth. Review the *strengths* and *weaknesses* of the country in the "Global Insights" section of globalEDGE under country risk subsection. Evaluate the country risk and business climate ratings. Get ready to discuss the strategies you believe would benefit the company most with your top management.

2. In the "by Industry" sub-section of the "Global Insights" section on globalEDGE, select an industry of your choice and examine the industry's profile. What is the level of fragmentation in the industry and what are the demand and profitability drivers for that industry? Now review the corporations in that industry. Would these factors impact the pressures the companies in this industry face and as such their choice of international strategies? How?

MINICASE

THE GLOBALIZATION OF WALMART

Founded in Arkansas in 1962, Walmart became the dominant firm in the U.S. retail industry by leveraging high levels of service, strong inventory management, and purchasing economies. After rapid expansion during the 1980s and 1990s, Walmart faced limits to growth in its home market and was forced to look internationally for opportunities.

When Walmart opened its first international location in 1991, many skeptics claimed its business practices and culture could not be transferred internationally. Yet, the company's globalization efforts progressed at a rapid pace. Its more than 6,360 international retail units employ 800,000 associates in 27 countries, and the company sources its products from more than 100 nations. International sales accounted for 24 percent of Walmart's $500 billion in revenues for 2018, a level that is projected to increase substantially over the next decade.

Globalizing Walmart: Where and How to Begin?

When Walmart began to expand internationally, it had to decide which countries to target. The European retail market was large, but success would require taking market share from established competitors. Instead, Walmart deliberately selected emerging markets as its starting point for international expansion. In the Americas, it targeted nations with large, growing populations—Mexico, Argentina, and Brazil—and in Asia, it aimed at China. Lacking the organizational, managerial, and financial resources to simultaneously pursue all of these markets, Walmart focused first on the Americas rather than the more culturally and geographically distant Asian marketplace.

For its first international store, opened in 1991 in Mexico City, Walmart used a 50-50 joint venture to help manage the substantial differences in culture and income between the United States and Mexico. Its partner, the retail conglomerate, Cifra, provided learning opportunities and expertise in operating in the Mexico market. Leveraging its Mexican learning, in 1996 Walmart entered Brazil by taking a majority position in a 60-40 venture with a local retailer, Lojas Americana. When subsequently entering Argentina, Walmart did so on a wholly owned basis. By 2018, Walmart's 2,358 units in Mexico accounted for half of all supermarket sales in Mexico.

The Challenge of China

The lure of China proved too great to ignore and Walmart set up operations there in 1996. Beijing restricted operations of foreign retailers, including requirements for government-backed partners and limits on the number and location of stores. Walmart formed a venture with two politically connected Chinese partners, with Walmart holding a controlling stake. Pressured to appease the government's desire for local sourcing of products, while maintaining the aura of being an American shopping experience, Walmart sourced about 85 percent of the Chinese stores' purchases from local manufacturers but heavily weighted purchasing toward locally produced American brands (such as products from Procter & Gamble's factories in China). Walmart also learned the importance of building relationships with the central and local governments and with local communities. Bureaucratic red tape, graft, and lengthy delays in the approval process proved to aggravate, but the company learned ways to curry favor with local officials. By 2018, Walmart operated 443 retail units in China and estimated its Chinese operations could be nearly as large as in the United States within 20 years.

India: Anticipating the Opening Up of a Billion-Person Market

Although one of the world's five largest retail markets, at more than $500 billion, and having 400 million people with disposable income, the inefficiency of the Indian retail sector is well known. More than 95 percent of retail sales are made through nearly 15 million tea stands, newspaper stalls, and mom-and-pop stores. To exploit the potential of India, Walmart needed to manage a notoriously frustrating bureaucracy, highly protectionist and anti-capitalist political parties, a bad road system, frequent power outages, difficulties acquiring appropriate plots of land, and lack of adequate distribution and cold-storage systems, among other concerns. The country's diversity is also problematic, with 18 official languages, 6,000 castes and subcastes, and widely varying regional consumer cultures. Savvy new Indian chains, such as Provogue and Shoppers' Stop, had started to emerge, and nationalistic sentiments continue to produce much consternation for expansion efforts of foreign companies such as Walmart.

As part of its market-opening strategy, Walmart began establishing relationships with Indian suppliers, distributors, and consumers. In 2007, Walmart established Bharti Walmart, a 50-50 joint venture with Bharti Enterprises, a leader in mobile telecommunications, and their first store opened in 2009. Due to constraints on retailing, this venture was technically focused on the wholesale market, selling only to large institutional or wholesale buyers while the company built up its infrastructure and skills for eventual liberalization of the retail market. By 2018, the venture had opened 20 BestPrice Modern Wholesale stores, with plans to open additional stores and ultimately be in a market leadership position. Also in 2018, Walmart spent $16 billion to purchase a majority holding in Flipkart, a leading Indian e-commerce firm, in order to enhance its competitiveness in India and abroad. Clearly, to succeed when the Indian market finally opens up, Walmart will need to understand the political and market dynamics and exploit the lessons it has learned from entering other emerging markets.

Critical Thinking Questions

1. Why has Walmart viewed international expansion as a critical part of its strategy?

2. What did Walmart do to enable the company to achieve success in Latin America and China?

3. What should Walmart do—or not do—to help ensure that the company achieves success in India?

Sources: "Our Business," *Walmart*, 2018, www.corporate.walmart.com; "2018 Annual Report," *Walmart*, January 31, 2018, www.stock.walmart.com; Jon Russell, "Walmart Completes Its $16 Billion Acquisition of Flipkart," *Tech Crunch*, April 30, 2018, www.techcrunch.com; Vijay Govindarajan, and Anil Gupta, "Taking Wal-Mart Global: Lessons from Retailing's Giant," *Strategy+Business*, June 19, 2002, www.strategy-business.com; and Mark Landler, and Michael Barbaro, "Wal-Mart Finds that Its Formula Doesn't Fit Every Culture," *New York Times*, August 02, 2006, www.nytimes.com.

NOTES

1. Kenichi Ohmae, *The Mind of the Strategist: The Art of Japanese Business*, Oakland, CA: Mcgraw-Hill, 1982, 36.

2. For an overview discussion of strategy, see Michael E. Porter, "What Is Strategy?" *Harvard Business Review*, November–December 1996, 61–78; and Costas Markides, "What Is Strategy and How Do You Know If You Have One?" *Business Strategy Review*, vol. 15, no. 2, 2004, 5–12.

3. Jay B. Barney, "Looking Inside for Competitive Advantage," *Academy of Management Executive*, vol. 9, 1995, 49–61; M. A. Peteraf, "The Cornerstones of Competitive Advantage: A Resource-Based View," *Strategic Management Journal*, vol. 14, no. 3, 1993, 179–91; B. Wernerfelt, "A Resource Based View of the Firm," *Strategic Management Journal*, vol. 5, no. 2, 1984, 171–80; and Jay Barney, *Gaining and Sustaining Competitive Advantage*, 2nd ed., Upper Saddle River, NJ: Prentice Hall, 2002.

4. Quote by Benjamin Franklin.

5. Darrell Rigby, and Barbara Bilodeau, "Management Tools and Trends," *Bain & Company*, https://www.bain.com, accessed October 30, 2018.

6. Hai Duong, "Will China's Rivals Benefit from the Trade War?" *The Economist*, https://www.economist.com, accessed October 30, 2018.

7. Ibid.

8. Martin Hirt, and Sven Smit, "Economic Conditions Snapshot, March 2017: McKinsey Global Survey Results," https://www.mckinsey.com, accessed October 30, 2018.

9. Thomas A. Stewart, *The Wealth of Knowledge: Intellectual Capital and the Twenty-first Century Organization*, Danvers, MA: Crown Publishing Group, 2007, 32.

10. Alan G. Lafley, and Roger Martin, *Playing to Win: How Strategy Really Works*, Massachusetts, US: Harvard Business Press, 2013, 260.

11. Reggie Van Lee, Lisa Fabish, and Nancy McGaw, "The Value of Corporate Values," *Strategy+Business*, no. 39, https://www.strategy-business.com, accessed October 30, 2018; and Len Sherman, "Corporate Mission Statements Don't Really Matter, Unless You Want to be a Great Leader," *Forbes*, https://www.forbes.com, accessed October 30, 2018.

12. Google, "Our Company," https://www.google.com, accessed October 30, 2018.

13. Amazon.com, *Amazon.com 2017 Annual Report*, http://phx.corporate-ir.net, accessed October 30, 2018.

14. Samsung, "Vision 2020," https://www.samsung.com, accessed October 30, 2018.

15. Mitsubishi Corporation, "MC Group Corporate Vision," https://www.mitsubishicorp.com, accessed October 30, 2018.

16. Kiva, "About Us," https://www.kiva.org, accessed October 30, 2018.

17. Anadolu Agency, "Quatar Petroleum Becomes the Exclusive Marketer of All Quatari Crude Oil Exports," January 03, 2018, http://www.aa.com.tr.

18. Qatar Petroleum, "Strategy and Values," https://www.qp.com.qa, accessed October 30, 2018.

19. Intel Corporation, "Where Can I Find Intel's Mission Statement, Values, and Objectives," https://www.intel.com, accessed October 30, 2018.

20. Alessandro Giudici, and Marianna Rolbina, Pankaj *Ghemawat's Distance Still Matters: The Hard Reality of Global*, Abingdon, UK: Taylor & Francis, 2018, 112.

21. Intel Corporation, "Corporate Responsibility at Intel, Summary 2017–2018," https://csrreportbuilder.intel.com, accessed October 30, 2018.

22. Brad Stone, "Xiaomi's Phones Have Conquered China. Now It's Aiming for the Rest of the World," *Bloomberg Businessweek*, https://www.bloomberg.com, accessed October 30, 2018; Manish Singh, "Chinese Smartphone Makers Are Winning in India—The Fastest Growing Market," *Venturebeat*, https://venturebeat.com, accessed October 30, 2018; Katie Canales, and Shayanne Gal, "Chinese Smartphone Maker Xiaomi Has Grabbed a Healthy Slice of the Smartphone Market at an Impressively Quick Pace," *Business Insider*, https://www.businessinsider.com, accessed October 30, 2018; and Chao-Ching Shih, Tom M. Y. Lin, and Pin Luam, "Fan-Centric Social Media: The Xiaomi Phenomenon in China," *Business Horizons*, vol. 57, no. 3, May–June 2014, 349–59.

23. Alan M. Rugman, and Alain Verbeke, "A Perspective on Regional and Global Strategies of Multinational Enterprises," *Journal of International Business Studies*, vol. 35, no. 1, 2004, 3–18; J. Michael Geringer, Paul W. Beamish, and Richard C. DaCosta, "Diversification Strategy and Internationalization: Implications for MNE Performance," *Strategic Management Review*, vol. 10, no. 2, 1989, 109–19; UNCTAD, World Investment Report 2017, 27–30, https://www.unctad.org, accessed October 30, 2018; Lei Li, "Is Regional Strategy More Effective Than Global Strategy in the U.S. Service Industries," *Management International Review*, vol. 45, special issue (2005), 37–57; Pankaj Ghemawat, "Semiglobalization and International Business Strategy," *Journal of International Business Studies*, vol. 34, no. 2, 2003, 138–52; Eden Yin, and Chong Ju Choi, "The Globalization Myth: The Case of China," *Management International Review*, vol. 45, 2005, 103–20; Allen J. Morrison, David A. Ricks, and Kendall Roth, "Globalization versus Regionalization: Which Way for the Multinational?" *Organizational Dynamics*, vol. 19, no. 3, 1991, 17–29; and Pankaj Ghemawat, "Regional Strategies for Global Leadership," *Harvard Business Review*, December 2005, 98–108.

24. Shell Global, "New Lens on the Future," https://www.shell.com, accessed October 30, 2018.

25. Peter Schwartz, *The Art of the Long View—Planning for the Future in an Uncertain World*, New York: Doubleday, 1996.

26. Sanjay Kalavar, and Mihir Mysore, "Are You Prepared for a Corporate Crisis," *McKinsey Quarterly*, https://www.mckinsey.com, accessed October 30, 2018.

27. Bob Pisani, "A Cyberattack Could Trigger the Next Financial Crisis, New Report Says," *CNBC*, https://www.cnbc.com, accessed October 30, 2018.

28. Cornelius A. de Kluyver, and John A. Pearce II, *Strategy: A View from the Top*, 2nd ed., Upper Saddle River, NJ: Pearson Prentice Hall, 2006, 9.

29. 3M, *Annual Report 2017*, https://investors.3m.com, accessed October 30, 2018; and H.C. Shin, "International Operations," https://s2.q4cdn.com/974527301/files/doc_events/2016/Shin_International.pdf, accessed October 30, 2018.

30. Frederick W. Gluck, "A Fresh Look at Strategic Management," *Journal of Business Strategy*, Fall 1985, 6.

31. Gary Hamel, "Strategy as Revolution," *Harvard Business Review*, July–August 1996, 70.

32. Eric D. Beinhocker, and Sarah Kaplan, "Tired of Strategic Planning?" *McKinsey Quarterly*, 2002, https://www.mckinsey.com, accessed October 30, 2018.

10 Organizational Design and Control

> **We are in the midst of a major transition. . . . We'll see our top organizations grow and shed a variety of structures and models to suit their changing circumstances.**
>
> —*Jim Clemmer, in "High Performance Organization Structures and Characteristics"*[1]

©Alex-VN/Alamy Stock Photo.

LEARNING OBJECTIVES

After reading this module, you should be able to:

LO 10-1   **Explain** why the design of organizational structure is important to international companies.

LO 10-2   **Identify** the various organizational dimensions managers must consider when selecting organizational structures.

LO 10-3   **Explain** how decision making is allocated between parent and wholly owned subsidiaries in an international company.

LO 10-4   **Discuss** how an international company can maintain control of a joint venture or of a company of which it owns less than 50 percent of the voting stock.

LO 10-5   **List** the types of information an international company's units around the world need to report to the parent company.

Restructuring to Enhance Global Competitiveness: The Walt Disney Company's Reorganization

In early 2018, The Walt Disney Company announced an immediate strategic reorganization of its operations worldwide, focused on enhancing global reach, technological innovation, and greater ease for business partners. The newly created Direct-to-Consumer and International business segment focuses on providing a global, multiplatform vehicle for distributing world-class, Disney-created content, including the company's stake in Hulu and partnership with ESPN for the ESPN+ streamed content. It will also include Disney's direct-to-consumer streaming service, scheduled to launch in 2019 with video-on-demand content from Disney, Marvel, Pixar, and Lucasfilm. Global advertising sales activities were also moved to this segment to make it easier for advertisers to reach audiences worldwide.

Under the new Parks, Experiences, and Consumer Products segment, consumer products, retail, and e-commerce are brought together to ensure strong and consistent global branding across all products and services. "We are strategically positioning our businesses for the future, creating a more effective, global framework to serve consumers worldwide, increase growth, and maximize shareholder value," explained Robert Iger, chairman and chief executive officer of The Walt Disney Company.

The company had previously operated with more segments, a structure that could complicate efforts to have a consistent, timely, and effective competitive presence globally. A big push for the reorganization was increasing competition with tech giants Amazon, Apple, and Netflix, particularly the latter company's rapid expansion into more than 190 countries. With customers dropping cable in exchange for streaming services, much of Disney's content could no longer reach consumers through traditional channels. Having one segment cater to Disney's new streaming and direct-to-consumer services highlights the company's desire to focus on this competitive area, along with the acquisition of a 60 percent stake in Hulu.

Disney has reiterated key points throughout the reorganization, including being a "one-stop shop" for media services and advertisers, fitting into the global framework, and positioning the company for future growth. Disney's enhanced focus on technological innovations is a way to achieve these goals. For consumers, Disney CEO Iger made it clear what this new Disney structure plans to offer: choice, personalization, and convenience.

With $55 billion in global revenues, Disney is also the largest licensor worldwide. Its six park locations, with multiple other resorts, a cruise line, vacation club, and tours to six continents have helped Disney become one of the most influential global brands among entertainment products. While the company's stock has struggled recently due to factors such as the low performance of ESPN, this reorganization sets up Disney for strong future global growth, ready to handle new direct-to-consumer channels and give customers a universal, cohesive "Disney" experience globally.

Sources: "The Walt Disney Company Announces Strategic Reorganization," *The Walt Disney Company*, March 14, 2018, www.thewaltdisneycompany.com; Sarah Perez, "Disney Announces a Strategic Reorganization of Its Business, Ahead of the Launch of Its Netflix Rival," *TechCrunch*, 2018, www.techcrunch.com; Will Ashworth, "Walt Disney Co Reorganization Good for Disney Stock," *InvestorPlace*, April 03, 2018, www.investorplace.com; and Christine Wang, "Disney Announces Strategic Reorganization, Effective Immediately," *CNBC*, March 14, 2018, www.cnbc.com.

Organizations exist to enable a group of people to effectively coordinate their collective activities and accomplish objectives.[2] **Organizational structure** is the way an organization formally arranges its domestic and international units and activities and the relationships among these components. A company's structure helps determine where formal power and authority will be located within the organization. This structure is what we typically see in a company's organization chart.

Creating and developing the structure of an international company (IC) over time are fundamental tasks of senior management. All the company's managers work within the context created by this structure. Managers also need to structure the activities within their area of responsibility in a manner consistent with the company's overall structure. Aspiring IC managers must understand that the different ways in which ICs can be structured and the relative strengths and weaknesses of each way is an essential analytical skill for them to develop.

organizational structure
The way an organization formally arranges its domestic and international units and activities, and the relationships among these components

In this module, we discuss the different organizational forms an IC can adopt, and key strategic issues managers must address in choosing among them. We also identify concerns managers have about how to control the international activities of their companies.

How Does Organizational Design Impact International Companies?

Organizational design is a process that determines how a company should be organized to ensure its worldwide business activities are integrated in an efficient and effective manner. As suggested in Figure 10.1, it is essential that an IC's structures and systems be consistent with each other, with the environmental context in which the organization is operating, and with the strategy the IC is utilizing. The size of the organization and the complexity of its business operations also influence its organizational design. We can think of this consistency as "organizational fit."

The structure of an IC needs to be able to evolve over time. This capability is essential because it allows the IC to respond to change and to efficiently and effectively reconfigure the way in which its competencies and resources are integrated within and across the company's various business units. Such flexibility is also a major challenge for ICs, especially as their activities become increasingly dispersed across the globe and subject to rapid and ongoing environmental and strategic change. Failure to successfully deal with this challenge threatens the organization's performance, however, and indeed, its long-term survival.

Does structure follow strategy? Yes, in that the IC's strategic planning process, which includes an analysis of the firm's external environments as well as its strengths and weaknesses, often discloses a need to alter the organization. Yet, while changes in an IC's strategy may require changes in the organization, the reverse is also true. For instance, the IC may acquire a company in another country or in another area of business activity. Strategic planning and organizing are so closely related that usually management treats the structure of the organization as an integral part of the strategic planning process.

What are the main issues to consider in designing an IC's structure? Two that management faces are (1) departmentalizing to most effectively take advantage of efficiencies gained from specialization of labor and (2) coordinating the resulting departments' activities to meet the firm's overall objectives. As all managers know, these two goals can conflict with each other; that is, the gain from increased specialization of labor may sometimes be nullified by the increased cost of coordination. The search for an optimal balance between them often leads to a reorganization of the IC's structure.

What elements need to be considered when designing the structure of an IC? There are four:

1. *Product and technical expertise* for the company's different businesses.
2. *Geographic expertise* on the countries and regions in which the company operates.
3. *Customer expertise* to gauge the similarity of client groups, industries, market segments, or population groups that transcend the boundaries of individual countries or regions.
4. *Functional expertise* in the company's value chain activities.

“WHEN ORGANIZATIONAL STRATEGY CHANGES, STRUCTURES, ROLES, AND FUNCTIONS SHOULD BE REALIGNED with THE NEW OBJECTIVES. THIS DOESN'T ALWAYS HAPPEN . . . (SO) RESPONSIBILITIES CAN BE OVERLOOKED, STAFFING CAN BE INAPPROPRIATE, AND PEOPLE—AND EVEN FUNCTIONS—CAN WORK against EACH OTHER.”

—Gill Corkindale, executive coach and former management editor of the Financial Times[3]

ICs structure and integrate these four elements differently, and no one structure is best for all companies and contexts. Rather, managers have to consider the nature of their company's international operating

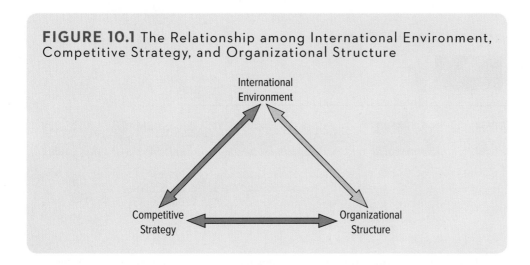

FIGURE 10.1 The Relationship among International Environment, Competitive Strategy, and Organizational Structure

environment and strategy—both currently and how they might look in the future—when deciding on the IC's structure.[4] In the following sections, we discuss the most common types of organizational designs for ICs. In reality, due to the complex nature of their operating environments and nuances of their historical origins and evolution, the structure of many ICs may deviate from these basic organizational designs. Yet understanding these basic designs can help managers select an organizational structure appropriate for their current and anticipated circumstances.

> **"THE NEGLECTED LEADERSHIP ROLE IS THE DESIGNER of THE SHIP."**
>
> —*Peter Senge, author and founding chair of the Society for Organizational Learning*

Evolution of International Company Structure

How do the organizational structures of ICs evolve over time? Companies often enter foreign markets first by exporting and then, as sales increase, by forming overseas sales companies and eventually by setting up manufacturing facilities. As international activities grow and change, the IC's structure also tends to change. In this section, we discuss the most common IC structures.

LO 10-2
Identify the various organizational dimensions managers must consider when selecting organizational structures.

INTERNATIONAL DIVISION STRUCTURE

At first, a firm might have *no one* responsible for international business; its marketing department might fill the export orders. Next, the firm might create an export department, possibly within the marketing department. If the company begins to invest in various overseas locations, it might then form an international division to take charge of all overseas activity. An international division is a division in the organization that is at the same level as the domestic division and is responsible for all non-home-country activities. Many larger firms, such as Walmart, have organized their international divisions on a regional or geographic basis (Figure 10.2). Today, we still see companies—both the relatively modest in size and some of the largest in the world—that are organized into a primary domestic division and an international one to coordinate and promote the company's activities outside the home country.

Unfortunately, the use of an international division structure can result in conflicts within the firm. For example, there may be disagreements and power struggles between the domestic operations and the international division over product designs, priority in scheduling of production, or the prices that the domestic unit charges to the international unit. The challenges of managing the international division effectively as the size of this division and the range of products, markets, and activities increase, can be substantial, which can result in rising inefficiency.

international division
A division in the organization that is at the same level as the domestic division and is responsible for all non-home-country activities

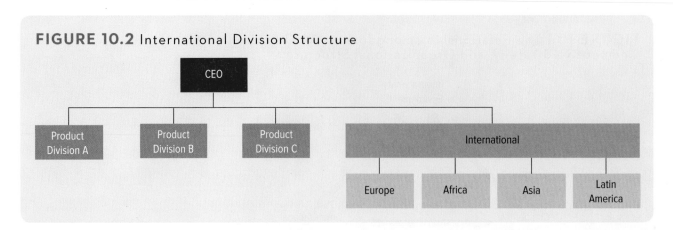

FIGURE 10.2 International Division Structure

Therefore, as the company's overseas operations increase in importance and scope, management often eliminates international divisions in favor of worldwide organizational structures based on *product, region, function,* or *customer classes.* At second, third, and still lower levels, these four characteristics—product, region, function, and customer classes—plus process, national subsidiary, and international or domestic, provide the basis for subdivisions.

As they grow over time, most ICs move away from the use of international divisions and instead implement one of the global structures we present later in this module based on either global product or global geographic factors. For example, at the end of 2016, General Mills announced a move away from an international structure to a global structure based on geography.[5] Figure 10.3 combines these paths for the IC's design and evolution with the international stages model of organizational structures.[6]

When an IC's managers choose one of these designs for the organization's structure, they usually expect that their company will now (1) be more capable of developing competitive strategies to confront increasing global competition; (2) obtain lower production

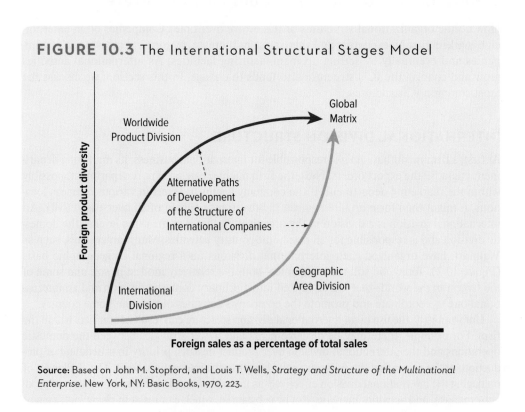

FIGURE 10.3 The International Structural Stages Model

Source: Based on John M. Stopford, and Louis T. Wells, *Strategy and Structure of the Multinational Enterprise.* New York, NY: Basic Books, 1970, 223.

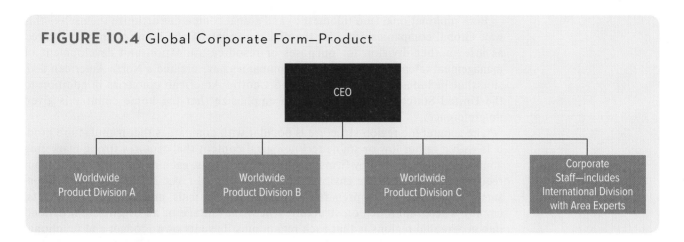

FIGURE 10.4 Global Corporate Form—Product

costs by promoting worldwide product standardization and manufacturing rationalization; and/or (3) enhance technology transfer and the allocation of company resources.

INTERNATIONAL PRODUCT STRUCTURE

An international product structure represents a return to pre-export department times in that the domestic product division is given responsibility for global line and staff operations. Product divisions are then responsible for the worldwide operations, such as marketing and production, of those products and services under their control. Each division generally has regional experts, so while this organizational form avoids the duplication of product experts common in a company with an international division, it does create a duplication of area experts. Occasionally, to avoid placing regional specialists in each product division, the IC will have a group of managerial specialists in an international division who advise the product divisions but have no authority over them (see Figure 10.4). For example, General Electric's businesses are managed through a global line-of-business structure, and investment opportunities are identified and assessed on a global basis by managers within each of these business areas. Procter & Gamble uses a structure based on 10 category-based global business units, with the category business units having full authority for decisions involving their respective businesses.[7]

GEOGRAPHIC REGION STRUCTURE

Firms in which geographic regions are the primary basis for organizing their operations put the responsibility for all activities under geographic area managers who report directly to the chief executive officer. This kind of organization simplifies the task of directing worldwide operations because every country in the world is clearly under the control of someone who is in contact with headquarters (see Figure 10.5).

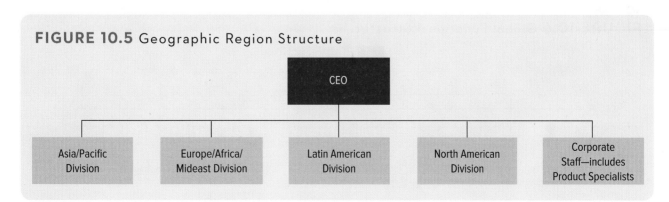

FIGURE 10.5 Geographic Region Structure

Both multinational (multidomestic) and global companies organize themselves this way. Global companies consider the division in which the home country is located as just another division for purposes of resource allocation and development of management talent. Some U.S. global companies have created a North American division that includes Canada, Mexico, and Central American countries in addition to the United States, possibly in part to emphasize that the home country is given no preference.

The geographic region structure is popular with companies that manufacture products with a rather low or stable technological content that requires strong marketing ability. It is also favored by firms with diverse products, each having different product requirements, competitive environments, and political risks. Many producers of consumer products, such as prepared foods, pharmaceuticals, and household products, employ a geographic region structure. The disadvantage of an organization divided into geographic regions is that each region must have its own product and functional specialists, so although the duplication of area specialists found in international product division structures is eliminated, duplication of product and functional specialists is necessary.

Production coordination across regions presents challenges, as does global product planning. To address these, ICs often place specialized product managers on the corporate headquarters staff. Although these managers have no line authority, they do provide input to corporate decisions concerning products.

GLOBAL FUNCTIONAL STRUCTURE

Few ICs are organized by function at the top level. Those that are believe worldwide functional expertise is more significant to the firm than is product or area knowledge. In this type of organization, those reporting to the CEO might be the senior executives responsible for each functional area (production, marketing, finance, and so on), as shown in Figure 10.6. The common factor among the users of the functional form is a narrow and highly integrated product mix, such as that of aircraft manufacturers or oil refining companies. Ford Motor Company modified its company to a global functional structure in May 2017.[8]

HYBRID ORGANIZATIONAL STRUCTURES

hybrid organization
A structure organized by more than one dimension at the top level

A **hybrid organization** is a structure organized by more than one dimension at the top level. In a hybrid organization, the top level is a mixture of the organizational forms described above, and the lower levels may or may not be. Figure 10.7 illustrates a simple hybrid form. Starbucks uses a hybrid structure, with functional units (e.g., for finance, human resources, and marketing), geographical units (e.g., the Americas, China and Asia-Pacific, and

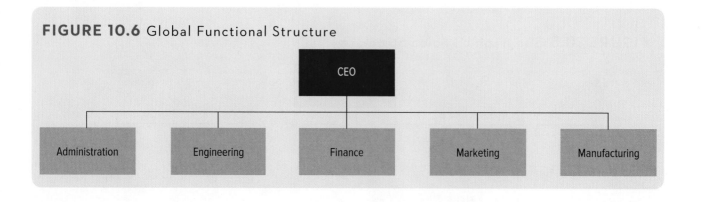

FIGURE 10.6 Global Functional Structure

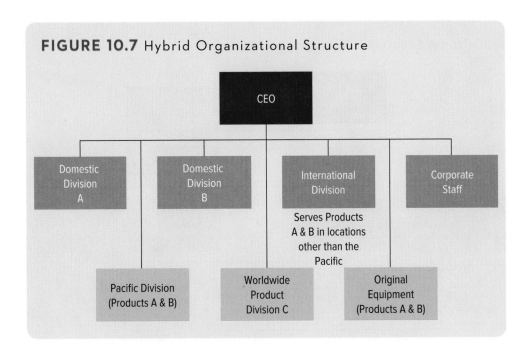

FIGURE 10.7 Hybrid Organizational Structure

Europe, Middle East and Africa), and product divisions (e.g., coffee and related, baked goods, and merchandise).[9]

Hybrid structures are often the result of a regionally organized company having introduced a new and different product line that management believes can best be handled by a worldwide product division. A firm that acquires a company with distinct products and a functioning marketing network may be integrated into the organization as a product division even though the rest of the firm is organized on a regional basis. Later, after corporate management becomes familiar with the operation, this acquired unit may be regionalized.

A mixed structure may also be used when an IC is selling to a sizable, homogeneous class of customers. Special divisions for handling sales to the military or to original equipment manufacturers, for example, are often established at the same level as regional or product divisions.

MATRIX ORGANIZATIONS

The **matrix organization** is an organizational structure composed of one or more superimposed organizational structures in an attempt to mesh product, regional, functional, and other expertise. The matrix organization has evolved from management's attempt to mesh product, regional, and functional expertise while still maintaining clear lines of authority. It is called a matrix because an organizational structure based on one or possibly two dimensions is superimposed on an organization based on another dimension. In an organization of two dimensions, such as area and product, both the geographic area managers and the product managers will be at the same level, and their responsibilities will overlap. An individual manager—say, a marketing manager in Germany—will have a multiple reporting relationship, being responsible to the manager overseeing the geographic area that includes Germany and also to an international or worldwide marketing manager at headquarters. Figure 10.8 illustrates an extremely simple matrix organization based on two organizational dimensions. Note that the country managers are responsible to both the area managers and the product-line managers.

matrix organization
An organizational structure composed of one or more superimposed organizational structures in an attempt to mesh product, regional, functional, and other expertise

FIGURE 10.8 Regional–Product Matrix

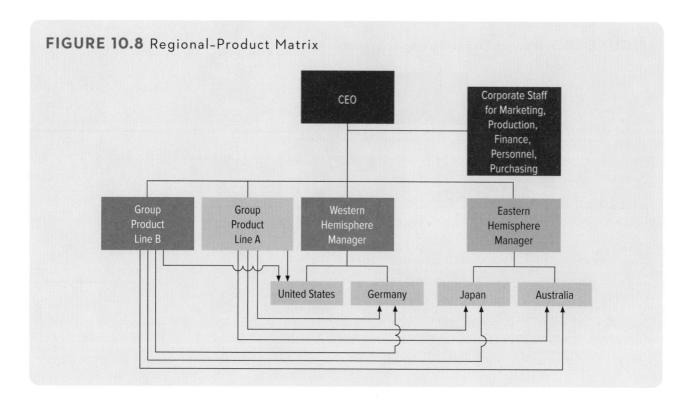

> **"To ENSURE THAT LEADERSHIP IS MORE EFFECTIVE, YOU NEED ORGANIZATIONAL CLARITY."**
>
> *—Guido Quelle, managing partner, Mandat GmbH*[10]

matrix overlay
An organization in which top-level divisions are required to heed input from a staff composed of experts of another organizational dimension in an attempt to avoid the double-reporting difficulty of a matrix organization but still mesh two or more dimensions

Although it once seemed the matrix organizational form would let firms simultaneously access the advantages of product, regional, and functional forms, you might be asking yourself whether its multiple reporting relationship might be a problem. In fact, the disadvantages of the matrix form have kept most worldwide companies from adopting it. One problem with it is that the two managers (or three, if it is a three-dimensional matrix) must agree on a decision. This can lead to less-than-optimal compromises, delayed responses, and power politics in which more attention is paid to the process than to the problem. When the managers cannot agree, the problem goes higher in the organization and takes top management away from its duties. Starbucks operates under a corporate matrix structure that coordinates across regional divisions and product divisions.

Because of these difficulties associated with the matrix structure, many firms have maintained their original organizations based on product, function, geographic region, or international divisions and have built into the structure accountability for the other organizational dimensions; this organization is called a **matrix overlay**.

MATRIX OVERLAY

The matrix overlay is an organization in which top-level divisions are required to heed input from a staff composed of experts of another organizational dimension in an attempt to avoid the double-reporting difficulty of a matrix organization but still mesh two or more dimensions. The matrix overlay attempts to address the problems of the matrix structure by requiring accountability of all functions in the organization while avoiding the management complications of a pure matrix structure. We have already seen that a firm organized by product may have regional specialists in a staff function, who have input to product decisions. They even may be organized in an international division. In a regional organization, product managers on staff would provide input to regional decisions.

STRATEGIC BUSINESS UNITS

An organizational form in which product divisions are defined as if they were distinct, independent businesses makes use of strategic business units (SBUs), self-contained business entities, each with a clearly defined market, specific competitors, the ability to carry out its business mission, and a size appropriate for control by a single manager. Most SBUs are based on product lines. For example, Nestlé's SBUs are organized by specialization, such as powdered and liquid beverages, chocolate and confectionery, water, and pet care.[11] BP's business units are organized on a global basis.[12] If a product must be modified to suit different markets, a worldwide SBU may be divided into a few product/market SBUs serving various markets or groups of countries.

strategic business unit (SBU) A self-contained business entity with a clearly defined market, specific competitors, the ability to carry out its business mission, and a size appropriate for control by a single manager

CURRENT ORGANIZATIONAL TRENDS

The rapidly changing business environment caused by increased global competition, a growing customer preference for custom-made rather than mass-produced products, and faster technological change is pressuring companies to step up their search for organizational forms that enable them to act more quickly, reduce costs, and improve the quality of product offerings. The ability to maintain an alignment between the organization and its global and hypercompetitive environment has become a fundamental determinant of an organization's ability to survive. Three key trends that support alignment or fit are evident in organizational design: reengineering, virtual corporations, and horizontal corporations.

Reengineering One result of ongoing pressures for change in international companies is that changes in organizational form, often called reengineering, have become an almost constant process. Reengineering involves redesigning organizational structure, hierarchy, business systems, and processes in order to improve organizational efficiency. Not only are companies mixing older, established forms of organization, they are also changing to different forms, many of which are modified versions of long-established forms with new names.

reengineering Redesigning organizational structure, hierarchy, business systems, and processes in order to improve organizational efficiency

Reengineering is often accompanied by a significant reduction in middle management staff, restructuring of work processes across functional departments, and improvement in the speed and quality of strategy execution. CEOs are striving to make their organizations lean, flat, fast to respond, and innovative.

Virtual Corporation Another trend that we see in the design of international companies is the increasing use of the virtual corporation. A virtual corporation, also called a *network corporation* or a *modular corporation,* is an organization that coordinates economic activity to deliver value to customers using resources outside the traditional boundaries of the organization. In other words, it relies to a great extent on third parties to conduct its business. Outsourcing once was used for downsizing and cost reduction, but now companies are using it to obtain specialized expertise they don't have but need in order to serve new markets or adopt new technology. Wikipedia, the free Internet encyclopedia whose entries are contributed by a large and fluid collection of collaborative volunteers located around the world, is an example of a virtual organization.

Telecommuting, home offices, and flexible working practices have contributed to the increase in virtual corporations. Global networking on the Internet has made worldwide outsourcing possible for firms of all sizes. Inditex, the Spanish multinational clothing company that owns retail brands such as Zara, uses competencies in information technology and tight integration with its international network of suppliers and garment makers to design, cut, assemble, and deliver fashionable clothing to its branded retail chains within days of receiving an order, without carrying large volumes of expensive inventory that can lose value quickly through fashion obsolescence.[13]

virtual corporation An organization that coordinates economic activity to deliver value to customers using resources outside the traditional boundaries of the organization

Working in a Global Virtual Organization

Automattic, Inc. is a web development corporation best known for Wordpress.com, the free blogging service. Automattic previously had offices in San Francisco, where the company was founded in 2005, yet a decision to close the facility was made in 2017 due to the space staying mostly unused. Clearly, employees were taking full advantage of their workspace freedom. The company now has 814 employees who work in 69 countries and speak 84 different languages. As a distributed company, employees are encouraged to work remotely, with Automattic allocating funds for employees to set up home offices, encouraging co-working offices, and even going so far as to pay for an employee's Starbucks drink if they choose to work at the coffeehouse.

Automattic seeks employees who are, "curious, driven, compassionate, tenacious, autonomous, friendly, independent, collaborative, communicative, supportive, self-motivated, and amazing with .gifs." The hiring process is unique, yet not surprising when one considers Automattic's structure as a virtual corporation. Employees are almost always hired without ever meeting the hiring manager, or even speaking on the phone. First, a prospective employee is contacted via Skype to respond at their convenience, and after an impromptu messaging interview, they may be given a trial project. Receiving hourly pay for the assignment, applicants generally finish the project in about a month and communicate with the manager over a private blog. If the applicant is approved after both rounds, they are referred to CEO Matt Mullenweg and messaged for the final interview. In perhaps the most unusual aspect of the whole process, Mullenweg himself sorts through the applicants first and sends his recommendations to the hiring manager.

The focus that Automattic places on employees working outside of the office clashes with the practices of tech-giants such as Hewlett Packard or IBM, which have moved away from remote work in recent years. Research has been conducted for both sides of the work-from-home argument, examining whether workers are more productive away from the office, where there are fewer co-worker distractions.

While some companies are pressing to keep employees in the office, distributed companies prove there are advantages. Money saved on office space can be spent elsewhere, such as Automattic's large annual employee events. Low overhead, along with high employee

Employees in virtual organizations conduct their business in a variety of locations, including airports.
©Chris Kober/robertharding/Getty Images.

retention and access to talent from all over the globe, makes a strong argument for the company's virtual organization model. Mullenweg keeps a blog where he shares business-related content both involving and separate from Automattic, such as a piece that discusses his company's office-less work environment, which can be found here: https://ma.tt/2018/02/no-office-workstyle. If Automattic's experience is any indication, we may be seeing even more international companies adopting a virtual organization structure.

Critical Thinking Questions

1. What do you think might be the greatest strengths and weaknesses of working in a virtual organization like Automattic?
2. Based on Automattic's success, why might companies like IBM choose the traditional face-to-face hiring process and in-office structure? What differences among the companies could be attributed to this?
3. Would you enjoy working in a virtual organization like Automattic? Why or why not?

Sources: "All Around the World, Building a New Web, and a New Workplace. Join Us!," *Automattic*, 2005; "Work with Us," *Automattic*, 2018; Leibowitz Glenn, "This CEO Runs a Billion-Dollar Company with No Offices or Email," *Inc.*, 2018; Julie Bort, "$1 Billion Startup Automattic Is Closing Its San Francisco Office and Having Everyone Work from Home," *Business Insider*, June 12, 2017; Angelica Cabral, "The Company Behind WordPress Is Shutting Its Office Because Too Many Employees Work Remotely," *Slate*, June 13, 2017; Julie Bort, "Billion-dollar Startup Automattic Hires Employees Without Ever Meeting Them or Talking to Them on the Phone," *Business Insider*, June 05, 2016; and Susan Caminiti,"The Dream Job That's All the Rage Across America," *CNBC*, April 03, 2018.

Although the name is new, the virtual corporation concept has existed for decades. Construction firms, each with a special area of expertise, often form a consortium to bid on projects, a contract for constructing a road or a sports stadium, for example. After finishing the job, the consortium disbands. Other examples of network organizations are clothing and athletic shoe marketers such as DKNY, Nike, and Reebok.

The virtual corporation concept has several potential benefits. In particular, it permits greater flexibility than other corporate structures. Rather than building competence from the ground up and incurring high start-up costs that could limit future production decisions, virtual corporations form a network of dynamic relationships that allows them to take advantage of the competencies of other organizations in order to respond rapidly to changing circumstances. However, this form of organization can have disadvantages, including the potential to reduce management's control over the corporation's activities; networks are vulnerable to the opportunistic actions of partners, including cost increases, unintended "borrowing" of technical and other knowledge, and departure from the relationship at inappropriate times. From the standpoint of employees, the virtual organization may replace the security of long-term employment and the promise of ever-increasing salaries with the insecurity of a global market.

horizontal corporation
A form of organization characterized by lateral decision processes, horizontal networks, and a strong corporate-wide business philosophy

Horizontal Corporation Another organizational form, the horizontal corporation, has been adopted by some large technology-oriented global firms in highly competitive industries such as electronics and computers. A horizontal corporation is a form of organization characterized by lateral decision processes, horizontal networks, and a strong corporate-wide business philosophy. Firms such as 3M have chosen this organizational form to foster the flexibility to respond quickly to advances in technology and be product innovators. In many companies, *teams* are drawn from different departments to solve a problem or deliver a product.

The horizontal organization has been characterized as anti-organization because its designers are seeking to remove the constraints imposed by the more conventional organizational structures. Employees worldwide create, build, and market the company's products through a carefully cultivated system of interrelationships. In a horizontal corporation, marketers in Great Britain would speak directly to production people in Brazil without having to go through the home office in Germany, for example.

Why might ICs adopt the horizontal organization format? Its proponents claim lateral relationships spark innovation and new product development and place more

 CULTURE FACTS @internationalbiz

Reflecting a greater tendency toward collectivism than we see in the more individualistic United States, Japanese companies tend to present organizational charts as systems of collective units such as departments or sections, rather than as networks of individual positions. #collectivism

SOCIAL MEDIA

decision-making responsibility in the hands of middle managers and other skilled professionals who do not have to clear each detail with higher-ups. The objective of the horizontal organization form is to substitute cooperation and coordination, which are in everyone's interest, for strict control and supervision. Pursued effectively, this approach can help develop international communities of skilled workers that create and exploit valuable intangible assets.

REQUIREMENTS FOR THE FUTURE OF INTERNATIONAL COMPANIES

What might the future have in store for IC's organizational structures? Managers in many ICs can expect to make greater use of the *dynamic network structure* that breaks down the major functions of the firm into smaller, more agile companies coordinated by a downsized headquarters organization.[14] Business functions such as marketing and accounting may be provided by separate organizations—some owned partially or fully by the IC, some not. To attain the optimal design and level of control, a firm must focus on its core business. Anything not essential to the business can often be done cheaper, faster, and better by outside suppliers.

As we watch ICs engage in the global battles of the 21st century, we must remember that organizations, like people, have life cycles. In their youth, they are small, fast growing, and tend toward the entrepreneurial. However, as they age, they often become big, complex, and out of touch with their markets. The ICs of tomorrow must learn how to be both large and entrepreneurial.[15] As one CEO told us, "It is not smaller firms that are better; rather, it is focused firms that are."

LO 10-3

Explain how decision making is allocated between parent and wholly owned subsidiaries in an international company.

Where Decisions Are Made in Wholly Owned Subsidiaries

Every successful company uses controls to put its plans into effect, evaluate the plans' effectiveness, make desirable corrections, and evaluate and reward or correct executive performance. The challenges associated with achieving effective control are more complicated for an IC than for a one-country operation. Different languages, cultures, and attitudes; different taxation and accounting methods; different currencies, labor costs, and market sizes; different degrees of political stability and security for people and property; and many other factors contribute to these challenges. Yet ICs need controls even more than domestic operations do.

Before we proceed further in our discussion of the challenges of control, we need to clarify a bit of terminology. The terms *subsidiary* and *affiliate* are sometimes used interchangeably, but here we would like to be more precise. Subsidiaries are companies controlled by other companies (known as parent companies) through ownership of enough voting stock to elect a majority of the voting members on the company's board of directors. Affiliates are companies controlled by other companies, but less-than-majority owners may exercise control by a variety of means, both those involving stock ownership and those involving non-ownership mechanisms.

We first examine the control of companies in which the parent has 100 percent ownership, known as wholly owned subsidiaries. Where should control be located, that is, where should decisions be made in these companies? There are three possibilities. Theoretically, all decisions could be centralized at the IC headquarters or decentralized to the subsidiary level. However, common sense dictates that some decisions be made at headquarters, some at subsidiaries, and—the third possibility—some cooperatively. Many variables determine which decision is made where. Some of the more significant are (1) the degree of standardization of the company's product and equipment; (2) the competence of subsidiary management and the degree of

subsidiaries
Companies controlled by other companies (known as parent companies) through ownership of enough voting stock to elect a majority of the voting members on the company's board of directors

affiliates
Companies controlled by other companies, but less-than-majority owners may exercise control by a variety of means, both those involving stock ownership and those involving non-ownership mechanisms

headquarters' reliance on it; (3) the size of the IC and the length of time it has conducted global operations; (4) the headquarters' willingness to benefit the whole enterprise at the subsidiary's expense; and (5) the subsidiary's degree of frustration with its limited power. We discuss each of these variables that contribute to the location of decision making in the sections that follow.

STANDARDIZATION OF THE COMPANY'S PRODUCTS AND EQUIPMENT

CULTURE FACTS @internationalbiz

National culture may influence the extent to which decisions are centralized in an IC. For example, cultures with relatively higher uncertainty avoidance, such as Germany, tend to have more centralization of operating decisions and increased emphasis on planning and rule setting, than do lower uncertainty avoidance cultures like the United Kingdom. #nationalculture

Some large global manufacturers of consumer products, such as Procter and Gamble (P&G) and Colgate, are developing products that are standardized from the outset for global or regional markets. In these situations, the affiliates have to follow company policy. Of course, representatives of the affiliates may have an opportunity to contribute to the design of the product, which is typically introduced first in the home market. After the production process has been stabilized, the specifications are sent to the affiliates for local production, where adaptations can be made if local management deems them necessary for their markets, which are called second markets.

In firms without a global product policy, operations managers at headquarters typically have preferred to standardize the product, or at least the production process, in as many overseas plants as possible. A subsidiary that can demonstrate higher overall profit potential if the product is tailored for its own market is usually allowed to proceed, however. Of course, the decision is then cooperative, in that the parent has the power to veto or override the subsidiary's choice.

Kellogg has standardized some of their products for global markets, like these familiar brands in a Chinese supermarket.
©Education & Exploration 1/Alamy Stock Photo.

COMPETENCE OF SUBSIDIARY MANAGEMENT AND HEADQUARTERS' RELIANCE ON IT

The extent to which an IC relies on subsidiary management to make decisions can depend on how well the executives know company policies and each other, on whether headquarters management thinks it understands host country conditions, on the distance between the home country and the host country, and on how big and how old the parent company is. Let's briefly look at each of these factors.

Many ICs regularly transfer managers between headquarters and subsidiaries, and among subsidiaries. Thus, managers learn headquarters policies firsthand and know the problems they might encounter when putting them into effect at subsidiary levels. One result of such transfers, which is difficult to measure yet important, is a network of intra-IC personal relationships. These relationships tend to increase executives' confidence in one another and make communication among them easier and less subject to error. Some ICs also have moved their regional executives into headquarters to improve communications and reduce cost.

Another contributor to the degree of headquarters' reliance on subsidiary management is its familiarity with conditions in the subsidiary's host country, including culture. The less familiar or the more different from home headquarters management perceives conditions in the host country to be, the more likely headquarters is to rely on subsidiary management.

Headquarters' reliance on subsidiary management also depends on how far away the host country is. A U.S. parent company is likely to place more reliance on the management of an Indonesian subsidiary than on the management of a Canadian subsidiary for two reasons: U.S. management typically perceives that it understands management conditions in Canada more easily than conditions in Indonesia, and Indonesia is much farther from the United States than Canada is—not merely geographically but also in terms of culture, institutions, politics, and other variables.

SIZE AND AGE OF THE IC

As a general rule, a large company can afford to hire more specialists, experts, and experienced executives than can a smaller one. The longer a company has been an IC, the more likely it is to have a number of experienced executives who know company policies and have worked both at headquarters and in the field. Successful experience builds confidence. In most ICs, the top positions are at headquarters, and the ablest and most persistent executives will typically get positions there eventually. Thus, over time, the headquarters of a successful IC is run by experienced executives who are confident of their knowledge of the business in the home and host countries.

It follows that in larger, older ICs, more decisions are made at headquarters and fewer are delegated to subsidiaries. Smaller companies, in business for shorter periods of time, tend to be able to afford fewer internationally experienced executives and will not have had time to develop them internally. Smaller, newer companies often have no choice but to delegate decisions to subsidiary managements. However, with the increasing pace of change and intensity of competition in many markets of the world, as well as continued differences across many markets, even large and experienced companies are finding the need to delegate at least some decision-making authority to subsidiary managements who can effectively sense pressures for adaptation, develop and communicate innovation, and promote effective execution of strategy.

HEADQUARTERS' WILLINGNESS TO BENEFIT THE ENTERPRISE AT THE SUBSIDIARY'S EXPENSE

An IC has opportunities to source raw materials and components, locate factories, allocate orders, and govern intrafirm pricing that are not available to a non-IC. Such activities may be beneficial to the enterprise yet harm the subsidiary. We look at each of them next.

An IC may decide to move factors of production from one country to another, or to expand in one country instead of another. In addition to the cost, availability, and skill levels of labor, other possible reasons for such a move include corporate tax rates, market conditions, currency fluctuation, and political instability. It is understandable that the subsidiary from which factors are being taken will be unenthusiastic about giving up control over existing activities, and its management slow, at best, to cut capacity or to downsize or eliminate local operations. Headquarters will typically have to make such decisions. Intel headquarters recently announced that it has chosen to expand its emphasis on China as a location to invest in new semiconductor production facilities, rather than the West or other Asian countries where it has facilities it could have expanded. Intel wants to invest where its future customers are, and that is China, the largest market for smartphones and home of the world's largest pool of Internet users.[16] This is a decision that the other Asian subsidiaries in Hong Kong, Japan, and Malaysia would not have made because it works against their own interests.

Similarly, say an order from an Argentine customer could be filled by a subsidiary in France, another in South Africa, and a third in Brazil; parent headquarters might decide which subsidiary gets the business. Among the considerations in the decision would be production costs, transportation costs, comparative tariff rates, customers' currency restrictions, comparative order backlogs, governmental pressures, and taxes. Making such a decision at IC headquarters avoids price competition among members of the same IC group.

The market in a single country is often too small to permit achieving economies of scale in manufacturing an entire industrial product or offering a full range of services for that one market. An example is Ford's production of a light vehicle for the Asian market. Ford negotiated with several countries, with the result that particular components will be manufactured in individual countries, with the output shared and assembly done in each country. Thus, one country makes the engine, a second country has the body-stamping plant, a third makes the transmission, and so forth. Each specialized operation achieves the efficiency and cost savings of economies of scale. This kind of multinational production demands a high degree of control and coordination by the IC headquarters.

In certain circumstances, an IC may have a choice of two or more countries in which to declare profits, such as happens when two or more units of the IC cooperate in supplying components or services under a contract with an external customer. Headquarters might then have one unit or subsidiary charge the customer higher prices than the other, with the result that one books more profit than the other. If the host country of one of the subsidiaries has lower taxes than the other host countries, the IC will try to maximize profits in the lower-tax country and reduce them in the higher-tax country. Other factors that affect the allocation of profit among host countries include country differences in currency controls, labor relations, political climate, and social unrest. It is sensible to direct as much profit as reasonably possible to subsidiaries in countries with the fewest currency controls, the best labor relations and political climate, and the least social unrest.

Intrafirm transactions may also give a company choices regarding profit location. Pricing established for transactions between members of the same enterprise is referred to as transfer pricing, and while IC headquarters could permit undirected, arm's-length price negotiations between itself and its subsidiaries, this might not yield the best results for the enterprise as a whole. Price and profit allocation decisions like these are usually best made at parent-company headquarters, which is supposed to maintain the overall view, looking out for the best interests of the enterprise as a whole. Naturally, however, subsidiary management does not gladly make decisions to accept lower profits, largely because its evaluation may suffer as a result of the apparent reduction in performance.

How might transfer pricing work in practice? The following Tables 10.1 and 10.2 illustrate how the total IC enterprise may profit even though one subsidiary makes less. Assume a cooperative contract by which two subsidiaries of a major industrial equipment manufacturer are selling products and services to an outside customer for an agreed-upon price. The host country of IC Alpha levies company income taxes at the rate of 50 percent, whereas IC Beta's host country taxes its income at 20 percent. The customer is in a third country, has agreed to pay a set sales price (one that the IC has calculated will yield a pretax profit level of $100 million), and is indifferent to how Alpha and Beta share the money from the sale.

Table 10.1 shows the enterprise's after-tax income if Alpha is paid an amount that will yield $60 million in profits in its country, and Beta is paid an amount that will yield $40 million in profits in its country. Thus, after tax, the IC as a whole realizes $62 million in profit.

transfer pricing
Pricing established for transactions between members of the enterprise

❝THE VERY NATURE of TRANSFER PRICING IS TRANSACTING across **BORDERS AND THEREFORE COMPANIES NEED to ENSURE THEY ADEQUATELY MEET BOTH THEIR LOCAL AND GLOBAL REPORTING RESPONSIBILITIES.❞**

—Paul Brindle, managing director, Thomson Reuters[17]

TABLE 10.1 Example of Transfer Pricing and Taxes

	Pretax Profit Received ($ millions)	Tax Paid ($ millions)	After-Tax Profit ($ millions)
Alpha	$60	$30	$30
Beta	40	8	32
			$62

The Table 10.2 shows the after-tax income if Alpha is paid in a manner that will yield $40 million in profit in its country, and Beta is paid in a manner that will yield $60 million in profit in its country. After taxes, the IC realizes $68 million in profit from this payment approach.

TABLE 10.2 Example of Transfer Pricing to Reduce Taxes

	Pretax Profit Received ($ millions)	Tax Paid ($ millions)	After-Tax Profit ($ millions)
Alpha	$40	$20	$20
Beta	60	12	48
			$68

These simple examples illustrate that the IC will be $6 million better off, after taxes, if it can shift $20 million of the profits from Alpha to Beta, while the customer is no worse off because it pays the same overall price in either case. Alpha, having received $20 million less in payment, is $10 million worse off after taxes, but Beta is $16 million better off—and the enterprise is $6 million ahead on the same contract. Given the number of countries and tax laws in the world, there are countless ways to realize such savings. Financial management awareness and control are the keys to successfully managing these situations.

We do not mean to leave the impression that the host and home governments are unaware of or indifferent to transfer pricing and profit allocation by ICs operating within their borders. The companies must expect questioning by both governments and be prepared to demonstrate that prices or allocations are reasonable. Management needs to show that other companies charge comparable prices for the same or similar items or, if there are no similar items, show that costs plus profit have been used reasonably to arrive at the price. As to allocation of profits, the IC in our example would try to prove the volume or importance of the work done by Beta, or the responsibilities assumed by Beta—such as financing, after-sales service, or warranty obligations—to justify the higher amount being paid to it. Of course, the questions in this instance would come from the host government of Alpha if it got wind of the possibility of more taxable corporate income going to Beta's country and less to itself.[18]

THE SUBSIDIARY'S FRUSTRATION WITH ITS LIMITED POWER

An extremely important consideration for parent-company management is that the management of its subsidiaries is motivated and loyal. If all the big decisions are made, or are perceived to be made, at IC headquarters, the managers of subsidiaries can lose incentive and prestige with their employees and community. These managers may grow hostile and disloyal.

Should Companies Be Allowed to Profit from International Transfer Pricing?

Transfer pricing and its impact on corporate profits and tax revenue generation by countries has become an important issue, as suggested by recent cases involving global giants such as Apple, Starbucks, Fiat, and Microsoft. Consider this disguised case of a leading competitor in the international computer software industry, BigSoft.

The company is headquartered in the United States and has subsidiaries in more than 100 countries. More than 80 percent of BigSoft's long-lived assets are located in the United States, and 60 percent of its revenues of $58 billion are generated from the U.S. operations. However, 60 percent of the company's $25 billion of income before taxes is generated in international markets, much of it from nations with corporate tax rates lower than the 21 percent tax rate BigSoft is subject to in the United States.

One way BigSoft has reduced the level of taxes it pays is through the careful and legal use of transfer pricing. Here's an example of how transfer pricing can work to the company's advantage. BigSoft established a subsidiary in Ireland, where the corporate tax rate in 2018 was only 12.5 percent, one of the lowest in Europe. This subsidiary, called Emerald Isle Enterprises (EIE), licenses BigSoft's software to European customers. Although most of BigSoft's software development occurs in the United States, the U.S. organization licenses this software to EIE at a relatively low rate. The outcome of this transfer pricing decision is that BigSoft's U.S. operations earn a lower level of revenues—and correspondingly lower taxable income—from EIE's activities. As a result, BigSoft pays a smaller amount of taxes in the United States than would be the case if it charged a higher license fee to EIE.

Although EIE licenses BigSoft's software from the parent company at a relatively low rate, EIE charges a much higher fee for it to BigSoft's other European subsidiaries. This approach to pricing allows EIE to have a high level of revenues and taxable income in Ireland, where the tax rate is low. The high license fee also reduces the level of taxable income in the other European subsidiaries, which are located in nations with higher tax rates than Ireland. Due to tax treaties, the after-tax profits of EIE are not subject to further taxation when they are transferred to the company's headquarters in the United States.

Through the creative use of transfer pricing techniques such as this, BigSoft has been able to reduce its worldwide tax bill by more than an estimated $500 million per year. Yet, another way to understand this tax maneuver is that BigSoft is depriving governments, in this case, the U.S. government, of tax revenues. The licensed product BigSoft is underpricing to EIE was developed in the United States and is part of U.S. commercial activity. Its corporate headquarters are located in the United States and the company enjoys benefits conferred on residents by U.S., state, and city governments such as transportation and communication infrastructures, political stability, rule of law, and protection of property. If the corporation were considered a person in this case, it would be taxed on its global income, the way U.S. expatriates are. There are precedents for treating corporations like people, such as protection of corporate free speech, leading to their right to make political statements through independent communications (*Citizens v. the Federal Election Commission*, 558, U.S. 2010). Should the transfer pricing tax maneuver ICs regularly use to limit their tax liability in high-tax environments be blocked? What do you think?

Critical Thinking Questions

1. If you were a shareholder in BigSoft, would you support the company's approach to transfer pricing? Why or why not?

2. If you represented the government of Ireland, would you support BigSoft's approach to transfer pricing? Why or why not?

3. If you represented the U.S. government, or the government of one of the other nations in Europe, would you support BigSoft's approach to transfer pricing? Why or why not?

Sources: "Ireland's Tax Regime," *IDA Ireland*, 2016; Rochelle Toplensky, "Europe Points Finger at Ireland over Tax Avoidance," *The Irish Times*, March 07, 2018; and Rochelle Toplensky, "Multinationals Pay Lower Taxes than a Decade Ago," *The Irish Times*, March 12, 2018.

Therefore, even though there may be reasons for an IC's headquarters to make decisions, it should delegate as many as is reasonably possible to the subsidiary. Management of each subsidiary should be kept thoroughly informed and be consulted seriously about decisions, negotiations, and developments in its geographic area. The trend among many ICs to shift power away from subsidiaries toward the parent has caused predictable frustration to subsidiary management, sometimes followed by resignations.

LO 10-4

Discuss how an international company can maintain control of a joint venture or of a company in which it owns less than 50 percent of the voting stock.

Where Decisions Are Made in Joint Ventures and Subsidiaries Less Than 100 Percent Owned

A joint venture may be a corporate entity whose ownership is shared between an IC and local owners, a corporate entity owned by two or more companies foreign to the area where the joint venture is located, or one company working on a project of limited duration (such as constructing a dam) in cooperation with one or more other companies. The other companies may be subsidiaries or affiliates, but they may also be entirely independent entities.

All the reasons we looked at earlier for making decisions at IC headquarters, at subsidiary headquarters, or cooperatively also apply to joint-venture situations. However, headquarters will almost never have as much freedom of action and flexibility in a joint venture as it has with subsidiaries that it owns 100 percent.

LOSS OF FREEDOM AND FLEXIBILITY

Why might an IC experience a loss of freedom and flexibility in joint ventures and subsidiaries that are less than 100 percent owned? If shareholders outside the IC have control of the affiliate, they can block any IC headquarters' efforts, for example, to move production factors away or to fill an export order from another affiliate or subsidiary. Even if outside shareholders are a minority and cannot directly control the affiliate, they can bring legal or political pressures on the IC to prevent it from diminishing the affiliate's profitability for the IC's benefit. Likewise, the local partner in a joint venture is highly unlikely to agree with measures that penalize it for the IC's benefit. Factors such as these can substantially reduce the control an IC might be able to exercise over such subsidiaries and their activities. But can the IC still achieve some degree of control in such situations?

CONTROL CAN BE HAD EVEN WITH LIMITED OR NO OWNERSHIP

With less than 50 percent of the voting stock and even with no voting stock, an IC can exercise control over a subsidiary's decisions and activities. Some methods of maintaining control include:

- Drawing up a management contract.
- Retaining control of the finances.

Mary Barra, Chairwoman and CEO of General Motors.
©Mark Wilson/Getty Images.

- Retaining control of the technology.
- Putting people from the IC in important executive positions.

As you might expect, ICs have encountered resistance from their joint-venture partners or from host governments when they have attempted to put their own people in important executive positions within a joint venture or a subsidiary in which the IC has less than 100 percent ownership. The natural desire of these partners and governments is to protect their own interests, such as by having their nationals in equally important positions, ensuring the local staff get training and experience in the technology and management, or providing the local operations with expertise in developing and supplying foreign markets for their products or services.

Reporting

LO 10-5
List the types of information an international company's units around the world need to report to the parent company.

For decision making and control of organizational resources to be effective, all operating units of an IC must provide headquarters with timely, accurate, and complete reports, including (1) financial, (2) technological, (3) market opportunity, and (4) political and economic reports.

FINANCIAL REPORTING

A surplus of funds in one subsidiary often is retained there for investment or contingencies. On the other hand, such a surplus might be more useful at the parent company, in which case, the parent would pay the subsidiary a dividend. Or perhaps another subsidiary or affiliate needs capital, and the surplus could be lent or invested there. Obviously, parent headquarters must know of the existence and size of a surplus to determine its best use.

TECHNOLOGICAL REPORTING

New technology is constantly being developed, and when it happens locally, the subsidiary or affiliated company is likely to learn about it before IC headquarters, hundreds or thousands of miles away. If headquarters finds the innovation potentially valuable, it can gain competitive advantage by being the first to contact the developer for a license to use it, or perhaps by purchasing the developing company outright to gain ownership and control over the new technology.

REPORTING ABOUT MARKET OPPORTUNITIES

The affiliates in various countries may spot new or growing markets for some product of the enterprise. This could be profitable all around, as the IC sells more of the product while the affiliate earns sales commissions. Of course, if the new market is sufficiently large, the affiliate may begin to assemble or produce the product under license from the parent company or from another affiliate.

Other market-related information that should be reported to IC headquarters includes competitors' activities, price developments, and new products of potential interest to the IC group. Also of importance is information about the subsidiary's market share and whether it is growing or shrinking, together with explanations.

POLITICAL AND ECONOMIC REPORTING

Not surprisingly, reports on political and economic conditions have multiplied mightily in number and importance in recent years as revolutions—some peaceful, some not—have toppled and changed governments. Democracies have replaced dictatorships, one dictator has replaced another, countries have broken apart or reunited—changes have occurred on almost every continent. Therefore, the receipt of timely reports of information about political and economic conditions is of key importance to IC management.

SARAH WARTINGER IN PERU: Embracing the Challenges of New Environments

Courtesy of Sarah Wartinger.

As an undergraduate, Sarah Wartinger pursued a double major in Spanish and global studies, with a Latin American focus. She also completed a minor in geography and certificates in European studies and international business. This vignette summarizes some of her experiences internationally while pursuing her studies.

My first experience abroad was during the spring semester of my sophomore year when I did a study abroad in Costa Rica. After my junior year, I accepted a position with AIESEC as an English education intern in Peru. After my last abroad experience in Costa Rica, I thought I would be fine in this new position: I spoke Spanish, I thought I was prepared for culture shock, and I was confident that I was well-versed and independent as a traveler.

Despite my confidence, this internship proved quite challenging at first. I was exhausted from jet lag that never seemed to go away. Each workday, I had an hour and a half commute on public transit, a tiny bus packed with people inches apart and many hanging out of the windows. I had never taken public transit in a foreign country before and being so close to the locals made me hyper-aware of my differences and how much I stood out. This, in addition to a full day of introductions, lesson planning, and execution in the classroom, meant that initially, I went home to my host family feeling defeated.

Weeks went by and nothing changed. I was still exhausted, I kept getting on the wrong bus and I was making simple Spanish mistakes that I couldn't help but play over and over in my mind. So the thoughts poured in, "What am I doing here?" "Is this really something I should be doing?" and "Does it even matter?"

I decided to start taking the moments of mindfulness that I found so relieving and tried to incorporate them throughout my day. I would close my eyes for a moment and set an intention: focus on the now. I would focus on what I was seeing, smelling, or feeling and connect with that feeling rather than focusing on how uncomfortable the bus was or how I couldn't seem to get it all right. I began being selective about where I exerted my energy as to not focus on how uncomfortable my cultural integration was. I started taking the time to remind myself where I was and what I was doing in that exact moment and accepted the challenges I had been facing as a way to reflect upon myself and my ability to overcome. I knew I wanted to be there and that I was doing something I felt strongly about. My intentions were purposeful, but I wasn't getting immediate gratification from my day's work. It was my ability to reflect on the challenges I was faced with that allowed me to celebrate and begin to love the community I was in.

Culture shock comes in waves, and within each wave are phases. The honeymoon phase is where you find the new culture to be fun and exciting, and transitioning to the rejection phase, where the realities of life become overwhelming. The regression phase is where you may retreat back to your own culture, try to seek comfort in what you know and surround yourself with familiarity. The recovery phase is where you are working through regression to accept and feel accepted by the new culture. Then finally, one may go through a phase of reverse culture shock upon return to one's own culture. My experience in Peru was a beautiful learning experience, but I have only been able to say that after deep reflection and acceptance. The truth is that you will not always be in a position where everything goes as planned, or where comfortability with the context comes easily; maybe you skip the honeymoon phase and jump straight to rejection. What is important is that you are aware of the possibility of challenges when deciding to work and live internationally in different cultures. International business is a valuable field, where you will be able to experience so much more than those who don't travel abroad. Accepting challenges such as culture shock will make you stronger as an individual and a stronger applicant for future endeavors if you are able to reflect on such challenges as a form of growth.

Source: Sarah Wartinger.

SUMMARY

LO 10-1
Explain why the design of organizational structure is important to international companies.

The structure of an international organization involves how its domestic and international units and activities are arranged and where formal power and authority will be located inside the company. It helps determine how efficiently and effectively the organization will be able to integrate and leverage its competencies and resources within and across various units of the enterprise, and thus it contributes to successful implementation of the company's strategy. The organizational structure selected for a company must be consistent with the organization's capabilities and resources, as well as with the environmental context in which the organization operates and with its strategy. In selecting an organizational structure, managers of an IC must consider the requirements for expertise in terms of product and technology, geography, customer, and function.

LO 10-2
Identify the various organizational dimensions managers must consider when selecting organizational structures.

Companies may (1) have an international division; (2) be organized by product, function, or region; or (3) have a mixture of them (hybrid form). To attain a balance between product and regional expertise, some companies have tried a matrix form of organization. Its disadvantages, however, have caused many companies to put a matrix overlay over a traditional product, regional, or functional form instead of using the matrix.

LO 10-3
Explain how decision making is allocated between parent and wholly owned subsidiaries in an international company.

Several considerations govern where decisions are made in an IC family of organizations. They include the desirability of standardizing products as opposed to differentiating them for different markets; the competence of organization managements; the size and age of the IC; the benefit of one part of the family to the detriment of another; and the building of confidence or avoidance of management frustration.

LO 10-4
Discuss how an international company can maintain control of a joint venture or of a company of which it owns less than 50 percent of the voting stock.

Control can be maintained over a joint venture or a company in which the IC owns less than 50 percent of the voting stock by several devices, including a management contract, control of the finances, control of the technology, and placement of people from the IC in key executive positions.

LO 10-5
List the types of information an international company's units around the world need to report to the parent company.

Subsidiaries should report to the IC information about financial conditions, technological developments, market opportunities and developments, and economic and political conditions.

KEY TERMS

affiliates 278
horizontal corporation 277
hybrid organization 272
international division 269
matrix organization 273

matrix overlay 274
organizational design 268
organizational structure 267
reengineering 275
strategic business unit (SBU) 275

subsidiaries 278
transfer pricing 281
virtual corporation 275

CRITICAL THINKING QUESTIONS

1. Why is organizational structure an important issue for international companies?

2. What are the main strengths and weaknesses of using an international division as part of a company's organizational structure? Under what circumstances might such a structure be an appropriate choice for a company?

3. Compare and contrast geographic and product structures for international companies.

4. Your company's matrix organization isn't working; decisions are taking too long, and it seems to you that instead of the best solutions, you're getting compromises. What can your company's CEO do to address this problem?

5. You are the CEO of Mancon Incorporated, and you have just acquired Pozoli, an Italian small-appliance maker (electric shavers, small household and personal care appliances). It has been in business for more than 40 years and has manufacturing plants in Italy, Mexico, Ireland, and Spain. Its output is sold in more than 100 markets worldwide, including the United States. Your company is now organized into two product groups—shaving and personal care—along with an international division at the top level. How are you going to include Pozoli in your organization? Explain your rationale.

6. It is obvious that in formulating new strategies, management may uncover a need to change its organization. Can you describe some situations in which the reverse may be true?

7. In choosing whether decisions will be made by the parent company or by its subsidiaries, what should management consider when equipment and products are standardized worldwide? What about when they are tailored to individual national circumstances and markets?

8. Regarding issues of control in an international company:

   a. What are some decisions that could result in detriment for a subsidiary but greater benefit for the enterprise as a whole?

   b. In such circumstances, where will the decision be made—at IC headquarters or at the affected subsidiary?

9. What measures can be utilized to control subsidiaries that are less than 100 percent owned by the firm or partnerships in which the firm has no ownership?

10. Some companies use the same control systems for each unit or operation worldwide. For example, Starbucks, Kentucky Fried Chicken, or McDonald's apply the same rigid quality controls throughout all aspects of their organizations, even as they expand internationally. Why would a company impose rigorous corporate quality standards, regardless of the country in which it operates? What modifications in these quality standards, if any, should the company permit because of differences across nations or regions of the world? Why is the company allowing these modifications to occur?

globalEDGE RESEARCH TASK   http://globalEDGE.msu.edu/

Use the globalEDGE website (http://globalEDGE.msu.edu/) to complete the following exercises:

1. Your company, which is in the machine manufacturing industry, plans to reorganize its operations in the Asia-Pacific region and build an international division that will take control of that region. As a top executive, you oversee identifying the best country to locate the headquarters of this division. You decided to compare the *global manufacturing competitiveness* of the countries in the region to make the right selection. Pick the top three competitive countries in the Asia-Pacific region and prepare a table to compare the main indicators used to calculate their global manufacturing competitiveness ranking. Prepare to discuss those values/indicators with your manager, suggest a country for the regional headquarters, and explain your reasoning.

2. Pick two industries from the "Global Insights" section of globalEDGE: one more likely to standardize products and equipment globally and another more likely to use less standardization. Prepare a class briefing to define some product groups from both industries, share common features of those product groups, and explain the reasons why one industry is more likely to standardize products and equipment and why the other is not.

MINICASE

ELECONNECT, INC.—MUST IT REORGANIZE?

Eleconnect, Inc. manufactures specialized electronic and electrical connectors used on such diverse products as computers, home appliances, telecommunications, mining equipment, and the airbag and antiskid systems of automobiles. The company has been in business for more than 50 years. The accompanying table provides a summary of the important financial information for the last five years.

For some time, Eleconnect has been exporting to South America, where its major markets are Brazil, Argentina, Chile, Colombia, and Peru. When its foreign sales were confined to exports, the company functioned well with an export department whose manager reported to the company's marketing manager. In 2017, however, another U.S. firm tried to enter the Brazilian market as that country began to emerge from an economic recession, and there were rumors that a Brazilian firm from a related industry was searching for a licensor in the United States to supply it with manufacturing technology. As a result, Eleconnect decided to set up its first foreign plant in Brazil. When it did, Eleconnect hired financial and marketing people with experience in South America and established an international division at headquarters to oversee the Brazilian operation. The company's president felt that the situation would be repeated in Chile, Colombia, and perhaps other nations. These were all good export markets at the time, but it was reasonable to suppose that some competitor would soon set up manufacturing facilities in one or more

of them, which could dramatically affect the potential for exporting to these markets. Having a small international division with some South American expertise responsible for monitoring these markets would help the firm avoid being surprised by a competitor's move.

After the Brazilian Eleconnect plant was in production, more firms in that nation were willing to do business with the company than when it had served the market through exports. In fact, the major portion of the 2018 sales increase was due to improved sales to Brazil. However, the new customers also brought the company into a new, higher level of competition than it had known before. Other Brazilian competitors were bringing out new products at a considerably faster rate than Eleconnect. The company's president wondered if horizontal linkages across functions, such as the linkages automakers have used to reduce their design time, might help his firm. Also, on his trips to Brazil, the marketing people told him things about the market and the competitors that were not being sent to the Eleconnect home office.

It was obvious to the president that overseas production and growth in overseas sales demanded a reorganization of the firm. Even though the company had only one plant overseas, in Brazil, the president was confident that other plants would soon be needed. How should the company be organized to handle the new foreign production facilities? How can Eleconnect reduce the time needed to bring new designs to market?

	Eleconnect Five-Year Financial Highlight Summary ($ millions)				
	2018	**2017**	**2016**	**2015**	**2014**
Net sales	$353.00	$298.20	$271.90	$257.40	$231.10
Gross profit	134.1	116.3	110.3	106.7	94.9
Selling, general, and administrative expenses	70.5	61.2	55.8	51.8	45.1
Income from operations	63.6	55.1	54.5	54.9	49.8
Income taxes	23.9	20.9	20.9	21.8	20.9
Effective tax rate (%)	37.6	37.9	38.3	39.7	42
Net income	39.7	34.2	33.6	33.1	28.9

NOTES

1. Jim Clemmer, "High Performance Organization Structures and Characteristics," *The Clemmer Group*, 2018. www.clemmergroup.com.

2. Nitin Nohria, *Note on Organization Structure*, Boston: Harvard Business School, 1991.

3. Gill Corkindale, "The Importance of Organizational Design and Structure," *Harvard Business Review*, February 11, 2011, www.hbr.org.

4. For example, see Nirmalya Kumar and Phanish Puranam, "Have You Restructured for Global Success?" *Harvard Business Review*, October 2011, 123–128.

5. Monica Watrous, "General Mills Announces New Global Organizational Structure," *FoodBusiness News*, https://www.foodbusinessnews.net, accessed November 01, 2018.

6. John M. Stopford, and Louis T. Wells, *Strategy and Structure of the Multinational Enterprise*, New York: Basic Books, 1972.

7. Procter & Gamble, "Corporate Structure," https://us.pg.com, accessed November 01, 2018.

8. Michael Martinez, "Why Ford's New Structure Might Make Sense," *Automotive News*, https://www.autonews.com, accessed November 01, 2018.

9. Pauline Meyer, "Starbucks Coffee's Organizational Structure & Its Characteristics," *Panmore Institute*, http://panmore.com, accessed November 01, 2018.

10. Guido Quelle, managing partner, Mandat GmbH.

11. Nestlé, *Annual Report 2017*, https://www.nestle.com, accessed November 01, 2018.

12. BP p.l.c., *Annual Report 2017*, https://www.bp.com, accessed November 01, 2018.

13. Inditex, "Who We Are," https://www.inditex.com, accessed November 01, 2018.

14. For example, see Judith Heerwagen, Kevin Kelly, and Kevin Kampschroer, "The Changing Nature of Organizations, Work, and Workplace," *WBDG*, https://www.wbdg.org, accessed November 01, 2018; Joe Aki Ouye, "Five Trends That Are Dramatically Changing Work and the Workplace," *Knoll Workplace Research*, https://www.knoll.com, accessed November 01, 2018; Josh Bersin, Tiffany McDowell, Amir Rahnema, and Yves Van Durme, "The Organization of the Future: Arriving Now," *Deloitte Insights*, https://www2 .deloitte.com, accessed November 01, 2018; and Lynn A. Karoly, and Constantijn W.A. Panis, *The 21st Century at Work: Forces Shaping the Future Workforce and Workplace in the United* States, Santa Monica, California: Rand Corporation, 2004.

15. Wouter Aghina, Aaron De Smet, and Suzanne Heywood, "The Past and Future of Global Organizations," *McKinsey Quarterly*, https://www.mckinsey.com, accessed November 01, 2018.

16. Ma Si, "Intel Expects Chinese Tech to See Growth," *China Daily*, http://www.chinadaily.com.cn, accessed November 01, 2018.

17. Paul Brindle, managing director, Thomson Reuters.

18. Prem Sikka, and Hugh Willmott, "The Dark Side of Transfer Pricing: Its Role in Tax Avoidance and Wealth Retentiveness," *Critical Perspectives on Accounting*, vol. 21, no. 4, April 2010, 342–356; and Smitha Francis, "Transfer Pricing and Tax Evasion: Beyond the Trans-Atlantic Furore," http://www .networkideas.org, accessed November 01, 2018.

11 Global Leadership Issues and Practices

> " Global leaders become who they are by cultivating particular ways of looking at the world, thinking about problems and opportunities and acting with integrity in pursuit of solutions. "
>
> —*Financial Times Lexicon*[1]

©Lissa Harrison.

LEARNING OBJECTIVES

After studying this module, you should be able to:

LO 11-1   **Discuss** the importance of creating a company "global mind-set."

LO 11-2   **Describe** what distinguishes the practice of global leadership from domestic leadership.

LO 11-3   **Identify** the competencies required for effective global leadership.

LO 11-4   **Distinguish** among the approaches for selecting and developing effective global leaders.

LO 11-5   **Describe** global team leadership skills.

LO 11-6   **Identify** some of the challenges of leading global change.

Lindsay Levin's Quest for International Leaders

Lindsay Levin is definitely a leader. She has been the CEO of a British conglomerate in auto dealerships, property, and residential health care facilities. Ernst and Young named her an Entrepreneur of the Year. As her career developed an international context, she became concerned about international leadership and the potential for everyone to make a difference. She founded the nonprofit social organization Leaders' Quest, operating programs in 26 nations, whose mission is to catalyze change across international borders by helping people build the skills they need to lead. Viewing the ability to bridge divides, such as those between nations, cultures, perspectives, and sectors, as a core requirement for successful change, Levin connects leaders from all disciplines to develop solutions for today's biggest challenges.

FIGURE 11.1 Fuller or Dymaxion Projection Map

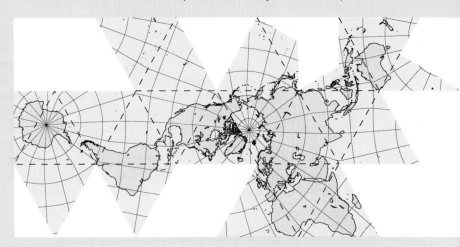

Levin's involvement stems from her concern about what it means, in a shared and increasingly complex, ambiguous, and interconnected world, to be a responsible business. This question arose for her while she was an economics student at Cambridge University in the United Kingdom. Her desire to lead such business efforts and then apply them to fight poverty, malnutrition, and other world problems soon followed. Levin described sitting under a tree in Kenya talking with some local farmers after a meeting. The farmers wanted to know, "How is it that when the financial crisis came to Europe and America that some of us had our goats and shacks repossessed?" The question brought home to her that decisions made in London and New York could reverberate to influence the lives of rural Kenyan goat farmers. She realized that, despite our technical brilliance that has led to vaccines and solar power and made vast amounts of knowledge widely available at minimal effort; despite a remarkable century of achievements in understanding ourselves and our planet that have taken us from a hot air balloon in France to the far side of the moon, we still face many challenges: We are frightened of strangers. We are unable to feed, clothe, and educate everyone.

Leaders' Quest sponsors a fellowship program and has an active corporate and nongovernmental organization (NGO) training program. Levin has recognized that the core ability to bridge divides may lead to unlikely partnerships and collaborations. For example, Aaron Sonson, a South Londoner and co-founder of the Stop & Search app, which keeps track of police-search incidents, partnered with Bill Leask, product director at PR Newswire Europe, to develop an ITV London News feature. The Leaders' Quest approach involves a new way of seeing called active hope, based on three skills: asking questions by letting go of judgment and embracing uncertainty; listening; and building the courage to act. The Leaders' Quest world is portrayed as a Fuller projection map (Dymaxion map), which shows the earth as a 20-faced icosahedron shape, connected through 12 points (Figure 11.1). With the Fuller map, the Earth is a closely connected landmass and we can see our connectedness, rather than our separation, as with the more familiar Mercator projection.

"One of the things I love about this work is the privilege to keep learning and exploring," Levin said. "You have to keep your mind open and keep your eyes open. I love the fact that certainty gets challenged all the time if you're learning." Levin describes her founding of Leaders' Quest and her own development in the 2013 book *Invisible Giants: Changing the World One Step at a Time*. Invisible giants are individuals who emerge, often against great odds, to inspire confidence and commitment to change in those around them. Her thoughts on what is required to be a "bold" leader are presented in a November 2016 address to the Business for Social Responsibility conference (found at https://leadersquest.org/blog/bsr-conference-2016-be-bold-series). Check it out: You might want to get involved. As she observes, "In my experience, people have infinite potential to grow and to create."

Sources: "Lindsay Levin: Showreel of Talks Around the World," *Youtube*, www.youtube.com; Molly Callahan, "International Leader, Entrepreneur Lindsay Levin to Deliver CPS Graduation Address," *News@Northeastern*, May 10, 2017, www.news.northeastern.edu; Frederick Denver, "Lindsay Levin of Leaders' Quest and the Philosophy Behind Compassion X," *The Business of Giving*, August 24, 2016, www.denver-frederick.com; and "Make amazing things happen," *British Airways*, www.britishairways.com.

Can you be a global leader? If so, what will you need to do to prepare yourself for such a role? As we investigate leadership in the context of international business to help you answer these questions, we need to recognize that the leadership challenge varies by company and context. There is no universal approach to selecting and developing global leaders. However, we know that a strong grasp of the business fundamentals that underlie international business is an important first step. Experiences in different cultures, languages, and other unfamiliar areas may also help you develop the "right stuff" to meet the complex international challenges that global leaders confront.

Although many international business opportunities exist, most companies do not have the leaders they need to exploit these opportunities. Our first step in this module's exploration of global leadership is to investigate the concept of *global mind-set*. Then we look at global leadership, how it differs from leadership in the domestic context, and why it is important, along with a closer look at some of the current global leaders. We identify some of the competencies an effective global leader needs, as well as some of the issues associated with candidate selection for global leadership positions and how companies develop global leaders. Then we look at the leadership of global teams and the most critical challenge global leaders often face, the management of global change.

global mind-set
A set of ideas and attitudes that combines an openness to and an awareness of diversity across markets and cultures with a propensity and ability to synthesize across this diversity

LO 11-1
Discuss the importance of creating a company "global mind-set."

The Global Mind-Set

Research indicates that many CEOs feel developing a company global mind-set is a "prerequisite for global industry dominance."[2] Global mind-set is defined as a view "that combines an openness to and awareness of diversity across cultures and markets with a propensity and ability to synthesize across this diversity."[3] Global mind-set has two key components: (1) intellectual intelligence, which includes business acumen, and (2) global emotional intelligence, which includes self-awareness, cross-cultural understanding, cultural adjustment, and cross-cultural effectiveness.[4] These two components form the foundation of the behavioral skills that constitute a person's global leadership style. The manager with a global mind-set is open to understanding others from different backgrounds, is less judgmental about people from other cultures, and is eager to approach issues from multiple perspectives.

> **❝IN TODAY'S WORLD, SUCCESS FOR ANY LEADER IS ABOUT BEING A GOOD INFLUENCER. . . . IF YOU IMPOSE YOUR METHOD, IF YOU'RE NOT SENSITIVE OR AWARE OF THE OTHER PERSON'S METHOD, EITHER YOU WON'T COME TO A DECISION OR YOU WON'T GET BUY-IN.❞**
>
> —*Sunil Nayak, CEO of Sodexo's Corporate Services Asia-Pacific*[6]

Percy Barnevik, who served as the leader for the merger of the Swedish firm Asea AB with the Swiss company BBC Brown Boveri Ltd. to create the global engineering and manufacturing giant ABB, observed that "Global managers have exceptionally open minds. They respect how different countries do things, and they have the imagination to appreciate why they do them that way. But they are also incisive; they push the limits of the culture. Global managers don't passively accept it when someone says, 'You can't do that in Italy or Spain because of the unions,' or 'You can't do that in Japan because of the Ministry of Finance.' They sort through the debris of cultural excuses and find opportunities to innovate."[5] Developing a cadre of managers and a company culture that embrace a global mind-set is a key challenge for global leaders. This challenge helps to highlight what is different and important about global leadership.

LO 11-2
Describe what distinguishes the practice of global leadership from domestic leadership.

leadership
The behaviors and processes required for organizing a group of people in order to achieve a common purpose or goal

Global Leadership: What It Is and Why It Matters

Leadership is a complex multidisciplinary concept with many definitions. Among the ways we can understand it are to consider an individual's traits and behaviors, the way the individual uses power to influence, the context of the leadership situation, and a combination of these approaches. Even a cursory review of the academic and managerial works of literature reveals the existence of many different definitions of leadership.[7] Our working definition of leadership refers to the behaviors and processes required for organizing a group of people in order to achieve a common purpose or goal.

Most experts agree that leadership is not the same thing as management, although they overlap.[8] Warren Bennis, one of the leading scholars of leadership and management, made the following helpful distinctions:

- The leader innovates; the manager administrates.
- The leader develops; the manager maintains.
- The leader challenges the status quo; the manager accepts it.
- The leader has a long-range perspective; the manager has a short-term perspective.
- The leader asks "what?" and "why?"; the manager asks "how?" and "when?"
- The leader's eye is on the horizon; the manager's eye is always on the bottom line.
- The leader originates; the manager imitates.
- The leader inspires; the manager controls.[9]

Given these distinctions between leadership and management, we now consider what is different about leadership at the global level.

> **"MANAGEMENT IS DOING THINGS RIGHT; LEADERSHIP IS DOING THE RIGHT THINGS. "**
>
> *—Peter F. Drucker*[10]

HOW GLOBAL LEADERSHIP DIFFERS FROM DOMESTIC LEADERSHIP

The leadership competencies needed in a domestic setting are also important in global contexts. Yet global leaders confront more and different contexts than do domestic leaders. This suggests that global leaders must be attuned to how things work in local cultural contexts, how things differ between different contexts, and whether and how to modify principles and practices in response to those differences. When they examined the work characteristics of more than 12,000 global leaders, researchers from CEB, a subsidiary of Gartner, found that in comparison to their peers who operated in single markets, global leaders:

- Worked with 17 percent more people that they did not manage directly.
- Were 32 percent less likely to possess accurate market information.
- Had a 74 percent broader span of responsibilities.
- Worked with 160 percent more stakeholders.[11]

As these results clearly suggest, global managers confront a dramatically different leadership context than do their domestic peers.

Scholars have identified four overlapping dimensions of complexity that are relevant to globalization and the challenge confronting global leaders: (1) *multiplicity*, which refers to the geometric growth in the volume and nature of issues global leaders deal with; (2) *interdependence*, which recognizes that although dispersed geographically, different units of the company are systematically linked to each other and increasingly dependent on external organizations; (3) *ambiguity*, which refers to the challenge of dealing with information that lacks clarity and incorporates both quantitative and qualitative dimensions, hindering the understanding of cause-and-effect relationships and the effectiveness of subsequent problem-solving efforts; and (4) *dynamism*, which recognizes that the international system itself is constantly changing.[12]

Globalization increases the complexity of the firm's external environment—(geographic and cultural), as well as its internal environment—consisting of the broader range of backgrounds and motivations among employees. As a result, globalization places an increased emphasis on the recruitment and development of managers who can operate successfully in such a challenging environment.[13] In Project GLOBE, an important global study of leadership using data from 17,300 middle managers from 951 organizations in the food processing, financial services, and telecommunications services industries, researchers found that people in different nations had some similar and many dissimilar understandings of the traits of leaders.[14] The 22 leadership traits that were universally *acceptable* included being decisive, informed, honest, dynamic, administratively skilled,

CULTURE FACTS @internationalbiz

In low-power-distance cultures like the United Kingdom, the United States, the Netherlands, Germany, and Scandinavia, people tend to negotiate their performance goals. In high-power-distance cultures like Belgium, France, and Italy, such goals tend to be dictated by senior managers. #lowpowerdistance #highpowerdistance #performancegoals

SOCIAL MEDIA

able to coordinate, just, a team builder, an effective bargainer, dependable, a win–win problem solver, a forward planner, intelligent, and a seeker of excellence. Eight leadership traits were universally *unacceptable*: being ruthless, egocentric, asocial, nonexplicit, irritable, noncooperative, dictatorial, and a loner.

Project GLOBE—more commonly known as the House study, after its initiator, Robert J. House—found that the largest number of leadership traits were contingent on cultural context. These included enthusiasm, readiness to self-sacrifice, openness to risk taking, sincerity, ambition, sensitivity, self-effacement, compassion, uniqueness, and willfulness. Follow-up studies by the same research team developed country clusters based on leaders' styles. Here are the six styles with their focuses[15]:

- *Performance-oriented*: high standards, decisiveness, innovation vision, and core values.
- *Team-oriented*: pride, loyalty, collaboration, team cohesiveness, and a common purpose.
- *Participative*: input from others in decision making and implementation; delegation and equality.
- *Humane*: compassion, generosity, patience, and support; well-being of others.
- *Autonomous*: independent, individualistic, and self-centric.
- *Self-protective*: procedural, status-conscious, face-saving, safety, and security.[16]

Table 11.1 summarizes the findings of this second study,[17] grouping the country clusters by their preference for leader styles. Each of the clusters differs significantly from the others, but there is no significant difference within the cluster. These studies highlight the context-specific aspect of global leadership and the traits of global leaders.

Although most of the competencies found in domestic leadership success are also required for global leadership, the degree of difference between the two activities is so great—and the nature of the possible outcomes within a global context can be so profoundly greater—that many scholars regard global leadership as different in kind from domestic leadership.[18] As one team of researchers noted, global leadership

> differs from domestic leadership in degree in terms of issues related to connectedness, boundary spanning, complexity, ethical challenges, dealing with tensions and paradoxes, pattern recognition, and building learning environments, teams, and community, and leading large-scale change efforts—across diverse cultures.[19]

THE CHALLENGE OF FINDING GLOBAL LEADERS WITH THE "RIGHT STUFF"

Globalization is not only creating many new business opportunities; it also is creating opportunities for a new breed of leaders who can operate in an increasingly globalized world. Rapid economic growth in emerging markets, particularly the BRIC nations (Brazil, Russia, India, and China), is creating large new markets for consumer and industrial goods.

The revolution in communications and computer technology, including the Internet, social media, smartphones, and other developments, enables diverse and geographically dispersed groups of employees to collaborate in their work and to learn from and with each other. Developments in shipping and logistics are heightening pressure on companies to reconfigure their international value chains in order to maintain competitiveness. An expanded geographic scope of operations is exposing companies to different regulatory environments, a more diverse set of suppliers and competitors, and a variety of unfamiliar risks.

International companies require a new type of leader to compete successfully in this complex and dynamic global environment. In addition to proficiency in business, these leaders must have cultural understanding and adaptability; be able to understand and reflect upon the meaning of their own culture and how that influences their leadership behavior and effectiveness, and be able to work with and inspire individuals from a range of nations and cultures.[20]

Tidjane Thiam, Chief Executive of Swiss bank Credit Suisse.
©Moritz Hager/REUTERS/Newscom.

TABLE 11.1 Project GLOBE's Societal Clusters and Preference for Leadership Styles

Performance	Team	Participative	Humane	Autonomous	Self/Group Protective
Higher					
Anglo Germanic Nordic SE Asian L. European L. American	SE Asian Confucian L. American E. European African L. European Nordic Anglo Middle Eastern Germanic	Germanic Anglo Nordic	SE Asian Anglo African Confucian	Germanic E. European Confucian Nordic SE Asian Anglo African Middle Eastern L. European L. American	Middle Eastern Confucian SE Asian L. American E. European
Mid-Range					
Confucian African E. European		L. European L. American African	Germanic Middle Eastern L. American E. European		African L. European
Lower					
Middle Eastern		E. European SE Asian Confucian Middle Eastern	L. European Nordic		Anglo Germanic Nordic

Where are such global leaders found? They can come from anywhere in the world. An Iranian–American son of Iranian immigrants (Arash Ferdowsi) founded Dropbox. A Cote d'Ivoire born son (Tidjane Thiam) is CEO of the Switzerland-based bank Credit Suisse. And a woman born in Cuba (Geisha Williams) who immigrated to the United States with her parents when she was 5 years old is president and CEO of a gas and electricity utility company (PG&E). With the right preparation, global leaders with the "right stuff" can come from anywhere on the planet.

What Competencies Are Required for Effective Global Leadership?

LO 11-3

Identify the competencies required for effective global leadership.

What competencies should a global leader have to perform successfully? Research conducted by Aperian Global, a consulting company whose goal is to open the world for its clients, identified five abilities returning expatriates thought necessary for a successful global leadership assignment. These are the ability to:

- *See differences*, a self-awareness in cultural contexts. Leadership patterns are shaped by culture, and other ways exist to get things done.
- *Make connections* because, in the global environment, relationships are a prerequisite for getting things done. "Results through relationships" is a key observation.
- *Adjust*, a kind of "frame-shifting" that requires cognitive flexibility to see differences and adjust behavior quickly.
- *Integrate and lead change*, a complex ability to adjust to some local practices while selling other practices into the local environment, a combination of adapting and questioning the status quo.
- *Localize*, an ability to develop local talent.[21]

Management scholar Henry Mintzberg and others have identified a range of roles that a global leader may need to take, including:

- *Monitor*—scanning environments, seeking information, monitoring different units of the company.
- *Spokesperson*—advocating and representing the company, communicating with different levels of internal and external stakeholders.
- *Liaison*—networking, coordinating, spanning internal and external boundaries.
- *Leader*—motivating and coaching individuals and teams, building and maintaining corporate culture.
- *Negotiator*—making deals, managing conflict.
- *Innovator*—seizing opportunities, generating new ideas, promoting a vision for the company.
- *Decision maker*—troubleshooting, making decisions.
- *Change agent*—taking action, developing and implementing change plans.[22]

CULTURE FACTS @internationalbiz

Only 19.9 percent of board of directors' positions in the United States are held by women. Norway, France, and Sweden each have over 30 percent women in these roles, and Japan has 3.5 percent. #womeninleadership #boardofdirectors

This broad range of duties suggests that global leaders require a complex mix of competencies in order to be effective.

Research by scholars at the Center for Creative Leadership suggests that global leaders are more challenged in the areas of emotional stability, ability to learn, and decision-making and negotiating roles than are domestic leaders[23] due to the impact of cultural differences. In addition, Project GLOBE researchers concluded that a global mind-set, cultural adaptability and flexibility, and tolerance for ambiguity are attributes global leaders needed in order to be effective.[24] From a survey of the research on global leadership, Alan Bird has collected over 220 competencies and divided them into three categories: those needed to manage the business, to manage people and relationships, and to manage the self.[25] The three parts of Table 11.2 summarize these leadership competencies by type, with examples of behavior associated with each.[26]

In contrast to the lists of leadership competencies, the five-level Pyramid Model of Global Leadership presented in Figure 11.2 attempts to identify a progression of

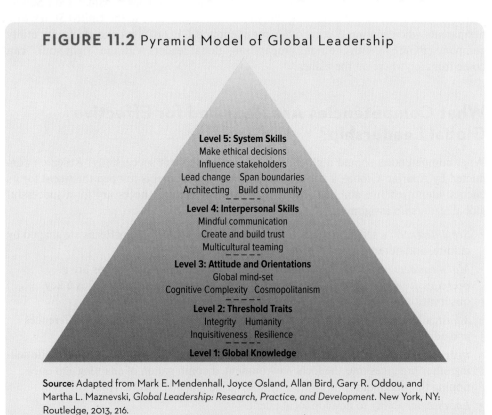

FIGURE 11.2 Pyramid Model of Global Leadership

Source: Adapted from Mark E. Mendenhall, Joyce Osland, Allan Bird, Gary R. Oddou, and Martha L. Maznevski, *Global Leadership: Research, Practice, and Development.* New York, NY: Routledge, 2013, 216.

TABLE 11.2A Business Competencies

Vision and Strategic Thinking	Intellectual intelligence, able to deal with complexity, oscillation between details and big picture, environmental scanning, frame-shifting
Business Savvy	Business acumen, results orientation, global capitalist, technical savvy, finding creative solutions, third-way solutions
Managing Communities	Customer orientation, stakeholder orientation, building partnerships and alliances, influencing stakeholders, building community, boundary spanning
Organizational Savvy	Total organizational acumen, designing and aligning, architecting, managing a budget on a worldwide basis
Leading Change	Catalyst for strategic change, catalyst for cultural change, lead change

TABLE 11.2B People Competencies

Cross-Cultural Communication	Communication skills, culture bridger, cultural interest and sensitivity, cultural understanding, mindful communication, cultural self-awareness
Interpersonal Skills	Emotional intelligence, influencing, urgent listening, relationship interest, social flexibility, results through relationships
Valuing People	Skilled people reading, understand actors, cultural acumen, respectful modernizer, respect for others, pragmatic trust
Empowering Others	Being able to empower others, energizing, rewarding and feedback, connective teaching, sharing leadership
Teaming Skills	Team building, multicultural teaming, managerial ability, with an emphasis on teamwork and interpersonal skill

TABLE 11.2C Self-Competencies

Resilience	Stress and emotional resilience, resourceful, optimistic, energetic, self-confidence, personal management, life balance
Character	Integrity, maturity, exhibit character, honesty, conscientiousness, self-identity, core values and flexibility, make ethical decisions, tenacity
Inquisitiveness	Inquisitiveness, curiosity and learning, aggressive insight, open-mindedness, openness to experience, inviting the unexpected, nonjudgmentalness, confident humility, motivation to learn (also mistakes)
Flexibility	Thinking agility, authentic flexibility, open-minded and flexible in thought and tactics, interest flexibility, tolerance for ambiguity, embrace duality
Global Mind-Set	Global mind-set cosmopolitanism, cognitive complexity, thinking globally

Source: Andrea Straub-Bauer, consultant, "Overview of Global Leadership Competencies," http://di.dk/-globalleadershipacademy/newsandarticles/insights/Pages/GlobalLeadershipCompetenciesanoverview. aspx, accessed February 08, 2015.

Are Global Leadership Positions What Corporations and Women Have Been Waiting For?

The World Bank has stated that a core development objective is to achieve gender equality and the full participation of women in business, particularly in developing nations. Despite this, as noted by Nancy Adler, most of the research on leadership has focused on men, with only a minor portion addressing the potential of women as leaders. Research has continued to show uneven participation of women in leadership roles in business.

Here's a summary of the situation for women CEOs in the United States. Although they occupy more than 51 percent of the managerial and professional positions in U.S. organizations, there are relatively few women in the top tier of corporate leadership. Women CEOs such as Phebe Novakovic at General Dynamics and Vicki Hollub at Occidental Petroleum represent a very small minority of the leadership in publicly held corporations. Most of the women who serve as CEOs in the United States have started their own firms or have taken over the leadership of a family business. As of 2018, only 4.8 percent of chief executive officers in S&P 500 companies were women, despite comprising 44.7 percent of all employees in those firms. Slightly more encouraging is that 26.5 percent of all executive/senior level managers and officials were women, suggesting that the number of women CEOs in the United States might expand in the future, given their numbers in the executive pipeline.

Research has shown that women's and men's typical leadership styles differ. For example, women tend to view leadership as an opportunity to empower their subordinates and enhance their potential to excel; men tend to see their leadership position as a chance for exerting control over their subordinates. Adler argues for more women in global leadership positions, due in part to research suggesting that

traits and qualities typically associated with women are consistent with those linked to effective global leadership. She found that global leaders who were women:

- Came from diverse backgrounds, with no predictable pattern associated with their route to leadership positions.
- Were not selected for leadership positions by only women-friendly companies or countries.
- Symbolized hope, change, and unity through their selection as leaders, particularly in light of their position as outsiders who were going against the odds, thereby suggesting the potential for organizational or societal change.
- Were driven to achieve success based on vision, rather than desire for hierarchical status.
- Relied upon broad-based, popular support or support directly from the marketplace, instead of traditional, hierarchy-based support.
- Pursued paths to power that involved lateral transfers within their organizations, instead of the more traditional path up the hierarchy common among men.
- Leveraged the enhanced visibility that they received due to their status as women or as "the first woman." This special status led to more attention from the media, and they were able to use this visibility as a platform to enhance their position and performance.

Consistent with Adler's work, other research has found that women tend to have a leadership style that is more participative, interactional, and relational, with greater levels of emotional intelligence and empathy, than is the case for men. These are attributes of successful global leadership, and some research has

Phebe Novakovic, Chairman and CEO of General Dynamics. (left) Vicki Hollub, President and CEO of Occidental Petroleum Corporation. (right)
©Ron Sachs/Pool via CNP - NO WIRE SERVICE/dpa picture alliance/ Alamy Stock Photo;
©F. Carter Smith/Bloomberg/ Getty Images.

shown that multinationals experience significantly improved profitability when they increase their hiring of women, particularly at the senior management level. Women also have been found to attribute greater importance to the areas of social responsibility, inclusion and diversity, and global skills—and women were believed to be better prepared in these areas as well—than was the case for men. They also tend to use leadership styles that are more participative and democratic and less directive and autocratic than the leadership styles that tend to be used by men.

The idea that women should be recruited to lead global efforts of companies is a logical consideration, given the research. What do you think? Would such a human resource strategy bring companies competitive advantage? Would it bring women the corporate leadership positions they seek?

Critical Thinking Questions

1. The research findings suggest that women might be better suited than men for the challenges of global leadership. Yet how could this be true, given the small number of women occupying executive leadership positions?

2. What options might be available for increasing the level of women's participation in global leadership positions?

3. Are there certain industries, nations, or other contexts in which it would be inappropriate or undesirable to have women as leaders? Why or why not?

Sources: "Women CEOs of the S&P 500," *Catalyst Inc*, October 03, 2018, www.catalyst.org; "Women CEOs of the S&P 500," *Catalyst Inc*, October 03, 2018, www.catalyst.org; Jordan Siegel, Lynn Pyun, and B. Y. Cheon, "Multinational Firms, Labor Market Discrimination, and the Capture of Outsider's Advantage by Exploiting the Social Divide," *Administrative Science Quarterly*, April 02, 2018; Nancy Adler, "Global Leadership: Women Leaders," *Management International Review*, vol. 37, no. 1, 1997, 171–96; Mark E. Mendenhall, Torsten M. Kühlmann, and Gunter K. Stahl, *Developing Global Business Leaders: Policies, Processes and Innovations*. Westport, CT: Quorum Books, 2001, 73–97; J. B. Rosener, "Ways Women Lead," *Harvard Business Review*, vol. 68, no. 6, 1990, 119–25; N. Fondas, "Feminization Unveiled: Management Qualities in Contemporary Writings," *Academy of Management Review*, vol. 2, no. 1, 1997, 257–82; Marc A Brackett., Susan E. Rivers, Sara Shiffman, Nicole Lerner, and Peter Salovey, "Relating Emotional Abilities to Social Functioning: A Comparison of Self-Report and Performance Measures of Emotional Intelligence," *Journal of Personality and Social Psychology*, vol. 91, no. 4, 2006, 780–95; and Alice H. Eagly, and Blair T. Johnson, "Gender and Leadership Style: A Meta-Analysis," *Psychological Review*, vol. 108, no. 2, 1990, 573–98.

skills required for effective global leadership. At the bottom level is a baseline of necessary global knowledge. Building on this knowledge is the second level of four threshold traits: humility, integrity, inquisitiveness, and resilience. Level 3 includes attitudes and orientations that affect the way global leaders perceive and interpret their world, while the fourth level includes interpersonal skills that enable global leaders to effectively cross cultures. Level 5, the very apex of the pyramid, includes system skills that enable global leaders to effectively influence people and systems inside and outside the company.

The broad array of global leadership competencies we have covered highlights the complex and diverse nature of global leaders' challenges. Research in this area began in the 1990s and is still in its infancy.

Selecting and Developing Effective Global Leaders

The process of selecting and developing global leaders has been evolving along with our understanding of global leadership. Here we look at how companies select and develop their global leaders. We look at the way competencies are assessed, then review models for developing global leaders, and finally, review the way global leadership competencies are developed.[28]

ASSESSING GLOBAL LEADERSHIP COMPETENCIES

A key challenge confronting companies faced with the need for developing global leaders is assessing the competencies of candidates. Since the study of global leadership is in its

> **"WE ARE *NOT* TALKING about GLOBAL BUSINESS *EFFICIENCY*. WE'RE TALKING about CULTURAL COMPETENCY DEVELOPMENT LEADING to GLOBAL BUSINESS *EFFECTIVENESS*."**
>
> —*Cornelius Grove*[27]

LO 11-4
Distinguish among the approaches for selecting and developing effective global leaders.

infancy, there are many competing models for its skills and attributes, and the variations across these models complicate assessment.

There are many assessment instruments available to assess global leadership competencies. Among the most widely respected are the Cross-Cultural Adaptability Inventory (CCAI),[29] the Intercultural Development Inventory (IDI),[30] the Global Competencies Inventory (GCI),[31] and the Global Executive Leadership Inventory (GELI).[32] The CCAI is a tool for self-assessment of cross-cultural adaptability. It can be used to assess an individual's capability to adjust to a new culture and to design a training program to enhance success in relocating to another culture. The IDI identifies the competencies associated with intercultural sensitivity, and it often is used to assess the ability to modify cultural perspective and to adapt behavior to different cultural contexts. The GCI assesses personality predispositions linked with effective intercultural behavior and global managerial skills. It addresses competencies in 16 areas, categorized within perception management, relationship management, and self-management. The GELI is a 360-degree feedback approach for identifying leadership competencies and gaps. Each of these instruments can help people understand aspects of their global leadership competencies.

MODELS FOR DEVELOPING GLOBAL LEADERS

An important issue facing international companies is the need to understand how to develop effective global leaders. Are candidates just "born global," with a special set of skills and attributes that makes them effective in global leadership contexts, or do these capabilities get developed over time, as a result of some interplay among personal attributes, experience, and other factors? Most experts in the field think global leadership effectiveness is the result of a developmental process rather than innate capability, at least in part.[33] As a result, various models of global leadership development have been proposed. Understanding these models may assist the international company in developing appropriate processes for developing its cadre of global leaders. This section discusses two models: the Global Leadership Expertise Development (GLED) model and the "right stuff" model.

The Global Leadership Expertise Development (GLED) Model A model designed for developing the expertise of global leaders, the GLED model (Figure 11.3) emphasizes the process by which expertise is developed.[34] It begins with antecedents for the development of global leaders and their expertise, divided among four categories: individual characteristics, cultural exposure, global education, and project novelty. The level of global leadership expertise is thought to be determined by four dependent variables: cognitive processes, global knowledge, intercultural competence, and global organizing expertise. The model assumes a transformational process influences the relationship between the initial conditions and the outcomes that result. This transformational process consists of the set of experiences, interpersonal encounters, decisions, and challenges related to the global leader's expertise, and it is thought to be the primary cause of the different levels of global leadership expertise we observe among leaders with global responsibilities.

The "Right Stuff" Model The "right stuff" model (Figure 11.4) focuses on developing global leaders that have the "right stuff" in terms of what they have learned and what they are able to do as leaders. Producing leaders with the right stuff is the result of interaction and partnership between the leader and the organization. The basic talent of the leadership candidates, combined with their developmental experiences and the context in which these experiences occur, help produce the global leader's skills and capabilities, the right stuff for the company in a particular context. This model argues that the company's global business strategy is a major determinant of the relevant lessons and skills the leader needs. Because it is strategy-dependent, the right

FIGURE 11.3 The Global Leadership Expertise Development (GLED) Model

Antecedents

Individual Characteristics
Nonjudgmentalness • Tolerance of ambiguity • Cosmopolitanism • Relationship interest • Interpersonal initiation • Emotional sensitivity • Self-awareness • Behavioral flexibility • Optimism • Self-confidence • Self-identity • Emotional resilience • Non-stress tendency • Stress management • Interest flexibility • Emotional intelligence

Cultural Exposure
Cross-cultural experience (years, type) • Cultural involvement (buffering) • Cultural novelty • Language

Global Education
Global knowledge • Seminars • Courses • Coaching • Mentoring

Project Novelty
Multicultural team • Virtual group • Globe scope

↓

Transformational Process
Multiplicity of experience, encounters, decisions, challenges that vary in degree of: • Complexity • Development significance • Intensity of emotional affect

↓

Level of Expertise

| Cognitive Processes | Global Knowledge | Intercultural Competence | Global Organizing Expertise |

Global Knowledge

High ←————————————————————————→ Low

stuff for a global leader will vary across organizations. For example, a company whose strategy depends on extensive use of alliances with external organizations will require leaders with skills and experience in working with entities beyond the firm's formal boundaries. A decision to compete in a broad array of less-developed nations, for instance, will help determine the number and range of cultural capabilities the company's leaders will require as well.

FIGURE 11.4 The "Right Stuff" Model

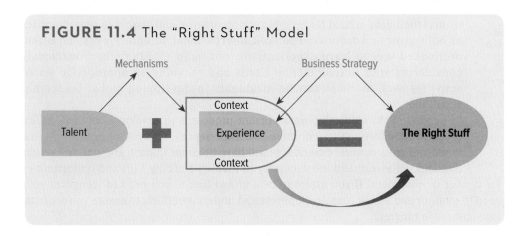

Nelson Mandela, first post-apartheid president of the Republic of South Africa.
©Susan Winters Cook/Hulton Archive/Getty Images.

As our discussion so far suggests, the development of global leaders is a complex process that demands flexibility in order to match the individual, organizational, and external contexts in which the leaders need to learn and perform. A standardized approach applied to all leadership candidates and across all contexts is unlikely to be successful in developing effective global leaders.

TOOLS AND TECHNIQUES FOR DEVELOPING GLOBAL LEADERSHIP SKILLS

How can individuals develop the required skills and experiences of global leaders? Recognize first that it is a nonlinear process that may include all sorts of diverse experiences. Differences in personal backgrounds and attributes, as well as in the companies and their contexts, suggest that development efforts need to be individualized. Global leaders require strong training in business fundamentals, including international business. Knowledge of history, geography, and political science, among other topics, is valuable because these areas enhance international understanding and performance. Training in language and culture is also valuable.

Much of this learning may come through traditional channels, such as university study, intensive international business simulations, and short executive courses and seminars.[36] However, a deeper, nuanced understanding of the complex issues of global leadership is seldom achieved solely through traditional learning methods. To develop the skills necessary to deal effectively with the complex, ambiguous, high-level challenges that global leaders face requires an array of techniques and experiences. Some of these can occur during or shortly after university studies. Future leaders can live with a host family while studying abroad in order to enhance language and cultural fluency; take on international internships both paid and unpaid; undertake personal and business travel to international locations; identify and participate in short- or long-term expatriate assignments within international markets; develop effective networks from contacts at university or work and other contexts; pursue opportunities to work within multicultural and international teams (including virtual teams); pursue mentoring and coaching opportunities as both giver and receiver; and seek international volunteer work, an often-overlooked way to learn experientially and build global skills. Consciously considering your developmental needs and pursuing an appropriate set of activities such as these can be invaluable in developing global leadership capability.

The goal of the leadership development process is to develop global leadership experientially through transformational experiences. Of course, not all international and cross-cultural experiences will have the same impact, and ongoing reflection and self-assessment are necessary to identify learning gaps and opportunities for further development. If you aspire to be a global leader, you need to recognize your need to monitor and assess your development and undertake efforts to ensure you are making substantive progress.

> **"REMEMBER TO BE CURIOUS ABOUT OTHER CULTURES AND ENJOY THE CHALLENGES OF COMMUNICATING IN A COMPETITIVE, FAST-PACED GLOBAL BUSINESS ENVIRONMENT."**
>
> —*Maya Hu-Chan, Alliant University's Global Leadership Development Center*[35]

CULTURE FACTS @internationalbiz

Leaders in emerging markets, with communal cultures that value hierarchy, particularly India and China, are inclined to focus heavily on hands-on management, operational process, and control of individual performance. Leaders in the individualist and low-power-distance Benelux and Nordic countries tend to focus more heavily on planning, strategy, and communication. #communalcultures #individualist #lowpowerdistance

SOCIAL MEDIA

Volunteer Assignments Build Global Leadership Skills

Students and recent graduates often wonder how they can get a start on building their international leadership skills when they may not have international experience or jobs with international responsibilities. Management scholar Paula Caligiuri describes a recent development in corporate social responsibility programs that might offer a way forward.

A growing number of corporate employees are taking volunteer assignments in international corporate social responsibility (CSR) programs that range from three to six months, with release time and compensation sponsored by the company. The programs team up corporate employees from companies such GlaxoSmithKline, Dow Corning, PepsiCo, FedEx, and IBM with nongovernmental organizations (NGOs) in order to build employees' corporate social responsibility values and other skills fundamental to global leadership. We know that "to work effectively in different cultures and with culturally diverse others, responsible global leaders require cross-cultural competencies [that include] a tolerance of ambiguity, perspective taking, humility, and resilience." Caligiuri's analysis of these CSR programs and her assessment of their benefits suggest they are an effective way to build global leadership skills.

Caligiuri and her colleague, Christian Thoroughgood, suggest that to build responsible global leadership skills, the experience should have five key features. First, it should include *meaningful collaboration with peers across cultures*, since such activities build cultural agility and empathy and interest in the needs of the target population. Volunteer assignments should also be a *cultural stretch for your functional skills*. The experience should test the limits of cultural knowledge and assumptions so you can know the limits to which you are culture-bound. You can then further push these limits through your volunteer experience.

The opportunity to *practice cultural humility* is a third suggested feature of participation in an international volunteer program whose goal is to build global leadership skills. Cultural humility is the extent to which you appreciate contributions of host nationals and recognize that you have something to learn from their country. It allows you to understand how your behavior is interpreted by the host country members with whom you interact.

The fourth feature of any program to which you commit to building your global leadership skills is that it should *positively reinforce corporate social responsibility behavior* with meaningful projects. Caligiuri points out that "neuroscientists have discovered that when acting with generosity and altruism, the human brain responds" with the sensation of pleasure. That may be why volunteer programs are able to develop responsible global leaders: "Doing good also feels good." The final feature Caligiuri recommends is that the programs *encourage empathy*. Empathy, the ability to understand and share another's feelings, is fostered by the opportunity to observe the effects of your altruism on others.

Organizations to help you find placements likely to have the five features Caligiuri recommends and sort through the many volunteer and internship options include NGO Abroad, Volunteer Match, AIESEC, and One World 365. If you decide to, you can strengthen your global leadership skills the corporate way.

Sources: P. Caligiuri, C. Thoroughgood, "Developing Responsible Global Leaders through Corporate-Sponsored International Volunteerism Programs," *Organizational Dynamics*, vol. 44, no. 2, April–June, 2015, 138–145; and P. Caligiuri, Ahsiya Mencin, and Kaifeng Jiang, "Win–Win–Win: The Influence of Company-Sponsored Volunteerism Programs on Employees, NGOs, and Business Units," *Personnel Psychology*, vol. 66, no. 4, November 03, 2012, 825–860.

Leading Global Teams

Global teams with members in more than one country are an increasingly common approach in international work. Such teams are characterized by high levels of diversity, geographic dispersion, and virtual rather than face-to-face interaction. Several dimensions add to their complexity, including members from different national cultures whose locations are in different time zones with different communication technologies available, and different corporate, cultural, and economic contexts in which team members are embedded. We begin with a discussion of team leadership in general,

LO 11-5
Describe global team leadership skills.

global team
A team characterized by a high level of diversity, geographic dispersion, and virtual rather than face-to-face interaction

examining the three activities in which team leaders usually engage, and then we address the added challenges global teams bring to leadership, including their performance management.

LEADING TEAMS

Leading teams in almost any context includes three main activities: establishing the team, coaching team members, and setting team norms.[37] Each has an enhanced aspect when the context is global.

The first leadership activity is to establish the team itself. In this process, the leader encourages strong member identification with the team and its norms, because this identification leads to better performance. When team members see one another as each member sees himself or herself, and when team members feel their team is distinctive, even when it is very diverse, high levels of motivation are likely to exist.[38] An environment where these positive team norms can come into play is especially useful in global teams, where high levels of diversity challenge team members to grasp one another's self-concepts, which are influenced by subtle levels of cultural values.

The next group leader activity is coaching team members. When faced with diversity, co-workers who are unfamiliar with the work of a group member tend to expect that person to perform poorly. Such expectations occur regardless of the person's actual skill level and can be self-fulfilling.[39] The team leader can confront this bias by publicizing the strengths of team members. Motivational coaching is also important as the team begins its task, and strategic coaching may be valuable when strategic choices come into play, later in the team's evolution.

Setting team norms is the third key activity for all team leaders. **Team norms** are defined as "legitimate, shared standards against which the appropriateness of behavior can be evaluated."[40] They greatly influence the dynamics of the team, especially in two areas, cooperation and consideration. Cooperation is critical, especially when team members are not located in the same place. Often in work life, face-to-face interaction takes priority, and responding to requests from a nearby co-worker may be much easier than responding to the geographically distant team member who is also in a different time zone. One way to support cooperation in a global team is to increase the level at which team members see one another as members of their in-group. Reward structures also can encourage group cooperation.

Norms of consideration—sensitivity to others or what is sometimes described as good manners—are also important to teams, and especially global teams. For example, when potentially offensive language is self-censored, diverse groups tend to build trust more quickly. The sooner that happens, the sooner the team can move to a constructive focus on the task at hand.

team norms
Legitimate, shared standards against which the appropriateness of behavior can be evaluated

COMPLEXITY FOR TEAMS IN THE GLOBAL CONTEXT

In addition to these traditional team leader roles, the global team leader is acting within the context of globalization. As we described earlier in this module, globalization brings a great shift toward increasing complexity. The three specific conditions identified in the international context that contribute to globalization's complexity are increased multiplicity, increased interdependence, and increased ambiguity.[41] We look at these forces a bit more closely to understand the complexity that global team leaders face.

Multiplicity arises from the increased number of players in the game. Globalization brings more competitors, more stakeholders, and more customers, creating many more relationships to manage and viewpoints to consider. Multiplicity contributes to increased levels of interdependence, including economic interdependence, interdependence among the various activities of the firm's value chain, and interdependence among alliance partners. Along with multiplicity and interdependence comes increased ambiguity, which results from the multiple ways we have to interpret an increasing amount of data. Yet the more data we have, the less clear the path for interpreting these data. Cause-and-effect relationships are not clear; there are many plausible ways to interpret the same data, and the information itself may not be clear. We are left not knowing how to interpret the data we do have in a way that will guide decisions.

GLOBAL TEAM LEADERSHIP AND CULTURE

Global team leaders have to address the basic conditions of team performance—organization, social processes, and task processes—as well as the issues that accompany an international context. A major part of this context is culture. Global team members bring different cultural expectations to the team environment, including the way they think of the team at deep levels. (Is the team a family? A tribe? A collection of friends? A sports team?) Explicitly addressing these differences in cultural expectations can lead to superior performance. Researchers have pointed out, though, that the inclination in diverse teams is to suppress differences and focus on what team members have in common.[42]

As you study the impact of cultures, you will learn that they influence the way people think about defining and managing roles and identifying acceptable communication and conflict resolution norms. In cultures with high power distance—for example, most Asian and Latin American cultures—team members will expect a clear hierarchy and a single leader with decision-making power. They may not be fully aware of their expectations (like most of us). In Scandinavian cultures, a more fluid leadership model is expected; leadership is shared and also shifts around, depending on the task and the leader's ability. In individualistic cultures such as the United States or Britain, task roles are clearly defined and responsibility is allocated, with individual rewards assumed. Contrast this to more collectivist cultures such as Malaysia and Thailand, where accountability and rewards are assumed to occur at the group level. Addressing these differences openly builds a foundation for understood and agreed-upon roles in the team.

Global teams also need to explicitly address their communication and conflict norms. Compare some Latin countries—where speaking up at any time is fine, even when someone else is talking—to some Asian countries, where people respond only to direct questions and silence is a comfortable way to communicate. How do cultural predispositions operate in the virtual world? How do team members from different cultures deal with disagreement? Is open disagreement appropriate? Or is harmony so valued that disagreement is suppressed? The team needs to be able to resolve conflict constructively, but as you can imagine, reaching the point where they can do so may take some work.

One way to get at understanding the various cultures of team members is to use the map-bridge-integrate (MBI) model. Developed by Martha Maznevski, the MBI model is a process that can open up the cultural assumptions team members may have.[43] *Mapping*, the first step, lets the team members discuss their differences and similarities; that is, they map their relevant characteristics. This is followed by a *bridging* effort. Here, team members communicate with each other about the differences and establish how they will work with one another. Bridging includes decentering—seeing the other person's point of view, a bit akin to empathy—and avoiding blame. Effective bridging also enables *integration*, which is the process of managing the various differences, so team members begin to understand the expectations and assumptions of their peers, as well as their backgrounds and skills. The application of the MBI steps takes time, yet it can enable teams to function better and achieve improved performance.

Multicultural team in meeting. ©Ute Grabowsky/Photothek/Getty Images.

VIRTUAL AND GEOGRAPHICALLY DISPERSED TEAMS

Many global teams are geographically dispersed and communicate through technology. Leading a team whose members are on different continents and in different time zones, and who connect through technology such as texting, e-mail, or videoconferencing, creates unique leadership challenges. Virtual communication, even with video content, lacks the richness of face-to-face communication. Research suggests that initial face-to-face meetings for teams that plan to subsequently work virtually are a good way to build trust among team members, and trust is critical for the team's functioning.[44] Most teams meet face-to-face at their launch and during crises. Maznevski points out that virtual teams with high performance actually schedule regular face-to-face meetings to discuss progress and issues and to further develop their relationships. Such regular meetings create a kind of heartbeat. "[T]eams that have a strong heartbeat can manage all other tasks virtually in between their face-to-face meetings, and . . . this is both less expensive and more effective than getting together 'whenever we need to.'"[45]

PERFORMANCE MANAGEMENT IN GLOBAL TEAMS

What do we understand about rewarding global team performance in culturally diverse, geographically dispersed virtual global teams? Researchers suggest that the one factor accounting for many of the failures of global teams is ineffective reward and recognition strategies.[46] The questions that are critical for global team effectiveness include:

- Are rewards based on individual performance, team performance, or a combination of the two?
- What factors come into play with team-based pay?
- What role can recognition play?

Individual-based rewards are most common in virtual global teams, despite the fact that individual contributions are difficult to discern, especially in a virtual environment. Team-based rewards are thought to encourage social loafing, the tendency of some people to put forth less effort when they are members of a group. Many researchers see a combination of individual and group rewards as a good way to avoid

social loafing
Tendency of some people to put forth less effort when they are members of a group

this problem. There are five areas to consider when establishing a balance of team and individual rewards:

1. What is the nature of the task? How interdependent is it? The greater the task interdependence, the higher the portion of team-based rewards should be.

2. How stable is the team membership? If the team boundaries are fluid or if membership changes are frequent, appropriate team rewards will be difficult to determine.

3. What are the national cultures of the team members? The individualism-collectivism dimension of the cultures needs to be considered. High levels of team rewards are appropriate for teams whose members are from collectivist cultures, and high levels of individual rewards are appropriate for teams whose members are from more individualist cultures. With high levels of cultural diversity, the team should be included in the development of the reward system.

4. What are the labor laws that affect employee compensation? In many locations, salary levels are set by local or national laws or by labor unions, and their flexibility is constrained.

5. What are the available reward options? In addition to financial rewards, recognition is a valued reward. These rewards are most successful when they incorporate national cultural values of team members.[47]

Remember that performance appraisal for global teams will also be influenced heavily by national culture, and by the other team variables mentioned in our discussion of rewards and recognition.

Global team leadership is an evolving skill whose importance will increase as the internationalization of business increases. Early research suggests that global teams require the same leadership skills basic teams need, plus the increased awareness and more subtle leadership skills that help the team build on its diversity and its geographic dispersion, all in a context that is increasingly complex.

Leading Global Change

LO 11-6
Identify some of the challenges of leading global change.

Leading organizational change is always a difficult process, largely because it deals with changing individual behaviors. Jim Clawson believes change is the central part of leadership. He writes that leadership has three elements: "(1) seeing what needs to be done; (2) understanding all the underlying forces at play in the situation; and (3) having the courage to initiate actions to make things better."[48] Key players in the successful change process have to alter their behavior, which rests on their assumptions, values, beliefs, perceptions, tasks, and roles.[49] If the scope of the change global managers hope to effect is global, then the process becomes exponentially difficult. The difficulty comes from the size of the organization, its geographic dispersion, and, most significantly, the varying expectations and values that surround personal assumptions about change in different national-level cultures.

> **"INDIVIDUALLY, WE ARE ONE DROP. TOGETHER, WE ARE AN OCEAN."**
>
> —*Ryunosuke Satoro*[50]

CHANGE MODELS

Research on global change is in its early stages, and it builds on the more general study of change. Here, we look at two models for change and its leadership, and then at the aspects of culture that may influence global change leadership. Each of the models describes the *process* of change and its stages.

Probably the best-known change model, developed by Kurt Lewin, is a three-stage process of unfreezing, moving, and refreezing.[51] The first stage, *unfreezing*, requires overcoming inertia and preparing people for change, including dealing with

CHAD HENRY: Developing Global Leadership Skills and Experience, Beginning with an Internship in Croatia

Chad Henry's development of global leadership skills began in Croatia.
Courtesy of Chad Henry.

I went to college on a football scholarship, and after completing my degree, I was searching for direction. I wanted to do something different with my life. I didn't see myself as a traditional "finance guy" and thought these traditional career paths would not bring me personal fulfillment. I sought to step into a new frontier, the opportunity to work and live abroad.

I accepted an AIESEC internship to Croatia (see AIESEC.org), a place I knew almost nothing about. I gathered as much information as possible before leaving, a bit like cramming for an exam. My main preparation focused on understanding where I was going, ensuring that it was safe, and preparing information for my parents.

My internship was for 12 months, but I ended up becoming fluent in Croatian, had a range of jobs, and stayed for 10 years. Croatia was in the midst of change, and it was an exciting time. I lived in Split, Varaždin, and Zagreb and traveled throughout Europe. My work was in export development, strategic development, and foreign direct investment. I also played professional baseball for a Croatian team and coached a team playing American football.

The keys to my adjustment included keeping a very open mind and maintaining my determination to succeed. These qualities helped me deal with challenges as they presented themselves. The biggest challenge I confronted was learning to accept things as they are without making value judgments, remembering that things are relative rather than absolute. While as individuals we learn through our cultures a certain way to do things or approach situations, this doesn't make it right or wrong. When you can learn to accept different viewpoints and see the value in them—even if not necessarily agreeing with them—then it allows you to enjoy and adapt to the culture in which you are immersed.

My rewards from my time in Croatia included learning to manage people who have intrinsically different work values; finding a way to work with people that brings out their best, and being accepted by friends in another culture. I learned to see and understand things from multiple perspectives and to adapt and react to adverse and sometimes hostile situations.

Here are my recommendations for life abroad:

- Make sure you understand the perspective of others while you are abroad. This perspective is developed by cultural differences and values. Without understanding them, you won't be able to resolve differences and disputes or motivate others.
- Learn the local language.
- Have a general understanding of the history of the country.
- Ask questions.

Have a lot of fun and enjoy the privilege, not always an easy one, of learning another culture.

Source: Chad Henry.

---

defense mechanisms against the proposed change. At this point, there is stress, tension, and recognition of the need for change. The second stage is *moving* the proposed behaviors into practice, a period often characterized by confusion. *Refreezing* is the final stage when the new behaviors are either accepted and institutionalized or rejected.

Expanding the level of description found in Lewin's model, John Kotter's approach to change suggests eight steps:

1. Increase urgency, so that people are inspired to move toward real and relevant objectives.
2. Develop the guiding team, so that those involved in leadership are the right people, with high emotional commitment and the right combination and levels of skills.

3. Develop a change vision and strategy.

4. Communicate the vision for buy-in.

5. Empower broad-based action by removing obstacles.

6. Generate short-term wins that are rewarded.

7. Don't let up; foster determination and persistence.

8. Make the change stick through leadership development and succession.[52]

These models might be misconstrued to imply that change is an orderly process and that the steps are nicely sequential. In practice, whether incremental or transformative, change is not neat and orderly, largely because it rests on human behavior. Often it includes a lot of learning through trial-and-error approaches.

CHANGE AND CULTURE

Not surprisingly, aspects of culture are related to the process of change. These include cultural traits that govern our tolerance of ambiguity, power distance, attitude toward planning, communication styles, and flexibility. Recent research suggests that the influence of national culture on change efforts is stronger than the influence of organizational culture.[53] In her work on the implementation of change, Joyce Osland looks closely at this issue, and our discussion is informed by her observations.[54] Cultures characterized by a high tolerance of ambiguity—that is, cultures that have low uncertainty avoidance—are likely to be more change-friendly. The United States is a prime example. Cultures with high uncertainty avoidance are inclined to avoid change. To lead change in cultures such as Japan, Germany, and France, the process has to be very well outlined and communicated with frequency.

CULTURE FACTS @internationalbiz

Cultures that have high uncertainty avoidance are inclined to avoid change. #highuncertaintyavoidance #avoidchange

SOCIAL MEDIA

People from cultures characterized by high power distance will feel most comfortable with hierarchy and will want top managers to make decisions and issue directives. Likewise, cultures that strongly respect the past are likely to resist change. The influence of these cultural variables suggests that an ability to communicate across cultural borders and build trust is essential for global managers as they drive global change in their organizations.

SUMMARY

LO 11-1

Discuss the importance of creating a company "global mind-set."

A global mind-set "combines an openness to and awareness of diversity across cultures and markets with a propensity and ability to synthesize across this diversity." It has two key components: (1) intellectual intelligence, which includes business acumen, and (2) global emotional intelligence, which includes self-awareness, cross-cultural understanding, cultural adjustment, and cross-cultural effectiveness. The manager with a global mind-set is open to understanding others from different backgrounds, is less judgmental about people from other cultures, and is eager to approach issues from multiple perspectives.

LO 11-2

Describe what distinguishes the practice of global leadership from domestic leadership.

Global leadership is leadership behavior that occurs in a more complex global context, where the challenge is heightened by multiplicity, interdependence, ambiguity, and dynamism. The difference between domestic and global leadership in the level of demands on skills and their applications is so great, and the possible outcomes in a global context can be so profoundly greater, that we can regard global leadership as being different in kind from domestic leadership.

LO 11-3
Identify the competencies required for effective global leadership.

Global leaders require a complex mix of competencies. Various researchers have identified different sets of these, including business acumen; adaptability across cultures; ability to develop individuals from and across diverse cultures; global strategic thinking; ability to establish business in new markets; ability to build global teams; competency in interacting with local political interests; emotional stability; ability to learn; decision-making and negotiating ability; global mind-set; cultural adaptability and flexibility; and tolerance for ambiguity. Others have argued for the importance of (1) a high level of cognitive complexity in order to collect and comprehend contradictory data from a variety of sources and to subsequently make effective decisions; (2) excellent interpersonal skills to enable individuals to understand how to behave within particular countries and situations; (3) capability for learning from experience; and (4) advanced capacity for moral reasoning in order to comprehend ethical dilemmas. The Pyramid Model of Global Leadership identifies five levels of competencies: global knowledge, threshold traits, attitudes and orientations, interpersonal skills, and system skills.

LO 11-4
Distinguish among the approaches for selecting and developing effective global leaders.

The Global Leadership Expertise Development (GLED) model suggests that existing conditions and transformational processes interact to produce global leadership expertise. The "right stuff" model suggests that the basic talent of leadership candidates, combined with their developmental experiences and the context, will help produce the right stuff in terms of skills and capability. However, this model argues that the company's global business strategy is a major determinant of the relevant lessons the global leader needs to learn and the skills that will be developed, and thus what represents the right stuff for a global leader will vary across organizations.

LO 11-5
Describe global team leadership skills.

Global team leadership is an evolving skill. Research suggests it requires all the basic team leadership needs plus the increased awareness and more subtle leadership skills that help the team build on its diversity and its geographic dispersion—all in a context that is increasingly complex. A tool to support understanding of the various cultures of team members is the map-bridge-integrate (MBI) model. An ability to create trust in virtual teams is also an important skill for leaders of global teams.

LO 11-6
Identify some of the challenges of leading global change.

Leading organizational change is always a difficult process, largely because it deals with changing individual behaviors. Global change also requires an ability to quickly grasp cultural differences in an environment characterized by increased levels of multiplicity, interdependence, ambiguity, and flux.

KEY TERMS

global mind-set 294	leadership 294	team norms 306
global team 305	social loafing 308	

CRITICAL THINKING QUESTIONS

1. How can a student with no international experience work on global mind-set, and why is it important to do so?

2. Are good managers also good leaders? Why or why not?

3. A co-worker jealous of her friend's work travel claimed that leadership is just leadership and there is no need to make global leadership a separate category requiring additional training and development. Agree or disagree, explaining your position.

4. Develop a short scenario in which a global leader needs to take three different types of roles.

5. Given what you have learned in this module, would you say that leaders in the international context are born or made? That is, can we train people to be global leaders?

6. Compare and contrast the GLED model and the "right stuff" model of leadership development.

7. What are some things that an aspiring global leader might be able to do to develop his or her global leadership skills?

8. Describe global teams and comment on what makes them more challenging than teams with members from a single nation.

9. Explain the elements that lead to the increased complexity of globalization.

10. How might national culture affect readiness to change? Give an example.

globalEDGE RESEARCH TASK   http://globalEDGE.msu.edu/

Use the globalEDGE website (http://globalEDGE.msu .edu) to complete the following exercises:

1. You've been assigned as the Asia Region Business Manager to your company's offices in China. Find the *culture crossing guide* for China in the "Culture" page of the "Global Insights" section of globalEDGE and review the basic and business-related culture facts for China. Considering the range of roles of a global leader Henry Mintzberg and others identified, as discussed in this chapter, discuss which and how the cultural aspects of China would affect the ways these roles of the global leader are executed in the business environment. What are some of the challenges likely to arise while executing these roles?

2. As the business manager in charge of the Latin American operations of your medical devices company, you are asked by the top management to make a choice between Brazil and Chile and decide on the country your company should invest and build a new manufacturing facility in. Leaving all other aspects of the business aside, compare the different risk factors of two countries in the "By Classification" section of the "Global Insights" of globalEDGE and get ready to discuss your decision and your reasoning with the top management. Explain to them what do the risk factors listed on this page mean and which of them are crucial for your industry and why.

MINICASE

JUSTIN MARSHALL: A FAILED GLOBAL LEADERSHIP OPPORTUNITY?

Justin Marshall earned a bachelor's degree in business, with honors, from a prominent midwestern state university in the United States. After graduation, he worked for two years in finance for a consumer products company and then for two additional years in business development, consistently receiving excellent performance reviews. He then pursued an MBA at one of the top-ranked U.S. universities, ultimately graduating in the top 5 percent of his class. He was recruited by several corporations and accepted a generous offer to work for Compcorp, a prominent computer software and services company. Justin quickly worked his way up the corporate hierarchy. By the age of 31, he had been promoted to divisional vice president for the United States, where he oversaw the transformation of his division from a mediocre performer to one of Compcorp's most profitable units.

Justin's performance as division VP caught the eye of the company's senior executives, and he was offered the opportunity to become VP of the Asia-Pacific region. This division had sales growth but had underperformed major competitors in recent years. Compcorp's executives told Justin they wanted him to replicate his earlier success and transform the Asia-Pacific unit's performance.

Justin leaped at this opportunity. He dreamed of living and working abroad, and he felt confident he could quickly diagnose the unit's problems and turn it around. Within a month, he had transitioned out of his former position, packed up his family, and moved into an apartment near the Hong Kong headquarters of his division. Applying the skills and experiences he had honed in earlier positions, Justin began an aggressive evaluation of his new division. He pored over the financial statements and other documentation, met with dozens of key people throughout the division, and quickly initiated changes to help ratchet up performance. Rigorous reporting requirements and performance reviews were implemented, and Justin met with each of his country managers and other key executives to agree on a set of ambitious cost-cutting and revenue growth targets. He instituted close monitoring of individual unit performance, with results shared across the unit's top managers. As he expected, performance showed a strong uptick during his second quarter as division VP. When he traveled back to headquarters for a quarterly review meeting with his superiors and the heads of other divisions, he proudly pointed out his unit's performance improvements and projected even stronger results for upcoming quarters. He basked in the positive feedback and attention his achievements received from his bosses and was delighted with a substantial performance bonus. Justin felt it was only a matter of time until he was promoted again, perhaps into a senior VP position back at headquarters.

During the months after he returned to Hong Kong, results for his third quarter in office declined slightly, and he was surprised to receive resignation letters from several of his key managers. A few took comparable positions with competitors, and rumors of morale problems began to filter back to the Hong Kong offices. Despite his efforts to turn the situation around, staff departures and performance decline trends continued into Justin's fourth quarter on the job. A team from the U.S. headquarters visited the region several times, meeting with Justin and a number of his executive team members and other subordinates, trying to discern the problem and how to resolve it.

Justin realized he needed to do something soon to reverse the performance trend or his position would be at risk. He initiated a number of rapid changes, yet performance did not improve. Shortly after his unit reported subpar performance for his fifth quarter, he was invited back to company headquarters for a meeting with the company's president. Justin was informed he was being reassigned to a VP position in one of Compcorp's less prestigious domestic units, and that a replacement was being appointed to lead the Asia-Pacific region.

Although it was termed a lateral transfer, Justin knew his reassignment was viewed in the company as a demotion and that his once high-flying career had encountered serious turbulence. Despite his efforts to focus on his new position and reestablish his visibility in the company, he felt his actions were not paying off. Within a year of his transfer back to the States, he left the company to pursue opportunities with a different organization.

Critical Thinking Questions

1. What might explain Justin's failure to perform well in his new leadership role as the head of the Asia-Pacific division?

2. What might Compcorp have done to increase prospects for Justin's successful performance? What might Justin himself have done to enhance the likelihood of success in his new assignment and to help avoid derailing an otherwise highly promising career in Compcorp?

NOTES

1. "Definition of Global Leader," *Financial Times*, 2018. www.lexicon.ft.com.

2. C. A. Bartlett, and S. Ghoshal, *Managing Across Borders: The Transnational Solution*, Boston: Harvard Business School Press, 1989; Vijay Govindarajan, and Anil Gupta, *The Quest for Global Dominance: Transforming Global Presence into Global Competitive Advantage*, San Francisco: Jossey-Bass, 2001, 106; and M. F. R. Kets de Vries, and E. Florent-Treacy, "Global Leadership from A to Z: Creating High Commitment Organizations," *Organizational Dynamics*, vol. 30 (2002), 295–309.

3. Govindarajan and Gupta, *The Quest for Global Dominance*, 111.

4. S. Rhinesmith, "Basic Components of a Global Mindset," in *The Many Facets of Leadership*, eds. M. Goldsmith, V. Govindarajan, and A. Vicere, Upper Saddle River, NJ: Financial Times Prentice Hall, 2003.

5. Govindarajan and Gupta, *The Quest for Global Dominance*, 111.

6. Sunil Nayak, CEO of Sodexo's Corporate Services Asia-Pacific.

7. As identified and reviewed in G. Yukl, *Leadership in Organizations*, 6th ed. (Upper Saddle River, NJ: Pearson Prentice Hall, 2006).

8. Ibid., 6–7.

9. Warren Bennis, *Learning to Lead: A Workbook on Becoming a Leader*, New York: Perseus Books, 1997, 9.

10. Quote by Peter F. Drucker.

11. Executive Insight, *Strengthening the Global Leadership Pipeline*, https://executiveinsight.typepad.com, accessed November 05, 2018.

12. H. W. Lane, M. L. Maznevski, and M. E. Mendenhall, "Hercules Meets Buddha," in *The Handbook of Global Management: A Guide to Managing Complexity*, eds. H. W. Lane, M. Maznevski, M. E. Mendenhall, and J. McNett, Oxford: Blackwell, 2004, 3–25.

13. For example, J. Osland, A. Bird, M. E. Mendenhall, and A. Osland, "Developing Global Leadership Capabilities and Global Mindset: A Review," in *Handbook of Research in International Human Resource Management*, eds. G. K. Stahl and I. Bjorkman (Cheltenham, UK: Edward Elgar, 2006), 197–222; and Ernest Gundling, Terry Hogan, and Karen Cvitkovich, *What Is Global Leadership? 10 Key Behaviors that Define Great Global Leaders*, Boston: Nicholas Brealey Publishing, 2011.

14. D. N. Den Hartog, R. J. House, P. J. Hanges, S. A. Ruiz-Quintanilla, P. W. Dorfman, and Associates, "Culture Specific and Cross-Culturally Generalizable Implicit Leadership Theories: Are Attributes of Charismatic/Transformational Leadership Universally Endorsed?" *Leadership Quarterly*, vol. 10, no. 2, 1999 219–56.

15. This summary is adapted from Michael Hoppe, "Culture and Leader Effectiveness: The GLOBE Study," https://www.inspireimagineinnovate.com/PDF/GLOBEsummary-by-Michael-H-Hoppe.pdf, accessed November 05, 2018.

16. Michael H. Hoppe, "Culture and Leader Effectiveness: The GLOBE Study," *Inspire Imagine Innovate*, September 18, 2007. www.inspireimagineinnovate.com.

17. R. J. House , P. J. Hanges, M. Javidan, P. W. Dorfman, and V. Gupta, *Culture, Leadership, and Organizations: The GLOBE Study of 62 Societies*, Thousand Oaks, CA: Sage, 2004. The follow-up study is *Strategic Leadership Across Cultures: GLOBE Study of CEO Leadership Behavior and Effectiveness in 24 Countries* (Thousand Oaks, CA: Sage, 2014).

18. M. E. Mendenhall, J. S. Osland, A. Bird, G. R. Oddou, and M. L. Maznevski, *Global Leadership: Research, Practice, and Development*, New York: Routledge, 2008, 17.

19. J. S. Osland, and A. Bird, "Global Leaders as Experts," in *Advances in Global Leadership*, vol. 4, ed. W. Mobley and E. Weldon, Stamford, CT: JAI Press, 2006, 123–42.

20. Jenny Paister-Ten, "Leading Across Cultures: Developing Leaders for Global Organizations," Routledge Transpersonal Leadership Series: White Paper Four, https://www.routledge.com/posts/11399, accessed November 05, 2018.

21. Aperian Global, http://www.aperianglobal.com/newsletter_archive/publications_newsletter042.asp, accessed February 8, 2015.

22. H. Mintzberg, *The Nature of Managerial Work*, New York: Harper and Row, 1973; J. P. Kotter, "What Leaders Really Do," *Harvard Business Review*, vol. 68, no. 3, 1990, 103; and J. S. Osland, "The Multidisciplinary Roots of Global Leadership," in *Global Leadership: Research, Practice, and Development*, M. E. Mendenhall, J. S. Osland, A. Bird, G. R. Oddou, and M. L. Maznevski, New York: Routledge, 2008, Ch. 2.

23. J. B. Leslie, M. Dalton, C. Ernst, and J. Deal, *Managerial Effectiveness in a Global Context*, Greensboro, NC: CCL Press, 2002, 63, https://www.ccl.org/wp-content/uploads/2015/04/ccl_managerialeffectiveness.pdf, accessed November 05, 2018.

24. M. Javidan, P. Dorfman, M. Sully de Luque, and R. House, "In the Eye of the Beholder: Cross Cultural Lessons in Leadership from Project GLOBE," *Academy of Management Perspectives*, February 2006, 67–90.

25. A. Bird, and M. J. Stevens, "Mapping the Content Domain of Global Leadership Competencies," in *Global Leadership: Research, Practice, and Development*, M. Mendenhall, J. Osland, A. Bird, et al. London, UK: Routledge, 2013.

26. Andrea Straub-Bauer, consultant, "Overview of Global Leadership Competencies," http://di.dk/globalleadershipacademy/newsandarticles/insights/Pages/GlobalLeadershipCompetenciesanoverview.aspx, accessed February 08, 2015.

27. Cornelius Grove, "Develop Global-Minded Managers without Expensive Expat Assignments," Grovewell, 2018.

28. Kozai Group, "Intercultural Effectiveness Scale (IES)," https://www.kozaigroup.com, accessed November 05, 2018.

29. C. Kelley, and J. Meyers, *The Cross-Cultural Adaptability Inventory*, Minneapolis, MN: National Computer Systems, 1995.

30. M. R. Hammer, M. J. Bennett, and R. Wiseman, "Measuring Intercultural Sensitivity: The Intercultural Development Inventory," *International Journal of Intercultural Relations*, vol. 27, no. 4, 2003, 421–43.

31. Kozai Group Inc. *The Global Competencies Inventory*, St. Louis, MO: Author, 2002; and Kozai Group, "Global Competencies Inventory (GCI)," https://www.kozaigroup.com, accessed November 05, 2018.

32. M. F. R. Kets de Vries, P. Vrignaud, and E. Florent-Treacy, "Global Executive Leadership Inventory: Development and Psychometric Properties of a 360-Degree Feedback Instrument," *International Journal of Human Resource Management*, vol. 15, no. 3, 2004, 475–92.

33. See, for example, M. W. McCall Jr., and G. P. Hollenbeck, *Developing Global Executives: The Lessons of International Experience*, Boston: Harvard Business School Press, 2002.

34. J. Osland, A. Bird, M. E. Mendenhall, and A. Osland, "Developing Global Leadership Capabilities and Global Mindset: A Review," in *Handbook of Research in International Human Resource Management*, eds. G. K. Stahl and I. Björkman (Cheltenham, UK: Edward Elgar, 2006), 197–222; and J. S. Osland, and A. Bird, "Process Models of Global Leadership Development," in *Global Leadership: Research, Practice, and Development*, M. E. Mendenhall, J. S. Osland, A. Bird, G. R. Oddou, and M. L. Maznevski, New York: Routledge, 2008, Ch. 5.

35. Maya Hu-Chan, Alliant University's Global Leadership Development Center.

36. J. Michael Geringer, and W. R. Pendergast, "CEO Views on the Value of International Business Skills and Education," *International Journal of Management and Business*, vol. 1, no. 1, 2010, 12–35.

37. J. Chatman, and J. Kennedy, "Psychological Perspectives on Leadership," in *Handbook of Leadership Theory and Practice*, eds. N. Nohria and R. Khurana, Boston: Harvard Business Press, 2010, 159–83.

38. M. Swann, L. Milton, and J. Polzner, "Should We Create a Niche or Fall in Line? Identity Negotiation and Small Group Effectiveness," *Journal of Personality and Social Psychology*, vol. 79, no. 2, 2000, 238–50.

39. Chatman, and Kennedy, "Psychological Perspectives on Leadership," 166; Tsedal Neeley, "Global Teams That Work: A Framework for Bridging Social Distance," *Harvard Business Review*, October 2015; and V. Govindarajan and A.K. Gupta, "Building an Effective Global Business Team," *Sloan Management Review*, vol. 42, no. 4, Summer 2001.

40. A. Birenbaum, and E. Sagarin, *Norms and Human Behavior*, New York: Praeger, 1976 as referenced in Chatman and Kennedy, "Psychological Perspectives on Leadership"; and V. Govindarajan and A.K. Gupta, "Building an Effective Global Business Team," *Sloan Management Review*, vol. 42, no. 4, Summer 2001.

41. Maznevski Lane, and Mendenhall, "Globalization: Hercules Meets Buddha," 3–25. This portion of the discussion draws on the introduction to the handbook.

42. M. L. Maznevski, "Leading Global Teams," in *Global Leadership: Research, Practice and Development*, M. Mendenhall et al. (London: Routledge, 2008), 94–113. The discussion on global teams is strongly influenced by Maznevski's work. See also Tsedal Neeley, "Global Teams That Work: A Framework for Bridging Social Distance," *Harvard Business Review*, October 2015; and V. Govindarajan and A.K. Gupta, "Building an Effective Global Business Team," *Sloan Management Review*, vol. 42, no. 4 42(4), Summer 2001.

43. H. Lane et al., *International Management Behavior: Leading with a Global Mindset*, Chichester, UK: Wiley, 2009, 79.

44. Tsedal Neeley, "Global Teams That Work: A Framework for Bridging Social Distance," *Harvard Business Review*, October 2015.

45. M. Maznevski, "Leading Global Teams," 108.

46. B. L. Kirkman, and D. N. Den Hartog, "Performance Management in Global Teams," in *The Handbook of Global Management: A Guide to Managing Complexity*, eds. H. W. Lane, M. Maznevski, M. E. Mendenhall, and J. McNett, Oxford: Blackwell, 2004, 250-67; and Tsedal Neeley, "Global Teams That Work: A Framework for Bridging Social Distance," *Harvard Business Review*, October 2015.

47. These suggestions are drawn from the work of Kirkman and Den Hartog, "Performance Management in Global Teams" and Tsedal Neeley, "Global Teams That Work: A Framework for Bridging Social Distance," *Harvard Business Review*, October 2015.

48. J. Osland, "Leading Global Change," in *Global Leadership: Research, Practice and Development*, M. Mendenhall et al., London: Routledge, 2008, 131; and J. G. Clawson, *Level Three Leadership: Getting Below the Surface*, Upper Saddle River, NJ: Prentice Hall, 2006, 6. Joyce Osland's work on international change management has greatly influenced this discussion of change leadership.

49. M. Maznevski, "Global Leadership Issues and Practices," in *International Management Behavior: Leading with a Global Mindset*, H. Lane et al., Chichester, UK: Wiley, 2009, 250.

50. Quote said by Ryunosuke Satoro.

51. K. Lewin, "Frontiers in Group Dynamics," *Human Relations*, vol. 1, 1947, 5-40.

52. J. Kotter, "8 Steps to Accelerate Change," https://www.kotterinc.com, accessed November 05, 2018.

53. T. Savolainen, "Challenges of Intercultural Management: Change Implementation in the Context of National Culture," *Proc. 12th International Conference on ISO 9000 & TQM*, 2007, ed. Samuel Ho, http://www.academia.edu, accessed November 05, 2018.

54. J. Osland, "Building Community through Change," in *The Blackwell Handbook of Global Management: A Guide to Managing Complexity*, eds. H. W. Lane, M. Maznevski, M. E. Mendenhall, and J. McNett, 143-51.

12 International Markets: Assessment and Entry Modes

©Rawpixel.com/Shutterstock.

LEARNING OBJECTIVES
After reading this module, you should be able to:

LO 12-1   **Review** the steps of market screening and techniques for environmental analysis.

LO 12-2   **Discuss** the value of trade missions and trade fairs.

LO 12-3   **Describe** some of the problems market researchers encounter in foreign markets.

LO 12-4   **Explain** international market-entry methods.

Marketing to the Millennials: Global Trends and Differences

Business owners and marketing professionals pay attention to changing demographics and their potential impact on consumer behavior and market opportunities within and across nations and regions of the world. An important target market internationally is the group commonly referred to as "millennials"—those individuals born from about 1982 to 2004. Of course, millennials share many attributes with other populations of consumers, such as baby boomers or generations X or Z. However, market analysts have also identified some interesting traits and trends associated with millennials, as well as how these attributes may vary across countries or regions of the world.

InSites Consulting, an international marketing research firm with offices on four continents, identified "five paradoxical trends" among millennials: (1) amortality (an anti-aging trend reflected in developments such as health and fitness apps and "sportainment" sporting holidays); (2) sharconomy (or shortcut society, reflected in the growth of MOOC [massive open online course] companies like Coursera; Uber ride-sharing; and peer-to-peer lodging such as AirBnB); (3) cloaking (creation of private pages or closed groups on social media sites such as Facebook; desharing and unselfies (deleting or use of self-destructing messages and use of anonymous dark websites); (4) predictable consumer behavior (integrating and analyzing data from online searches and choices to predict consumer preferences and behavior); and (5) serendipity (enjoying "surprises" such as those obtained through coincidental discoveries on social networks or through surprise boxes of cosmetics and skin care products from Bespoke Post or Birchbox).

GlobalWebIndex, a London-based firm collecting and analyzing consumer data, examined the digital behavior of about 37,000 millennials across 40 nations. Among their findings: (1) nearly all millennials owned a smartphone and used it as their most important device for accessing the Internet, with this preference ranging from 55 percent in Europe and 56 percent in North America to 77 percent in the Middle East and Africa and 76 percent in the Asia Pacific; (2) millennials used an average of 2.8 different devices, including phones, computers, and tablets, to spend nearly 4 hours online daily; (3) despite their substantial online activity, broadcast television still consumes more of millennials' daily time; (4) millennials spend 2 hours and 38 minutes per day on social media, with an average of nine social media accounts per user; and (5) while social media activity is an important channel for millennials to conduct product research, traditional commerce sites remain the primary option for online purchase transactions.

GlobalWebIndex also discovered some interesting regional differences in millennials' online activity. In terms of streaming TV, Netflix's penetration was 77 percent in Latin America and 82 percent in North America, but was used in the past month by less than 25 percent of European respondents. iQiyi was the leader for streaming content in the Asia Pacific region, Shahid.net in the Middle East and Africa, and national providers like the BBC's iPlayer in the United Kingdom and France's MYTF1 were the leaders in Europe. While Spotify was the dominant service for music streaming in North America, Latin America, and Europe, QQ Music and Kugou were the leaders in the Asia Pacific. For online gaming, 25 percent of respondents worldwide owned game consoles, with the popularity of these devices being greatest in North America (56 percent), followed by Europe and Latin America at 35 percent each. In contrast, the Asia Pacific and the Middle East and Africa reported the greatest tendency to use smartphones for gaming, at 75 and 74 percent, respectively, versus a low of 59 percent in Europe. While 46 percent of millennials in the Asia Pacific used ad-blocking software monthly, in North America and Europe the percentages were 27 and 25, respectively.

In the United States alone, millennials account for one-quarter of the overall population and, by 2020, worldwide this group will spend $1.4 trillion annually. What might demographic traits and trends such as these mean to businesspeople and marketers trying to identify the best markets worldwide for their products and services? How could these insights be best used in order to focus market entry or expansion efforts?

Sources: Philip Bump, "Here Is When Each Generation Begins and Ends, According to Facts," *The Atlantic*, March 25, 2014, www.theatlantic.com; "InSites Consulting," *InSites nv*, 2018, www.insites-consulting.com; "Millennials: Examining the Attitudes and Digital Behaviors of Internet Users Aged 21–34," *Trendstream Limited*, 2018; Dan Schawbel, "10 New Findings About the Millennial Consumer," *Forbes*, January 20, 2015; and Cassandra Wade, "Marketing to Millennials: Trends You'll See in 2018," January 08, 2018, www.universalwilde.com.

market screening
A modified version of environmental scanning in which the firm identifies desirable markets by eliminating the less desirable ones

environmental scanning
A procedure in which the firm scans the world for changes in the environmental forces that might affect it

Market Screening Approaches and Techniques

International environmental forces can complicate our efforts to assess the attractiveness of foreign markets for potential expansion. While companies have used a range of approaches to assess foreign markets, many of them tend to be unsystematic and prone to error. Here we offer a more systematic, structured approach to the international market screening process.

Market screening is an application of environmental scanning in which the firm identifies markets by using analysis of the environmental forces active in markets to eliminate the less desirable ones. **Environmental scanning** is a broader procedure in which a firm scans the world for changes in the environmental forces that might affect it.[2] For some time, environmental scanning has been used by managers during the strategic planning process to provide information about world threats and opportunities that could influence the context in which the firm operates. Those who do environmental scanning professionally may belong to organizations such as the Society of Competitive Intelligence Professionals (www.scip.org). If the firm does not have the internal capability, environmental scanning services are available from a number of private firms such as Smith Brandon International (www.smithbrandon.com) and Stratfor (www.stratfor.com).

In market screening, the firm reviews markets based on the market's basic need potential and the external environmental forces in the market, such as economic, financial, political, legal, and cultural conditions. Although these forces may be placed in any order in a screening, the arrangement suggested in Figure 12.1 progresses from the least to the most difficult analysis based on the accessibility and subjectivity of the data. In this way, the smallest number of candidates is left for the final, most difficult—and hence, most costly—screening.

Market screening is useful both for the firm selling exclusively in the domestic market but aware that it possibly might increase sales by expanding into foreign markets, and for the firm that is already an international company (IC) and wants to avoid missing potential new markets. In both situations, market screening provides an ordered, relatively fast method of analyzing and assessing the nearly 200 countries (and multiple market segments within countries) to pinpoint the best prospects.

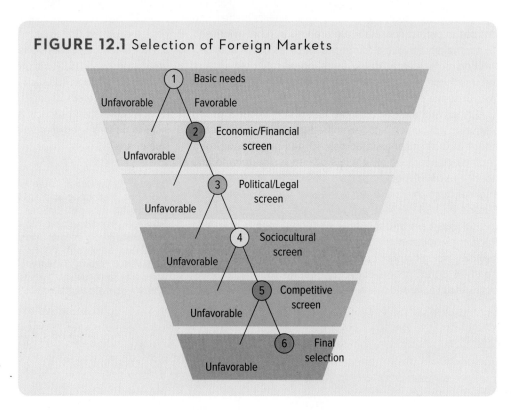

FIGURE 12.1 Selection of Foreign Markets

In this module, we will look at two levels of market screening: **country screening**, using countries as the relevant unit of analysis, and **segment screening**, using a within-country analysis of groups of consumers. The initial screening is for the basic needs potential and eliminates countries that do not have a basic need for the product under consideration.

INITIAL SCREENING—BASIC NEEDS POTENTIAL

An initial screening based on the basic need potential is a logical first step because if the need for the good or service is lacking, no reasonable expenditure of effort and money will enable the firm to successfully market goods for which there is no need potential. For example, the basic need potential of some goods depends on various physical forces, such as climate, topography, and natural resources. If the firm produces air conditioners, the analyst will look for countries with warm climates. Makers of large farm tractors might not consider Switzerland a likely prospect because of its mountainous terrain. Builders of large yachts might consider a landlocked country such as Paraguay to be an unattractive potential market, and areas known to have humid climates are not likely markets for humidifiers. In areas such as Singapore, where there are small apartments known as shoe-boxes, there may be a market for low-profile, small-scale furniture.

The basic need potential of some goods is easy to assess. For example, producers of specialized industrial materials or equipment such as heavy-duty snow-removal equipment find little difficulty in assessing their basic need potential. With less specialized products that are widely consumed, assessing basic need potential can be more challenging. For example, establishing a basic need for chocolate, consumer robots, or movies in ultra HD is difficult, because for these products we are addressing desires rather than needs.

There are many public sources for data to use in establishing the basic need potential. A list of firms in an industry is available from the industry's association and from specialized trade media. A builder of cement kilns can obtain the names and addresses of cement plants worldwide through the website of the Portland Cement Association. Analysts who want to know where U.S. competitors are exporting their products can go to the International Trade Administration (ITA) at www.trade.gov. The U.S. Department of Commerce also has the report, *U.S. Exports of Merchandise*, on the National Trade Data Bank (NTDB), which is available online by subscription. This report's information is especially useful because it includes both units and dollar values, permitting the analyst to calculate the average price of the unit exported. Many national government trade or commerce offices compile foreign trade statistics. The U.S. Department of Commerce releases a monthly report, *U.S. International Trade in Goods and Services*, commonly referred to as the FT900. In addition, *country market surveys* published by many countries indicate products for which there is an established market in a given country. For example, the data office of the European Union (Eurostat) publishes an annual, *External Trade*, and JETRO (the Japanese External Trade Organization) publishes a wide assortment of trade and industry data.

Be aware, though, that imports do not completely measure a market's potential. Trade flows show the magnitude of current sales, but imports may not be the whole story on market potential. There could be poor marketing, lack of foreign exchange, and high prices (potentially caused by transportation, duties, and markups). Nor can imports give much indication of the potential demand for a brand new product.

Import data indicate only that a market has been buying certain products from abroad, and are no guarantee that these imports will continue. A competitor may decide to produce locally, which, in many markets, will cause imports to cease. Change in a country's political situation also may reduce or eliminate imports, as in present-day Syria or Yemen. Nevertheless, import data do provide the firm with a conservative estimate of the immediate market potential at the going price. If local production is being considered and calculations show that goods produced in the country could be sold at a lower price, the firm might reasonably expect to sell more than the quantity currently being imported.

country screening
A screening that uses countries as the basis for market selection

segment screening
A screening that uses market segments, a within-country analysis of groups of consumers, as the basis for market selection

SECOND SCREENING—FINANCIAL AND ECONOMIC FORCES

After the initial screening, the analyst will have a much smaller list of prospects. Then a second screening based on financial and economic forces further reduces the list of potential markets. The major areas of concern here are trends in inflation, currency exchange rates, and interest rates. Other financial factors, such as credit availability, paying habits of customers, and rates of return on similar investments, are also important. This screening, though, is not a complete financial analysis. That occurs later if the market analysis and assessment disclose that a country has sufficient potential for capital investment.

Two measures of market demand based on economic data are especially useful at this point: *market indicators* and *market factors.* In addition, *trend analysis* and *cluster analysis,* both of which depend on economic data, may be used to estimate demand.

Over the next few years, the number of online shoppers in Latin America is expected to grow annually by more than 10 percent. According to Table 12.1A and Table 12.1B, Brazil has the largest number of online buyers and also the largest overall e-commerce market.

Economic data that serve as yardsticks for measuring the relative market strengths of various geographic areas are known as **market indicators**. As an example, an analyst might develop an index of e-commerce potential for Latin America and key markets within that region by collecting and ranking data of the sort found in Tables 12.1A, 12.1B, and 12.1C, so that the countries in the region could be compared. The data would include indicators of the strength and growth rate of the overall economy, as well as factors related more

market indicators
Economic data used to measure relative market strength of countries or geographic areas

TABLE 12.1A Latin America E-Commerce Market Growth, 2018–2022 (US$ billions)

	2018	2019	2020	2021	2022
Total Retail Sales (US$ billions)	1,988	2,094	2,189	2,270	2,354
Number of E-Commerce Buyers (millions)	131	142	153	163	174
Average E-Commerce Revenue per Buyer (U.S. dollars)	290.2	304.9	318.0	329.6	342.5

TABLE 12.1B B2C Sales in Latin America, by Country, 2018–2022 (US$ billions)

	2018	2019	2020	2021	2022
Argentina	5.0	5.7	6.3	6.9	7.4
Brazil	21.3	23.9	26.6	29.2	31.7
Mexico	10.3	12.0	13.6	15.3	16.9

TABLE 12.1C Number of Digital Buyers in Latin America, by Country, 2018–2022 (millions)

	2018	2019	2020	2021	2022
Argentina	26	26	26	27	28
Brazil	73	80	87	95	101
Mexico	40	43	46	49	51

Sources: eMarketer, *Latin America E-commerce 2018,* https://www.emarketer.com, accessed November 10, 2018; "Latin American Commerce," https://www.eshopworld.com/blog/latin-american-e-commerce, accessed November 10, 2018; Statista, https://www.statista.com, accessed November 10, 2018; and author estimates.

specifically to e-commerce or communications that would aid the growth of e-commerce. Three indices suggest themselves for this analysis, with each indicator given equal weight:

$$\text{Market size} = \text{Size of urban population} + \text{Electricity consumption}$$

$$\text{Market growth rate} = \text{Average growth rate in commercial energy use} + \text{Real GDP growth rate}$$

$$\text{E-commerce readiness} = \text{Mobile phones per 1,000} + \text{PCs per 1,000} + \text{Internet hosts per million people}$$

The rankings on these three indexes could then be used to form a composite ranking.

Market factors are similar to market indicators except they tend to correlate highly with the market demand for a given product. If analysts of a foreign market have no factor for that market, they may be able to use one from the domestic market or a comparable subsidiary to provide an approximation for the foreign market. To be able to transfer these relationships to the country under study, the analysts must assume that the underlying conditions affecting demand are similar in the two markets. This process, called *estimation by analogy*, can be quite helpful. If, for example, we are a smartphone supplier and know that one in five Ugandans replaces his or her smartphone each year, we might use the same relationship to estimate demand for replacement tablets in a new, similar market. If there are 3 million existing smartphones in the new market, we might forecast that 3 million × 0.20, or 600,000, replacement tablets will be sold annually. The constant in the country under study may be somewhat different, but the estimates will represent a reasonable approximation and a base from which further analysis can be conducted. Many such factors exist, and generally, research personnel are familiar with them.

When analysts know the historical growth rates of either the relevant economic variables or the imports of a product, they can forecast future growth by means of **trend analysis**, a statistical technique used to estimate future values by successive observations of a variable at regular time intervals that suggest patterns. In trend analysis, a time series similar to a regression model, or the arithmetic mean of past growth rates, may be applied to historical data. When using growth rates, remember to make adjustments or develop alternate scenarios, because trend analysis assumes that past conditions affecting the dependent variable will remain constant. If the average annual growth rate is applied mechanically, in just a few years, the dependent variable may reach an incredible size. For example, a 5 percent growth rate, compounded annually, will result in a doubling of the original value in only 15 years.

As multinationals expand their presence to more markets, managers are searching for ways to group countries and geographic regions by common characteristics. **Cluster analysis** divides objects (market areas, individuals, customers, and other variables) into groups so that the variables within each group are similar. A team of college softball players sitting at a table in a restaurant might constitute a small cluster, while users of iPhones and Android phones might be two different clusters. Marketers use cluster analysis to identify a group of markets where a single promotional approach can be employed; attorneys use it to group nations according to similarities in certain types of laws, and anthropologists use it to group similar cultures. In other words, cluster analysis is used to classify a "mountain" of information into meaningful "piles."

THIRD SCREENING—POLITICAL AND LEGAL FORCES

The elements of the political and legal forces that can eliminate a market from further consideration or make it more attractive are many. We review those that most impact the IC, including barriers to entry, government controls, stability of government policy, and political stability.

Entry barriers to ICs may be established by the host government. Import restrictions can be positive or negative, depending on whether managers are considering whether to

market factors
Economic data that correlate highly with market demand for a product

trend analysis
Statistical technique used to estimate future values by successive observations of a variable at regular time intervals that suggest patterns

cluster analysis
Statistical technique that divides objects into groups based on similarity

Should Africa Be the Next Priority Market for International Companies?

The population of the 50 countries designated by the United Nations Statistics Division as comprising sub-Saharan Africa exceeded 1 billion people in 2018. By 2060, the region's population could reach 2.7 billion, nearly four times Europe's projected population of 702 million, and it will be home to the ten nations globally that have the youngest average population age. This population growth rate reflects traditionally high birth rates combined with declining rates of infant mortality and increased life expectancy. The population of Nigeria alone is projected to exceed that of the United States by 30 million people in 2060. Compared to projections of declining populations for many developed nations, some view the sub-Saharan region as poised for an exciting future, one rich with opportunity for achieving economic growth, attracting foreign investment to employ the abundant pool of working-age adults, and meeting the infrastructural and consumer needs of a large and expanding population.

The World Bank projected an economic growth rate of 3.4 percent in 2018 for sub-Saharan Africa, sustaining the region's position as among the two most rapidly growing economic areas in the world. About one-third of the sub-Saharan nations have been posting growth rates of 6 percent or more, and another 40 percent have been growing 4 to 6 percent annually. Although about 60 percent of the region's GDP is currently concentrated in three nations—Nigeria, South Africa, and Angola—the World Bank expects most nations in the region will achieve "middle income" status by 2025 and that the combined GDP will be $29 trillion by 2050. Continued policy developments targeted toward structural areas, including governance, education, health, labor market, and business climate reform, could help enhance the attainment of the region's growth potential. Many people believe the region has reached a critical tipping point where the rich natural resource base, the abundant population of working-age people, and the rapid pace of technological innovation combine to fuel a sustained growth phase similar to that experienced by East Asia's Tiger economies.

However, the diverse set of nations comprising the region suggests that growth will be uneven across countries. Many nations in the region suffer from severe poverty, low levels of education, inadequate housing stock, underdeveloped transportation infrastructure, lack of clean water or adequate sanitation, and a history of corruption, weak legal systems, and other institutional gaps. Foreign investment and international support will be essential for leveraging domestic capabilities and achieving the region's potential as an attractive market for international

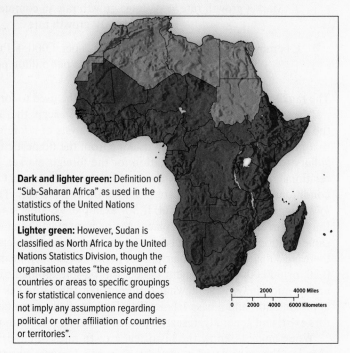

Dark and lighter green: Definition of "Sub-Saharan Africa" as used in the statistics of the United Nations institutions.
Lighter green: However, Sudan is classified as North Africa by the United Nations Statistics Division, though the organisation states "the assignment of countries or areas to specific groupings is for statistical convenience and does not imply any assumption regarding political or other affiliation of countries or territories".

companies. As noted by Chief of the International Monetary Fund's Regional Studies Division Papa N'Diaye, "weak private investment has weighed on growth." Director of the Macroeconomic Policy Division at the Economic Commission for Africa Adam Elhiraika stated, "Mobilizing domestic revenue and private investment is critical for Africa, given the infrastructure gaps and rising cost of external borrowing."

Critical Thinking Questions

1. What might make sub-Saharan Africa an attractive market for entry by international companies? Which types of firms or products might be expected to do best? Why?

2. What arguments could be made for why sub-Saharan Africa would not represent an attractive market for entry by international companies? Explain your reasoning.

Sources: David Canning, Sangeeta Raja, and Abdo S. Yazbeck, *Africa's Demographic Transition: Dividend or Disaster?* Washington, DC: World Bank Publications, October 22, 2015; "Sub Saharan Africa Population 2018," *World Population Review*, November 10, 2018; and "Growth in Sub-Saharan Africa Projected at 3.4 Percent in 2018," *United Nations Economic Commission for Africa*, 2018, www.uneca.org.

serve the market by exporting (can the firm's products enter the country?) or by setting up a foreign plant (will competitive imports be kept out?). If an entry objective includes 100 percent ownership, will the nation's laws permit it, or is some local participation required? Put another way, will the government accept minority local ownership, or does the country require that a minimum percentage of the subsidiary be controlled by nationals? Are there laws that reserve certain industries for either the government or its citizens?[4] Is the host government demanding that the foreign owner turn over technology to its proposed affiliate that the foreign owner prefers to keep at the home-country plant? Perhaps the host government has local content restrictions that the prospective investor considers excessive. There may be a government-owned company that would compete with the proposed plant. Depending on the circumstances and how strongly management wishes to enter the market, any one of these conditions may be sufficient to eliminate a nation from further consideration.

When there are no objectionable barriers to entry, a market may still be excluded if management believes there are undue restrictions on the repatriation of earnings. For example, the host government may set limits on allowable repatriation of profits linked to the amount of foreign investment or other criteria, or the nation may have a history of inability to provide foreign exchange for profit remittances.

Stability of government policy is another consideration. Is there continuity in policy when a new leader takes office, for example? What is the political climate? Is the government stable, or is there infighting among government leaders? Public life must also be examined. Is there visible unrest? Do the armed forces have a history of intervention when there are public disturbances? Business can adapt to any form of government and thrive, as long as the conditions are stable. But instability creates uncertainty, and this complicates planning. An often-heard complaint is, "They've changed the rules again." Note the distinction between *political stability* and *policy stability*. Rulers may come and go, but if the policies that affect businesses do not change very much, these political changes really may not affect the firm. In fact, if we measure political stability in terms of changes in leadership at the top, the United States is politically unstable compared with many countries, since top leadership can change every four years! Sources for political and policy stability analysis are many, such as Stratfor (www.stratfor .com); Business Environment Risk Intelligence S.A. (www.beri.com); the Economist Intelligence Unit (www.economist.com); and the PRS Group (www.prsgroup.com), all of which publish rankings that compare countries on the issue of political risk.

U.S. manufacturer Vogmask wants to sell fashion face masks in Asia.
©Bobby Yip/REUTERS/Newscom.

FOURTH SCREENING—CULTURAL FORCES

A screening of the remaining candidates on the basis of cultural factors is next and is often an arduous process. First, recognition of cultural factors is a fairly subjective and interpretive process. The analyst, unless a specialist in the country, must rely on the perceptions and opinions of others. Second, data are difficult to assemble, particularly from a distance. Fortunately, consultants who are "old hands" with experience in the country or region are available. Some may have a particular methodology, such as Clotaire Rapaille, whose approach is described in the minicase at the end of this module. Professional organizations and universities also hold seminars to explain the cultural aspects of doing business in a particular area or country.

After the fourth screening, the analyst should have a list of countries for which an industry demand appears to exist. Now we want to know which of these potential markets seems to offer the best prospects for the firm's products. A fifth screening based on the competitive forces will help provide this information.

FIFTH SCREENING—COMPETITIVE FORCES

In this screening, we examine markets on the basis of competitive forces such as:

1. The number, size, and financial strength of the competitors.
2. Their market shares.
3. Their marketing strategies.
4. The apparent effectiveness of their promotional programs.
5. The quality levels of their product lines.
6. The source of their products—imported or locally produced.
7. Their pricing policies.
8. The levels of their after-sales service.
9. Their distribution channels.
10. Their coverage of the market. (Could market segmentation produce niches that are currently poorly served?)

Examining regional or ethnic subcultures in a particular foreign market may be important, as the topic of market coverage suggests. These subcultures may be natural or at least identifiable segments for which specific marketing programs may be successful. For example, 1.5 million Japanese descendants live in Brazil, about half of all the ethnic Japanese outside of Japan. There is also a significant ethnic-Brazilian presence in Japan. In this screening, we eliminate countries where research shows that strong competitors would make a profitable operation difficult to attain unless the firm is following a strategy of being present wherever its global competitors are or believes entering a competitor's home market will distract the competitor's attention from that market.

FINAL SELECTION OF NEW MARKETS

Although much can be accomplished through analysis, there is no substitute for personal visits to markets that appear to have the best potential. An executive or company team should visit those countries that still appear to be good prospects, having reviewed the screening data along with any new information that the researcher can supply. Preparing a list of points on which they wanted to gather more information on their visit would be useful here. The goal of the visit is to corroborate what was learned from the five screenings, the desk research phase. A trip report would include firsthand observations on the market, including competitive activity, appraisal of the suitability of the firm's current marketing mix, and availability of support services (such as warehousing, media agencies, and credit).

This field trip should not be hurried as much time as should be allotted to this part of the study as would be spent on a similar domestic field trip. The point is to develop a feel for what is going on, and this cannot be accomplished quickly. The need is to see what is there and not operate on assumptions. For example, while Japanese youths model themselves after American basketball stars by wearing Nike sneakers, an observer of athletic shoe use in Japan might notice that these kids change into off-brand sneakers when they actually play basketball. Or it seems to be relatively more common for men to shop in grocery stores in Chile, as compared with elsewhere in Latin America. And in East Asia, there is not much of a tradition of men taking on the "do-it-yourself" home improvement projects for which Home Depot and similar brands are famous. These types of observations are not likely to be available without actual, substantive visits to the potential new market.

In many cases, the field trip report will provide the final data for the decision. Sometimes, though, the company's required financial and people commitments are so

Uniqlo Tries to Succeed in U.S. Fashion Clothing Market

Uniqlo, known for providing high-quality private-label casualwear at low prices, is a wholly owned subsidiary of Fast Retailing Company Ltd. of Japan. The biggest apparel chain in Asia with about 800 retail sites, Uniqlo is currently opening about 100 stores per year in China and expects to have over 1,000 stores there by 2021. The brand's designs are simple, reflecting Japanese minimalist traditions and the company's philosophy of "Made for All."

In 2017, Fast Retailing had revenues of $17.3 billion and profits of $1.6 billion, with Japan contributing 44 percent of total revenues. *Forbes* reported that Uniqlo has a brand value of $7 billion, placing the company 91st among the world's most valuable brands. Uniqlo aims to achieve sales of $28 billion by 2020, based largely on international expansion. If it achieves this target, Uniqlo would become the world's largest apparel company.

Uniqlo store in Tokyo, Japan.
©Mark Eite/Aflo Co. Ltd./Alamy Stock Photo.

When a brand achieves a position of leadership in its home country and region, a logical next step is to seek opportunities for expansion in other regions. This is especially the case for Uniqlo, which targeted the United States as an expansion priority. Up until now, however, Uniqlo has experienced considerable challenges in extending its brand within the highly competitive U.S. market.

The label's first effort to crack the U.S. market came in 2005, with stores opening in three different suburban New Jersey shopping malls. This effort failed and the stores were closed two years later.

Uniqlo changed tack and opened a store in New York's trendy SoHo fashion district, followed by two additional, large New York sites in 2011. At the time, the company announced a goal of 200 stores and $10 billion in U.S. sales by 2020. Uniqlo rapidly opened new stores, including many in shopping malls, reaching 20 locations by 2014. Still, performance fell short of expectations, leading to the closure of several mall-based stores.

The company reflected on its second failed market expansion effort before developing and launching a third assault on the U.S. market. Although viewed as a market Uniqlo must be present in, Chief Marketing Officer Masahiko Nakasuji stated, "We have a very, very low presence" in the United States. The brand has once again tweaked its strategy for becoming a mainstay in the American shopping scene. In addition to retreating from its previous goal of 200 U.S. stores, the retailer shuttered stores in suburban malls in favor of larger locations in cities like Boston, Chicago, and Washington, D.C. "That's probably the best way to let the people understand what we are selling," said Nakasuji, "We have a very big brand in Asia, but in the U.S. . . . we need to let the people know about our product."

One problem is that Uniqlo doesn't do a great job communicating the quality and functionality of their products to the American consumer. Because prices are comparable to fast-fashion competitors like H&M, Zara, and Forever 21, many consumers assume Uniqlo's products are also low quality and disposable. When the company attempted to raise prices in 2015 to reflect their higher quality, customers balked and sales flattened. Meanwhile, the brand has a limited number of styles and size ranges, and consumers often complain that Uniqlo's clothes are designed for Asian body types. American consumers often have a different, larger body structure, making it harder to find Uniqlo apparel that fits well. Uniqlo's minimalist approach to clothing design may also need to be modified. As Chief Executive Tadashi Yanai said, "unless [the clothing] shows sexiness, it doesn't really sell" in the United States. But reworking Uniqlo's designs for the U.S. market may complicate international production and logistical practices and undercut profitability.

The challenge of Uniqlo's restart in the United States is compounded by its timing. Not only are online retailers like Amazon taking a larger share of the market, but the fast-fashion space is crowded. Despite having 53 U.S. stores at the end of 2018, the company's brand is still relatively unknown outside of major urban areas. Uniqlo's success in extending its international reach into the critical U.S. market may rest upon its ability to break out from the competition.

Sources: Krystina Gustafson, "As Retailers Close Stores, the World's Third-largest Apparel Player Takes Another Run at the U.S.," *CNBC*, March 29, 2017, www.cnbc.com; Adrianne Pasquarelli, "Why Uniqlo Is Done Chasing Trends and How It Will Conquer U.S. Consumerism," *Advertising Age*, March 30, 2017, www.adageindia.in; "Uniqlo: The Strategy Behind the Global Japanese Fast Fashion Retail Brand," *Martin Roll*, July 2018, www.martinroll.com; and Kathy Chu, Ken Brown, and Mayumi Negishi, "Uniqlo's Parent Presses to Become World's Top Retailer," *The Wall Street Journal*, March 05, 2014, www.wsj.com.

great that management will want to have data gathered in the potential market rather than depend solely on desk research and field reports. This could be the position of a consumer products manufacturer that plans to enter a large competitive market of an industrialized country. It might also be the recommendation of the manager making the field trip if the market conditions are seen to be substantially different from those to which the firm has been accustomed. In face-to-face interviews, information is often revealed that would never be written. In these situations, research in the local market will supply information about market definition and its future projection and will also assist in the formulation of an effective marketing mix.

SEGMENT SCREENING

When a company intends to do business in several countries, managers can choose two broad market screening approaches: country or segment. In the first approach, Brazil may be viewed as a target market segment. Using the second approach, while Brazil is the physical location of a large group of consumers, the important variables for segmentation are shared needs and wants among consumers *across nationalities*. These consumers may reside in different countries and speak different languages, but they have similar desires for a product or service. From this perspective, age, income, and psychographics (lifestyles) are the essential means of identifying market segments. The relevant marketing question is not where consumers reside but whether they share similar wants and needs. The targeted consumers might be global teens, middle-class executives, or young families with small children; each of these segments may share wants and needs across borders.

When we identify and assess segments, it is important that they be:

1. *Definable.* We should be able to identify and measure segments. The more we rely on lifestyle differences rather than socioeconomic indicators, the more difficult this becomes, but the more accurate the resulting analysis is likely to be.

2. *Large.* Segments should be large enough to be worth the effort needed to serve a segment and have the potential for growth in the future. Of course, as we adopt 3D printer manufacturing, the need to find large segments is beginning to recede for some products, including clothing and other consumer products, perhaps leading to a further wave of localization.

3. *Accessible.* If we cannot reach our target segment for either promotional or distribution purposes, we will be unsuccessful.

4. *Actionable.* If we cannot bring into play the components of marketing programs (the 4 Ps of product, promotion, place, and price), we may not be successful. For example, in Mexico, the price of tortillas was formerly controlled by the government. Therefore, competition on the price variable was impossible. Foreigners could not penetrate the Mexican market for the standard tortilla by offering a lower price.

5. *Capturable.* Although we would love to discover market segments whose needs are completely unmet, in many cases these market segments are already being served. Nonetheless, we may still be able to compete. Where segments are completely captured by the competition, however, our task is much more difficult.

In the final analysis, our view of the rest of the world tends to be organized along national lines. However, attempting to leave that viewpoint behind when examining international markets may be useful. With the increasing recognition of subcultures *within* nations and similarities among subcultures *across* nations, we may wish to expand our horizon beyond the conventional view of the nation as the relevant unit of analysis.

Trade Missions and Trade Fairs

When government trade specialists perceive a foreign market opportunity for an industry, they may organize a **trade mission**, a market visit by businesspeople and/or government officials in search of business opportunities. The purpose is to send executives from firms in the industry to a country or group of countries to learn firsthand about the market, meet important customers face-to-face, and make contact with people interested in representing their products. Because of discounted airfares, hotels, and hospitality during the visit, the cost to the firm may be less than if the firm's managers visited on their own. Moreover, the impact of a group visit often is greater than that of an individual company's visit. Before the mission's arrival, consulate or embassy officials will have publicized the visit and made contact with local, interested companies. A country's federal government, state governments, trade associations, chambers of commerce, and other export and development-oriented organizations also organize trade missions.

Many nations hold periodic **trade fairs**, large exhibitions at which companies promote the sale of their products. Trade fairs are open to the public, but during certain hours (generally mornings), entrance is limited to businesspeople interested in doing business with the exhibitors.

Many fairs in developing countries are general, with displays of many kinds of products, such as the China Import and Export Fair in Shanghai, China, which in 2018 had over 25,000 exhibitors and over 200,000 buyers in 1.2 million square meters of exhibition space.[6] In contrast, fairs in Europe are usually specialized. Several examples are the CeBIT computer trade fair, the Paris Air Show, and the Frankfurt Book Fair.

In addition to making contact with prospective buyers and agents (direct sales are often made during these meetings), most exhibitors use these trade fairs to learn more about the market and gather competitive intelligence. They also receive feedback from visitors to their exhibits and have the opportunity to observe their competitors in action.

LO 12-2
Discuss the value of trade missions and trade fairs.

trade mission
A market visit by business people and/or government officials (state or federal) in search of business opportunities

trade fair
A large exhibition at which companies promote the sale of their products

The CeBIT trade fair is the largest computer expo, held annually in Hanover, Germany.[5]
©John Macdougall/AFP/Getty Images.

LO 12-3
Describe some of the problems market researchers encounter in foreign markets.

Research in the Local Market and as Practiced

When a firm's research personnel have had no experience in the targeted country, often management brings in a local research group to do the work. Generally, home-country research techniques may be used, though they may need to be adapted to local conditions. The person in charge of the project needs to have experience either in that country or in one that is culturally similar and preferably in the same geographic area. If secondary data are unavailable in the market, the researchers must collect primary data, and here they face other complications caused by cultural problems and technical difficulties.[7]

If the researchers are from one culture and are working in another, they may encounter a series of cultural problems. When they are not proficient in the local language or dialect, the research instrument or the respondents' answers must be translated. A number of languages may be spoken in a country (for example, there are 31 endangered languages in Italy), and even in countries where only one language is used, a word's meaning may change from one region to another.[8] For example, the Spanish word "chucha" is used in Colombia to describe armpit odor that is bad, while the same term in Argentina refers to a woman's reproductive organ and, in Chile, something that is distant may be referred to as "esta a la chucha."[9] The meaning of the Spanish term "buzo" is diver, but it refers to sweatpants in Chile and Costa Rica, a sweatshirt in Argentina, and in Guatemala, it refers to someone with expertise at doing a task.

Researchers encounter other cultural problems as they try to collect data. Low levels of literacy may make the use of mail questionnaires virtually impossible. If a husband is interviewed in a market where the wife usually makes the buying decisions, the data obtained from him may be worthless. Nor is it always clear who should be interviewed. Respondents sometimes refuse to answer questions because of their general distrust of strangers. In other instances, the respondent's desire to please may lead to answers calculated to please the interviewer; this is known as **social desirability bias**.

Often, people have practical reasons for not wanting to be interviewed. In some countries, income taxes are based on the apparent worth of individuals as measured by their tangible assets. In such countries, when asked if there is a stereo or TV in the household, the respondent may suspect the interviewer of being a tax assessor and refuse to answer. To overcome such a problem, experienced researchers often hire college students as interviewers because their manner of speech and their dress correctly identify them as what they are.

Researchers may also encounter various technical difficulties. Up-to-date maps are often unavailable. The streets chosen for sampling may have three or four different names along their length, and the houses may not be numbered. In Japan, a grid system is used for addresses rather than street names and numbers, and it is said in Tokyo only cab drivers can find street addresses. In Venice, Italy, street signs can be 600 years old and impossible to read.[11]

Despite the many hindrances encountered in carrying out foreign market research, marketers persist. As you might assume from the availability of secondary data, marketing research is highly developed in many areas where markets are large and incorrect decisions are costly. Among the approaches are collaborative online research communities and the use of big data.

Online research communities (known under a variety of names such as Market Research Online Communities or MROCs) are a new trend in market research. These are online platforms that connect a company with a group of interested consumers to collaborate with them in qualitative research projects. InSites Consulting, discussed in the opening vignette, found that consumers are ready to help co-create the future of brands and products/services. InSites also found that in Asia, a mobile app increases engagement: mobile users logged in 2.3 times more, viewed 1.4 more pages, and made 65 percent more contributions to the discussion than nonmobile participants.[12]

SOCIAL MEDIA

social desirability bias
The respondent's desire to please that leads to answers designed to please the interviewer rather than reflect the respondent's true beliefs or feelings

Many of us live in international markets, yet the art of catering to multiple cultures has yet to be perfected, and we face multiple barriers in our attempts to market to an international audience. Identifying a market need, a basic element of starting a business, becomes more complex in a foreign country. After all, these countries have different cultures, priorities, and needs for their day-to-day lives than a typical domestic consumer, and just as in the home market, those needs will vary among communities. As one of the largest pizza chains in the world, Pizza Hut has some experience in the international arena, with more than 16,000 restaurants in over 100 nations.[13] In the chain's recent efforts to boost profits, it gathered data about customers' preferences and then broke down its customer base into clusters and microclusters based on consumer purchasing habits, characteristics, and other behaviors. These microgroups can then be targeted with specific engagement programs across channels, such as in Pizza Hut restaurants or the chain's website.

The increasing ability of firms to access vast amounts of data on customers and market trends is creating an opportunity often described as "big data." **Big data** refers to the massive sets of data, both structured and unstructured, that businesses are collecting, which can be analyzed with advanced data analysis methods such as predictive analytics or user behavior analytics to provide valuable insights into consumer needs and trends. Retailers are using data analytics to improve their market positioning efforts. For example, the top management team in one business unit of an Asian retailer devoted 60 to 70 percent of its time over the course of a decade to visiting over 3,000 potential store locations.[14] This time expenditure was an inefficient use of senior managers' time and skills. So the company developed an artificial intelligence–powered modeling tool to identify factors associated with high- and low-performing retail locations. Applying this tool, within only a few weeks the company was able to identify over 1,000 potential store locations, saving valuable time and expense. The company then used this big-data approach to scan for retail locations in other markets.

Ironically, big data analytics will also play a part in literally personalizing the shopping experience. This trending form of analytics in fashion and other consumer goods will be able to identify each visitor and customize the experience accordingly. The online e-commerce platform is able to suggest products that link to the history of purchases and to the profile of the customer making the purchase.

Banks know a lot about their customers, too. As the ability to process large amounts of data becomes ubiquitous, banks are discovering that big data can be good for far more than fighting fraud. One way of using data is to try to sell customers more products. Santander sends out weekly lists to its branches of customers who it thinks may be interested in particular offers from the bank, such as home insurance. Some of the products banks are offering through this targeted process are not even financial. In Singapore, Citigroup keeps an eye on customers' card transactions for opportunities to offer them discounts in stores and restaurants. Citi opened a new innovation lab in Singapore that brings together those data analysts with big institutional customers and a large analytics center in Bangalore.

Several forward-thinking governments in the developing world are demonstrating how government can catalyze the development of the ecosystem through the opening of its own datasets and the active management of big data use. Kenya developed an innovative Open Data Portal (http://www.opendata.go.ke), which includes a full digital edition of the country's census, detailed government expenditure data, government household income surveys, energy and infrastructure information, and the location of schools and health facilities, among other data. The portal provides unlimited data access on the web and through mobile phones to researchers, web and software developers, journalists, students, civil society, and the general public. Civic organizations, mobile application developers, and media groups are already using the data to improve understanding of population patterns, increase the transparency of governments, and map public services.[15]

big data
The massive sets of data, both structured and unstructured, that businesses are collecting, which can be analyzed with advanced data analysis methods such as predictive analytics or user behavior analytics to provide valuable insights into consumer needs and trends

LO 12-4

Explain international market-entry methods.

What Methods Are Available for Entering Foreign Markets?

Once a company has decided to enter into a foreign market, it must decide which of the many different options for market entry would be the best strategic fit for the company. An example of Starbucks entering into China shows how Western companies can adapt successfully to local markets. In China, Starbucks faced cultural entry barriers, given China's thousands of years drinking tea and a strong, traditional tea culture. Yet today, many Chinese drink coffee at Starbucks, which in 2018 had more than 3,300 stores in 141 Chinese cities. Building on this momentum, the company plans to open an additional 2,700 stores over the next four years, or a new store every 15 hours.[16] It successfully connected a coffee way of life with the younger, emerging Chinese middle class, while incorporating respect for tea traditions into its offerings, including space to sip, chat, and check iPhones. Starbucks in China illustrates that global brands can adapt their offerings to local markets and succeed. The ability to think differently, implement good strategies, adapt to local markets, and commit long term are all important steps to being successful in international markets.

We now turn to ways ICs can enter new markets, market-entry modes. They are described in terms of whether equity is part of the IC's commitment to the new market, as summarized in Figure 12.2. We look first at nonequity-based modes, which tend to have less risk but also less control of their product in the market, and then at equity modes, which have more risk and also more control.

NONEQUITY MODES OF ENTRY

If a company wishes to enter foreign markets without equity investments in the market entry, a number of alternatives are available. In this section, we discuss exporting, turnkey projects, licensing, franchising, management contracts, and contracted manufacturing.

Most firms begin their involvement in international business by exporting—that is, by selling some of their regular production beyond their domestic market. This method requires little investment and is relatively free of risks. It is an excellent way to get a feel for international business without committing significant resources.

A **turnkey project** is an export of technology, management expertise, and, in some cases, capital equipment. The contractor agrees to design and erect a plant, supply the process technology, provide the production inputs, and then train the operating personnel. After a trial run, the facility is turned over to the purchaser. The exporter of a turnkey project may be a contractor that specializes in designing and erecting plants in a particular industry, such as petroleum refining or steel production. The turnkey

turnkey project
An export of technology, management expertise, and possibly capital equipment where a contractor agrees to design and erect a plant, supply the process technology, provide the production inputs, train the operating personnel, and, after a trial run, turn the facility over to the purchaser

FIGURE 12.2 Modes of Market Entry

Nonequity-Based Modes of Market Entry
Exporting
Turnkey project
Licensing
Franchising
Management contract
Contracted manufacturing

Equity-Based Modes of Market Entry
Wholly owned subsidiary
Joint venture

supplier earns money from its expertise by delivering a plant ready to run rather than merely selling its technology. Once they build the turnkey installation, companies often provide work training as well.

Frequently, worldwide companies are called on to furnish technical assistance to firms that have sufficient capital and management strength. By means of a **licensing** agreement, one firm (the licensor) will grant to another firm (the licensee) the right to use any kind of expertise, such as manufacturing processes (patented or unpatented), marketing procedures, and trademarks for one or more of the licensor's products. The licensee generally pays a fixed sum when signing the licensing agreement and then a royalty of 2 to 5 percent of sales over the life of the contract (five to seven years with an option for renewal is one common way to structure such agreements). The exact amount of the royalty will depend on the amount of assistance given and the relative bargaining power of the two parties. In 2017, the World Bank reported that charges for the use of intellectual property totaled more than $48 billion in the United States, and more than $403 billion worldwide.[17]

In recent years, courts in the United States and the European Union increasingly have been enforcing patent protection laws. Apple sued Korea's Samsung Electronics for copying patented features of its iPhone, with a U.S. jury ordering Samsung to pay $539 million in damages.[18] As a result of increased enforcement of patent laws, more companies at home and abroad have begun to obtain licenses, as an alternative to making illegal copies, at least in some cases.

Technology is not the only thing that is licensed to support a firm's market entry. In the fashion industry, a number of designers license the use of their names. Ralph Lauren, one of the largest such licensors, reported an average of $173 million per year in licensing revenues from 2013 through 2017 for a broad range of items within apparel, home, fragrance, and accessories categories.[19]

Despite the opportunity to obtain a sizable income from licensing, many firms, especially those that produce high-tech products, still will not grant licenses. They fear that a licensee will become a competitor when the agreement expires or that the licensee will seek to market the products aggressively outside its home territory. At one time, licensors routinely inserted a clause in the licensing agreement that prohibited exports, but most governments will no longer accept such a prohibition.

Firms have also gone international with a different kind of licensing—**franchising**. Franchising is a form of licensing in which one firm contracts with

A Polo Ralph Lauren store in Busan, South Korea. ©Heorshe/Alamy Stock Photo.

another to operate under a specific set of rules, permitting the franchisee to sell products or services under a well-publicized brand name and a well-proven set of procedures with a carefully developed and controlled marketing strategy. Fast-food operations (such as Subway, McDonald's, KFC, and Burger King) are the most numerous. Other types of franchisers are hotels (Intercontinental), business services (The UPS Store), fitness (Jazzercise), building maintenance (ServiceMaster, Nationwide Exterminating), car rental and dealers (Hertz, Europcar), and real estate (ReMax). More than 400 U.S.-based franchisors have international operations, generating more than $6 billion in franchise fees from these foreign sites.[20] A survey of International Franchise Association members showed that 61 percent have international franchisees or international operations, with 16 percent generating 25 to 35 percent of their overall revenues from international activities.[21]

licensing
A contractual arrangement in which one firm grants access to its patents, trade secrets, or technology to another for a fee

 CULTURE FACTS @internationalbiz

Franchising is a form of business popular in the West, where individualistic cultures reward the individual over the group. It is also a popular form in more collectivistic or communal cultures. The world's top three franchising countries are the United States, Japan (at over 220,000 units in both franchised and corporate units), and Canada. Japan's culture measures high on communalism on many cultural frameworks. #franchising #individualisticcultures #unitedstates #japan #canada

 SOCIAL MEDIA

franchising
A form of licensing in which one firm contracts with another to operate a business under an established name according to specific rules

management contract
An arrangement by which one firm provides management to another firm

The **management contract** is an arrangement under which a company provides management in some or all functional areas to another party for a fee that typically ranges from 2 to 5 percent of sales. International companies make such contracts with firms in which they have no ownership (e.g., Hilton Hotel provides management for foreign hotels that use the Hilton name, and Delta provides management assistance to foreign airlines); joint-venture partners; and wholly owned subsidiaries. The last arrangement allows the parent to siphon off some of the subsidiary's profits. This becomes important when, as in some foreign exchange–poor nations, the parent firm is limited in the level of profits it can repatriate. Moreover, because the fee is an expense, the subsidiary is likely to receive a tax benefit in the IC's home country. This practice may also allow the parent firm to better manage its corporate-wide tax burden by reducing profits within higher-tax nations by moving them to countries with lower tax rates.

contracted manufacturing
An arrangement in which one firm contracts with another to produce products to its specifications

International firms employ **contracted manufacturing**, an arrangement in which one firm contracts with another to produce products to its specifications, in order to enter a foreign market or to subcontract work there. Entering a foreign market via contracted manufacturing does not require an investment in plant facilities, so it is sometimes thought of as foreign direct investment without investment. The contracting firm's sales organization markets the products under its own brand. With the subcontract, when the international firm is the largest or only customer of the subcontractors, there is, in effect, a new company created in the host nation that generates employment and foreign exchange. Frequently, the international firm will lend capital to the foreign contractor in the same way that a global or multinational firm will lend funds to its subsidiary. From the home country point of view, this practice is often politically sensitive and known as outsourcing.

EQUITY-BASED MODES OF ENTRY

When management does decide to make a foreign direct investment, it usually has several alternatives available, though not all of them may be feasible in a particular country. They include the wholly owned subsidiary and joint venture. We also mention here the strategic alliance, which may be either an equity or a nonequity way to enter a market.

A company that wishes to own a foreign subsidiary outright may start from the ground up by building a new plant (greenfield investment) or acquiring a going concern. With an acquisition, a company might purchase its distributor, thus obtaining a distribution network familiar with its products. Historically, ICs making foreign direct investments have preferred wholly owned subsidiaries when possible. However, foreign investors in the United States have demonstrated a preference for acquiring going concerns for the instant access to the market they provide. Moreover, they also have one less competitor after the purchase. Sometimes it is not possible to have a wholly owned subsidiary in a foreign market because the host government may not permit it, the firm may lack the capital or expertise to undertake the investment alone, or there may be tax and other advantages that favor another form of investment, such as a joint venture.

joint venture
A cooperative effort among two or more organizations that share a common interest in a business undertaking

A **joint venture** may be a corporate entity formed by an international company and local owners, by two international companies for the purpose of doing business in a third market, a corporate entity formed by a government agency (usually in the country of investment) and an international firm, or a cooperative undertaking between two or more firms for a limited-duration project. Large construction jobs such as a dam or an airport are frequently joint ventures. Often these joint ventures are **strategic alliances**, which are collaborations with competitors, customers, and/or suppliers. Strategic alliances may take other forms as well and are a response to growing global competition in an environment of increased research, product development, and marketing costs. A strategic alliance can provide faster market entry and start-up; gain access to new

strategic alliance
Collaboration with competitors, customers, and/or suppliers that may take nonequity or equity form

ELLA MICHELICH IN ROMANIA: Keep an Open Mind When Entering a New Culture

Ella Michelich in Romania.
Courtesy of Ellen Michelich.

After entering college with no major in mind, I finally decided on international business and analytics. I was drawn to the creativity, curiosity, and empathy that are required in international business and I saw how the hard skills of analytics complemented that.

My first experience with international business, even before coursework, was my job as a research assistant to an international business and strategy professor. Through my research work, I have been exposed to more ideas, areas of study, and various challenges that accompany research than I would have been exposed to through classroom learning alone. The projects I worked on are what pushed me to want to go abroad while still in college. I have been learning about global issues and contributing to international databases without ever leaving my small area of the Midwest, let alone the country. I wanted to take the skills I gained as a research assistant and apply them internationally, but I wasn't sure how I could do it.

At one point, I had considered changing my international business major. I was scared I could not afford the international immersions required for my major, as I had always heard about how expensive studying abroad is. The typical study abroad trip also did not appeal to me; I would still be surrounded by my own culture and not pushed out of my comfort zone if my trip involved traveling, living, and studying with other students from my own school or country. Then the professor I was working for recommended that I volunteer abroad through AIESEC, the world's largest youth-run nonprofit, which partnered with the United Nations. So I took his advice and applied for an AIESEC internship.

The summer after my sophomore year, I spent six weeks in Romania, working at an educational summer camp for young children. My co-workers, who were also international students, and I crafted and delivered English language lessons, created science experiments, and prepared other workshops to teach the children about cultures around the world. While at times the work was difficult and tiring, the passion of my Romanian bosses is what kept me pushing forward. They were a group of three older Romanians whose dream was to change the educational system in their country and shape learning into a positive experience for students. Their hope was to eventually turn their summer camp into a full-fledged school.

To prepare myself to go to Eastern Europe, when my only prior international travel was on a childhood trip to Mexico, was a bit overwhelming initially. I tried to have few expectations about the country, the culture, or my living situation. I tried to keep an open mind and accept that there is no such thing as "weird" when entering a new culture, only "different." Romanians proved that these differences, while substantial, did not equate to "bad." I felt so welcomed into the lives of everyone I met in Romania and I am so grateful to have made wonderful friends who shaped my trip into such a positive and caring experience. I did begin to experience burnout about a month into the trip when the language barriers (I spoke no Romanian and picked up only a few words during my internship) and complete upheaval of my normal life became more and more apparent to me. However, after realizing the importance of body language and nonverbals and how far they went in communication, and creating a routine for each day, I began to feel much more at home.

Back at school in the U.S., I feel more confident in myself and my ability to adapt. Now, I'm hungry for new challenges and hopefully another—longer—assignment abroad. I am exploring a potential career in consulting and hopefully one day international project management, but I also have an interest in joining the Peace Corps so I can apply what I've learned throughout my undergraduate career and push myself further to be a global citizen.

Source: Ella Michelich.

products, markets, and technologies; and share costs, resources, and risks. We are probably aware of airlines' code-sharing alliances. Other examples include Starbucks partnering with Barnes & Noble to provide coffee shops in bookstores and the giant pharmaceutical Eli Lilly's more than 100 strategic alliances aimed at discovery, development, and marketing.

SUMMARY

LO 12-1
Review the steps of market screening and techniques for environmental analysis.

The screening process examines the various forces in succession, eliminating countries at each step. The sequence of screening is (1) basic need potential; (2) financial and economic forces; (3) political and legal forces; (4) sociocultural forces; (5) competitive forces; and (6) personal visits. Each step reduces the number of prospects, and research at each successive stage is more difficult and expensive. Environmental analysis is a review of external, environmental forces. The two basic approaches are country screening and segment screening.

LO 12-2
Discuss the value of trade missions and trade fairs.

Trade missions and fairs allow potential buyers and sellers to explore market potential for the products they are selling and to explore import opportunities if they are seeking products. They also offer opportunities for networking and direct observation of competitors.

LO 12-3
Discuss some of the problems market researchers encounter in foreign markets.

Both cultural and technical difficulties await the market researcher in foreign markets. Language and dialect issues may be present. A social desirability bias may be in operation. Technical difficulties such as unreliable mail service or unreadable street names may be present as well. Luckily, Internet-based research is helping to lessen these difficulties.

LO 12-4
Explain international market-entry methods.

Nonequity-based modes of entry include exporting, turnkey projects, licensing, franchising, management contract, and contracted manufacturing. Equity-based modes of market entry include wholly owned subsidiaries and joint ventures. Strategic alliances can take nonequity or equity forms of involvement.

KEY TERMS

big data 331
cluster analysis 323
contracted manufacturing 334
country screening 321
environmental scanning 320
franchising 333
joint venture 334

licensing 333
management contract 334
market factors 323
market indicators 322
market screening 320
segment screening 321
social desirability bias 330

strategic alliance 334
trade fair 329
trade mission 329
trend analysis 323
turnkey project 332

CRITICAL THINKING QUESTIONS

1. Select a country and a product that you believe your firm can market there. Make a list of the sources of information you will use for each screening.

2. What is the logic for the order of the screenings? Can you suggest a time when the order might change?

3. A firm's export manager examines the UN's *International Trade Statistics Yearbook* and finds that the company's competitors have begun to export. Is there a way the manager can learn to which countries the U.S. competitors are exporting?

4. Do a country's imports completely measure the market potential for a product? Why or why not?

5. What are three examples, either real or hypothetical, of political and legal barriers that may eliminate a country from further consideration?

6. Trade missions are political junkets that get the taxpayer to fund a politician's vacation. Do you agree or disagree with this assertion, and why?

7. What are some of the complications that researchers may face when they collect primary data in a foreign market? Give examples.

8. Consider the market segment screening method. Take a lifestyle segment—say, people who like do-it-yourself home decorating. How would the segment screening method suggest that you go about identifying potential foreign markets?

9. You are a consultant to the developers of the latest Spider-Man video game, responsible for telling the Gameloft CEO where the likely international markets are. What do you do?

10. Assume that your academic unit (probably a college of business) wants to open a campus in a foreign country and that the dean has asked you to prepare a list of possible countries. How would you go about fulfilling the dean's request?

globalEDGE RESEARCH TASK   http://globalEDGE.msu.edu/

Use the globalEDGE website (http://globaledge.msu.edu/) to complete the following exercises:

1. The U.S. Commercial Service prepares a series of reports titled the *Country Commercial Guide* (or, CCG) for each country of interest to U.S. investors. Utilize this guide to gather information on South Africa. Imagine that your company is in the machinery industry and is considering entering this country. Select the most appropriate entry method and discuss its advantages and disadvantages. Be ready to support your decision with the information collected from the commercial guide.

2. Your company is in the construction industry and plans to expand to new international markets. You are selected as the project manager and you need to come up with a plan to evaluate the market potential of countries. First, find the "Market Potential Index" on globalEDGE and review the dimensions measured and indicators (measures) that are used to measure those dimensions. Now, considering the characteristics of the construction industry, design an industry-specific market potential index. What are the dimensions you would measure, and which indicators would you use to measure those dimensions?

MINICASE

CLOTAIRE RAPAILLE: CHARLATAN OR CODE BREAKER EXTRAORDINAIRE IN INTERNATIONAL MARKET RESEARCH?

Clotaire Rapaille could be either a grand charlatan—or an advisor your company simply cannot do without. Originally a psychologist treating autistic children in Europe, Rapaille now operates from a mansion in upstate New York, where top management seeks his advice on "the code" that will allow them access to the Indian, French, or Norwegian psyche. This insight should help the firm understand the motivations that will draw these people to buy its products.

Rapaille's earlier breakthrough insights came in the process of comparing French and American attitudes toward cheese. For the French, he says, cheese is alive, and the French would not put cheese in the refrigerator any more than put the cat there. Rapaille's insight is that for U.S. consumers cheese is "dead," so they seal it in a plastic "casket" and put it in a refrigerator, which is really a "morgue." They are more concerned about safety and control of sanitation than about taste; the French reverse these preferences. As a result, more French than U.S. consumers die from eating

cheese. However, U.S. consumers eat a relatively sterile and tasteless product, while the French enjoy a variety of cheeses U.S. consumers can barely fathom. The cultural archetype that this code suggests connects at a deep—Rapaille would say reptilian—level with U.S. concerns about sanitation and cleanliness as a primary yet unstated psychological factor, the "why" in buying choices and decisions. The French, in contrast, have a greater implicit concern for the sensual experience and have a relatively more relaxed approach to cleanliness. The archetype is found in cheese: individually plastic-wrapped slices of Kraft processed cheese versus a creamy, runny brie left on the counter after dinner for the next morning's baguette.

Rapaille's clients include JPMorgan, NASA, LEGO, Seiko, Absolut Vodka, and Samsonite and at least 50 of the Fortune 100 firms. In 2015, Rapaille released a book titled, *The Global Code: How a New Culture of Universal Values Is Transforming Business and Marketing.* This book is aimed at uncovering the new phenomenon of "global unconscious," or core values and feelings that are imitated worldwide, as a result of constant interconnectedness.

Teams under Rapaille's direction have "broken the code" for "anti-Americanism," "China," "seduction," the "teen Internet," and more. An excursion to India led him to pronounce that the caste system was simply a "practical" way of signaling to all their places in society. "It's not a problem, it's a solution," he summarized.

From this process, he discovers cultural archetypes, which are long-lasting, compared to opinions, which may change more readily. Some former clients have scoffed at him, using "the cheese is dead" as a constant mantra, mocking his methods. For others, the idea that complex attitudes can be summarized in a word or phrase (such as the German code for Americans, which is "John Wayne") is, well, silly. Yet many of the same established clients come back to him—P&G has returned 35 times.

Critical Thinking Questions

1. Is Rapaille's code system a short-cut code to understanding the complexities in culture and a way to make market research easier? Or is it a superficial hoax sold by a charlatan? Explain your answer.

2. As a manager, would you hire Clotaire Rapaille or his company to assist you in assessing and interpreting international market opportunities?

Sources: Adam Hanft, "The Man Behind the Culture Code," *Fast Company*, January 26, 2007, www.fastcompany.com; "Clotaire Rapaille," IPFS, 2018, www.ipfs.io; Clotaire Rapaille, *The Global Code: How a New Culture of Universal Values Is Reshaping Business and Marketing*, New York, NY: St. Martin's Press, September 29, 2015; "Interview: Clotaire Rapaille," *Frontline*, November 09, 2004, www.pbs.org; and Danielle Sacks, "Crack This Code," *Fast Company*, April 01, 2006, www.fastcompany.com.

NOTES

1. Om Malik, "The New Land of Opportunity IT'S A GLOBAL ECONOMY," *Business 2.0*, July 01, 2004.

2. An example of scanning the environment, by the American Hospital Association, is the "2018 Environmental Scan," at https://www.aha.org, accessed November 10, 2018; and the segment screening approach was inspired by Masaaki Kotabe and Kristiaan Helsen, *Global Marketing Management*, New York: Wiley, 2014.

3. Julie Jargon, "Campbell Soup to Exit Russia," *Wall Street Journal*, https://www.wsj.com, accessed November 10, 2018.

4. Virtually all governments have barriers to foreign direct investment and at the same time offer a variety of incentives to potential foreign investors. For example, Mexico currently restricts foreign investment in the petroleum industry. See, for example, UNCTAD's annual World Investment Reports, https://unctad.org, accessed November 10, 2018.

5. You can see information about CeBIT 2019 at https://www.cebit.de/en, accessed November 10, 2018.

6. Canton Import and Export Fair, "Statistics—123rd Canton Fair," http://www.cantonfair.org.cn, accessed November 10, 2018.

7. Secondary data and sometimes primary data will be gathered on a field trip, but the visitor rarely has the time or ability to conduct a complete field study.

8. Janet Harkness, and Alicia Schoua-Glusberg, "Questionnaires in Translation," https://www.ssoar.info/ssoar/handle/document/49733, accessed November 10, 2018.

9. "10 Spanish Words with Multiple Meanings," Lingoda GmbH, https://www.lingoda.com, accessed November 10, 2018.

10. Janet Harkness and Alicia Schoua-Glusberg, "Questionnaires in Translation."

11. "Finding Your Way in Venice," *Italy Heaven*, http://www.italyheaven.co.uk, accessed November 10, 2018.

12. Tom De Tuyck, Erica Van Lieven, and Anouk Willems, "Running Research Communities in Asian Markets," *InSites Consulting*, https://www.insites-consulting.com, accessed November 10, 2018.

13. "Pizza Hut," http://www.yum.com/company/our-brands, accessed November 10, 2018.

14. Paul McInerney, Marcus Roth, and Tunnee Sinburimsit, "Advanced Analytics: Poised to Transform Asian Companies," *McKinsey Analytics*, https://www.mckinsey.com, accessed November 10, 2018.

15. Kenya ICT Authority, "Kenya Open Data," http://www.opendata.go.ke, accessed November 10, 2018.

16. "Starbucks Has an Eye-Popping New China Plan: Open a Store Every 15 Hours for 4 Years," *Fortune*, http://fortune.com, accessed November 10, 2018; and Wang Zhuoqiong, "Starbucks Aims to Increase Stores, Revenue in China over 5 Years," *China Daily*, http://www.chinadaily.com.cn, accessed November 10, 2018.

17. The World Bank, "Charges for the Use of Intellectual Property, Payments (BoP, current US$)," https://data.worldbank.org/indicator/BM.GSR.ROYL.CD, accessed November 10, 2018.

18. "Jury Awards Apple $539 Million in Samsung Patent Case," *New York Times*, https://www.nytimes.com, accessed November 10, 2018.

19. "Top 150 Global Licensors," *License Global*, https://www.licenseglobal.com, accessed November 10, 2018; and "Ralph Lauren Corp (RL)," *Reuters*, https://www.reuters.com, accessed November 10, 2018.

20. International Franchise Association, "FAQs About Franchising," https://www.franchise.org, accessed November 10, 2018; and U.S. Commercial Service, U.S. Department of Commerce, *Franchising Industry: A Reference for U.S. Exporters*, 2018 Edition, https://www.franchise.org, accessed November 10, 2018.

21. "Franchising," Export.gov, https://2016.export.gov, accessed November 10, 2018.

13 Marketing Internationally

> **A global company should always go about its business in a way that's responsive to the major differences from one country to another, in terms of, for example, how retailing or distribution or payment systems work. But the core product or service should remain unchanged, since that is what is 'globalized.'**
>
> —*Theodore Levitt, author of the landmark* Harvard Business Review *article on standardization, "The Globalization of Markets"*[1]

©Lou-Foto/Alamy Stock Photo.

LEARNING OBJECTIVES

After reading this module, you should be able to:

LO 13-1 **Discuss** why international marketing managers may wish to standardize the marketing mix.

LO 13-2 **Distinguish** among the total product, the physical product, and the brand name.

LO 13-3 **Compare** the way consumer and industrial products and services are modified for international sale.

LO 13-4 **Identify** the product strategies that can be formed from three product alternatives and three kinds of promotional messages.

LO 13-5 **Discuss** some of the effects the Internet may have on international marketing.

LO 13-6 **Explain** "glocal" advertising strategies.

LO 13-7 **Define** pricing and distribution strategies.

The forces of social media are rippling through international marketing, even as the old marketing standbys refuse to go away. In China's large market for luxury brands, the traditional focus on flawless in-store pampering experiences by salespeople is being supplemented or replaced by digitally enhanced experiences—both in stores and online—including a heavy reliance on social media that particularly appeals to free-spending millennial shoppers. In Beijing, British luxury fashion house Burberry is outfitting its 59 stores with digital technology, including customer touchscreens the size of full-length mirrors and iPads for its staff. Burberry, Pepsi, and McDonald's are using WeChat, a Chinese-language version of WhatsApp with added elements of Facebook and Instagram and more than 800 million active monthly users, to communicate one-on-one with Chinese consumers.

More than 50 percent of Chinese consumers, versus 14 percent of consumers globally, use their mobile phone daily or weekly to shop. Developments in big data and artificial intelligence are enabling brands to collect and analyze customer data and provide more personalized shopping experiences. To enhance and personalize the shopping experience, Burberry, Chanel, and Lane Crawford, among others, have begun offering client-centric apps and product catalogs for use on mobile phones and other digital devices. Some companies now enable customers to walk through their stores with virtual reality goggles, trying on items without ever physically touching them.

Perhaps because they distrust official information, Chinese consumers rely heavily on peer reviews. Research has shown that they write, and act on, online reviews of products and services to a much greater extent than Westerners do. A PwC survey found that 79 percent of Chinese consumers report that positive interactions on social media with brands have resulted in them endorsing the brand more (versus 46 percent globally), and 71 percent have subsequently spent more money (versus 44 percent globally). Millions of online shoppers follow the thoughts of key opinion leaders (or KOLs), such as Zhang Dayi, Zhu Chenhui, Papi Jiang, Wang Tao, Fil Xiaobai, Ma Jianguo, and Angelababy, all who have emerged as trusted and reliable sources of information about the latest fashions and lifestyle trends, as well as de facto ambassadors for the brands they favor. These KOLs post recommendations nearly every day on social media sites such as Instagram or on Weibo, as well as engage in events like livestreaming and Q&A sessions that promote "see now, buy now" e-commerce sales. Their likes and dislikes can make or break products.

India is one of the fastest-growing markets for instant messaging applications. Of the 1.5 billion WhatsApp users, 200 million are in India. Facebook bought WhatsApp for $19 billion in 2014, its largest acquisition to date. Luxury and premium brands such as Cartier, Armani, and Diesel as well as many small and medium entrepreneurs use WhatsApp to keep in touch with their customers in India and elsewhere around the world.

These examples highlight just a few of the new opportunities for marketing goods and services that barely existed 5 or 10 years ago. In this module, we examine methods, both established and new, for reaching consumers wherever they might be, from Ulan Bator in Mongolia to Chicago and from Doha to Bangalore.

Sources: "eCommerce in China—The Future Is Already Here," *PwC*, 2017, www.pwccn.com; Farah Mastor, and Donny Kwok, "Global Luxury Brands Again Chase China's Young, Rich and Spendthrift," *Reuters,* August 20, 2018, www.reuters.com; Elizabeth Paton, and Sui-Lee Wee, "Luxury Sales Are Rebounding in China. Just Not in Stores," *The New York Times,* June 07, 2018, www.nytimes.com Cate, "Inside the Retail Strategy of Burberry," *Insider Trends,* January 16, 2018, www.insider-trends.com; Daniel Newman, "Top Five Digital Transformation Trends in Retail," *Forbes,* March 14, 2017, www.forbes.com; and "Whats Trotor, App Now Has 1.5 Billion Monthly Active Users, 200 Million Users in India," *Financial Express,* February 01, 2018, www.financialexpress.com.

Differences between Domestic and International Trade

LO 13-1
Discuss why international marketing managers may wish to standardize the marketing mix.

Marketers everywhere must know their markets; develop products or services to satisfy their customers' needs; price the products or services so that they are readily acceptable in the market; make them available to buyers; and inform potential customers, persuading them to buy. Further, as Table 13.1 illustrates, both new customers and new means of reaching them are available. But whether a product or service is first

TABLE 13.1 Method/Location Matrix for Reaching Consumers

	Established Methods	New Methods
Established Locations	TV ads in Chicago	Social media in Paris
New Locations	Retail stores in Ulan Bator	Mobile phone ads in Bangalore

designed for global use and adapted for local markets, or the idea comes from the home country and then is exported overseas, international marketers must recognize the possible differences, large and small, between marketing domestically and marketing internationally.

Although the basic functions of domestic and international marketing are the same, international markets often differ widely because of great variations among nations in the uncontrollable environmental forces they face—sociocultural, resource and environmental, economic and socioeconomic, legal, and financial. Moreover, even the forces we think of as controllable vary across markets. For example, the distribution channels to which we are accustomed in the United States may be unavailable elsewhere. Certain aspects of the product may need to be different, for reasons that range from taste and aesthetic preferences to voltage patterns and altitude issues. Then, too, the promotional mix often must change, to accommodate language and other differences. Finally, distinct cost structures of specific markets may require that different prices be set.

The international marketing manager's task is thus complex. It requires planning and controlling a variety of marketing strategies, rather than a unified or standardized one, and then coordinating and integrating those strategies into a single marketing program. Even marketing managers at global firms, who may want to use a single worldwide strategy, realize that doing so is nearly impossible. They must know enough about the uncontrollable variables to be able to make quick and decisive changes when necessary.

The Marketing Mix

marketing mix
A set of strategic decisions made about the product and its promotion, pricing, and distribution in order to satisfy the needs and desires of customers in a target market

The **marketing mix** is a set of strategic decisions made about the product and its promotion, pricing, and distribution in order to satisfy the needs and desires of customers in a target market. The number of variables in these strategic decisions is large, making hundreds of combinations possible. Often a company's domestic operation has already established a successful marketing mix, and the temptation to follow the same strategies and tactics overseas is strong. On the other hand, digital tools have brought personalization more easily within reach, even across vast distances. Yet the question the international marketing manager must answer for each market is, "Can we standardize worldwide, should we make some changes, or should we formulate a completely different marketing mix?"

STANDARDIZE, ADAPT, OR START FROM SCRATCH?

Often, top management would prefer to standardize the marketing mix globally, using the same marketing mix in all the firm's markets because standardization can produce significant cost savings. If the domestic product and marketing mix can be exported as is, then regardless of where the product is made, the firm can plan longer production runs, which lower manufacturing costs. In addition to these economies of scale, the longer experience curve, or learning curve, can create economies as well: it's usually true that the more experience we have doing

> **"But WHEN IT COMES to QUESTIONS of TASTE AND, ESPECIALLY, AESTHETIC PREFERENCE, CONSUMERS DO NOT like AVERAGES.... THE LURE of A UNIVERSAL PRODUCT IS A FALSE ALLURE."**
>
> *—Kenichi Ohmae, corporate strategist and author*[2]

something, including marketing, the better we get at that activity. For example, rather than vary the fit country by country, Levi's standardized the fit of its 501 jeans worldwide and launched its first global ad campaign (although it also introduced Denizen jeans targeted to younger Asian consumers, then to the U.S. and other consumers).

When advertising campaigns, promotional materials (point-of-purchase displays), websites and social media, and sales training programs can be standardized, the expensive creative work and artwork need to be done only once. A standardized corporate visual identity (CVI), consisting of the firm's name, logo, color, and slogan with graphics, can help project a consistent image around the world.[3] Other identity elements such as jingles or music and even odors can also be standardized. Standardized pricing strategies for firms that serve markets through several different subsidiaries can prevent the embarrassment of quoting different prices for the same product.

In spite of the advantages of standardization, almost all firms find it is seldom as easy as it sounds. Many firms must modify their domestic marketing mix or develop a new one. The extent of the changes depends on the type of product, the environmental forces, and the degree of market penetration desired. Further, because the very concept of standardization is in a state of tension with the marketing principle—which centers on the needs of the buyer, not the seller—we probably should not be too disappointed that the economies that would come with complete standardization are seldom available to the seller, especially the seller of consumer goods.

Even The Coca-Cola Company, the firm often portrayed as the exemplar of the standardized product, found that its increasingly standardized strategy had run its course. According to the company's former chair, Douglas Daft, "As the [20th] century was drawing to a close, the world had changed course, and we had not. The world was demanding greater flexibility, responsiveness and local sensitivity, while we were further centralising decision making and standardising our practices. . . . The next big evolutionary step of 'going global' now has to be 'going local.'"[4] As an example of this effort, the company introduced Coca-Cola Plus in Japan, a cola that includes a laxative and is marketed as a government-certified health food.[5]

Similarly, the need to rethink old brands reflects a new reality, as companies like Johnson & Johnson are increasingly trying to appeal to the local cultures, appetites, and customs of new markets. There is the alcohol-free Listerine Zero, popular in Muslim countries where spirits are forbidden; Green Tea Listerine, made specifically for Asian markets; and Listerine Naturals, a mouthwash geared toward Americans' obsession with nonsynthetic ingredients that was introduced first in the United States and could expand overseas.[6]

Product Strategies

The product or service is the central focus of the marketing mix. If it fails to satisfy the needs of consumers, no amount of promotion, price-cutting, or convenient distribution will persuade people to buy. Consumers will not repurchase a detergent, for example, if clothes do not come out as clean as commercials say they will.

In formulating product strategies, international marketing managers must remember that the product is more than a physical object. The total product, which is what the customer buys, includes the physical product, brand name, accessories, after-sales service, warranty, instructions for use, company image, and package (see Figure 13.1). That means product adaptation can be less expensive and easier than altering the product's physical characteristics. Different package sizes and promotional messages, for example, can create a new total product for a distinct market. This is one reason that products sold globally are more standardized physically than we might expect. They can be localized by changes to the package, brand name, accessories, after-sales service, warranty, instructions for use, and company image.

corporate visual identity (CVI)
A firm's name, logo, slogan, graphics, color, and typeface that help identify the firm to consumers and other interested constituents

LO 13-2
Distinguish among the total product, the physical product, and the brand name.

total product
What the customer buys, including the physical product, brand name, accessories, after-sales service, warranty, instructions for use, company image, and package

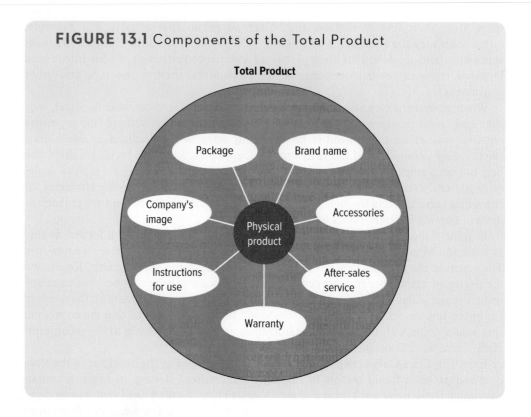

FIGURE 13.1 Components of the Total Product

Total Product

Physical product

Package
Brand name
Accessories
After-sales service
Warranty
Instructions for use
Company's image

©Imagine China/Newscom.

To illustrate the concept of the total product, let's consider three consumer products: tonic water, chocolate, and instant coffee. As a physical product, tonic water is global because it is the same everywhere, but as a total product, it is multidomestic because people in different markets buy it for different reasons. The French drink it straight, while the English mix it with alcohol. Chocolate is neither a global physical product nor a global total product; it is eaten as a snack in some areas, put in sandwiches in others, and eaten as a dessert elsewhere. Because of strong local preferences, it also varies greatly in flavor, from bitter to quite sweet or even spicy depending on what is added to it. In the case of coffee, Nestlé produces different blends sold in nearly 200 countries under the same brand name, Nescafé, the same unified look, and the same slogan, "It all starts with a Nescafé."[7] For this company, the brand name is global while the physical product is local.

Modifying Types of Products

LO 13-3
Compare the way consumer and industrial products and services are modified for international sale.

The degree of change a company should make in a product or service is affected by whether it is sold in the consumer or industrial market, and by environmental forces overseas. Generally, consumer products require greater adaptation than do industrial products, especially if they are stylish or the result of a fad, as shown in Figure 13.2.

INDUSTRIAL PRODUCTS

As Figure 13.2 suggests, many industrial products can be sold unchanged worldwide. Memory chips, for example, are used wherever computers are manufactured, and there is no cultural content in nuts and bolts.

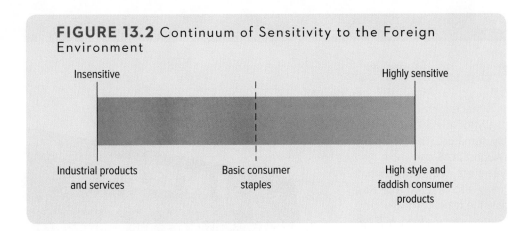

FIGURE 13.2 Continuum of Sensitivity to the Foreign Environment

Insensitive   Highly sensitive

Industrial products   Basic consumer   High style and
and services   staples   faddish consumer
                                                          products

Adaptations are occasionally necessary to meet local legal requirements, such as those that govern noise, safety, or emissions. To avoid the need to change the product, some manufacturers design it to meet the most stringent laws even though it will be overdesigned for the rest of its markets. In some instances, governments have passed strict laws with the intent of protecting a local manufacturer from import competition. When this occurs, the company may prefer to design the product for the country with the next-most stringent laws and stay out of the first market.

CONSUMER PRODUCTS

Although consumer products generally require greater modification to meet local market requirements than do industrial products, some, especially luxury products such as champagne and perfume, can be sold unchanged to certain market segments that have similar characteristics across countries, including foreign-educated and well-traveled citizens and expatriates. Many products and services new to local tastes and preferences have been successfully introduced in a number of countries by first being marketed to these similar groups. Gradually, members of other market segments purchase them until consumption becomes widespread. Some technology products, such as Apple's iPhones, have been offered unchanged across borders, with the exception of the power supply, pricing, and technical specifics associated with local telecommunications carriers. According to a recent marketing article, "Customers adapt to Apple, Apple does not adapt to customers."[8]

While wealthy consumers may have much in common across countries, marketers tend to find greater dissimilarities in social and cultural values as they go down the economic strata in each country. It follows from this that, in general, the deeper the desired immediate market penetration is, the greater must be the product modification. This does not necessarily mean the *physical* product has to be changed. Perhaps a modification of one of the other elements of the total product is sufficient—a different size or color of the package, a change in the brand name, or a new positioning. A different emphasis in after-sales service may also be important. For example, Mars faced a drop in Bahrain's imports of candy when it was ready to launch M&M's there. Fortunately, the company's marketing research group discovered that Bahrainis consider the peanut to be a health food, so it repositioned its peanut M&M's as a health food. Mars also was able to turn the hot Gulf climate to its advantage by emphasizing the packaging with its traditional slogan, "M&M's melt in your mouth, not in your hand." In the case of home furnishings company Ikea, while its simple product designs are generally standardized across nations, it has modified elements of the total product for local cultures. For example, when entering India, Ikea stores for the first time offered on-site assembly services in recognition of that country generally placing less emphasis on a do-it-yourself approach.[9]

 CULTURE FACTS

Sandwich varieties are endless. Mexico, the Netherlands, and Scotland make varieties of chocolate sandwiches; Britain has a cheese and pickle sandwich; a donkey burger is popular in China; Japan has the *Katsu sando* consisting of breaded and deep-fried pork cutlets; and Denmark offers a smoked herring and raw egg yolk concoction called *Sol over Gudhjem*. #sandwich varieties #consumerproducts

 CULTURE FACTS @internationalbiz

Japan may be one of the world's perennial early adopters of new technologies, but its continuing attachment to the CD (and vinyl) puts it sharply at odds with the rest of the global music industry. While CD sales are falling worldwide, in Japan they still account for a hefty percentage of sales, compared with some countries, like Sweden, where online streaming is dominant. This difference has been explained by the relatively large number of audiophiles in Japan.[10] #CDsalesinJapan #onlinestreamingdominates #audiophiles

Ikea Adapts to Enter the Indian Market

Ikea, the iconic Swedish company that is the world's largest furniture retailer, is known globally for low-priced, innovatively designed, self-assembly furniture. The company opened its first store in India in August 2018, after more than a decade of planning and five years after receiving approval from Indian officials. The company encountered repeated delays as it attempted to navigate the famously challenging Indian political and economic bureaucracy, along with the need for adapting to local needs, but ultimately Ikea persevered. The initial store, 400,000 square feet in size and located on 13 acres in the outskirts of the southern city of Hyderabad, employs 950 employees. "They've been very patient about India. In terms of the amount of effort and time that they have taken to launch the first store, it's unusual actually," said Arvind Singhal from Technopak Advisors. "It shows to me a determination to get it right in the market."

Although India's GDP is only one-quarter the size of China's, India's 1.3 billion people and growing middle class makes it a potentially massive market to penetrate. India was projected to grow faster than any other major economy in 2018 and the Indian market for furniture, lighting, and household items was estimated at $30 billion annually. However, many idiosyncrasies of the Indian market caused Ikea to adopt a slower pace for entry, taking more time to learn about the market and adapt accordingly.

Ikea is famous for offering flat-packed furniture that requires assembly by consumers themselves. However, Indian culture generally places less emphasis on a do-it-yourself approach. Instead, reflecting a "do-it-for-me" preference, furniture is typically custom ordered from one of the thousands of small local furniture vendors and delivered to consumers fully assembled. To adapt to local preferences, Ikea established a 150-person on-site team to help customers assemble products.

Before deciding on product offerings, Ikea personnel visited about 1,000 Indian homes to observe how people lived and what they needed. Accustomed to spending much time together as a family, including multiple generations under the same roof, Indians also frequently have relatives stop by. As a result, Ikea added more flexible seating to its product line, like folding chairs and stools. Because children often share the same bedroom as their parents until entering elementary school, Ikea's displays include a child's bed among the other bedroom furniture. Some displays feature cabinets and countertops with lower heights, acknowledging the shorter average stature of Indian women compared to American and European counterparts. Furniture designs were modified to include risers to keep furniture off the floor, reflecting Indian practices of frequently using water to clean floors.

©Sanjay Borra/Alamy Stock Photo.

Product pricing also was modified. "Indians are very price–sensitive, but they're also value–sensitive. You can't give them substandard quality at cheaper rates. They want both," says Paresh Parekh, partner at Ernst & Young. Reflecting India's lower income levels, 1,000 of the 7,500 items in the product line are priced below $3. Many items are sourced locally, to avoid high import tariffs and keep prices low.

Ikea also modified the in-store restaurant to fit local palates. Acknowledging local religious sensitivities, Ikea doesn't offer meatballs made with beef or pork, only chicken and vegetarian ones. Local favorites like biryani, dal makhani, and samosas also appear on the menu. The restaurant has 1,000 seats, the most of any Ikea store, to accommodate the more leisurely pace that Indian families enjoy while dining.

Ikea has already committed to investing $1.5 billion into India, including plans to open a second store in Mumbai in 2019, followed by Bangalore and Delhi in 2020. The company aims for 25 stores by 2025. Ikea also plans to move vigorously into online commerce for serving Indian customers. Ikea Group CEO Jesper Brodin stated, "This is our next really big market," although he also cautioned that it would take many years before significant profits would be seen. "The investments are high and the time until which you reach an economy of scale will be a stretch for us, but we will try to endure."

Sources: Justina Crabtree, "Ikea Finally Opens First Store in What CEO Calls a 'More Open India'," USA Today, 2018, www.usatoday.com; Warren Shoulberg, "Why Ikea Succeeds Around the World While Other Retailers Falter," Forbes, July 30, 2018, www.forbes.com; "Ikea Set to Adapt as It Opens First India Store," The National, June 14, 2018, www.thenational.ae; Vindu Goel, "Ikea Opens First India Store, Tweaking Products But Not the Vibe," The New York Times, August 07, 2018, www.nytimes.com; and Yogita Limaye, "Will the First Ikea in India Succeed?" BBC, August 09, 2018, www.bbc.com.

SERVICES

The marketing of services, like the marketing of industrial products, is generally less complex globally than is the marketing of consumer products. The consulting firm Accenture, for instance, has more than 435,000 employees in over 120 countries offering the same kinds of business expertise it provides in the United States.[11]

However, laws and customs sometimes do mandate that providers alter their services. Manpower Inc. cannot operate in some markets because private employment agencies are against the law there. Accounting laws vary substantially among nations, but the large accounting firms operate globally, making local adaptations where necessary. The Sereno Spa on the west coast of India offers the same general sort of pampering as other expensive spas, but it also uses its location to draw on local expertise in yoga and ayurvedic medicine.[12] VISA, MasterCard, and American Express are examples of successful companies in the global credit card industry. They had combined billings of $1.7 trillion in 1996; by 2017, VISA alone had $10.2 trillion in total volume, including payments and cash volume.[13]

FOREIGN ENVIRONMENTAL FORCES

We've reviewed international businesses' marketing strategies based on the type of product. Next, we'll look at a few concrete examples of how some environmental forces abroad, such as sociocultural, economic, and legal factors, might also affect product and service offerings.

Sociocultural Forces   Cultural patterns often require changes in the physical product or in aspects of the total product. Appliance makers, for instance, find variations in consumer preferences for washing clothes. The French tend to want top-loading washing machines, and the British tend to want front-loaders; the Germans prefer high-speed machines that remove most of the moisture in the spin-dry cycle, but the Italians prefer slower spin speeds because they prefer to let the sun do the drying. Thus, Whirlpool must produce a variety of models, although after buying Philips's appliance business and acquiring Maytag, the company took huge steps to integrate these independent national companies into regional manufacturing facilities and product platforms. For example, its European organization emphasizes sharing across a few common platforms. Whirlpool's CEO at the time argued that national differences are exaggerated: "This business is the same all over the world. There is great opportunity to leverage that sameness."[14]

After a painful restructuring in which the company closed a Spanish plant, laid off 2,000 workers, centralized inventory control, and reduced its 36 European warehouses to 8, both sales and operating margins in Europe improved. In fact, Whirlpool created a "world washer," called Duet in the United States and Dreamspace in Europe, combining the U.S. preference for large-load capacity, the European preference for front-loading machines, and sensor technology that selects wash time and water consumption.[15]

While some international firms, such as Campbell's, have been extremely successful in employing the same brand name, label, and colors worldwide, other firms learn they must change names, labels, or colors because of cultural differences. Gold appears frequently on packages in Latin America because Latin Americans view it as a symbol of quality and prestige. Procter & Gamble found that a gold package has value in Europe, too, after it launched its silver-boxed Crest Tartar Control Formula in the United Kingdom, which was followed two months later by Colgate's equivalent in a gold box. P&G officials agreed that Colgate's choice of gold was better than their silver, even though their product was packaged in silver in the United States. The German multinational Henkel had to abandon its blue and yellow Bref Duo Stick toilet bowl freshener because the product looked uncannily like the flag of neighboring Ukraine. In Europe, McDonald's uses hunter green for the background of its golden arches logo, rather than the red used in the United States, to project an eco-friendly image.

The meaning colors convey in different cultures is also a marketing consideration. For example, in the Netherlands blue is considered warm and feminine, but the Swedes consider it masculine and cold. In Belgium, blue is used to represent baby girls and pink for baby boys, the exact opposite as for the United States.[16] While red signifies a drop in prices in North American stock markets, in East Asia it indicates stock price increases. Purple is associated with sorrow and unhappiness in India, but freedom or peace in France and royalty in the United Kingdom and China.

Even if the colors can remain the same, instructions on labels must be translated into the language of the local market. Firms selling in areas where two or more languages are spoken, such as Canada, Switzerland, Belgium, and the United States, may need to use multilingual labels. Where instructions are not required, as with some consumer or industrial products whose use is well known, there is an advantage to printing the label in the language of the country best known for the product. For example, a French label on a perfume helps strengthen the product's image in the United States.

A perfectly good brand name may have to be scrapped because of its unfavorable connotations in another language. A U.S. product failed to survive in Sweden because its name translated as "enema." Procter & Gamble changed the name of its "Vicks" brand of cough drops to "Wick" in Germany because Germans pronounce the letter V as F and the word "ficks" is translated as a sexual act.[17] In Latin America, a product had to be taken off the market when the manufacturer found the name meant "jackass oil."[18]

One common story about names turns out not to be true. The story is that Chevrolet reportedly couldn't sell Novas in Spanish-speaking countries because *no va* means "doesn't go" in Spanish. But the pronunciation is different—*Nova* has the accent on the first syllable, whereas the accent for *no va* falls on the *va*. To someone speaking Spanish, the words have different meanings, and *nova* might well connect with "star," which is probably what Chevrolet had in mind. You may be surprised to learn that Pemex, Mexico's government-owned petroleum monopoly, once called its regular gasoline *Nova*. So the story of the Chevy Nova is an urban legend, but there are legions of other examples.

CULTURE FACTS @internationalbiz

Japanese *keiretsus* span and use their brand name across multiple industries. Mitsubishi, among other things, sells food, automobiles, electronics, and heavy construction equipment.[19] U.S. firms observed that Japanese consumers closely examined American products if they could not immediately find a major brand name on the package. It is required as a sign of quality.
#keiretsus #brandnamequality

SOCIAL
MEDIA

An important difference in social forces to which U.S. marketers are not accustomed is a preference in other nations for making daily visits to small neighborhood specialty shops and large, open markets where consumers can socialize while shopping. More frequent buying requires smaller packages, which is important to a shopper who has no automobile in which to carry purchases. However, this custom is changing in Europe, where consumers are demanding the kinds of assortments that only a large store can offer. Shopping frequency is also slowing as European women, who traditionally did the food shopping, are finding they have less free time than before. One solution is the huge combination supermarket–discount house (*hypermarché* in France) with ample parking, typically located in the suburbs.

Legal Forces Legal forces can be a formidable constraint in the design of products because if the firm fails to adhere to a country's laws governing the product, it will be unable to do business in that country. Laws concerning pollution, consumer protection, and operator safety have been enacted in many parts of the world and limit the marketer's ability to standardize the product mix internationally. For example, U.S. machinery makers exporting to Sweden have found that Swedish operator-safety requirements are stricter than those required by the Occupational Safety and Health Act (OSHA) in the United States, so if they wish to market in Sweden, they must produce a special model. Of course, product standards set to protect a nation's citizens can also be effective in protecting indigenous industry from foreign competitors.

Food and pharmaceuticals are especially influenced by laws regulating product purity and labeling. Food products sold in Canada, whether imported or produced locally, are subject to strict rules that require both English and French on the labels as well as metric and inch/pound units. The law even dictates the space permitted between the number and the unit—"16 oz." is correct, but "16oz." is not. The Venezuelan government has decreed that the manufacturer or the importer must affix to the package the maximum retail price at which many products can be sold, and India has a roughly similar price regime. Because of local desire to avoid food that contains pork, the label of any product containing animal fat or meat sold in Saudi Arabia must identify the kind of animal used or state that no swine products were used.

Legal forces may also prevent a worldwide firm from employing its brand name in all its overseas markets. Managers accustomed to U.S. law, which establishes the right to a brand name by order of use, are surprised to learn that in most countries, a brand belongs to the person registering it first. The company's long-established brand name at home may have been registered abroad by someone who is employing it legitimately for his or her own products, or it may have been pirated by someone who hopes to profit by selling it back to the originating firm.

To avoid this predicament, the firm must register its brand names in every country in which it wants to use them, now or in the future, and quickly. The Paris Convention grants a firm that has registered a name in one country only six months to register it elsewhere. To be certain it has enough names for new products, Unilever, the English–Dutch manufacturer of personal-care products, has more than 100,000 trademarks registered throughout the world, most of which are not in use but are being kept in reserve.

The use of Internet domain names shows these problems have not faded away. A study found that American Express, for example, had registered the domain name "americanexpress" in 19 countries, but in 11 others the name was already registered to someone else. In a more extreme example, CBS found that it could complete 4 registrations of its name, but other people and organizations had secured 46. When Japanese characters became an option for registering Japanese domain names, tiny Web Japan Co. got a head start by registering some 100 domain names, including those of major corporations. When Google's parent company was renamed "Alphabet," it was unable to obtain the domain name alphabet.com because BMW owns it. Nissan has spent 20 years trying to obtain the domain Nissan.com from a man named Uzi Nissan, and it took Apple 16 years to obtain the domain apple.co.uk from the British company Apple Illustrations.[20] The law is even more confusing about patents. The United States followed a "first to invent" policy for decades until in 2013 it changed to a "first to file" system, which brings the country in line with most of the world.[21]

Economic Forces The disparity in income throughout the world is an obstacle to worldwide product standardization. Some products are priced too high for some consumers in developing nations, and firms must adjust to consumers' ability to pay. Sometimes they can achieve this by simplifying or repackaging the product. Procter & Gamble sells shampoo packaged for individual use in India, in addition to the regular bottle size. In addition, many consumers throughout the world buy cell phone airtime by purchasing prepaid cards worth only a few dollars, or even by renting cell phones from intermediaries and paying per call. But consumers' aspirations can run high. The Boston Consulting Group CEO tells the story of a Chinese woman who built a house with outlets for air conditioners and a two-car garage, even though she didn't have either air conditioners or a car.[22]

In some cases, the foreign subsidiary cannot afford to produce as complete a product mix as does the parent company. Automobile manufacturers may assemble a less expensive and higher-volume line locally and broaden their local product mix by importing luxury models. International firms practice this marketing technique whenever possible because a captive foreign sales organization is available to promote the sales of the home organization's exports and because the revenue derived helps pay the subsidiary's overhead. Yet, GM has been successful in China by first introducing the Buick as a premium brand and then moving to mid-range and economy vehicles. The company held nearly 15 percent of the Chinese market in January 2018, edging out Volkswagen for the No. 1 position among foreign brands.[23]

Physical Forces Physical forces, such as climate and terrain, also work against international product standardization. Manufacturers of clothes washers have found success in India by "hardening" their machines against heat, dirt, and power outages. The heat and high humidity in many parts of the tropics require that electrical equipment is built with extra-heavy insulation. Consumer goods that are affected by moisture must be specially packaged to resist its penetration, so pills may be wrapped in foil or blister packs.

High altitudes frequently require product alteration. Food manufacturers have found they must change their cooking instructions for people who live at high altitudes because cooking takes longer there. The thinner atmosphere requires that producers of cake mixes include less yeast as well.

Promotional Strategies

LO 13-4
Identify the product strategies that can be formed from three product alternatives and three kinds of promotional messages.

promotion
Any form of communication between a firm and its publics, including advertising, public relations, sales promotions such as rebates and "buy one get one," and events and experiences, such as sponsoring events to both yield purchases in the short term and confidence in the firm in the long run

Promotion, one of the basic elements of the marketing mix, is communication between a firm and its publics to bring about a favorable buying action and achieve confidence in the firm and the product or service it provides. Note that this definition employs the plural "publics" because promotional efforts must be directed to more than just the ultimate consumers; they also reach retailers and other members of the distribution channel.

Promotion both influences and is influenced by the other marketing mix variables. Marketers can devise nine promotion strategies by choosing different combinations of three product options: (1) market the same physical product everywhere; (2) adapt the physical product for foreign markets; and (3) design a different physical product with (*a*) the same, (*b*) adapted, or (*c*) different messages.[24] Here we examine the six most common promotion strategies of the nine.

1. *Same product–same message.* When marketers find that target markets vary little with respect to product use and consumer attitudes, they can offer the same product and use the same promotional appeals in all markets. Avon uses this strategy, so does Apple.

2. *Same product–different message.* The same product may satisfy a different need or be used differently elsewhere, meaning it can be left unchanged but requires a different message. Honda's early "You meet the nicest people on a Honda" campaign appealed to U.S. consumers who used their motorcycles as pleasure vehicles, but in Brazil Honda stressed the use of motorcycles as basic transportation. Honda has now captured about 90 percent of the Brazilian motorcycle market.

3. *Product adaptation–same message.* When the product serves the same function but must be adapted to different conditions, the changed product can carry the same message. In Japan, Lever Brothers puts Lux soap in fancy boxes because it is often purchased as a gift.

4. *Product adaptation–message adaptation.* In some cases, both the product and the promotional message must be modified for foreign markets. In Latin America, Tang is especially sweetened, premixed, and ready to drink in pouches, and in the Middle East, it comes in a pineapple flavor.[25] Mondelez International (formerly part of Kraft Foods) adapts the vitamins in Tang to meet local needs, for example, by adding iron in Brazil and the Philippines.

5. *Different product–same message.* In many markets, potential customers cannot afford the product as manufactured for developed markets. To overcome this obstacle, companies frequently produce a very distinct product for these markets. Substituting a low-cost plastic squeeze bottle for an aerosol can and a manually operated washing machine for an automated one are two examples. The promotional message, however, can be very similar to what is used in developed markets if the product performs the same functions.

6. *Different product for the same use–different message.* Frequently, the different product requires a different message as well. Developing-country governments faced with high unemployment might be persuaded by a message emphasizing the job-creating possibilities of labor-intensive processes rather than the labor-saving operation of highly automated machinery. In this case, low-tech welding torches might suit better than welding robots.

The tools for communicating these messages—the promotional mix—are advertising, personal selling, sales promotion, public relations, and publicity. Just as in the case of the product strategies, the composition of the promotional mix will depend on the type of product, the environmental forces, and the amount of market penetration desired.

Businesses see real and measurable benefits from using social media to promote their products and services, and companies are hiring social media strategists or full-time social media managers. Worldwide, Facebook leads the pack in terms of the number of active monthly users (2.2 billion at last count), YouTube has 1.9 billion, WhatsApp has 1.5 billion, Instagram has 1 billion, and Twitter has 336 million monthly users.[26] Among more Asia-focused platforms, WeChat (1 billion million monthly users), QQ (0.8 billion), and QZone (0.6 billion) are in a brisk competition for social media users.

> **❝ JEANS ARE about SEX. THE ABUNDANCE of BARE FLESH IS THE LAST GASP of ADVERTISERS TRYING to GIVE REDUNDANT PRODUCTS A NEW IDENTITY. ❞**
> —*Calvin Klein*[27]

ADVERTISING

Among all the promotional mix elements, advertising may be the one that changes the least around the world. **Advertising** is any paid, nonpersonal presentation of ideas, goods, or services by an identified sponsor. U.S. ad agencies have followed their corporate customers into the global realm through wholly owned subsidiaries, joint ventures, and working agreements with local agencies.

advertising
Paid, nonpersonal presentation of ideas, goods, or services by an identified sponsor

The decision whether to advertise globally, as Apple has with the iPad, or locally or regionally, as an increasing number of iPad application developers have done or as the energy drink brand Red Bull does, is not an easy one, but localization seems to be a common trend of late.[28]

Cultural dimensions play a major role in these decisions. Here is a summary of their influence, adapted from work by the researcher Lars Perner[29]:

- *Directness versus indirectness.* U.S. advertising tends to be direct. What are the product benefits? Bluntness may be considered too pushy by Japanese consumers, who can read it as arrogance. How could the seller presume to know what the consumer would like?
- *Comparison.* Comparative advertising is banned in most countries and would probably be counterproductive in Asia, where it could be seen as an insulting instance of confrontation and bragging, even if it were allowed. In the United States, comparison advertising has proven effective (although its implementation can be tricky).
- *Humor.* Although humor is universal, what is considered funny differs greatly across cultures, so pretesting is essential. The British use irony in their jokes, and while U.S. consumers usually understand, they are much less likely to use irony in their own humor.
- *Gender roles.* One study found that women in U.S. advertising tended to be shown in more traditional roles than in Europe or Australia. Some countries are more traditional than the United States. African television ads are also more likely to show women in traditional roles.
- *Explicitness.* Europeans tend to tolerate more explicit advertisements, often with sexual overtones, than do U.S. consumers.

- *Sophistication.* Europeans, particularly the French, demand a considerable level of sophistication, while U.S. shoppers may react more favorably to emotional appeals. U.S. ads seem more likely to use animal personifications than advertising in other cultures.
- *Popular versus traditional culture.* U.S. ads tend to employ contemporary, popular culture, often including current music, while those in more traditional cultures tend to refer more to older roots.
- *Information content versus fluff.* U.S. ads often contain puffery, which was found to be ineffective in eastern European countries because it resembled communist propaganda. The eastern European consumer instead wants facts.

Global and Regional Advertising Manufacturers are increasingly using global or regional advertising for a number of reasons:

1. Cost—A standardized campaign is cheaper. By producing one TV commercial for use across a region, a firm can save up to 50 percent of the production costs.
2. Quality—There is a better chance of obtaining one regional source to do high-quality work than of finding sources in several countries that will work to the same high standard.
3. Brand image—Some marketing managers believe their companies must have a single image throughout a region.
4. Regional organization—Companies are establishing regionalized organizations in which many functions, such as marketing, are centralized.
5. Ease of transmission—Global and regional satellite and cable television are widely available.
6. Economies of scale—Identical products are easier to make.

Brands are science and psychology brought together as a promise.[30] Products may have life cycles, but brands outlive products. They convey a uniform quality, credibility, and experience. And they are valuable. Many companies put the value of their brand on their balance sheet. Look at the dollar value placed on the world's most valuable global brands (including their value in the home market and abroad) (Table 13.2).[31]

Global or National Advertising The debate continues among international marketers about whether to promote their brands as global, regional, or national. Nestlé is an example of a large global firm that achieves consumer familiarity and marketing

TABLE 13.2 Comparing Global Brand Values, 2010–2018

Rank 2018	Rank 2010	Brand, HQ Country	Value ($M), 2018
1	17	Apple, United States	$214,480
2	4	Google, United States	155,506
3	36	Amazon, United States	100,764
4	3	Microsoft, United States	92,715
5	1	Coca-Cola, United States	66,341
6	19	Samsung, S. Korea	59,890
7	11	Toyota, Japan	53,404
8	12	Mercedes-Benz, Germany	48,601
9	N/A	Facebook, United States	45,168
10	6	McDonald's, United States	43,417

Sources: "Best Global Brands 2018 Rankings," *Interbrand*, 2018, www.interbrand.com; and "Best Global Brands 2010 Rankings," *Interbrand*, 2010, www.interbrand.com.

efficiency by using two brands on a single product, a local brand that may be familiar and appeal only to a small group of consumers, and a corporate strategic brand such as Nestlé or Nescafé. In some markets, including Asian ones, product quality across many categories is suggested by a shared brand. The Coca-Cola Company launched a "one brand" approach to advertising the company's beverages, highlighting the consistency world-wide of the company's brand while acknowledging the many variations in its product line. "We are reinforcing that Coca-Cola is for everybody," said Chief Marketing Officer Marcos de Quinto. "Coca-Cola is one brand with different variants, all of which share the same values and visual iconography. People want their Coca-Cola in different ways, but whichever one they want, they want a Coca-Cola brand with great taste and refreshment."[32]

Media Availability Satellite TV broadcasters make it possible for numerous programming networks to provide service to millions of households in dozens of countries and in many languages. International print media include local, national, and regional editions. The *International New York Times*; the Asian and European editions of the *Wall Street Journal*; and the international editions of the *Guardian* and the *Financial Times* are newspapers with wide circulation. Digital ads will lead the way for global media growth in the next four years, with mobile ad spending estimated to reach a level twice that of television advertising spending by 2022. Instagram alone is expected to generate $5.5 billion in ad revenues in the United States in 2018, with online advertising reaching 40 percent of the world's total ad spend.[34] There is some indication that advertisers are confronting the irony of having digital ads becoming more expensive, yet reaching fewer customers, thus impacting the efficiency of ad spending choices.[35]

Advertisers can also go to other media to reach their markets. Cinema advertising is heavily used in many parts of the world (including Norway, Austria, the United Kingdom, and Brazil) and revenues are expected to rise by nearly half a billion dollars between 2015 and 2019, reaching $3.1 billion.[36] In a number of developing countries, automobiles equipped with loudspeakers circulate through the cities announcing products, and street signs are furnished by advertisers whose messages hang on them. Homeowners can get a free coat of paint by permitting advertisers to put ads on their outside walls. Buses and trains carry advertisements. One of the most ingenious campaigns was launched by a tea company that gave away thousands of printed prayers to pilgrims bound for Mecca. A tea advertisement was printed on the other side.

The point is that multiple media are available in every market, and the local managers and advertising agencies are familiar with the advantages of each kind. Media selection is challenging for international advertising managers who try to standardize their media mix from the home office. The variation in media availability is a strong reason for leaving this part of the advertising program to the local organization.

Media Availability and Internet Advertising

The Internet is valuable as a marketing research tool, and as an advertising medium as well. Among its advantages in international advertising are the following:

1. The Internet reaches an affluent, accessible audience. Many users in a wide variety of countries read English or other common languages well, although most users prefer native-language sites.
2. Internet ads can be inexpensive, or not. Here are some examples:
   - LinkedIn = $6.05 cost per thousand impressions (CPM)
   - Twitter-promoted trending topic = $200,000 for a day
   - Twitter = $5.76 CPM
   - Facebook = $9.06 CPM
   - Instagram = $6.70 CPM

> **❝ MORE THAN HALF of CONSUMERS ARE WILLING to PAY MORE IF YOU ARE WILLING to GIVE THEM INFORMATION in THEIR OWN LANGUAGES. ❞**
>
> *—Nataly Kelly, VP of Market Development at Smartling, the cloud-based enterprise translation management company*[33]

LO 13-5
Discuss some of the effects the Internet may have on international marketing.

> **❝ THE INTERNET IS BECOMING THE TOWN SQUARE for THE GLOBAL VILLAGE of TOMORROW. ❞**
>
> *—Bill Gates*[37]

- Hulu in-stream ads = $30 CPM
- Foursquare actions = 40 cents
- Spotify ads = $5 CPM, $25,000 minimum per campaign or $250 minimum for individual ads
- BuzzFeed-sponsored article = $100,000
- Branded mobile app = $125,000[38]

3. Advertising online is sometimes less heavily regulated than other advertising forms. In Europe, where direct advertising of prescription drug products is banned, Internet sites about these drugs (with a disclaimer that the information is for U.S. audiences only) are a way to provide potential consumers with product information.

4. Unlike TV or newspaper ads, Internet communications are interactive, and consumers can choose which messages and information they receive. For this reason, company web offerings can be tailor-made for the user. This customization increases the application of the marketing concept.

5. Internet and smartphone advertising can be a valuable means to reach certain groups such as teenagers, who spend less time watching TV than any other demographic group and who prefer to use social media or play video games. Two-thirds of U.S. adults over 65 use the Internet and at least 37 percent use social media such as Facebook.[39] The number of Internet users in Bangladesh grew an astounding 80,383 percent between 2000 and 2018.[40]

Thus, in a variety of ways, the Internet and social media have quickly become an important necessity for the global advertiser.

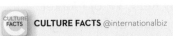

CULTURE FACTS @internationalbiz

Although Indians are avid phone users, many need to limit their usage to keep fees down. According to one estimate, 65 percent of India's 860 million mobile subscribers use purposely missed calls to convey short messages determined in advance, like "Thinking of you" or "Call me back."[41] #limitphoneusage #lowerfees #callmeback

©Kerstin Geier/Gallo Images/Getty Images.

TYPE OF PRODUCT

Buyers of industrial goods and luxury products usually act on the same motives the world over; thus, industrial and luxury products lend themselves to a standardized approach. This standardization enables manufacturers of capital goods, such as General Electric and Caterpillar, to prepare international campaigns that require very little modification in their various markets. Certain consumer goods markets are similar, too, and firms can use the same appeals and sales arguments worldwide when the product is low priced, is consumed in the same way everywhere, and is always bought for the same reasons. Examples of such products are gasoline, soft drinks, detergents, cosmetics, and airline services.

FOREIGN ENVIRONMENTAL FORCES

Like variations in media availability, foreign environmental forces act as deterrents to the international standardization of advertising, and as you would expect, among the most influential of these forces are sociocultural factors.

A basic cultural decision for the marketer is whether to position and advertise the product as foreign or local. The choice often depends on the country, the product type, and the target market. In Germany, for example, consumers are not at all impressed by a carmaker that announces it has "American" know-how. At the same time, such purely U.S. products as bourbon, fast food, and jeans have made tremendous inroads there and in the rest of Europe. Similarly, in Japan and elsewhere in Asia, the national identity of some consumer products enhances their image. The current rage among Chinese teenagers, and even in the United States and beyond, is skincare products and popular music (K-pop) from Korea.[42] Pandakorea.com, a Korean online retailer selling Korean goods to foreigners, is taking advantage of this situation by selling a range of products to teens in China and elsewhere. Korean soaps have also gained a foothold in Turkey. Some speculate this is due to the Korean emphasis on romantic, rather than openly sexual, themes.

U.S.-based fast-food restaurants such as McDonald's (Japan's largest restaurant business), KFC (the third largest), Dairy Queen, and Mister Donut account for half the total restaurant business in Japan. KFC has zeroed in on an even larger Asian market—it has over 5,000 restaurants in 1,100 Chinese cities—despite accusations that it served tainted food in 2013 and 2014.[43] One explanation is that the Chinese have less and less time for preparing meals at home. KFC is also the largest fast-food chain in South Africa and the largest foreign chain in Nigeria. One of its attractions there, given Nigeria's spotty public power grid, is its outlets' continuous wi-fi signal, supplemented by power generators.[44]

The experience of suppliers to the youth market indicates that this, too, is an international market segment, much like the market for luxury goods. A former director of MTV Europe observed that teenagers in places like Paris have more in common with their peers in New York than they do with their own parents. They watch the same movies, buy the same products, drink the same colas, and listen to the same music.[45] This similarity suggests that marketers can formulate global advertising campaigns for these consumers that will require little more than a translation into the local language, unless the product strategy requires a foreign identity. That decision should be made with local input.

Because communication is impossible if the two parties don't share a language, translations must be made into the language of the consumers. Yet the same word may be perfectly apt in one country while connoting something completely different in another. Experienced advertising managers therefore use back-translation (translating the translated copy back into the original language to double-check that the meaning is as intended) and keep the copy short with plenty of illustrations.

Because a nation's laws generally reflect public opinion, cultural forces tend to be closely aligned with legal forces, which exert a strong and pervasive influence on advertising. We have seen how laws affect media availability; they also restrict the kinds of products marketers can advertise and the ad copy they can use.

In 1995 PepsiCo launched a series of TV commercials, the Pepsi Challenge campaign, to test the comparative advertising laws of 30 countries. PepsiCo's head of marketing said the company "intended to push the envelope on comparison advertising in markets around the world."[46] The ads presented the competitor's product in a way that some countries specifically prohibit as unfair advertising. Because of this and other conflicts over comparative advertising, some Latin American countries found their laws to be inadequate. In Europe, the EU Commission authorized comparative advertising subject to restrictions because some member countries permitted it while others did not.

Advertisers in the Islamic countries face limitations, although these vary widely across the Middle East. Women appear about as often in Lebanese and Egyptian TV ads as in U.S. ads, but only half as often in Saudi ads. They are just as likely to be dressed "immodestly" (that is, roughly, in Western dress) in Lebanese as in U.S. ads, although less often in Egyptian and never in Saudi ads.[47]

With so many obstacles to international standardization, what should the international advertising manager do? The opinion of some experts is that good brands and good products can cross international borders, but each may have to be adjusted for the local market. Let's examine this situation more closely.

A global product and a global brand, such as Apple's iPad, can reach many markets unchanged or virtually unchanged, leading to valuable cost savings.[48] Such products tend to be innovations. A global product with a local brand is often the result of mergers. Germany's Henkel—maker of Right Guard, Dial Soap, and other consumer

Entering Cuba: Pipe Dream or Real Opportunity?

After Fidel Castro overthrew Cuba's U.S.-backed regime in 1959, the two countries had decades of acrimonious relations. Cuba was subjected to economic and diplomatic sanctions from the United States longer than any other nation. Estimates by the Cuban government suggest that U.S. trade embargoes cost Cuba a total of $126 billion.

In 2009, the Obama administration initiated efforts to improve diplomacy between the nations, including a relaxation of restrictions on travel and remittances. President Raul Castro also began to liberalize portions of Cuba's heavily state-controlled economy, enabling the number of self-employed workers to nearly triple between 2009 and 2013. In 2014, it was announced that full diplomatic ties would be restored between the two nations, the culmination of 18 months of secret diplomacy on the part of Catholic Pope Francis. The Obama administration subsequently removed Cuba from the U.S. list of terrorism sponsors and announced that the United States would loosen certain restraints on financial transactions with Cuba, remove some restrictions on U.S. citizens traveling to Cuba, and authorize the export of more goods to the Cuban private sector. The announcements signaled the first steps toward reestablishing formal relationships between the two governments and reopening Cuba to trade and travel with the United States. In 2016, commercial U.S. airlines were able to commence service to Cuba for the first time in over 50 years. Many U.S.-based firms, including Google, Starwood Hotels & Resorts, and Airbnb, subsequently made heavy investments in Cuba.

Havana has much to gain from improved relations with the United States, especially when its regional partner, Venezuela, faces severe instability. Cuba also transitioned to a new regime as the ruling Castro brothers passed from the scene and were replaced by President Miguel Diaz-Canel. When it comes to business, Cuba's cars are of 1950s' vintage, there are opportunities for tourism going in both directions, sellers of farm and construction and food manufacturing equipment see possibilities, and Cuba imports huge quantities of long-grain rice, a specialty of southern states in the United States.

In late 2017, the recently elected Trump administration announced new regulations that impacted U.S. companies attempting to conduct business in Cuba. Changes included prohibition of new business activity with certain entities owned or controlled by Cuban intelligence, security, or military services that are included on a new Cuba Restricted List prepared by the U.S. State Department. Additional restrictions were imposed to limit individual travel to Cuba. These new rules were mostly expected to impact Cuba's tourism sector, as well as projects being considered for Cuba's new Special Economic

Making cigars in Havana. Some Americans look for easier access to Cuban cigars. ©Luis Acosta/AFP/Getty Images.

Source: Julie Creswell, "U.S. Companies Clamor to Do Business in New Cuban Market," *The New York Times,* December 18, 2014, https://www.nytimes.com, accessed November 13, 2018.

Development Zone at the port of Mariel, due to significant investments in these areas by Cuba's Armed Forces' holding company. The new rules did not force existing business activities in Cuba to be unwound, however, even if they involved entities on the new Cuba Restricted List.

The Trump administration hinted that further changes might occur in the future. In the meantime, the new rules allow opportunities to be pursued in many areas, including food production, construction, energy and waste management, agricultural trade, consumer electronics, fashion, sports, and music, among others.

Critical Thinking Questions

1. Should U.S. marketers continue to gear up for trade and investment with Cuba, or adopt a go-slow approach and wait for the political situation to clarify? Defend your answer.

2. Does Cuba present sufficient opportunities to foreign exporters? Why or why not?

3. What problems could the political climate in Cuba give U.S. exporters or investors?

Sources: Claire Felter, and Danielle Renwick, "U.S.–Cuba Relations," *Council on Foreign Relations,* January 19, 2018, www.cfr.org; Anya Landau French, "Despite Policy Changes, Many Opportunities Remain for US Businesses in Cuba," *The Hill,* January 09, 2018, www.thehill.com; Damien Dave, "Focusing on the Future, Cuba Leaves Fidel Castro to History," *The New York Times,* December 18, 2014, www.nytimes.com; Julie Creswell, "U.S. Companies Clamor to Do Business in New Cuban Market," *The New York Times,* December 18, 2014, www.nytimes.com; and Stratfor, "The United States and Cuba Begin Restoring Relations," *Stratfor Global Intelligence,* www.stratfor.com.

products—has kept local packaging and standardized the physical product, its soap powder, making manufacturing efficiencies possible. The final option, a local product with a local brand, is the most localized approach and is appropriate when, for perhaps cultural reasons, the product that sells well in one country will not transfer to another or does so for quite a different set of purposes. Dish soaps that are adjusted for the hardness of local water and sell under local names are an example. P&G's Fairy Liquid, a dishwashing soap that is a leading brand in the United Kingdom, similar to Joy in the U.S. market, is localized on both brand and content. Remember, too, that, as the director of multinational accounts at McCann-Erickson claims, social classes across different countries have shared sensibilities: "A male middle executive in Italy has more in common with a male middle executive in the U.K. than with a farmer in Italy. It is those shared sensibilities that make global branding possible."[49]

Such global branding approaches look for similarities across segments and countries to capitalize on them by providing promotional themes with worldwide appeal. A second approach suggests that even though human nature is the same everywhere, it is also true that a Spaniard will remain a Spaniard and a Jamaican a Jamaican. In this view, it is preferable to develop separate appeals to take advantage of the differences among customers in different cultures and countries.

Neither Purely Global nor Purely Local

LO 13-6
Explain "glocal" advertising strategies.

You probably have already gathered that for most firms neither a purely global nor a purely local campaign is the best way to handle international advertising. In fact, companies at either end of the global–local spectrum, with purely global campaigns or only local campaigns, tend to be moving toward the middle, with a "glocal" (combined *global* and *local*) approach that allows them to develop a cost-effective common strategy for large regions. Coca-Cola says simply, "Think globally, but act locally." Another example is Samsung, which in India builds a sari program into its washers so that 5-foot-long saris will not become tangled. Other appliance makers selling in India such as Bosch also have this feature.

Gillette organizes its advertising in regional and cultural clusters: pan-Latin America, pan-Middle East, pan-Africa, and pan-Atlantic. The company believes it can identify the same needs and buying motives among consumers in regions or countries linked by culture, consumers' habits, and level of market development for its products. Gillette might use the same European-style advertising for Australia and South Africa, but in Asia, it would link developing economies such as the Philippines, Indonesia, Thailand, and Malaysia. The company introduced a modified version of its Mach 3 Turbo razor in India using a local marketing agency. The agency parked modified trucks with shaving booths, sound systems, and female marketers outside call centers and shopping malls. The trial led many consumers to switch immediately to the Gillette razor, giving up the traditional double-edged razor that is still common in India. After stumbling with the Vector shaver in 2002 (Gillette had used Indian MIT students as their focus group rather than Indians living in India), the Guard razor seems to be a success. It stresses safety more than closeness and is one-bladed.[50] With its regional-where-possible approach to marketing, Gillette moved toward a global marketing strategy in the markets where such an approach might be appropriate, while allowing for regional and national differences.

The **programmed-management approach** is another middle-ground advertising strategy in which the home office and the foreign subsidiaries agree on marketing objectives, after which each subsidiary puts together a tentative advertising campaign. This is submitted to the home office for review and suggestions. The campaign is then market-tested locally, and the home office reviews the results and offers comments. The subsidiary then submits a complete campaign to the home office for review. When the

programmed-management approach
A middle-ground advertising strategy between globally standardized and entirely local programs

home office is satisfied, the budget is approved and the subsidiary begins implementing the campaign. The result may be a highly standardized campaign for all markets or one that has been individualized to the extent necessary to cope with local market conditions. The programmed-management approach gives the home office a chance to standardize those parts of the campaign that can be standardized but still permits flexibility in responding to different marketing conditions. You can read more about the programmed-management approach here: https://www.ibm.com/developerworks/rational/library/4751.html.[51]

PERSONAL SELLING

Along with advertising, personal selling constitutes a principal component of the promotional mix. Its relative importance compared with advertising depends to a great extent on the cost of each, the funds available, media availability, and the type of product sold. Manufacturers of industrial products rely more on personal selling than on advertising to communicate with their overseas markets. However, producers of consumer products may also emphasize personal selling overseas, especially in developing countries.

Evidence suggests that the Internet, when used to build trust through the advertiser's consumer orientation, competence, dependability, candor, and likability,[52] can be an effective tool in personal selling. Its value may be enhanced by face-to-face communication as well. Approaches to trust building in a virtual environment are evolving that seem to be working, such as the London-based Depop peer-to-peer social shopping or the HelloFresh meal-kit provider.

Many companies keep the organization of their overseas sales force, their sales presentation, and their training methods very similar to those employed in the home country whenever possible. Avon was following the same plan of person-to-person selling in its major markets when China outlawed door-to-door selling in 1998, citing concerns about consumer safety and fraudulent pyramid schemes.[53] Avon China then shifted to a retail model and in 2006 provided products through a network of 6,000 beauty boutiques and 1,000 beauty counters. China later approved Avon for person-to-person selling and the company resumed its successful model. However, the company was fined $135 million by the U.S. Securities and Exchange Commission in 2014 for bribing Chinese officials in order to resume door-to-door selling.[54] Under the U.S. Foreign Corrupt Practices Act, companies cannot pay money or otherwise provide anything of value to foreign officials in order to gain or retain business.

Avon has also been successful in Mexico, but when it entered the market, local experts predicted it would fail because Mexican middle-class women tend to be away from the home during the day. However, Avon made some small but important changes. It mounted a massive advertising campaign to educate Mexicans about what they could expect from the visits, using its standardized U.S. advertising with some added information about the selling approach. In addition, Avon recruited educated, middle-class women as sales representatives and trained them well. They were encouraged to visit their friends, too. In both China and Mexico, changing the U.S. plan as necessary for legal reasons and cultural differences supported Avon's entry. However, the rise of online sales is causing Avon to explore changes to its strategy and increase its involvement in e-commerce.[55]

Recruiting salespeople in foreign countries is at times more difficult than recruiting them at home because sales managers may have to cope with the stigma attached to selling that exists in some areas. It is also necessary to hire salespeople who are culturally acceptable to customers and channel members. This can be challenging if a market is small and subdivided into several distinct cultures with different customs and languages.

SALES PROMOTION

Sales promotion provides the selling aids for the marketing function and includes activities such as the preparation of point-of-purchase displays, contests, premiums, trade show exhibits, celebrity-embraced promotion, money-off offers, and coupons. Couponing is a good example. A Nielsen report surveyed consumers on cost-saving measures that would move them to increased coupon use.[56] In the United States, 46 percent of consumers stated that they would increase coupon use, while the global average was only 19 percent. Couponing has also been affected by the Internet, with many offers available online.

When marketers are considering transferring sales promotion techniques to other markets, they must consider some cultural constraints. For example, a premium must be meaningful to the purchaser. A kitchen gadget might be valued by a U.S. consumer but may not be particularly attractive in Latin America, where a consumer of similar economic status is likely to have a housekeeper.

Contests, raffles, and games have been extremely successful in countries where people love to play the odds. If people will buy a lottery ticket week after week, hoping to win the grand prize despite odds of 500,000 to 1, why shouldn't they participate in a contest that costs them nothing to enter? Point-of-purchase displays are well accepted by retailers, although many establishments are so small that there is simply no place to put all the displays offered to them. The marketing manager who prepares a well-planned program after studying the constraints of the local markets can expect excellent results from the time and money invested.

sales promotion
Any of the various activities, such as preparation of point-of-purchase displays, contests, premiums, trade show exhibits, celebrity-embraced promotion, money-off offers, and coupons

PUBLIC RELATIONS

Public relations is the firm's methods of communicating with its various publics, including the governments where it operates, to secure a favorable impression. As one writer has put it, "Public relations is the marketing of the firm." Ford Motor Company is one firm whose public relations reach is broad. The Ford Foundation, a philanthropy begun by Edsel Ford and two company executives, has an international graduate fellowships program that has provided $280 million in graduate fellowships for students from Africa, the Middle East, Asia, Latin America, and Russia since 2001.[57] Wells Fargo donated $286.5 million in 2017 to various entities, including affordable housing and homeowner education programs, the Red Cross, military and veterans, scholarships, and environmental grants. In addition, Wells Fargo gives employees paid vacation days to volunteer on significant nonprofit projects of their choice.[58] This activity involved local economies and communities around the world.

Although U.S. firms have had organized public relations programs for many years at home, some have paid less attention to this important function elsewhere in the world and have failed to inform their local publics about what they are doing. Nationalism and a public-opinion backlash against multinationals in many countries have made it imperative that companies improve their communications to their nonbusiness publics with more effective public relations programs. International pharmaceutical manufacturers are viewed with suspicion by the public in developing nations because, although their products may alleviate suffering, they do so at a profit made from the poor. To improve their images, major pharmaceuticals have begun programs related to disease globally. For example, in 2014 Sanofi was praised for developing a vaccine for dengue fever, which mainly plagues the poor in developing countries. Years earlier the Bill & Melinda Gates Foundation (B&MGF) had purchased shares of nine Big Pharma companies, valued at nearly $205 million. This signaled a shift in Bill Gates's personal investment strategy to becoming an influence on the operations of his foundations. It was an important step in convincing the rich to donate their personal fortunes to B&MGF: a sort of leadership by example for those who need their conscience stroked, or their image restored or improved.[59]

public relations
Various methods of communicating with the firm's publics to secure a favorable impression, rather than immediate sales

One of the biggest challenges for firms is dealing with critics of their operations and motives. Some try to defuse criticism by holding open public meetings at which topics of interest are regularly debated. Others prefer to meet with critics privately, although they may find themselves caught in a never-ending relationship in which the critics continually escalate their demands.

A strategy some firms have employed successfully is to address a contentious issue by working with international or governmental agencies instead of dealing directly with critics. For example, in China a number of foreign firms that have achieved success recently—among them Toshiba, Philips, and Canon—have found themselves under fire in the Chinese media for a number of reasons. If the coverage is too unbalanced, firms should complain to the central party's Propaganda (now Publicity) Department. Although the department is not actually part of the government, it is a committee of the Central Committee of the Communist Party of China.[60]

Another alternative is to do nothing. If the criticism receives no publicity, it may die from lack of interest. Yet sometimes a libeled company chooses to defend its reputation in court. McDonald's decided it was the victim in London when Helen Steel and Dave Morris distributed leaflets accusing the company of starving the countries of the Third World, exploiting children in its advertising, and destroying the Central American rainforests. McDonald's was also cruel to animals, they alleged, because at times chickens were still conscious when their throats were cut. McDonald's sued Steel and Morris in 1994. It became the longest libel trial in English history, ending two and a half years later. McDonald's was awarded $98,000 in damages in a case it had spent $16 million to pursue, although McDonald's has never collected the money.[61]

LO 13-7

Define pricing and distribution strategies.

Pricing Strategies

Decisions about pricing, the third element of the marketing mix, affect other corporate functions, directly determine the firm's gross revenue, and therefore influence profits. Most pricing research has been done on North Americans, and this raises serious problems for its generalizability. U.S. shoppers like sales, for example, while consumers in countries where goods are more scarce may attribute sales to low quality rather than a desire to gain market share. There is some evidence that perceived price–quality relationships are quite high in Britain and Japan. Thus, discount stores have had difficulty in both these markets. In developing countries, there is less trust of outsiders in the market. Cultural differences may influence the effort a buyer puts into evaluating deals in these markets, where buying decisions rest on relationships. Those consumers in some economies who are usually paid weekly rather than biweekly or monthly may influence the effectiveness of shaping the context for pricing as well. "A dollar a day" is a much bigger chunk from a weekly than from a monthly paycheck.

Effective price setting consists of more than mechanically adding a standard markup to a cost. To obtain the maximum benefits, management must regard pricing in the same manner as it does other controllable variables—as an element of the marketing mix that can be varied to achieve the marketing objectives of the firm.

For instance, if the marketer wishes to position a product as a high-quality item, setting a relatively high price will reinforce promotion that emphasizes quality. However, combining a low price with a promotional emphasis on quality could result in a contradiction that will hurt credibility with the consumer. Pricing can also affect the choice of intermediaries, because if the firm requires a wholesaler to take title to, stock, promote, and deliver the merchandise, it must give the wholesaler a much larger trade discount than would be demanded by a broker, whose services are much more limited.

These examples illustrate one of the reasons for the complexity of price setting: the interaction of pricing with the other elements of the marketing mix. In addition, two other sets of forces influence this variable: environmental forces, and the interaction between marketing and the other functional areas of the firm. Consider the following:

1. The finance people want prices that are both profitable and conducive to steady cash flow.
2. Production supervisors want prices that create large sales volumes, which permit long production runs with their associated lower cost benefits.
3. The legal department worries about possible antitrust violations when different prices are set according to type of customer. It also worries about global trademark protection and intellectual property issues.
4. The tax people are concerned with the effect of prices on tax loads.
5. The domestic sales manager wants export prices to be high enough to avoid having to compete with company products that are purchased for export but then diverted to the domestic market. If export prices are too low, this provides gray-market resellers with the opportunity to buy the product abroad and re-export to the country of manufacture.

The marketer must address all these concerns and also consider the impact of legal and other environmental forces as well.

STANDARDIZING PRICES

Companies that pursue a policy of unified, global corporate pricing know that pricing is acted on by the same forces that inhibit the international standardization of the other marketing mix components. Pricing for the overseas markets is more complex because managements must be concerned with two kinds of pricing: **foreign national pricing**, which is local pricing in another country, and **international pricing** for exports, which sets prices for goods produced in one country and sold in another.

foreign national pricing
Policy that sets local pricing based on market forces in another country

international pricing
Policy that sets prices of goods produced in one country and sold in another

FOREIGN NATIONAL PRICING

Prices can vary because of cost differentials on opposite sides of a border. One government may levy higher import duties on imported raw materials or may subsidize public utilities, while another may not. Differences in labor legislation cause labor costs to vary. Competition among local suppliers may be intense in one market, permitting the affiliate to buy inputs at better prices than those paid by an affiliate in another market.

Introducing a product into a new market may induce some firms to employ a price-skimming strategy, setting a high price to quickly recover development costs. Early adopters simply want the product and will pay a premium. Other firms take a penetration pricing strategy, where the price is set very low in order to quickly establish the product in a new market. Apple seems to follow a skimming strategy, while its competitors use a penetration strategy. Ultra HDTV makers are switching from skimming to a penetration pricing model.

INTERNATIONAL PRICING

International pricing sets prices for goods produced in one country and sold in another. A special kind of exporting, *transfer pricing*, is common among large companies that want their subsidiaries to specialize in the manufacture of some products and import others. Their imports may be components that are assembled into the end product, such as computer chips made in one country that are mounted on boards built in another, or they may be finished products imported to complement the product mix of an affiliate.

Increasingly, the Internet is redefining pricing options. It is a tremendous tool for comparing prices—already sites can scan hundreds of outlets for prices on certain goods—and so national boundaries may mean less and less. In a sense, world prices for consumers may be on the way to being achieved. The effect extends to business-to-business pricing as well.

LO 13-7
Define pricing and
distribution strategies.

Distribution Strategies

The development of distribution strategies is challenging in the home country and even more so internationally, where marketing managers must concern themselves with two functions rather than one: getting the products *to* foreign markets (exporting) and distributing the products *within* each foreign market.

Distribution decisions are often interdependent with the other marketing mix variables. For example, if the product requires considerable after-sales servicing, the firm will want to sell through dealers with the facilities, staff, and capital to purchase spare parts and train service people. Channel decisions are critical because they are long-term decisions; once established, they are far less easy to change than those made for price, product, and promotion. The Coca-Cola Company made a major decision to change its channel system in China; at great cost, it moved from using a traditional channel, where competing interests of the channel members were slowing up the company's connection to the market, to building relationships with its small retail sellers.

STANDARDIZING DISTRIBUTION

Although management would prefer to standardize distribution patterns internationally, there are two fundamental constraints on doing so: the variation in the availability of channel members among the firm's markets and the environmental forces present in these different markets. International managers have found flexibility around an overall policy to be effective. The subsidiaries implement the distribution policy and design channel strategies to meet local conditions.

As a starting point in their channel design, local managers have the successful distribution system used in the domestic operation. Headquarters' support for a policy of employing the same channels worldwide will be especially strong when the entire marketing mix has been built around a particular channel type, such as a direct sales force or franchised operators. McDonald's is an example of a firm that relies primarily on franchise operators at home and abroad.

FOREIGN ENVIRONMENTAL FORCES

Basic geographic differences matter greatly in distribution. Just think about dealing with Switzerland's mountainous terrain. Changes caused by cultural forces generally occur over time, but those caused by legal forces can be radical and quick. To illustrate, hypermarkets are changing distribution patterns everywhere, including Europe, but European governments have experimented with such laws as the Royer and Raffarin laws to restrict construction permits for supermarkets and hypermarkets.

Another restriction of distribution has been tried in the European Union. Manufacturers have attempted to prevent distributors from selling across national borders, but the EU Commission has prohibited them from doing so by invoking antitrust laws. In effect, a firm that has two factories in the European Union with different costs, and thus distinct prices, is nearly powerless to prevent products from the lower-cost affiliate from competing with higher-cost products from the other affiliate.

Economic differences also make international standardization difficult in distribution, although marketers can adapt. In Japan, many women no longer have time to shop and prepare traditional Japanese foods. They fill their needs by purchasing more convenience foods advertised on TV; there are more than 50 chains of convenience stores, and home delivery is also available. The largest chain, 7-Eleven, has more than 20,000 stores, many of which are run by former small shopkeepers.

Can retailing be globalized? Retailers such as France's Carrefour, with 12,300 stores in 30 countries worldwide, think it can. So do Safeway, Gucci, Cartier, and Benetton, which have made aggressive penetration in Canada, Europe, Hong Kong, and Singapore. Walmart, now with operations in 28 countries, is learning that global retailing takes localization.

Disintermediation is the unraveling of traditional distribution structures and is most often the result of firms' ability to combine the Internet with fast delivery services

disintermediation
The unraveling of traditional
distribution structures,
popularly called "cutting out
the middlemen"

NICOLE KISSAM: Consider a Career in International Marketing

Courtesy of Nicole Kissam.

Nicole Kissam holds a BS in business administration with a concentration in international management. She speaks Czech and Spanish in addition to English and lived and worked in Prague for three years as account manager for an independently owned ad agency with multinational clients. Here are her comments:

I completed an internship through AIESEC International after I graduated from university. This internship is what originally took me to a small town in the Czech Republic for a four-month assignment. The assignment was with an umbrella holding company that owned many types of businesses. My role there as an intern was to research the marketing potential of a few of their products. I highly recommend using an international student organization such as AIESEC to do an internship right when you graduate from college. The contacts and experience I gained through my internship transitioned me into finding another job in Prague for a longer expat experience. Although I eventually chose to come back to America, working for the smaller agency was a great first work experience and could have easily been a stepping stone to a larger multinational corporate role.

Interesting for me was learning the protocols around different levels of friends and how interaction is structured. For example, in adult life in America, we tend to call or make appointments to see each other, rather than just stop by. Czech people, if they knew each other very well and were good friends, would always just stop over at each other's houses and apartments unannounced. When you did so, it was like a pleasant and welcoming reunion of friends. There would always be a pot of hot tea, shot of distilled spirits, and some bread and cheese available to nibble on and converse over for a half hour or so. It was common to show up and have meals together without notice as well.

Czech people also have a custom of always bringing something to share with them when they visit, such as chocolate, tea, bread, etc. I carry this custom over into my life in America with friends and sometimes close business associates.

Success is really determined on your ability to perform quality work, of course, but also to be able to adapt to a foreign culture enough to get people to like you and give you what you want/need to do your job. Language skills are not necessarily essential at this point because most businesspeople around the world speak English. However, if you are talented in learning other languages, it will deepen your experience in a foreign country a thousandfold.

Working in the Czech Republic showed me a lot I never knew about my own capacity and abilities. I learned the language in less than six months and was successful at planning and implementing advertising campaigns in a foreign country. Working across cultures was also amazing. The approach to working and work life is different in every country and can sometimes take some getting used to.

My most memorable experience was really just the day-to-day experience of living and working in Prague. I walked from my apartment to my office every day, rode the metro to visit clients in various European cities, and enjoyed the beauty of Prague while getting my first work experience.

Source: Nicole Kissam.

such as FedEx and UPS. Increasingly, disintermediation is shaking up traditional distribution channels and making rapid service possible with or without a formal distribution structure. Our increasing ability to ship products quickly may mean that the lack of dedicated channels makes less difference over time. On the other hand, the Internet has also provided new channel structures, such as eBay, Etsy, Depop, and Folksy.

SUMMARY

LO 13-1
Discuss why international marketing managers may wish to standardize the marketing mix.

As a whole, firm executives are interested in the potential cost savings of using the same product and promotional mix. It is also easier to control the program and less time needs to be spent on the marketing plan.

LO 13-2
Distinguish among the total product, the physical product, and the brand name.

Each of the components of the total product can be altered as part of product adaptation. A brand name may be the same while the product is changed. On the other hand, sometimes the brand name is inappropriate and should be changed while the physical product may be fine without alteration.

LO 13-3
Compare the way consumer and industrial products and services are modified for international sale.

Industrial products (for example, concrete) contain little or no "cultural input" and there are few personal preferences. On the other hand, consumer products reflect personal preferences. Notice that, for example, at the fashion end of the consumer market, there again may be few differences in country preferences. A Louis Vuitton luxury purse may be the same all over the world.

LO 13-4
Identify the product strategies that can be formed from three product alternatives and three kinds of promotional messages.

Six commonly used promotional strategies can be formulated by combining the same, adapted, or newly designed product with the same, adapted, or different promotional message.

LO 13-5
Discuss some of the effects the Internet may have on international marketing.

Among others, the Internet makes more pricing information available, increases the possibilities of distribution (for example, the Burberry stores in China can broadcast runway events, and clerks are equipped with iPads to instantly order unstocked sizes), and can make the offering much more personal in terms of sizing and other variables.

LO 13-6
Explain "glocal" advertising strategies.

The idea is to design an international program and then make local adjustments that local managers find necessary.

LO 13-7
Define pricing and distribution strategies.

A pricing strategy considers segments, competitors, industries, market conditions, and costs. Distribution is how the product reaches the end user.

KEY TERMS

advertising 351
corporate visual identity (CVI) 343
disintermediation 363
foreign national pricing 361

international pricing 361
marketing mix 342
programmed-management approach 357
promotion 350

public relations 359
sales promotion 359
total product 343

CRITICAL THINKING QUESTIONS

1. Former Louis Vuitton CEO Yves Carcelle said, "One to two thousand people is all you need. You can't judge by average income—average doesn't mean anything." Although he was speaking about the luxury goods market, do you think his comments about averages apply to other segments of the market as well? Why or why not?

2. What future do you see for global advertising?

3. What advantages and disadvantages may result from standardizing the marketing mix worldwide?

4. As people become more educated and living conditions improve, do their product preferences become more similar? Why or why not?

5. Under what conditions would a "glocal" approach not be useful?

6. Assume you are a consultant to Sony, shortly before the introduction of PlayStation 4. What advice would you give Sony about making the device attractive to various foreign customers?

7. What cultural problems might you encounter in introducing the search and discovery application Foursquare in foreign markets?

8. Candy Crush Saga is a simple game with 2.73 billion downloads and more than 1 trillion rounds of the game played since its launch, but only about 16 percent of its fan base is in the United States. What elements of Candy Crush Saga do you think appeal to consumers from many different cultures?

 globalEDGE RESEARCH TASK http://globalEDGE.msu.edu/

Use the globalEDGE website (http://globalEDGE.msu.edu) to complete the following exercises:

1. You work for a food company, and your company plans to export to the growing Chinese market. You are in the process of identifying any regulations you need to meet to export, any product customization you may need to consider, promotion channels you may use, and the trade shows you may need to attend. Visit the "Resources" page of the "Global Insights" section of globalEDGE and review all the resources listed there. Which of those resources may be helpful in answering your questions? Make a list of the information you can think of that will help you market your products in China and match with the resources listed on this page that you may use to find that information you need.

2. Understanding the overall identity and characteristics of a country may help in understanding the needs and expectations of the consumer base in that country. Find the FutureBrand's "Country Brand Index" in globalEDGE and review the latest report on the external site. How is the identity of a country measured? What dimensions are used, and how relevant do you think they are? Review the summary of the top-ranked country in the report and considering how the top country is ranked on different dimensions, comment on some of the possible consumer needs and expectations you can think of.

MINICASE

WILL DOLLAR SHAVE CLUB'S EDGINESS WORK ABROAD?

Michael Dubin launched Dollar Shaving Club (DSC) in 2012 as a mail-to-home razor blade subscription company costing members as little as $1 a month. A key element in the successful U.S. launch was an edgy video that introduced Dollar Shave Club to the world by opening with Dubin at a desk, pitching his razors. He then stands up and asks, "Are the blades any good?" After responding, "No," he stops beside a sign that says "our blades are f***ing great." The video then turns into a hilariously slapstick pitch, with Dubin driving a forklift, dancing with a guy in a bear costume, and scattering dollar bills into the air with a leaf blower. The video proved an instant success, going viral and crashing the company's server but generating 12,000 orders the first day. The video has since been watched about 26 million times on YouTube (https://www.youtube.com/watch?v=ZUG9qYTJMsI).

More than 3 million people subscribed to DSC, and the company's $152 million in sales in 2015 represented nearly 50 percent of the online razor market in the United States. In 2016, Unilever, the giant British-Dutch consumer goods multinational, purchased DSC for $1 billion, one of the largest deals in e-commerce history. Despite the steep acquisition price, Unilever vowed to allow the company to retain its autonomy in order to preserve its edginess and close affinity with customers. Alan Jope, Unilever's president of beauty and personal care, claimed that rather than intervening in DSC's affairs, Unilever would instead learn from the newly acquired unit, particularly regarding the brand's approach to lifestyle marketing and advertising.

DSC represents a disruptive force in a personal care sector that has traditionally been characterized by high priced competition and traditional approaches to product positioning. "American men are evolving in their bathroom routine," Dubin says. "Five years ago, if you spent time in front of the mirror, people would have called you a metrosexual. We now live in the age where it's okay to hug guys and compliment and give advice." To help establish itself as a lifestyle brand rather than just a purveyor of shaving supplies, DSC has expanded into a broad range of toiletry items, including skincare and body washes, hair creams, and toothbrushes and toothpaste, with discussion of further expansion into vitamins, hair color, and makeup for men. Despite the expanded product line, DSC tries to retain its quirky image. A video released in mid-2018 featured a range of people preparing for a night out, including a drag queen shaving her legs, men shaving their privates, a woman shaving her head, and DSC's CEO stuffing his underwear with toilet paper (https://www.youtube.com/watch?v=QEU-MAZRhJs).

While DSC has had success in the U.S. market, a key question is whether and to what extent it can successfully apply its business approach in international markets. While the company ships some product to Australia and Canada, the range of products being sold has been limited, as have sales. In 2018, the company announced that it would expand to Europe, initially to the United Kingdom. The company was coy about other European markets they might target, while suggesting there was strong growth potential in the region. The company has also hinted at an interest in other areas, such as Brazil and India. But penetrating new cultures could prove challenging. DSC's success to date has been based on a keen understanding of the American man, but penetration of foreign markets will require detailed understanding of grooming standards elsewhere, some of them quite different. Will DSC's wacky, sometimes raunchy humor work abroad? "We'll test it and see what happens," Dubin said of the company's future overseas marketing efforts.

Critical Thinking Questions

1. View one or more of DSCs videos online. Did you find the videos funny? Uncomfortable? Offensive? Please explain your reaction.

2. Do you think Dollar Shaving Club's approach will be successful in international markets? Why or why not? What changes, if any, do think the company would have to make in order to enhance its success in international markets?

Sources: Ann-Marie Alcantara, "Once the Brand of Bros, Dollar Shave Club Is Now Aiming to Conquer the Wellness Market," *Ad Week*, September 23, 2018, www.adweek.com; Dave Paresh, "Dollar Shave Club Succeeded with Razors, But the Rest of the Bathroom Is a Challenge," *Los Angeles Times*, September 01, 2017, www.latimes.com; Shomara Roosblad, "Unilever's Dollar Shave Club to Expand to Europe in 2018," *Fashion Network*, October 13, 2017, www.uk.fashionnetwork.com; Jaclyn Trop, "How Dollar Shave Club's Founder Built a $1 Billion Company That Changed the Industry," *Jaclyn Trop*, www.jaclyntrop.com; and Entrepreneur, www.entrepreneur.com.

NOTES

1. Theodore Levitt, The Globalization of Markets, New York, NY: Harvard University, 1983.

2. Kenichi Ohmae, "Managing in a Borderless World," *Harvard Business Publishing*, May–June 1989, www.hbr.org.

3. T. C. Melewar, and John Saunders, "International Corporate Visual Identity: Standardization or Localization?," *Journal of International Business Studies*, Third Quarter 1999, 583–98; and Adesegun Oyedele, Osama J. Butt, and Michael S. Minor, "The Extent of Global Visual Identity as Expressed in Web Sites: An Empirical Assessment," working paper, 2014; "What Is Corporate Visual Identity?," http://www.wisegeek.com, accessed November 13, 2018.

4. Douglas Daft, "Back to Classic Coke," *Financial Times*, March 27, 2000, 16.

5. Suryatapa Bhattacharya, "Things Go Better with Coke, Laxative Edition," *The Wall Street Journal,* https://www.wsj.com, accessed November 13, 2018.

6. Rachel Abrams, "Adapting Listerine to a Global Market," *The New York Times,* https://www.nytimes.com, accessed November 13, 2018.

7. Nestlé, "Nescafe," https://www.nescafe.com, accessed November 13, 2018.

8. Francoise Hovivian, "Globalization: Apple's One-Size-Fits-All Approach," *Brand Quarterly,* http://www.brandquarterly.com, accessed November 13, 2018.

9. Warren Shoulberg, "Why Ikea Succeeds Around the World While Other Retailers Falter," *Forbes,* https://www.forbes.com, accessed November 13, 2018.

10. Ben Sisario, "CD-Loving Japan Resists Move to Online Music," *The New York Times,* https://www.nytimes.com, accessed November 13, 2018; and Makiko Itoh, "Why Do People in Japan Still Buy Physical Media?," https://www.quora.com, accessed November 13, 2018.

11. Accenture, "Accenture Reports Strong First Quarter Fiscal 2018 Results," *Business Wire,* https://www.businesswire.com, accessed November 13, 2018.

12. "Sereno Spa," https://www.hyatt.com, accessed November 13, 2018; "Review of Sereno Spa," https://www.tripadvisor.com/ShowUserReviews-g312681-d1751658-r126844193-Sereno_Spa-Cansaulim_South_Goa_District_Goa.html, accessed November 13, 2018.

13. Visa, *Annual Report 2017,* https://s1.q4cdn.com/050606653/files/doc_financials/annual/2017/Visa-2017-Annual-Report.pdf, accessed November 13, 2018.

14. Patrick Oster, and John Rossant, "Call It Worldpool," *BusinessWeek,* November 27, 1994, https://www.bloomberg.com, accessed November 13, 2018.

15. Peter Marsh, "The World's Wash Day," *Financial Times,* April 29, 2002, 6; "Front-Load Washing Machines—Whirlpool," https://www.whirlpool.com, accessed November 13, 2018; and Whirlpool Corporation, "Whirlpool Corporation Announces Changes at Several Manufacturing Facilities in North America," October 03, 2006, https://investors.whirlpoolcorp.com, accessed November 13, 2018.

16. Aelee Lee, "An International Guide to the Use of Color in Marketing and Advertising," *SixDegrees,* https://www.six-degrees.com, accessed November 13, 2018.

17. Jurgita Simeleviciene, "Famous Brands That Are Called Differently in Different Countries," *Business Fondue,* http://www.businessfondue.com, accessed November 13, 2018.

18. "Cross-Cultural Marketing Bloopers in Translation," https://www.onehourtranslation.com, accessed November 15, 2018.

19. Lars Perner, "Product Issues in International Marketing," http://www.consumerpsychologist.com/intl_Product.html, accessed November 13, 2018.

20. Alan Dunn, "The World Is Running Out of Domain Names—What Will We Do When They're All Gone?" *Quartz,* https://qz.com, accessed November 13, 2018.

21. Sam Holmes, and Christopher Rhoads, "Web Addresses Enter New Era," *The Wall Street Journal,* https://www.wsj.com, accessed November 13, 2018; and Ashby Jones, "Inventors Race to File Patents," *The Wall Street Journal,* https://www.wsj.com, accessed November 13, 2018.

22. Leslie Kwoh, "Wrangling Big Issues to Draw Clients," *The Wall Street Journal,* https://www.wsj.com, accessed November 13, 2018.

23. John Rosevear, "As Ford Slumps in China, General Motors Keeps Cruising," *The Motley Fool,* https://www.fool.com, accessed November 13, 2018.

24. Warren J. Keegan, "Multinational Product Planning Strategic Alternatives," *Journal of Marketing,* January 1969, 56–62, combines these strategies to formulate five product and promotional strategies.

25. Belay Seyoum, *Export-Import Theory, Practices, and Procedures,* 3rd ed., New York: Taylor & Francis, 2014.

26. Hootsuite, "Digital in 2018: Q3 Global Digital Statshot," https://www.slideshare.net, accessed November 13, 2018.

27. Quote by Calvin Klein.

28. Geoffrey Fowler, "Intel's Game: Play It Local but Make It Global," *The Wall Street Journal,* https://www.wsj.com, accessed November 13, 2018; and Nitin Pangarkar, and Mohit Agarwal, "The Wind Behind Red Bull's Wings," *Forbes,* https://www.forbes.com, accessed November 13, 2018.

29. Lars Perner, "International Marketing," http://www.consumerpsychologist.com/international_marketing.html, accessed November 13, 2018.

30. Scott Goodson, "Why Brand Building Is Important," *Forbes,* https://www.forbes.com, accessed November 13, 2018.

31. Note that the top brands are technology companies. Google was 38th in 2005 and was not in the first 100 in 2004. Facebook was not listed among the top 100 in 2010.

32. Jay Moye, "'One Brand' Strategy, New Global Campaign Unite Coca-Cola Trademark," https://www.coca-colacompany.com, accessed November 13, 2018.

33. Nataly Kelly, "Speak to Global Customers in Their Own Language," *Harvard Business Review,* August 03, 2012, www.hbr.org.

34. CMO Council, "Facts & Stats," https://www.cmocouncil.org, accessed November 13, 2018.

35. Fark Fahey, "Digital Ads: More Expensive But Reaching Fewer Consumers," *CNBC,* https://www.cnbc.com, accessed November 13, 2018.

36. Statista, "Global Cinema Advertising Revenue from 2015 to 2019 (in billion U.S. dollars)," https://www.statista.com, accessed November 13, 2018.

37. Quote by Bill Gates.

38. Maxwell Gollin, "How Much Do Ads Cost on Facebook, Instagram, Twitter, and LinkedIn in 2018?," https://www.falcon.io, accessed November 13, 2018; Nicole Grodesky, "How to Advertise on Spotify," https://www.powerdigitalmarketing.com, accessed November 13, 2018; Valerie Turgeon, "Native Advertising vs. Sponsored Content: What's the Difference," *Brandpoint,* https://www.brandpoint.com, accessed November 13, 2018; Dan Shewan, "The Comprehensive Guide to Online Advertising Costs," *Wordstream,* https://www.wordstream.com, accessed November 13, 2018; and Garett Sloan, "#Newlook: Twitter Eyes Redesign to Promoted Trend Ads," *AdAge,* https://adage.com, accessed November 13, 2018.

39. Pew Research Center, "Digital Media Fact Sheet," http://www.pewinternet.org, accessed November 13, 2018; and Pew Research Center, "Internet/Broadband Fact Sheet," http://www.pewinternet.org, accessed November 13, 2018.

40. Internet World Stats, "Top 20 Countries with the Highest Number of Internet Users—December 31, 2017," https://www.internetworldstats.com, accessed November 13, 2018.

41. A.A.K., "Marketing a Missed Call," *The Economist,* https://www.economist.com, accessed November 13, 2018.

42. Kang Hyun-kyung, "Rise of K-Pop—Comparable to 1960s 'British Invesion'?," *The Korea Times,* http://m.koreatimes.co.kr, accessed November 13, 2018; and Hugh McIntyre, "Is America Ready to Embrace K-Pop? It Already Has; You Just May Have Missed It," *Forbes,* https://www.forbes.com, accessed November 13, 2018.

43. "Chinese Supplier Repackages Expired Meat, Sells to McDonald's," *Inc.,* https://www.inc.com, accessed November 13, 2018; and Harrison Jacobs, "KFC Is by Far the Most Popular Fast Food Chain in China and It's Nothing like the US Brand—Here's What It's Like," *Business Insider,* https://www.businessinsider.com, accessed November 13, 2018.

44. Chris Kay, "KFC Follows Nigerian Fast Food Pioneer in African Growth," *Bloomberg Business,* https://www.bloomberg.com, accessed November 13, 2018.

45. Referenced in Marieke de Mooij, *Consumer Behavior and Culture: Consequences for Global Marketing and Advertising,* Los Angeles, CA: Sage, 2011, 9.

46. "PepsiCo's New Campaign to Knock Rival Coca-Cola," *Financial Times,* January 19, 1995, 12.

47. Morris Kalliny, Grace Dagher, Michael S. Minor, and Gilberto de los Santos, "Television Advertising in the Arab World: A Status Report," *Journal of Advertising Research,* June 2008, 215–23.

48. Gerrit Wiesmann, "Brands That Stop at the Border," *Financial Times,* October 06, 2006, 10, https://www.ft.com.

49. Rachel Kaplan, "Ad Agencies Take on the World," *International Management* vol. 49, no. 3, April 1994, 50–52.

50. "How Gillette Execs Spent a Fortune Developing a Razor for India Using MIT Student Focus Groups . . . Without Considering the Country's Lack of Running Water," *Daily Mail,* https://www.dailymail.co.uk, accessed November 13, 2018; and Eric Pfanner, "On Advertising: A Race to Connect in India," *The New York Times,* https://www.nytimes.com, accessed November 13, 2018.

51. Michael F. Hanford, "Program Management: Different from Project Management," *IBM DeveloperWorks,* May 14, 2004, https://www.ibm.com/developerworks/rational/library/4751.html, accessed November 13, 2018.

52. Stephen X. Doyle, and George Thomas Roth, "Selling and Sales Management in Action: The Use of Insight and Coaching to Improve Relationship Selling," *Journal of Personal Selling & Sales Management,* Winter, 1992, 62.

53. Melissa Campanelli, "Avon's Calling in China," *Direct Marketing News,* https://www.dmnews.com, accessed November 13, 2018.

54. "US Watchdog Fines Avon $135m for China Bribes," *BBC News,* https://www.bbc.com, accessed November 13, 2018.

55. "Avon's CEO Shares Plan to 'Open Up Avon'," *Beauty Packaging,* https://www.beautypackaging.com, accessed November 13, 2018.

56. "Our Social Lives and Personal Image the First to Suffer When the Going Gets Tough," *ACNielsen,* https://my.nielsen.com, accessed November 13, 2018.

57. Ford Foundation, "International Fellowships Program," https://www.fordfoundation.org, accessed November 13, 2018.

58. Wells Fargo, "Community Giving," https://www.wellsfargo.com, accessed November 13, 2018.

59. John LaMattina, "Cleveland Clinic Survey Shows Big Pharma Innovation Renaissance," *Forbes,* https://www.forbes.com, accessed November 13, 2018; Carolyn Y. Johnson, "A Big Pharma-Funded Charity That Helps Patients Pay for Drugs Just Sued the Government," *Washington Post,* https://www.washingtonpost.com, accessed November 13, 2018; and Ruben Rosenberg Colorni, "Bill Gates, Big Pharma, Bogus Philanthropy," https://newsjunkiepost.com, accessed November 13, 2018.

60. U.S. Congressional Executive Commission on China, "Agencies Responsible for Censorship in China," https://www.cecc.gov, accessed November 13, 2018.

61. "McDonald's Wins Its Libel Case against Two Activists in the UK," *The Wall Street Journal,* June 20, 1997, B2; and McSpotlight, "The McLibel Trial," https://www.mcspotlight.org, accessed November 13, 2018.

14 Managing Human Resources in an International Context

> **Globalization is focused on talent, searching the world for intellectual capital, driven by the knowledge that the team that fields the best talent from any source wins.**
>
> —*General Electric, "Key Growth Initiatives"*[1]

©Norbert Eisele-Hein/imageBROKER/Alamy Stock Photo.

LEARNING OBJECTIVES

After studying this module, you should be able to:

LO 14-1   **Identify** several of the major factors that may affect the quantity and quality of labor in a nation.

LO 14-2   **Explain** the relationship between competitive strategies (international, multidomestic, global, and transnational) and international human resource management approaches (ethnocentric, polycentric, regiocentric, and global).

LO 14-3   **Compare** recruitment and selection considerations for home-country, host-country, and third-country nationals as international company executives.

LO 14-4   **Distinguish** among the training and development considerations for home-country, host-country, and third-country nationals as international company executives.

LO 14-5   **Identify** some of the challenges and opportunities of an expat position.

LO 14-6   **Describe** some of the complications of compensation packages for expatriate executives.

Should You Pursue an Opportunity to Work Internationally?

Your boss has called you into her office and said, "We have a problem in Asia that we need you to solve." You have been performing well with your company, in a job that requires familiarity within your home country, but now the company has discovered markets away from home and wants to take advantage of these opportunities. Although you have often daydreamed of going abroad, you haven't personally been out of the country since you and your college friend backpacked through the rainforests of Costa Rica after graduation from college. There was a total of more than 66 million expatriates worldwide in 2017, including about 7 million corporate executives working overseas, a number expected to grow to 87.5 million by 2021. Now you have the chance to join that group! As you leave your boss's office, you can hardly wait to phone your family with the news.

You are about to become an **expatriate**, which is a person living outside his or her country of citizenship. Your family will love it, you'll learn a new language and immerse yourself within another culture, and the foreign experience will be your passport to your company's top executive positions. Your career will be made. Right?

Maybe. You must be very careful. For too many employees who take foreign assignments, it is "out of sight, out of mind," and you may find yourself well out of the loop back at the company's home-country operations. On the other hand, however, these assignments can be passports to the top if you take the right steps before you make the move.

If at all possible, arrange to have someone fairly high in the company hierarchy be your mentor, ideally a person who has also served in an expatriate role so you can draw from his or her international experience. That home-country mentor should keep you advised of changes and developments in the company back at home and keep your name in consideration so you won't be forgotten while you are on your assignment abroad. You might also consider finding a mentor in the host country who can assist you in understanding the local culture, introduce you to valuable business contacts, and help you interpret situations you encounter in your position abroad.

Before you take the job, you should insist that your bosses tell you exactly what the company expects you to accomplish. Are you to get a plant up and running, install systems or practices that are currently in use in the home country, arrange customer financing, negotiate investment, or perhaps groom a host-country replacement? Will this be an extended on-site assignment, such as two to four years in length, or will it merely involve a few short-term assignments where you are primarily expected to work on a specific problem or transfer specific knowledge?

Of course, there is the chance that despite all your efforts and precautions, your company will forget or not value you. Realizing this possibility, you should make sure to profit from your foreign assignment by doing your job well; learning about new markets; gaining proficiency in the local language, which will permit you to better understand the culture; using your international experiences to develop creative new ways of seeing the world and understanding challenges and opportunities; developing important new life skills associated with adapting to new situations; and actively building up your international network of contacts. You can network by being active in such things as local chambers of commerce, social clubs, and sports clubs.

All this will make you valuable to other companies and make them aware of you. In essence, by going abroad you have received a million dollars' worth of training paid for by your company, and you and other companies can utilize it. After all, active expats are an important source of globally skilled executives for businesses worldwide.

Sources: Finaccord, "Global Expatriates: Size, Segmentation and Forecast for the Worldwide Market," http://www.finaccord.com, accessed November 16, 2018; and Finaccord, *Global Expatriates: Size, Segmentation and Forecast for the Worldwide Market,* http://finaccord.com, accessed November 16, 2018.

The effectiveness of every organization depends to a great extent on the nature of its workforce and how well its human resources are utilized. Their effective use depends on management's policies and practices. Management of a company's human resources is a shared responsibility. The day-to-day supervision of people on the job is the duty of the operating managers, who must integrate human, financial, and physical resources into an efficient production system. However, the formulation of policies and procedures for (1) estimation of workforce needs, (2) recruitment and selection, (3) training and development, (4) motivation, (5) compensation, (6) discipline, and (7) employment termination is generally the responsibility of human resource managers working in cooperation with executives from marketing, production and operations, and finance, as well as the firm's lawyers.

expatriate
A person living outside his or her country of citizenship

Finding the right people to manage an organization can be difficult under any circumstances, but it is especially difficult to find good managers of overseas operations. Such positions require more and different skills than do purely domestic executive jobs. The right persons need to be bicultural, with knowledge of the business practices in the home country plus an understanding of business practices and customs in the host country. And to fully understand a culture, any culture, it is usually necessary to speak the language of its people. Only with a good grasp of the language can one understand the subtleties and humor and know what is really going on in the host country. Although difficult to locate, such managers do exist, and they may be found in (1) the home country, (2) the host country, or (3) a third country. A key precursor for undertaking such a selection process is an examination of labor conditions and trends.

Worldwide Labor Conditions

LO 14-1
Identify several of the major factors that may affect the quantity and quality of labor in a nation.

labor market
The pool of available potential employees with the necessary skills within commuting distance from an employer

When a foreign company enters a new nation, it must take what it finds in terms of the local **labor market**, which refers to the pool of available employees with the necessary skills who are within commuting distance of an employer. However, the quantity and quality of labor vary across nations and regions of the world and also over time, so a prudent company will study the labor market when considering whether to invest in another country. Among the many information sources is the *Yearbook of Labor Statistics*, published by the United Nations International Labor Office in Geneva, Switzerland. This section provides a brief review of several dimensions associated with labor conditions, including the overall size of the workforce, the aging of populations, urbanization of workforces, immigration, and labor unions.

OVERALL SIZE OF THE WORKFORCE

We begin by looking at the overall situation in the world in terms of some very macro demographic data. In 2018, the world had 7.5 billion inhabitants, 33 percent of whom were under the age of 20.[2] Due to high birthrates and a decline in the rate of infant mortality, populations in the developing nations tend to be growing as well as becoming younger. More than 34 percent of the world's 15- to 24-year-olds, a key source of new workers over the next decade, live in just two developing countries: India and China.[3]

CULTURE FACTS @internationalbiz

Reflecting differences in cultural practices regarding appropriate roles for women, 70 percent of women in China are employed or seeking employment versus only 25 percent of women in India. #differences #culturalpractices #womenroles

SOCIAL MEDIA

In contrast, populations in many developed countries are projected to decline in the coming years, due to factors such as low birthrates and low levels of immigration. For example, between 2015 and 2050, Japan's population is projected to decline from 127 million to 108 million; Russia's from 144 million to 129 million; and Germany's from 81 million to 76 million.[4] Countries that have admitted large numbers of immigrants—such as the United States, the United Kingdom, Canada, and Australia—are projected to have continued population growth due to the younger age and higher birthrates of their immigrant populations. For example, between 2015 and 2050, the U.S. population is projected to grow from 322 million to 388 million, and Canada's from 36 million to 44 million.[5]

AGING OF POPULATIONS

In addition to examining population as a whole, we need to consider the effects of an aging population on the workforce, a trend impacting many nations worldwide. The rapid increase in the proportion of the world's population that is age 65 or older has received much attention in recent years. While the population of people aged 65 or older was 609 million in 2015, by 2050 this group will be about 2.5 times larger, or over 1.5 billion.[6]

The aging of populations is more pronounced in developed countries than in developing nations, as shown in Figure 14.1. The percentage of the population aged 65 or over in developed countries is projected to grow from 12 percent in 2010 to over 25 percent by 2050.[7] An aging population in most of the developed countries has implications for labor

FIGURE 14.1 Population Aged 65 and Above, 2017

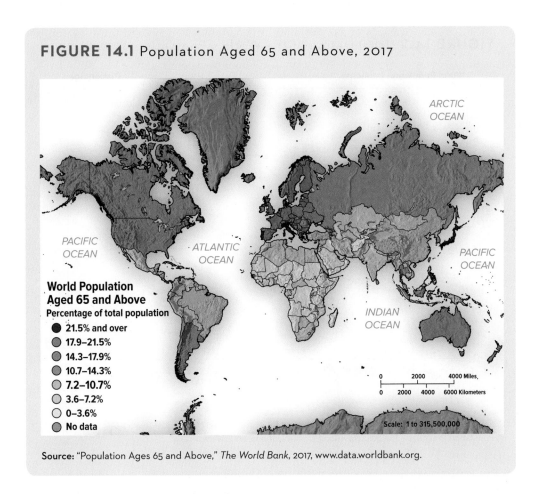

World Population Aged 65 and Above
Percentage of total population

- 21.5% and over
- 17.9–21.5%
- 14.3–17.9%
- 10.7–14.3%
- 7.2–10.7%
- 3.6–7.2%
- 0–3.6%
- No data

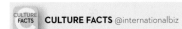

Scale: 1 to 315,500,000

Source: "Population Ages 65 and Above," *The World Bank*, 2017, www.data.worldbank.org.

force size and skill; for policies regarding immigration; for economic growth; and a range of political issues related to pension plans, health care, and other key social, economic, and political factors in those nations. For example, the European Union's share of world output could be cut in half by 2050, to 15 percent, unless major policy changes are undertaken, including population-related changes.[8] In contrast, a more youthful United States could expand its world output share during the same time, as will the economically developing countries. Compared to developed countries, the developing countries will have only about one-half the proportion of people aged 65 and older. Take India for example. A much larger proportion of Indians will be of traditional working age, 20 to 64 years old, than will be the case for most of the rest of the world, especially the developed countries. That may have important implications for international companies considering where to locate production as well as those seeking markets for products that target working-age adults.

URBANIZATION OF WORKFORCE

The population and labor force worldwide have been shifting dramatically from rural to urban during the past century. As shown in Figure 14.2, nearly 30 percent of the world's population lived in urban areas in 1950. By 2010, more than half of the world's population was urban, and this proportion is projected to increase to over 60 percent by the year 2030. Although the level of urbanization is higher in developed countries, the level of urbanization increased nearly six times faster in developing countries from 1975 to 2015 as the developing nations experienced rapid increases in population as well as increasing economic development.

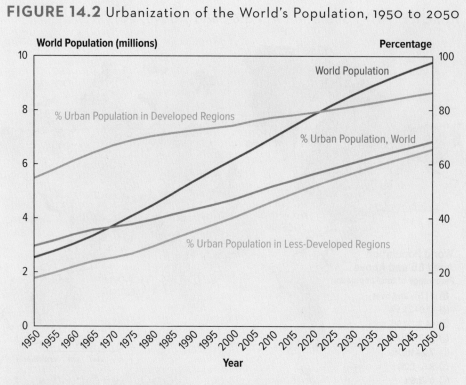

FIGURE 14.2 Urbanization of the World's Population, 1950 to 2050

Sources: "World Urbanization Prospects: The 2018 Revision," *United Nations*, 2018, www.un.org; and "World Population Prospects: The 2012 Revision," *United Nations*, 2012, www.un.org.

As populations migrate from rural areas to urban areas, particularly within developing nations, they also move from agriculturally based employment to employment in industry and service sectors. Often, this influx of labor from rural areas creates a pool of low-cost, low-skilled workers, a large portion of which may be classified as part of the vulnerable workforce, those at most risk of losing their jobs. While labor trainers for international companies in developing nations have found that people learn industrial skills rapidly, a more difficult challenge is teaching new workers who come from farms and villages how to adjust socially and psychologically to modern work life demands in industrial or service sectors.

labor mobility
The movement of people from country to country or area to area seeking jobs

©Pacific Press/Alamy Stock Photo.

IMMIGRANT LABOR

Labor mobility refers to the movement of people from country to country or area to area seeking jobs. Although classical economists assumed that labor was immobile, we now know that labor mobility does exist, as shown in Figure 14.3. When possible, people move to secure better economic situations, regardless of their socioeconomic level, and immigration is at least partly the result of the relative supply of and demand for labor as well as regulations influencing those factors. For example, at least 60 million people left Europe to work and live overseas between 1850 and 1970. During part of that time, between the end of World War II and the mid-1970s, some 30 million workers from southern Europe and North Africa flowed into eight northern European

FIGURE 14.4 Share of a Country's Nationals with a University Degree Living in Another Nation

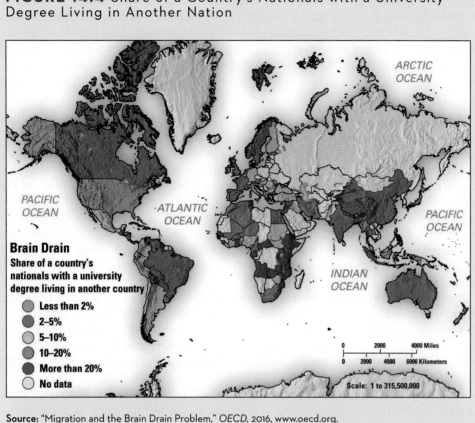

Brain Drain
Share of a country's nationals with a university degree living in another country

- Less than 2%
- 2–5%
- 5–10%
- 10–20%
- More than 20%
- No data

0   2000   4000 Miles
0   2000   4000   6000 Kilometers
Scale: 1 to 315,500,000

Source: "Migration and the Brain Drain Problem," *OECD*, 2016, www.oecd.org.

scientists and engineers from other countries, and these immigrants have become an essential element for the health of the U.S. economy. For example, almost 25 percent of college-educated workers in the United States are foreign-born, as are more than 56 percent of workers with doctorates in engineering.[23] Roughly 53 percent of international students remain in the United States after receiving doctorates in science. Studies have shown that immigrants to the United States create new businesses at a rate 30 percent greater than do native-born citizens, contributing to job creation and economic growth.[24] Immigrants own one-third of businesses in Washington, D.C. and California.[25] Half of all company founders in Silicon Valley are immigrants, as are 25 percent of the founders of all new businesses in the United States.[26] The National Venture Capital Association found that immigrants created 25 percent of the venture capital-backed public companies in the United States, including Google, Intel, Yahoo, and eBay.[27]

Reverse brain drain, which refers to the return home of highly skilled immigrants who have contributed to their adopted country, has recently become a concern of educators, public policy makers, and businesspeople. It is a trend related to the growth of outsourcing and the willingness of some governments to allow or even encourage "controversial" scientists to move to other countries.[29] Some developing countries have begun to sponsor reverse-brain-drain programs to bring these workers home. For example, Beijing has launched the Thousand Talents Program in a bid to recapture talent that has emigrated from China. The program offers top scientists grants of 1 million yuan (about $146,000), high salaries, and generous lab funding. In the United States, the extent of brain drain has also been worsened by limitations on the number of work visas being offered to foreign workers and long waits for naturalization. The growth of outsourcing in developing economies such

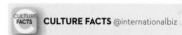

CULTURE FACTS @internationalbiz

Although Kenya is considered a collectivistic society, which suggests an individual would be loyal and committed to one's group, a high masculinity orientation with its emphasis on achievement and material rewards may account for the estimated 80 to 90 percent of doctors trained in Kenya's public hospitals who subsequently emigrate, leaving many areas of the country without adequate medical care.[28]
#kenya #collectivisticsociety #doctorsleaving

SOCIAL MEDIA

reverse brain drain
The return home of highly skilled immigrants who have made a contribution in their adopted country

as India is also pulling talented Indian professionals back home. International companies contribute aggressively to this aspect of reverse brain drain as they outsource knowledge work—engineering, software, product design, and development—to such countries as China, India, and Russia. In some controversial areas of science where the U.S. government has tried to limit research efforts, such as stem cell research, scientists—both native and non-native— have moved to environments where such cutting-edge research receives greater support.

LABOR UNIONS

labor union
An organization of workers, formed to advance the interest of its members

collective bargaining
The process in which a union represents the interests of workers bargaining in negotiations with management

Labor unions, which are organizations of workers, vary significantly from country to country. They tend to be more effective in developed countries, but even comparing Europe, the United States, and Japan, it is apparent that labor unions in various countries serve different purposes and influence employee matters differently. Labor legislation in the United States has mostly confined itself to the framework of **collective bargaining**. Collective bargaining is the process in which a union represents the interests of everyone in a bargaining unit (which may include both union members and nonmembers) in negotiations with management. In Europe, government's role is more active, with wages and working conditions frequently legislated. Many Latin American governments are also active in employer–employee relationships, frequently because the unions are weak and the union leaders inexperienced.

In contrast to the adversarial relationship usually found between unions and management in Europe and the United States, Japanese unions tend to identify strongly with the interests of the company. For example, if Japanese unions are convinced a high wage increase would hurt the company's competitiveness, they tend to not ask for much of a pay raise. Japanese unions are also enterprise based rather than industrywide as in the United States.

The level of union membership varies substantially across countries, from single digits in some nations to more than 80 percent in others. Figure 14.5 indicates the percentage of selected nations' workers who are members of trade unions, and how this percentage has been changing in recent years.

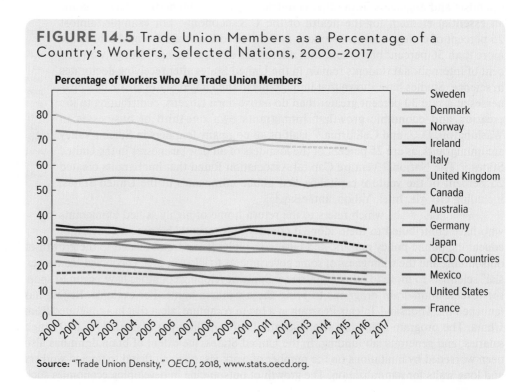

FIGURE 14.5 Trade Union Members as a Percentage of a Country's Workers, Selected Nations, 2000–2017

Source: "Trade Union Density," *OECD*, 2018, www.stats.oecd.org.

For the past four decades, there has been a decline in the number of union members in most developed countries, especially among workers in industrial sectors. There are several reasons for this trend, including:

- Employers have made efforts to keep their businesses union-free, including putting employees on business boards and instituting profit-sharing plans. This co-optive approach has had its desired effect in many cases.
- More women and teenagers have joined the workforce, and because theirs are usually secondary incomes, they accept lower wages and have little loyalty toward organized labor.
- The unions have been successful. Their results have led to wage increases, but sometimes this has also led to higher costs and lower competitiveness of their employers, which have led to layoffs, downsizing, and movement of jobs to lower-cost locations. So in this sense, unions have been the victims of their own success.
- As developed countries transition to a knowledge economy, their industrial jobs that have formed the core of union membership are declining.

Despite a general decline in union members in industrial sectors, unions in some nations have successfully organized workers in the expanding service sectors of their post-industrial economies, helping to limit the overall level of decline in the proportion of unionized workers.

National unions have begun to perceive opportunities for companies to escape the organizing reach of unions through the relatively simple step of international outsourcing, transferring production to another country. Unions see such steps as dangerous. To combat those dangers, national unions have begun to (1) collect and disseminate information about companies; (2) consult with unions in other countries; (3) coordinate with those unions' policies and tactics in dealing with some companies; and (4) encourage international company codes of conduct. Such multinational labor activity is likely to increase, although unions are divided by ideological differences and are frequently strongly nationalistic. Vastly more effort and money have been spent on lobbying for the protection of national industries than on cooperating with unions in other countries.

The Strategic Approach to International Human Resource Management

Two competing forces—the pressure to achieve global integration and reduce costs and the pressure to respond to local differentiation—determine which of four alternative competitive strategies (home replication, multidomestic, global, or transnational) a company should adopt.[30] A company's competitive strategy should, in turn, drive the organization's approach to international human resource management (IHRM).

David Heenan and Howard Perlmutter developed a model that considers these four competitive strategies to determine whether the organization's IHRM policies for hiring and promoting employees should be ethnocentric, that is, based on the parent company's home-country frame of reference; polycentric, based on the specific local context in which the subsidiary operates; regiocentric, based on the specific regional context in which the subsidiary operates; or geocentric, based on ability and experience without considering race or citizenship.[31] Employees may be classified into one of three categories: (1) home-country national or parent-country national (PCN), a citizen of the nation in which the parent company is headquartered; (2) host-country national (HCN), a citizen of the nation in which the subsidiary is operating, which is different from the parent company's home nation; or (3) third-country national (TCN), a citizen of neither the parent company nation nor the host country. These relationships are illustrated in Table 14.1.

ethnocentric policy
A policy of hiring and promoting based on the parent company's home-country frame of reference

polycentric policy
A policy of hiring and promoting based on the specific local context in which the subsidiary operates

regiocentric policy
A policy of hiring and promoting based on the specific regional context in which the subsidiary operates

geocentric policy
A policy of hiring and promoting based on ability and experience without considering race or citizenship

home-country national
Same as parent-country national

parent-country national (PCN)
Employee who is a citizen of the nation in which the parent company is headquartered; also called *home-country national*

LO 14-2
Explain the relationship between competitive strategies (international, multidomestic, global, and transnational) and international human resource management approaches (ethnocentric, polycentric, regiocentric, and global).

host-country national (HCN)
Employee who is a citizen of the nation in which the subsidiary is operating, which is different from the parent company's home nation

third-country national (TCN)
Employee who is a citizen of neither the parent company nation nor the host country

TABLE 14.1 Strategic Approach, Organizational Concerns, and the International Human Resource Management Approach to Be Used

Aspects of the Enterprise	Human Resource Policy Orientation			
	Ethnocentric	**Polycentric**	**Regiocentric**	**Geocentric**
Primary strategic orientation/ stage	Home replication	Multidomestic	Regional	Transnational
Perpetuation (recruiting, staffing, development)	People of home country developed for key positions everywhere in the world	People of local nationality developed for key positions in their own country	Regional people developed for key positions anywhere in the region	Best people everywhere in the world developed for key positions everywhere in the world
Complexity of the organization	Complex in home country, simple in subsidiaries	Varied and independent	Highly interdependent on a regional basis	"Global Web," complex, independent, worldwide alliances/ network
Authority, decision making	High in headquarters	Relatively low in headquarters	High regional headquarters and/or high collaboration among subsidiaries	Collaboration of headquarters and subsidiaries around the world
Evaluation and control	Home standards applied to people and performance	Determined locally	Determined regionally	Globally integrated
Rewards	High in headquarters, low in subsidiaries	Wide variations, can be high or low rewards for subsidiary performance	Rewards for contribution to regional objectives	Rewards to international and local executives for reaching local and worldwide objectives based on global company goals
Communication, information flow	High volume of orders, commands, advice to subsidiaries	Little to and from headquarters, little among subsidiaries	Little to and from corporate headquarters, but may be high to and from regional headquarters and among countries	Horizontal, network relations
Geographic identification	Nationality of owner	Nationality of host country	Regional company	Truly global company, but identifying with national interests ("glocal")

Source: Adapted from David A. Heenan, and Howard V. Perlmutter, *Multinational Organization Development*, Boston, MA: Addison-Wesley, 1979, 194.

Recruitment and Selection of Employees

LO 14-3
Compare recruitment and selection considerations for home-country, host-country, and third-country nationals as international company executives.

The recruitment and selection of employees, frequently referred to as *staffing*, should be determined in a manner consistent with one of the four IHRM approaches the organization is pursuing, as we discuss next.[32]

ETHNOCENTRIC STAFFING POLICY

Companies with a primarily international strategic orientation (characterized by low pressures for cost reduction and low pressures for local responsiveness) may adopt an ethnocentric staffing policy. In this approach, most decisions are made at headquarters, using the home country's frame of reference. International companies (ICs) utilize citizens of their own countries, or PCNs, in key foreign management and technical positions. Labor negotiators and other specialists may be sent to troubleshoot such problems as product warranty, international contracts, taxes, accounting, and reporting. Teams may be sent from the home country to assist with new plant start-up, and they would probably stay until subsidiary staff were trained to run and maintain the new facilities.

At first, PCNs usually are not knowledgeable about the host-country culture and language. Many such expatriates have adapted, learned the language, and become thoroughly accepted in the host country, although it is also common that such managers encounter difficulty both in overcoming the biases of their own cultural experience and in being able to understand and perform effectively within the new operating context, especially early in their assignment when their lack of host-country knowledge is greatest.

An advantage of employing home-country citizens abroad is expanding their experience in preparation for their becoming high-level managers at headquarters. Firms earning a large percentage of their profits from international sources require top executives who have a worldwide perspective, both business and political. It is difficult or impossible to acquire that sort of perspective without living and working abroad for a substantial period.

If new technology for the subsidiary is involved, the parent company will probably station at least one of its technologically qualified experts at the subsidiary until its local personnel learn the technology. In this way, the home office can be confident that someone is immediately available to explain headquarters' policies and procedures, see that they are observed, and interpret what is happening locally for the IC's management. Positions that an IC must take or demands that it must make are sometimes not popular with a host government. It can seem unpatriotic for a host-country national to do such things, whereas the host government can understand, and sometimes accept, such positions or demands from a foreigner.

A drawback of ethnocentric staffing policies is that it can be expensive to use employees from the home country. In addition to their salaries, which may be higher than for corresponding host-country managers, there may be additional expenses associated with relocating these employees and their families. Home-country managers may also find it difficult to be effective in the host country, due to differences in language and culture as well as other environmental forces.

POLYCENTRIC STAFFING POLICY

When the company's primary strategic orientation is multidomestic, with low pressures for cost reduction and high pressures for local responsiveness, a polycentric approach may be used. Polycentric staffing relies on human resource policies that are created at the local level for the specific context of the local operations. Companies primarily hire HCNs for subsidiaries and PCNs for headquarters' positions; movement from the local subsidiaries to headquarters' positions is uncommon.

ICs often must manage employees from multiple nations.
©Gallo Images/age fotostock.

When the IC staffs a subsidiary with HCNs, there is no problem of their being unfamiliar with local customs, culture, and language. Furthermore, the first costs of employing them are generally lower (compared with the costs of employing home-country nationals and paying to move them and their families to the host country), although considerable training costs are sometimes necessary in order for the HCNs to understand the IC and its way of doing things. If there is a strong feeling of nationalism in the host country, having nationals as managers can make the subsidiary seem less foreign.

The government development plans and laws of some countries demand that employment in all sectors and at all levels reflect the racial composition of the society. In other words, more skilled and managerial slots must be given to the local people. If foreign-owned firms in Indonesia fail to hire enough *pribumi* (indigenous Indonesians), those firms might encounter difficulties with reentry permits for foreign employees as well as with other government licenses and permits that they need. Bribery requests have been known to increase until more pribumi are hired and promoted.

A disadvantage of hiring local managers is that they are often unfamiliar with the home country of the IC and with its corporate culture, policies, and practices. As Liu Zhengrong, head of human resources for the German chemical group Lanxess, said of hiring local managers, "You lose something in terms of communication with the headquarters, but you get more hints about the local marketplace."[33] Differences in attitudes and values can cause these locally hired managers to act in ways that surprise or displease headquarters. Also, local managers may create their own upward immobility if, because of strong cultural or family ties, they are reluctant to accept promotions that would require them to leave their home country to work abroad at parent headquarters or at another subsidiary.

> **66 IF YOU LOOK at CAPITAL INVESTMENT STRATEGY, MARKETING, RESEARCH AND DEVELOPMENT, THOSE TYPES of ACTIVITIES ARE INTERNATIONAL. But IF YOU TALK about PEOPLE, HUMANS, IT IS QUITE LOCAL in NATURE. 99**
>
> —*Fujio Mitarai, chair and CEO of Canon*[34]

Foreign-owned companies that hire and train local, host-country people frequently experience a common, and disruptive, IHRM problem. In many countries, there is a shortage of talented, experienced managers and other skilled employees. The best of these people may be pirated away by local firms or other IC subsidiaries, as local executive recruiters are constantly on the lookout to make raids and entice the most talented employees to leave the original IC and join another firm that is seeking to overcome its own shortage of skilled personnel.

Finally, there can be a conflict of loyalty between the host country and the employer. For example, the host-country national may give preference to a local supplier even though imported products may be less expensive or of better quality. Local managers may oppose headquarters' requests to set low transfer prices that might benefit the IC by causing lower levels of taxes to be paid to the host government.

REGIOCENTRIC STAFFING POLICY

Companies with a regional strategic approach (with slightly higher pressures for cost reduction and slightly lower pressures for local responsiveness than is the case for the multidomestic strategy) can employ a regiocentric staffing approach. In this approach, regional employees are selected for key positions in the region, meaning the IC will employ a variety of HCNs and TCNs to meet its staffing needs.

Executives with a Global Skill Set Are in Big Demand

Executives with a global skill set are increasingly in demand worldwide. PwC predicts that there will be a 50 percent increase in the number of international assignments by 2020, and the need is particularly great in developing economies. You can look at China and Latin America for examples.

The Chinese operation of one U.S. consumer products company brought in Western managers who were excellent at the technical aspects of their jobs. Nevertheless, they failed because they did not understand the Chinese culture. In an attempt to solve the problem, the U.S. company recruited Chinese-speaking staff from other countries in Asia. But there were still cultural considerations, and unforeseen problems arose from the actions of managers skilled in the Chinese language but not in Chinese values.

Local hires in China are less costly than expatriates, and they often have a better understanding of the Chinese market and customers. Having a boss who is a local can be motivating to ambitious junior employees and can enhance communication and morale. As Walmart China executive Du Limin says about the response of her Chinese employees, "They take me as their big sister and they confide their family issues with me. That is impossible if you're an expatriate." Yet finding adequate numbers of local candidates, at an adequate quality level, in emerging markets such as China can be difficult for international companies. Even if an IC wants to localize its workforce, the majority of the local mainland Chinese will not have experience with global principles. The imbalance between demand and supply is not likely to change in the near future.

Similarly, hundreds of non-Latin American businesses trying to operate in that region have openings for bilingual executives. Fluency in the language does not mean that prospective employees have the skills required for a particular position, however. These companies are looking for people who can operate in a dual mode, combining U.S. efficiency and business culture with the Latin way of doing things, which is more personal and requires knowledge of Spanish or Portuguese. Ignacio Kleiman of I-Network.com provides an example of cultural contrast.

A U.S. business executive might try to complete a deal over the phone, he observes, but in Latin America a typical approach is to take a plane ride to the customer's country, share a lunch, and talk about family and soccer. "Afterward, that Latin customer is going to feel closer to you. If there is no personal chemistry, there is likely to be no business."

How can you develop the skills and experience to be effective in a foreign posting? First, it is important not to become insulated from the local culture. "Managing in a global environment means you manage people who are separated not only by time and distance, but also by cultural, social, and language differences," says S. Devarajan, the Bangalore, India-based managing director of Cisco Systems' Global Development Center. "You need to build a relationship and have frequent interaction and communication among your team members," he says. When arriving in a country, many expats choose to pursue a comfort zone familiar to them: they live in sections of a city favored by American visitors, travel everywhere in a chauffeured sedan with a driver who speaks English, and frequent stores, restaurants, and bars that cater to U.S. visitors. Such managers are often termed "Teflon expatriates," because they are living abroad but nothing about the local culture sticks to them. As a result, they are not likely to develop the capability for working effectively with partners in the local culture.

Critical Thinking Questions

1. What kinds of skills or experience are needed in order to succeed in a foreign assignment?
2. How might a company go about assessing whether or not a candidate has the proper set of such skills and experiences?

Sources: Cui Rong, "Firms in China Think Globally, Hire Locally," *The Wall Street Journal,* February 27, 2006, ww.wsj.com; Chris Kraul, "Latino Talent Pinch Hobbling U.S. Firms' Expansion Plans," *Los Angeles Times,* June 25, 2000, www.latimes.com; and Glenn Rifkin, "The Soft Skills of Global Managers," *Harvard Business School Working Knowledge,* 2018, www.hbswk.hbs.edu.

The disadvantages often encountered when using employees from the home or host country can sometimes be avoided by sending third-country nationals to fill management posts. A Chilean going to Argentina may have little cultural or language difficulty, but IC headquarters should be careful not to rely too heavily on similarities in language as a guide to similarities in other aspects of cultures. Mexicans, for example,

ICs that use a regiocentric approach will select regional employees for key positions and use a variety of HCNs and TCNs to fill staffing needs. ©FatCamera/Getty Images.

"PEOPLE from DIFFERENT CULTURES TEND to MISUNDERSTAND EACH OTHER'S BEHAVIORS OR STEREOTYPE PEOPLE from OTHER COUNTRIES. IT IS ESSENTIAL to RECOGNIZE THE DISCREPANCIES between CULTURES in ORDER to WORK TOGETHER EFFECTIVELY. "

—S. Devarajan, managing director of Cisco Systems' Global Development Center in Bangalore, India[35]

may have to make considerable adjustments if they are transferred to Argentina, and they would find a move to Spain even more difficult. This is because the Mexican culture, in general, differs considerably from that of both Argentina and Spain. Although Argentina and Chile are certainly not identical, they do have many similarities. A fair generalization is that after an executive has successfully adapted once to a new culture and language, a second or succeeding adaptation is easier.

An employer should not count on cost savings in using third-country nationals. Although they may come from countries where salary scales are lower, in such countries as Brazil and most of the nations of northwestern Europe, salaries for experienced managerial and technical personnel may be higher than what is being paid in many developed countries, such as the United States.

GEOCENTRIC STAFFING POLICY

Companies with a transnational strategic orientation, driven simultaneously by high pressures for cost reduction and high pressures for local responsiveness, often follow a geocentric staffing policy. These organizations select the best person for each job without considering national origin and can, therefore, capitalize on the advantages of each staffing policy. With a geocentric staffing policy, HRM strategy tends to be consistent across all subsidiaries, borrowing best practices from wherever they may be found across the company's worldwide network of operations rather than showing preference only to the practices used at headquarters or within a local context. However, employees with the strongest set of skills also tend to be more difficult to hire and retain, due to the value and relative scarcity of their skill sets and their attractiveness to a range of potential employers, which can increase the costs and other challenges of pursuing such a staffing policy. Agreeing on what the best practices may be for various aspects of the company's activities, across the different alternatives being employed in various parts of the world, may also be a challenge for companies pursuing this strategy.

Training and Development of Employees

LO 14-4

Distinguish among the training and development considerations for home-country, host-country, and third-country nationals as international company executives.

Training and development activities include efforts to help employees acquire job-related knowledge, behavior, and skills. The training and development of managers and other key IC employees vary somewhat, depending on whether the candidate is from the home country, the host country, or a third country, as we discuss in this section.

HOME- OR PARENT-COUNTRY NATIONAL

Although the majority of employees sent abroad continue to be assignees from the home country, relatively few recent college graduates are hired for the express purpose of being sent overseas.[36] Usually, they spend a number of years in the domestic (parent) company, and they may get into the company's international operations by design and persistence, by luck, or by a combination of those elements. For example, they may first be assigned to the international division at the firm's headquarters, where they handle problems submitted by foreign affiliates and meet visiting overseas personnel.

If the company is likely to send PCNs abroad, then prior to going abroad, the company will frequently encourage the PCNs to study the language and culture of the country to which they may go. Prior to embarking on their expat assignment, the PCNs may be sent on short trips abroad to handle special assignments and to be exposed to foreign surroundings. Newly hired PCNs with prior overseas experience may undergo similar but shorter training periods.

Increasingly, U.S. ICs supplement their in-house training for overseas work with courses in U.S. business schools. In recognition of the growing importance of international business, those schools are expanding the number and scope of international business courses they offer. In addition, a number of university-level business schools are now operating in other countries, and some schools offer programs that enable students to get applied business experience such as consulting or internship activity within foreign contexts.

A major concern for employers is the families of executives transferred overseas. Even though the employee may adapt to and enjoy the foreign experience, the family may not, and an unhappy family can sour the employee on the job or even damage the marriage. In such cases, the company may have to send the family and its possessions home at great expense. Consequently, many companies try to assess whether the executive's family can adapt to the foreign ambience before assigning the executive abroad. This is part of the subject of expatriates that we will deal with later in this module.

HOST-COUNTRY NATIONAL

The same general criteria for selecting home-country employees apply to host-country nationals. Usually, however, the training and development activities undertaken for HCNs will differ from those used for home-country nationals in that host-country nationals are more likely to lack knowledge of advanced business techniques, particularly those that are specific to business applications and operations of the IC, and knowledge of the company as a whole. As a result, training programs will need to be developed to enable host-country nationals to more fully understand and perform effectively within the IC.

HCNs Hired in the Home Country Many multinationals try to solve the business technique problem by hiring host-country students upon their graduation from home-country business schools. After being hired, these new employees are usually sent to IC headquarters to receive indoctrination in the firm's policies and procedures as well as on-the-job training in a specific function, such as finance, marketing, logistics, or production. However, while away from the host country attending business school and indoctrination at headquarters, the HCNs may become distanced from the developments and relationships back in their home country. For example, many emerging (and more developed) markets are undergoing rapid political and economic change, and someone who lives abroad for several years may experience some challenges when reintegrating into his or her home country.

HCNs Hired in the Host Country Because the number of host-country citizens graduating from home-country universities is limited, multinationals must also recruit locally for their management positions. To impart knowledge of business techniques, the company may do one or more things. It may set up in-house training programs in the host-country subsidiary, or it may utilize business courses in the host-country's universities. The IC may also send new employees to home-country business schools or to home-country training programs offered by the parent company. In addition, employees who show promise may be sent repeatedly to the parent-company headquarters, divisions, and other subsidiaries to observe the various enterprise operations and meet the other executives with whom they will be communicating during their careers. Such visits are also learning opportunities for the home office and the other subsidiaries.

THIRD-COUNTRY NATIONAL

Hiring employees who are citizens of neither the home country nor the host country is often advantageous. TCNs may accept lower wages and benefits than will employees from the home country, and they may come from a culture similar to that of the host country. In addition, they may have worked for another unit of the IC and thus be familiar with the company's policies, procedures, and people. This approach can simplify the training and development requirements for such recruits. The use of TCNs has become particularly prevalent in developing countries because of shortages of literate, skilled local employees. It can be an advantage to get someone who already resides in the country and has the necessary work permits and knowledge of the local languages and customs.

However, if the host government emphasizes the employment of its own citizens, third-country nationals will not be welcomed any more than will home-country people. Third-country nationals could face an additional obstacle in obtaining necessary work permits. For example, the host government can understand that the German parent company of a subsidiary would want some German executives to look after its interests in the host country. It may be harder to convince the government that a third-country native is any better for the parent than a local executive would be.

We must be careful with generalizations about third-country personnel, partly because people achieve that status in different ways. They may be foreigners hired in the home country and sent to a host-country subsidiary either because they have had previous experience there or because that country's culture is similar to their own. Third-country nationals may have originally been home-country personnel who were sent abroad and became dissatisfied with the job but not with the host country. After leaving the firm that sent them abroad, they take positions with subsidiaries of multinationals from different home countries. Another way in which TCNs can be created is by promotion within an IC. For instance, if a Spanish executive of the Spanish subsidiary of an Italian multinational is promoted to be general manager of the Italian firm's Colombian subsidiary, the Spanish executive is then a third-country national.

As multinationals increasingly take the *geocentric* view toward promoting (according to ability and not nationality), we are certain to see greater use of TCNs. This development will be accelerated as more executives of all nationalities gain experience outside their native lands. Another, and growing, source for third-country nationals is the heterogeneous body of international agencies such as various units of the United Nations and the World Bank. These agencies deal with virtually every field of human endeavor, and member-countries send their nationals as representatives to the headquarters and branch office cities all over the world. Many of those people become available to or can be hired away by international companies.

LO 14-5
Identify some of the challenges and opportunities of an expat position.

Expatriates

International markets are becoming increasingly important to success for even small and medium-sized companies. To exploit these international opportunities, the staffing of positions in international operations is an important strategic issue. Although many of the employees may be hired in the host country (sometimes called *inpatriates*), ICs have continued to send employees on foreign assignments. Some of the international positions, especially those that deal with addressing a specific technical problem or transferring specialized knowledge, will be staffed with home- or third-country employees who are on short-term assignments (called *flexpatriates*). Yet companies will continue to staff many key positions with expatriates, employees who are relocated to the host country from the home country or a third country, with the assignment lasting for an extended period of time (two to five years is a common length of time for an expatriate assignment).[37] In fact, about 80 percent of medium- and large-sized companies have employees working abroad and 86 percent of surveyed companies reported that their number of employees on international assignments would either remain the same or increase in the next five years.[38] Companies are sending expats to a broader range of countries than ever before, and surveys suggest that the average age of expats is declining, with more than half now being under 40 years old, versus the historical average of 41 percent.[39] It is viewed as a positive that millennials tend to have a more entrepreneurial mindset, are comfortable with technology, and have a lower level of ties such as spouses and children. In addition, a higher proportion of expatriates are women, around 27 percent, versus the historical average of 15 percent.[40]

Why hire expatriates rather than local employees? Expatriates can bring technical or managerial skills that are scarce in the host country; they can help transfer or install companywide systems or cultures; they may provide a trusted connection for facilitating oversight or control over foreign operations, whether it is a new endeavor or an operation that is already in existence; or the international assignment may enable the expat to develop the skills and experiences that will allow a subsequent promotion into leadership positions of greater scope and responsibility within the IC. The most effective leaders in an increasingly complex and internationalizing world tend to be those who can understand and interact effectively with a variety of stakeholders, despite differences in culture or location. Expat assignments can demonstrate such skills, including the development of political and social capital, and these assignments have been reported to lead to faster promotions.[41] Experience with international assignments has been found to result in over 40 percent faster promotions within companies and over a quarter of responding companies report that international work experience is a prerequisite to joining their global leadership team.[42] Indeed, about 80 percent of respondents consider the primary purpose of expatriate assignments to be the development of leadership and management skills.[43]

> "Out of **OUR SENIOR MANAGEMENT CADRE of A HUNDRED PEOPLE, ONLY A FEW HAVE NEVER WORKED** outside **THEIR HOME COUNTRY.**"
>
> —*Ian Cloke, vice president of Global Mobility at KPMG UK*[44]

The costs of using expatriates are substantial, estimated at $50 billion annually for U.S. companies and an average of about $250,000 per employee, so the performance of expatriates is an important issue for ICs.[45] Yet various studies report that failure rates for expatriate assignments—including failing to achieve performance targets for an international assignment or prematurely returning from the assignment—range from 25 to 45 percent.[46] Approximately one-quarter of expats leave their firms during their overseas assignment, and an additional 38 percent leave their

culture shock
The anxiety people often experience when they move from a culture that they are familiar with to one that is entirely different

companies within a year of their return from abroad and 50 percent within two years of return, hindering the IC's ability to retain and leverage the skills and experience that the expatriate has gained from the international assignment.[47] Despite the investment in expats, 61 percent of surveyed companies do not track the proportion of workers who leave their company within two years of completing an expat assignment, and 75 percent fail to track expats' careers after their return from abroad.[48]

One important cause of expatriate performance problems is culture shock, which is the anxiety people often experience when they move from a familiar culture to one that is entirely different.[49] Because familiar signs and symbols are no longer present in the new

Although moving to a new country for work can be exciting, it can also cause culture shock, the anxiety people feel when they become part of an entirely different culture as part of their job. ©George Doyle/Stockbyte/Getty Images.

> **❝THE INITIAL PERIOD in A NEW POSTING INVOLVES CONSIDERABLE PERSONAL TRAUMA. THE MAIN REASON for EXPATRIATE FAILURE IS LACK of ADAPTABILITY, OR THE FAMILY UNIT'S LACK of ADAPTABILITY.❞**
>
> *—Brian Friedman, founder of the Forum for Expatriate Management*[50]

culture, a person experiencing culture shock tends to feel lack of direction or inadequacy from not knowing what to do or how things are done in the new culture. Physical and emotional discomfort and feelings of disorientation and confusion are a common experience for people who go to other nations to study, live, or work. Many expatriates and members of their families are affected by culture shock, sometimes to a very great degree. Ironically, once a person has grown accustomed to a new culture, returning to one's home culture can produce a similar experience, referred to as *reverse culture shock.*

Researchers have identified three dimensions associated with cross-cultural adjustment.[51] The first is associated with the work context, such as the extent of job clarity, inherent conflict in the person's role, and the amount of discretion associated with completing the job tasks. Adjustment to the general environment, the second dimension, is associated with reacting to differences in housing, food, education, health, safety, and transportation. The third dimension, interaction with local nationals, involves adjusting to differences in behavioral norms, ways of dealing with conflict, communication patterns, and other relationship issues that can produce anger or frustration. An expatriate can experience some degree of culture shock associated with any or all of these three dimensions.

To enhance expatriate performance, ICs should consider the support that they provide to the employee during predeparture, while away on assignment, and upon repatriation.[52] "As businesses continue to expand into more countries, or even more remote locations in relatively more established countries, second- and third-tier cities in China, for example, the future of international assignment success will depend on the combination of individually tailored support and a more adaptable, flexible and qualified assignee," says Scott Sullivan, managing director at Graebel Asia Pacific.[53]

During the predeparture phase, the focus of support efforts should be on ensuring that the expatriate has the skills needed for successful performance in the foreign assignment, including language and cultural training, career counseling, and any needed technical or other skill development. Support during assignment includes the use of mentors (both home- and host-country), career counseling, and communication strategies to ensure that the expatriate remains connected to the IC's strategy, people, policies, and culture. Repatriation support, including management of the relocation to the home or other nation and reintegration into the company, is discussed later in this section. Organizational support has been shown to be a predictor of the success of expatriates' adjustment to their international postings.[54] Such support can enhance expatriate motivation, improve adjustment to challenging international work environments, and improve performance.[55]

> **❝INCREASINGLY, A FAMILY'S HAPPINESS AND ABILITY to ADJUST ARE nearly AS IMPORTANT to THE SUCCESS of A JOB RELOCATION AS THE EMPLOYEE'S OWN JOB PERFORMANCE.❞**
>
> *—Matt Spinolo, executive vice president of Cartus Corporation*[57]

THE EXPATRIATE'S FAMILY

Studies examining the failure of expatriates suggest that as many as 9 in 10 such failures are family-related, and more than 75 percent of the employees who declined relocations in recent surveys cited family concerns as the basis for their decision.[56] In contrast to immigrants, who typically commit themselves to become part of their new country of residence, expats usually are living only temporarily in the new nation, so they often fail to adopt the host country's culture and seldom attempt to gain citizenship in that nation.

Cultural adaptation pressures may be particularly difficult for the accompanying spouses. Although many spouses are highly educated and pursuing professional careers, they often are unable to work in the host country and may experience more challenges with regard to their personal identity. Spouses also typically need to interact more extensively with the local host community than do their expatriate partners, for such things as shopping, schools, and the management of domestic help,

Why Aren't More Women Selected for International Assignments?

Businesses consistently report they have a growing need for competent global leaders but difficulty in finding the talent. Although women make up about 47 percent of the workforce in the United States, at only 27 percent they represent a relatively small (though growing) fraction of the population of expatriates. Why does this difference exist, especially with the pressing need for finding and developing competent global leaders? Professor Nancy Adler examined three myths about women in international management:

Myth 1: Women do not want to be international managers.
Myth 2: Companies refuse to send women abroad.
Myth 3: Foreigners' prejudice against women renders them ineffective.

When Adler tested these myths empirically, neither the first nor the third was supported, but the second one was. Adler's research suggested that 70 percent of her sample of international companies were hesitant to select women for expatriate assignments. Why? Among the reasons expressed were that women in dual-career relationships would experience problems with international assignments; that gender-based prejudice would limit women's performance in many challenging countries or cultures; that women might feel lonely and isolated in an international assignment or be subjected to sexual harassment; or that the men making selection decisions regarding international assignments were biased by traditional views and stereotypes regarding the appropriateness of assigning women to expatriate positions.

Is reluctance to select women for international assignments justified? Research has shown that women are just as eager to go abroad as are men, sometimes more so. Gender is not related to the performance ratings of expatriates, to their adjustment to the host-country context, or to their intention to leave their ICs. Studies have shown that women are not at a disadvantage relative to men in terms of working in a foreign country, especially in nations or industries where women are already well accepted within the workforce. Recent studies have even suggested that the skills and identity typically associated with women (attentiveness to personal aspects of business, comfort with ambiguity, willingness to share information and power, and skill in building interpersonal relationships) may give women an edge over men for some expatriate assignments and thus make them more desirable hires.

In addition, rather than serving as a barrier to the effectiveness of female expats, as has sometimes been argued, sexist cultural attributes may confer an advantage for women in international roles. Indeed, women may be able to divert attention from gender by demonstrating individualized sources of legitimacy and power, such as functional expertise and experience, and thereby enhance their effectiveness in international assignments. Research has suggested that women may benefit from a halo effect, in which foreigners assume a female expat must be particularly well-qualified in order to be selected over a male for a particular expatriate position. Similarly, although studies have reported that women assigned to countries where females have lower social status often have a more difficult time adjusting, they are nevertheless rated as being equally effective as men at their jobs. Some Japanese even refer to female expats as "the third gender" because they are accorded a different role and status than local women. Many expatriate women have reported similar experiences in other contexts, such as Saudi Arabia, where foreign women can be effective as managers even if local women may have few or no opportunities to pursue such positions. A recent Australian study showed that childless single women were most likely to take expatriate roles because they did not encounter the same role conflicts and social pressures that married women or women with children might face. Female expatriates who are married are much less likely to take a partner overseas with them than are male expatriates. Among expats, 49 percent are men who are married or partnered, while 19 percent are women who are married or partnered. Only 16 percent of women bring partners, versus 57 percent for male expatriates. Research suggesting that men may be less willing than in the past to accept international assignments may also be opening additional opportunities for women to successfully seek, and perform effectively within, expatriate roles.

To reduce barriers women may face in pursuing expatriate opportunities, Sapna Welsh and Caroline Kersten of Leverage HR recommend the following steps:

- Build awareness within management about benefits women can bring to expat positions and barriers they may face in being chosen for these roles.
- Build awareness among women with high potential about potential benefits of expat roles.
- Develop women's capability to overcome external and self-imposed barriers, develop competencies for expat success, and create support networks for those accepting expat assignments.

Critical Thinking Questions

1. Should ICs select more women for expatriate assignments? Why or why not?

2. Are there circumstances in which you believe female expatriates should be most strongly considered, or in which they should not be considered at all? Why?

3. How can companies help ensure that more high-potential women are encouraged to pursue international assignments, and that their expat experiences will be supported and leveraged effectively?

Sources: Nancy J. Adler, "Women Do Not Want International Careers: And Other Myths about International Management," *Organizational Dynamics*, vol. 13, no. 2, 1984, 66–80; Paula M. Caligiuri, and Wayne Cascio, "Can We Send Her There? Maximizing the Success of Western Women on Global Assignments," *Journal of World Business*, vol. 33, no. 4, 1998, 394–417; Rosalie Tung, "Female Expatriates: The Model Global Manager?," *Organizational Dynamics*, vol. 33, no. 3, August 2004, 243–53; Phyllis Tharenou, "Disruptive Decisions to Leave Home: Gender and Family Differences in Expatriation Choices," *Organizational Behavior and Human Decision Processes*, vol. 105, no. 2, March 2008, 183–200; Ann Pomeroy, "Outdated Policies Hinder Female Expats," *HR Magazine*, December 2006, 16; Yochanan Altman, and Susan Shortland, "Women and International Assignments: Taking Stock—A 25-Year Review," *Human Resource Management*, vol. 47, no. 2, 2008, 199–216; Jeremy Smerd, "More Women, Young Workers on the Move," *Workforce Management*, August 2007; Jan Selmer, and Alicia Leung, "Are Corporate Career Development Activities Less Available to Female than to Male Expatriates?," *Journal of Business Ethics*, vol. 43, no. 1, 2003, 125–36; Susan Shortland, "Gender Diversity in Expatriation: Evaluating Theoretical Perspectives," *Gender in Management: An International Journal*, vol. 24, no. 5, 2009, 367–69; Sapna Welsh, and Caroline Kersten, "Where Are Women in the Expatriate Workforce?," *Society for Human Resource Management*, January 01, 2014, www.shrm.org; BGRS, "Closing the Gender Gap and Talent Mobility's Role," *Building the Business Case for Mobility Transformation*, 2017, www.bgrs.com; Corinne, Purtill "Expat Couples Do Best When They've Moved for the Woman's Job," *Quartz*, December 06, 2017, www.qz.com; and Susan Shortland, "Networking: A Valuable Career Intervention for Women Expatriates," *Career Development International*, vol. 16, no. 3, 2011, 271–92.

and these related issues increase adjustment pressures.[58] The stress an overseas move places on spouses and children will ultimately affect employees no matter how dedicated they may be to the company. Even worse, if family-related factors cause an expatriate employee to request to return to the home country early, the company is losing a "million-dollar corporate-training investment" in the executive. On the other hand, expatriates tend to have better satisfaction and performance when their spouses and other family members are able to adjust well to the new host-country context.[59] Although repeated studies have shown that companies consider cross-cultural training to be highly valuable and recognize that such training can have important implications for performance, only about one in five companies require such training for their expats or their families.[60]

Trailing Spouses in Two-Career Families While about 80 percent of expats are accompanied by a spouse or partner, the number of two-career families is growing. That is a major factor affecting expatriate adjustment and performance, and it can complicate matters when one spouse is offered a really good job opportunity abroad.[61] About 82 percent of expat spouses have university degrees and about two-thirds were working prior to their partner's assignment.[62] Yet, in many countries the employee's spouse does not have the legal right to work, as work permits for foreigners may be difficult or nearly impossible to acquire. As a result, as few as 8 percent of spouses were employed during the course of the expat assignment, which can increase financial pressures and strain relationships before, during, and after the expatriate assignment.[63] The trailing spouses must often make major adjustments in lifestyle, family balance of power, and self-image. They often experience stages of grief from the derailment of their careers that is similar to the loss of a loved one—going through shock, denial, and anger—and sometimes fail to reach the reconciliation stage of adjustment.[64] Indeed, concern about the implications of an international assignment for the employee's partner and the partner's career prospects represented the second highest reason for refusing an expatriate assignment, behind family concerns (such as children's education, family adjustment, resistance by the partner, difficult location for assignment, cultural adjustments, length of the assignment, and language).

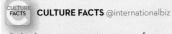

CULTURE FACTS @internationalbiz

Only about 30 countries, many of which rank relatively high on individualism, allow the spouse or partner of an expatriate to work freely, including the United Kingdom, Canada, New Zealand, Denmark, Finland, Australia, and the Netherlands.
#individualism #expatriates

SOCIAL MEDIA

In efforts to ease the problem, some companies are starting programs that give trailing spouses more help in adjusting. Such help may take the form of assisting with job hunting in the host country, providing support for résumé preparation, arranging language and cultural training, identifying career opportunities, or giving tips on local interview techniques. Many companies have made greater use of shorter international assignments, under the belief that this can be less disruptive to the expatriate family's lives while still permitting benefits from the international assignment of personnel.[65]

Another option many companies are pursuing is to hire people for expat assignments who are single and often younger as well, with over 40 percent of such positions being filled by unmarried personnel.[66] It should be noted that the hiring of single people for expatriate positions is not without its own set of potential concerns.

Challenges for Expatriate Children Although an overseas stint may be seen as critical for career advancement of a parent, children are an important but often overlooked consideration when planning for an international move, even though 26 percent of expats have dependent children while abroad.[67] Children can benefit in many ways from joining parents on an expatriate assignment, such as meeting people from all over the world, becoming familiar with many cultures, learning to speak multiple languages, developing more cosmopolitan approaches to the world, and getting a head start on developing a global mind-set. Also, some people suggest that children are likely to be more flexible in adjusting to new environments than might be the case for their parents.

Although children can benefit from participating in their parents' expatriate experiences, these assignments can also wreak havoc upon children's lives. Children are seldom involved in the initial decision-making process associated with a move abroad. This can result in the children experiencing many feelings, such as insecurity, frustration, and powerlessness, from being uprooted from friends and many of the sources of their own identity. A move does not merely involve changing schools; there are also new systems, new learning styles, new language, and so forth to which the child must adjust. Sometimes these children are referred to as *third-culture kids* (or TCKs) because they often speak several different languages, hold passports from more than one country, and have difficulty explaining where they are from (i.e., where "home" is). As a consequence of these challenges, companies are increasing their focus on easing the disruptions faced by children.

©Kali Nine LLC/Getty Images.

PREPARATION FOR THE TRANSITION: LANGUAGE TRAINING

The English language has become the *lingua franca* of the world; in effect, it is everybody's second language. Nevertheless, foreign language skill has been shown to be a critical factor influencing the effective adjustment of expatriates and their family members within the host country. When you are trying to sell to potential customers, it is much better to speak their language. Having at least some ability to speak the language of your customer can not only allow you to understand her and her culture better, but it may also enhance your ability to establish trust and a good working relationship. As English speakers try to sell abroad, it is far more likely that their customers will speak English than that the English speakers will be able to speak the customers' language. Customers can then hide behind their language during negotiations. While only 25 percent of native-born Americans are reported to be able to speak in two or more languages, and less than half of those reporting that they can speak the second language "very well," 56 percent of the citizens of the European Union are multilingual.[68] If your career relates to international business—and few can avoid at least some exposure to it—it is likely to suffer if you speak only English.

EXPATRIATE SERVICES

Although most U.S. expatriates currently continue health coverage with their company's domestic plans, we can expect that to change in the near future as expatriate health care programs are being created to assist companies and expatriates with claims administration, language translations, currency conversions, and service standardization. Similarly, banks are developing expatriate services, allowing expatriates to sign up for services online and providing 24-hour assistance to their customers, regardless of where in the world the expatriate is working.

In recognition of expatriate family issues, some companies have begun to prepare and assist these families. Assistance may take the form of realistic job previews for expatriates (and sometimes for their family members); training in the culture and language of the host country; assistance in finding suitable schools or medical specialists; or even arranging for long-distance care for elderly relatives or parents while the family is living abroad. House-hunting help may be given, and the new transplants should be taken on grocery and hardware shopping trips with locals and expats who have been in the host country for a while. Locals can teach you the social norms and where to shop and not to shop. Expats can teach you how to get things only expats want. Websites that focus on expatriate issues and can assist you in preparing for, adjusting to, or returning from an expatriate assignment include Internations.org, Expat.org, and Expatfocus.com.

REPATRIATION—THE SHOCK OF RETURNING HOME

As mentioned earlier, an expatriate returning home often experiences reverse culture shock. He or she will have gained new skills and knowledge, and the company's attitudes and people will have changed. Expatriates who have become accustomed to high levels of autonomy while abroad often struggle with the more restrictive work context when they return home, as well as experiencing the common frustration of failing to be promoted or having their job expectations fulfilled after repatriation. If fully utilized, the repatriate can provide the company with rare, difficult to imitate, and competitively valuable knowledge and skills.

That is why planning for an expat's return should start well before the overseas assignment even begins. The assignee and the employer should discuss up front how the assignment will fit the employee's long-range career goals and how the company will handle the return. Challenges of repatriation should be discussed even before departure, and a mentor program should be considered between the expat and a mentor back home. During the assignment, expats should be encouraged to make regular visits back to the home-country offices to help "stay in the loop" and feel part of the organizational network. When expats come back, companies have to understand that they are going to be different and should try to harness their new knowledge.[69] Upon return, 61 percent of expats felt they were not provided with opportunities to apply their foreign experience and 75 percent felt that the position they move into upon return represented a demotion from their position abroad.[70] Efforts should be made to help repatriates find appropriate positions that use their newly developed skills and to help the expat and the family members re-acculturate, including access to counseling and other forms of support, in order to promote adjustment success and build company loyalty. "It has become increasingly acknowledged, that returning home can be even more difficult than moving to a foreign country. Yet, organizations do not have the answers to the question 'what makes coming home so difficult?' The question has been identified as a serious management concern because it culminates with repatriates resigning," states Ida Stilling.[71] Nevertheless, while about three-quarters of companies with expatriate programs have formal policies regarding repatriation, only one-fifth discuss repatriation prior to sending an employee on assignment.[72] Indeed, 68 percent of expatriates report that they do not have any guaranteed position in their IC after the end of their international assignment.[73] "We are seeing rapid globalization, and it's going to become a real problem to find people who are willing and qualified to go overseas if everyone hears about people who were not satisfied" after they are repatriated, said Lisa Johnson, the director of consulting services for Cendant Mobility.[74]

Compensation for International Assignments

Establishing a compensation plan that is equitable and consistent and yet does not overcompensate the overseas executive is a challenging, complex task, especially since a "one-size-fits-all" approach does not match up well with the reality of diverse company and country assignments. Because more companies are sending employees on expatriate assignments, there is a greater need to keep pace with the cost of living changes. To ensure that companies receive a good return on their investment and employees are compensated fairly, expatriate programs must be managed proactively. If ICs are not able to compensate in a manner that is perceived to be fair and attractive, it will become even more difficult to attract the quantity and quality of potential expatriates needed to satisfy the company's international requirements. This can also fundamentally affect the extent to which a company's future leaders are shaped by such experiences and have developed the skills and experiences needed to lead effectively in an increasingly complex and internationalizing business environment.

The method traditionally favored by the majority of American ICs is the balance sheet approach, whereby the expatriate is paid a base salary equal to that of a domestic counterpart and then, in the belief that no one should be worse off for accepting foreign employment, to add a variety of allowances and bonuses.[76] This approach can work well for expatriates who are at mid- or senior levels of an organization. The expatriate is not put at a disadvantage relative to domestic counterparts in the same or similar positions, and it may facilitate easier movement between expatriate and domestic assignments. However, this approach can be complex and expensive for a company to administer, particularly if the IC is involved with many such positions across a range of nations and regions. Table 14.2 provides an example of some of the compensation costs for sending an American manager on a three-year assignment to Moscow, Russia. Many international assignments will entail significantly higher levels of additional costs when compared with those in the home country, than suggested by this example.

Because of the high cost typically associated with expatriate assignments, some companies have attempted various schemes to help reduce these costs. In terms of salaries and other benefits, some companies have localized their workforce, replacing expatriates with qualified but lower cost locals if such personnel are available. In other instances, an expatriate may begin with a higher salary and benefits package, but then have some but not all of this extra "expatriate package" phased out over time, creating a hybrid compensation scheme (e.g., key benefits such as children's schooling or housing subsidies may be maintained while other perks are eliminated).

Alternatively, some companies provide a lump-sum approach, beginning with a home-country–based salary and then providing an additional sum the expatriate may choose to allocate across various categories such as housing, education, and so forth.[77] This practice allows the company to avoid paying for things the expat does not value, but calculating the appropriate lump sum can require complex analyses. A modification of the lump-sum approach is sometimes referred to as the "cafeteria approach," in which the company provides a limited set of options from which the expatriate can choose, such as

LO 14-6
Describe some of the complications of compensation packages for expatriate executives.

"IT HAS BECOME INCREASINGLY ACKNOWLEDGED, THAT RETURNING HOME CAN BE EVEN MORE DIFFICULT THAN MOVING TO A FOREIGN COUNTRY. YET, ORGANIZATIONS DO NOT HAVE THE ANSWERS TO THE QUESTION 'WHAT MAKES COMING HOME SO DIFFICULT?' THE QUESTION HAS BEEN IDENTIFIED AS A SERIOUS MANAGEMENT CONCERN BECAUSE IT CULMINATES WITH REPATRIATES RESIGNING. "

—Ida Stilling, Global Mobility Consultant[75]

TABLE 14.2 Total Compensation Costs for Sending an Expatriate American Manager to Russia

The following compensation costs are illustrative of those an IC might encounter annually when sending an American manager and his or her family (spouse, two school-age children) to Moscow, Russia, for a three-year assignment.

Compensation Component	Annual Cost (US$)
Base salary	$ 170,000
Incentive plan	34,000
Location differential (hardship premium)	25,500
Housing (three-bedroom apartment)	96,000
Cost-of-living allowance	42,500
Automobile allowance	36,500
Home leave	25,000
Educational assistance	30,800
Relocation/repatriation expenses	25,000
Total compensation before tax	**$ 485,300**
Tax assistance	77,060
Total compensation expense	**$ 562,360**
Other Expenses	
Preparation services (passports, visas, language training, etc.)	$ 10,000
Settling-in services	8,500
Emergency leave	15,000
Total annual cost for expatriate	**$ 595,860**
Total cost over three-year assignment	**$1,787,580**

Sources: Author estimates and relocation experts.

a company car or company-paid tuition for a spouse or children, rather than a monetary sum. Another approach is to eliminate all expatriate compensation and benefits premiums, substituting a "local terms" package identical to what would be paid to an indigenous manager. This localization approach may be used from the point of initial recruitment or be applied after a certain trigger point is reached (such as time since the initial appointment of the expat).[78]

SALARIES

The practice of paying home-country nationals the same salaries as their domestic counterparts permits worldwide consistency for this part of the compensation package. Because of the increasing use of third-country nationals, those personnel are generally treated in the same way.

Some firms take the equal-pay-for-equal-work concept one step further and pay the same base salaries to host-country nationals. In countries that legislate yearly bonuses and family allowances for their citizens, a local national may receive what appears to be a higher salary than is paid to the expatriate, although companies usually make extra payments to prevent expatriates from falling behind in this regard. In many nations, particularly those with high tax rates on personal income, it is a common practice to pay executives relatively lower salaries and to provide them with expensive perquisites, such as chauffeured automobiles, premium housing, elite education for spouses or children, and club memberships.

ALLOWANCES

Allowances are employee compensation payments added to the base salaries of expatriates because of higher expenses encountered when living abroad. The most common allowances are for housing, cost of living, tax differentials, education, and moving.

allowances
Employee compensation payments added to base salaries of expatriates because of higher expenses encountered when living abroad

Housing Allowances Housing allowances are designed to permit executives to live in housing comparable to the level of quality they had at home. However, in many foreign locations, particularly major urban areas, it is not financially viable or logistically practical to provide the same size housing as an expatriate may have enjoyed in the home country, particularly if the expatriate is from a nation where large suburban homes are common.[79] The size of the employee's family is a key factor influencing the type of housing to be provided. Although a commonly used rule of thumb has been for the IC to pay all the rent in excess of 15 percent of the expat's salary, the decision depends on whether the expat is expected to continue paying for housing in the home country during the term of the foreign assignment. Indeed, about two-thirds of ICs have moved away from requiring their expats to pay for housing abroad in order to minimize situations in which employees had to sell or rent their property in order to afford their foreign housing, a hurdle that reduces incentives for accepting foreign postings as well as creating a range of financial and logistical challenges for both the company and the expat.

Cost-of-Living Allowances Cost-of-living allowances are based on differences in the prices paid for food, utilities, transportation, entertainment, clothing, personal services, and medical expenses overseas compared with the prices paid for these items in the IC's headquarters city. Many ICs use the U.S. Department of State index, which is based on the cost of these items in Washington, DC, but have found it is not altogether satisfactory. For one thing, critics claim this index is not adjusted often enough to account for either the rapid inflation in some countries or the changes in relative currency values. Another objection is that the index does not include many cities in which the firm operates. As a result, many companies take their own surveys or use data from the United Nations, the World Bank, the International Monetary Fund, or private consulting firms. Figures and comparisons on costs of living, prices, and wages can also be found in private publications. Table 14.3 provides a ranking of the 10 cities with the highest cost of living, as well as a ranking of 5 cities with the highest quality of living in 2018.

Allowances for Tax Differentials ICs often pay tax differentials when the host-country taxes are higher than the taxes that the expatriates would pay on the same compensation and consumption at home; a practice often referred to as "tax protection" or "tax equalization" policies.[80] The objective is to ensure that expatriates will not have less after-tax take-home pay in the host country than they would at home. This can create a considerable extra financial burden on a parent company, however. For example, the U.S. Internal Revenue Code treats tax allowances as additional taxable income and expatriates from the United States may be subject to tax even if they live and work full-time in another country.[81] Other countries, such as China, may tax certain employer-provided benefits and bonuses.[82]

Education Allowances Expatriates are naturally concerned that their children receive educations at least equal to those they would get in their home countries, and many want their children taught in their native language. Primary and secondary schools with teachers from most industrialized home countries are available in many cities around the world,

TABLE 14.3 Cost-of-Living and Quality-of-Living Rankings of Top 10 and Top 5 Cities, Respectively, 2018

Cost-of-Living Rank	City	Country	Quality-of-Living Rank	City	Country
1	Hong Kong	Hong Kong, SAR	1	Vienna	Austria
2	Tokyo	Japan	2	Zurich	Switzerland
3	Zurich	Switzerland	3	Auckland	New Zealand
4	Singapore	Singapore	4	Munich	Germany
5	Seoul	South Korea	5	Vancouver	Canada
6	Luanda	Angola			
7	Shanghai	China			
8	Ndjamena	Chad			
9	Beijing	China			
10	Bern	Switzerland			

Note: Cost-of-living index includes cost of housing. Base City, New York City, USA = 100.
Sources: Mercer Human Resource Consulting, *2018 Cost-of-Living Survey*, https://www.mercer.com, accessed November 16, 2018; and Mercer Human Resource Consulting, *2018 Quality of Living Survey*, https://www.mercer.com, accessed November 16, 2018.

but these are private schools and therefore charge tuition. ICs either pay the tuition or, if there are enough expatriate children, operate their own schools. For decades, petroleum companies in the Middle East have maintained schools for their employees' children. A survey indicated that 53 percent of companies provide an education allowance for dependent children of their long-term expatriates.[83] Education expenses can be substantial in many locations, up to $100,000 per child in some private schools in China, for example, and whether the company adequately covers these expenses can be a deciding factor in an employee's accepting an expatriate posting.[84]

Moving and Orientation Allowances Companies generally pay the total costs of transferring their employees overseas.[85] These costs include transporting the family, moving household effects, and maintaining the family in a hotel on a full expense account until the household effects arrive. Some firms find it less expensive to send the household effects by air rather than by ship because the reduction in hotel expenses more than compensates for the higher cost of air freight. It has also been found that moving into a house sooner raises the employee's morale. Increasingly, ICs will pay for a relocation service, in the home or host countries or both, to assist expats and their families in moving and getting acclimated to the new country. Companies may pay for some orientation of the employees and their families to facilitate successful relocation. Companies frequently pay for language instruction, and some will provide the family with guidance on the intricacies of everyday living, such as shopping, hiring domestic help, finding new or used appliances, locating expatriate associations or social groups and churches, and helping to find and gain admission to appropriate schools for the expat's children.

BONUSES

Bonuses (or *premiums*), unlike allowances, are expatriate employee compensation payments in addition to base salaries and allowances because of hardship, inconvenience,

bonuses
Expatriate employee compensation payments in addition to base salaries and allowances because of hardship, inconvenience, or danger

TABLE 14.4 Hardship Differential Pay Premiums for Selected Cities and Countries, 2018

City and Country	Differential Pay Premium (%)
Kabul, Afghanistan	35
Dhaka, Bangladesh	35
La Paz, Bolivia	20
São Paulo, Brazil	10
Phnom Penh, Cambodia	25
Wuhan, China	25
Cairo, Egypt	20
Tbilisi, Georgia	15
Port-au-Prince, Haiti	25
Kolkata, India	25
Jakarta, Indonesia	25
Baghdad, Iraq	30
Nairobi, Kenya	20
Mexico City, Mexico	15
Peshawar, Pakistan	35
Manila, Philippines	15
Riyadh, Saudi Arabia	25
Kiev, Ukraine	20
Caracas, Venezuela	30
Harare, Zimbabwe	20

Source: "Post (Hardship) Differential (DSSR 500), Percentage of Basic Compensation," *U.S. Department of State*, December 09, 2018, https://aoprals.state.gov.

or danger that expatriates and their families undergo while living abroad. Bonuses include overseas premiums, contract termination payments, and home leave reimbursement.

Overseas Premiums Overseas premiums are additional payments to expatriates and are generally established as a percentage of the base salary. They typically range from 10 to 25 percent. If the living conditions are extremely disagreeable, the company may pay larger premiums for hardship posts. The U.S. Department of State maintains a list of hardship differential pay premiums that is often used as a reference by ICs and expats. Table 14.4 shows the hardship differentials for 20 selected cities as of November 2018.

Contract Termination Payments These payments are made as inducements for employees to stay on their jobs and work out the periods of their overseas contracts. The payments are made at the end of the contract periods only if the employees have worked out their contracts. Such bonuses are commonly used in industries such as the petroleum and construction sectors and by other firms that have contracts requiring work abroad for a specific period of time or a specific project. They may also be used if the foreign post is a hardship or not a particularly desirable one.

Home Leave ICs that post home-country—and sometimes third-country—nationals in foreign countries make it a practice to pay for periodic trips back to the home country by such employees and their families.[86] The reasons for this are at least threefold.[87] One, companies do not want employees and their families to lose touch with the home country and its culture. Two, companies want to have employees spend at least a few days at company headquarters to renew relationships with headquarters' staff and catch up with new company policies and practices. Three, providing a break from a host-country location, particularly those considered "hardship postings," may be essential to the emotional health of an expatriate and family. A survey by *The Economist* revealed that 56 percent of companies gave regular, paid trips back home for their expatriate staff.[88] Some firms grant three-month home leaves after an employee has been abroad about three years, but it is a more common practice to give two to four weeks' leave each year. All transportation costs to and from the executive's hometown are paid, and all expenses during the executive's stay at company headquarters. As workforces become more diverse, a complicating factor for ICs is determining where "home" is for intercultural families of expats. In addition, the emergence of new technologies such as videoconferencing (Skype, FaceTime, Zoom), e-mail, and a range of social networking options have changed the nature and frequency of such travel.

COMPENSATION PACKAGES CAN BE COMPLICATED

One might think from the discussion to this point that **compensation packages**, while costly—the extras frequently total 50 percent or more of the base salary—are fairly straightforward in their calculation. Nothing could be further from the truth. Compensation packages for expatriate employees can incorporate many types of payments or reimbursements and must take into consideration exchange rates and inflation.

compensation packages
For expatriate employees, packages that can incorporate many types of payments or reimbursements and must take into consideration exchange rates and inflation

What Percentage of the Base Salary? All allowances and a percentage of the base salary are usually paid in the host-country currency. What should this percentage be? In practice, it varies from 65 to 75 percent, with the remainder being banked wherever the employee wishes. One reason for such practices is to decrease the local portion of the salary, thereby lowering host-country income taxes and giving the appearance to government authorities and local employees that there is less difference between the salaries of local and foreign employees than is actually the case. Another reason is that expatriate employees have various expenses that must be paid in home-country currency. Such expenses may include professional society memberships, purchases during home leave, payments on outstanding debts in the employee's home country (e.g., mortgage, school loans), and tuition and other costs for children in home-country universities.

What Exchange Rate? Most of the expatriate's compensation is usually denominated in the host-country currency, but it is established in terms of the home-country currency. To achieve comparable compensation throughout the enterprise, a currency exchange rate must be chosen. In countries whose currencies are freely convertible into other currencies, this presents no serious problem, although the experienced expatriate will argue that an exchange rate covers only international transactions and may not represent a true purchasing power parity between the local and home-country currencies. For instance, such items as bread and milk are rarely traded internationally, and living costs and inflation rates may be much higher in the host country than in the home country. International companies attempt to compensate for such differences in the cost-of-living allowances.

More difficult problems must be solved in countries that have exchange controls and nonconvertible currencies. Those currencies are generally overvalued at the official rate, and if the firm uses that rate, its expatriate employees are certain to be shortchanged. Reference may be made to the free market rate for the host-country currency in free currency markets in, for example, the United States or Switzerland or to the black market rate in the host country, but these do not give the final answers. In the end, all companies must pay their expatriate employees enough to enable them to live as well as others who have similar positions in other firms, regardless of how the amount is calculated.

A common compensation component at many U.S. companies is a stock plan that gives employees opportunities to acquire the company's stock on favorable terms. Such programs are designed to increase loyalty and productivity. However, these programs sometimes run into problems outside the United States. Share ownership is unknown or restricted in numerous countries, and efforts to implement such programs often encounter a host of challenging differences with respect to laws governing accounting, taxation, and securities practices.[89] DuPont, for example, discovered it could not give stock options in 25 of 53 nations, primarily because those countries' laws ban or limit ownership of foreign shares.

COMPENSATION OF THIRD-COUNTRY NATIONALS

Although some companies have different compensation plans for third-country nationals, there is a trend toward treating them the same as home-country expatriates. In either event, there are areas in which problems can arise. One of these areas is the calculation of income tax differentials, such as when an American expatriate is compared with an expatriate from another country. This results from the unique American government practice of taxing the income of U.S. citizens even though they live and work abroad and treating tax differential payments made to those citizens as additional taxable income.[90] No other major country taxes its nationals in those ways.

Another possible problem area is the home leave bonus. Two of the commonly stated purposes of home leave are to prevent expatriates from losing touch with their native cultures and having them visit IC headquarters. A third-country national must visit two countries instead of only one to achieve both purposes, and the additional costs can be substantial. For example, compare the cost of sending an Australian employee home from Mexico with that required to send a U.S. executive home from Mexico to Dallas.

Regardless of problems, the use of third-country nationals is growing in popularity. As businesses race to enlarge their ranks of qualified international managers, third-country nationals are in greater demand. They often win jobs because they speak several languages and know an industry or country well. As the number of TCNs employed as executives by ICs continues to grow, the possible combinations of nationalities and host countries are virtually limitless, further complicating compensation efforts.

INTERNATIONAL STATUS

In all of this discussion, we have been describing compensation for expatriates who have been granted international status. Merely being from another country does not automatically qualify an employee for all the benefits we have mentioned. A subsidiary may hire home-country nationals or third-country nationals and pay them the same as it pays host-country employees. However, managers have found that although a U.S. employee, for example, may agree initially to take a job and be paid on the local scale, sooner or later bad feeling and friction will develop as that person sees fellow Americans enjoying international status perquisites to which he or she is not entitled.

international status
Entitles the expatriate employee to all the allowances and bonuses applicable to the place of residence and employment

Sometimes firms promote host-country employees to international status even without transferring them abroad. This is a means of rewarding valuable people, putting them at a level comparable to their peers from other countries, and preventing them from leaving the company for better jobs elsewhere.

Thus, international status means being paid some or all of the allowances and bonuses we have discussed, and there can be other sorts of payments as individual circumstances and people's imaginations combine to create them. Compensation packages for expatriates and other international executives are sufficiently important and complicated to have become a specialization in the human resource management field; at one firm, the title is "international employee benefits consultant." Help is also available from outside the IC. From time to time, the large consulting firms publish pamphlets advising about the transfer of executives to specific countries.

PERKS

Perks originated in the perquisites of the medieval lords of the manor, whose workers paid parts of their profits or produce to the lords to be allowed to continue working. Today, perks are symbols of rank in the corporate hierarchy and are used to compensate executives while minimizing taxes. Among the most common perks are:

- Cars, which may include chauffeurs, especially for senior-level executives
- Private pension plan
- Retirement payment
- Life insurance
- Health insurance
- Emergency evacuation services (for medical or other reasons)
- Kidnapping, ransom, and extortion insurance
- Company house or apartment
- Directorship of a foreign subsidiary
- Seminar holiday travel
- Club memberships
- Hidden slush fund (such funds may be illegal, but some corporations are said to have them)

WHAT'S IMPORTANT TO YOU?

When considering a relocation abroad, whether for a few months or many years, it is important for you to consider what elements of compensation and benefits are important to you. Common considerations include cost of living, safety of personnel, medical facilities, housing, and schools. They may also include availability of good restaurants, sports facilities, shopping facilities, and quality theaters or other entertainment venues. See Table 14.3 again for a ranking of the top five cities in the world for quality of life; none of these cities is located in an emerging country.

Also important to many employees may be the number of vacation days they are likely to receive annually. For example, the average number of vacation days in the United Kingdom is 37; 36 in France and Spain; 33 in Germany; 30 in Chile and South Korea; 28 in Australia, 25 in Japan; 21 in Israel; 19 in Canada; and 13 in Mexico.[91] In the United States, the average is 10 days, all public holidays, half of what Canadians enjoy and just over a quarter of what the British receive. Nearly 25 percent of all U.S. workers receive no paid holidays or vacations.[92]

Also of importance in decisions on where to locate a business operation are considerations such as cost of living, business environment, and office rents. Despite labor market problems and less attractive market opportunities, the quality of the business environment in western European and North American countries remains higher than that in most emerging markets because those countries possess sophisticated institutions, such as advanced financial sectors, reliable legal systems, and political stability, that companies value. See again Table 14.3 for cost-of-living comparisons for a number of the world's cities. The survey compares the prices of goods and services typically consumed by the families of executives being sent abroad. You will note that several of the cities ranked in the top 10 are located in emerging countries.

"THE UNITED STATES IS THE ONLY ADVANCED ECONOMY in THE WORLD THAT DOES NOT GUARANTEE ITS WORKERS PAID VACATION DAYS AND PAID HOLIDAYS. "

—John Schmitt, senior economist at the Center for Economic and Policy Research[93]

Laura Gunderson

Courtesy of Laura Gunderson.

I first caught the travel bug at age six, as a result of growing up in Jakarta, Indonesia, as part of an expatriate family. Upon return to the United States, I spent my life traveling, living, and studying all over the country, and then the world in places such as Australia, Mexico, New Zealand, and the United Kingdom. I had no idea that I could satisfy this craving for travel and international perspective while earning a living.

Once I got to university, it quickly became apparent that regardless of what level you were as a student taking business courses such as finance, accounting, economics, business law, or marketing, a common thread appeared among them all. This commonality was the incredible complications that arose when a business wanted to expand in any way internationally. This realization struck me, and I wanted to understand how all these aspects of business work together to create the best solutions—beyond the United States. When it came time to select a concentration for my undergraduate degree, I distinctly remember thinking, "How could I *not* do international business?"

I embarked on my newfound educational course, taking all classes related to how to resolve the issues posed by doing business internationally. International human resource management (IHRM), in particular, captured my interest. Although I didn't know how, I knew I wanted to work

with a company to leverage its greatest assets, its people, to achieve business success. I could combine my passion for people with my passion for business success (dating back to my childhood summer sidewalk lemonade café business venture). As I was graduating at one of the most difficult economic times the country had seen in decades, making this dream a reality seemed near to impossible. However, after much hard work and preparation, I have now worked in IHRM coordinating expatriate, repatriate, and host-to-host assignees on three different continents for a Fortune 100 company. My experience has been working with assignees, business leaders, and HR colleagues across all functions and located around the country and globe. Throughout my experience, I faced numerous challenges specific to IHRM supporting business success, including but not limited to:

Relocation How do we coordinate an employee's immigration and tax considerations? How do we prepare them for the cultural differences they will experience?

Talent management How do we best leverage the experiences and knowledge of individuals who have gone on assignment? How do we avoid the dreaded "out of sight, out of mind" experience felt by many assignees upon repatriation?

Recruitment Based on what criteria are we selecting candidates?

Employee development Are we a culture that supports assignments as a career steppingstone? How do we ensure that assignees are still receiving equal access to HR programs and support as domestic employees?

Compensation How can we properly incentivize employees to live and work in less desirable areas, especially if they have a family?

Labor relations Does a union-represented environment affect an employee's ability or desire to go on an assignment?

Information systems How are we managing employee data in countries where our typical infrastructure or software systems may not exist?

Considering the economic climate, cost considerations were a huge component of every single decision: What is the best option to balance what is best for the company strategically and what is best for the assignee personally, while keeping the bottom line in mind. In addition, many of these challenges were completely unique, and our team had to stretch to use all resources available to take action, usually on a short timeframe. I learned the best way to resolve these situations was to ask as many questions as possible and to continuously learn from my own and others' experience. As an entry-level professional, no one will expect you to be an expert; otherwise, they would have hired one, and you don't get to be an expert without starting somewhere. A large majority of the lessons learned during my college courses were directly applicable from my first day on the job, so believe it or not, it was incredibly helpful to keep my course notes and textbooks available.

An inspiring mentor of mine explained to me that luck was nothing more than being prepared for an opportunity when it arises, which allows you to make the most of any situation. I have found this to be true in every situation, which is why as an HR professional and as someone who recently went through the long and exhausting job search process, my strongest advice is to be prepared. This doesn't mean you have to have a dozen internships abroad or speak five languages, because I didn't, though it certainly wouldn't hurt. I suggest that you apply and interview for as many positions as possible in order to gain comfort and experience speaking with recruiters. Send

your résumé to everyone, including teachers, mentors, alumni, family, and friends for editing and review; it may even open unexpected doors and networks. If you are currently employed and an IHRM position is not readily available, volunteer or suggest HR projects related to your international business and learn as much as possible about your firm's international programs. Continue to build your networks and communicate your interests to as many people as possible; there is always an opportunity out there. It is imperative to advertise yourself and your interests while doing as much as possible to prepare for when that great IHRM job does present itself.

Although challenging and sometimes stressful, working in IHRM has always been incredibly rewarding. I feel I am truly helping people and program success by finding the best solutions for both the company and the individual employee. By stretching me in so many ways, both personally and professionally, working in IHRM has given me a great international business foundation because I truly understand how HR directly supports international business ventures. Everyone can gain from this experience and take their careers as far as possible—the sky is the limit, and I hope to see you there!

Source: Laura Gunderson.

SUMMARY

LO 14-1
Identify several of the major factors that may affect the quantity and quality of labor in a nation.

Forces that affect the quantity and quality of labor in a nation include such characteristics of the population as age, urbanization, immigrant labor availability, guest workers, brain drain, and unionization.

LO 14-2
Explain the relationship between competitive strategies (international, multidomestic, global, and transnational) and international human resource management approaches (ethnocentric, polycentric, regiocentric, and global).

Two competing forces—the pressure to achieve global integration and reduce costs and the pressure to respond to local differentiation—determine which of four

alternative competitive strategies (home replication, multidomestic, global, or transnational) a company should adopt. Recognize that competitive strategy should be a primary determinant of the IHRM policies that an IC will use, because it determines the things that must be done, and done well, in order for the firm to succeed. Therefore the four approaches to international human resource management must correspond with the strategy of a firm. Table 14.1 provides a concise summary of the link between a firm's strategic approach, key organizational concerns, and the appropriate international human resource management approach that should be used.

LO 14-3
Compare recruitment and selection considerations for home-country, host-country, and third-country nationals as international company executives.

Sources of IC executives may be the home country, host countries, or third countries, and their differing culture, language, ability, and experience can strengthen IC management. Ethnocentric staffing policies are common for companies with a primarily international strategic orientation, with most decisions made at headquarters and using the home country's frame of reference. Multidomestic strategies often use a polycentric approach to staffing, using PCNs for positions at headquarters and HCNs for positions in subsidiaries in order to leverage local knowledge in situations where that is important. Regional strategies are often accompanied by a regiocentric approach to strategy, using a mix of HCNs and TCNs for key positions within a region. Companies with a transnational strategic orientation tend to follow a geocentric staffing policy, selecting the best person for each job without consideration of national origin.

LO 14-4
Distinguish among the training and development considerations for home-country, host-country, and third-country nationals as international company executives.

The training and development of managers and other key IC employees vary somewhat, depending on whether the candidate is from the home country, the host country, or a third country. Although PCNs may know the IC and its practices, they often lack knowledge and experience in a foreign country and this can indicate a focus for their training and development, including language and cultural preparation. The same general criteria for selecting home-country employees apply to host-country nationals. Usually, however, the training and development activities undertaken for HCNs will differ from those used for home-country nationals in that host-country nationals are more likely to lack knowledge of advanced business techniques, particularly those that are specific to business applications and operations of the IC, and knowledge of the company as a whole. Hiring TCNs, personnel who are citizens of neither the home country nor the host country, may involve individuals who come from a culture similar to that of the host country. In addition, they may have worked for another unit of the IC and thus be familiar with the company's policies, procedures, and people. This can simplify the training and development requirements for such recruits. We must be careful with generalizations about training and development requirements for TCNs because people may achieve that status in different ways.

LO 14-5
Identify some of the challenges and opportunities of an expat position.

Expat positions allow employees to work in foreign locations, providing a foundation for learning and growth, both personally and professionally, and a basis for movement upward in an IC's hierarchy. Expats can also find themselves "out of sight, out of mind," with unclear performance objectives and bases for performance evaluation. The families of many expats find the adjustment to a foreign posting difficult to manage successfully.

LO 14-6
Describe some of the complications of compensation packages for expatriate executives.

Expatriate manager compensation packages can be extremely complicated. Among other sources of complications are fluctuating currency exchange rates and differing inflation rates. Basic elements of those packages are salaries, allowances, and bonuses.

KEY TERMS

allowances 395
bonuses 396
brain drain 376
collective bargaining 378
compensation packages 398
culture shock 387
ethnocentric policy 379

expatriate 371
geocentric policy 379
guest worker 376
home-country national 379
host-country national (HCN) 379
international status 399
labor market 372

labor mobility 374
labor union 378
parent-country national (PCN) 379
polycentric policy 379
regiocentric policy 379
reverse brain drain 377
third-country national (TCN) 379

CRITICAL THINKING QUESTIONS

1. What are the implications for international companies of trends toward aging populations in many developed countries and rapid urbanization in many emerging nations? What changes are ICs likely to make to successfully respond to these trends?

2. Explain arguments against allowing immigrant labor into nations. Who would benefit most from limiting the number of immigrants into a country? What are the primary arguments associated with allowing immigrant labor into a nation?

3. Why might brain drain be beneficial for a country whose skilled people move to other nations? How might a country maximize the benefits from brain drain, while reducing the potential damage from this mobility of labor?

4. Why might an international company encounter challenges in trying to establish a linkage between the international human resource management approaches it uses and its competitive strategy? How might these challenges be managed successfully?

5. Why has there been an increasing use of third-country nationals in the foreign operations of ICs? Do you think this trend will continue? Why or why not?

6. International companies often encounter performance problems with expatriation, where problems arise due to issues associated with the expatriate's family. What advice would you provide to an IC regarding how to avoid such problems?

7. What are some of the quality-of-life issues that employees should consider before taking their families abroad as part of an expatriate experience?

8. Why are expatriate employees frequently paid more than their colleagues at equivalent job levels in the home office? Do you think this premium is justified?

9. Suppose you are the CEO of an American multinational. On your staff and in the U.S. operating divisions of your company are several bright, able, dedicated female executives. They are also ambitious, and in your company, international experience is a must before an executive can hope to get into top management. An opening comes up for the position of executive vice president in the company's Middle East subsidiary, headquartered in Saudi Arabia. One of the women on your staff applies for the position, and she is well qualified for the job, better than anyone else in the company. Would you give her the position? What are the arguments pro and con?

10. Using the company example in question 9, suppose another position becomes available, this one as treasurer of the Japanese subsidiary. The chief financial officer of the company's California division applies for this job. She has performed to everyone's satisfaction, and she seems thoroughly qualified to become the treasurer in Japan. In addition, she speaks and writes Japanese. She is the daughter of a Japanese mother and an American father, and they encouraged her to become fluent in both English and Japanese. Would you give her the job? Why or why not?

global**EDGE** RESEARCH TASK   http://globalEDGE.msu.edu/

Use the globalEDGE website (http://globalEDGE.msu .edu) to complete the following exercises:

1. The company you work for is in the services industry and looking into options to outsource some of its service businesses. The availability of a skilled and educated workforce in a country, as well as its financial attractiveness and business environment, are important factors that will affect your decision while selecting the best country to outsource. Review the *Global Services Location Index* and find the top five countries most favorable for offshoring

services. Also, read the highlights of the report. Be ready to discuss your selection criteria and the trends highlighted in the report.

2. A colleague of yours and you are going to move to China as expats to represent your company and you are interested in finding some practical information about living in China. Locate China under the "Global Insights" section of globalEDGE and open "Kwintessential Language and Culture Specialists" in a new tab. Now read the "Expat Advice" subsection for China and prepare a summary to share with your colleague.

MINICASE

JAYDEN WHITE: SHOULD HE ACCEPT AN EXPAT ASSIGNMENT TO CHINA?

Jayden White, a 32-year-old manager with Techtonics International, had just returned to his office early on a Thursday afternoon. During a lunchtime meeting in the company's executive lunchroom, his boss had just offered him a chance to move to Shanghai, China, where he would be in charge of establishing the company's new office for the East Asia region. As he sat at his desk looking out over the urban skyline, he was filled with a mix of excitement and trepidation. Should he accept the position he was offered? Or should he pass on this opportunity and wait for something else in the future? What factors should he consider in making this important decision?

White had joined Techtonics 10 years ago as an assistant sales manager, shortly after completing his bachelor's degree in business at Howard University. Since then, he had been promoted several times and was now the vice president in charge of North American operations for one of Techtonics's main business areas, overseeing a workforce of more than 2,100 people and sales in excess of $700 million. Identified as one of the "rising stars" in Techtonics, and mentored by one of the senior vice presidents of the company, he seemed to have no limits to his career path.

White had always dreamed of living and working abroad. As a student, he studied abroad for a semester in London and spent a month afterward traveling around Europe with several friends. After graduation, he worked on a six-month internship with AIESEC, working for a small exporting company based in Spain. Since joining Techtonics, his international experience had primarily consisted of business trips to Canada or the Caribbean, attending several conferences and visiting a few selected client companies in Europe and Asia, and going on two

extended vacations: one to Thailand and another to Germany. When his boss mentioned the possibility of going to China, he could barely contain his enthusiasm!

However, White also began to think about his family and how an international assignment might affect them. His wife, Aretha, was an accountant in the local office of a large accounting firm. Although she had a successful career, he thought that she might be open to a change. He also had two children: Jayden Jr., who was eight, and Chantoya, who was five. How would they respond to moving to a new country? Would now be a good time for such a move, or would it be better to wait for a few years?

And what if he was to accept the offer to go to China? What issues would he need to discuss with the company regarding the implications of a move to China? His boss said that he would like to have White's decision within about a week and that he would need to move to Shanghai within four to six months if he accepted the job.

As he watched the traffic begin to jam up on the freeway outside his office building, White thought about reaching for his cell phone and calling his good friend for advice on how to deal with the job opportunity that he had been offered.

Critical Thinking Questions

1. If you were a good friend of Jayden White, what recommendation would you give regarding whether he should accept the international assignment that has been offered to him?

2. What issues should he focus on in making such a decision?

NOTES

1. General Electric, "Key Growth Initiatives."

2. U.S. Census Bureau, International Data Base, "World Population by Age and Sex," https://www.census.gov, accessed November 16, 2018.

3. United Nations, "Population Aged 15–24," https://data.un.org, accessed November 16, 2018.

4. The World Bank, "Population Estimates and Projections," http://databank.worldbank.org, accessed November 16, 2018.

5. Ibid.

6. Ibid.

7. National Institute on Aging, U.S. Department of Health and Human Services, "World Population Aging," http://www.nia.nih.gov/research/dbsr/world-population-aging, accessed February 02, 2015.

8. European Commission, *Global Europe 2050*, https://ec.europa.eu, accessed November 16, 2018.

9. OECD, "Is Migration Good for the Economy?," *Migration Policy Debates*, no. 2, May 2014, http://www.oecd.org, accessed November 16, 2018.

10. The World Bank, "Migration and Remittances," https://web.worldbank.org, accessed November 16, 2018; and United Nations, *International Migration Report 2017*, http://www.un.org, accessed November 16, 2018.

11. United Nations, *International Migration Report, 2017*.

12. Ibid.

13. The World Bank, "Population, Total," https://data.worldbank.org, accessed November 16, 2018; United Nations, *International Migration Report, 2017*.

14. Sabrina Tavernise, "U.S. has Highest Share of Foreign-Born Since 1910, with More Coming from Asia," *The New York Times*, https://www.nytimes.com, accessed November 16, 2018; and United States Census Bureau, "Current Population Survey (CPS)," https://www.census.gov, accessed November 16, 2018.

15. Jeffrey S. Passel, and D'Vera Cohn, "Immigration Projected to Drive Growth in U.S. Working-Age Population Through at Least 2035," http://www.pewresearch.org, accessed November 16, 2018.

16. Ibid.

17. Eric Beauchesne, "Immigration Cuts Wages; StatsCan Study Finds 7% Slide at Top of Pay Scale," *National Post*, May 26, 2007, FP7.

18. Eric A. Ruark, and Matthew Graham, *Immigration, Poverty and Low-Wage Earners: The Harmful Effect of Unskilled Immigrants on American Workers*, Washington, DC: Federation for American Immigration Reform, May 2011, http://www.fairus.org, accessed November 16, 2018.

19. Frederic Docquier, Calar Ozden, and Giovanni Peri, "The Wage Effects of Immigration and Emigration," Working Paper, no. 16646, December 2010, Cambridge, MA: National Bureau of Economic Research, https://www.nber.org, accessed November 16, 2018.

20. "OECD," https://en.wikipedia.org, accessed November 18, 2018.

21. OECD, "Migration and the Brain Drain Phenomenon," http://www.oecd.org, accessed November 16, 2018.

22. Ibid.

23. National Science Foundation, *National Center for Science and Engineering Statistics, Scientists and Engineers Statistical Data System (SESTAT)*, 2010, http://www.nsf.gov, accessed November 16, 2018.

24. Diana Furchtgott-Rott, "The Economic Benefits of Immigration," Manhattan Institute for Policy Research, Issue Brief No. 18, February 2013, https://www.manhattan-institute.org, accessed November 16, 2018; and Jason Furman, and Danielle Gray, "Ten Ways Immigrants Help Build and Strengthen Our Economy," *The White House Blog*, https://obamawhitehouse.archives.gov, accessed November 16, 2018.

25. Walter Ewing, "Immigrants Are Founding a Quarter of New Businesses in the United States," http://immigrationimpact.com, accessed November 16, 2018.

26. Ibid.

27. Stuart Anderson, *American Made 2.0: How Immigrant Entrepreneurs Continue to Contribute to the U.S. Economy*, Washington, DC: National Venture Capital Association, 2013.

28. Trudy Mbaluku, "Doctor Brain Drain Damages Kenya's Healthcare," *Internews in Kenya*, http://www.internewskenya.org, accessed November 16, 2018; "Africa Economy: EU Foreign Ministers Bid to Stop Africa's Brain-Drain," *EIU ViewsWire*, New York, March 30, 2006; Paul Yonga, "Medical Brain Drain Among Doctors in Africa: A Neglected Global Health Component," http://globalmedicine.nl/issues/issue-16/medical-brain-drain-among-doctors-in-africa-a-neglected-global-health-component, accessed February 02, 2015; and "What about Kenya?" https://www.hofstede-insights.com, accessed November 16, 2018.

29. Alan M. Webber, "Reverse Brain Drain Threatens U.S. Economy," *USA Today*, February 23, 2004, https://www.usatoday.com, accessed November 16, 2018; and Vivek Wadhwa,

"Beware the Reverse Brain Drain to India and China," *Tech Crunch*, October 17, 2009, https://techcrunch.com, accessed November 16, 2018.

30. These four strategy types are discussed in Module 9.

31. David A. Heenan, and Howard V. Perlmutter, *Multinational Organization Development*, Boston: Addison-Wesley, 1979.

32. Consistency between mind-set and IHRM practices was reported in Linda K. Stroh, and Paula M. Caligiuri, "Strategic Human Resources: A New Source for Competitive Advantage in the Global Arena," *International Journal of Human Resource Management*, vol. 9, no. 1, 1998, 1–17.

33. Geoff Dyer, "A Spun-Out Tale of Two Corporate Cultures," *Financial Times*, May 22, 2006, https://www.ft.com.

34. David Pilling, and Francesco Guerrera, "We Are a Mixture: Western Style in Management but with an Eastern Touch," *Financial Times*, September 26, 2003, 13.

35. S. Devarajan, managing director of Cisco Systems' Global Development Center in Bangalore, India.

36. Kalpana Pathak, "Over 70% of Companies to Increase Short-Term Assignments of Expatriates in 2013," *Business Standard*, April 18, 2013, https://www.business-standard.com.

37. *Up or Out: Next Moves for the Modern Expatriate*, London: The Economist Intelligence Unit, 2010, http://graphics.eiu.com/upload/eb/LON_PL_Regus_WEB2.pdf.

38. Aperian Global, "Developing Cultural Competency for International Assignments: What We Can Learn from Expatriate Challenges," https://www.aperianglobal.com, accessed November 16, 2018; BGRS, *Global Relocation Trends 2012 Survey Report*, https://www.td.org/insights/global-relocation-trends-for-2012; Pathak, "Over 70% of Companies to Increase Short-Term Assignments of Expatriates in 2013"; Sapna Welsh, and Caroline Kersten, "Where Are Women in the Expatriate Workforce?," *Society for Human Resource Management*, https://www.shrm.org, accessed November 16, 2018; and Mary G. Tye, and Peter Y. Chen, "Selection of Expatriates: Decision-Making Models Used by HR Professionals," *Human Resource Planning*, vol. 28, no. 4, 2005, 15–20.

39. David Shadovitz, "Targeting Millennials for International Assignments," *Human Resource Executive*, http://hrexecutive.com, accessed November 16, 2018; BGRS, *Global Relocation Trends 2012 Survey Report*; Sue Shortland, "The Changing Nature of Expatriate Demographics," *Relocate Magazine*, https://www.relocatemagazine.com, accessed November 16, 2018; and "Expatriate Workforce Demographics," *HR Magazine*, vol. 51, no. 5, May 2006, 16.

40. BGRS, "Closing the Gender Gap and Talent Mobility's Role," https://www.bgrs.com, accessed November 16, 2018; and Welsh, and Kersten, "Where Are Women in the Expatriate Workforce?"

41. Michael Harvey, and Milorad Novicevic, "The Development of Political Skill and Political Capital by Global Leaders through Global Assignments," *International Journal of Human Resource Management*, November 2004, 1173–88; and BGRS, *Global Relocation Trends 2012 Survey Report*.

42. BGRS, "Closing the Gender Gap and Talent Mobility's Role"; and BGRS, "Global Mobility Trends."

43. Cartus Corporation, *2014 Trends in Global Relocation: Global Mobility Policy and Practices*, https://www.cartus.com, accessed November 16, 2018.

44. *Up or Out: Next Moves for the Modern Expatriate*, 7.

45. Steven Kilfedder, "Survey Shows What You'll Spend on Expat Managers," *TLNT*, https://www.tlnt.com, accessed November 16, 2018; and John C. Beck, "Globalization: Don't Go There . . . ," http://www.accenture.com/SiteCollectionDocuments/PDF/going_global_pov_rev.pdf, accessed February 02, 2015.

46. Juan I. Sanchez, Paul E. Spector, and Cary L. Cooper, "Adapting to a Boundaryless World: A Developmental Expatriate Model," *Academy of Management Executive*, vol. 14, no. 2, May 2000, 96–106; and A. Esther Joshua-Gojer, "Cross-Cultural Training and Success versus Failure of Expatriates," *Learning and Performance Quarterly*, vol. 1, no. 2, 2012.

47. GMAC Global Relocation Services, *Global Relocation Trends 2007 Survey Report*; and Ida Stilling, "Repatriation Turnover—This Is Why Repatriates Leave Their Companies," https://www.linkedin.com, accessed November 16, 2018.

48. Cartus Corporation, *2014 Trends in Global Relocation*.

49. Lalervo Oberg, "Culture Shock and the Problem of Adjustment to New Cultural Environments," http://www.worldwide.edu/travel_planner/culture_shock.html, accessed November 16, 2018.

50. *Up or Out: Next Moves for the Modern Expatriate*, 12.

51. Margaret A. Shaffer, David A. Harrison, and K. Matthew Gilley, "Dimensions, Determinants, and Differences in the Expatriate Adjustment Process," *Journal of International Business Studies*, vol. 30, no. 3, 1999, 557–81.

52. Pei-Chuan Wu, and Siah Hwee Ang, "The Impact of Expatriate Supporting Practices and Cultural Intelligence on Cross-Cultural Adjustment and Performance of Expatriates in Singapore," *International Journal of Human Resource Management*, vol. 22, no. 13, 2011, 2683–2702; Deirdre McCaughey, and Nealia S. Bruning, "Enhancing Opportunities for Expatriate Job Satisfaction: HR Strategies for Foreign Assignment Success," *Human Resource Planning*, vol. 28, no. 4, 2005, 21–29; and Jie Shen, "International Training and Management Development: Theory and Reality," *Journal of Management Development*, vol. 24, no. 7, 2005, 656–66.

53. BGRS, *Global Relocation Trends 2012 Survey Report*.

54. Shaffer et al., "Dimensions, Determinants, and Differences in the Expatriate Adjustment Process"; and Wu Ang, "The Impact of Expatriate Supporting Practices and Cultural Intelligence on Cross-Cultural Adjustment and Performance of Expatriates in Singapore."

55. Brady Firth, Gilad Chen, Bradley Kirkman, and Kwanghyun Kim, "Newcomers Abroad: Expatriate Adaptation During Early Phases of International Assignments," *Academy of Management Journal*, vol. 57, no. 1, 2014, 280–300.

56. Cartus Corporation, *2014 Trends in Global Relocation*.

57. "Cartus 2014 Global Relocation Trends Survey: It's All About Family When It Comes to the Success of a Costly Job Transfer," *PR Newswire*, https://www.prnewswire.com, accessed November 16, 2018.

58. Margaret A. Shaffer, and David A. Harrison, "Forgotten Partners of International Assignments: Development and Test of a Model of Spouse Adjustment," *Journal of Applied Psychology*, vol. 86, no. 2, 2001, 238–54.

59. Riki Takeuchi, Seokhwa Yun, and Paul E. Tesluk, "An Examination of Crossover and Spillover Effects of Spousal and Expatriate Cross-Cultural Adjustment on Expatriate Outcomes," *Journal of Applied Psychology*, vol. 87, no. 4, August 2002, 655.

60. Hsiu-Ching Ko, and Mu-Li Yang, "The Effects of Cross-Cultural Training on Expatriate Adjustment," *International Communication Studies*, vol. 20, no. 1, 2011, https://web.uri.edu/iaics/files/12Hsiu-ChingKoMu-LiYang.pdf; and GMAC Global Relocation Services, *Global Relocation Trends 2007 Survey Report*.

61. Sue Shortland, "The Changing Nature of Expatriate Demographics," *Relocate Magazine*, https://www.relocatemagazine.com, accessed November 16, 2018; Cartus Corporation, *2014 Trends in Global Relocation*; GMAC Global Relocation Services, *Global Relocation Trends 2003/2004 Survey Report*, http://www.nftc.org; and GMAC Global Relocation Services, *Global Relocation Trends 2007 Survey Report*.

62. Corinne Purtill, "Expat Couples Do Best When They've Moved for the Woman's Job," *Quartz*, https://qz.com, accessed November 16, 2018; and *Up or Out: Next Moves for the Modern Expatriate*, 14.

63. Michael Harvey, "Dual-Career Expatriates: Expectations, Adjustment and Satisfaction with International Relocation," *Journal of International Business Studies*, vol. 28, no. 3, 1997, 627–58; Susan Shortland, "The Changing Nature of Expatriate Demographics"; Cartus Corporation, *2014 Trends in Global Relocation: Global Mobility Policy and Practices*, http://www.cartus.com, accessed November 16, 2018; and Perri Capell, "What 'Trailing Spouses' Can Do," *The Wall Street Journal*, May 02, 2006, B6.

64. Alison Langley, "Always Beginning Again," *Financial Times*, November 03, 2006, https://www.ft.com.

65. BGRS, *Global Relocation Trends 2012 Survey Report*; and Cartus Corporation, *2014 Trends in Global Relocation*.

66. Cartus Corporation, *2014 Trends in Global Relocation*; Pathak, "Over 70% of Companies to Increase Short-Term Assignments of Expatriates in 2013"; and Jeremy Smerd, "More Women, Young Workers on the Move," *Workforce Management*, August 2007, 9–10, https://www.workforce.com.

67. Philipp von Plato, "Expat Insider 2017," *Expat Insider*, https://cms-internationsgmbh.netdna-ssl.com, accessed November 16, 2018; and Expatica, "How Children View Moving Abroad," https://www.expatica.com, accessed November 16, 2018.

68. Dorie Clark, "English—the Language of Global Business?" *Forbes.com*, October 26, 2012, accessed February 02, 2015; and Kat Devlin, "Learning a Foreign Language a 'Must' in Europe, Not So in America," http://www.pewresearch.org, accessed November 16, 2018.

69. Alan Paul, "Combating the Repatriation Blues," *The Wall Street Journal*, March 20, 2009, https://www.wsj.com; Expat Info Desk, "Coming Back Home: Repatriating," https://www.expatinfodesk.com, accessed November 16, 2018; Annette Haddad, and Scott Doggett, "Road Home Hard after Working Overseas," *Los Angeles Times*, March 13, 2000, C2, https://www.latimes.com; and Leslie Gross Klaff, "The Right Way to Bring Expats Home," *Workforce*, July 2002, 40–44, https://www.workforce.com.

70. Nathaniel Richards, and Todd Averett, "How to Make the Most of Your Returning Expat Workers," https://www.radiusworldwide.com, accessed November 16, 2018.

71. Ida Stilling, "Repatriation Turnover—This Is Why Repatriates Leave Their Companies."

72. Sarah Waters, "Top 6 Considerations for Successful Employee Repatriation," https://rsmus.com, accessed November 16, 2018.

73. Kathryn Tyler, "Retaining Repatriates," *HR Magazine*, vol. 51, no. 3, March 2006, 97–102, https://www.shrm.org, accessed November 16, 2018.

74. Ibid.

75. Ida Stilling, "Repatriation Turnover—This Is Why Repatriates Leave Their Companies."

76. Society for Human Resource Management, "Global: Expatriate: How Should We Compensate an Employee on a Foreign Assignment?," https://www.shrm.org, accessed November 16, 2018.

77. Ibid.

78. *Up or Out: Next Moves for the Modern Expatriate*, 9.

79. Andrea Duxbury, "Getting Your Expatriate Housing Policy Right," *ECA International*, https://www.eca-international.com, accessed November 16, 2018.

80. GTN, 2018, "*Taxation of U.S. Expatriates*," https://www.gtn.com, accessed November 16, 2018.

81. Ibid.; Expat Info Desk, "Negotiating Relocation Packages," https://www.expatinfodesk.com, accessed November 16, 2018.

82. Dezan Shira and Associates, "How to Calculate Your 2013 Expatriate Individual Income Tax in China," *China Briefing*, http://www.china-briefing.com, accessed November 16, 2018.

83. *Up or Out: Next Moves for the Modern Expatriate*, 11; Viola Lloyd, "DHRs: Are You Expatriate Savvy?" *The HR Director*, http://www.thehrdirector.com, accessed November 16, 2018.

84. Rob Budden, "How Does Your Expat Package Stack Up?," *BBC*, http://www.bbc.com, accessed November 16, 2018.

85. Lloyd, "DHRs: Are You Expatriate Savvy?"; Expat Info Desk, "Negotiating Relocation Packages."

86. Some writers regard paid home leave as an allowance, but our experience convinces us that it is a bonus because ICs consistently give more frequent or longer home leaves to employees working in less desirable assignments.

87. "Managing Expatriate Reward: Home Leave," *Expatica*, https://www.expatica.com, accessed November 16, 2018.

88. *Up or Out: Next Moves for the Modern Expatriate*, 11.

89. Scott E. Landau, and Bradley A. Benedict, "Going Global with U.S. Employee Stock Plans," Pillsbury, Winthrop Shaw Pittman LLP, https://www.pillsburylaw.com, accessed November 16, 2018.

90. American Citizens Abroad, "U.S. Taxes Abroad for Dummies (Update for Tax Year 2017)," https://www.americansabroad.org, accessed November 16, 2018; and Internal Revenue Service, "Taxpayers Living Abroad," https://www.irs.gov, accessed November 16, 2018.

91. Niall McCarthy, "Vacation: Americans Get a Raw Deal," https://www-statista-com.proxy.library.ohio.edu, accessed November 16, 2018.

92. Tanya Mohn, "U.S. the Only Advanced Economy That Does Not Require Employers to Provide Paid Vacation Time, Report Says," *Forbes*, https://www.forbes.com, accessed November 16, 2018.

93. John Schmitt, Rebecca Ray, and Milla Sanes, "No-Vacation Nation Revisited," *Center for Economic and Policy Research*, May 2013, www.cepr.net.

15 International Accounting and Financial Management

> 66 **Quick decisions are unsafe decisions.** 99
>
> —*Sophocles, 496–406 BC*[1]

©NicolasMcComber/Getty Images.

LEARNING OBJECTIVES

After reading this module, you should be able to:

LO 15-1   **Outline** the major accounting issues international firms face when operating in foreign currencies.

LO 15-2   **Outline** the benefits and limitations of triple-bottom-line accounting.

LO 15-3   **Compare** the capital structure choices open to international firms and their significance.

LO 15-4   **Describe** why ICs move funds and the utility of an international finance center.

LO 15-5   **Identify** foreign exchange risks the IC faces and ways to address them.

LO 15-6   **Describe** taxation as an international financial force.

Sovereign Wealth Funds: Globalization at Work

Sovereign wealth funds are investment funds controlled by governments. The funds themselves may be from national reserves, pension funds, and other monies owned by the government. Recently, the steady growth of sovereign wealth funds in China and the oil-rich nations has created pools so large, easily in the trillion-dollar range, that their owners can influence global markets in areas they target and readily acquire business assets in the developed world. In August 2018, the Sovereign Wealth Funds Institute listed Norway as having the single largest fund, at just over $1 trillion, followed by China at $941 billion. UAE-Abu Dhabi and Kuwait follow, with individual funds of $683 and $592 billion, respectively. The Sovereign Wealth Funds Institute tracks individual funds under management, so these amounts don't reflect the total picture of a nation's sovereign wealth. China, for example, has several funds in the top rankings. If consolidating different funds listed within the top 30 largest worldwide, China's funds total $2.2 trillion and UAE funds total $1.2 trillion.

Governments invest to get a return on their assets for their citizens and to diversify their national risk. For example, if the country's main earnings are in the oil sector, investments in nonrelated industries will protect it from a down oil market. In one such diversification attempt, the armed forces of Qatar, a country rich in oil and natural gas reserves, bought the five-star Renaissance Hotel in the center of Barcelona from Marriott International, Inc., which will stay on as manager.

"What's the problem?" you might ask. Why not use Norwegian, Arab, and Chinese wealth to leverage growth in the developed world? Investments by sovereign wealth funds often present several interesting issues to developed nations. First of all, they represent a somewhat odd twist on the current trend toward privatization. Except for dire situations such as the recent financial crisis in which governments bailed out some private companies, the developed nations tend to preach that business should be controlled by private risk takers. Keep the government out. Yet sovereign wealth fund investments actually represent a foreign government's ownership.

In addition to the countertrend aspect of sovereign wealth funds' interests being purely commercial, they might choose objectives other than maximizing returns to the shareholder. For example, as a majority stakeholder, the Chinese Investment Corporation, one of China's major sovereign wealth funds, might choose to influence firms' procurement decisions, favoring China's companies over less costly suppliers on the basis of national self-interest. Or a government's economic policy could encourage investing in a firm that's important to national defense or choosing job creation over profitability. Once government ownership of a firm has been established, the firm's business decisions may be influenced by political objectives or other objectives not in its best economic interests. Further, sovereign wealth funds are private funds and have limited transparency, so assessing what the fund managers are doing with the money can be difficult.

Many of these concerns have been addressed by government legislation that limits foreign investment directly, requires disclosure, or requires the approval of foreign investments by various government bodies. There are many examples of government-owned businesses, both domestic and foreign. In the United States, public pension funds constitute more than 40 percent of the government's institutional investment. Four of the five largest oil companies in the world are state-owned.

There's still another noteworthy point to be made about sovereign wealth funds. They represent a global shift—a trend toward a transfer of ownership away from the United States, Europe, and Japan and toward developing nations. Sovereign wealth funds represent globalization at work. In addition, they provide benefits for the developed world because they encourage continued growth and provide a means to cushion financial crises. Remember, developing country assets are growing around twice as fast as those in the developed nations. A Global Development Horizons report predicts that, by 2030, 60 percent of the world's global investments will be by developing countries, triple the level in 2000.

Sources: "Sovereign Wealth Fund Rankings: August 2018," *Sovereign Wealth Fund Institute*, November 2018, www.swfinstitute.org; Benjamin Elisha Sawe, "Biggest Oil Companies in the World," *worldatlas*, December 05, 2018, www.worldatlas.com; "Developing Countries to Dominate Global Saving and Investment, But the Poor Will Not Necessarily Share the Benefits, Says Report," *World Bank*, May 16, 2013, www.worldbank.org; Stephen Burgen, "Qatar's Armed Forces Pay Euro 78.5 for Barcelona's Renaissance Hotel," *The Guardian*, January 31, 2014, www.theguardian.com; and James Surowiecki, "The Financial Page: Sovereign Wealth World," *The New Yorker*, November 26, 2007, www.newyorker.com.

International managers regularly face financial challenges in their daily operations. These include fluctuating currency values, currency exchange controls, taxation, and inflation and interest rates. They also must follow the accounting practices of their host government as well as those of the United States, if they work for a U.S.-based company. We now look at some of the methods international managers have developed to deal with challenging forces, some of which are imaginative and elegant, and all of which are legal.

International finance can be complex, but you do not need an advanced background in accounting or finance to understand that financial issues are at the core of the way companies work—and often make the difference between moderate and outstanding results. We begin with accounting because it is a fundamental tool of financial management, and because accounting practices and standards change across national borders. First, we look at the differences in the way countries record stored value (the essence of accounting). Fortunately, there is a strong movement toward a convergence of accounting standards, which will soon make the process much easier for the international company (IC).

The second half of this module reviews the major issues in IC financial management. We begin with the way an IC's capital is structured and then move on to cash management techniques. Finally, we discuss some aspects of taxation. Our goal is to describe these areas in an understandable way so that you can appreciate their contributions to the IC's success.

Accounting and Foreign Currency

LO 15-1

Outline the major accounting issues international firms face when operating in foreign currencies.

There are only two points at which operating in a foreign currency raises accounting issues: when transactions are made in foreign currencies, and when branches and subsidiaries operate in foreign currencies and their results need to be made a part of the parent company's financial reports. We look first at the general purpose of international accounting; then at transactions, translation, and the process of consolidation; then at the process of convergence of accounting standards across the world; and close with an exploration of the role of culture in accounting.

THE PURPOSE OF INTERNATIONAL ACCOUNTING

The purpose of accounting in all countries is to provide managers with financial data for use in their decision making and to provide external constituencies (investors, governments, lenders, suppliers, and others) with the quantitative information they seek to inform their decisions. Accounting also provides the data governments need to levy taxes. If you think back to what you know about how cultural values vary across nations, you won't be surprised that what is considered useful accounting data varies from country to country. For example, in many countries that follow code or civil law such as Germany, the primary users of financial information tend to be creditors; they care about the firm's financial stability. So accounting in these countries will tend to be conservative and focus on the balance sheet and the company's assets. By contrast, in common law countries such as the United States, individual investors tend to be major users of financial information, and they care most about the future prospects of the company. They look to the income statement as a sign of the company's future and are less interested in the balance sheet than are the Germans, while their financial statements tend to be more optimistic.[2]

FOREIGN CURRENCY TRANSACTIONS

When the U.S.-based company has foreign currency-based transactions such as sales, purchases, and loans (made and taken), they need to be recorded in the United States as revenues, expenses, assets, or liabilities. Here's an example.

Suppose a U.S.-based company buys Swiss watches in Geneva for 25,000 Swiss francs (CHFs) on June 1. Because the company's books are in U.S. dollars, the transaction is entered in dollars at the exchange rate on June 1. Let's say it's $0.963149/CHF. That is, 1 CHF buys $0.963149. The purchase entry will be $24,078.73. Accounts payable will also be $24,078.73 and the exchange rate notation "CHF 25,000 @ $0.963149" is made.

Now, if the payment is immediate or stipulated in U.S. dollars (US$), that will be the end of it. But suppose there is a time lag, and the CHF payment is made on August 1.

In the meantime, the exchange rate has changed. Because the transaction was made in CHF, the underlying dollar value of the purchase will change. Let's say the Swiss franc weakens against the dollar, moving to $0.94300/CHF on August 1, when the payable is due. Now the U.S. company has to pay $23,575, which is $503.73 less than its original purchase entry. This difference constitutes a foreign exchange gain. In this case, the journal entries will remain the same, and the gain (or loss) will be recorded in the U.S. company's income statement.

This process is described by U.S. Financial Accounting Standards Board (FASB) Statement 52 (FASB 52), which requires that companies record foreign currency–based transactions at the spot rate (the exchange rate for delivery within two business days) at the time of the transaction. Any gains or losses from changes in exchange rates for items carried as payables or receivables are posted in the income statement. The International Accounting Standards Board (IASB), the international accounting standards organization that most of the rest of the world follows and that we'll soon discuss when we look at the convergence of accounting standards, has the same rule.

FOREIGN CURRENCY CONSOLIDATION: TRANSLATION AND FUNCTIONAL CURRENCY

Now we move to our second concern about foreign currencies in accounting operations, brought about when the IC translates results of its foreign subsidiaries back to its headquarters and home currency. When a U.S. IC's foreign subsidiary reports its subsidiaries' results, they can't be consolidated at headquarters in Saudi riyal, Chinese renminbi, or Peruvian sol. The results need to be translated into the parent company's operating currency—in our discussion, dollars—following the U.S. generally accepted accounting principles (GAAP). The process of aggregating these various results from foreign subsidiaries into one financial report is called **consolidation**.

Once again, questions arise about exchange rates. What exchange rate should the U.S. company use, the one on the day of the consolidation or the one in effect on the day of the transaction? There are two basic approaches to this translation, the current rate method and the temporal method. They both have as their objective to accurately reflect the business results.

The **current rate method** translates current assets and liabilities at the rate in effect the day the balance sheet is produced, except for the equity accounts such as stockholder's equity. (These are translated at their historical rates, the ones in effect on the day of the transaction.) The **temporal method** translates monetary items such as cash, receivables, and payables at the current exchange rate. Fixed assets and long-term liabilities are translated at the rates in effect the date they were acquired or incurred.

So when is each of these translation methods used? The choice hinges on the currency in which the operation denominates its local cash flows, pricing, expenses, and financing, in other words, its **functional currency**. Usually, the functional currency is the local one, but every once in a while, an IC will use its parent currency in a foreign location. All the details for the translation process are in FASB 52 and IASB 21. Figure 15.1 summarizes the implications of using the local and the parent company currency as the functional currency.

INTERNATIONAL ACCOUNTING STANDARDS ON THE PATH OF CONVERGENCE

There are now two main accounting standards at play in the global arena, one followed by most of the world and one followed by the United States. The private nonprofit organization charged by the U.S. Securities and Exchange Commission (SEC) with establishing accounting standards in the United States is the seven-member Financial Accounting Standards Board (FASB). FASB's standards are recognized by the SEC and known as the generally accepted accounting principles (GAAP).

consolidation
The process of translating subsidiary results and aggregating them into one financial report

current rate method
An approach in foreign currency translation in which assets and liabilities are valued at current spot rates

temporal method
An approach in foreign currency translation in which monetary accounts are valued at the spot rate and accounts carried at historical cost are translated at their historic exchange rates

functional currency
The primary currency of a business

FIGURE 15.1 Functional Currency and Translation Methods

When Functional Currency Is:	Local Currency	Parent Company Currency
Translation method is:	Current method	Temporal method
Assets are translated at:	Spot rate on date balance sheet prepared	Spot rate for monetary assets Historic cost for fixed assets
Income statement is translated at:	Average exchange rate for reporting period	Cost of goods sold and depreciation at historic rates Average exchange rate for reporting period Other items at average rate for period
Owner's equity is translated at:	Rates in effect when stock issued	Rates in effect when stock issued
Retained earnings are translated at:	Rates in effect when earnings posted	Rates in effect when earnings posted

The international accounting standards body is the International Accounting Standards Board (IASB), whose standards are the International Financial Reporting Standards (IFRS). In 2002, the U.S. FASB and IASB agreed in principle to harmonize standards and converge. Convergence will create a standard for a global market, increase comparability, and allow ICs to list stock in foreign stock markets, so they can tap into their potential as a new source of shareholders. This would increase the efficiency of global capital markets.

Today there is general political agreement to move toward the IASB standards (IFRS), and negotiations have made progress in the areas of business combinations, noncontrolling, and fair value measurement to date. However, although progress has been achieved, the pace has been slower than anticipated. Earlier expectations of a 2015 deadline on convergence have been recognized as unrealistic because the process itself is complex. The worldwide recession also slowed the move toward convergence. In 2007, the SEC decided that foreign companies listing their shares in the United States no longer needed to restate their financial statements to comply with FASB standards. A technical plan now divides the remaining work into projects and establishes deadlines for the submission of suggestions for stakeholder comment. You can review this plan at www.fasb.org and you can review a list of completed IASB/FASB convergence projects, including outcomes and whether improvement was achieved, at https://www.iasplus.com/en/projects/completed/other/iasb-fasb-convergence.

One of the major differences between GAAP and the IFRS is their general approaches. GAAP relies on rules and regulations; it is a formal institution, and compliance is based on expedience. That is, we follow GAAP because we don't want to face the legal outcomes of not following GAAP. In marked contrast, the IFRS relies strongly on shared principles. It is a normative guide, with compliance based on social obligation. IFRS principles also allow for interpretation and reasoned judgment. With GAAP, the principle is to apply the rules.

Reconciling these different approaches suggests that GAAP-trained accountants will have to learn a new way of thinking, with more focus on the process of accounting than they are used to.

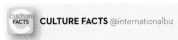
CULTURE FACTS @internationalbiz

@Italy In Italy, *ragioneria* is often translated into English as "accounting," but it actually conveys the idea of reiteration or going forward and going back, not the English accounting's sense of control. Often the payment of corporate taxes in Italy is a process of discussion and compromise, an example of this difference in understanding the meaning of the term "accounting" that affects all international managers.
#accounting #goingforward #goingback #differentmeaning

With convergence, financial markets around the world will be more integrated, and investors and others will be able to compare company performance across borders, companies will no longer have to restate their financials, and the complex process of consolidation will be much easier. These features of standardization will mean substantial cost reductions for companies and better information for everyone.

ACCOUNTING AND CULTURE

An international company such as the Indian Tata Group, the Chinese household appliance company Haier Group, or the U.S. consumer goods company Procter & Gamble has to address transactions in foreign currencies, with an obvious impact on the practice of accounting. It is not surprising that countries' different needs for accounting information have led to variations in financial statements across the globe. There is another source of variation in accounting, and this goes more directly to cultural differences. The assumptions that underlie the country's legal, political, and economic systems, as well as the country's history, influence its domestic companies' shared understanding of the purpose of accounting. Thus culture plays a significant role in the practice of accounting.

Researcher Sidney Gray measures how two aspects of accounting, the information companies provide and their valuation of assets, are influenced by culture. The accounting terms for these functions are *disclosure practices* and *accounting measurement*. Gray's study, summarized in Figure 15.2, classifies countries on two dimensions, secrecy-transparency and optimism-conservatism.[3] The dimension of secrecy–transparency measures the degree to which companies disclose information to the public. Germany, Japan, and

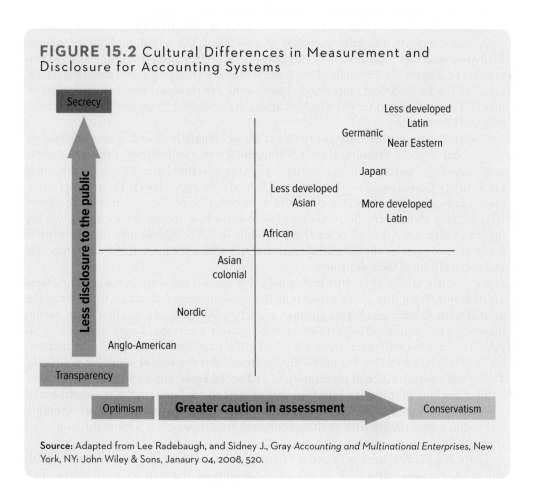

FIGURE 15.2 Cultural Differences in Measurement and Disclosure for Accounting Systems

Source: Adapted from Lee Radebaugh, and Sidney J., Gray *Accounting and Multinational Enterprises*, New York, NY: John Wiley & Sons, Janaury 04, 2008, 520.

Switzerland are countries that tend to value secrecy or privacy over transparency. In the United Kingdom and the United States, there is more disclosure and less privacy.

Gray's second dimension, optimism–conservatism, measures the degree to which a company is cautious in its valuing of assets and measuring of income. Accounting reports in countries with conservative asset-valuing approaches tend to understate assets and income, while those in countries whose asset-valuing approach is more optimistic tend toward overstatement. In France, Germany, and Japan, we find a conservative approach to asset-valuing. In these countries, public companies' capital structure tends to depend more on debt than on equity, with banks being a major source of that debt. Banks are concerned with liquidity. A conservative statement of profits may reduce tax exposure and dividend payouts, contributing to cash reserves that can be tapped for debt service. On the optimism measure, in the United States and in a more restrained way in the United Kingdom, companies want to show impressive earnings that will attract investors and raise the share value sooner rather than later.

Triple-Bottom-Line Accounting

LO 15-2

Outline the benefits and limitations of triple-bottom-line accounting.

As environmental sustainability increasingly becomes important to businesses and consumers, companies have made efforts to report to their stakeholders on their environmental, social, and financial results. The focus of this reporting framework has been termed the *triple bottom line (3BL)*, a term credited to John Elkington. In his 1997 book, *Cannibals with Forks: The Triple Bottom Line of 21st Century Business*,[4] Elkington argued that capitalism can become civilized. His metaphor asserts that capitalists can be taught to eat with forks, they can be civilized, as a result of consumer pressure and other social forces. Corporate capitalism can become sustainable capitalism.

Sustainability is a systems concept only recently associated with capitalism that has three major aspects: the environmental or ecological, the social, and the economic. Elkington describes eight drivers of this potential transformation from capitalism to sustainable capitalism: the demands of consumers; markets; changing values about the importance of the environment; increased expectations for transparency; breakthroughs in life-cycle technology; wider partnerships across stakeholders; time; and the influence of corporate governance.

Currently, we measure business results at the economic level and, where required by government or social pressure, at the environmental level (for instance, emission controls and hazardous waste) and the social level (for instance, the Equal Employment Opportunity Commission's enforcement of federal civil rights laws). Yet in the environmental and social areas, we still tend to know more about the problems than about company-level thinking about them. Stakeholders need to know how companies are acting and the impact of their actions in all three areas, not only in the economic area. Consensus has grown that companies should provide stakeholders with a measure of the environmental and social effects of their decisions.

Even critics of 3BL agree that ecologically and socially responsible business practices are desirable. What they claim, however, is that measurement will not get us closer to the desired state. Researchers Wayne Norman and Chris MacDonald argue that social performance and environmental impact cannot be objectively measured in ways that are comparable to our economic measurements of a firm's activities.[5] They point out that the rhetoric may be appealing, but no widely implementable framework exists for measuring a company's performance in environmental and social areas, although there are high levels of consulting in these areas. In fact, they suggest that a focus on the measurement of these activities may well detract from efforts to figure out ways to combine sustainability and social responsibility with positive economic results, which is a more difficult challenge, by far.

There is a parallel here with codes of ethics: what matters is what a company actually does, not whether a code of ethics is hanging on the wall of every office. The poster is rhetoric; putting it up is not taking ethical action. Decisions in the field that implement ethical standards are what matter, as well as how the organization's members understand the company's values and what those values say about their duties to stakeholders.[6]

Perhaps such reporting requires a reframing of how we think about organizational outcomes, processes that are both incremental and subtle. Interest in 3BL has continued to grow, not only in for-profit companies but also in governmental and nonprofit sectors, and many organizations have developed or adopted 3BL frameworks.[7] Notable efforts to develop a framework that supports substantive reporting on the environmental, social, and financial aspects of business have been made by the Global Reporting Initiative (GRI), an international network of more than 20,000 stakeholders from thousands of organizations, including private-sector businesses, nongovernmental organizations, and government organizations, both local and international. GRI is independent and collaborates with the United Nations Environment Programme (UNEP). You can find details at https://www.globalreporting.org.

International Financial Management: Capital Structure of the Firm

LO 15-3
Compare the capital structure choices open to international firms and their significance.

We now look at how the firm manages funds across borders. This process of transferring value internationally includes many variables, among them exchange rates between currencies, varying restrictions on the movement of funds, differing tax systems, and differing economic environments. You might think of this challenge as a complex process merging the management of risk, opportunity, and complexity.

We begin our financial management review with a focus on the capital structure of the firm and then move on to cash flow management across borders, looking at both the financial flows themselves and the techniques used to move them. Foreign exchange (FX) risk management follows. We close with a look at taxation issues. Our goal is to introduce you to the types of challenges international financial managers face as they manage their firm's cash flows across borders and how they resolve these challenges.

We have seen that firms are becoming increasingly international in their markets and their sourcing in order to exploit attractive opportunities. These global opportunities are also available for the capital structure of the firm, and increasingly chief financial officers (CFOs) have been tapping international financial markets, both public and private. Because financial markets are not globally integrated, though they are increasingly interconnected, varying opportunities arise among them, and with varying costs. If a CFO can raise capital in a foreign market at a lower cost than in the home market, such an opportunity may be attractive as a way to increase shareholder value.

The firm raises capital from two sources: internally, through retained earnings, and externally, through either equity (issuing of shares) or debt (leveraging). When equity securities (stock shares) are issued, part of the firm's ownership is being sold. No money is being borrowed that must be repaid, as is the case when debt securities (bonds) are issued.

Many firms choose to use equity, and they may issue stocks in foreign markets, in part to tap into a broader investor pool beyond their home country's financial market, which can increase the firm's stock price and reduce the firm's cost of capital. Selling stock in foreign markets may have a significant marketing advantage, too, by raising the profile of the firm's brand name abroad. Among the foreign companies that have issued shares in the United States are Unilever, Fujifilm, Canadian Pacific, KLM, Sony, Toyota, Banco Santander, and Cemex. Smaller, high growth start-up companies that have too short an operating history or are too small to raise money in the traditional capital markets find venture capital—private capital in return for equity—another source of capital. Venture capital is most active in the United States (where it first developed) and the European Union and has been growing in developing economies such as China, Vietnam, and India.

American depository receipts (ADRs)
Foreign shares held by a custodian, usually a U.S. bank, in the issuer's home market and traded in dollars on the U.S. exchange

Sometimes foreign shares are traded directly on the U.S. stock markets, but many times they are traded in the form of American depository receipts (ADRs). These receipts represent shares that are held by a custodian, usually a U.S. bank, in the stock's home market. They are denominated in dollars and traded on the U.S. exchange, eliminating the need to have a broker in the country of issue and to make a currency exchange. J.P. Morgan developed this program in New York in 1927 with a listing for the famed British department store Selfridges. You can visit the ADR database at https://www.adr.com. There are deposit receipt programs in other countries as well, including Luxembourg, India, and the EU countries.

The sale of large amounts of a firm's stock in foreign stock markets may raise concerns that foreigners have too much control of domestic assets. This is more likely when the relevant industry sectors are perceived as essential to national security. In these cases, governments may restrict foreign ownership of equity, a response that is more prevalent in developing countries. For example, in China, India, Mexico, and Indonesia, foreign ownership in specific sectors is limited. Some sectors in developed nations are also protected from foreign ownership, often through an approval process. Such an example in the United States is the airline industry. U.S. airlines must be directed and operationally controlled by a U.S. citizen. In addition, foreign acquisitions are approved by the U.S. Treasury's Committee on Foreign Investment in the United States (CFIUS), with the final decision made by the president. In 2018, China-owned Ant Financial's bid to acquire MoneyGram International Inc., a U.S.-based firm involved in money transfer, was derailed due to concerns raised by CFIUS.[8] The acquisition would have provided Ant Financial with access to about 350,000 MoneyGram outlets, including locations in nearly every nation worldwide.

Debt markets are the other source of capital for the firm, and increasingly the tendency is to tap local markets first. That may mean a foreign subsidiary of the Japanese firm Toyota would look first to its market in the United States for funds to use in its U.S. operations. Multinational corporations, in addition to obtaining funds at the corporate level, can explore borrowing in their domestic and international debt markets, increasing their opportunities to reduce the cost of capital. They also have access to offshore financial centers, also known as tax havens, locations that specialize in financing by nonresidents, where the taxation levels are low and the banking regulatory environment is loose. Hong Kong, Switzerland, the Cayman Islands, and the Bahamas are examples of offshore financial centers.

offshore financial center
Location that specializes in financing nonresidents, with low taxes and few banking regulations

The commonly shared belief is that debt financing is less expensive than equity financing, because the interest paid on the debt is usually tax deductible, while dividends paid to investors are not. Yet the firm's balance between debt and equity financing is also influenced by local practice. Firms in the United States, the United Kingdom, and Canada tend to rely on equity more heavily than do companies in many other countries. In both Japan and Germany, banks traditionally play a more central role than do the stock markets in the financing picture. In Japan, we find the *keiretsu*, a network in which related companies in a larger family—such as Mitsubishi, Sumitomo, or C. Itoh—are connected through interlocking ownership of stocks and bonds, with the company bank at their center. Essentially, this structure eliminates the stakeholder conflicts between bondholders and stockholders, an appropriate characteristic for a national culture in which harmony is an important cultural value.

CULTURE FACTS @internationalbiz

@Britain Many of the world's offshore financial centers are former British colonies or territories, a cultural legacy of Britain's leadership in the development of global banking. The former colonies have been influenced by their colonizers' values, on both obvious and subtle levels. #offshoring #globalbanking @culturallegacy

The way the local government treats taxes may also influence how the IC structures its capital. If the local tax rate is high and the interest paid on debt is tax deductible, debt may be a way to partially protect profits from taxes. National policies also influence this decision. For example, exchange controls, restrictions on the exchange of a country's currency, may limit dividend payments to foreign equity holders, and national policies designed to encourage local reinvestment may control the payment of dividends. In summary, local practices, taxation, and other country-level policies may influence the firm's capital structure. Figure 15.3 shows capital structure percentages for selected countries.

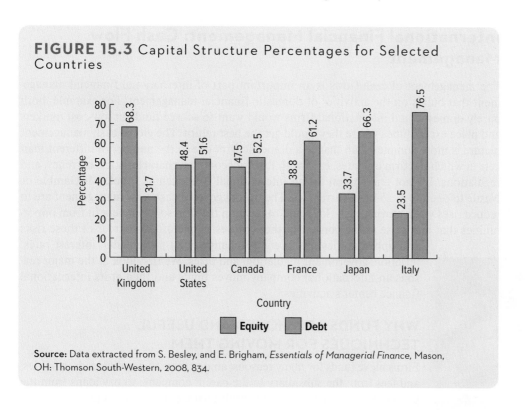

FIGURE 15.3 Capital Structure Percentages for Selected Countries

Source: Data extracted from S. Besley, and E. Brigham, *Essentials of Managerial Finance*, Mason, OH: Thomson South-Western, 2008, 834.

Decisions a financial manager will make in the process of raising capital are as follows:

1. In what currency should the capital be raised, considering an estimate of its long-term strength or weakness? For example, if trendy Norwegian clothing designer Lisbeth Løvbak Berg wanted to enter the U.S. market with a wholly owned store in late 2018, she would likely have tried to raise her capital in her home currency, the Norwegian krone, since that currency was forecast to appreciate against the U.S. dollar through at least March 2020.

2. How should the raised capital be structured between equity and debt? A small family-owned porcelain business with a good credit rating that is expanding from Mexico into the United States might be hesitant to use equity financing because family members want to retain control of the business.

3. What sources of capital are available? Money can be borrowed from a commercial bank by an ordinary loan; from a bank as part of a swap (a matching of different currencies to reduce the risk of exposure due to exchange-rate fluctuations); from another company as part of a swap; from another part of the MNC; or through a public offering of stock, either an IPO or an offering of additional shares in one of the world's capital markets, for example, in the New York or European Union's bond market.

4. If the firm decides to use one of the world's capital markets, in which market can management achieve its objectives at the lowest cost?

5. Are other sources of money available? For example, a joint-venture partner, an offer of private capital, or a host government may be possible sources. A host government may be a source of funds or tax abatement if the company's planned move into that country is expected to bring the IC's technology and management knowledge, or if local jobs will be created.

6. How much money does the company need and for how long? For instance, if the company is moving into a new market or product, there will probably be a period during product introduction or plant construction when the new venture will need more capital than it can generate on its own.

International Financial Management: Cash Flow Management

The management of cash flows is an important part of international financial management that builds on the activities of domestic financial management. For example, both purely domestic and international firms would want to source funds in low-cost markets and place excess funds where they would get the best return. The global cash management picture is more complex than that of a domestic firm due to the number of different markets in which the firm operates, each with its own economic characteristics, currency, and regulations. It's not uncommon for an international firm such as Procter & Gamble or Nestlé to operate in 25 local currencies. The overall goals of cash flow management are to reduce risks when moving cash flows and to position the firm so it can benefit from opportunities that may arise in the context of these moves. Some of the sources of these risks and opportunities are foreign exchange (FX) movements, interest rates, inflation, government regulation, and taxes. We first look at the major reasons an international company moves funds and then at its international finance center's activities.

WHY FUNDS ARE MOVED AND USEFUL TECHNIQUES FOR MOVING THEM

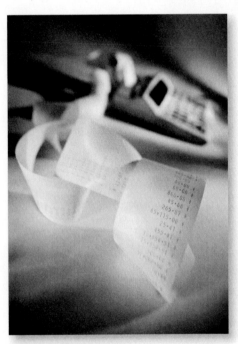

©Stockbyte/Getty Images.

Firms move funds for many reasons, among them to pay dividends, royalties, and fees from the subsidiary to the parent company; to pay loans from the parent to the subsidiary or among subsidiaries; and to carry out transfer pricing of sales between subsidiaries and the parent company. Dividends result from the parent company's equity interest in the subsidiary, while royalties and fees are payments made for the use of company assets such as trade names, technology, consulting, and management systems. These payments are important to the business in and of themselves, and they may also be useful in cash flow management in several ways. They may serve as a vehicle for moving profits from subsidiaries in high-tax environments to lower-tax environments. They may be a way to move profits out of countries where repatriation of profits is blocked or limited. They may also be a way to reduce FX risk by moving currency from environments that have a high risk of devaluation to lower-risk ones. Note, too, that these payments are business expenses, so they can affect tax liability.

fronting loan
A loan made through an
intermediary, usually a bank,
from parent company to
subsidiary

A loan also may be a useful technique in cash flow management. Parent companies can loan funds directly to the subsidiary, but the host government may restrict the subsidiary's remittances, including the loan payments, back to the parent. A **fronting loan** is an approach that achieves the same objective for the firm with much less risk. In a fronting loan, the parent company deposits money in an international bank, which then lends to the subsidiary, *fronting* for the parent company. The host government is less inclined to restrict subsidiary loan payments than other remittances, especially when the payment is to a major international bank. There is a small cost to the parent company, while the bank has no risk because it is holding a fully collateralized loan. If the deposit is made from a tax haven, there will be tax advantages as well. Such loans may also get around a host government's blocking of funds, which is a way the host can protect its balance of payments position.

transfer pricing
Pricing established for
transactions between
members of the enterprise

One additional method of transferring funds within the firm that may serve as a cash management technique is **transfer pricing**, which sets the price of transactions between members of the same business enterprise. Such transactions are common within globally dispersed firms, making up 60 percent of world trade. Because the sale that creates the transfer is internal, its costs are somewhat flexible. In this flexibility lies the potential to move funds from high-tax, weak-currency environments in ways that are beneficial to the firm. Transfer pricing can also circumvent host-country currency transfer controls and tariffs.

BANKING IN AFRICA: Mobile Money Leads the Way

While storefront bank branches and online banking are ubiquitous in most developed nations, only a small fraction of the population in less-developed countries is served by banking services. Africa has the world's lowest level of bank branch penetration, averaging less than half as many as the emerging markets of Asia and less than a third of the level in the Middle East and Latin America.

Mobile banking, which allows customers to use their mobile phones to not only pay bills but also access services including loans, insurance, and savings, are one way to overcome this gap. Africa has emerged as the global leader in mobile banking, thanks to the development of an innovative array of services provided by telecom companies along with mobile phone prices that have dropped below $20. There are over 100 million active mobile money accounts in Africa, or about 2.5 times the number of users in the second largest region, South Asia.

First appearing in the Philippines in 2001, mobile banking skips the use of debit or credit cards and enables customers to send, receive, and store money using a mobile phone. A bank typically holds the underlying funds in a dedicated or linked account. A person usually sends a payment by text to the recipient's phone number. The recipient then obtains the payment from an authorized local agent, often a mom-and-pop retailer that also sells prepaid mobile phone cards. Coffee growers in Kenya routinely use text messages to pay field workers, and customers of Tanzania's national electric utility can pay their bills by text. For many customers, mobile banking is having a significant, positive impact on their lives because it is the first time they have been able to connect to critical banking services.

Although banks have recently begun entering Africa's mobile money market, telecom companies dominate this sector. The five largest telecoms have 60 percent of all mobile customers in Africa, creating enormous scale economies. The largest telecom, MTN, has over 170 million customers while even the largest African banks generally have less than 15 million clients. Telecoms also dominate in the area of distribution channels, with registered mobile money agents per nation averaging more than 10 times the number of branches offered by banks. For example, Kenya's Safaricom has over 130,000 agents while that country's leading banks have only 15,000 agents. Mobile money transactions are also simpler for clients, who can conduct

Mobile phones can allow a farmer in a developing nation to check commodity prices and perform other tasks. ©thonephoto/Shutterstock.

transactions virtually anywhere and require as few as three inputs and six clicks to send money, with no transaction fees charged on bill payments. Banks face other competitive challenges as well, including fees that are unaffordable for low-income clients, high-cost business models, and an ingrained preference for cash rather than digital transactions.

The number of mobile money users in Africa has been growing by about 30 percent annually in recent years, with annual revenues approaching $29 per active user. Margins on mobile money payments in Africa, at about 2 percent of transaction value, remain among the highest in the world. With sub-Saharan Africa's population projected to swell to 2.7 billion by 2060 and availability of mobile money services still uneven across markets, there is ample room and incentive for continued growth in this sector.

Sources: O'Brien, Kevin J., "Mobile Banking in the Emerging World," *The New York Times*, November 28, 2018. www.nytimes.com; "Digital Financial Services: Challenges and Opportunities for Emerging Market Banks," *International Finance Corporation, World Bank Group*, August 2018. www.ifc.org/thoughtleadership; Chironga, Mutsa, Grandis, Hilary De, and Zouaoui, Yassir, "Mobile Financial Services in Africa: Winning the Battle for the Customer," *McKinsey & Company*, September, 2017. www.mckinsey.com; Canning, David, Raja, Sangeeta, and Yazbeck, Abdo S., *Africa's Demographic Transition: Dividend or Disaster?*. Washington, DC: World Bank and L'Agence Francaise de Developpement, October 22, 2015; and Dahir, Abdi Latif, "Mobile Money Is the Key to Growing Africa's Banking Sector," *Quartz*, April 03, 2018. www.qz.com.

Transfer pricing can raise ethical issues, too, because the maneuvers, although they may be legal, are often not in the spirit of the host-country tax and monetary laws. Host-government authorities carefully review transfer pricing for potential lost tax revenues, for example. The OECD and the U.S. Internal Revenue Service have issued guidelines on transfer pricing. Some firms now voluntarily agree with the host country in advance on their approach to internal (within the firm) pricing. Such agreements, in addition to offering ethical guidelines to decision makers, reduce the firm's legal and tax audit risks.

INTERNATIONAL FINANCE CENTER

> **" In OUR VIEW, DERIVATIVES ARE FINANCIAL WEAPONS of MASS DESTRUCTION CARRYING DANGERS THAT, WHILE LATENT, ARE POTENTIALLY LETHAL. "**
>
> *—Warren Buffett*[9]

The increasing complexity of global financing, combined with rising global competition, has encouraged firms to pay more attention to financial management. In many firms, this increased awareness has led to the centralization of the finance operation as a profit center, a bit like a company bank. Other factors include (1) floating exchange rates, whose fluctuations are sometimes volatile; (2) growth in the number of capital and foreign exchange markets, where the firm can shop for lower interest costs and better currency rates; (3) different and changing inflation rates from country to country; (4) advances in electronic cash management systems; (5) realization by financial managers that through innovative management of temporarily idle cash balances of company subsidiaries, they can increase yields and thereby profit; and (6) the explosive growth of derivatives (contracts whose value is determined by the value of underlying assets) to protect against commodity, currency, interest rate, and other risks.

Centralized finance centers can tap capital markets, manage inflation rate risk, manage cash management technological innovation, manage derivatives use, handle internal and external invoicing, help a weak-currency subsidiary, strengthen subsidiary evaluation and reporting systems, and balance and *hedge* currency exposures. **Hedging** is the process of holding assets (taking a position) in one market in order to offset exposure to price changes in the opposite position. This technique is widely used to cover risk. We now move to cash flow management and look at multilateral netting and leading and lagging as two approaches the firm's finance center may use to manage cash flows.

hedge
To hold assets (to take a position) in one market in order to offset exposure to price changes in an opposite position

MULTILATERAL NETTING

multilateral netting
Strategy in which subsidiaries transfer net intracompany cash flows through a centralized clearing center

There are many possible types of cash flows between subsidiaries and their parent company and among subsidiaries. The parent company makes loans to the subsidiary and may increase investment in the form of equity capital. In the other direction, cash from sales, dividends, royalties, and fees move from the subsidiary to the parent. Flows also exist among subsidiaries. One common strategy finance centers use to manage and optimize these flows is **multilateral netting**. This is a centralized approach in which subsidiaries transfer their net cash flows within the company to a cash center that disperses cash to net receivers. A single transaction to or from each member settles the net result of all cash flows. The structure is essentially the wheel-and-spoke model.

Why do companies consider multilateral netting? First, the transfer of funds has a cost attached to it, the *transaction cost*, and while the funds are in transit, they present an opportunity cost: they are not working for the company. In addition, FX costs are incurred. Reducing the number of transfer transactions means there is less inactive time for funds, the actual transfer costs are reduced, and fewer FX transactions are needed. As an example, consider multilateral netting among the Chinese, German, Mexican, and Indian subsidiaries of a firm. Each subsidiary with a net payable position would transfer its funds to a central account at scheduled intervals, say, once a month, where the central account manager would then transfer funds to the net receivers. Compare the two approaches in Figure 15.4. Without netting, reconciling the positions

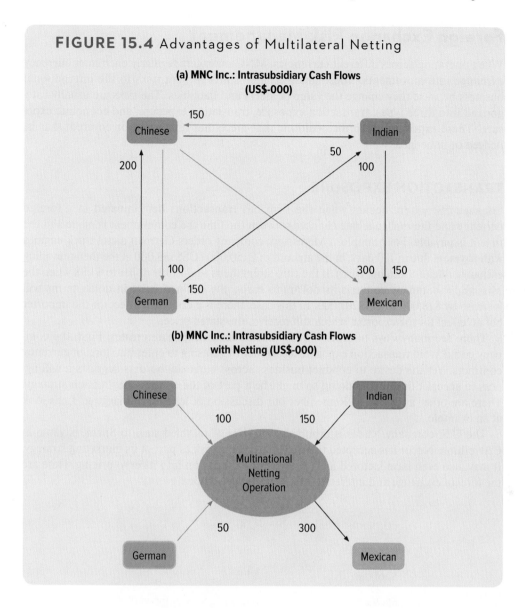

FIGURE 15.4 Advantages of Multilateral Netting

(a) MNC Inc.: Intrasubsidiary Cash Flows (US$-000)

(b) MNC Inc.: Intrasubsidiary Cash Flows with Netting (US$-000)

would require eight transactions and $1.2 million in transit. With netting, there are four transactions and $600,000 in transit. Plus, the foreign exchange transaction costs are reduced.

LEADING AND LAGGING

Currency exchange rates that float, as do today's, create a risk for the multinational firm because currency values can change without warning. To minimize such a risk, one useful technique is leading and lagging, which times the collection and payment of funds. This is actually a simple technique that you may practice already: collect payments as early as possible (lead) and pay out as late as possible (lag). In the international arena, leading and lagging can also limit FX risk. A *lead* approach is to collect receivables early when the foreign currency is expected to weaken and to fund payables early when the foreign currency is expected to strengthen. A *lag* approach is to collect receivables late when the currency is expected to strengthen and to fund payables late when the currency is expected to weaken. If we now think about combining the multilateral netting approach with leading and lagging, we can see that IC subsidiaries can coordinate to reposition funds and help compensate for blocked funds or funds about to be blocked.

leading and lagging
Timing payments early (lead) or late (lag), depending on anticipated currency movements, so that they have the most favorable impact for the company

LO 15-5
Identify foreign exchange risks the IC faces and ways to address them.

Foreign Exchange Risk Management

When operating across different currencies, MNC managers regularly encounter currency exchange rate movements. These unanticipated shifts present risks to the international business because they change the value of assets and liabilities. The risks are usually categorized into three types: transaction exposure, translation exposure, and economic exposure. These exposures describe positions that are either uncovered or covered; that is, hedged or unhedged.

TRANSACTION EXPOSURE

transaction exposure
Change in the value of a financial position created by foreign currency changes between the establishment and the settlement of a contract

Transaction exposure occurs when the firm has transactions denominated in a foreign currency and the exchange rate changes between the time the commitment is made and the time it is payable. For example, a Mississippi company orders German diesel truck engines with payment due in 180 days, in the amount of €150,000 (US$189,000 at the then-prevailing exchange rate of $1.26 per euro). If the euro strengthens against the dollar to $1.38 when the Mississippi company converts its dollars to euros, the engines' price in dollar terms will increase by $18,000 to US$207,000. In this case, there is a cash flow effect for the importer but no effect for the exporter, which still receives the stated price.

There are many ways to cover the risk a transaction exposure creates. First, the company could avoid transaction exposure altogether by refusing to enter into foreign currency contracts. Yet the desire to conduct business across currency borders suggests a willingness to accept this risk and doing so might be a part of the contract negotiation strategy. There are other approaches. Remember our discussion of leading and lagging? Let's look at an example.

The U.S. company Nucor is exporting an order of recycled steel to Spain, payable as €20 million. Nucor has accepted the foreign exchange risk as part of its marketing strategy. It may also even have factored a currency shift expectation into its euro pricing. Here are the foreign exchange and interest data (they are hypothetical):

EU interest rate	4.00 percent
U.S. interest rate	5.00 percent
Spot rate	$1.534
Forward rate	$1.527 (one year forward)

Nucor faces transaction exposure in its receivable. There are six ways it can cover this risk. First, Nucor could lead its receivable, because the market indicates that the dollar may well strengthen against the euro. (Moving from a spot rate of $1.534 to a forward rate of $1.527 means that the market expects the euro to buy fewer dollars a year out. So the dollar is strengthening against the euro.) The Spanish customer may well want to lag the payment, though, if there is no incentive for early payment.

In a second way to hedge on transaction exposure through company actions, Nucor could follow a centralized practice similar to multilateral netting: *exposure netting*. The firm would run a centralized clearing account that matches and nets out foreign exchange exposures across currencies or across currency families. Working with currency families is a way to recognize that some currencies tend to move in lockstep with one another, such as the euro, U.S. dollar, and British pound moving in the same direction, or the U.S. dollar and the Swiss franc moving in the opposite direction. Many ICs follow this approach.

forward market hedge
Foreign currency contract sold or bought forward to protect against foreign currency movement

Third, a **forward market hedge** is a simple transaction. The company sells forward (contracts today to deliver currency at a specified rate on a specified future date) its foreign currency receivables for its home currency, matching the future date to the due date of the receivables. When the Spanish company pays, Nucor will deliver the amount to its bank, its partner in the forward market hedge contract. Nucor will not have been exposed to currency risk in the Spanish sale. Because the forward market hedge is a way to cover all the exposure in a given transaction, it is the most widely used approach, but it also eliminates the chance of gaining from a currency move in the company's favor.

A fourth approach to hedging an exposure while retaining the opportunity to gain from a currency appreciation is known as a *foreign currency option*. With a currency option hedge, you purchase an option to buy or sell a specific amount of currency at a specific time. These contracts are solicited through social media networks as well as through banks. The hedges are *calls* for, or contracts with an option to buy, foreign currency payables and *puts* for, or contracts to sell, foreign currency receivables. Because they are options, if the market works against you, you can exercise the contract. If the market works for you, you don't need to exercise the option.

For example, Nucor booked receivables today, payable in nine months, of 1 million Swiss francs (CHF). It wants to protect the dollar value of this payment, so, essentially, it creates an option to make the dollar transaction now. Assume that today one CHF buys $1.04. Nucor takes out a put option to sell the CHF for U.S. dollars at today's rate, known as the strike price. If, in nine months, the Swiss franc has strengthened to $1.0754, so that Nucor will make money on the transaction, then Nucor is not obligated to exercise its option contract. Its Swiss franc payment will yield $1,075,400. If the Swiss franc has weakened over the nine months to $0.99, Nucor has hedged its foreign currency risk and can exercise the option.

The money markets also offer an opportunity to hedge a foreign transaction. In a money market hedge, Nucor would borrow euros in the European money market in the amount of the receivables from the Spanish sale. The idea here is to match the balance sheet asset (in this case, the amount of the sale) with a liability in the same currency. Here's how the money market hedge works. Nucor borrows the equivalent of $20 million in euros, or €13,035,300, for a period that matches the receivable's due date. Nucor then converts the euros to dollars at the spot rate and invests them. It will use the euros it receives from the Spanish company to close out the euro loan. Then the invested dollars plus their earned interest provide Nucor a dollar amount for the Spanish sale.

Swap contracts are the sixth way to hedge foreign currency exposure. A swap is an agreement to exchange currencies at specified rates and on a specified date or sequence of dates. Swaps are quite flexible and may be undertaken for long periods, much longer than contracts available in the forward market. If Nucor had a series of sales in the European Union over the next 10 years, all denominated in euros, it could enter into a series of swaps, so it would know the exchange rate or series of exchange rates in advance.

Many of these hedging techniques involve interest payments. Since one of the pillars of Islamic banking is that commercial relationships must not involve the payment of interest because interest earns a return without accompanying risk, a series of Islamic hedging instruments is available. These instruments are designed to share risk equitably, in compliance with Sharia, the moral and legal code of Islam.

TRANSLATION EXPOSURE

Translation exposure occurs when subsidiary financial statements are consolidated at the corporate level for companywide financial reports. Because the foreign subsidiaries operate in non-dollar currencies, amounts in their financial reports must be translated to the parent company's currency during the corporate consolidation process. Exchange rate movements can have a substantial impact on the value of these financial statements, which may affect per-share earnings and stock price. Take a U.S. company that has subsidiaries in Brazil, Japan, Spain, and the United Kingdom. Each subsidiary will prepare financial reports in its own currency, so amounts in four currencies will need to be translated. Any changes in the exchange rates will affect the dollar values of these results. Such changes, either gains or losses, are not reflected in cash flow; they are paper or unrealized changes.

currency option hedge
An option to buy or sell a specific amount of foreign currency at a specific time in order to protect against foreign currency risk

money market hedge
A method to hedge foreign currency exposure by borrowing and lending in the domestic and foreign money markets

swap contract
A spot sale/purchase of an asset against a future purchase/sale of an equal amount in order to hedge a financial position

translation exposure
Potential change in the value of a company's financial position due to exposure created during the consolidation process

LENDING TO THE POOR: Charitable Activity or For-Profit Business?

©Ute Grabowsky/Photothek/
Getty Images.

You might think it is foolish to lend money to the poor in a developing country. How will borrowers pay it back? But a tiny, or *microfinance*, loan to a new small-business owner or entrepreneur—a vegetable peddler, tailor, or candle maker—can make both good charitable and good business sense. Development organizations around the world are finding that some of the world's poorest entrepreneurs, many of whom are women, repay their debts at rates approaching 100 percent.

Microloans give thousands of small entrepreneurs small spurts of working capital when they need it, allow them to establish credit, and let them borrow again in hard times. The money helps them start or expand their business and boosts the local economy. The microcredit concept was developed by Muhammad Yunus, a U.S.-trained Bangladeshi economist, through the Grameen Bank in Bangladesh, which he established to administer his program, and by ACCION, a U.S. microcredit organization. Dr. Yunus was awarded the Nobel Peace Prize in 2006 for his work fighting poverty.

Performance on microloan repayment shines when compared with the repayment rates of some sovereign nations. It also looks very good compared with a default rate of 10.8 percent within three years of beginning loan repayment, among U.S. recipients of federally guaranteed student loans. ACCION reports a default rate over the life of its program of 3 percent. A Mexican microloan bank, Compartamos Banco, is the largest microfinance lender in Latin America, with more than 2.5 million customers. It reports a 1 percent default rate. Critics point out, though, that one microloan is not going to pull a budding entrepreneur out of poverty, let alone a whole country. A series of loans is probably necessary, combined with training and support.

Recently, because of their success, several nonprofit microloan programs such as Compartamos have become banks, and some have gone public, selling shares to investors. The move to private ownership that seeks a return on investment changes the microloan business model substantially, from *charity* to for-profit business. The charity model uses donated funds and funds from international financial institutions such as the World Bank and the European Bank for Reconstruction and Development, and it has relatively low interest rates. Compartamos now charges its credit customers in the range of 100 percent (on an annualized basis) to cover loan interest, fees, and taxes, three times the cost of borrowing from other microcredit lenders. To make matters a little more complicated, many of the shareholders who profited greatly from the Compartamos IPO are themselves microlenders, such as ACCION.

Is it right to profit from loans to the poor? Dr. Yunus thinks not and "refuses to mention the words *Compartamos* and *microfinance* in the same breath." The founders of Compartamos, in contrast, suggested that money exists in poor countries but the problem is distribution. By inserting the potential for profit, private capital is quickly and efficiently brought in touch with the people who need it, aligning the world's wealth with the world's poor.

View a PBS video that explores this issue further at http://www.pbs.org/now/shows/338.

Critical Thinking Questions

1. Is profiting from lending to the poor an ethical business model?
2. Is for-profit microlending a way to reach more of the poor more effectively, or a mistaken development?

Sources: Andrew Kreighbaum, "Student Loan Default Rate Declines Slightly," *Inside Higher Ed*, September 27, 2018, www.insidehighered.com; Compartamos Banco, 2018, www.compartamosnet.com.mx; Muhammad Yunus, "Sacrificing Microcredit for Megaprofits," *New York Times,* Januray 14, 2018, www.nytimes.com; Kentaro Toyama, "Lies, Hype, and Profit: The Truth About Microfinance," *The Atlantic,* Januray 28, 2018, www.theatlantic.com; and Jason Hickel, "The Microfinance Delusion: Who Really Wins?," *The Guardian,* June 10, 2018, www.theguardian.com.

The key question related to translation exposure is what currency exchange rate to use for the translation. We reviewed the two basic approaches to translation, the current rate method and the temporal method, and their exchange rate use rules earlier in this module in our discussion of international accounting. Approaches to translation exposure differ by country.

Many organizations do not hedge translation exposure because translation gains and losses do not represent cash flows. Also, hedging a translation exposure can actually increase transaction exposure. For example, if the translation exposure is hedged through a matching foreign exchange liability, such as a debt, then that debt would be an exposure at the transaction level.

ECONOMIC EXPOSURE

Economic exposure occurs at the operations level and results from exchange rate changes on projected cash flows. Unlike transaction exposure, which addresses the individual transaction, economic exposure is firm-wide and long term. For example, when the dollar strengthens, as it did in 2017–2018, U.S. export prices increase in terms of other currencies. U.S. exported goods become less price-competitive in foreign markets, so sales are likely to decline. Yet when the dollar weakens, U.S. export prices become more attractive in foreign markets. These changes are examples of the possible effects of economic exposure. Economic exposure can affect both the dollar value of the company's foreign assets and liabilities and the company's cash flow because it has an impact on foreign sales. Asset exposure includes the firm's fixed assets as well as their financial assets. The exposure of cash flow to currency fluctuation is known as *operating exposure.* Operating exposure is difficult to measure because it affects both the cash flows and the larger commercial context, the competitive conditions connected to obtaining inputs and selling. The management of economic exposure draws on the hedging and swap contracts we have discussed as ways to manage transaction exposure, on flexibility in sourcing, and on a portfolio approach to foreign market involvement.

economic exposure
The potential for the value of future cash flows to be affected by unanticipated exchange rate movements

Taxation

LO 15-6
Describe taxation as an international financial force.

Taxation is an external financial force that affects decisions international managers make because it affects revenues. In the United States, corporate taxes are paid on the business revenue's less current expenses (including wages and interest), deductions for the cost of inventory, and depreciation of capital investments. This is an income tax. Until tax law changes in 2017 dropped the maximum rate to 21 percent, most resident U.S. corporations were subject to a maximum rate of 35 percent. At the time of that change, corporate taxes represented the third largest U.S. source of revenue, next to individual income taxes and payroll taxes.

The international tax picture can be complex if you focus on the details of taxation in individual countries, but there are just three major types of taxation that governments around the world use—income tax, value-added tax, and withholding tax. Income tax is a direct tax levied on earnings, as in the U.S. example. Value-added tax (VAT) is an indirect tax, in that the tax authority collects it from the person or firm that adds value during the production and marketing process, not from the owner of the item taxed. The ultimate user of the product pays the full amount of tax, which is rebated to the others in the value chain. The withholding tax is also an indirect tax, levied on passive income such as royalties, dividends, and interest. It is paid by the business that makes the royalty, dividend, or interest payment. In the United States, wages are taxed, and the income tax payment is withheld by the employer and paid to the government on the employees' behalf. These are individual income taxes, not corporate taxes.

income tax
Direct tax levied on earnings

value-added tax (VAT)
Indirect tax collected from the parties as they add value to the product

withholding tax
Indirect tax paid by the payor, usually on passive income

As for what territories a government's tax covers, there are two approaches to this jurisdiction issue, worldwide and territorial. A worldwide approach taxes residents of a country on their worldwide income. The United States follows a policy of worldwide taxation, and it can be argued convincingly that, despite tax treaties, such taxation puts U.S. firms operating foreign subsidiaries at a disadvantage compared with their foreign domestic competitors.[10] A territorial taxation policy taxes income earned within the nation's borders. In the United States, tax credits reduce or eliminate double taxation for U.S. residents and companies, as long as the foreign tax liability is less than the U.S. equivalent would be.

The way the foreign operations of a company are organized is key to its U.S. tax liability on foreign earnings. If the operation is a branch, that is, an extension of the parent company

branch
Legal extension of the parent company

BRYAN GOLDFINGER: Microfinance in Latin America with Kiva

Courtesy of Bryan Goldfinger.

In my third year of university, I studied abroad in Puntarenas, Costa Rica, where I lived with a Spanish-speaking host family and took Spanish classes. During that year, I became infatuated with travel and the Latin people and culture and gained fluency in Spanish and a desire to help those less fortunate. When I got home, I changed my major to international business management with a concentration in accounting. When I graduated I had a contract to begin auditing with KPMG. The months between graduation and entering the "real world" I spent taking an overland trip from Nicaragua to Argentina, an experience that proved to be more valuable than I could have imagined.

My plan at KPMG was to complete the CPA examinations, spend two years auditing, and then complete an international rotation at one of its overseas offices. At the end of my first year, I began to feel my work was not helping others and, frankly, the public accounting lifestyle was not for me. So I left KPMG.

In conversation about my future, a friend asked me to describe my ideal dream job. I realized that it would include international business travel, allow me to use Spanish, involve more time in the field and less in an office, and be socially fulfilling. Two days later, he sent me an e-mail about a friend who was working in Paraguay with a company called Kiva, and he included a link to the website (https://www.kiva.org). Kiva's mission is to connect people through lending to help alleviate poverty. Individuals like you and me provide funds in increments of $25 via the organization's website to entrepreneurs in developing countries and the United States. Kiva then sends the funds to its partner microfinance institutions (MFIs), which provide the loans.

I applied for a Kiva fellowship. Kiva fellows are volunteers who work closely with partner institutions to help them implement Kiva policies, meet and interview borrowers, and complete verifications of the information the MFIs provide to Kiva. Essentially, the Kiva fellows are Kiva's eyes and ears in the field who connect all four stakeholders involved with Kiva: the borrowers, the lenders, the MFIs, and Kiva headquarters. The actual work of a Kiva fellow varies greatly, depending on experience, skill set, and the partner institution.

I completed two placements as a Kiva fellow, as a roamer in Peru and then in Managua, Nicaragua. The primary objective of my placement in Peru was borrower verification. I would select a small sample of loans from several MFIs, visit the borrowers, and verify that the information Kiva's partner had filed was consistent with what was actually taking place in the field. During these visits, I also would write a short journal entry on the progress of the borrowers that would be uploaded to the Kiva website and sent out to everyone who had lent money to that particular borrower. In Nicaragua, I worked primarily with one MFI to complete a review of its social performance. Social performance monitoring is a new and growing subject in microfinance, and there are a variety of tools and companies whose purpose is to monitor social performance. The goal is to review and identify the strengths and weaknesses of an MFI's social performance. More specifically, what is the mission statement of the MFI and is the mission being applied in the field?

Due to their different locations and duties, Kiva fellows tend to have wildly different experiences, challenges, and rewards. For me, the most rewarding part was visiting and interviewing borrowers and having the opportunity to witness, firsthand, the effects of microfinance. To trek out into the field with a loan officer to a place you would likely never go otherwise, meet people you would likely never meet otherwise, ask them in-depth questions about their businesses and lives, and at the end ask, "What are your hopes and dreams?" is an experience I found rewarding.

Aside from the anticipated challenges of learning how to work in the cultures of new countries and MFIs, I was lucky to have very few difficulties as a Kiva fellow. The biggest challenge I experienced, particularly during my placement in Peru and the first half of my placement in Nicaragua, was loneliness and lack of a social network. Although an incredibly rewarding and valuable experience, work travel is not the same as tourist travel or a study abroad experience. You don't have the built-in support group that is often present in a study abroad program or the free time and lodging situations that "tourist" travel provides—which are helpful in facilitating social interactions. That said, by the end of each placement, I found myself wishing I did not have to leave so soon. The most important thing to do when in such a situation is to not resort to crawling into a ball and secluding yourself. The Internet and comforts of home can easily become a crutch to lean on, which ultimately serve no purpose in alleviating the situation. Go out by yourself, put your pride on the line, meet random people, and be willing to experience situations you normally would never dream of.

My advice to anyone who wishes to pursue international work is to get as much international experience as possible before entering the workforce. Whether it is through study abroad; international internships; small jobs abroad like working at a restaurant, bar, or hostel; or just flat-out travel, you gain knowledge and experience that cannot be taught in any classroom.

Source: Bryan Goldfinger.

and not a separate legal entity incorporated in the foreign country, the parent company can deduct its losses from its U.S. taxable income. If the foreign entity is a subsidiary, that is, a separate legal entity incorporated in the foreign country, its ownership by the IC may be a minority share, that is, between 10 and 50 percent. Such minority company income, both active (wages) and passive (rent, dividends, royalties), is taxed only when it is remitted to the parent company. If the foreign subsidiary is actually controlled by a parent company that has more than 50 percent ownership, it is known as a *controlled foreign corporation (CFC)*. Its active income is taxed in the United States when that income is remitted to the parent company, but its passive income (royalties, licensing fees, dividends, service fees) is taxed as it occurs.

subsidiary
Separate legal entity owned by the parent company

When deciding where to locate and how to structure a foreign operation, IC managers review the tax rates of possible locations and also consider what legal form their operations should take. Often, start-ups have several years of losses, so the establishment of a branch rather than a subsidiary might generate losses that are valuable for the parent from a tax point of view. Transfer pricing, which we discussed earlier, offers international businesses another way to reduce tax liability.

Some ICs are remarkable for their ability to manage their tax exposure. The *New York Times* reported that GE paid no U.S. taxes in 2010 on U.S. profits of $5.1 billion and actually claimed a tax benefit (for taxes paid in other countries) of $3.2 billion.[11] In ensuing years, GE controlled its U.S. tax liability by not repatriating profits.[12] Reduction of taxes was also one of the reasons for the U.S. pharmaceutical company Pfizer's recent aborted attempt to buy the British firm AstraZeneca PLC. Pfizer planned to move its headquarters abroad and leave New York, saving at least $1 billion in taxes every year. This process, called *inversion*, would have meant moving at least 20 percent of the company's shares to foreign ownership and then establishing a legal home in a low-tax area.[13] In fall 2014, the United States Treasury Department took steps to limit U.S. inversions by reducing their tax-limitation attractiveness. The new regulations constrain the use of corporate cash parked abroad to defer U.S. taxes and make the spinning off of foreign subsidiaries more difficult.[14] The rules limit the extent to which large firms can deduct royalties and interest expenses paid to foreign parents by their U.S. subsidiaries.[15] Some firms that moved offshore through inversions have subsequently considered returning to the United States now that domestic tax rates have been reduced and tax policing has become more rigorous abroad.[16]

SUMMARY

LO 15-1

Outline the major accounting issues international firms face when operating in foreign currencies.

The purpose of international accounting is to provide managers with financial data for use in their decision making and to provide external constituencies (investors, governments, lenders, suppliers, and others) the quantitative information they seek to inform their decisions. Accounting also provides the data governments need to levy taxes. International firms face major accounting issues including those related to foreign currency, such as which values to be used to translate currencies during regular operations and consolidation,

the current rate or the temporal rate, and choosing the functional currency.

Convergence of accounting standards will create a standard for a global market, increase comparability, and allow ICs to list stock in foreign markets, so they could tap into their potential as a source of shareholders. The U.S. approach is a collection of rules and regulations, while the European approach tends to work from principles.

It is helpful to remember that accounting is influenced by culture, because it exists in a context that is influenced by a country's legal, political, and economic systems, as well as the country's history, and its assumptions rest fundamentally on understandings about human behavior and the need to control.

LO 15-2
Outline the benefits and limitations of triple-bottom-line accounting.

Currently, we measure at the economic level and, increasingly more frequently, at the environmental level (as with emission controls and hazardous waste) and at the social level (as with the Equal Employment Opportunity Commission's enforcement of the federal civil rights laws). Yet in the environmental and social areas, we tend to know more about the problems—what is reported in the media—than about the company-level thinking on these important issues. Reporting the triple bottom line, or 3BL, shares the environmental and social effects of the firm's decisions along with the economic ones. This is, in summary, the major benefit of 3BL. Its major limitation is neither a substantive disagreement with the desirability of ecologically responsible business practices that support sustainability nor a disagreement with the idea of business being socially responsible; rather, it is the critics' claim that measurement of these dimensions will not move us closer to the desired state.

LO 15-3
Compare the capital structure choices open to international firms and their significance.

The firm raises capital through its retained earnings, and then, externally, through equity, the issuing of shares, or debt (leveraging). Firms may choose to issue stocks in foreign markets, in part to tap into a broader investor pool, which can raise the stock price and reduce the cost of capital. Debt markets are the other source of capital for the firm, and increasingly the tendency is to tap local markets first. Offshore financial centers, where taxation is low and banking regulations are slim, are also a source of debt financing. Debt financing is usually less expensive than equity financing, but local practices and taxation are also considerations.

LO 15-4
Describe why ICs move funds and the utility of an international finance center.

Firms move funds to pay dividends, royalties, and fees from the subsidiary to the parent company; to make loans from the parent to the subsidiary or among subsidiaries; and to pay for the transfer price of sales between subsidiaries and the parent company. An international finance center can operate as a profit center to balance and hedge currency exposures, tap capital markets, manage inflation rate risk, manage cash management technological innovation, manage derivatives use, handle internal and external invoicing, help a weak-currency subsidiary, and strengthen subsidiary evaluation and reporting systems.

LO 15-5
Identify foreign exchange risks the IC faces and ways to address them.

Unanticipated currency exchange rate movements present risks to the international business. These risks are categorized into three types: transaction exposure, translation exposure, and economic exposure. Transaction exposure occurs when the firm has transactions denominated in a foreign currency. The exposure is due to currency exchange rate fluctuations between the time the commitment is made and when it is payable. Translation exposure arises when subsidiary financial statements are consolidated at the corporate level for the companywide financial reports. Economic exposure is at the operations level and results from exchange rate changes on projected cash flows. Unlike transaction exposure, which addresses the individual transaction, economic exposure is firm-wide and long term.

There are many ways to cover the risk a transaction exposure creates. The company could hedge through leading and lagging, exposure netting, currency options, a forward market hedge, a money market hedge, or a swap. The key goal is to cover the exposure to foreign currency. (The company could avoid transaction exposure altogether by refusing to enter into foreign currency contracts.) Translation exposure is another story. Many organizations do not hedge translation exposure because translation gains and losses do not represent cash flows. Also, hedging a translation exposure can actually increase transaction exposure. Economic exposure is a result of firm-wide long-term decisions and external forces. Its management draws on the hedging and swap contracts we have discussed as ways to manage transaction exposure, on flexibility in sourcing, and on a portfolio approach to foreign market involvement.

LO 15-6
Describe taxation as an international financial force.

Taxation is an external financial force that affects decisions international managers make because it affects revenues. There are three major types of taxes governments use: income, value-added, and withholding.

KEY TERMS

American depository receipts (ADRs) 418
branch 427
consolidation 413
currency option hedge 425
current rate method 413
economic exposure 427
forward market hedge 424

fronting loan 420
functional currency 413
hedge 422
income tax 427
leading and lagging 423
money market hedge 425
multilateral netting 422
offshore financial center 418

subsidiary 429
swap contract 425
temporal method 413
transaction exposure 424
transfer pricing 420
translation exposure 425
value-added tax (VAT) 427
withholding tax 427

CRITICAL THINKING QUESTIONS

1. The only difference between accounting in the domestic arena and accounting in the international one is that international transactions may be in foreign currencies that have to be translated into dollars. Comment on this observation.

2. How might you expect the practice of accounting to be different in another country?

3. Does the process of convergence of accounting standards present any benefits to U.S. firms that already operate internationally?

4. How might adopting triple-bottom-line accounting influence the competitiveness of U.S. firms in foreign markets?

5. You are a CFO establishing your firm's first overseas subsidiary. As you consider how to capitalize your business, what are your concerns about using the local and home-country debt and equity markets?

6. A local business new to exporting has signed a sales contract with a buyer in Riyadh that specifies payment of $3 million in Saudi riyals in six months.

Discuss the hedge options you would advise the exporter to consider.

7. One of the characteristics of centralized structures is that they are slow and reduce innovation. Given that a globalized business needs increasingly quick responses, why would an MNC set up a centralized cash management operation?

8. U.S. corporations use three major tactics to keep their tax bills low: they avoid repatriating their foreign earnings; they are careful about how they organize their foreign operations; and they have explored inversions. Which of these tactics would you choose to be the most reliable for the corporation?

9. Could transaction exposure be avoided if the revenues generated by foreign sales were transferred to the home company's currency at the end of every business day?

10. When accounting systems are fully harmonized and convergence is achieved, will the company's functional currency matter? Why or why not?

globalEDGE RESEARCH TASK   http://globalEDGE.msu.edu/

Use the globalEDGE website (http://globalEDGE.msu.edu/) to complete the following exercises:

1. Your company had some difficulties *paying taxes* in some of the international markets it operates due to challenges in the taxation systems in place. Therefore, your manager has assigned you the task of analyzing countries to find out how easy it is to pay taxes. Choose a country of your choice under the "Global Insights" section of globalEDGE and find the most relevant indicator/index in the "Indices" page you can utilize for this purpose. Review the "Heat Map" to see how countries are ranked and visit the external link to learn more.

Prepare a summary of your findings to explain how the rankings are calculated and what indicators are used and present the highest and lowest ranked countries.

2. As the CFO of your global company, which frequently exports products to Australia, you are requested to a presentation to the top executives about the payment methods, the banking system, and the foreign exchange controls in Australia. Visit the *Country Commercial Guide* of Australia and review the "Trade & Project Financing" section. Prepare a summary of your findings for your presentation.

MINICASE

DEALING WITH TRANSACTION RISK IN A RENMINBI CONTRACT

You are the finance manager of a U.S. multinational firm that has sold US$6 million of high-tech product to a Chinese importer. Because of stiff competition for the contract with European and other U.S. companies, you agreed that the negotiators could sign a renminbi-based contract, although this is not standard practice for your firm.

The sales contract calls for the Chinese importer to make three equal payments at 6, 12, and 18 months from the date of delivery, which is in 60 days. Your plan is to translate the renminbi to dollars on their receipt; your company has no operations in China and no need for Chinese currency. You realize, though, that this arrangement incurs transaction exposure. How could you cover this risk?

NOTES

1. Quote by Sophocles.

2. Ryan Teeter, "Worldwide Accounting Diversity," https://www.youtube.com/watch?v=qsvpB7wijo4, accessed November 11, 2018; and Timothy Doupnik, and Hector Perera, *International Accounting*, 3rd ed., Chapter 2, New York, McGraw-Hill, 2011.

3. Sidney J. Gray, "Towards a Theory of Cultural Influence on the Development of Accounting Systems Internationally," *Abacus*, vol. 24, no. 1, 1998, 1–15.

4. John Elkington, *Cannibals with Forks: The Triple Bottom Line of 21st Century Business*, Gabriola Island, BC, Canada: New Society Publishers, 1997.

5. Wayne Norman, and Chris McDonald, "Getting to the Bottom of Triple Bottom Line," *Business Ethics Quarterly*, vol. 14, no. 2, 243–262.

6. A good example of this is the energy company BP. For years it ran an advertising campaign based on the company's sensitivity to the environment. In fact, BP's observed behavior through crises in the first decade of the 21st century in Texas, Alaska, and the Gulf of Mexico shows different priorities: 1993–1995, Hazardous substance dumping in Alaska; 2006–2007, Prudhoe Bay Alaska pipeline corrosion; 2010, Texas City chemical leak (two weeks before oil spill); and 2010 Gulf of Mexico Oil Spill (https://en.wikipedia.org/wiki/BP).

7. Timothy F. Slaper, and Tanya J. Hall, "The Triple Bottom Line: What Is It and How Does It Work?" *Indiana Business Review*, vol. 86, no. 1, Spring 2011, http://www.ibrc.indiana.edu, accessed November 11, 2018.

8. John P. Barker, John B. Bellinger III, Charles A. Blanchard, Ronald D. Lee, Claire E. Reads, Nancy L. Perkins, and Nicholas L. Townsend, "CFIUS Scrutiny of Foreign Investment Intensifies with Broadening Scope," https://www.arnoldporter.com, accessed November 11, 2018.

9. Quote by Warren Buffett.

10. Daniel Mitchell, "Job Creation and the Taxation of Foreign Earned Income," *Executive Memorandum*, vol. 911, The Heritage Foundation, 2004.

11. David Kocieniewski, "G.E.'s Strategies Let It Avoid Taxes Altogether," *The New York Times*, https://www.nytimes.com, accessed November 11, 2018.

12. Kevin Drawbaugh, and Patrick Temple-West, "Many Big U.S. Corporations Pay Very Little in Taxes: Study," *Reuters*, https://www.reuters.com, accessed November 11, 2018.

13. Liz Hoffman, "Pfizer Sees Tax Savings from Deal, Leaving U.S.," *The Wall Street Journal*, https://www.wsj.com, accessed November 11, 2018.

14. John McKinnon, and Damian Paletta, "The Obama Administration Issues New Rules to Combat Tax Inversions," *The Wall Street Journal*, https://www.wsj.com, accessed November 11, 2018.

15. Jonathan D. Rockoff, and Nina Trentmann, "New Tax Law Haunts Companies That Did 'Inversion' Deals," *The Wall Street Journal*, https://www.wsj.com, accessed November 11, 2018.

16. David Morgan, "U.S. Tax Cuts Prompt Rethink by Some 'Inverted' Companies," *Reuters*, https://www.cnbc.com, accessed November 11, 2018.

A International Institutions from a Business Perspective

> ❝No institution can possibly survive if it needs geniuses or supermen to manage it. It must be organized in such a way as to be able to get along under a leadership composed of average human beings.❞
>
> —Peter Drucker[1]

Issouf Sanogo/AFP/Getty Images.

LEARNING OBJECTIVES

After reading this module, you should be able to:

LO A-1   **Explain** the importance of major international institutions to business decision makers.

LO A-2   **Describe** institutions, drawing on new institutional theory.

LO A-3   **Describe** the United Nations as an institution and its relevance to international managers.

LO A-4   **Describe** the purposes of the two monetary institutions, the IMF and the World Bank.

LO A-5   **Discuss** the resources of the Organisation for Economic Co-operation and Development and the World Trade Organization.

LO A-6   **Identify** the types of trading blocs by their level of economic integration, with examples.

United Nations Peacekeeping: An Institution at Work

The United Nations (UN) became involved in peace-keeping in 1948 when the UN Security Council sent military observers to the Middle East to monitor the armistice agreement between Israel and Arab nations. Then in 1949, the United Nations was called on again to monitor the ceasefire between India and Pakistan. The job was to monitor and observe truces, and peacekeepers were mostly unarmed.

These first two peacekeeping operations took place during the Cold War, when the UN Security Council was unable to make decisions because two of its five permanent members, who hold veto power—the United States and Russia (the others being China, France, and the United Kingdom)—could not come to an agreement on ways to respond to crises. Peacekeeping operations were a way for the UN to monitor and stabilize tense, dangerous situations when the Security Council was unable to pass a resolution.

Sometimes the peacekeeping forces have taken a more active, armed role. In the 1956 Suez Crisis, when Israel, France, and Britain invaded Egypt in response to Egyptian President Nasser's nationalization of the Suez Canal, the Security Council again could not decide on action. This time, France and Britain vetoed resolutions calling for them to withdraw from Egypt. In response to this deadlock, the General Assembly held its first emergency session and passed a resolution for a ceasefire (997 ES-1). The Assembly sent in the first UN Emergency Force to expedite withdrawals, an arms embargo, and a clearing of the Suez Canal so that it could be reopened. The troops went only to the Egyptian side of the demarcation line because Israel refused to allow UN troops on its territory. Under this pressure from the United Nations, with the Soviet Union and the United States jointly and strongly backing it, Britain,

France, and Israel withdrew from Egypt. The way the United Nations worked, in this case, was exactly the way it was designed to: a peacekeeping operation was carried out with the consent of the parties to the conflict. The peacekeepers had a force of 6,000, from Brazil, Canada, Colombia, Denmark, Finland, India, Indonesia, Norway, Sweden, and Yugoslavia. They lost 109 peacekeepers in the Suez operation.

Since 1956, the UN peacekeeping force has been called on to support peace in some of the most dangerous and difficult conflicts on our globe. In the past decade, it has generally protected civilians rather than monitoring and observing truces, as in the early involvements, or entering a conflict directly, as in the Suez Crisis. For example, during the civil war in Côte d'Ivoire which divided that nation in half, the United Nations in 2004 deployed more than 6,000 peacekeepers, eventually increasing the number to 11,792 in 2011. The peacekeepers protected civilians, promoted inclusive political discussions between the warring parties, and provided support to the Ivorian government in demobilizing, disarming, and reintegrating former combatants before departing the country. As a result, Côte d'Ivoire became a safer nation that has emerged as one of the most rapidly growing economies in Africa, achieving annual growth of over 9 percent.

The peacekeepers aim to provide the difference between war and peace: security, justice, stability, and human rights. See the UN video at https://www.youtube.com/watch?v=jAXVbtdBu10&feature=share&list=PL49CE20981558F582&index=1.

Sources: "Our Successes," *United Nations Peacekeeping*, June 30, 2017, www.peacekeeping.un.org; "UN Peacekeeping," *Better World Campaign*, 2018, www.betterworldcampaign.org; and "Past Peacekeeping Operations," *United Nations Peacekeeping*, 2018, www.peacekeeping.un.org.

In a world where the atmosphere is warming, the global economy lurches from crisis to crisis, and massively destructive civil wars erupt, we need to learn how to use our global institutions better, because our problems are too complex for individual nations to solve. So says Mark Malloch Brown, former deputy secretary-general of the United Nations, in his book *The Unfinished Global Revolution*, a call for institutions to rise to meet the challenges we face.[2] Brown's main point is of special note: as the world becomes more closely connected, it becomes less governable at the national level.

What are international institutions and how do they influence the firm? We explore these questions in this module and then examine the institutions most important to the international manager, beginning with those that focus on global cooperation (such as the United Nations, the World Trade Organization, and the International Monetary Fund) and then those whose concerns are mainly regional (such as trade alliances).

LO A-1
Explain the importance of major international institutions to business decision makers.

What Are Institutions, and Why Are They Useful?

Strong institutions are important for international decision makers because they allow for problem solving before confrontations reach the level of overt hostility. For example, consider the roles of China and the United States on the global stage: one is a superpower, the other a rapidly developing nation moving into a major global role. They must cooperate.[3] Yet look at their differences: one is a democracy, the other an autocracy; one is "a child of the enlightenment,"[4] the other an emerging industrial empire. Although working together will not be easy for either country, international institutions such as the World Trade Organization and the United Nations encourage such efforts and make them more likely to succeed because they develop multilateral solutions in which all nations collaborate. Institutions shift the frame of the communication between nations, so it is cooperative and not a matter of *us versus them*. Will the United States be ready to accept a solution to an issue China has raised about trade between the two nations that is worked out in the World Trade Organization, where members cooperate to solve problems, than if Washington negotiated with China directly, putting international status and "face" at stake, with winners and losers?

Institutions are important to business decision makers because they provide ways to settle conflict and resolve disagreements. They also provide support and infrastructure for decision makers. Before we go on to examine these institutions, we take a look at recent institutional theory.

LO A-2
Describe institutions, drawing on new institutional theory.

Institutional Theory

Institutions are organizations that a group, society, or culture construct to "provide stability and meaning to social life,"[5] a collection of norms that "regulate the relations of individuals to each other."[6] Consider the institutions you deal with daily and how they contribute to the structure of your life. School, government, religious groups, sports groups—the list could go on—all help us give meaning to and build stability in our social lives. Institutions are socially constructed—meaning a group, society, or culture builds them—and they *limit* behavior. This approach to understanding institutions, called **new institutional theory**, suggests that institutions are important for business because they provide the basic rules and codes of conduct, written and unwritten, that limit and direct the decisions firms can make. In a way, they provide managers with the *rules of the game*, thereby reducing uncertainty in the firm's external environment.[7]

new institutional theory
Understanding of institutions as social constructs, a collection of norms that structure the relations of individuals to one another

TYPES OF INSTITUTIONS

Scholars have identified two basic types of institutions, formal and informal, a distinction that provides a helpful way of thinking about subtleties in the practice of international business.

Formal Institutions **Formal institutions** operate through laws and regulations to influence behavior. Any organization that uses the threat of force to achieve compliance is formal, such as a government, the police, and even a club that threatens sanctions if members fail to observe club rules. We often comply with the norms of formal institutions for fear of reprisal.

formal institutions
Institutions that influence behavior through laws and regulations

Informal Institutions **Informal institutions** use norms, values, customs, and ideologies to mold behavior rather than laws.[8] Much of our social behavior is the result of norms and customs. Conventional good manners are a part of the informal institution of

informal institutions
Institutions that influence behavior through norms, values, customs, and ideologies

social interaction that reduces ambiguity in our social interactions, for example. There is no legal penalty for noncompliance, yet we conform in order to fit in. Many professional organizations that establish processes and standards are informal institutions. In accounting, no police enforce standards. We follow the conventions of the generally accepted accounting principles (GAAP) not because we'll go to jail if we don't, but because there is wide agreement that these principles are the best way to ensure professionalism and keep the discipline strong, or because we don't want to be seen as not fulfilling a social obligation to conform.

Informal institutions can be further divided, based on their main focus, into normative and cognitive entities. Informal *normative* institutions establish standards, "propagate principles, and broadly represent 'humanity.'"[9] Professional organizations and nongovernmental organizations (NGOs) that influence behavior through shared norms and values are examples of normative institutions. GAAP, the American Institute of Chartered Public Accountants (AICPA), the United Nations, and the World Trade Organization (WTO) are examples of informal normative institutions. UN members agree to abide by the UN's resolutions because they have publicly committed to doing so; they have accepted social obligations.

The informal *cognitive institution* is also important to the international manager. Cognitive institutions are collections of shared ideas that define reality by means of conceptual frameworks, or schema, that are usually neither explicit nor tangible. Examples abound, including duty, motherhood, good manners, and gender roles. In fact, cultures themselves are collections of cognitive institutions, the invisible aggregations of norms and values that often lie hidden in our minds without our explicit awareness. A lack of understanding of cognitive institutions contributes greatly to the challenges international managers face. Because informal cognitive institutions are so important, we look at two examples here: the Chinese concept of *guanxi* and the understanding of the supplier relationship found in Japanese and U.S. business practices.

Guanxi (guan-SHEE) is a Chinese collection of values, an informal cognitive institution that describes a relationship combining social capital and mentoring. *Guanxi* relationships carry obligations that may be stronger than civic responsibilities and seemingly rational understandings of business situations. From a Western perspective, these relationships may be difficult to understand, and the observed behaviors of delivering on a *guanxi* obligation, which may be inaccurately construed by outsiders as conferring favoritism, might not make sense to someone without knowledge of the cognitive institution. Yet, they make perfect psychological and moral sense to the Chinese businessperson. When it comes to cognitive institutions of a foreign culture, remember that you don't know what you don't know. Postpone attributing meaning while you seek advice from a trusted local.

Two additional examples of cognitive institutions that often influence international managers are found in Japanese and U.S. supplier relationships, which contrast greatly. Remember that institutions set the rules of the game. The "supplier game" in Japan calls for the supplier to build a trusting relationship with the potential buyer. Such a relationship allows both firms to learn about one another's reliability and organizational cultures, both of which may be important in a crisis. Price is not likely to be high on the Japanese list of criteria in the purchase decision.

In contrast, in supplier relationships in the United States, the game is played differently. Price plays a more prominent initial role and at times may be the top criterion in the purchase decision. In addition, the U.S. custom is to share drinks *after* the deal is sealed because drinks are a reward, a celebration. In Japan, the drinks occur *before* the deal occurs, as a way to build the relationship, and they are continued during and after, as part of relationship maintenance.

CULTURE FACTS @internationalbiz

Cultures are vast collections of cognitive institutions that are invisible to the outsider, so learning about them and how to operate within them are complex challenges for the international business manager. #cognitiveinstitutions #invisible #complexchallenges

CULTURE FACTS @internationalbiz

As an example of a cognitive institution at work, Westerners unaware of Japanese cultural values sometimes misunderstand the Japanese interest in getting to know suppliers before striking a deal as an attempt to exert undue influence on the deal's terms. Westerners are thinking mainly about price, while the Japanese are thinking about building relationships, especially trust. #westerners #japaneseculturalvalues #buildingrelationships #trust

Much of the behavior we see in supplier relationships in Japan and the United States reflects these different understandings, but nowhere are the rules of these "games" written out in procurement guidelines. You know the approach of your firm, and you may think it is normal, even though you may be aware of the differences. The behaviors that contribute to establishing a supplier relationship are institutionalized and usually operate below our level of awareness because, if we are members of the culture, we know how the game is played. If we are outsiders, we are not aware of these rules, and we see behavior that may seem unusual or puzzling. Cognitive institutions around supplier relationships in both Japan and the United States have evolved to limit behavior choices and reduce uncertainty. Being aware that they might exist gives the international manager an advantage in understanding a trading partner's actions.

These examples illustrate that informal institutions operate a bit like the mind's software, as Geert Hofstede observed.[10] They can exert a powerful influence on how decision makers in the firm understand their environment, and thus on the choices open to the firm in international activities. Scholar Mike Peng notes that in developing economies, informal institutions tend to play a greater role than in developed economies. He suggests that informal institutions emerge to bring added order to the chaotic, unstructured environment in the developing economy, which lacks well-developed formal institutions.[11]

Richard Scott developed the framework we use to describe the types of institutions international managers encounter. Figure A.1 describes these types of institutions in more detail, including the basis of compliance to their rules or norms, the way they institutionalize, their inherent logic, the basis of their legitimacy, and their indicators or evidence.[12] Figure A.2 illustrates how institutions influence firms, managers, and the behavior of firms.

We now take a closer look at some of the major international institutions that are important to international business, beginning with the United Nations and then moving to international monetary institutions like the World Trade Organization, the Organisation for Economic Co-operation and Development, and the various groups created by economic integration agreements.

FIGURE A.1 New Institutional Theory: Characteristics of Institutions

Institution type:	Formal	Informal	
Social agreement is:	**Regulative**	**Normative**	**Cognitive**
Compliance based on	Expedience	Social obligation	Predisposition (taken for granted)
Institutionalization based on	Coercion	Norms	Imitation
Logic based on	Means to an end	Appropriateness	Conformance, orthodoxy
Legitimacy based on	Legal enforcement	Moral governance	Cultural support, concept correctness
Indicators/ Evidence	Rules, laws, sanctions,	Certification, accreditation	Prevalence, similarity

(Attributes)

Source: J. McNett after W. R. Scott, *Institutions and Organizations*, Thousand Oaks, CA: Sage, 1995, 10.

FIGURE A.2 Influence of Institutions on Firms, Managers, and Firm Behavior

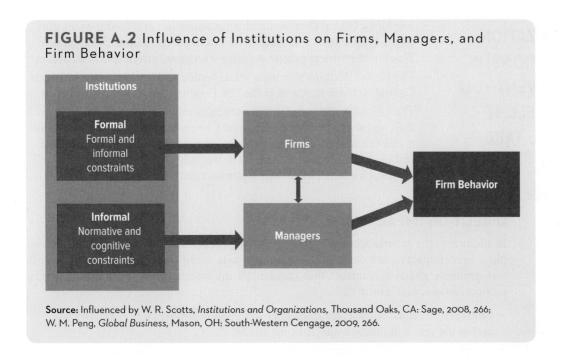

Source: Influenced by W. R. Scotts, *Institutions and Organizations*, Thousand Oaks, CA: Sage, 2008, 266; W. M. Peng, *Global Business*, Mason, OH: South-Western Cengage, 2009, 266.

The United Nations

The United Nations (UN) is probably the best-known worldwide organization, and its 193 member-nations (nearly all the countries in the world) are dedicated to the promotion of peace and global stability. Given its stabilizing force in the world economy, the United Nations contributes to creating the conditions under which international business thrives. Many of its activities affect business and the infrastructure on which business operations depend. As an institution, the United Nations operates with voluntary agreements among members based on their shared norms, an informal normative institution.

GENERAL UN SUPPORT OF BUSINESS

The United Nations is responsible for international agreements that affect commercial relationships, including much of the body of international law. Here are some general areas, often not recognized, in which the United Nations plays a significant role in international business:

- UN agreements set technical standards and norms. These standards and norms function as the "soft infrastructure" for the global economy. The United Nations Center for Trade Facilitation and Electronic Business (UN/CEFACT) has standardized trade documents and developed standards for electronic data exchange.

- UN efforts prepare the ground for investment in emerging economies and the development of their workforce through a focus on areas such as health, education, governance, and political stability. The United Nations Educational, Scientific and Cultural Organization (UNESCO) promotes literacy for the world's approximately 775 million adults and children over 15 who cannot read and write. About 8.5 percent of the world's youth cannot read and write.[13]

- Various UN agencies address the downsides of globalization, such as terrorism, crime, drugs, and arms traffic. Treaties have been developed that focus on terrorist activities such as the taking of hostages so that agreed-upon responses among UN members exist.

- UN efforts to seek solutions to global environmental problems include the work of the UN Environment Programme (UNEP), the agency that laid the groundwork for the Climate Change Convention, leading to the 1997 Kyoto Protocol to reduce greenhouse gases, which came into effect in 2005. The UNEP has developed many initiatives that support sustainable business practices.

LO A-3
Describe the United Nations as an institution and its relevance to international managers.

United Nations (UN)
Organization of 193 countries dedicated to the promotion of peace and stability of the world

> **"THIS ORGANIZATION [THE UNITED NATIONS] IS CREATED to PREVENT YOU from GOING to HELL. IT ISN'T CREATED to TAKE YOU to HEAVEN."**
>
> *—Henry Cabot Lodge, Jr.*[14]

- The UN's Global Compact addresses education and health issues that require global-level solutions arrived at in partnership with businesses. This effort partners private industry with groups in developing nations.
- The United Nations promotes social justice and human and labor rights. Central to these concerns is the UN Economic and Social Council.
- The United Nations builds the cornerstones of an interdependent world: trust and shared values. The Global Compact, a sustainability initiative, is one example of this. The Global Compact provides a framework for sustainable business based on 10 universally accepted principles in areas such as the environment, human rights, labor, and anticorruption.

DIRECT UN IMPACT ON BUSINESS

In addition to the general areas of impact on business described above, the United Nations has a direct impact on the conduct of business in quite specific ways because UN committees negotiate global agreements that standardize the international exchanges of goods, services, money, and information.

- Ships are protected by rules legitimized in UN conferences when they sail freely across the seas and through international straits.
- Commercial airlines have the right to fly across borders, and to land in case of emergency, due to agreements negotiated by the International Civil Aviation Organization, part of the UN system.
- The World Health Organization sets criteria for pharmaceutical quality and standardizes drug names.
- Universal Postal Union protocols prevent losses and allow the mail to move across borders.
- The International Telecommunication Union allotment of frequencies keeps the airwaves from becoming hopelessly clogged, thus avoiding interference among radio transmissions.
- Data collected and redistributed from member-states by the World Meteorological Organization make possible worldwide and country-specific weather forecasts.
- The UN Sales Convention and the UN Convention on the Carriage of Goods by Sea help establish rights and obligations for buyers and sellers in international commercial transactions.

In terms of direct business engagement with the United Nations, the site https://business.un.org lists collaborations with business, so you can see how many firms, including Ikea, Intel, Philips, and Bank of America, partner with the United Nations. Now that we've seen the United Nations from a business perspective, we look briefly at its structure.

UN ORGANIZATION

General Assembly
Deliberative body of the United Nations made up of all member-nations, each with one vote regardless of size, wealth, or power

Security Council
Main peacekeeping body of the United Nations, composed of 15 members including 5 permanent members

The work of the United Nations is carried out through five bodies, called *organs*, in UN terminology. All UN member-nations belong to the **General Assembly**, the main deliberative body in which each nation has one vote regardless of its size, wealth, or power. The General Assembly adopts resolutions that express the will of the member-nations. These decisions are normative and carry the heavy weight of world opinion, yet they have no legally binding force for governments or citizens of the member-nations. The 73rd session of the General Assembly met in September 2018, and its open meetings are available via webcast. The *Journal of the United Nations* reports the daily business of the General Assembly, available at https://journal.un.org in the six UN languages: Arabic, Chinese, English, French, Russian, and Spanish.

The UN **Security Council** has the responsibility for maintaining international peace and security. Its membership is 5 permanent members—China, France, the Russian Federation, the United Kingdom, and the United States—each having veto power, and 10 nonpermanent

The UN Security Council in session. Note the room's circular arrangement. ©lev radin/Alamy Stock Photo.

members elected by the General Assembly and representing specific regions. Historian Mark Mazower argues that the Security Council was established by the Allies to ensure their continued political and economic domination after WWII, and that it has achieved just the opposite, the support of minorities and human rights.[15] Currently, the Security Council's peacekeeping operations are active in 16 locations in Africa, Europe, Asia and the Pacific, the Caribbean, and the Middle East.[16]

The **Economic and Social Council (ECOSOC)** is concerned with issues you would expect from its name: trade, transport, industrialization, economic development, population growth, children, housing, women's rights, racial discrimination, illegal drugs, crime, social welfare, youth, the human environment, and food. ECOSOC makes recommendations on how to improve education and health conditions and promotes human rights and freedom of people everywhere. These actions contribute to the development of a high-quality workforce across nations.

The **International Court of Justice (ICJ)**, also known as the *World Court*, makes legal decisions involving disputes between national governments and gives advisory opinions. Because only nations litigate before the court, governments often intervene on behalf of corporations and individuals in their countries. Even though the court has worldwide jurisdiction to hear disputes between governments, it hears relatively few cases. There are currently 2 cases being heard and 17 pending.[17] Current cases involve a range of issues, including territorial disputes (e.g., Somalia vs. Kenya, Chile vs. Bolivia, Nicaragua vs. Columbia), relocation of the U.S. embassy to Jerusalem (Palestine vs. the United States), and armed aggression and genocide (e.g., the Democratic Republic of the Congo vs. Uganda). The ICJ, headquartered in The Hague, Netherlands, has 15 judges from different countries elected by the General Assembly and Security Council, serving nine-year terms.

The **Secretariat**, headed by the secretary-general of the United Nations, is the UN's staff. The General Assembly appoints the secretary-general on the recommendation of the Security Council for a five-year renewable term. The ninth secretary-general, António Guterres of Portugal, began his term in 2017. About 40,000 people from around the world made up the UN Secretariat staff at the end of 2017.[18]

Economic and Social Council (ECOSOC)
UN body concerned with economic and social issues such as trade, development, education, and human rights

International Court of Justice (ICJ)
UN body that makes legal decisions involving disputes between national governments

Secretariat
The staff of the United Nations, headed by the secretary-general

"EVERY INSTITUTION NOT ONLY CARRIES within IT THE SEEDS of ITS OWN DISSOLUTION, but PREPARES THE WAY for ITS MOST HATED RIVAL."

—Dean William R. Inge, 1860–1954, dean of St Paul's, London[19]

That is a brief picture of the United Nations. Some of its activities are quite significant for international managers. You also might note that the United Nations and its agencies spread around the globe could be interesting institutions in which to begin an international career.

International Monetary Institutions

LO A-4
Describe the purposes of the two monetary institutions, the IMF and the World Bank.

Bretton Woods
1944 conference at which Allied nations' treasury and central bank representatives met to establish the International Monetary Fund and the World Bank

International Monetary Fund (IMF)
Institution that fosters global monetary cooperation, financial stability, international trade, high employment and sustainable economic growth, and reduction of poverty

World Bank
Institution that lends money for development projects focused on reducing poverty

There are two major global monetary institutions, the International Monetary Fund and the World Bank, both established at the UN-convened conference held at Bretton Woods, New Hampshire, in 1944. Representatives of 44 nations allied against the Axis Powers (Germany, Italy, and Japan) met near the end of World War II to work on monetary issues. Bretton Woods, as the resulting agreement is known, is significant because it was the world's first negotiated agreement among independent nations to support trade through monetary institutions. The meetings set up the two major global monetary institutions, the International Monetary Fund (IMF), to establish rules for international monetary policies and their enforcement, and the World Bank, to lend countries money for development.

INTERNATIONAL MONETARY FUND

The premise of the International Monetary Fund, which operates as a collaboration of nations, is that the common interest of all nations in a workable international monetary system far transcends their conflicting national interests.[20] The IMF promotes international monetary cooperation, including orderly exchange rate arrangements and payments systems, and makes funds available for balance-of-payments corrections.

Although the IMF officially deals solely with governments, it also collaborates with many other international institutions, especially monetary institutions and organizations that share similar interests, such as the United Nations, trade unions, nongovernmental organizations, governments, religious organizations, and other civic groups, in order to build financial stability to create the conditions necessary to reduce poverty. IMF policies and actions have a profound impact on international business worldwide.

Each of the 189 IMF members contributes funds, known as *quotas*, determined by the nation's relative size in the world economy. The nation's quota also determines its number of votes for IMF decision making. Currently, the quota formula is a weighted average of GDP (50 percent), openness (30 percent), economic variability (15 percent), and international reserves (5 percent).[21] Quotas are continuously under review in order to reflect changes in developing countries. Under the present quota system, China has 6.09 percent of the total votes, while the United States has 16.52 percent, Germany 5.32, and Japan 6.15.[22]

special drawing rights (SDRs)
An international reserve asset established by the IMF

Special Drawing Rights Special drawing rights (SDRs) are a reserve asset established by the IMF, its "currency," so to speak. SDRs are also the IMF's unit of account, so quotas are denominated in SDRs. They are an interesting creation, like a paperless currency, except—and this is the interesting part—they are not a claim on the IMF. Rather, they are a claim on the currencies of IMF members. The SDR's value is linked to a basket of currencies made up of five international currencies: the euro, Japanese yen, pound sterling, Chinese renminbi, and U.S. dollar.[23] The exchange equivalent of the SDR for these four currencies is posted daily on the IMF's website; the SDR dollar value on November 18, 2018, was $1.382320.[24] The aggregate quotas form a pool of money used to fund IMF lending. The United States has the largest IMF quota (or dues); currently, 17.46 percent or SDR 83.0 billion (about $114.7 billion), and the Polynesian island nation of Tuvalu has the smallest, at 0.0001 percent or SDR 1.8 million (about $2.5 million).[25]

par value
Stated value

IMF and Exchange Rates The IMF Articles of Agreement, which took effect in 1945, set up fixed exchange rates among member-nations' currencies, with par value or stated value based on gold and the U.S. dollar, valued at $35 per ounce of gold. Previously, the gold standard, which used gold as the common denominator among currencies, had undergone severe pressure caused by increasing demand in the face of stable supplies, especially during the Great Depression (1929–1933). In the Bretton Woods system, par value for the British pound was set at US$2.40, the French franc at US$0.18, and the German mark at US$0.2732. There was an understanding that the U.S. government would redeem dollars for gold and that the dollar was the only currency to be redeemable for gold. This system, which lasted from 1944 to 1971, was a dollar-based gold exchange standard in which the U.S. dollar became both a means of international payment and a reserve currency. President Nixon took the United States off the gold standard in 1971 when he closed the gold window at the U.S. Treasury, where people would queue to exchange currency for gold. Today, as the IMF struggles with core issues related to its purpose in a changing world, some economists think that it might play a renewed role with exchange rates, offering a buffer to the market's volatile movements.

Criticism of the IMF The IMF has been widely criticized. The Nobel economist Joseph Stiglitz, who has served as chief economist of the World Bank and sees many potentially positive aspects to globalization, wrote *Globalization and Its Discontents* to explain his critique of the IMF, along with the World Bank and the World Trade Organization. In the 1980s, when Ronald Reagan and Margaret Thatcher advocated free markets in the United States and the United Kingdom, they used the IMF and the World Bank as "missionary institutions" through which they forced free-market policies on poor countries that badly needed IMF loans.[26] True, the financial leaders of the developing countries cooperated, but Stiglitz points out that they hardly had a choice, given the high levels of poverty and their drastic need for funding. These IMF loans increased both poverty and political and social chaos.

Stiglitz cites Bolivia, and after the 1997 Asian crisis, Indonesia and Thailand as examples where the IMF got it wrong. He points out that neither IMF nor World Bank leadership represents the nations they serve, and that development experience is not a prerequisite for either leadership position. By custom, the IMF managing director is a European, and the World Bank president, an American. Currently, Christine Lagarde, a lawyer and former French finance minister, is the managing director of the IMF, while Jim Yong Kim, a Korean American physician and anthropologist, heads the World Bank. Some of the IMF criticism does seem deserved, and the IMF, in its response, appears to be intent on learning from its mistakes.

Current IMF Issues In its support of international monetary cooperation, the IMF works to help nations manage the risks inherent in globalization, such as globalized capital markets, whose unpredictable and rapid changes challenge economies. IMF economists focus on providing technical assistance with exchange rate issues, macroeconomic policy and financial sector stability, serving as a lender of last resort. And therein lies one of the IMF's problems.

IMF aid is often tied to a country's following IMF advice for achieving increased financial stability. This advice—which isn't advice but rather a loan condition—frequently includes the requirement to reduce both budget deficits and inflation. Such measures, monetarist in their approach in that they focus on the money supply, tend to increase local poverty immediately in the short term. They also get in the way of significant progress in longer-term areas of social development, such as public health, poverty reduction, and education. For example, when past borrowers took IMF advice to devalue their currency, it created domestic problems such as political unrest resulting from increased poverty. China argues this IMF approach was the leading cause of Japan's decline as a global power.[27] IMF intervention has also led to significant social unrest, as in Argentina and Kenya.

The IMF is also in the midst of a stand-off between Western countries and the larger developing countries, frustrated with their limited influence and voice in the IMF. The political economists Wade and Vestergaard recently pointed out that the BRIC economies (Brazil, Russia, India, and China) produced 22.9 percent of the world's GDP in 2017, while the four largest European economies (Germany, France, the United Kingdom, and Italy) yielded 13.4 percent combined.[28] The BRICs have 13.54 percent of the IMF vote power, while the four European economies weigh in at 16.40 percent.[29] One of the stumbling blocks to a more equitable quota reform is a difference between the U.S. and European view on how quotas should be determined. The United States supports an increased role for GDP, which would mean increased quotas for many developing economies, while the Europeans argue that these nations need to increase their transparency and democratic approaches. Discussions have reportedly reached a stalemate.

Some have criticized the IMF's role in helping to strengthen the economies of dictatorial regimes, thereby contributing to the growth of markets attractive to U.S. and European multinational firms. This critique appears to be accurate. The IMF does not apply a political litmus test when it acts, but rather an economic one.

The IMF appears to have recognized at least partial validity of these criticisms and is addressing them. Figure A.3 illustrates a map of the IMF global growth forecasts.

THE WORLD BANK

The World Bank was established along with the IMF at the Bretton Woods meeting in order to address economic development. Organized into two major and three smaller institutions, it functions as a nonprofit cooperative for its member-nations, able to pass on to developing nations its ability to borrow funds at low rates. Nations choose to join World Bank Group institutions by need. The two major institutions, the International Bank for Reconstruction and

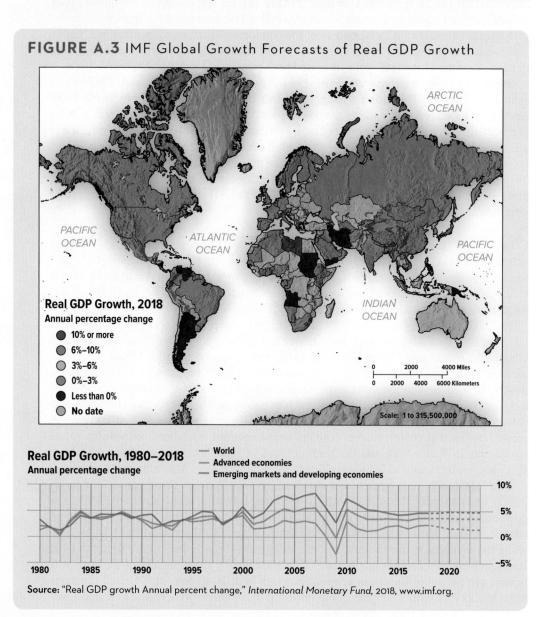

FIGURE A.3 IMF Global Growth Forecasts of Real GDP Growth

Source: "Real GDP growth Annual percent change," *International Monetary Fund*, 2018, www.imf.org.

The Kajaki hydroelectric dam, which will provide power and irrigation for Afghanistan's Helmand Province, was funded by USAID and the World Bank. U.S. State Department/Alamy Stock Photo.

Development (IBRD)—known simply as the World Bank—and the International Development Association (IDA) have 189 and 173 members, respectively.[30] Both institutions lend to countries to support development as a way to reduce poverty. The IBRD's focus is on middle-income nations with GDPs from $1,000 to $10,000 per capita, where 70 percent of the world's poor are located, and on creditworthy poor nations. The IDA helps the world's 75 poorest nations, 39 of which are in Africa, and represents the largest single source of donor funds for basic social services in these nations.[31] IDA provides interest-free loans and grants for development projects in areas such as water, sanitation and flood protection, transportation, health, education, agriculture, and law and justice.

Begun in 1960, IDA can take a long view, with many projects having a 25- to 45-year payback period, saving lives and improving standards of living for hundreds of thousands of people. In the fiscal year of 2018, IDA commitments reached a total of $24 billion, including guarantees, including about $5 billion in grants.[32] The healthy growth of the nations targeted for IDA commitments is important to business because millions of people are joining the world economy as their living standard rises. Developing nations account for more than half the increase in import demand since 2000. At the World Bank interactive map (http://maps.worldbank.org/p2e/mcmap/map.html) you can find map, satellite, and hybrid views of current World Bank projects. The World Bank projects underway to reduce poverty are impressive.

Frustrated with the dominance of developed nations in the IMF and World Bank, the BRICS group (BRIC nations plus South Africa) of vibrant emerging economies announced its members were forming their own development bank, the New Development Bank. This bank began its formal legal existence in July 2015 and is headquartered in Shanghai, China. The bank's initial authorized capital totaled $100 billion, targeted to support the needs of developing nations.[33] Each of the five founding members, Brazil, China, India, Russia, and South Africa, has an equal 20 percent shareholding in the bank. Such an institutional effort might make an important contribution to development and at the same time create leverage for the BRICS to have greater participation in the IMF and World Bank.

Three more institutions that participate in the World Bank Group may be of use to international managers. The International Finance Corporation (IFC) invests in companies and financial institutions in developing countries to build domestic capital markets so that local entrepreneurs have access to funding. The Multilateral Investment Guarantee Agency (MIGA) encourages FDI in developing economies and guarantees private-sector investment through political risk insurance, technical assistance, and dispute mediation. Finally, the International Centre for the Settlement of Investment Disputes (ICSID) helps resolve disputes between governments and foreign investors, and, in that way, helps build foreign direct investment. Currently, 715 cases are being heard, and their procedural details are available for review online at https://icsid.worldbank.org.

World Development and Trade Organizations

The Organisation for Economic Co-operation and Development (OECD) and the World Trade Organization (WTO) are two global membership institutions that focus on economic development for a broad range of economies.

ORGANISATION FOR ECONOMIC CO-OPERATION AND DEVELOPMENT (OECD)

The **Organisation for Economic Co-operation and Development (OECD)** supports governments in their efforts to increase economic growth, fight poverty, maintain financial stability, and help nonmember-nations' economic growth. Today the OECD provides information on economic and other activities within its member-nations and serves as a forum for discussion of shared economic and social policy issues. OECD publishes extensive research on a wide variety of international business and economic subjects that is a well-regarded source for desk research related to international business. OECD's highly regarded individual country surveys are a good complement to the Central Intelligence Agency's *World Factbook* (https://www.cia.gov/library/publications/the-world-factbook/) for reliable demographic and economic information, as well. In addition, recent studies include the pension markets in OECD countries, global pension statistics, insurance market trends, a market study for green cars, and broadband penetration rates.[34] Table A.1 contains OECD current members.

The OECD has been instrumental in many areas, including encouraging member-nations to eliminate bribery, to establish a code of conduct for multinational companies, and to propose the adoption of specific legislation. The Business and Industry Advisory Committee (BIAC) of OECD, created in 1962 to represent business and industry in OECD discussions, works in various areas that concern business, such as trade liberalization, sustainable development, e-commerce, taxation, and biotechnology.

LO A-5
Discuss the resources of the Organisation for Economic Co-operation and Development and the World Trade Organization.

Organisation for Economic Co-operation and Development (OECD)
Group of developed countries dedicated to promoting their own and other nations' economic expansion

TABLE A.1 OECD Member Countries

Australia	France	Korea	Slovenia
Austria	Germany	Luxembourg	Spain
Belgium	Greece	Mexico	Sweden
Canada	Hungary	Netherlands	Switzerland
Chile	Iceland	New Zealand	Turkey
Czech Republic	Ireland	Norway	United Kingdom
Denmark	Israel	Poland	United States
Estonia	Italy	Portugal	
Finland	Japan	Slovak Republic	

Source: "OECD Watch," *OECDwatch.org,* November 18, 2018.

WORLD TRADE ORGANIZATION

The World Trade Organization (WTO), a rules-based, member-driven organization with decisions negotiated by all the member governments, is the only global international organization designed to establish and help implement rules of trade between nations. Begun in 1995, the WTO aims to reduce or eliminate trade barriers and restrictions worldwide in order to reduce costs of doing business for producers of goods and services, exporters, and importers. By limiting the possible actions governments may take in their trade relationships, the WTO is an institution that increases trade flows. It currently has 164 members, representing 98 percent of all world trade.[35] All WTO members sign on to every WTO agreement. Notable among the nonmembers, some of whom have observer status, are Algeria, Ethiopia, Iran, Iraq, Uzbekistan, North Korea, and Libya.

WTO Principles In WTO negotiations, members have established six basic principles, norms on which the global trade system rests[36]:

1. *Trade without discrimination.* The most-favored nation (MFN) principle, or trade without discrimination, requires that nations treat all WTO members equally. If one nation grants another a special trade deal, that deal has to be extended to all WTO members, and the goods of foreigners and locals should be treated equally. This means that imported goods should not face market discrimination.

2. *Freer trade, gradually, through negotiation.* Lower trade barriers encourage trade growth. WTO agreements establish "progressive liberalization" through gradual changes and developing economies have longer to make adjustments.

3. *Predictability, through binding and transparency.* Predictability helps businesses know what their real costs will be. The WTO operates with tariff "bindings," or agreements, to not raise a specific tariff over a given time period. Such promises are as good as lowering a tariff because they give businesspeople realistic data. Transparency, making trade rules as clear and accessible, also helps businesspeople anticipate a stable future.

> **"THE NATIONS MUST BE ORGANIZED INTERNATIONALLY AND INDUCED to ENTER into PARTNERSHIP, SUBORDINATING in SOME MEASURE NATIONAL SOVEREIGNTY to WORLDWIDE INSTITUTIONS AND OBLIGATIONS."**
>
> —*Arthur Henderson, Nobel Laureate and founder of the British Labour Party*[37]

World Trade Organization (WTO)
An international organization that establishes and helps implement rules of trade between nations

Business plays an active role in development. ©Nick Hawkins/SSPL/Getty Images.

4. *Promoting fair competition.* Although many describe the WTO as a "free trade" organization, and it certainly does work toward trade liberalization, the WTO also recognizes that trade relationships among nations can be exceedingly complex. Many WTO agreements support fair competition in agriculture, services, and intellectual property, and discourage subsidies and the dumping of products at prices below the cost of their manufacture.

5. *Encouraging development and economic reform.* Three-quarters of WTO members are developing economies and those transitioning to market economies, and they are active in the WTO's current Doha Development Agenda or extended conference.

6. *Protecting the environment.* Members are permitted to engage in measures to protect the environment, including the health of the public, animals, and plants, but to apply these measures in the same manner to both domestic and foreign businesses.[38]

Doha Development Agenda
WTO extended conference on trade, also known as the Doha Round

Doha Development Agenda Talks known as the Doha Round began in 2001 in Doha, Qatar, to work on an agenda of trade-related issues between developed and developing economies. Developing nations face constraints that limit their ability to benefit from the WTO trading system, especially on trade issues related to textiles, clothing, agriculture, and fish. Doha talks held in 2003 in Cancun, Mexico, collapsed when delegates from developing nations walked out of the meeting over a disagreement with developed nations on agricultural issues. In 2007, the WTO launched the Aid for Trade initiative to assist the least-developed WTO members, for infrastructure, technical support, and productive capacity—three areas that affect a developing nation's ability to gain from trade agreements. All WTO members approved Aid for Trade by 2008, and in 2013, more than $200 billion had been mobilized for Aid for Trade funding.

In late 2013 meetings in Bali, the Bali Package agreement on market access for goods from the least-developed countries and increases in technical assistance was proposed and is now being approved by members. Developed countries also have begun duty-free and quota-free imports for many products from these least-developed countries, but agriculture remains a difficult area in which to build agreement. In 2005, Brazil sued the United States in the WTO over cotton subsidies, and the WTO ruled in Brazil's favor in 2009. Discussions between Brazil and the United States resulted in an agreed settlement in 2014. Doha discussions on member countries' food supplies are ongoing. In Nairobi in 2015, an agreement was reached for developed nations to end export subsidies immediately and for developing nations to end their subsidies by the end of 2018.

trade-related intellectual property rights (TRIPS)
The WTO agreement that protects copyrights, trademarks, trade secrets, and other intellectual property matters

In addition to agriculture, intellectual property rights remain a difficult negotiation area for WTO members. Discussion of WTO's trade-related intellectual property rights (TRIPS) has led to the acceptance of the duty to enforce property rights on 20-year patents and 50-year copyrights. Yet, intellectual property rights violations remain endemic in several industries, such as music, software, and pharmaceuticals, and they tend to occur in a small group of developing countries, with music and software piracy frequent in China and pharmaceutical patent violations legendary in India, China, and Brazil. The WTO has negotiated a basic agreement that property rights should not take precedence over public health, and any country that adopts TRIPS will have the right to copy drugs patented before 1995. The WTO has also established a system of compulsory licensing that mandates that copyright holders license producers in developing countries, and the WTO is offering courses to government officials on intellectual property rights in partnership with the World Intellectual Property Organization, a UN agency.

The Doha Round's discussions have continued to be contentious and were slowed down by the global financial crisis and subsequent slow recovery. Yet, the major players are still talking and have committed to moving Doha forward. They have not dropped out of the discussions, and the 2013 Bali Package and 2015 Nairobi agreement are evidence that progress is achievable, even if it happens slowly.

UN Millennium Development and Sustainable Development: Business Models at Work, Generating Progress

The United Nations established the Millennium Development Goals (MDGs) at the turn of the century, with a target date of 2015 for the world to end poverty, provide primary education for all, build gender equality, reduce child mortality, increase maternal health, combat HIV/AIDS and malaria, build environmental sustainability, and build global partnerships for development. These eight stretch goals have motivated many in the world, and some of them were achieved by the end of 2015 when they were replaced by the Sustainable Development Goals (SDGs), which are also known as the Global Goals.

The 17 SDGs build on the MDGs. Briefly, the goals include (1) no poverty; (2) zero hunger; (3) good health and well-being; (4) quality education; (5) gender equality; (6) clean water and sanitation; (7) affordable and clean energy; (8) decent work and economic growth; (9) industry, innovation, and infrastructure; (10) reduced inequalities; (11) sustainable cities and communities; (12) responsible consumption and production; (13) climate action; (14) life below water; (15) life on land; (16) peace, justice, and strong institutions; and (17) partnerships for the goals. The goals are interconnected. Often, achieving success on one goal will be linked directly with addressing issues associated with another of the goals. All the goals serve as a foundation for future development commitments.

Businesses are an important part of the critical push to eradicate dehumanizing hunger. "How?" you might ask. It's all in the value chain. Inclusive businesses take steps to include poor people in their value chains as producers, employees, and consumers. This is easier said than done, however, since slums and small villages often lack basic market infrastructures, such as roads, market information, and business support services. Supply chains reaching the markets can be deep and complex, so ensuring appropriate work standards and quality can be challenging. In addition, there's usually no legal, banking, and technology access. Many poor people can't afford the registration and legal documents necessary to open a business either.

These are significant challenges, and companies have stepped up with enthusiasm. More is needed than pushing corporate social responsibility—the poor's participation in the value chain has to be institutionalized. We know this can be done. RugMark International established Goodweave, a certification program for rug weaving that operates at the village level, providing jobs and market access, while protecting workers and attempting to eliminate child labor in global supply chains. As a result, more than half a million weaving jobs that were held by children are now held by adults, and the children are in school. Anglo American, the largest private-sector employer in South Africa, runs an HIV/AIDS medical program with guaranteed jobs for those members of its workforce that test positive. The Fairtrade Labelling Organization, whose logo you probably know, is an association of producers, labeling, and marketing organizations that sets standards for goods produced by the world's poorest, including their work conditions. Fairtrade allows you to participate in this important effort, too, through your buying choices.

Check out the Sustainable Development Goals, recent activities, and progress toward their achievement, and ways that you or your company might help in promoting the advancement of these goals at https://www.un.org/sustainabledevelopment.

Critical Thinking Questions

1. Should businesses participate in such efforts as the Sustainable Development Goals, or should their focus be on the bottom line and returning dividends to shareholders?
2. How might a local business include poor people in its value chain? Think of a specific local business and offer ways it might join the Sustainable Development Goals initiatives.

Sources: "Our Mission," *GoodWeave,* 2018, www.goodweave.org; "Unravelling HIV/AIDS," *AngloAmerican,* 2018, www.angloamerican.com; "About Fairtrade," *Fairtrade International,* 2018, www.fairtrade.net; "Millennium Development Goals and Beyond 2015," *United Nations,* September 20, 2018, www.un.org; and "Sustainable Development Goals," *United Nations,* November 18, 2018, www.un.org.

WTO Going Forward In addition to agriculture and intellectual property rights, there are many issues of concern for WTO members, including the rights of farmers, women, and entrepreneurs, all trying to build success in developing economies. WTO members realize that for global trade to work, the rising tide must lift all boats. The future growth of world trade and the economic health of developed nations depend on getting globalization right so that all participants benefit from trade. New markets, an educated workforce, economic growth, and political stability in emerging nations are all important for international business.[39] Both China and India offer a sense of the WTO's possibilities. Together they account for one-third of the global population, and in both countries, as a result of increased trade, absolute poverty has declined.

A more critical view of the WTO exists. It may be the case that the current problems in many international institutions, including the WTO's inability to resolve the problems and conclude the Doha Round, along with the IMF's lack of effectiveness, and issues with the World Bank, are signs of the final efforts of the major post–World War II powers to maintain control of the global economy. If that is the case, true multilateralism lies ahead of us with the fuller participation of India and China. Alternatively, recent developments such as the Trump administration's threats to have the United States withdraw from the WTO and to block new appointments to the WTO's Appellate Body have created uncertainty about whether this multilateral institution can continue to meet its objectives, or even continue as a workable entity.[40]

Recently, in part, because WTO progress on trade liberalization and the inequities of globalization has been slow, regional trade agreements (RTAs) have grown to fill the institutional gap. The WTO reports that in 2018, there were 290 regional trade agreements currently in existence worldwide, as well as more than 170 additional agreements that had been announced or for which notifications had been issued.[41] Every WTO member is a member of at least one RTA, and some members belong to as many as 30. There are two ways to think about RTAs. The European Union and the North American Free Trade Agreement may weaken the WTO because they disrupt or limit the trade of excluded nations. On the other hand, perhaps they are intermediate steps toward greater reduction of trade barriers. Next, we look at these trade agreements and the process of economic integration.

Economic Integration Agreements

LO A-6
Identify the types of trading blocs by their level of economic integration, with examples.

Economic integration represents attempts by nations to create agreements that lead to improved trade conditions for parties to the agreement. Economic integration agreements are informal normative institutions that rely on agreements among members, and their development has tended to follow a general pattern, from free trade area through the common market to economic integration.

FREE TRADE AREA

Economic cooperation often begins with an agreement for a free trade area, such as the North American Free Trade Agreement (NAFTA) among Canada, Mexico, and the United States.[42] In a **free trade area (FTA)**, members trade with one another without tariffs or quotas, while each member maintains its own external tariffs on goods arriving from countries in the rest of the world. Within the FTA, restrictions generally remain on the movement of services (such as accounting, insurance, and legal services), people (labor), and capital. Another example of an FTA is the one established by the Association of Southeast Asian Nations, known as ASEAN. There are many other FTAs, both operating and proposed. Figure A.4 shows the current FTAs and customs unions.

An FTA often develops into a **customs union**, an agreement that adds common external tariffs to the FTA. The Southern African Customs Union (SACU), the oldest of all customs unions, was established in 1910, with South Africa, Lesotho, Namibia, Swaziland, and Botswana as members. Other examples are the **Common Market of the South (Mercosur or Mercosul)**, with the participation of Argentina, Brazil, Paraguay, Uruguay, and Venezuela (suspended since 2016); and the Andean Community, consisting of Chile, Peru, Ecuador, Bolivia, and Colombia.

free trade area (FTA)
Area in which tariffs among members have been eliminated, but members keep their external tariffs

customs union
Collaboration that adds common external tariffs to an FTA

Common Market of the South (Mercosur or Mercosul)
Currently a South American customs union of Argentina, Paraguay, Brazil, Uruguay, and Venezuela (suspended since 2016), with associate members Chile, Bolivia, Colombia, Ecuador, and Peru

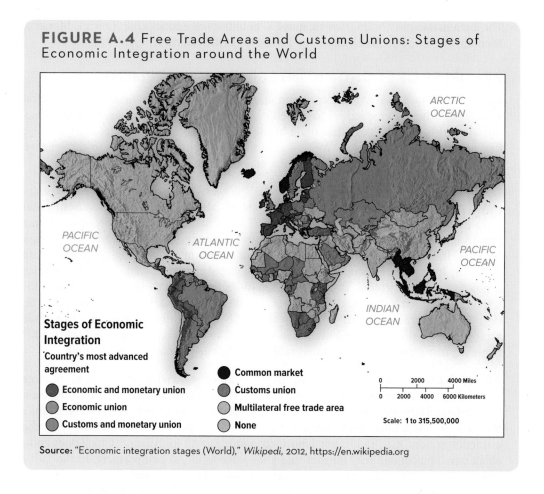

FIGURE A.4 Free Trade Areas and Customs Unions: Stages of Economic Integration around the World

Stages of Economic Integration
'Country's most advanced agreement

- Economic and monetary union
- Economic union
- Customs and monetary union
- Common market
- Customs union
- Multilateral free trade area
- None

Scale: 1 to 315,500,000

Source: "Economic integration stages (World)," *Wikipedi,* 2012, https://en.wikipedia.org

COMMON MARKET

Progressing from the FTA and the customs union, the next level of economic integration is a **common market**, created when a customs union lifts restrictions on the mobility of services, people, and capital among the member-nations. A common market is essentially a single market, so all the barriers to trade, such as standards, borders, and taxes, become common to all members. To achieve this level of economic integration, common market members establish common economic policies, an achievement that requires political will. Mercosur is developing in this direction. The CIS (formerly, the Soviet Union) nations of Russia, Belarus, Kazakhstan, Armenia, and Kyrgyzstan established a common market known as the Eurasian Economic Union.[43]

ECONOMIC INTEGRATION

Eventually, a common market agreement may move toward an agreement for **economic integration**, as has happened with the European Union. Such integration requires a high degree of political integration, since member-nations surrender important elements of their sovereignty. In the European Union, for example, a central bureaucracy is responsible for coordinating and harmonizing tax rates, labor systems, education systems, and other social and legal systems for all EU members, while the European Central Bank develops the monetary policy for all members who have elected monetary union. A single currency, the euro, has been established to replace member-nations' currencies and is used in 19 of the 28 member-states.

common market
Customs union that includes mobility of services, people, and capital within the union

economic integration
Integration on economic and political levels

> **"EACH [of THE BRICS] IS EAGER to REAP THE BENEFITS of A LARGER TRADE GROUP—AND ALL ARE FEARFUL of BEING FLOODED with PRODUCTS from THE OTHERS, ESPECIALLY CHINA."**
>
> *—Patrick McGroarty,* Wall Street Journal *columnist*[44]

The euro is also used by at least six non-EU countries or entities (the Vatican, Monaco, Montenegro, Andorra, San Marino, and Kosovo) as official currency.

EXAMPLES OF ECONOMIC INTEGRATION AGREEMENTS

Trading blocs such as FTAs and common markets affect the international firm in several ways. They bring cost reductions to those firms inside the integrated area, through reductions in tariffs, quotas, and other trade barriers. They also bring cost increases to those firms outside the trading bloc. We now take a closer look at some of these agreements. Table A.2 compares the relative sizes of the major trading blocs and trading nations.

North American Free Trade Agreement (NAFTA)
Agreement creating a free trade area among Canada, Mexico, and the United States

North American Free Trade Agreement The North American Free Trade Agreement (NAFTA) created a free trade area among Canada, Mexico, and the United States that came into existence on January 1, 1994. NAFTA has paved the way for strong economic growth and prosperity based on liberalized trade among its three members. Through NAFTA, the three countries have created one of the world's largest free trade zones and one of the most powerful productive forces in the global economy. Trade in North America is now just about tariff-free. The initial negotiations included a carve-out or exception for Canadian agricultural goods in the dairy, poultry, egg, and sugar sectors. In 2018, negotiations were conducted to modify the NAFTA, resulting in a revised free trade arrangement called the United States-Mexico-Canada Agreement (or USMCA).[45] However, that agreement still required ratification by each of the member-nations.

African Trade Groups African countries have formed regional trade groups to promote economic growth throughout the continent. Most African countries, though, have their main trade relationships with developed countries, often their former colonial powers. China's dramatically increasing involvement in African aid, trade, and FDI, especially in the extraction sectors, may lead to substantive economic growth for Africa.[46] China does know about development and may transfer that knowledge to its African partners. In the 1970s when China began its current reforms targeted toward development, it was poorer than Africa is today and faced more challenging institutional, education, and agricultural issues.[47]

Except for South Africa and Nigeria, African economies are small and underdeveloped, and therefore marginalized in the world trade scene. Their unstable environments are not conducive to economic growth, yet their economic collaborations persevere, despite the daunting challenges their governments face: infrastructure development; public health needs connected to HIV/AIDS, tuberculosis, and malaria; corruption; and insurgencies and civil wars. Five of these groups are the 15-member Economic Community of West

TABLE A.2 Major Regional Trading Blocs and Trading Nations

Regional Bloc	Area (sq km)	Population	GDP (US$, PPP)	GDP per Capita (US$, PPP)
European Union	4,479,968	516,195,432	$20.85 trillion	40,900
NAFTA	21,782,562	491,097,329	23.727 trillion	48,314
China	9,596,960	1,384,688,986	23.21 trillion	16,600
India	3,287,263	1,296,834,042	9.474 trillion	7,200
Russia	17,098,242	142,122,776	4.016 trillion	27,900
Canada	9,984,670	35,881,659	1.774 trillion	48,400
Mexico	1,964,375	125,959,205	2.463 trillion	19,900
United States	9,833,517	329,256,465	19.49 trillion	59,800
World	510.072 m	7,405,107,650	127.8 trillion	17,500

Sources: "The World Factbook," *CIA*, 2018, www.cia.gov. and author calculations.

African States (ECOWAS); the 21-member Common Market for Eastern and Southern Africa (COMESA); the 14-member Southern African Development Community (SADC); the 26-member African Free Trade Zone (AFTZ); and the 55-member African Union (AU), formerly the Organization of African Unity (OAU).

Latin American Trade Groups In South America, Central America, and the Caribbean, we find several vital economic integration agreements. *Mercosur* (Spanish) or *Mercosul* (Portuguese) is an acronym for the Common Market of the South, whose members are Argentina, Brazil, Paraguay, and Uruguay, with associate members Chile, Bolivia, Colombia, Ecuador, and Peru. Venezuela was a full member until that nation was suspended in 2016. At this point an FTA, the alliance seeks common market status, and it has made substantive progress. Most trade within Mercosur is tariff-free, and members have adopted a common external tariff on most products. Figure A.5 shows the regional trade agreements in Central and South America.

FIGURE A.5 Regional Trade Agreements in Central and South America

The Dominican Republic-Central American Free Trade Agreement (DR-CAFTA) includes the United States, Guatemala, Honduras, Nicaragua, El Salvador, Costa Rica, and the Dominican Republic. Although there is criticism of DR-CAFTA because it is asymmetrical (the aggregate GDP of the Central American members is equal to under 1 percent of the U.S. GDP), trade figures report substantial growth in the DR-CAFTA economies, a solid portion of which is attributable to the influence of this free trade area. DR-CAFTA is the first U.S. trade agreement with a group of developing economies. Other South American trade agreements include the Andean Community (CAN), which functions as a customs union among Colombia, Peru, Ecuador, and Bolivia.

Asian Trade Groups In Asia, the 10-member Association of Southeast Asian Nations (ASEAN) was formed in 1967 to foster peaceful relations among members and offer mutual protection against political threats, especially the growth of communism in that region. It began as a cooperative military and security arrangement, in the context of the conflict in what was then known as Indochina. Since military alliances have an impact on trade, it is not surprising that ASEAN's security cooperation has led to economic cooperation. Since Southeast Asia is one of the fastest-developing and most dynamic economic regions in the world, ASEAN (Brunei, Cambodia, Indonesia, Laos, Malaysia, Myanmar [formerly Burma], the Philippines, Singapore, Thailand, and Vietnam) has increasing significance and has grown into the free trade area, AFTA. ASEAN's initial agreement to noninterference in each other's internal affairs has allowed them to overcome conflict and to build the cohesion and mutual values needed for a common market. A subsidiary group, ASEAN+3 adds China, Japan, and South Korea to foster Asian cooperation and financial stability. Figure A.6 shows ASEAN's membership.

The European Union The European Union has developed from a customs union to a common market and then beyond, with added political integration creating a regional government. We look briefly at the European Union's development, then its basic organization, and finally, its impact and prospects.

In the devastation created by World War II, Europeans recognized that their economic and political institutions had failed them. This awareness slowly developed into a tentative but persistent willingness to relinquish some aspects of national sovereignty in order to achieve greater economic and political stability. In 1950, French foreign minister Robert Schuman integrated the coal and steel industries into the European Coal and Steel Community (ECSC). The initial six members—Belgium, West Germany, France, Italy, Luxembourg, and the Netherlands—signed the Treaty of Rome in 1957, establishing a common market with coal and steel. By 1967, this core group had broadened the common market and established the European Community (EC), with a European Parliament, a European Commission, and a Council of Ministers. Then, in 1993, the EC members signed the Maastricht Treaty, which established the European Union (EU), with three areas of integration: economic, foreign policy, and domestic affairs.

Denmark, Ireland, and the United Kingdom joined the European Union's six founding members in 1973, followed by Greece in 1981; Spain and Portugal in 1986; and Austria, Finland, and Sweden in 1995. The European Union welcomed 10 new countries in 2004: Cyprus, the Czech Republic, Estonia, Hungary, Latvia, Lithuania, Malta, Poland, Slovakia, and Slovenia. In 2007, Bulgaria and Romania joined. Croatia joined in 2013. Currently, there are six candidate countries: Albania, Macedonia, Iceland, Turkey, Montenegro, and Serbia; Bosnia and Herzegovina and Kosovo are in talks to join the candidates. Today the European Union's 28 member-countries embody most of the economic, industrial, and population strengths of Europe.[48] The European Union's population is about 516 million people, 7 percent of the world's population, and 55 percent larger than the United States. It is the world's largest exporter and second-largest importer, with about a 17 percent share of global trade. In comparison, the United States is the second-largest trader, with about a 15 percent share.[49] Notable are the Western European countries that have rejected EU

Association of Southeast Asian Nations (ASEAN)
Agreement among Southeast Asian nations that began as a security agreement, grew to a free trade agreement, and is continuing toward a common market, known as AFTA

European Union (EU)
A body of 28 European countries committed to economic and political integration

FIGURE A.6 ASEAN Members

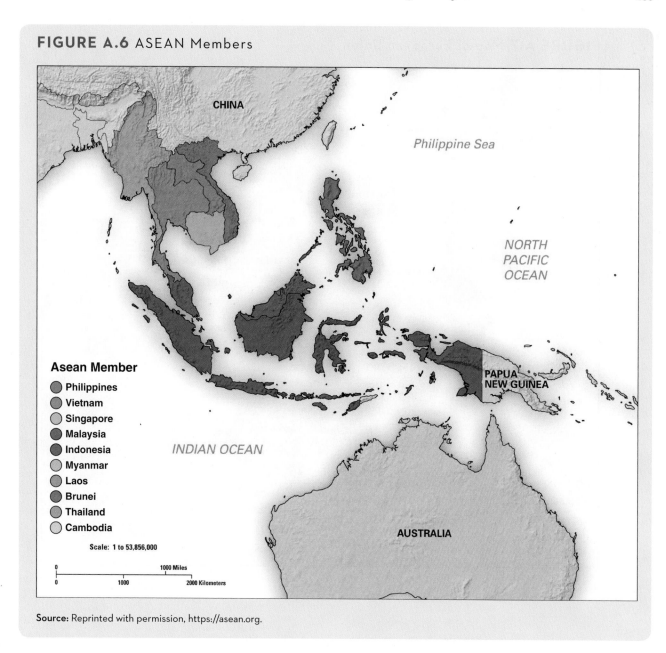

Asean Member
- Philippines
- Vietnam
- Singapore
- Malaysia
- Indonesia
- Myanmar
- Laos
- Brunei
- Thailand
- Cambodia

Scale: 1 to 53,856,000

Source: Reprinted with permission, https://asean.org.

membership, Switzerland and Norway, both of which made the decision not to join based on national elections. In addition, the United Kingdom voted in 2016 to terminate its membership in the European Union, with its departure slated to become official on March 29, 2019. Figure A.7 shows a map of the present European Union.

The European Union has become a regional government, moving forward with integration in the economy, foreign affairs, security, and justice. Its **Economic and Monetary Union (EMU)**, also known as the European Monetary Union, has established the euro (€), which has become a reserve currency second to the dollar. On the international front, the European Union represents its members at the WTO and both the European Commission and the European Council presidents participate at the G20, a group involving the finance and central bank directors representing 19 nations and the EU and accounting for 80 percent of world trade; and the European Court of Justice has the power to impose fines and other sanctions on individuals, companies, and member-nations found to violate EU agreements.

Economic and Monetary Union (EMU)
EU group that established use of the euro in the 18-country euro zone

FIGURE A.7 Map of European Union

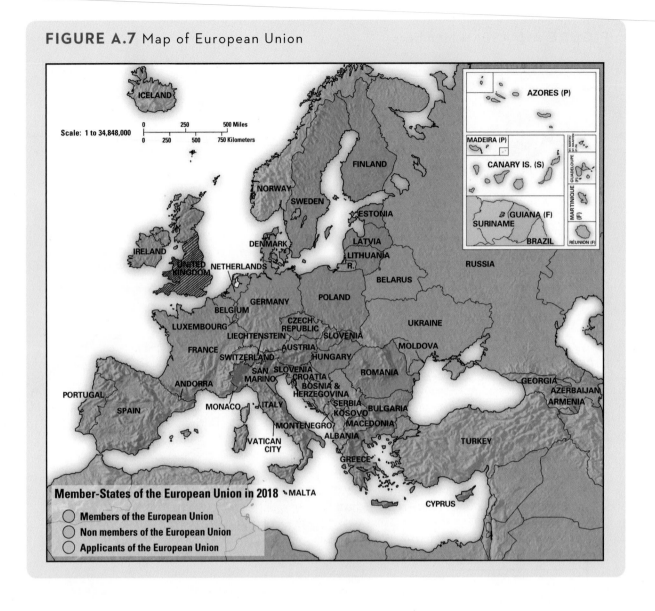

Member-States of the European Union in 2018

- Members of the European Union
- Non members of the European Union
- Applicants of the European Union

European Parliament
EU legislative body whose members are popularly elected from member-nations

Council of the European Union
The European Union's primary policy-setting institution

European Commission
Body responsible for the European Union's day-to-day operations

The European Union is organized into nine institutions with functions similar to those performed by a national government. The **European Parliament** represents the *people* of Europe and is elected from member-states. Its sessions are available live at http://www.europarl.europa.eu/portal/en. The **Council of the European Union** represents the *member-states* and is the primary policy-setting institution of the European Union. When the Council meets, the nation's minister who represents the specific area being discussed serves as the representative of the member-nation. For example, when financial matters are discussed, the 28 finance ministers of member-nations participate. Council decisions are set forth in regulations and directives and they are supranational.

The **European Commission** administers the daily operations of the European Union. It consists of 28 commissioners, one from each member-nation. Countries nominate their Commission members, appointed by the Commission president-elect, and then approved by a vote of the European Parliament. The remaining six EU institutions focus on financial and social issues and include the European Central Bank (ECB) and the European Court of Justice (ECJ).

INTERNATIONAL INSTITUTIONS: A Dangerous Path for the Nation-State, or a Way to Cope with Globalization?

In most nations, major forces oppose the global institutions we've reviewed in this module. One of the foremost issues of concern is that these institutions weaken national sovereignty, the nation's authority to govern itself. The supranational agreements they foster are seen as an assault on the nation's independence. The United States, for example, has refused to ratify the UN Convention on the Rights of the Child, joining only Somalia, a nation that currently does not have a functioning government. The issue in the United States is that ratifying the treaty would uphold international law over state and federal laws protecting the rights of parents to make decisions related to their children's upbringing and education. The 2015 Paris climate agreement, which the Trump administration announced in 2017 that the United States would withdraw from, is another example. The argument here is that such an international agreement on emissions would modify the power of the state and federal governments to regulate in this area. Local control is important to many citizens.

The major counterargument to protect-our-sovereignty objections is that the benefits of supranational agreements far outweigh their trade-offs. This is especially the case with issues not defined by international borders, such as climate change and pollution. With globalization, increasingly the global becomes local and borders dissolve. We need regional and global organizations to address issues related to climate change, pollution, and terrorism

Critical Thinking Questions

1. Do international institutions such as the United Nation promote harmony, or do they violate the sovereignty and thereby reduce the power of nation-states? Defend your reasoning.

2. Would a world without international institutions be a good or better world? Why or why not?

3. Do the ends (the achievements of international institutions) justify the means (supranational agreements)?

The European Union has become a major world political and economic force. Its directives supersede 28 sets of national rules and harmonize hundreds of thousands of national standards, labeling laws, testing procedures, and consumer protection measures covering everything from toys to food, stock brokering to teaching. The 28 nations have scrapped more than 60 million customs and tax formalities at their shared borders and are implementing a harmonized patent system. The introduction of the euro is one of the most significant achievements of the European Union.

International managers need to pay attention to the European Union because it significantly impacts how they can conduct business. The common currency and common import and export processes have reduced the cost of doing business within the European Union. EU standards are advanced, especially in environmental and sustainability requirements, and, because of its market size, a number of EU regulations have major impacts in the United States, Japan, China, and elsewhere. For example, in an effort to reduce electronic equipment waste, the European Union requires manufacturers to provide recycling for all the equipment they sell, including cell phones, computers, household appliances, and televisions.

In general, the European Union requires a higher standard of data privacy than found in the United States, reflected in the European Union's General Data Protection Regulation.[50] For example, EU law requires any e-business website to obtain a computer user's informed consent before placing a cookie on the user's machine.

Microsoft is an example of a company whose business practices have been substantially influenced by the European Union. In 2004, the European Commission ordered the company to pay a fine of €497 million (about $607.8 million), share its software code with competitors, and offer an unbundled version of the Windows operating system. Microsoft complied. Then, in 2005, the European Union ruled that Microsoft would be fined $2.37 million per day if the software code it provided competitors didn't have better documentation. In 2008, the European Union imposed a $1.35 billion fine, because

KATIE EMICK: International Experience Targets Growth, Intellectual and Spiritual

Katie Emick in the field. Courtesy of Katie Emick.

While majoring in international business, I studied with Semester-at-Sea, where I witnessed the context and concepts of what I was studying firsthand. We visited 13 countries and 30 major cities, many of which face the challenges of poverty and overpopulation. To prepare for the voyage, I researched where I would be traveling and made a guide for myself. I also spoke with personal contacts who had experience in these countries and who gave me travel advice. I approached the voyage with adequate preparation and set off confidently with an open mind. In order to make the most out of an international experience, we need to enter foreign cultures filled with anticipation rather than expectation.

One of the biggest challenges I faced abroad was transportation within the countries, particularly the densely populated cities with weak infrastructure. The language barriers present complications, and the chaotic flow of traffic can be overwhelming. Even in advanced countries such as Japan, language barriers presented significant challenges. In many places, Westerners are targets for exorbitant pricing by locals, and it is difficult to dispute prices while avoiding confrontation. In some cases, I quickly learned the public transit systems and used them effectively to get around the large cities. However, I spent many times trying to cope with being utterly lost and trying to communicate using only gestures and drawings. Like learning foreign transit systems, most of the challenges I confronted abroad are ones that can be understood and appreciated only through firsthand experience.

Looking back, my greatest enjoyment was not bungee jumping off the tallest bridge in the world, shark diving with 18-foot great whites, sky-diving over the townships of South Africa, tobogganing down the Great Wall of China, or riding camels and ATVs through the Sahara Desert. Although these were exhilarating, they do not compare to the profound interactions I shared with people around the world, which indescribably influenced me. Two visits worth mentioning are the townships of South Africa and the slums of India.

In both countries, I went on unofficial visits to these areas, despite the risks. I went with another student, and in both cases, we were taken to the homes of our cab drivers. In retrospect, I see how great the risk was, and I would not have done it again. It was sketchy, to say the least, as we got further from the relative safety of the city and deeper into the maze of shantytowns. In South Africa, we were treated as celebrities throughout the neighborhood and spent the afternoon with the locals, sharing beers at the tavern, playing jump rope with the kids, and visiting the one-room shacks that serve as homes. This township is crime-ridden, so residents were not accustomed to visits by foreigners.

In Chennai, we also visited the home of our cab driver, deep in the slums. The tuk-tuk taxi made its way in the dark through a maze of narrow corridors lined with people. We shared hours in the company of the residents, who invited us into their one-room homes. Interacting with the children was so moving. I held a one-month-old baby who had her face painted, danced with the toddlers, played with a baby goat, and left the neighborhood singing the ABCs with a trail of kids following us. It was a surreal and amazing experience that left an indelible mark on me.

During my travels, I learned more about myself than I did about the people and places I visited, and I learned a lot about them. One of my greatest learning points is just that—learn! There is an infinite amount of knowledge out there to discover and endless opportunities to explore. Each of us has the potential to create a positive impact and change the world for the better. Here are my recommendations for your international career development:

- Remove all self-imposed limitations and be wholeheartedly open to self-discovery.

- Embark on your journey with anticipation, not expectation!

- Be respectful and considerate of your surroundings. Understand fully where you are and be fully engaged in the setting. Don't be distracted by the trivial, irrelevant, or inconvenient—let your imagination take hold of the international experience and live in the moment.

- Keep a journal. Try to interpret events and record thoughts about intangible experiences. Photos can tell the story of what you did; use the journal to tell what you learned.

Source: Katie Emick.

Microsoft had not complied fully with its 2004 order to share code. In 2009 the European Union announced that it would investigate Microsoft's bundling of Internet Explorer with the Windows operating systems, an investigation that was settled when Microsoft agreed to allow consumers to choose from among 12 competing browsers, including Explorer, all accessible on a choice screen. In March 2013, the European Union fined Microsoft another $732 million for failing to implement the agreement not to bundle that it had made in 2009. The point is clear: if foreign companies want access to the EU market, they must conduct business by the European Union's rules, often at the global level as well as within the European Union.

Institutions matter because they operate to limit the international manager's available choices, thereby simplifying and codifying the environment. An international manager can benefit greatly by being aware of their strengths, limitations, and contributions.

SUMMARY

LO A-1
Explain the importance of major international institutions to business decision makers.

Institutions exist to limit and direct choices decision makers can make, so they limit the choices open to the firm. Institutions accomplish this constraint by simplifying the external environment. Whether the institution is formal or informal (normative or cognitive), it establishes rules, ways of acting, and ways of thinking that achieve compliance through various means and have the effect of reducing the number of options open to the firm or establishing the rules of the game. Their value to business is that they simplify the external environment, which can help businesses better understand and operate in it.

LO A-2
Describe institutions, drawing on new institutional theory.

Institutions are divided into formal and informal, based on how they influence behavior. Formal institutions use laws and regulations, while informal institutions use customs and ideologies. Informal institutions may be either normative or cognitive. Normative institutions work through values and norms, while cognitive institutions work through sets of shared assumptions that shape meanings. The United Nations, the World Trade Organization, and the two monetary institutions—the World Bank and the International Monetary Fund—are examples of global institutions. Many other global institutions exist, at all levels, including firms and nongovernmental organizations. Among these are the economic integration agreements. There are many other regional institutions such as economic cooperation agreements (OECD) and trade agreements (Mercosur, ASEAN, NAFTA)."

LO A-3
Describe the United Nations as an institution and its relevance to international managers.

The United Nations is an informal, normative institution. Governments comply with their UN agreements based on moral principles and social obligation. The UN's work is carried out through five main bodies. The General Assembly is a forum in which every nation has one vote; the Security Council focuses on peace and security; the Economic and Social Council addresses issues related to trade, education, health, and other economic and social issues; the International Court of Justice hears cases between nations; and the Secretariat, headed by the secretary-general, is the administrative arm of the United Nation. By providing a forum for governments to talk to each other, the United Nations contributes toward peace and stability, conditions that stimulate international business.

LO A-4
Describe the purposes of the two monetary institutions, the IMF and the World Bank.

The basic idea of the IMF is that a workable monetary system is in the interests of all nations. Its Articles of Agreement outline the purpose of the fund in six points: to promote international monetary cooperation, to facilitate the expansion and balanced growth of international trade, to promote exchange stability and orderly exchange arrangements among members, to assist in the establishment of a multilateral system of payments, to make the fund's resources available for balance-of-payments corrections, and to shorten the duration and lessen the disequilibrium of members' balance of payments. The World Bank, including the IBRD and the IDA, lends money for development projects in middle-income and creditworthy poor countries. In the poorest countries, it provides low-interest loans and grants for projects designed to help them develop infrastructure, health and education, and other areas connected to development.

LO A-5
Discuss the resources of the Organisation for Economic Co-operation and Development and the World Trade Organization.

The OECD conducts extensive research on a wide variety of international business and economic subjects, and it produces highly regarded individual country surveys. These resource materials are valuable to researchers and businesspeople as they develop an understanding of markets.

The WTO attempts to reduce trade barriers worldwide in order to facilitate trade. Its membership is composed of the world's major trading countries, so it has the potential to significantly influence world trade. The WTO routinely issues decisions on trade disputes between countries. The Doha Development Agenda of the WTO has been stalled and faces difficult negotiations in the areas of agricultural subsidies of developed nations, enforcement of rules and rulings, and intellectual property rights.

LO A-6
Identify the types of trading blocs by their level of economic integration, with examples.

The four major forms of economic integration are the free trade area (tariffs abolished among members); the customs union (a free trade agreement plus a common external tariff); the common market (a customs union plus mobility of services, people, and capital); and complete integration (a common market plus a common currency and additional economic and political integration). NAFTA is an example of an FTA, while Mercosur, whose goal is a common market, is at the customs union level. African economic integration efforts have faced difficulties, and they endure. The European Union has been markedly successful and able to weather the instability of the recent financial crisis and the ensuing fallout in its weaker economies, so far. Critics suggest it may be reaching its institutional limits.

KEY TERMS

Association of Southeast Asian Nations (ASEAN) 454
Bretton Woods 442
common market 451
Common Market of the South (Mercosur or Mercosul) 450
Council of the European Union 456
customs union 450
Doha Development Agenda 448
economic integration 451
Economic and Social Council (ECOSOC) 441
Economic and Monetary Union (EMU) 455

European Commission 456
European Parliament 456
European Union (EU) 454
formal institutions 436
free trade area (FTA) 450
General Assembly 440
informal institutions 436
International Court of Justice (ICJ) 441
International Monetary Fund (IMF) 442
new institutional theory 436
North American Free Trade Agreement (NAFTA) 452

Organisation for Economic Co-operation and Development (OECD) 446
par value 442
Secretariat 441
Security Council 440
special drawing rights (SDRs) 442
trade-related intellectual property rights (TRIPS) 448
United Nations (UN) 439
World Bank 442
World Trade Organization (WTO) 447

CRITICAL THINKING QUESTIONS

1. Choose a specific informal cognitive institution, discuss its characteristics, and comment on why they could be significant to international business managers.

2. The United Nation may be best known for its peacekeeping missions, but it also has many agencies that directly affect business. Choose a single trade transaction and describe the United Nation's influence on it.

3. Sovereign wealth funds and high levels of monetary reserves are held by many developing nations today,

the very same nations that had been the major market for IMF loans in the past. How might the IMF adjust to a world in which fewer countries need its loans?

4. In your judgment, do bilateral trade agreements such as NAFTA and Mercosur undercut the WTO? Explain your reasoning.

5. Companies that violate the European Union's General Data Protection Regulation (GDPR) are exposed to potential penalties up to 20 million euros or 4 percent of a company's annual global turnover, whichever is higher. This can occur from

noncompliance with the regulation, such as not using an approved approach to receiving consent for collecting, storing, and using data on consumers, even if the company involved is located in the United States or other non-EU nations. Do you think that the European Union should be able to apply such penalties to companies operating in other parts of the world? Explain.

6. Mercosur's main trading partner is the European Union rather than the United States. Why might this be the case?

7. Why is the OECD, known as "the rich man's club," important to countries beyond the cluster of rich ones?

8. Using concepts from new institutional theory, describe three international organizations.

9. What impact can the European Union have on businesses external to the European Union?

10. Criticism of international institutions such as the United Nation or the European Union often focuses on such organizations' perceived threats to national sovereignty, the authority of the state to govern itself. How might globalization affect a state's ability to govern itself?

 globalEDGE RESEARCH TASK   http://globalEDGE.msu.edu/

Use the globalEDGE website (http://globalEDGE.msu.edu) to complete the following exercises:

1. There are also institutions that focus on only one area or branch of business, such as those that focus on an industry. *World Energy Council* (WEC) is one of those institutions and its only focus area is the energy industry. Prepare a briefing about WEC to share in the classroom to help your friends learn more about WEC and include the following information: What are the main purposes of WEC? How many countries are members of WEC and who are represented in national member committees? What types of services are available on the WEC web site?

2. You are a researcher who is interested in finding the trade blocs with the highest levels of intra-bloc trade volumes. Visit the "By Trade Bloc" section of "Global Insights" on globalEDGE and review the major free trade agreements listed. Then drill down in the "Statistics" page of one of those blocs and review the intra-group trade rankings of all blocs. What are the top three blocs listed and their intra-bloc export volumes? How many members does each have and who are those members? Which one do you think is the main drive of the intra-bloc trade volume: the number of members in a bloc or the economic size of member countries?

MINICASE

GETTING HELP FROM GLOBAL INSTITUTIONS

You are an international manager of Vertbien, a French energy company that is committed to the development of alternative energy sources. Vertbien has been monitoring the increasing Chinese investments in African energy sectors and is concerned that the Chinese will control the development of large portions of the African wind, hydro, and solar markets. You are on a team that has been asked to research alternative energy direct foreign investment options in West African countries, either 100 percent owned or with a local partner. Which organizations discussed in this module would you look to for help in developing a list of investment alternatives and criteria for the ownership recommendation?

NOTES

1. Quote by Peter Drucker.

2. Mark Malloch Brown, *The Unfinished Global Revolution: The Limits of Nations and the Pursuit of a New Politics,* London: Allen Lane, 2012.

3. Martin Wolfe, "Why Washington and Beijing Need Strong Global Institutions," *Financial Times,* April 19, 2006, 13.

4. Ibid.

5. W. Richard Scott, *Institutions and Organizations,* 3rd ed., Thousand Oaks, CA: Sage, 2008, 48.

6. Talcott Parsons, "Prolegomena to a Theory of Social Institutions," *American Sociological Review,* vol. 55, 1934/1990, 319–39, as referenced by Scott (2008), 14.

7. Douglass North, *Institutions, Institutional Change and Economic Performance,* Cambridge: Cambridge University

Press, 1990, 4, as quoted in Scott (2008). Also see Gerry Everding, "Douglass North Prizes Economic History," *Washington University Record,* October 21, 1993, 3. Douglass North received the Nobel Prize, along with Robert Fogel, for work using economic theory to explain institutional change. Douglass C. North, *Understanding the Process of Economic Change,* Princeton, NJ: Princeton University Press, 2005.

8. Scott, *Institutions and Organizations.*

9. Ibid.

10. Geert Hofstede, *Cultures and Organizations: Software of the Mind,* San Francisco: Jossey-Bass, 1991.

11. M. W. Peng, "How Entrepreneurs Create Wealth in Transition Economies," *Academy of Management Executive,* vol. 15, 2001, 95–108, as cited in M. W. Peng, *Global Business,* Mason, OH: South-Western Cengage, 2009, 33.

12. Scott, *Institutions and Organizations,* 100, referencing John Boli, and George M. Thomas, "World Culture in the World Polity: A Century of International Nongovernmental Organization," *American Sociological Review,* vol. 62, 171–90.

13. The World Bank, https://data.worldbank.org, accessed November 18, 2018.

14. Quote by Henry Cabot Lodge, Jr.

15. Mark Mazower, *No Enchanted Palace: The End of Empire and the Ideological Origins of the United Nations,* Princeton, NJ: Princeton University Press, 2009.

16. "UN Peacekeeping," https://betterworldcampaign.org/un-peacekeeping, accessed November 18, 2018.

17. International Court of Justice, "Pending Cases," https://icj-cij.org, accessed November 18, 2018.

18. "Composition of the Secretariat: Staff Demographics," http://undocs.org/A/73/79, accessed November 18, 2018.

19. Quote by William R. Inge.

20. See International Monetary Fund, "The IMF at a Glance," https://www.imf.org, accessed November 18, 2018.

21. International Monetary Fund, "IMF Quotas," https://www.imf.org, accessed November 18, 2018.

22. International Monetary Fund, "IMF Members' Quotas and Voting Power, and IMF Board of Governors," https://www.imf.org, accessed November 18, 2018.

23. International Monetary Fund, "Special Drawing Right (SDR)," https://www.imf.org, accessed November 18, 2018.

24. International Monetary Fund, "SDRs per Currency Unit and Currency Units per SDR Last Five Days," https://www.imf.org, accessed November 18, 2018.

25. International Monetary Fund, "IMF Members' Quotas and Voting Power, and IMF Board of Governors," https://www.imf.org, accessed November 18, 2018.

26. Joseph Stiglitz, *Globalization and Its Discontents,* New York: Penguin Books, 2002, 12–19.

27. Alan Beattie, "Retread Required," *Financial Times,* December 01, 2009, 7.

28. The World Bank, "GDP (current US$)," https://data.worldbank.org, accessed November 18, 2018; Robert H. Wade, and Jakob Vestergaard, "The IMF Needs a Reset," *The New York Times, Opinion Pages,* https://www.nytimes.com, accessed November 18, 2018.

29. International Monetary Fund, "IMF Members' Quotas and Voting Power, and IMF Board of Governors."

30. World Bank, "Member Countries," http://www.worldbank.org/en/about/leadership/members, accessed November 18, 2018.

31. IDA, *International Development Association,* http://ida.worldbank.org, accessed November 18, 2018; and World Bank, "International Bank for Reconstruction and Development," https://www.worldbank.org, accessed November 18, 2018.

32. World Bank, "Financing," https://ida.worldbank.org, accessed November 18, 2018.

33. New Development Bank, "About Us," https://www.ndb.int, accessed November 18, 2018.

34. OECD, http://www.oecd.org/about/publishing/key-publications-online.htm, accessed November 18, 2018.

35. World Trade Organization, "The WTO," https://www.wto.org, accessed November 18, 2018.

36. World Trade Organization, "What We Stand For," https://www.wto.org, accessed November 18, 2018.

37. Quote by Arthur Henderson.

38. "What We Stand For," *World Trade Organization,* January 01, 2018.

39. See Yale Center for the Study of Globalization for resources on issues related to globalization and equity, https://ycsg.yale.edu.

40. Rachel Brewster, "Trump Is Breaking the WTO. Will China Want to Save It?" *Washington Post,* https://www.washingtonpost.com, accessed November 18, 2018; Larry Elliott, "Trump's WTO Threats Matter—Especially to a Post-Brexit Britain," https://www.theguardian.com, accessed November 18, 2018; and James Politi, "Donald Trump Threatens to Pull US Out of the WTO," *Financial Times,* https://www.ft.com, accessed November 18, 2018.

41. World Trade Organization, "Welcome to the Regional Trade Agreements Information System (RTA-IS)," https://trais.wto.org, accessed November 18, 2018.

42. In 2018, initial agreement was achieved on a modified agreement, renamed the United States Mexico Canada Agreement (USMCA), although ratification had not yet been formally made by the authorities in each of the three member-nations.

43. Wikipedia, "Eurasian Economic Union," https://en.wikipedia.org, accessed November 18, 2018; and Eurasian Economic Union, "About the Union," http://www.eaeunion.org, accessed November 18, 2018.

44. Patrick McGroarty, "BRICs Nations Take Steps on Currency Trade, Bank," *The Wall Street journal,* March 26, 2013, www.wsj.com

45. Office of the United States Trade Representative, "United States-Mexico-Canada Agreement Text," https://ustr.gov, accessed November 18, 2018.

46. OECD, "The China-DAC Study Group," http://www.oecd.org, accessed November 18, 2018.

47. "Is China Transforming Africa?" *The Atlantic,* https://www.theatlantic.com, accessed November 18, 2018; Center for Global Development, "How China Is Transforming Africa Into 'New World Factory,'" https://www.cgdev.org, accessed November 18, 2018; and Nick Van Mead, "China in Africa: Win–Win Development, or a New Colonialism," *The Guardian,* https://www.theguardian.com, accessed November 18, 2018.

48. See the EU website for information on accession: http://europa.eu, accessed November 18, 2018.

49. Figures from *The World Factbook,* CIA, https://www.cia.gov, accessed November 18, 2018.

50. Information on the EU General Data Protection Regulation (GDPR) can be found at https://eugdpr.org.

B Export and Import Practices

> " Fifty years on from the Beatles arriving in America, the music export growth scheme will give more talented young British artists the chance to be successful on the international stage. "
>
> —Lord Livingston, UK trade minister[1]

©Imagine China/Newscom.

LEARNING OBJECTIVES

After reading this module, you should be able to:

LO B-1   **Identify** sources of export counseling and support.

LO B-2   **Explain** the Incoterms, pricing, terms of sale, and payment.

LO B-3   **Describe** sources of export financing.

LO B-4   **Describe** export documentation.

LO B-5   **Identify** import sources.

Making China's Baijiu a Global Drink of Choice

The grain alcohol called baijiu has been distilled and consumed in its Chinese homeland for a millennium. The Chinese imbibe over 10 billion liters of the fiery spirit each year, or over one-third of all spirits consumed worldwide. Now China's baijiu makers want to transform their country's native spirit into a drink with global recognition and acceptance. "We want to see baijiu have its moment in the world," said Tony Tian, commercial director of Diageo Plc's China White Spirits unit. "Tequila had it. Vodka had it. Why not baijiu?"

Baijiu has traditionally been consumed straight up, and quickly, at government banquets, wedding receptions, and other celebratory events in China. Those unfamiliar with baijiu can be stunned by the drink's customary burn. A clear, flammable beverage averaging over 100-proof, journalist Dan Rather once referred to baiju as "liquid razor blades." Orson Salicetti, the co-founder of New York's Lumos bar, noted, "Baijiu is not a spirit you can just pour into a martini glass and grow an appreciation for its taste immediately."

Rather than referring to a single type of liquor, baijiu represents more than a dozen different, distinct grain-based spirits produced using traditional Chinese methods. Baiju College, a new, $58 million school in the Sichuan mountains, was created to enhance improved production and sales of the spirit. It is developing an English dictionary of baijiu terms so Western drinkers can learn how to order different styles. Flavor profiles range from "light aroma" or "heavy aroma" to "sauce aroma." Some varieties taste like soy sauce or sesame, for example, while others exhibit an essence of "fiery pineapple."

Baijiu's cheerleaders are searching for ways to make the beverage more acceptable to foreign palates and catapult baijiu upward on the global spirits market; the way margaritas did for tequila. Some companies are lowering the alcohol content, making it comparable to 80-proof spirits favored in the West. Others are infusing the spirit with flavorings, highlighting the antioxidant potential of the sorghum ingredient or creating mixed drink recipes. Baijiu maker Wuliangye, which posted $4.4 billion in sales in 2017, teamed up with Austrian crystal maker Swarovski to create wedding-themed baijiu bottles.

"We want to introduce our baijiu to Western drinkers slowly," Tian said. "We want people first to try it in the context of a cocktail. They may be intrigued by it and then slowly move up to the real version." But baijiu traditionalists have expressed some dismay at this approach. As noted by William Isler, CEO of baijiu maker Ming River, some people view the blending of baijiu into cocktails as "like if you had Chinese people in America taking hamburgers and blending them up into milkshakes."

For Baiju College student Luo Meixin, there can be a more fundamental and compelling role for baijiu. "I think this, part of our culture, could be a way to connect with others," she said, "connect with Americans." But with exports representing less than 1 percent of baijiu sales of 1.5 billion gallons, there remains much work before baijiu takes its place globally alongside whiskey and tequila.

Sources: Danielle Paquette, "China's New Booze University Wants to Change How Americans Drink," *Washington Post,* October 19, 2018, www.washingtonpost.com; "1,000-Year-Old Chinese Liquor Wants to Be the New Tequila," *Bloomberg,* October 06, 2016, www.bloomberg.com; and Julie Wernau, "World's Most Consumed Liquor Tries to Make It in the U.S.," *The Wall Street Journal,* October 14, 2018, www.wsj.com.

Sources of Export Information, Counseling, and Support

LO B-1
Identify sources of export counseling and support.

There are many reasons to export. But why do companies *not* export? Two major reasons are the preoccupation with the home market and the reluctance to embark on a new and unknown operation. When managers of non-exporting firms are probed further, they generally mention the following three areas in which they lack knowledge: identification of foreign markets, payment and financing procedures, and export procedures.

In many countries, national- and state-level departments of trade or commerce, banks, small business development centers, and private consultants are ready to offer assistance. In this module, we examine each of the areas that hinder managers in developing exporting capability: how foreign markets are found, how payment and financing procedures work, and how actual export procedures work.

> **❝THE COUNTRIES THAT ARE MOST CLOSED to TRADE TEND to BE THE POOREST in THE WORLD. COUNTRIES THAT HAVE REDUCED TRADE BARRIERS AND INCREASED THE SHARE of IMPORTS AND EXPORTS in THEIR ECONOMIES TEND to BE AMONG THE FASTEST-GROWING NATIONS. ❞**
>
> —Arnold Kling, author of Learning Economics[2]

The first step in locating foreign markets is to determine whether there is a need for the firm's products. This initial screening step may stymie those new to exporting. How do firms begin their foreign market research? They can answer this question by calling on an export assistance program for some guidance. Such programs are readily available in Japan, the European Union, and the United States. In addition, there is support from organizations and foundations for assisting potential exporters from less-developed nations. The Hinrich Foundation and the World Bank offer support targeted to building export capabilities in firms located in less-developed economies. Once the potential exporter has established that there may be a market for the firm's products, it's time to draft the export marketing plan.

We will look at sources of export counseling and support in the United States as examples. The national or federal governments of all major trading countries have comparable programs. Export.gov is the U.S. government's trade portal, where you can find almost everything from the federal government related to trade, including case studies of recent export successes and announcements of foreign trade missions and training programs. The site brings together resources on exporting from government agencies, including the Department of Commerce's International Trade Administration, U.S. Commercial Service, Export-Import Bank, Agency for International Development, Small Business Administration, Department of State, and Overseas Private Investment Corporation. The European Union's Trade Helpdesk (http://trade.ec.europa.eu/tradehelp) and Japan's Ministry of Economy, Trade and Industry known as METI (http://www.meti.go.jp) have similar resources, as do the main trade sites of many other countries.

For U.S. firms that already are exporting, the International Trade Administration (ITA) offers export promotion activities that include export counseling, analysis of foreign markets, assessment of industry competitiveness, and development of market opportunities and sales representation through export promotion events. The services of ITA are organized into three units.[3] The Global Markets Unit provides U.S. firms with specific country assistance on export promotion and advocacy for market access. Recently, it helped TCI International secure a $12.5 million contract to provide Macedonia's Agency for Electronic Communications a national system for monitoring their communications channels.[4] Then there is the Industry and Analysis Unit, which promotes the trade interests of U.S. industries by helping to shape industry-specific trade policies and promotion strategies, including trade missions, fairs, and seminars. The goal of the IAU is to increase U.S. exports. For example, the United States is the largest supplier of geothermal equipment and services, yet many foreign markets have underexploited geothermal sectors. The Industry and Analysis Unit promotes foreign geothermal sector development to help build a market for U.S. exports in this sector. The Enforcement and Compliance Unit monitors and enforces U.S. trade law and trade agreements. For example, it looks for dumping and subsidies that distort trade and helps U.S. companies that believe their trade problems stem from unfair practices seek compliance and remedies.

The Small Business Administration (SBA) offers business development and financial assistance through its Office of International Trade to encourage small businesses to export (see https://www.sba.gov/offices/headquarters/oit/). The National Export Initiative encouraged and supported the LaMotte Company of Charleston, Maryland, to pursue aggressive exporting of water-testing equipment.[5] The company has now entered into markets like Australia, South America, and Vietnam. SBA also has initiated a state-based financial grant program to support state efforts to build the export capacity of its businesses. This program, the State Trade and Export Program Grant (STEP), is a three-year pilot, the first two years of which delivered more than $60 million to the states for development of export capacity.

The U.S. Department of Education provides the Center for International Business and Research (CIBER program) to support education related to international business and trade in 17 universities. The program is buttressed with additional grant programs to support foreign language study, international study, international business research, and undergraduate international studies. These grants totaled $4.6 million for 2018 programs, and a description can be found at https://www2.ed.gov/programs/iegpscibe/funding.html#top, under CIBER.

The U.S. Department of Commerce also offers export-related help to businesses that want to begin or grow their exports. Among the Commerce programs are a matching service, bringing together potential exporters with business partners in specific markets, and an acquisitions support program that searches for suitable acquisitions in foreign locations. Commerce also sponsors trade events that are helpful in both locating foreign representatives and making sales.

Efforts to increase the export levels of smaller companies seem to be working. As the U.S. Census Bureau's 2017 report on exporting companies shows, small- and medium-sized companies constitute nearly 98 percent of all exporters and they continue recent trends to contribute more than one-third of the overall value of U.S. exports.[6] As Figure B.1 shows, these U.S. companies accounted for nearly 36 percent of the total value of exported goods in 2017. Exports of U.S. products overseas contribute to the economic health of the country, and these data highlight the significant role of small- and medium-sized companies.

In addition to the federal government, other sources of assistance available to the exporter include state governments, all of which have export development programs and many of which have export financing programs. In the private sector, the World Trade Centers Association, a membership organization active in 91 countries, provides networking opportunities and an online trading system. Industry-based trade groups are another source of export guidance. In summary, there are many resources for the beginning exporter, and the U.S. government is a good place for U.S. businesses to start building their export knowledge.

Once the firm knows that a potential market exists, it needs to choose between exporting indirectly through U.S.-based exporters or exporting directly using its own staff. If it

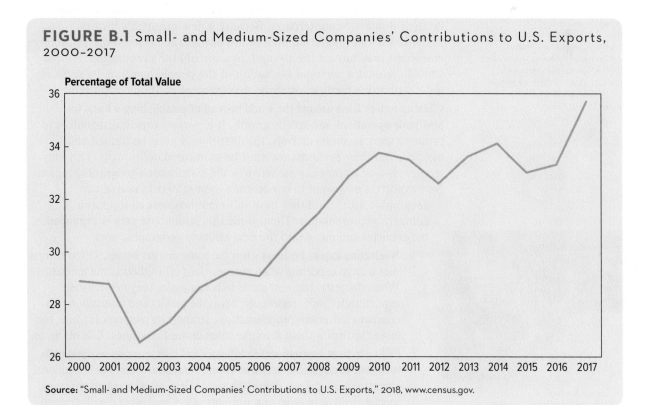

FIGURE B.1 Small- and Medium-Sized Companies' Contributions to U.S. Exports, 2000–2017

Source: "Small- and Medium-Sized Companies' Contributions to U.S. Exports," 2018, www.census.gov.

opts for indirect exporting as a way to test the market, a trade specialist, either from a consultancy or from one of the government programs, can provide assistance. If the firm sets up its own export operation, the next step is to find and establish overseas distribution. Here, the Export.gov portal could be useful for finding agents, distributors, or joint-venture partners.[7] Credit reporting agencies, such as Dun & Bradstreet, the Finance, Credit, and International Business Association (FCIB), and the exporter's bank are a source of credit information.

MISTAKES MADE BY NEW EXPORTERS

Here is a list of the 12 mistakes most commonly made by new exporters.[8] Review them to build a sense of where the actual pitfalls are when firms launch export programs.

1. **Failing to obtain qualified export counseling and to develop a master international strategy and marketing plan before starting an export business.** To be successful, a firm must first establish its export goals and objectives and develop a strategic plan for meeting those goals. Unless the firm is fortunate enough to possess a staff with export expertise, taking this crucial first step may require qualified outside guidance.

2. **Making an insufficient commitment to overcome the initial difficulties and financial requirements of exporting.** Establishing a firm in foreign markets usually takes more time than in domestic ones. Although the early delays and costs involved in exporting may seem difficult to justify compared to the costs of being in established domestic markets, the exporter needs to take a long-term view of this process and carefully monitor international marketing efforts through these early difficulties. If a good foundation is laid for export business, the benefits derived should eventually outweigh the investment.

3. **Taking insufficient care in selecting overseas sales representatives and distributors.** The selection of each foreign distributor is crucial. The complexity introduced by overseas communication and transportation requires that international distributors act with greater independence than do their domestic counterparts. Because a new exporter's history, trademarks, and reputation may be unknown in the foreign market, foreign customers may buy on the strength of a distributor's reputation. A firm should conduct a personal evaluation of the people handling its account, the distributor's facilities, and the management methods employed.

4. **Chasing orders from around the world instead of establishing a basis for profitable operations and orderly growth.** If exporters expect distributors to promote their accounts actively, the distributors must be trained and assisted, and their performance must be monitored continually. This may require placing a company executive in the distributor's geographic region. New exporters may want to concentrate their efforts in one or two geographic areas until they have sufficient business to support a company representative. Then, while this initial core area is expanded, the exporter can move into the next targeted geographic area.

5. **Neglecting export business when the home market booms.** Often companies turn to exporting when business falls off in their home market. When domestic business starts to boom again, they neglect their export trade. Such neglect can harm the profits and motivation of a company's overseas representatives, strangle its own export trade, and leave the firm without recourse when domestic business falls off again.

6. **Failing to treat international distributors and customers on an equal basis with their domestic counterparts.** Often, companies carry out institutional advertising campaigns, special discount offers, sales incentive programs, special credit term programs, warranty offers, and other distributor and

CULTURE FACTS @internationalbiz

@Barbie Barbie maker Mattel built a six-story Shanghai flagship mansion aimed at hyping Barbie up in China. But Mattel failed to realize that China's "Tiger Moms" prefer that their daughters focus on studies. Mattel closed the house and developed "Violin Soloist Barbie," complete with violin, bow, and sheet music, a Barbie more in line with Chinese self-discipline and achievement goals.[9] #mattel #violinistsoloistbarbie #barbiemodel

The Violin Soloist Barbie.
©Weng Iei/ICHPL Imaginechina/AP Images

BOTTLES OF AUSTRALIA: A Small Company Pursuing Export Opportunities

Bottles of Australia (BOA) is the leading manufacturer of custom-printed sports bottles in Australia. BOA launched in 1989 with a bank overdraft of $5,000, initially importing stickers from Hawaii for the bicycle industry. The company expanded into bottle manufacturing in 1992. Although BOA's primary focus has been serving its domestic market, exports became part of the company's efforts early in its business life. Anton Pemmer, BOA's former director, said, "We've been exporting, I suppose probably since about '93–'94. But I would call it more accidental exports. . . . When I say accidental, I mean someone's come across this somehow over the Internet or some sort of search, and they've wanted to place an order for some product, and we sent it to them. As opposed to us developing it and chasing a particular market."

In 2014, BOA undertook a concerted effort to identify and enter a new strategic market: South Korea. Surprisingly, the initial idea of targeting Korea for exports did not come from within the company. Rather, a group of students from the Australian National University (ANU), while participating in ANU's Business Plan competition, identified Korea as an attractive export market for BOA. The recently completed Korea–Australia Free Trade Agreement (KAFTA) eliminated tariffs on Australian products exported by BOA to Korea. Capturing the full potential of the Korean market, however, required commitment. In this case, BOA's commitment meant two years and four in-person visits to Korea, a significant cost for a company with fewer than 20 employees.

When exploring a potential new market, Pemmer advised, "Really get to know the country that you want to export to. If you're going to be targeting a particular country, then understand the culture. Understand the food, understand the people, even before you even think that you want to sell them anything. Really get to know what it's about. And if you're going to make an effort to target a particular country, and you're going to go there, make sure a simple thing like your business card's in the language of the country that you're visiting, that your price list and catalogues are in the language of the country that you're

visiting. . . . Taking the time to really familiarise yourself with some of the simple cultural differences in a country, to be able to say hello and goodbye in their language, to be able to say please and thank you. Those couple of things open up far, far more doors than you would ever imagine, and that would probably be the starting advice I would give to anybody who's even considering to export."

Gaining this level of understanding and preparation for a new market can quickly become expensive in terms of time and money. Properly done, including doing the required research, can help you produce results that more than outweigh the risks. According to Pemmer, within five years, BOA's export market sales increased from 1 percent to now nearly 10 percent of the company's overall business. By 2018, the company exported to 22 nations, including Korea, Germany, France, Russia, Canada, and the United States. Prominent clients include Puma, Warner Brothers, Shimano, and Giant Bicycles. A brief video about BOA's experience entering Korea can be found at https://www.youtube.com/watch?v=Doofa165y4w.

Critical Thinking Questions

1. Many companies engage in "accidental" exporting. Should companies avoid this practice? Why or why not?

2. What actions, besides those listed by Pemmer, could a company use to better understand a potential export market and improve the likelihood of success in entering that market?

Sources: Michael Gorey, "Canberra Business Bottles of Australia the Full Bottle on Exports," *The Sydney Morning Herald,* May 05, 2017, www.smh.com.au; Taikah Bretzke, "Secrets to Building a Thriving Export Business: Anton Pemmer, Bottles of Australia," *MyBusiness,* 2018, www.mybusiness.com.au; "Bottles of Australia Taking on the World," *Canberra Business Chamber,* November 14, 2018, www.canberrabusiness.com; "Bottles of Australia: Finding Export Success in Korea," *Australian Trade and Investment Commission,* September 2017, www.austrade.gov.au; "Bottles of Australia: Australian Made for 20 Years," *Australian Made,* 2018, www.australianmade.com.au; and Efic, "Bottles of Australia," 2018, www.efic.gov.au.

customer support in the home market but fail to make similar assistance available to their international distributors and customers. This mistake can destroy the vitality of overseas marketing efforts.

7. **Assuming that a given market technique and product will automatically be successful in all countries.** What works in one market may not work in others. Each market has to be treated separately until the company has sufficient knowledge about its export markets to generalize about them.

8. **Failing to modify products to meet regulations or cultural preferences of other countries.** Local safety codes and import restrictions cannot be ignored, nor can cultural preferences. If necessary modifications are not made at the factory, the distributor must make them, often at greater cost and perhaps not as well.

9. **Failing to provide service, sales, and warranty information in locally understood languages.** Although many people may speak English, they will want to read instructions and product information in their own language. This holds for both customers and distributors.

10. **Failing to consider the use of an export management company.** If a firm decides it cannot afford its own export department, it should consider the possibility of using an export management company (EMC).

11. **Failing to consider licensing or joint venture agreements.** Import restrictions in some countries, insufficient human or financial resources, or a too-limited product line can cause many companies to dismiss international marketing as unfeasible. Yet, many products that compete on a national basis in a home market can be marketed successfully in many markets of the world through licensing or joint-venture arrangements.

12. **Failure to provide readily available servicing for the product.** A product without the necessary service support can acquire a bad reputation quickly, potentially preventing further sales.[10]

EXPORT MARKETING PLAN

As soon as possible, the firm needs to draft its export marketing plan. An experienced firm will already have a plan in operation, but newcomers may need to wait until they have accumulated at least some information from foreign market research. Essentially, the export marketing plan takes the same approach as the domestic marketing plan. It should be specific about the markets to be developed, the marketing strategy for serving them, and the tactics required to carry out the strategy. Sales forecasts and budgets, pricing policies, product characteristics, promotional plans, and details on arrangements with foreign representatives are required. The export marketing plan spells out what must be done and when, who should do it, and what the costs are. A sample outline for an export marketing plan appears in the final section of this module.

LO B-2
Explain the Incoterms, pricing, terms of sale, and payment.

terms of sale
Conditions of a sale that stipulate the point at which costs and risks are borne by the buyer

Incoterms
Universal trade terminology developed by the International Chamber of Commerce

Incoterms, Pricing, Terms of Sale, and Payment

Firms beginning to export are often concerned about how to price, the terms of sale, and the payment process. Related to the first two of these, pricing and the terms of sale, are the export terms of sale, the conditions of sale that stipulate the point at which costs and risks are borne by the buyer, which is different from the process in the domestic market.

INCOTERMS

The International Chamber of Commerce created Incoterms, a series of 11 internationally standardized terms that describe the conditions of sale and the responsibilities of the buyer and seller in international trade transactions.[11] Any exporter will quickly become familiar with these terms.

Incoterms describe the three issues that arise in a commercial transaction: which party does which tasks, which party covers the costs, and which party bears the risk. For example, FOB (free on board) means the seller loads the goods on board the ship identified by the buyer and clears them for export, and both cost and risk transfer to the buyer at the ship's rail. The responsibilities for various types of foreign sales are more fully described in Table B.1.

TABLE B.1 International Chamber of Commerce Incoterms: Summary of Seller and Buyer Responsibilities by Incoterm Type of Sale

General Transportation Terms	Water Transport Terms
Ex-Works *(named place)*: Seller makes goods available at factory or warehouse, where risk passes.	FAS *(named loading port)*: Free alongside ship; seller clears the goods for export and places them by the ship, risk passes at rail.
FCA *(named place)*: Free carrier, seller hands over goods to carrier at a named place, where risk passes.	FOB *(named loading port)*: Free on board; seller loads goods, risk passes at rail.
CPT *(named destination)*: Carriage paid to destination, seller pays for carriage, while risk passes when goods handed to carrier.	CFR *(named destination port)*: Cost and freight; seller pays costs of freight to bring goods to destination port. This does not include insurance. Risk passes once goods are loaded.
CIP *(named place of destination)*: Carriage and insurance paid to destination, while risk passes when goods are handed to carrier.	CIF *(named destination port)*: Same as CFR, but also includes insurance. Risk still passes at ship's rail.
DAT: Delivered at terminal; seller pays for transport and insurance to terminal and has risk until goods loaded at terminal.	
DAP *(name of destination)*: Delivered at place; seller pays for carriage to the named place and assumes all risk until goods are unloaded.	
DDP *(destination place)*: Delivered, duty paid; seller delivers goods to destination and covers all duties, taxes, customs.	

Source: "Incoterms rules 2010," *International Chamber of Commerce*, 2010, www.iccwbo.org.

PRICING

On pricing, CIF and CFR terms of sale are more convenient for foreign buyers because to establish their cost, they merely have to add the import duties, landing charges, and freight from the port of arrival to their warehouse. New exporters need to remember the miscellaneous costs—wharf storage and handling charges, freight forwarder's charges, and consular fees—incurred in making a CIF shipment. The domestic marketing and general administrative costs included in the domestic selling price are frequently greater than the actual cost of making a CIF export sale.

For exporters, the preferred pricing method is the use of the factory door cost (production cost without domestic marketing and general administrative costs), to which are added the direct cost of making the export sale, a percentage of the general administrative

Cars awaiting export. ©Michael H/DigitalVision/Getty Images.

overhead, and a profit margin. This percentage can be derived from managers' estimates of the part of their total time spent on export matters. The minimum FOB, or Ex-Works, price is the sum of these costs plus the required profit margin. If research in a market has shown that either there is little competition or that competitive prices are higher, then, of course, the exporter is free to match the competition in that market (price skimming) or set a low price to gain market share (penetration pricing). The choice of pricing strategy will depend on the firm's sales objectives, just as in the domestic market.

TERMS OF SALE

In an export sale, the sales agreement needs to specify as simply as possible the duties of both the firm's foreign representative (the buyer) and the firm. Most of what is contained in the contract for a domestic representative can be used in export also, but two areas require special attention: the designation of the responsibilities for patent and trademark registration and the designation of the country and state or province whose laws will govern any contractual disputes. To be absolutely safe, the firm should register all patents and trademarks. Policing them may be left to the local representative; however, the firm should have the help of an experienced international attorney when drawing up an agreement. Exporters from any country are likely to prefer to stipulate the laws of their home country. Many nations, especially those of Latin America, follow the Calvo Doctrine, which holds that cases should be tried under local, and not foreign, law.

EXPORT PAYMENT PROCEDURES

Once new exporters build their understanding of the export process, including pricing and the sales agreement, they need to address the issues related to getting paid for their sale. We review the process of export payment and the terms used, approaches to export financing, and other government incentives that have been established to support exporters in the finance area.

Payment terms, as every marketer knows, are often a decisive factor in obtaining an order. As a grain exporter salesperson put it, "If you give credit to a guy who is broke, he'll pay any price for your product." This is an exaggeration, but customers will often pay higher prices when terms are more lenient, especially in countries where capital is scarce and interest rates are high. Among the payment terms exporters can offer to foreign buyers are cash in advance, open account, consignment, letters of credit, and documentary drafts. When the credit standing of the buyer is not known or is uncertain, cash in advance is desirable. However, very few buyers will accept these terms because part of their working capital will be tied up until the merchandise has been received and sold. Furthermore, they have no guarantee that they will receive what they ordered. Few customers will pay cash in advance unless the order is for a custom-made product.

When a sale is made on open account, the seller assumes all the payment-related risk, so such terms should be offered only to reliable customers. The exporter's capital is tied up until payment has been received. However, exporters that insist on less risky payment terms, such as a letter of credit, may find that they are losing business to competitors who do sell on open account. Well-known global firms such as Mercedes-Benz do not accept the extra cost of obtaining letters of credit and give their business to suppliers that will offer them open-account terms. To establish the buyer's credit, exporters can get credit reports and credit information on foreign firms from credit reporting firms such as Dun & Bradstreet, Experian, and Equifax.

In a sale made on consignment, goods are shipped to the buyer and payment is not made until they have been sold. All the payment risk is assumed by the seller, so such terms should not be offered without making the same extensive investigation of the buyer and country as that recommended for open-account terms. Multinationals frequently sell goods to their subsidiaries on this basis.

A **letter of credit (L/C)** is a document issued by the buyer's bank in which the bank becomes an intermediary in the sale, promising to pay the seller a specified amount under specified conditions. Only cash in advance offers more protection to the seller than does an L/C because payment will follow when the bank has received the stipulated documents by a specified time. Generally, the seller will request that the letter of credit is confirmed and irrevocable. In a **confirmed L/C**, a correspondent bank in the seller's country confirms that it will honor the issuing bank's letter of credit.

With an **irrevocable L/C**, once the seller has accepted the credit, the customer cannot alter or cancel it without the seller's consent. Figure B.2 is an example of a bank's confirmation of an irrevocable letter of credit. If the letter of credit is not confirmed, the correspondent bank (Merchants National Bank of Mobile) has no obligation to pay the seller

letter of credit (L/C) Document issued by the buyer's bank in which the bank promises to pay the seller a specified amount under specified conditions

confirmed L/C A confirmation made by a correspondent bank in the seller's country by which it agrees to honor the issuing bank's letter of credit

irrevocable L/C A stipulation that the L/C cannot be canceled without the seller's consent

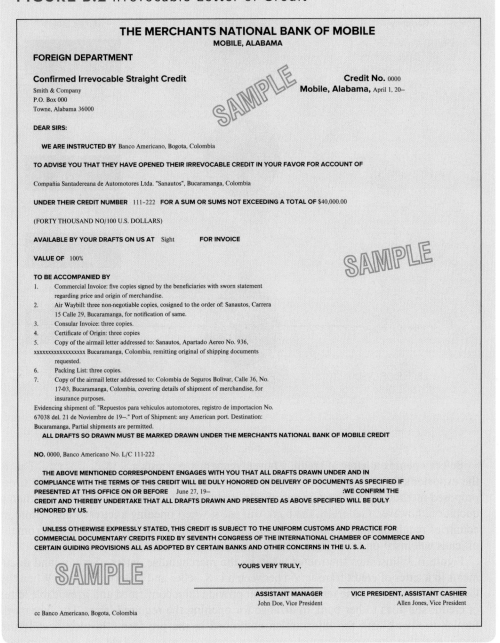

FIGURE B.2 Irrevocable Letter of Credit

THE MERCHANTS NATIONAL BANK OF MOBILE
MOBILE, ALABAMA

FOREIGN DEPARTMENT

Confirmed Irrevocable Straight Credit   **Credit No.** 0000
Smith & Company   **Mobile, Alabama,** April 1, 20–
P.O. Box 000
Towne, Alabama 36000

DEAR SIRS:

WE ARE INSTRUCTED BY Banco Americano, Bogota, Colombia

TO ADVISE YOU THAT THEY HAVE OPENED THEIR IRREVOCABLE CREDIT IN YOUR FAVOR FOR ACCOUNT OF

Compañia Santadereana de Automotores Ltda. "Sanautos", Bucaramanga, Colombia

UNDER THEIR CREDIT NUMBER 111-222 **FOR A SUM OR SUMS NOT EXCEEDING A TOTAL OF** $40,000.00

(FORTY THOUSAND NO/100 U.S. DOLLARS)

AVAILABLE BY YOUR DRAFTS ON US AT Sight   **FOR INVOICE**

VALUE OF 100%

TO BE ACCOMPANIED BY
1.   Commercial Invoice: five copies signed by the beneficiaries with sworn statement
      regarding price and origin of merchandise.
2.   Air Waybill: three non-negotiable copies, cosigned to the order of: Sanautos, Carrera
      15 Calle 29, Bucaramanga, for notification of same.
3.   Consular Invoice: three copies.
4.   Certificate of Origin: three copies
5.   Copy of the airmail letter addressed to: Sanautos, Apartado Aereo No. 936,
xxxxxxxxxxxxxxxxxx Bucaramanga, Colombia, remitting original of shipping documents
      requested.
6.   Packing List: three copies.
7.   Copy of the airmail letter addressed to: Colombia de Seguros Bolivar, Calle 36, No.
      17-03, Bucaramanga, Colombia, covering details of shipment of merchandise, for
      insurance purposes.
Evidencing shipment of: "Repuestos para vehiculos automotores, registro de importacion No.
67038 del. 21 de Noviembre de 19–." Port of Shipment: any American port. Destination:
Bucaramanga, Partial shipments are permitted.
      ALL DRAFTS SO DRAWN MUST BE MARKED DRAWN UNDER THE MERCHANTS NATIONAL BANK OF MOBILE CREDIT

NO. 0000, Banco Americano No. L/C 111-222

      **THE ABOVE MENTIONED CORRESPONDENT ENGAGES WITH YOU THAT ALL DRAFTS DRAWN UNDER AND IN
COMPLIANCE WITH THE TERMS OF THIS CREDIT WILL BE DULY HONORED ON DELIVERY OF DOCUMENTS AS SPECIFIED IF
PRESENTED AT THIS OFFICE ON OR BEFORE** June 27, 19–   **:WE CONFIRM THE
CREDIT AND THEREBY UNDERTAKE THAT ALL DRAFTS DRAWN AND PRESENTED AS ABOVE SPECIFIED WILL BE DULY
HONORED BY US.**

      **UNLESS OTHERWISE EXPRESSLY STATED, THIS CREDIT IS SUBJECT TO THE UNIFORM CUSTOMS AND PRACTICE FOR
COMMERCIAL DOCUMENTARY CREDITS FIXED BY SEVENTH CONGRESS OF THE INTERNATIONAL CHAMBER OF COMMERCE AND
CERTAIN GUIDING PROVISIONS ALL AS ADOPTED BY CERTAIN BANKS AND OTHER CONCERNS IN THE U. S. A.**

                              YOURS VERY TRULY,

        ASSISTANT MANAGER   **VICE PRESIDENT, ASSISTANT CASHIER**
        John Doe, Vice President   Allen Jones, Vice President

cc Banco Americano, Bogota, Colombia

(Smith & Co.) when it receives the documents listed in the letter of credit. Only the issuing bank (Banco Americano in Bogotá) is responsible. If sellers (Smith & Co.) wish to be able to collect from a U.S. bank, they will insist that such a bank confirms the credit. This confirmation is generally done by the correspondent bank, as it is in Figure B.2. When the Merchants National Bank of Mobile confirms the credit, it undertakes an obligation to pay Smith & Co. if all the documents listed in the letter are presented on or before the stipulated date. Note that nothing is mentioned about the goods themselves; the buyer has stipulated only that an **air waybill** issued by the carrier be presented as proof that the shipment has been made. Even if bank officials knew that the plane carrying the shipment had crashed after takeoff, they would still pay Smith & Co. Banks are concerned with documents, not merchandise.

air waybill
A bill of lading issued by an air carrier

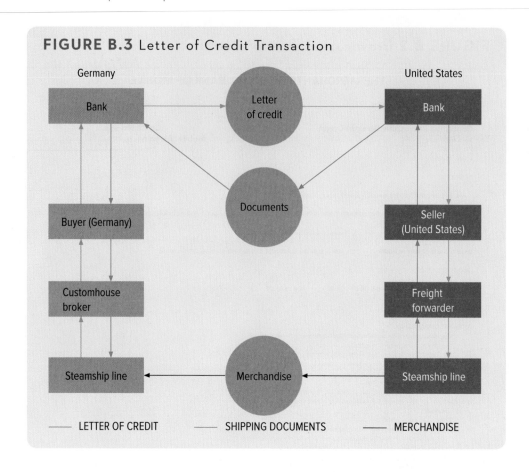

FIGURE B.3 Letter of Credit Transaction

pro forma invoice
Exporter's formal quotation, containing a description of the merchandise, price, delivery time, method of shipping, terms of sale, and points of exit and entry

Before opening a letter of credit, a buyer frequently requests a **pro forma invoice**. This is the exporter's formal quotation, a description of the merchandise, price, delivery time, proposed method of shipment, terms of sale, and ports of exit and entry. It is more than a quotation, however. Generally, the bank will use it when opening a letter of credit, and in countries requiring import licenses or permits to purchase foreign exchange, government officials will insist on receiving copies of the pro forma invoice.

Figure B.3 illustrates the routes taken by the merchandise, letter of credit, and documents in a letter of credit transaction between a U.S. seller and a German buyer. When the German buyer accepts the terms of sale that provide for a confirmed and irrevocable letter of credit, she goes to her bank to arrange for opening the required letter. The buyer will furnish the bank with the information contained in the pro forma invoice, specify the documents that the exporter must present to obtain payment, and set the expiration date for the credit. The concept of the L/C is a simple one: the bank as the intermediary between buyer and seller. In fact, though, a simple irrevocable L/C requires 11 steps to clear payment. Here are those steps[13]:

1. After the exporter and buyer agree on the terms of a sale, the buyer arranges for its bank to open a letter of credit that specifies the documents needed for payment. The buyer determines which documents will be required.

2. The buyer's bank issues, or opens, its irrevocable letter of credit, which includes all instructions to the seller relating to the shipment.

3. The buyer's bank sends its irrevocable letter of credit to a U.S. bank and requests confirmation. The exporter may request that a particular U.S. bank should be the confirming bank, or the foreign bank may select a U.S. correspondent bank.

4. The U.S. bank prepares a letter of confirmation to forward to the exporter along with the irrevocable letter of credit.

5. The exporter reviews carefully all conditions in the letter of credit. The exporter's freight forwarder is contacted to make sure that the shipping date can be met. If the exporter cannot comply with one or more of the conditions, the customer is alerted at once.

6. The exporter arranges with the freight forwarder to deliver the goods to the appropriate port or airport.

7. When the goods are loaded, the freight forwarder completes the necessary documentation.

8. The exporter (or the freight forwarder) presents the documents, evidencing full compliance with the letter of credit terms, to the U.S. bank.

9. The bank reviews the documents. If they are in order, the documents are sent to the buyer's bank for review and then transmitted to the buyer.

10. The buyer (or the buyer's agent) uses the documents to claim the goods.

11. A draft, which accompanies the letter of credit, is paid by the buyer's bank at the time specified or, if a time draft, may be discounted to the exporter's bank at an earlier date.

If the exporter believes the political and commercial risks are not sufficient to require a letter of credit, the exporter may agree to payment on a documentary draft basis, which is less costly to the buyer. An **export draft** is an unconditional order drawn by the seller on the buyer instructing the buyer to pay the amount of the order on presentation (sight draft) or at an agreed future date (time draft). Generally, the seller will ask its bank to send the draft and documents to a bank in the buyer's country, which will proceed with the collection as described in the letter-of-credit transaction.

Although documentary draft and letter-of-credit terms are similar, there is one important difference. A confirmed letter of credit guarantees payment to the seller if the seller conforms to its requirements. There is no guarantee with a documentary draft. An unscrupulous buyer could refuse to pay the draft when presented and then attempt to bargain with the seller for a lower price. The seller would then have choices: agree, try to find another buyer, pay a large freight bill to bring back the goods, or abandon them. If the seller were to choose the last alternative, customs would auction off the goods, and perhaps the original buyer would be able to acquire them at a bargain price. The seller would receive nothing. Figure B.4 illustrates that the risks and costs vary inversely among the various export payment terms.

export draft
An unconditional order drawn by the seller that instructs the buyer to pay the draft on presentation (sight draft) or at an agreed future date (time draft) and that must be paid before the buyer receives shipping documents

FIGURE B.4 Payment Risk/Cost Trade-Off

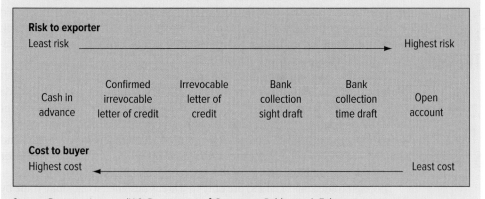

Source: Business America (U.S. Department of Commerce Publication), February 1995.

LO B-3
Describe sources of export financing.

banker's acceptance
A time draft with a maturity of less than 270 days that has been accepted by the bank on which the draft was drawn, thus becoming the accepting bank's obligation

factoring
The sale of an exporter's accounts receivable on ordinary goods, with the balance of the payment due upon delivery or soon after

forfaiting
The sale of an exporter's accounts receivable on capital goods, commodities, and other high-value goods, with the payment due at least 180 days out

> **❝ THE FACT THAT TRADE PROTECTION HURTS THE ECONOMY of THE COUNTRY THAT IMPOSES IT IS ONE of THE OLDEST but STILL MOST STARTLING INSIGHTS ECONOMICS HAS to OFFER. THE IDEA DATES BACK to THE ORIGIN of ECONOMIC SCIENCE ITSELF. ADAM SMITH'S *THE WEALTH of NATIONS*, WHICH GAVE BIRTH to ECONOMICS, ALREADY CONTAINED THE ARGUMENT for FREE TRADE: by SPECIALIZING in PRODUCTION INSTEAD of PRODUCING EVERYTHING, EACH NATION WOULD PROFIT from FREE TRADE. ❞**
>
> —*Jagdish Bhagwati, professor at Columbia University*[16]

Export Financing

Although exporters would prefer to sell on L/C terms because it is almost riskless, increased foreign competition forces them to offer credit. To do so, they need to be familiar with the available sources and kinds of export financing, both private and public.

Commercial banks have always been a source of export financing through loans for working capital and the discounting of time drafts. A bank may discount an export time draft, pay the seller and keep it until maturity or, if it is the bank on which the draft is drawn, accept it. By accepting a time draft, an action called a **banker's acceptance**, a bank assumes the responsibility for making payment at maturity of the draft. The accepting bank may purchase the draft at a discount. As commercial paper, it then can be bought and sold in the financial markets. If the bank does not choose to purchase the draft, the exporter can sell a banker's acceptance readily in the open market.

Factoring and forfaiting are two ways of financing exports that have their roots in ancient Mesopotamian international trade, as documented in the Code of Hammurabi, 1754 BC. **Factoring** is the sale of an exporter's accounts receivable on ordinary goods, with the balance of the payment due upon delivery or soon after. Factoring permits the exporter to be more competitive by selling on open account rather than by the more costly letter-of-credit method. This financing technique passes the risk to the factor, which may be a factoring house or a special department in a commercial bank. Under the export factoring arrangement, the seller passes its export order to the factor for approval of the importer's credit risk. Once the order has been approved, the exporter has complete protection against bad debts and political risk. The importer pays the factor, which, in effect, acts as the exporter's credit and collection department. The period of settlement generally is under 180 days. In contrast, **forfaiting** is the sale of an exporter's accounts receivable on capital goods, commodities, and other high-value goods, with the payment due at least 180 days out, and possibly extending to as long as five years. The forfaiter purchases the accounts receivable and discounts it for the entire credit period. Through forfaiting, the exporter can convert its long-term, credit-based sale into a cash transaction.

The **U.S. Export-Import Bank (Ex-Im Bank)** is the principal government agency that provides loans, guarantees, and insurance programs to support U.S. exporters. Ex-Im Bank provides direct loans to foreign buyers of U.S. exports and intermediary loans to responsible parties, such as a foreign government lending agency that relends to foreign buyers of capital goods and related services. Ex-Im Bank loans can be made for up to 85 percent of the value of the exported goods and services, with repayment terms of one year or more. Although Ex-Im Bank does not compete with institutions in the private sector, it does help small businesses obtain working capital to cover their export sales by guaranteeing private bank working capital loans. It also offers export credit insurance that helps an exporter reduce the political and commercial risks associated with an export sale. Ex-Im Bank has supported nearly $600 billion in export sales in its 80 years of existence, many of which were in developing countries. More than 90 percent of the bank's transactions in 2016 supported U.S. small businesses.[14]

Other government incentives for trade that are closely related to export financing are the Overseas Private Investment Corporation and the foreign trade zone.[15] The **Overseas Private Investment Corporation (OPIC)** is a government corporation formed to stimulate private investment in developing countries that offers investors insurance against expropriation, currency inconvertibility, and damages from wars or revolutions. OPIC also offers specialized insurance for U.S. service contractors and exporters operating in foreign countries.

Foreign trade zones (FTZs) are duty-free areas designed to facilitate trade by reducing the effect of customs restrictions. These areas may be free ports, transit zones, free perimeters, export processing zones, or free trade zones. In each instance, a specific and limited area is involved, into which imported goods may be brought without the payment of import duties. There are 3,000 of these zones in one form or another in more than 135 countries.[17] Of the five types, the free trade zone (FTZ), an area designated by a government as outside its customs territory, is the most common.

In an FTZ, foreign goods may be brought in for eventual transshipment, reexportation, or importation into the country. While the goods are in the zone, no import duties need be paid. Examples range from the Zhuhai Free Trade Zone, near Macao in China, to Chabahar in Iran. In the United States, free trade zones often are called foreign trade zones (the FTZ acronym is used for both). In other countries, they are called "special economic zones" or "free zones." Goods brought into the FTZ may be stored, inspected, repackaged, or combined with other components. Because of differences in the import tariff schedule, the finished product often incurs lower duty than would the disassembled parts. Importers of machinery and automobiles improve their cash flow by storing spare parts in an FTZ because duty is not paid until they are withdrawn from the free trade area.

Those are advantages to importers. Exporters can also benefit by using FTZs. If the exported goods qualify for excise tax rebates or customs drawbacks, that is, rebates on customs duties, moving the goods to FTZ can accelerate the rebate process because a product is exported as soon as it enters the FTZ. The federal government collects the tax when the item (e.g., tires, trucks, tobacco products) is manufactured. When the product is exported, the tax can be rebated. Although U.S. Customs has had the customs-drawback program in place since 1789, many firms do not use it. Each year about $2.4 billion of potential customs duty drawback rebates goes unclaimed.[18] FTZs offer another benefit to exporters, as well. When manufacturing or assembly is done in FTZs using imported components, no duties need ever be paid if the finished product is exported.

Export Procedures and Export Documents

Often those new to exporting are concerned about the complexity of export procedures, especially the documentation. Instead of dealing with the two documents used in domestic shipments—the freight bill and the bill of lading—export novices are confronted with five to six times as many documents, depending on the country. Table B.2 summarizes export documentation required for major locations and the United States.

U.S. Export-Import Bank (Ex-Im Bank)
Government agency that provides loans, guarantees, and insurance programs to support American exporters

Overseas Private Investment Corporation (OPIC)
A government corporation that offers U.S. investors in developing countries insurance against expropriation, currency inconvertibility, and damages from wars and revolutions

free trade zone (FTZ)
An area designated by a government as outside its customs territory

customs drawbacks
Rebates on customs duties

LO B-4
Describe export documentation.

TABLE B.2 Official Procedures for Exporting and Importing

Region or Economy	Documents for Export (number)	Cost to Export Documentary Compliance (US$)	Time for Export (hours)	Cost to Export (US$ per container)	Documents for Import (number)	Cost to Import Documentary Compliance (US$)	Time for Import (hours)	Cost to Import (US$ per container)
East Asia and Pacific	6	112.1	55.9	387.5	7	111.4	70.5	431
Eastern Europe and Central Asia	7	113.8	28	191.4	8	94.7	25.9	185.1
Latin America and Caribbean	6	110.4	62.5	526.5	7	119.5	64.4	684
Middle East and North Africa	6	243.6	62.6	464.4	8	266.2	112.3	540.7
OECD	4	35.4	12.7	149.9	4	25.6	8.7	111.6
South Asia	8	179.5	59.4	369.8	10	341.6	113.8	638
United States	3	60	1.5	175	5	100	1.5	175

Source: "Trading Across Borders," *World Bank*, 2018, www.doingbusiness.org.

"Exports move on a sea of documents" is a popular saying in the industry, and it seems an accurate description. Many firms give at least part of this work to a foreign freight forwarder, who acts as an agent for the exporter. Foreign freight forwarders prepare documents, book space with a carrier, and in general act as the firm's export traffic department. They also are a source of advice about markets, import and export regulations, the best mode of transport, and export packing, and will supply cargo insurance. After shipment, they forward documents to the importer or the paying bank, according to the exporter's requirements. We look now at the two basic elements of exporting, the paperwork and the actual transportation of goods. Then, in the next section, we look at import procedures, often the mirror image of export procedures.

Correct documentation is vital to the success of any export shipment, yet error rates reported for export and import documentation hover between 50 and 70 percent, largely because they are documents that are prepared by different parties, yet their data need to be consistent.[19] Think of what that statistic means: goods waiting in a container, on a dock, or in a warehouse, tying up working capital. We'll review the two sets of documents required to ship and collect goods.

Shipping documents are prepared by exporters or their freight forwarders so that the shipment can pass through U.S. Customs, be loaded on the carrier, and be sent to its destination. They include the bill of lading, the export packing list, the shipper's export declaration, the export licenses, the export bill of lading, and the insurance certificate. The bill of lading is a shipping document issued by the carrier that gives the title of the shipment to a specified party. The export packing list includes the packing details: seller, buyer, shipper, invoice number, date of shipment, mode of transport, carrier, quantity, description, type of package, number of goods, and gross weight. These first two documents are similar to those used in domestic traffic.

shipper's export declaration (SED)
U.S. Department of Commerce form used to control export shipments and record export statistics

The **shipper's export declaration (SED)** is a form required by the Department of Commerce to control exports and supply export statistics, containing the names and addresses of the shipper and consignee, the U.S. port of exit and foreign port of unloading, a description and value of the goods, the export license number and bill-of-lading number, and the name of the carrier transporting the merchandise. Shippers or their agents (foreign freight forwarders) deliver the SED to the carrier, which turns it in to U.S. Customs with the carrier's manifest (list of the vessel's cargo) before the carrier leaves the United States. The filing of this form is electronic.

Most exports from the United States do not require export licenses, but there is a small group of strategic goods that do require licensing, such as scarce materials, strategic goods, technology, and goods with military applications.

export bill of lading (B/L)
Document issued by the carrier that is a contract for the shipment, a receipt for the goods shipped, and a certificate of ownership

An **export bill of lading (B/L)** serves three purposes: (1) it is a contract for carriage between the shipper and the carrier; (2) a receipt from the carrier for the goods shipped; and (3) a certificate of ownership. B/Ls are either straight or to order. A straight bill of lading is nonnegotiable. Only the person stipulated in it may obtain the merchandise on arrival. An order bill of lading, however, is negotiable. It can be endorsed like a check or left blank. With an order B/L, the holder is the owner of the merchandise.

The insurance certificate is evidence that the shipment is insured against loss or damage while in transit. Unlike domestic carriers, oceangoing steamship companies assume no responsibility for the merchandise they carry unless their negligence causes the loss. Marine insurance may be arranged by either the exporter or the importer, depending on the terms of sale. The laws of some countries may require that the importer buy such insurance, thus protecting the local insurance industry and saving foreign exchange. If the exporter has sold-on-sight draft terms, the exporter carries the risk while the goods are in transit. In this case, the exporter should buy a type of coverage known as contingent interest insurance that will protect the exporter if the shipment is lost or damaged and collection from the buyer is not successful. An exporter selling on CFR terms (the buyer purchases the insurance) should also buy contingent interest insurance to protect itself in case the buyer's insurance does not cover all risks.

There are three kinds of marine insurance policies: (1) basic named perils; (2) broad named perils; and (3) all risks. Basic named perils include perils of the sea, fires, jettisons, explosions, and hurricanes. Broad named perils include theft, pilferage, nondelivery, breakage, and leakage in addition to the basic perils. All-risks marine insurance covers all physical loss or damage from any external cause and is more expensive than the other two types of policies. War risks are covered under a separate contract. Premiums depend on a number of factors, such as the goods insured, the destination, the age of the ship, whether the goods are stowed on deck or under deck, the volume of business, how the goods are packed, and the number of claims the shipper has filed. Brokers will sometimes admit that, much like in auto insurance, filing numerous small claims is not a great idea, even if justified, because the higher premiums charged for future shipments will exceed any money recovered.

In order to receive payment, the seller provides the buyer with collection documents that enable the buyer to receive the goods. These documents vary among countries and customers, but some of the most common are commercial and consular invoices, certificates of origin, and inspection certificates.

The commercial invoice used in export is similar to the domestic one, but includes additional information, such as the origin of the goods, export packing marks, and a clause stating that the goods will not be transshipped to another country. Invoices for letter-of-credit sales name the bank and the L/C number. Some importing countries require that the commercial invoice be in their language and be endorsed by their local consul. The consular invoice is a special form purchased from the consul, prepared in the language of the country, and then visaed (endorsed) by the consul. Along with the export invoice, many governments require a certificate of origin, which is usually issued by the local chamber of commerce and also visaed by the consul.

An inspection certificate is required frequently by buyers of grain, foodstuffs, and live animals. In the United States, inspection certificates are issued by the Department of Agriculture. Purchasers of machinery or products containing a specified combination of ingredients may insist that a U.S. engineering firm or laboratory inspect the merchandise and certify that it is exactly as ordered. The European Union requires the **Conformité Européene (CE) mark**, which indicates that merchandise conforms to European health, safety, and environmental requirements. It is the European "trade passport": once a product has this mark, it can travel to any other EU member country without modification.[20] The certification process has been streamlined, and most merchandisers can self-certify that their merchandise conforms to EU regulations. Inspection by authorized testing houses is required of hazardous goods.

Conformité Européene (CE) mark
EU mark that indicates that merchandise conforms to European health, safety, and environmental requirements

 CULTURE FACTS @internationalbiz

Argentina shows a high need for rules and systems on Hofstede's uncertainty avoidance measure. That may help explain why, although agriculture ought to be Argentina's strength, it has instead become a weakness because of government intervention meant to reduce inflation and make sure Argentines are fed (uncertainty avoidance). Increased export taxes and quotas on wheat designed to keep it home have done more than discourage exports; they have encouraged farmers not to plant.[21]
#hofstedesuncertaintyavoidance #agriculture #weakness #governmentintervention #reduceinflation

SOCIAL MEDIA

EXPORT SHIPMENTS

The physical movement of exported goods has been a welcome innovation in material-handling techniques that can help exporters reduce costs and perhaps reach markets they previously could not serve. Containerization, LASH, RO-RO, size, and air freight all offer increasingly cheaper, faster, and safer transportation solutions, shrinking our globe.

One means of reducing both theft and handling costs is to use containers, large boxes—8 feet by 8 feet by 10, 20, or 40 feet—that the seller fills with the shipment in the firm's warehouse. Once packed, the containers are then sealed; they are opened when the goods arrive at their final destination. Containers are transported by truck or rail from the warehouse to shipside for loading. From the port of entry, railroads or trucks deliver them, often unopened even for customs inspection, to the buyer's warehouse. In most countries, customs officials go to the warehouse to examine the shipment. This integrated process reduces handling time and the risk of damage and theft because the buyer's own employees unload the containers.

If the importer or exporter has a warehouse on a river too shallow for ocean vessels, the firm can save time and expense by loading containers on barges. *LASH* (lighter aboard ship) vessels provide direct access to ocean freight service for exporters and importers located on shallow inland waterways. Sixty-foot-long barges ("lighters") are towed to inland locations, loaded, and towed back to deep water, where they are loaded aboard anchored LASH ships. Another innovation in cargo handling is *RO-RO* (roll on–roll off) ships. Loaded trailers and any equipment on wheels can be driven onto these specially designed vessels. RO-RO service has brought the benefits of containerization to ports that have been unable to invest in the expensive lifting equipment required for containers.

In addition, ship size continues to expand. Until recently, the standard largest size was "Panamax," which fit through the Panama Canal's locks with only feet to spare. "New Panamax" ships were too big for the canal—nearly 44 feet too wide and more than 200 feet longer than the canal could accept. So, Panama expanded the canal with a set of larger locks, which became operational in 2016. However, the newest Triple-E ships and TI class supertankers, as well as some of the largest cruise ships, are too big for even the new canal locks.

Air freight has had a profound effect on international business because it permits shipments that once required 30 days to arrive in 1 day. Huge freight planes carry payloads of 200,000 pounds, most of which goes either in containers or on pallets. Airlines guarantee overnight delivery from New York to many European airports and claim that their planes can be loaded or unloaded in 45 minutes.

Newcomers to exporting might assume that ocean freight is a better choice than air freight because ocean freight is so much cheaper. Comparison of total costs of each mode may suggest otherwise. Total cost components that may be lower for air freight include insurance rates, because of a smaller chance of damage during shipment; packing costs, because the shipment does not need the heavier, more costly export packing, which is usually done by an outside firm; customs duties, when calculated on gross weights; replacement costs for damaged goods, again because of the reduced damage risk; and inventory costs, because rapid delivery by air freight often eliminates the need for expensive warehouses. For example, Brabus SLR McLaren modifies stock Mercedes-Benz cars for top performance and includes in the price air freight from Germany to anywhere in the world.[22] Another cost saving is that machinery shipped by air does not require a heavy coat of grease to protect it from the elements, as does machinery sent by ship. Table B.3 provides a sample comparison of the cost elements of ocean and air freight on a sample shipment of spare parts.

TABLE B.3 Sea–Air Total Cost Comparison, Shipment of Spare Parts

	Ocean Freight (with warehousing)	Air Freight (no warehousing)
Warehouse administrative costs	$1,020	—
Warehouse rent	1,680	—
Inventory costs		
Taxes and insurance	756	$ 396
Inventory financing	288	192
Inventory obsolescence	1,800	0
Seller's warehouse and handling costs	1,810	1,140
Transportation	420	2,400
Packaging and handling	300	120
Cargo insurance	72	36
Customs duties	132	127
Total	**$8,278**	**$4,411**

THE ETHICS OF EXPORTING: Do Home Values Apply?

In late 2018, Australia's Parliament debated legislation to ban the export of live Australian sheep after reports of cruelty in a shipment of the animals to the Middle Eastern market of Qatar. Australian Green party senator Mehreen Faruqi said that footage aired on the show *60 Minutes* of sheep dying by the thousands due to heat stress and overcrowded conditions, a situation incompatible with the animals' welfare. The images reflected ocean shipments of sheep, with Faruqi commenting about how strongly she was impacted by scenes of, "scared, confused and terrified animals knee-deep in excrement . . . Sheep desperately trying to escape pens as they are literally cooked alive. Carcasses piled up as they decay in the oppressive heat." The operator of the ship, on which 2,400 animals died due to heat stress, had its license for live animal exports suspended in the wake of the incident and was subjected to criminal investigation.

Arguing against the ban, Liberal senator Slade Brockman argued that if Australia shut down their live sheep exporting industry, other less scrupulous exporters would provide the sheep instead. "We don't just export live animals—we export Australian welfare standards," Brockman told the Senate. Each year, about 1.4 million sheep raised in Australia are shipped live to foreign markets. In referring to live animal exports as "an abject failure," Labor Party member of Parliament Josh Wilson states, "There has been no independent supervision of these 'death ships,' and no penalties in relation to the mass death and suffering of sheep."

Western Australia's minister of agriculture, Alannah MacTiernan, encouraged consideration of efforts to increase the level of onshore meat processing rather than live animal exports. Such domestic butchering of animals would help to "get more value out of our livestock and create more jobs in Western Australian abattoirs."

Yet there are consequences to this decision that harm Australians. Sheep ranchers in Queensland depend on the live export market for their sales. Sheep farmer Richard Brown said, "I would go broke (if there was a move from live animal exports to domestic meat processing) because I totally rely on the live export industry. It's my whole business."

Critical Thinking Questions

1. Should home-country ethics be applied to exports?
2. Should quality standards thought to be appropriate for the domestic market be maintained for export markets in areas such as pharmaceuticals? Should the United Kingdom, which has outlawed the death penalty, export execution drugs to the United States?
3. To what degree are ethics domestic and to what degree are they universal? What do you think?

Sources: Paul Karp, "Live Exports Ban: Labor Fails in Attempt to Debate Bill in Lower House," *The Guardian,* September 19, 2018, www.theguardian.com; Paul Karp, "Live Exports Licence Suspended for Australia's Biggest Operator," *The Guardian,* June 22, 2018, www.theguardian.com; Brendan Foster, "Australia Shocked by Death of 2,400 Sheep on Ship to Qatar," *New York Times,* April 09, 2018, www.nytimes.com.

Even when the total shipping costs are higher for air freight, shipping by air may still be advantageous for several reasons. First, the total cost may decrease. Getting the product to the buyer more quickly results in a more satisfied customer and faster payment, which speeds up the return on investment and improves cash flow. The firm's capital is released more quickly and can be invested in other profit-making ventures or used to repay borrowed capital, thus reducing interest payments. Production equipment may be assembled and sent by air so that it goes into production sooner, without the transit and setup delays associated with ocean shipments, a strong sales argument. These production and opportunity costs, although difficult to calculate, are part of the total cost. Then, too, either the firm or the product may be air-dependent. Perishable food products being shipped to Europe, Japan, and the Middle East are in this category, as are live animals (newly hatched poultry and prize bulls) and fresh flowers. Without air freight, firms exporting such products would be out of business. Rather than the goods being perishable, the market itself may be perishable, as is the case for high fashion. For goods with short life cycles, delivery speed matters. Finally, air shipments may strengthen the firm's competitive position. The sales argument that spare parts and factory technical personnel are available within a few hours is a strong one for an exporting firm competing with overseas manufacturers.

LO B-5
Identify import sources.

Importing

In one sense, importers are the reverse of exporters: they sell domestically and buy in foreign markets. However, many of their concerns are similar. As in the case of exporters, there are small firms whose only business is to import, and there are global corporations for which importing components and raw materials valued at millions of dollars is just one of their functions. We now examine sources for imports, the role of customhouse brokers, and the payment of import duties.

SOURCES FOR IMPORTS

Before importing, a firm may have difficulty determining whether the desired items exist and, if so, where to find them. How does the prospective importer identify import sources? There are a number of ways. First, similar imported products may already be in the market. By close examination, you can learn where they are made and often by whom. U.S. law requires that the country of origin be marked clearly on each product or its container if product marking is not feasible (e.g., individual cigarettes). The consul or embassy of the country of origin can help with names of manufacturers. One of the principal duties of all foreign government representatives is to promote exports, and they do this through newsletters, trade shows, industry shows, and collaborative events with their home-country chamber of commerce group and other organizations such as, for Japan, the Japan External Trade Organization (JETRO), which has a number of offices outside Japan. The process is the same if the product is not being imported. You simply have less information with which to begin.

Other sources of information are online bulletin boards. Accidental importing also occurs with some frequency. When you visit a foreign country, look for products that may have a market at home. Finding one could put you into a new business, one that makes your foreign travel tax deductible.

CUSTOMHOUSE BROKERS

customhouse brokers
Independent businesses that handle import shipments for compensation

bonded warehouse
An area authorized by customs authorities for storage of goods on which payment of import duties is deferred until their removal

Every nation has customhouse brokers, whose functions parallel those of foreign freight forwarders but on the import side of the transaction. As the agent for the importer, the customhouse broker brings the imported goods through customs, which requires knowledge of import regulations and the tariff schedule. Customhouse brokers also provide other services, such as arranging transportation for the goods after they leave customs if necessary and keeping track of import quotas and how much of the quota has been filled at the time of the import. Merchandise subject to import quotas can be on the dock of a U.S. port awaiting clearance through customs, but if the quota fills anywhere during the wait, those goods cannot be imported for the rest of the fiscal year. The would-be importer can put them in a bonded warehouse or a foreign trade zone where merchandise can be stored without paying duty and wait for the rest of the year, abandon them, or send them to another country. Importers of high-fashion clothing had lost millions of dollars when quotas became filled and they had a shipment that had not yet cleared customs. By the following year, their goods were out of fashion.

High-end brands attract Hong Kong shoppers. ©Maosant Ludovic/Hemis.fr/Alamy Stock Photo.

CAMERON MAUZY: Internationalizing through Learning a Language and Immersing Abroad

Cameron Mauzy on internship in China. ©Courtesy of Cameron Mauzy.

I am an international business and business economics major. Prior to starting my undergraduate degree, my scope of the world outside the United States was very limited. Growing up in rural southeastern Ohio, just the mere thought of moving to another state seemed like taking on a lot of risk. However, once I found my passion for learning a language, all of my plans for the future took a turn for the better.

Learning Chinese has helped me find more opportunities to go abroad and interact with people with a vastly different background from mine. When I started learning Mandarin Chinese, I knew then that I wanted to incorporate more international-related work into my courses and future endeavors. This realization also resulted in me changing my major from marketing to international business. After my change in major was official, I then started to look for any opportunities that could move me closer to my goal of going abroad. The first thing I did was look for any international programs that could send me to China. Subsequently, after speaking with some of my professors, I found a summer-long study abroad opportunity in Beijing, China. In Beijing, I was able to do an intensive Chinese language course at Beijing Language and Culture University. Every day, for the whole summer, I was able to interact with Chinese native speakers and receive one-on-one instruction from my language partner.

After coming back to the United States, I felt the aftereffects of an extended abroad experience that I was warned about prior to the program. The after-effect I was warned about was the urge to tell everyone about my experience. Consequently, these urges led me to become more involved in a number of student organizations with international relevance, including the Chinese Language Student Association. In this organization, I am surrounded by other students who share my interests. Thus, a large portion of the students have been to China to study abroad and everyone has had a very impactful experience that they have in common with the others. After becoming increasingly involved, I became one of the members on the association's executive board. My task became one where I could interact with the other international organizations, creating many relationships that way.

Throughout my sophomore year, I was looking for more of an applicable experience that could contribute to my progress as an international business student. After speaking with my faculty mentors, I was led to an abroad exchange through AIESEC. I was able to get an international internship in Shanghai, China. During the internship, we were assigned many different projects. These projects included consulting with local businesses and marketing the company we were working for, Dare to Dream. Each change in location throughout the Shanghai region also gave us the opportunity to give back to the local communities through volunteer work. The people I was working alongside during these projects were from all over the world. This international network that I was able to build during the internship was one of the most rewarding aspects. Upon finding out that I was the only student from the United States, thoughts of being on my own throughout the internship began to manifest. However, because all of us interns worked alongside each other, I never experienced such feelings. Over the course of my entire immersion in China, I was always with other interns. Those constant interactions are what led to the creation of friendships with Thais, Chinese, Italians, Malaysians, and many others.

The main takeaway from my experiences abroad is the need to be flexible in your environment. Whether I was studying in a university or working alongside more than 14 different nationalities, I was constantly being put in situations where I didn't have all the answers given to me on a silver platter. When I was forced to constantly overcome the challenges that come with being in an unfamiliar environment, dealing with problems in my home country felt much easier. Now that I have had those experiences abroad, I don't feel tethered to my hometown or afraid to encounter any new areas around the world that I have yet to visit.

Source: Cameron Mauzy.

IMPORT DUTIES

Every importer needs to know how U.S. Customs calculates import duties and the importance of the product classification system, the Harmonized Tariff Schedule of the United States (HTSA or HTSUS), the U.S. version of the global tariff code, the Harmonized System. The Harmonized System is a classification system for the more than 200,000 commodities traded internationally, and it includes interpretive notes that help determine the classifications.

In HTSA each product has a unique number. All member countries use the same system, so it is possible to describe the product in any language by using the first six digits of the product's number. The other four digits are for use in the United States. The HTSA also shows the reporting units, which U.S. Customs uses in its paperwork. The last three columns have to do with the rates of duty, which are broken down into three levels for each item—general, special, and a third-level for countries not considered friends of the United States. The HTSA is accessible at https://www.usitc.gov/tata/hts/index.htm.

New importers would do well to follow this advice: fully disclose to the U.S. Customs Service all foreign and financial arrangements before passing the goods through U.S. customs. The penalties for fraud are high. Get the advice of a customhouse broker before making the transaction. Frequently, a simple change in the product description can result in much lower import duty. For example, jeans carry higher duties if the label is outside the back pocket instead of under the belt. If the words on the label are stylized, the duties are higher as well. Any clothing that is ornamented has a higher duty. One importer brings in plain sports shirts and then sews on an animal figure after the products are in the United States. One last word of advice: carefully calculate the landed price in advance. If you are unsure of the import category, ask U.S. Customs to identify the category in advance and to put it in writing, just like an advance ruling from the Internal Revenue Service. At the time of importation, customs inspectors must respect this determination.

  CULTURE FACTS @internationalbiz

Global Blue, a retail-tourism company, found that for 82 percent of Chinese travelers, shopping was a crucial part of their travel plans. Chinese tourists have no problem buying Prada by day, but many want to sleep in two-star hotels by night.[23] Such choices reflect a cultural disposition toward restraint rather than self-indulgence (Hofstede). High-quality, well-designed goods are one thing, self-indulgent consumption another. #tourism #chinesetravelers #shopping #pradabyday #twostarhotelsbynight #restraint

SOCIAL MEDIA

SUMMARY

LO B-1

Identify sources of export counseling and support.

The Trade Information Center, Small Business Administration, Small Business Development Centers, and Department of Agriculture are some sources of export counseling. The Department of Commerce offers many programs covering all aspects of exporting.

LO B-2

Explain the Incoterms, pricing, terms of sale, and payment.

The International Chamber of Commerce created a series of terms standardized internationally, Incoterms, that describe the conditions of sale. Any exporter will become familiar quickly with these 11 three-letter trade terms that describe the responsibilities of the buyer and seller in international trade transactions. They are divided depending on the mode of transportation, either general or water. Incoterms describe the three issues that arise in a commercial transaction: which party does which tasks, which party covers the costs, and which party bears the risk.

The choice of pricing strategy will depend on the firm's sales objectives. Terms of sale have implications for pricing, as well.

The terms of sale, that is, the sales agreement, needs to specify as simply as possible the duties of both the firm's foreign representative (the buyer) and the firm. It should include who files for patent protection and where any dispute is to be litigated.

Payment options for exporters offered to foreign buyers are cash in advance, open account, consignment, letters of credit, and documentary drafts.

LO B-3
Describe sources of export financing.

Some sources of export financing are commercial banks, factors, forfaiting, the Export-Import Bank (Ex-Im Bank), and the Small Business Administration.

LO B-4
Describe export documentation.

Foreign freight forwarders act as agents for exporters. Shipping documents include export packing lists, export licenses, export bills of lading, shipper's export declaration, and insurance certificates. Collection documents include commercial invoices, consular invoices, certificates of origin, and inspection certificates.

LO B-5
Identify import sources.

Prospective importers can identify sources in a number of ways. They can examine the product label to see where the product is made and then contact the nearest embassy of that country to request the name of the manufacturer. Foreign chambers of commerce and trade organizations provide information on their countries' exporters. Online bulletin boards are also useful.

KEY TERMS

air waybill 473
banker's acceptance 476
bonded warehouse 482
confirmed L/C 472
Conformité Européene (CE) mark 479
customhouse broker 482
customs drawbacks 477
export bill of lading (B/L) 478

export draft 475
factoring 476
forfaiting 476
free trade zone (FTZ) 477
Harmonized Tariff Schedule of the United States (HTSA or HTSUS) 484
Incoterms 470
irrevocable L/C 472

letter of credit (L/C) 472
Overseas Private Investment Corporation (OPIC) 476
pro forma invoice 474
shipper's export declaration (SED) 478
terms of sale 470
U.S. Export-Import Bank (Ex-Im Bank) 476

CRITICAL THINKING QUESTIONS

1. In exporting, at what point does the risk of loss or damage pass to the buyer? Use Incoterms to explain your response.

2. Explain the protection the various export payment terms offer the seller.

3. How does the bank operate as an intermediary in an L/C transaction?

4. The manager of the international department of the Cape Cod Five Bank learns that the ship on which a local exporter shipped Wellfleet oysters in saltwater tanks to Spain has sunk in high seas. She has received all the documents required in the letter of credit and is ready to pay the exporter for the shipment. In view of the news about the ship, the manager now knows that the Spanish customer will never receive the goods. Should the manager pay the exporter, or should she withhold payment and notify the overseas customer? Explain your answer.

5. How might the use of a free trade zone impact the pricing of an imported good composed of French and domestic components that was assembled in the FTZ?

6. What are the consequences of losing an export bill of lading for a shipment you need to collect?

7. An importer brings plain sports shirts into the United States because the import duty is lower than it is for shirts with adornments. In New Jersey, the importer sews on a figure of a fox. Could the importer do this operation in a foreign trade zone with no cost impact?

8. How would you find sources for a product that you saw when traveling in Myanmar and want to import to sell in your design studio?

9. "Exporting is so complicated it's not worth the extra hassle." How might you respond to this statement made by your company's director of marketing?

10. Exporting contributes about 12 percent to the U.S. GDP, which is low compared to other developed nations. Why might this be the case?

globalEDGE RESEARCH TASK http://globalEDGE.msu.edu/

Use the globalEDGE website (http://globalEDGE.msu.edu) to complete the following exercises:

1. Assessing whether a company is ready to start exporting is considered as one of the first steps of engaging in global trade. globalEDGE provides a section called "Export Tutorials" to assist companies that are looking for help on how to start exporting. Review the "Export Readiness" section of these tutorials. What type of options are available for a company to assess whether they are ready to start exporting?

2. Your company is going to start exporting and you need to find out if your product needs a license to export. But first you will need to identify the government agencies that have jurisdiction over the goods and services exported. Visit the "Export Tutorials" section of globalEDGE to find those government entities. Once found, visit their websites and prepare a brief explanation of their missions and the product groups they have jurisdiction over.

MINICASE

NASHVILLE GUITAR STORE

Mark Bortz has an interesting business. Operating from a warehouse outside Nashville, Tennessee, he buys brand-name guitars from resellers. These guitars have been imported into the United States, but haven't passed inspection by their U.S. resellers, so they have been resold to Mark. He has them refurbished in the United States and then sells them to both foreign and domestic buyers through eBay. He started selling on the U.S. eBay website about 11 years ago.

Many of his guitars are now sold abroad, ranging between 10 and 40 percent per year according to Operations Manager Joel Grumblatt. So, the process is that these guitars are imported by someone else, he buys and refurbishes them, and he exports them to foreign buyers. He reports: "Some international buyers found us and we slowly began shipping to different countries. We now list on several foreign eBay sites. It has always surprised me that guitar players would buy a guitar without first playing it, especially buying a guitar from another country. It also surprises me that someone would purchase a guitar and then pay more than 50 percent of the purchase price to have it shipped to them. I know that some of the guitar models we sell are not available in other

countries, and that some foreign prices are inflated, making our prices attractive, even with the high shipping costs."

He noted, "Russian buyers tend to favor 'heavy metal/shredder' type guitars [and] Scandinavian countries (Denmark, Sweden, Norway) tend to favor white guitars. Most buyers in South America request that we change the value on the VAT tax form or mark the package as a gift. They do that to reduce or eliminate government taxes. We also find that most of the scam type communications we receive come from South American buyers. The Nashville Guitar Store has decided to no longer ship to SA."

Critical Thinking Questions

1. Can you think of other possible businesses that could use this import–add value–re-export strategy?
2. Are there ways Mark could vertically integrate to capture more of the value his business adds to the guitars?

Sources: http://www.nashvilleguitarstore.com, accessed November 19, 2018; e-mail interview with Mark Bortz (September 23, 2014); and e-mail correspondence with Joel Grumblatt (October 25, 2018).

SAMPLE OUTLINE FOR AN EXPORT MARKETING PLAN

I. Purpose—Why has the plan been written?

II. Table of contents—Include a list of any appendixes.

III. Executive summary—This is short and concise (no longer than two pages) and covers the principal points of the report. It is prepared after the plan has been written.

IV. Introduction—Explains why the firm will export.

V. Situation analysis.

   A. Description of the firm and products to be exported.

   B. Company resources to be used for the export business.

C. Competitive situation in the industry.

1. Product comparisons.
2. Market coverage.
3. Market share.

D. Export organization—personnel and structure.

VI. Export marketing plan.

A. Long- and short-term goals.

1. Total sales in units.
2. Total sales in dollars.
3. Sales by product lines.
4. Market share.
5. Profit and loss forecasts.

B. Characteristics of ideal target markets.

1. GNP/capita.
2. GNP/capita growth rate.
3. Size of target market.

C. Identify, assess, and select target markets.

1. Market contact programs.
   (a) U.S. Department of Commerce.
   (b) World Trade Centers.
   (c) Chamber of Commerce.
   (d) Company's bank.
   (e) State's export assistance program.
   (f) Small Business Administration.
   (g) Small Business Development Center in local university.
   (h) Export hotline directory.

2. Market screening.
   (a) First screening—basic need potential.
   (b) Second screening—financial and economic forces.
       (1) GNP/capita growth rate.
       (2) Size of target market.
       (3) Growth rate of target market.
       (4) Exchange rate trends.
       (5) Trends in inflation and interest rates.
   (c) Third screening—political and legal forces.
       (1) Import restrictions.
       (2) Product standards.
       (3) Price controls.
       (4) Government and public attitude toward buying American products.
   (d) Fourth screening—sociocultural forces.
       (1) Attitudes and beliefs.
       (2) Education.

(3) Material culture.
(4) Languages.

(e) Fifth screening—competitive forces.
    (1) Size, number, and financial strength of competitors.
    (2) Competitors' market shares.
    (3) Effectiveness of competitors' marketing mixes.
    (4) Levels of after-sales service.
    (5) Competitors' market coverage—Can market segmentation produce niches that are now poorly attended?

(f) Field trips to best prospects.
    (1) Department of Commerce trade mission.
    (2) Trade missions organized by state or trade association.

D. Export marketing strategies.

1. Product lines to export.
2. Export pricing methods.
3. Channels of distribution.
   (a) Direct exporting.
   (b) Indirect exporting.
4. Promotion methods.
5. After-sales and warranty policies.
6. Buyer financing methods.
7. Methods for ongoing competitor analysis.
8. Sales forecast.

VII. Export financial plan.

A. Pro forma profit and loss statement.
B. Pro forma cash flow analysis.
C. Break-even analysis.

VIII. Export performance evaluation.

A. Frequency.

1. Markets.
2. Product lines.
3. Export personnel.

B. Variables to be measured.

1. Sales by units and dollar volume in each market.
2. Sales growth rates in each market.
3. Product line profitability.
4. Market share.
5. Competitors' efforts in each market.
6. Actual results compared to budgeted results.

NOTES

1. Lord Livingston, UK trade minister.

2. Kling, Arnold, "International Trade," *The Library of Economics and Liberty*, 2018, www.econlib.org.

3. International Trade Administration, "About the International Trade Administration," https://www.trade.gov, accessed November 19, 2018.

4. Ibid.

5. International Trade Administration, "The LaMotte Company," https://www.trade.gov/success/lamotte.asp, accessed November 19, 2018.

6. United States Census Bureau, "Preliminary Profile of U.S. Exporting Companies, 2017," Release Number: CB 18–155, https://www.census.gov/foreign-trade/Press-Release/edb/2017/2017prelimprofile.pdf, accessed November 19, 2018.

7. The SBA has a book-length guide to the export process, "Breaking into the Trade Game: A Small Business Guide to Exporting," available at https://books.google.com.

8. U.S. Small Business Administration, "The 12 Most Common Mistakes Made by New Exporters," http://www.agmrc.org/business_development/operating_a_business/exporting/the-12-most-common-mistakes-made-by-new-exporters, accessed January 28, 2015.

9. Laurie Burkitt, "Mattel Gives Barbie a Makeover for China," *The Wall Street Journal*, https://www.wsj.com, accessed November 19, 2018.

10. U.S. Small Business Administration, "The 12 Most Common Mistakes Made by New Exporters," January 28, 2015.

11. International Chamber of Commerce, "Incoterms Rules 2010," https://iccwbo.org, accessed November 19, 2018. A recent technical study on the role of L/Cs and banks in world trade is Friederike Niepmann and Tim Schmidt-Eisenlohr, "International Trade, Risk, and the Role of Banks," Federal Reserve Bank of New York Staff Reports, https://www.newyorkfed.org, accessed November 19, 2018.

12. Mike Branom, "The Lucrative, Barely Legal Business of Shipping Luxury Cars to China," *The Daily Beast*, https://www.thedailybeast.com, accessed November 19, 2018; Joan Muller, "Millions of Dollars Seized Along with BMWs, Porsches and Mercedes in Government Crackdown on Vehicle Exports," *Forbes*, https://www.forbes.com, accessed November 19, 2018; and Matthew Goldstein, "U.S. Targets Buyers of China-Bound Luxury Cars," *New York Times*, https://dealbook.nytimes.com, accessed November 19, 2018.

13. "Sample Procedure for Letter of Credit Administration," https://www.crfonline.org, accessed November 19, 2018.

14. Export-Import Bank of the United States, "The Facts About EXIM Bank," https://www.exim.gov, accessed November 19, 2018.

15. More information about the Overseas Private Investment Corporation can be found at https://www.opic.gov, accessed November 19, 2018. Information about U.S. foreign trade zones, which are secure areas supervised by the U.S. Customs and Border Protection, can be found at "About Foreign-Trade Zones and Contact Info," https://www.cbp.gov, accessed November 19, 2018.

16. Jagdish, Bhagwati, *Protectionism*, Cambridge, MA: MIT Press, 1988.

17. "FTZs," https://www.knowyourcountry.com/free-trade-zones, accessed November 19, 2018.

18. Purolator, "Duty Drawback: Could Your Business be Eligible for a Duty Reimbursement?" https://www.purolatorinternational.com, accessed November 19, 2018.

19. Alliance International, https://alliancechb.com, accessed November 19, 2018.

20. "Aptean TradeBeam," https://www.aptean.com, accessed November 19, 2018.

21. "Against the Grain," https://www.economist.com, accessed November 19, 2018; Hofstede Insights, "Argentina," https://www.hofstede-insights.com, accessed November 19, 2018.

22. Joel Feder, "This Mercedes-Benz Brabus G63 6x6 Could Be Yours in the U.S. for $1.35M," *Motor Authority*, https://www.motorauthority.com, accessed November 19, 2018; and Jeff Glucker, "Brabus-tuned 2019 Mercedes-Benz G-Class Turns Up the Power, Baffles with Styling," *Motor Authority*, https://www.motorauthority.com, accessed November 19, 2018.

23. "China's Addiction to Luxury Goods," *The Economist*, https://www.economist.com, accessed November 19, 2018.

C Global Operations and Supply Chain Management

> **One of the most significant paradigm shifts of modern business management is that individual businesses no longer compete as solely autonomous entities, but rather as supply chains.**
>
> *—Douglas Lambert and Martha Cooper, in "Issues in Supply Chain Management"*[1]

Urbee 2, an ultra fuel-efficient, 3D-printed car at an auto show. ©Piero Cruciatti/Alamy Stock Photo.

LEARNING OBJECTIVES

After reading this module, you should be able to:

LO C-1   **Explain** the concept of supply chain management.

LO C-2   **Discuss** the relationship between design and supply chain management.

LO C-3   **Describe** the reasons for sourcing globally, the five global sourcing arrangements, and the benefits and challenges of global sourcing.

LO C-4   **Explain** why manufacturing systems and logistical elements may vary, even within the same company.

LO C-5   **Explain** the potential in, and challenges to, global standardization of production processes and procedures.

3D Printing: Will It Transform Global Manufacturing and Supply Chains?

Ever since the onset of the Industrial Revolution in the 1700s, manufacturing has typically been viewed as consisting of factories and mechanization. In recent years, manufacturing has evolved into a global network of integrated supply chains that source raw materials and components from locations around the world, assemble them into finished goods in globally efficient plants, and then ship to warehouses for ultimate delivery to customers in the consuming nations. Large plants able to achieve economies of scale in production often provide the foundation for modern global competitiveness.

This model of production may be changing, and in profound ways, due to the emergence of 3D printing. Sometimes called additive manufacturing, 3D printing uses a digital blueprint as a guide for creating a final product, "printing" the product by methodically adding material in a layer-by-layer manner. 3D printing can create products that are extremely detailed and intricate, including items that are difficult or impossible to make using more traditional production methods. Rather than subtracting material, as traditional manufacturing often does when it cuts, grinds, and otherwise reduces metals, wood, plastic, or other materials to their desired size and shape, 3D printing only adds the material necessary for creating the intended product. It can build products in an array of materials, including metal, plastics, ceramics, glass, and even food and human tissue. The aerospace company Boeing has printed more than 22,000 components for use in a range of aircraft. The Federal Aviation Authority approved Boeing's use of 3D-printed titanium structural parts on the 787 Dreamliner, possibly saving the company up to $3 million per jet.

Currently, prototyping is the most common application, accounting for about 55 percent of the 3D printing market. 3D printing allows rapid production of prototypes of new designs, enabling designers to test the feasibility and attractiveness of a new product quickly. Unlike traditional manufacturing, there is not likely to be a cost advantage to locating 3D printing sites abroad. By instead allowing production to be completed in close proximity to the customer, 3D printing facilitates just-in-time production close to the place of assembly or sale and reduces the need for large production runs and the time and money required for transporting and warehousing of products.

"Supply chains that support the flow of products and parts to consumers will vanish, to be replaced by supply chains of raw materials," argues Professor Yossi Sheffi of MIT. 3D printing allows production in batches of one, facilitating customiza-tion. For example, dental crowns, hearing aids, and personalized orthopedic joint replacements could be produced in a medical office, perhaps even while you are being seen by the doctor. 3D printing can also revolutionize the logistics of spare parts and service activities. Rather than maintaining an expensive inventory of different spare parts, a service person could simply download designs from the Internet and use a 3D printer in the back of a vehicle to produce the necessary parts on an as-needed basis.

Will 3D printing eliminate existing manufacturing and supply chain networks? That is unlikely in the short term. The size, speed, and precision of existing printers still limit the ability of 3D printing to produce many items in an efficient manner. Although 3D printers have been used experimentally to produce objects such as automobiles, most current printers allow production of only simple items produced from only one or two materials. The range of materials available for use in 3D printing is still somewhat limited and the costs much higher. The supply chains for producing and delivering these materials in a manner suitable for 3D printing are also still at an early stage of development. Because the blueprints used for 3D printing are digital, concern has been expressed about how to protect intellectual property rights of those who develop the blueprints, and there are concerns regarding who would have liability for the production of defective products. Nevertheless, while 3D printing is still at the initial stage of development, the technology has the potential to advance rapidly and to have a broad impact on the nature and location of manufacturing and supply chain activities worldwide. For example, the global 3D printing market was valued at under $8 billion in 2016 but projected to exceed $33 billion by the end of 2022. An analysis by A.T. Kearney projected that, within 10 years, 3D printing could impact up to 42 percent of production in automotive, consumer products, health care, aerospace, and industrials sectors; bring 3 to 5 million skilled jobs back to the United States, and generate up to $900 billion in economic value.

Sources: James Vincent, "3D-Printed Titanium Parts Could Save Boeing Up to $3 Million Per Plane," *The Verge*, April 11, 2017, www.theverge.com; Louis Columbus, "The State of 3D Printing 2016," *Forbes*, June 08, 2016, www.forbes.com; "Global 3D Printing Market by Type, Technology Used, Process, Industry, Geography, Trends and Forecast to 2022," *Orbis Research*, June 07, 2018, www.reuters.com; Laura Taylor-Kale, and Tim Simpson, "3D Printing and the Future of the US Economy," *ATKearney*, 2018, www.atkearney.com; Mark Patterson, "3D Printing and the Supply Chains of the Future," *eft*, February 18, 2013, www.eft.com; "3D Printing and the Future of Manufacturing," *Computer Sciences Corporation*, 2018, www.assets1.csc.com; and Natasha Clark, "Will 3D Printing Transform the Supply Chain?," *Business Reporter*, April 17, 2014, www.business-reporter.

As firms continue to enter global markets, global competition increases. This forces management of both international and domestic companies to search for ways to lower costs while improving their products or services in order to remain competitive. Sometimes the desired results are obtained through improvements within existing operations. Other times, improved competitiveness is pursued by having the company open new—or transfer existing—operations abroad or find alternative outside sources for labor, raw materials, or other inputs that it is currently sourcing from other organizations. A third option is outsourcing; that is, hiring others to perform some of the noncore activities and decision making in a company's value chain, rather than having the company and its employees continue to perform those activities. Commonly, outsourcing firms provide key components of data processing, logistics, payroll, and accounting, although any activity in the value chain can be outsourced. Management will often pursue some combination of these different options in their efforts to enhance their company's international competitiveness. The process of coordinating and integrating the flow of materials, information, finances, and services within and among companies in the value chain from suppliers to the ultimate consumer is often referred to as supply chain management. In this module, we discuss the topics of global supply chain management and critical issues in the management of global operations, including global sourcing, manufacturing systems, productivity and performance of international manufacturing operations, and issues associated with global standardization versus localization of international operations.

outsourcing
Hiring others to perform some of the noncore activities and decision making in a company's value chain, rather than having the company and its employees continue to perform those activities

supply chain management
The process of coordinating and integrating the flow of materials, information, finances, and services within and among companies in the value chain from suppliers to the ultimate consumer

LO C-1
Explain the concept of supply chain management.

Managing Global Supply Chains

Supply chain management has become an increasingly popular and strategically important topic in international business in recent years. *Supply chain* refers to the activities required to produce a company's products and services and the way these activities are linked together. Supply chain management applies a total systems approach to managing the overall flow of materials, information, finances, and services within and among companies in the value chain—from raw materials and components suppliers through manufacturing facilities and warehouses and on to the ultimate customer.[2] Supply chains are an integral part of global quality and cost management initiatives because a typical company's supply chain costs can represent more than 50 percent of assets and more than 80 percent of revenues.[3] Figure C.1 broadly illustrates the activities and links that transform initial designs at a U.S. laptop computer company into the finished goods and support services delivered to the consumer. These include product design, inputs from various suppliers, assembly and testing activities, warehousing and distribution of finished goods, and sales and technical support operations.

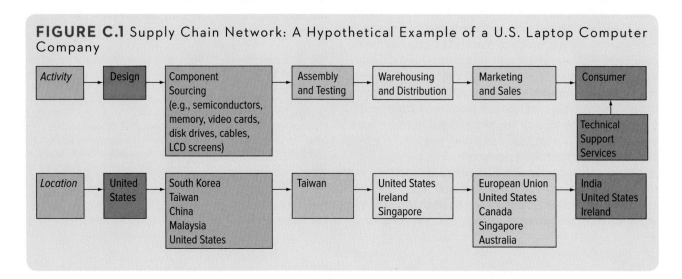

FIGURE C.1 Supply Chain Network: A Hypothetical Example of a U.S. Laptop Computer Company

| Activity | Design | Component Sourcing (e.g., semiconductors, memory, video cards, disk drives, cables, LCD screens) | Assembly and Testing | Warehousing and Distribution | Marketing and Sales | Consumer |

Technical Support Services

| Location | United States | South Korea Taiwan China Malaysia United States | Taiwan | United States Ireland Singapore | European Union United States Canada Singapore Australia | India United States Ireland |

Because inventory is carried at each stage in the supply chain, and because inventory ties up money, it has been argued that the ultimate goal of effective supply chain management systems is to reduce inventory, consistent with the prerequisites that the company's products be available when needed and at the desired level of quality and quantity. For that reason, it is critical that the operations at each stage in the supply chain are synchronized in order to minimize the size of these buffer inventories. Shorter, less predictable product life cycles, as well as the impact of unplanned economic, political, and social events, have placed further emphasis on the achievement of effective supply chain performance.[4] New technologies—including web-enabled tools for supply chain planning, execution, and optimization; machine learning; and artificial intelligence—have enhanced the availability of data and integration with suppliers and customers, helping to enhance the international competitiveness of companies that have adopted and mastered these technologies.[5]

As highlighted in the opening vignette on 3D printing, the IB in Practice box on Zara, the Global Debate box on Cognizant, and the Modern Millennials minicase at the end of this module, global supply chain management has been receiving increasing attention because many companies have achieved significant international competitive advantage as a result of the manner in which they have configured and managed their global supply chain activities. Some organizations, such as technology companies Apple and Dell, or retailers Walmart and Amazon, have reconfigured their international supply chains to substantially reduce or eliminate activities such as finished goods warehousing and retail stores, thus reducing costs and increasing effectiveness.[6] Other companies, such as the Hong Kong export trading company Li & Fung or logistics company FedEx, have transformed their operations to enter into new, value-adding activities in an industry's value chain.[7] Effective supply chain management can also enhance a company's ability to manage regulatory, social, and other environmental pressures, both nationally and globally.

Measurement of supply chain performance varies by industry and company because the way success is defined also tends to vary, and performance assessment should be aligned with a company's strategic objectives and the key factors for success. Typical measures include such metrics as the number of times inventory turns over in a year, the ratio of in-stock inventory versus the level of sales, the percentage of orders delivered on time, the level of defects per million, the proportion of orders fulfilled perfectly, and the number of orders that are unable to be filled due to stockouts.[8] Walmart, for example, reported that improved supply chain management increased inventory turns, reduced the level of stocking out of products, and reduced the time for replenishing stock from weeks to mere hours.

Design of Products and Services

LO C-2
Discuss the relationship between design and supply chain management.

An important factor in the structure and management of a company's global supply chain is the process of design. The design of a company's products and services has a fundamental relationship with the types of inputs that the company will require, including labor, materials, information, and financing. An important consideration in design is the extent to which the international company's products and services will be standardized across nations or regions or adapted to meet the different needs of various markets. The decision to standardize or localize is affected by a range of competitive, cultural, regulatory, and other factors.

As an example, Starbucks recognized the need to adapt the design of its coffee shops to local conditions, opening 18 different local design stores across the world to help identify the right mix of attributes to offer in each setting.[9] As a result, in Mexico the coffee shops are designed like a bar, to encourage discussions among groups of people. In China, Starbucks uses large community tables and movable furniture, since it is common for large groups to visit coffee shops together and linger for hours. In India, Starbucks uses hand-carved wooden screens and a range of decorations reminiscent of the mercantile past of Mumbai.

Indian version of Barbie. ©Alan Gillam/Alamy Stock Photo.

A traditional approach to product design is the "over the wall" approach. This takes a sequential approach to design: an initial step in which the designers prepare the product's design and then send it to the company's manufacturing engineers, who must address the production-related problems that often result from their exclusion from the initial design activity.

An alternative approach to design is to promote cross-functional participation in the design stage, thereby identifying and avoiding much potential sourcing, manufacturing, and other difficulties. Many companies also pull key customers into their design activities, to ensure that designs are consistent with the customers' needs. Using this type of concurrent engineering approach allows the proposed designs to undergo earlier assessments on cost, quality, and manufacturability dimensions, thereby enhancing the efficiency and effectiveness of subsequent manufacturing and supply chain management activities. Indeed, design decisions must often be integrated with assessment of the various supply chain considerations, such as whether and where the company can obtain the inputs needed for its operations, whether it will source locally or from foreign locations, and whether it has the capability to produce and deliver the product or service in a competitive manner.

A recent design process innovation is to solicit very broad input, increasingly from general customers. Examples include Dell's IdeaStorm site and Starbucks's suggestion site.

 **CULTURE FACTS** @internationalbiz

@Mattel To better fit with the local culture, the toymaker Mattel modified the popular Barbie doll for the Indian market, changing the U.S. version of a tall, tanned blonde to a dark-haired girl with slightly darker skin, bindi (Hindi forehead application), and traditional sari for clothing. #toymaker #barbiedoll #indianmarket #culture

 SOCIAL MEDIA

Within a week of Starbucks's opening of its MyStarbucksIdea.com site, more than 100,000 votes had been cast for various improvement ideas. Logitech's program for gathering customer feedback on its line of computer peripherals enabled it to redesign a Bluetooth keyboard in a way that sharply increased customer satisfaction. Other companies like Nike are finding that such activities also help engage the customer, possibly increasing loyalty.[10] As discussed in the opening vignette of this module, combining rapid prototyping through the use of 3D printing with quick feedback cycles from customers can allow companies to quickly and effectively develop and deliver new products that better meet market needs.

Sourcing Globally

Should a company source its inputs domestically or internationally? In this section, we discuss some of the reasons a firm may choose to source globally, different arrangements for global sourcing, and the importance of sourcing globally. We will also discuss the trend toward increased use of electronic purchasing for global sourcing.

REASONS FOR SOURCING GLOBALLY

Although the primary reason for sourcing globally is to obtain lower prices, there are other reasons. Perhaps certain products the company requires are not available locally and must be imported. Another possibility is that the firm's foreign competitors are using components of better quality or design than those available in the home country. To be competitive, the company may have to source these components or production machinery in foreign countries. The term **offshoring** describes a company's decision to relocate some or all of its activities or processes to a foreign location.

When deciding to source internationally, companies can either set up their own facilities abroad or outsource the production to other companies either at home or abroad. Outsourcing overseas is often called "offshore outsourcing." Outsourcing has become an increasingly common option for companies, as they try to focus scarce resources on their core capabilities and leverage the skills of other companies to reduce costs and capital investments, improve flexibility and speed of response, enhance quality, and provide other strategic benefits. Any part of the value chain can be outsourced, including product design, raw material or component supply, manufacturing or assembly, logistics, distribution, marketing, sales, service, human resources, or other activities.

Outsourcing decisions, including the decision to use global sources of supply, are extensions of the make-or-buy decisions of earlier eras. The pros and cons of these decisions usually include comparisons of costs as well as managerial control of confidential product design specifications, delivered quantity, quality, design, and delivery time and method. Other considerations include the manufacturing expertise required to make the raw material or components and the added cost of not being able to take advantage of the scale or larger volumes a vendor may have. In global purchasing, these issues are complicated by such factors as distance, different languages of buyers and sellers, and different national laws and regulations. Over time, many organizations have developed the ability to manage these obstacles fully or in part, thus enabling global outsourcing to become a viable option for an increasing number of firms. Many experts suggest that, when possible, it is better for companies to initially outsource simple activities and gradually outsource more complex activities as both the outsourcer and the service provider gain experience.

The lure of global sourcing is the existence of suppliers with improved competitiveness in terms of cost, quality, timeliness, and other relevant dimensions. For example, certain nations may provide access to lower-cost or better-quality minerals or other important raw materials or components compared to what might be available domestically (such as iron ore in Brazil or organic light-emitting diode [OLED] digital displays in South Korea). In addition, the existence of industrially less-developed countries with inexpensive and abundant unskilled labor may provide an attractive source of supply for labor-intensive products with low skill requirements. This helps explain why many relatively standardized and

LO C-3
Describe the reasons for sourcing globally, the five global sourcing arrangements, and the benefits and challenges of global sourcing.

offshoring
Relocation of some or all of a business's activities or processes to a foreign location

labor-intensive operations (such as the assembly of athletic shoes or men's casual shirts) have moved away from the more industrialized countries, where labor is more expensive, to more cost-effective locations in the developing areas of the world. Over time, many of these emerging economies have transitioned from high-labor-content products made with light, unsophisticated process equipment and lower labor skill requirements, to sophisticated processes and more complex, lower-labor-content machinery, or skill-intensive engineering and design services. This evolution often results in the low-skill, labor-intensive activities migrating to other countries that might be even less economically developed.

The ability to effectively and efficiently use global sources has been enhanced by the plummeting cost of communications, widespread use of standardized interfaces such as web browsers, and the increasing pace at which companies are automating and digitizing data. As more of a company's operational activities are automated, it becomes easier and more economical to outsource these activities. Increasing numbers of companies around the world have begun to compete for outsourcing business, and customers have become more accustomed to using these services.

GLOBAL SOURCING ARRANGEMENTS

Any of the following sourcing arrangements can provide a firm with foreign products:

1. *Wholly owned subsidiary.* May be established in a country with low-cost labor to supply components to the home-country plant, or the subsidiary may produce a product that either is not made in the home country or is of higher quality.
2. *Overseas joint venture.* Established where labor costs are lower, or quality higher, than in the home country to supply components or other inputs to the home country.
3. *In-bond plant contractor.* Production plant in the home country or another nation sends components to be machined and assembled, or just to be assembled, by an independent contractor in an in-bond plant.
4. *Overseas independent contractor.* Common in the clothing industry, in which firms with no production facilities, such as DKNY, Nike, and Liz Claiborne, contract with foreign manufacturers to make clothing to their specifications and with their labels.
5. *Independent overseas manufacturer.* A company contracts with an independent manufacturer in another country to provide it with products, often designed by the overseas manufacturer.

IMPORTANCE OF GLOBAL SOURCING

A strong relationship exists between global sourcing and ownership of the foreign sources. **Intrafirm trade**, in which trade occurs between a parent company and its foreign affiliates, accounts for an estimated 30 to 40 percent of exports of goods and 35 to 50 percent of imports in the case of the United States and can represent more than 70 percent of such trade in sectors such as automobiles, medical equipment, and scientific instruments.[11]

In U.S. industry, the proportion of externally purchased materials in the overall cost of goods sold has been rising for several decades, from an average of 40 percent in 1945 to 50 percent in 1960 and 55 to 80 percent today.[12] There are several reasons for this phenomenon, including greater complexity of products and increasing pressure for firms to focus on their core business and outsource other activities in which they lack strong competitive ability.

In addition, competitive pressures and reduced concept-to-market cycle times in many product and service sectors have resulted in a rapid increase in the number of new products that are made available to the market. It has been estimated that about one-third of companies' sales are generated by products that were not available five years ago, and this figure rises to about 50 percent for the best-performing companies.[13] This development has created additional pressure to locate suppliers worldwide that can provide inputs at competitive prices and quality levels and respond quickly to market changes.

intrafirm trade
Trade that occurs between a parent company and its foreign affiliates

THE INCREASING USE OF ELECTRONIC PURCHASING FOR GLOBAL SOURCING

Simply entering "exporter" and the name of the product in a search engine will bring up the websites of dozens if not thousands of exporters around the world that have online catalogs and information on how to order their products. There are also buyers, some of them from large companies, looking for products. In recent years, many firms have set up electronic procurement (e-procurement) exchanges, individually or in conjunction with other firms, to identify potential suppliers or customers and facilitate efficient and dynamic interactions among these prospective buyers and suppliers.

indirect procurement
The purchasing of goods and services that are not part of finished goods

Ambitious business-to-business (B2B) e-procurement projects have been announced in a range of industries, such as chemicals (ChemConnect .com), petroleum, and hospital supplies. E-procurement systems are also common in the public sector (e.g., B2G or business-to-government sites like ebidexchange.com). In some companies, the purchasing function was neglected for many years and often viewed as a prime candidate for outsourcing to other firms. However, purchasing is increasingly considered a strategic function, a trend encouraged by rapid developments in e-procurement.

While direct production-oriented goods have been the focus of management attention for many years, the purchasing of goods and services that are not part of finished goods—termed indirect procurement—is also critical. With such items as maintenance, repair, operating supplies, office equipment, and other services and supplies, indirect procurement can account for 50 to 70 percent of the total purchasing expenditures in an average company.[14] Although many organizations have continued to rely on traditional paper-based processes for indirect procurement despite their cost and inefficiency, new technologies are quickly encouraging change in this approach, even at small- and mid-sized companies.

> **"THE PROMISE of AN EXCHANGE IS THAT IT ALLOWS THEM [SMALLER COMPANIES] to LEVERAGE THEIR SIZE FURTHER AND GET into MORE MARKETS, ESPECIALLY GLOBALLY AND INTERNATIONALLY, THAN THEY EVER HAVE before."**
>
> —Amanda Mesler, General Manager, Enterprise Business of Microsoft Central and Eastern Europe[15]

Options for Global Electronic Procurement Among the most basic transactions that can occur over electronic purchasing exchanges are catalog purchases. Suppliers will provide a catalog of the products available and buyers can access, review, and place orders for desired items at a listed price. The supplier can keep the catalog updated in real time, adjusting prices according to inventory levels and the need to move particular products. Electronic exchanges can also permit buyers and suppliers to interact through a standard bid/quote system in which buyers can post their purchasing needs online for all prospective suppliers to view and the suppliers can then submit private quotes to the buyer. The buyer can then select among the submitted quotations on the basis of price, delivery times, or other factors. Industry-sponsored exchanges can also facilitate obtaining letters of credit, contracting for logistics and distribution, and monitoring daily prices and order flows, among other services.

Benefits of Global Electronic Procurement Systems The benefits of electronic purchasing initiatives can be substantial, allowing companies to streamline operations, cut costs, and improve productivity in supply chain management and customer response. Websites like Exostar.com help companies simplify and standardize procurement processes, streamline supply chains, reduce costs, improve productivity, and reach new markets.

Smaller companies are also using the Internet to purchase raw materials as well as to sell their products to customers, often on a worldwide basis. Developments such as e-procurement exchanges have opened the door for many smaller suppliers, which now have to spend very little time and money to get into the market, lowering barriers to entry to domestic and international market opportunities.

Overall, industry-based B2B exchanges can help optimize the supply chain across an entire network of organizations, not merely within a single company. These exchanges can create value by aggregating the purchasing power of buyers, improving process efficiency, integrating supply chains, enhancing content dissemination, and improving overall market efficiency within and across nations.

Problems with Global Sourcing Although global sourcing has become a standard procedure for most medium-sized and larger firms, it does have some disadvantages. Inasmuch as lower price is the primary reason companies make foreign purchases, managers may be surprised that what initially appeared to be a lower price is not really lower once all the costs connected to the purchase are considered. For example, the buyer must understand the terms of sale because international freight, insurance, and packing can add as much as 10 to 12 percent to the quoted price, depending on the sales terms. The following is a list of many common costs of importing:

1. International freight, insurance, and packing
2. Import duties
3. Customhouse broker's fees
4. Transit or pipeline inventory
5. Cost of letter of credit
6. International travel and communication costs
7. Company import specialists
8. Reworking of products that do not meet specifications

In addition to added costs, one disadvantage an importer does not want to experience is an increase in price because the home currency has lost value as a result of exchange rate fluctuation. For example, if a U.S. importer requires that the exporter quote dollar prices, the importer has no exchange rate risk. However, if the firm has a large volume of imports and the dollar is unstable, management may want a quotation in a foreign currency. In that case, the chief financial officer of the importing company probably will protect the company from exchange rate risk by using various financial hedging techniques. Hedging has been used for many years by companies that operate internationally, particularly if their raw materials include one or more of the commodities traded on established commodities markets.[16] In most cases, such hedging has been done not for speculative reasons but as a means of protecting the company from the risk of rapid price fluctuations.

For purchases of capital goods such as manufacturing equipment, many U.S. buying organizations now use "life cycle costing" to analyze purchasing decisions through the life of the purchased item, including trade-in or future estimated salvage value. Even on components, firms are increasingly including full costing, including the use of activity-based costing systems, to ensure that all the costs associated with foreign sourcing (transportation, insurance, increased inventory levels to insulate against delays in delivery) are fully recognized when they make purchasing decisions.[17] It is essential that global sourcing decisions be closely linked to the organization's strategy and that explicit objectives for suppliers (such as delivery times and cost objectives) be defined and incorporated in contracts, ideally with incentives for meeting or exceeding them. Cross-company teams should also be developed to enhance the likelihood that best practices can be effectively shared between the organization and its suppliers, in order to avoid supply problems.

The widespread adoption of e-procurement has also been accompanied by problems. E-procurement and electronic commerce as a whole cannot be isolated from the company's overall business system. Many early efforts at developing e-procurement systems were made in isolation and subsequently failed to deliver on their potential. Successful electronic commerce initiatives include connections to traditional systems for fulfilling procurement and other value chain activities, as well as considerations on how to manage the transition to new, electronic approaches. The traditional functions of purchasing—supplier determination, analysis, and selection—still have to be accomplished before the actual purchasing via e-procurement. In most instances, a company may be able to use the Internet for quicker data acquisition about possible suppliers and generally from a much broader information base than was previously available in a timely manner. Ensuring that a supplier is selected that can meet all the company's requirements for its raw materials in terms of quality, delivery, price, and so forth remains a challenge, particularly in a broad-scale e-procurement network including suppliers with which the company is not familiar. Suppliers located in emerging nations may also encounter difficulty in accessing and supporting sophisticated information technology (IT) infrastructures, which can affect e-procurement performance.

Security is often another significant concern for e-procurement. For B2B electronic commerce to achieve its full potential, access to the company's internal systems from outside is critical. Companies are wary of opening up the details of their business—including pricing, inventory, or design specifications—to competitors, to avoid risking the loss of brand equity and margins. In addition, exposing internal business systems to access via the Internet can expose the firm to a wide range of potential security issues, such as unauthorized entry (e.g., hacking) and fraudulent orders. Although extensive research and development efforts have been undertaken in encryption technology and other processes to ensure integrity, much progress still remains to be achieved before these systems can be considered fully secure. Different country standards are also of concern in attempting to implement international e-procurement systems. Governmental concerns with potential anticompetitive effects of collaboration among competitors may also cause problems for industrywide B2B exchanges.

CULTURE FACTS @internationalbiz

Although it is a common practice in North America to bring a lawyer to negotiations, in some cultures this practice would be interpreted as a signal that the company lacks trust in its partner. #nolawyers #trust

SOCIAL MEDIA

Manufacturing Systems and Logistics

Because international firms maintain manufacturing facilities in countries at various levels of development—facilities utilizing factors of production that vary considerably in cost and quality from one country to another—it is understandable that manufacturing systems and the logistical elements associated with coordinating the movement of materials within and across sites will also vary considerably, even within the same company. A single company may have a combination of plants that range from those with the most advanced production technology to those with far less advanced technology. The manufacturing and logistics systems in place within and across a company's international operations can have important implications for the way in which the company's global supply chain is set up and managed.

LO C-4
Explain why manufacturing systems and logistical elements may vary, even within the same company.

ADVANCED PRODUCTION TECHNIQUES CAN ENHANCE QUALITY AND LOWER COSTS

Growing international competition requires increasing efforts from companies to achieve efficiency and effectiveness in their international production activities. As a result, companies all over the world have pursued ways to improve their competitiveness, putting into place advanced production systems such as just-in-time supply chains or highly synchronized manufacturing systems. Others have installed computer-integrated manufacturing (CIM), utilizing computers and robots to improve productivity and quality further. Although these innovations can be a major challenge to implement successfully, their impact on international companies' competitiveness can be impressive.

Reducing Costs through Just-in-Time Manufacturing Systems When examining production activities, managers are quick to recognize that inventory costs are a major factor. Getting rid of inventory can lower labor cost by 40 percent or more, for example.[18] To operate without inventory, however, requires rigorous attention to the various activities within the manufacturing system and how these activities fit together effectively. **Just-in-time (JIT)** production systems were developed to enable firms to manage inventory cost and enhance quality. JIT is a balanced system in which there is little or no delay time and

just-in-time (JIT)
A balanced system in which there is little or no delay time and idle in-process and finished goods inventory

Use of robots alongside humans within an auto assembly plant. ©Monty Rakusen/Cultura/Getty Images.

idle in-process and finished goods inventory. Henry Ford incorporated elements of JIT in his moving automobile assembly lines in the early 1900s. For JIT to work effectively, manufacturers typically have to meet the following requirements:

1. Components, whether purchased from outside suppliers or made in the same plant, have to be defect-free, or the production line will be shut down while workers in all successive operations wait for usable inputs.

2. Parts and components have to be delivered to each point in the production process at the time they are needed, hence the name.

3. Customers everywhere want delivery when they make a purchase, and so sellers maintain inventories of finished products. How long do you want to wait for delivery of your new car or smartphone after you buy it? Sales often are made because one firm can supply the product from stock, but a competitor cannot. Eliminating inventories of finished goods while still responding quickly to customers' orders requires manufacturers to set up flexible production units, which necessitates rapid setup times.

4. It is also necessary to reduce process time. One way to do this is to lower the time needed to transport work in progress from one operation to the next. Grouping machines according to the workflow of a single product (having a separate

production line for each product) can virtually eliminate transport costs. Also, because parts are arriving immediately from one operation to the next, when the output of the preceding operation is defective, that operation can be stopped until the cause is rectified. Because each succeeding operation acts as quality inspection, this also lowers production costs because fewer defective parts are produced.

5. Flexible manufacturing allows product changes to be made rapidly, but each change in the production line still costs money. Therefore, many manufacturers have chosen to simplify product lines and design the products to use as many of the same parts as possible. This also contributes to company suppliers' acceptance of the JIT concept because they receive fewer but larger orders, which permits longer production runs that are less costly due to fewer production changeovers.

6. For JIT to be successful, manufacturers need to have the cooperation of their suppliers. They are often unable to follow the practice of having numerous vendors, which buyers have traditionally played against one another to obtain the best price. Instead, firms use fewer vendors and seek to establish close relationships with them, including calling them in during the design of the product.

7. To lower costs, improve quality, and lower production times, managers attempt to get product designers, production managers, purchasing people, and marketers to work together as a team. Getting these people together enables suppliers to suggest using lower-cost standard parts they regularly produce, manufacturing to indicate when a design change could simplify the production process, and marketing to contribute the customer's viewpoint, all before the first product is produced.[19]

Many manufacturers that attempted to transform their operations by adopting JIT principles mistakenly incorporated only one part of JIT: the narrow focus on managing goods inventories, sometimes called "little JIT." They failed to realize that what is important is "big JIT," a total system covering the management of people, materials, and relationships with suppliers (this total system is also called *lean production*).[20] Moreover, many did not understand that JIT requires a thorough and companywide commitment to managing quality, of which continuous improvement is an integral part.

Improving Quality through Total Quality Management To improve quality, everyone in the organization—from top management to workers—has to be committed to quality. This realization has led to the creation of total quality management (TQM), a companywide management approach in which the entire organization is managed so that it excels on all dimensions of product and services that are important to the customer. Teams are necessary for the implementation of TQM, and one useful kind of team is the quality circle. A creation of Kaoru Ishikawa, a Japanese quality expert, a quality circle is a small work group that meets periodically to independently discuss ways to enhance the quality of the company's product or service. Quality circles are used in all functional areas of an organization, not merely manufacturing. The quality circle is commonly led by an employee who has received training in quality control techniques. The activities of the overall quality circle are then divided among subgroups of circle members, each led by someone junior to the circle's leader.

The president of Komatsu, a Japanese competitor to the construction equipment company Caterpillar, describes the use of quality circles in his company in this way: "*Quality circle members are aware of the extent to which their achievement of their objectives will contribute to the results of their department, and also to the business of the company as a whole.*"[21] He described a situation in which outside callers to Komatsu were complaining about

total quality management (TQM)
A companywide management approach in which the entire organization is managed so that it excels on all dimensions of product and services that are important to the customer

quality circle
Small work group that meets periodically to discuss ways to improve its functional areas and the quality of the product

delays experienced in having their calls answered. A quality circle explored the situation, confirming that the delays were indeed occurring and that the average wait time for having a call answered was 7.4 seconds. After researching the standard for wait times for incoming calls, which was three seconds, the quality circle then explored ways to reduce the delays and achieve this three-second standard.

Enhancing Total System Performance through Synchronous Manufacturing Problems with JIT, especially the long time required for its installation in a manufacturing system, caused some firms to realize they needed something else to assist them in gaining market share. Many have turned to synchronous manufacturing, also called the *theory of constraints (TOC),* which is an entire manufacturing system with unbalanced operations that emphasizes total system performance. Synchronous manufacturing is a scheduling and manufacturing control system that seeks to locate and then eliminate or minimize any constraints to greater production output, such as machines, people, tools, and facilities. The system's output is determined by and limited to the output of the slowest operation, or bottleneck, that is working at full capacity. Thus a bottleneck is the operation in a manufacturing system whose output sets the limit for the entire system's output.

A computer program developed by Eli Goldratt, the originator of the TOC, schedules work, taking into consideration bottleneck and non-bottleneck operations. This makes scheduling much faster because it can be simulated on a computer instead of reached by trial and error, which is necessary with JIT. Also, once a bottleneck has been discovered, the operations manager can concentrate on increasing the production rate of that process. After resolving that issue, the manager can repeat the process on the next-slowest operation.[22]

Instead of attempting to achieve a balanced system like JIT, in which the capacities of all operations are equal, synchronous manufacturing aims to balance the *product flow* through the system, which leaves output levels of the various operations *unbalanced.* For example, with the bottleneck operation producing at full capacity, perhaps only 60 percent of capacity is needed at another operation. Because there is no reason for this operation to produce more than 60 percent of its capacity, it is stopped at that point; anything more would produce unwanted inventory. Because work is assigned to each operation rather than to the entire system, as in JIT, there is no need for more work in process than that which is actually being worked on. Inventory can also be placed near the bottleneck to avoid any shutdown in this crucial operation, and sometimes, unlike the case with JIT, there may even be a quality control inspector to check the bottleneck operation's input.

As we mentioned, management's attention is focused on the bottleneck rather than on the other operations because a production increase at the bottleneck means an increase for the entire production system; an increase in a non-bottleneck operation adds to only that machine's idle time.

Note another important difference between JIT and synchronous manufacturing: a defective part or component at any point in the production process can shut down a JIT system. But because a synchronous manufacturing system has excess capacity in all operations except at the bottleneck, any defective part produced before the bottleneck can be remade, and thus the entire system is not stopped.

Managing Costs and Customer Needs through Mass Customization Mass customization refers to a company's use of flexible, usually computer-aided, manufacturing systems to produce and deliver customized products and services for different customers worldwide. These systems typically combine the low unit costs and rapid production speeds associated with mass-production processes with the flexibility of customization for the demands of individual customers. As an approach to manufacturing, mass customization has been around since at least World War II, when Toyota began using it. Facilitated by continued advances in digital technology and electronic commerce, mass customization is now applied to varying degree by a range of companies in such fields as computers

---

synchronous manufacturing
An entire manufacturing system with unbalanced operations that emphasizes total system performance

bottleneck
Operation in a manufacturing system whose output sets the limit for the entire system's output

mass customization
The use of flexible, usually computer-aided, manufacturing systems to produce and deliver customized products and services for different customers worldwide

(Dell), greeting cards (Hallmark, Vistaprint), clothing (L.L.Bean, Cafepress, Levi Strauss), lighting (Lutron Electronics), footwear (Adidas, Puma), bags (Timbuk2), candy (M&M's), and cars (Land Rover).[23]

There are four basic approaches to mass customization: (1) collaborative—a company helps customers choose the required product features; (2) adaptive—the company offers a standard product that users can modify themselves; (3) cosmetic—only the product's presentation is customized, such as packaging or color; and (4) transparent—customers are provided with individualized product or service offerings without their knowing it, such as on website interfaces.[24]

Mass customization is usually appropriate in situations where it is feasible to delay differentiating the product for a particular customer until the last possible point in the supply network. This typically requires that the company reconceptualize the design of its product as well as the design and integration of the processes used for producing and delivering the product to customers. In practice, this means reconceptualizing and often reconfiguring the company's entire supply chain. But the benefits of such a comprehensive approach to operations are that the company will be able to function at maximum efficiency and to rapidly respond to customers' needs while maintaining a minimum level of inventory.

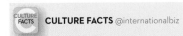

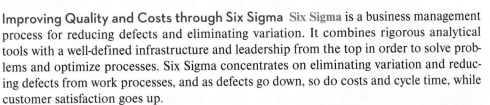

CULTURE FACTS @internationalbiz

North Americans often value speed of response when trying to solve problems in a plant. Reflecting their much higher score on the cultural dimension of pragmatism, Japanese managers often place more value on considering many alternatives for addressing the problem before action is taken.
#solvingproblems #speed #options

SOCIAL MEDIA

Improving Quality and Costs through Six Sigma Six Sigma is a business management process for reducing defects and eliminating variation. It combines rigorous analytical tools with a well-defined infrastructure and leadership from the top in order to solve problems and optimize processes. Six Sigma concentrates on eliminating variation and reducing defects from work processes, and as defects go down, so do costs and cycle time, while customer satisfaction goes up.

Six Sigma literally means a maximum of 3.4 defects per million occurrences, versus the two- or three-sigma level (more than 300,000 unsatisfactory experiences per million customer contacts) at which most businesses operate. It was once estimated that up to one-third of the work done in the United States consisted of redoing what has already been done, and that the cost of poor quality consumed 20 to 40 percent of the total effort expended in production.[25] Six Sigma attempts to overcome this problem.

The Six Sigma approach includes five steps: define, measure, analyze, improve, and control. It begins by defining the process, asking who the customers are and what their problems are. Key characteristics important to the customer are identified, along with the processes that support these characteristics. Next, Six Sigma focuses on measuring the process, including categorizing key characteristics, verifying measurement systems, and collecting data. The third step is analysis, converting raw data into information that provides insight into the process and identifies the fundamental and most important causes of defects or problems. Six Sigma then focuses on improving the process, including developing solutions to the problem, implementing the changes, and assessing whether additional changes are required. Finally, the process is put under control to monitor and sustain performance over time. In essence, Six Sigma is a method for creating a closed-loop system for making continuous improvements in business processes.

In selecting projects for Six Sigma, managers should look for a clear link between the project and the company's business priorities as reflected in its strategic and annual operating plans. A project should represent a breakthrough, offering significant improvements in both process and bottom-line results, with clear, quantitative measures of success. Projects should also be able to be completed within about three to six months (or be divided into subprojects of such duration), in order to maintain progress and company interest.

The CEO is often the driving force for implementing Six Sigma; seldom serves as the *champion*, who is the individual responsible for the project's success; provides the necessary resources; and breaks down organizational barriers. A major portion of a champion's bonus is typically tied to his or her success in achieving Six Sigma goals, helping ensure that the projects will have a substantial impact on the business. Project leaders are called

Six Sigma
Business management process for reducing defects and eliminating variation

"Black Belts" (BBs) and are typically individuals with a history of accomplishment and significant experience. Project team members are called "Green Belts" (GBs), and they do not spend all their time on Six Sigma projects. Both BBs and GBs tend to be change agents, and they should be open to generating and rigorously evaluating new ideas. Master Black Belts (MBBs), who are resources for project teams, are typically experienced BBs who have worked on many projects, have knowledge of advanced tools, have received business and leadership training, and have teaching experience. The primary responsibility of MBBs is training and mentoring new BBs.

The biggest advantage of Six Sigma among organizations using the methodology is increased cost savings, although the techniques are also associated with increased customer satisfaction, reduced defects, increased company growth, and increased quality. The Six Sigma methodology reevaluates the value-adding status of many elements of an organization, modifying some and discontinuing others. As a result, moving from two-sigma to Six-Sigma thinking often requires that companies rethink the way they do things and that they also adapt their culture, sometimes dramatically.

Successful culture change requires a concerted, long-term effort, particularly if the organization is multinational, with subsidiaries and offices around the world. The way organizations change is influenced by organizational and national culture, which affect such things as how companies ascribe status, recognize performance, structure reporting lines, and communicate internally. Increased acceptance may require that the organization (1) demonstrate the need for Six Sigma; (2) shape the vision of a Six Sigma culture and associated behaviors; and (3) identify and properly manage organizational resistance to Six Sigma, including technical, political, and organizational sources. At the same time, the Six Sigma methodology has been criticized as simply repackaging old ideas and for stifling creativity. Further, the 3.4 defects/million threshold may not be suitable for all processes. For heart pacemakers, that standard may be too low; for greeting cards, it may be too high.[26]

©Jill Braaten/McGraw-Hill Education.

LOGISTICS AND SUPPLY CHAINS

logistics
Managerial functions associated with the movement of materials such as raw materials, work in progress, or finished goods

Logistics are managerial functions associated with the movement of materials such as raw materials, components, work in progress, or finished goods. The effectiveness of supply chain management efforts is strongly influenced by the way a company manages the interface of logistics with sourcing and manufacturing, as well as with other activities such as design, engineering, and marketing.[27] Given the strong emphasis on minimization of inventory and handling in supply chains, the way a product (or the components and materials that will go into a product) is designed can significantly influence the cost of delivering the product. For example, packaging and transportation requirements for a product can significantly influence logistics costs, and these factors should be addressed during design as well as in other steps in the value chain.

Many companies have chosen to outsource their logistics needs to outside specialists, particularly for managing international logistics activities. Global logistics companies such as FedEx, DHL, and UPS have developed expertise in handling and tracking materials within and across nations, including sophisticated computer technology and systems for tracking shipments. For example, FedEx's website (www.fedex.com) allows a company to arrange pickups and then monitor the status of each item being transported, including information on the time the shipment was picked up; when and where it has been transferred within FedEx's network; and delivery location, time, and recipient. Many of these logistics companies have developed systems whereby their customers'

ZARA: Using Innovative Supply Chain Management to Transform the International Fashion Industry

Traditionally, leading designers of women's fashions looked to Paris and other European fashion centers for insight into what clothing to offer to the retail market. Fashion houses like Chanel and Gucci displayed their clothing lines twice a year in glamorous fashion shows. These designs, which often cost thousands of dollars, were affordable only for the very rich. The designs were subsequently copied by retailers and sold to the masses at lower prices, helping to ensure that consumer trends moved in sync with the fashion industry. The limited number of designs helped simplify planning and allowed clothing companies to survive even when they took six to nine months to bring a product from design to market.

That business model is disappearing rapidly as the international fashion industry evolves toward "fast fashion"—featuring up-to-the-minute fashion, low prices, and a clear market focus. Helping lead this revolution is a Spanish company called Zara, with over 2,200 clothing stores located in leading cities across more than 96 countries. Known for its fashionable and affordable clothing, Zara's competitive advantage comes from its world-class supply chain management skills.

The company's strategy of speed and flexibility has enabled Zara to dramatically shorten the fashion cycle. Store managers and roving observers use handheld devices to collect and send information regarding which designs are being well received by the buying public, which ones are not, and what will be the next hot trend. Zara's information systems also enable the company to better manage inventory, the primary cost of goods sold for clothing manufacturers and retailers. The textile manufacturers used by the company are mostly located close to Zara's headquarters in Spain, rather than lower-cost sources in the Far East that can lengthen the cycle time to market. Zara's use of information technology and advanced supply chain management techniques reduces cycle time from initial garment design to appearance in the company's retail stores to as little as 14 days—versus 3 to 15 months for most of its rivals' products. Rapid turnaround times also mean the company can keep its best-selling designs well stocked and limit excess inventory of designs that do not resonate with the consumer.

Zara ruthlessly removes its product lines, even ones that have been selling well, every two weeks or so. Zara's culture of reacting very quickly to new fashion trends means that each time a customer walks into a Zara store, she can get the feel of entering a new place, one with fresh styles on display. "When you went to Gucci or Chanel in October, you knew the chances were good that clothes would still be there in February," said Masoud Golsorkhi, editor of the London fashion magazine

Zara store in Tianjin, China. ©Lou Linwei/Alamy Stock Photo.

Tank. "With Zara, you know that if you don't buy it, right then and there, within 11 days the entire stock will change. You buy it now or never. And because the prices are so low, you buy it now." Customers have thus come to know Zara as a chain offering a steady stream of new, "gotta-have-it" merchandise. The limited availability of its merchandise promotes impulse purchases—a "grab it while you can" mentality among shoppers.

Zara's revolutionary approach to the fashion industry means that it dictates industry standards on such dimensions as time to market, order fulfillment, costs, and customer satisfaction, as well as the ability to manage the linkages between these factors. The result is high-end designers and fashion houses are being pressured to change their own operations and improve their ability to compete on speed. As Zara shows, effective supply chain management can indeed result in international competitive advantage.

Critical Thinking Questions

1. How does Zara's approach yield advantage over companies using more traditional approaches to logistics and supply chain management? What might make it difficult for competitors to imitate Zara's approach?

2. What factors might limit over time the international success of Zara's approach?

Sources: Graham Ruddick, "How Zara Became the World's Biggest Fashion Retailer," *The Telegraph*, October 24, 2014, www.telegraph.co.uk; Suzy Hansen, "How Zara Grew into the World's Largest Fashion Retailer," *The New York Times*, November 09, 2018, www.nytimes.com; "Financial Data," *Grupo Inditex*, 2018, www.inditex.com; "Zara Supply Chain Analysis—the Secret behind Zara's Retail Success," *TradeGecko*, June 25, 2018, www.tradegecko.com; and Kevin O'Marah, "Zara Uses Supply Chain to Win Again," *Forbes*, March 09, 2016, www.forbes.com.

in-house information systems are integrated with the logistics company's shipping and tracking systems. It is also common for logistics companies to offer a broad range of services beyond shipping, including warehousing, distribution management, and customs and brokerage services.

Standardization and the Management of Global Operations

LO C-5

Explain the potential in, and challenges to, global standardization of production processes and procedures.

standards
Documented agreements containing technical specifications or other precise criteria that will be used consistently as guidelines, rules, or definitions of the characteristics of a product, process, or service

Standards are documented agreements containing technical specifications or other precise criteria that will be used consistently as guidelines, rules, or definitions of the characteristics of a product, process, or service. International companies must address whether and to what extent they wish to pursue standardization in their global operations.

BENEFITS OF STANDARDIZATION OF GLOBAL OPERATIONS

Standards help ensure that materials, products, processes, and services are appropriate for their purpose. Credit cards and phone cards are produced to an accepted standard, including an optimal thickness of 0.76 mm, so that these cards can be used worldwide. The same symbols for automobile controls are displayed in cars throughout the world, no matter where the vehicles are produced.

In most countries, standards have been developed across product lines and for various functions. In the United States, for example, the standards developed by the American Society for Testing and Materials (ASTM) and other organizations are used in lieu of specific detailed requirements to ensure an expected level of use and quality. In Europe, the most popular standard for quality is the ISO 9000 collection. This is a set of universal standards for a quality-assurance system that has been agreed to by the International Organization for Standardization (ISO), a federation of standards bodies from 162 countries.[28] The intention is that ISO 9000 standards will be applicable worldwide, avoiding technical barriers to trade attributable to the existence of non-harmonized standards between countries. If a product or service is purchased from a company that is registered to the appropriate ISO 9000 standard, the buyer will have important assurances that the quality will be as expected. Indeed, registered companies have reported dramatic reductions in customer complaints as well as reduced operating costs and increased demand for their products and services. The ISO has also developed the ISO 1400 series of standards for managing environmental issues.

The most comprehensive of the standards is now ISO 9001, which the United States has adopted verbatim as the ANSI/ASQC Q9001 series for industries engaged in the design, development, manufacturing, installation, and servicing of products and services. The standards apply uniformly, regardless of company size or industry. In general, companies that want to do business in Europe must have at least ISO 9000 registration, and many companies also require registration from their suppliers to provide further assurance of compliance.

Although ISO 9000 has been widely adopted as a standard for quality, not all quality experts agree that it is superior to other alternatives: "The focus of the standards is to establish quality management procedures, through detailed documentation, work instructions, and record keeping. These procedures . . . say nothing about the actual quality of the product—they deal entirely with standards to be followed." Phil Crosby, a noted quality expert and the author of several books on quality, states, "It is a delusion that sound management can be replaced by an information format. It is like putting a Bible in every hotel room with the thought that occupants will act according to its contents."[29]

An example of standardization is provided by Intel, the worldwide leader in supplying semiconductor memory products and related computer components, which introduced an approach called "Copy Exactly" for achieving standardization in its factories.[30] "Copy Exactly solves the problem of getting production facilities up to speed quickly by duplicating everything from the development plant to the volume-manufacturing plant."[31] Managers from high-volume facilities participate in the development plant as new process technology is created. "Everything at the development plant—the process flow, equipment set, suppliers, plumbing, manufacturing clean room, and training methodologies—is selected to meet high-volume needs, recorded, and then copied exactly to the high-volume plant. Time after time, factory yields start at higher levels, and even improve when multiple factories come online using Copy Exactly."[32] In July 2018, Intel confronted potential supply problems with its processors, threatening the company's ability to meet customer demands. However, it was able to quickly shift

Worker in an industrial clean room ©Ian Lishman/Juice Images/Getty Images.

production to one of its Vietnamese plants to reduce the bottleneck problems, due to the Vietnamese plant operating under the Copy Exactly program and highlighting how that program enabled "faster production ramps that improve product availability and improved consistency to quality performance."[33]

In addition to those just mentioned, there are other important, although perhaps less obvious, reasons for global standardization. The following sections discuss some of them.

Organization and Staffing Some of the reasons for the global standardization of a firm's manufacturing systems are the effects on organization and staffing. For example, the standardization of production processes and procedures simplifies the manufacturing organization at headquarters because their replication enables the work to be accomplished with a smaller staff of support people. Fewer labor hours are needed for plant design because each new plant is essentially a scaled-up or scaled-down version of an existing one. The permanent group of experts that international companies maintain to give technical assistance to overseas plants can be smaller. Extra technicians accustomed to working with the same machinery can be borrowed from the domestic operation as needed.

Worldwide uniformity or standardization in manufacturing methods also increases headquarters' effectiveness in keeping the production specifications current. Every firm has hundreds of specifications, and those specifications are constantly being changed because of new raw materials or manufacturing procedures. If all plants, domestic and foreign, possess the same equipment, notice of a change can be given with one indiscriminate notification; there is no need for highly paid engineers to check each affiliate's list of equipment to see which ones are affected. Companies whose manufacturing processes are not unified have found that a current separate set of specifications for each of 15 or 20 affiliates is both more costly to maintain and more error-prone.

Standardization can also produce efficiencies associated with the supply and logistics activities. As we discussed earlier in this module, management has become increasingly aware that greater profits may be obtained by organizing all of its companies' production facilities into one logistical supply system that includes all the activities required to move raw materials, parts, and finished inventory from vendors, between enterprise facilities, and to customers. The standardization of processes and machinery provides a reasonable guarantee that parts manufactured in the firm's various plants will be interchangeable. This assurance of interchangeability enables management to divide the production of components among a number of subsidiaries in order to achieve greater economies of scale and take advantage of the lower production costs in some countries.

Standardization can also produce benefits associated with the rationalization of a company's operations. **Manufacturing rationalization** divides production among a number of production units, thus enabling each to produce only a limited number of components for all of a firm's assembly plants.[34] This strategy requires a change from a subsidiary's manufacturing only for its own national market to its producing a limited number of

manufacturing rationalization Division of production among a number of production units, thus enabling each to produce only a limited number of components for all of a firm's assembly plants

components for use by many or all of an international company's subsidiaries. For example, SKF, a major bearing manufacturer with headquarters in Sweden, was able to reduce the number of types of ball bearings produced in five major overseas subsidiaries from 50,000 to 20,000. Of the 20,000 remaining types, 7,000 were rationalized among the five plants, and the other 13,000 were produced solely by one or another subsidiary for its local customers.[35]

For manufacturing rationalization to be possible, the product mix must first be rationalized; that is, the firm must elect to produce products that are identical worldwide or regionwide. Once this has been done, each subsidiary can be assigned to produce certain components for other foreign plants, thus attaining a higher volume with a lower production cost than would be possible if it manufactured the complete product for its national market only. Obviously, this strategy may not be viable when consumers' tastes and preferences differ markedly among markets. For less differentiated products, however, manufacturing rationalization permits economies of scale in production and engineering that would otherwise be impossible.

Purchasing When foreign subsidiaries are unable to purchase raw materials and machinery locally, they generally look for assistance from the purchasing department at corporate headquarters. Because unified processes require the same materials everywhere, buyers can handle foreign requirements by simply increasing their regular orders to their usual suppliers and passing on the volume discounts to the subsidiaries. However, when special materials are required, purchasing agents must search out new vendors and place smaller orders, often at higher prices.

Control All the advantages of global standardization cited thus far also pertain to the other functions of management. For example, when production equipment is similar, home office control of quality in foreign affiliates is less difficult because management can expect all plants to adhere to the same standard. The home office can compare the periodic reports that all affiliates submit and quickly spot deviations from the norm that require remedial action, such as numerous product rejects. Separate standards for each plant because of equipment differences are unnecessary.

In addition, a single standard also lessens the task of maintenance and production control. The same machinery should produce at the same rate of output and have the same frequency of maintenance no matter where it is located. In practice, deviations will occur because of human and physical factors such as dust, humidity, and temperature. Nevertheless, the use of similar machinery permits the home office to establish standards by which to determine the effectiveness of local management. Furthermore, the maintenance experience of other production units in regard to the frequency of overhauls and the stock of required spare parts will help plants avoid costly, unforeseen stoppages from sudden breakdowns.

> **"PART of WHAT YOU NEED to DO in THE SUPPLY CHAIN IS to HELP YOUR COMPANY ANTICIPATE EVENTS, AND UNDERSTAND THE ENVIRONMENT YOU OPERATE in—PHYSICAL, POLITICAL, ECONOMIC— around THE GLOBE."**
>
> *—Fran Townsend, former Homeland Security advisor to President George W. Bush*[37]

Planning When a new plant can be a duplicate of others already functioning, the planning and design will be both simpler and quicker because they are essentially a repetition of work already done. For example:

1. Design engineers need only copy the drawings and lists of materials that they have in their files.
2. Vendors will be requested to furnish equipment that they have supplied previously.
3. The technical department can send the current manufacturing specifications without alteration.
4. Labor trainers experienced in the operation of the machinery can be sent to the new location without undergoing special training on new equipment.
5. Reasonably accurate forecasts of plant-building time and output can be based on experience with existing facilities.

In other words, the duplication of existing plants greatly reduces the engineering time required in planning and designing the new facilities and eliminates many of the start-up difficulties inherent in any new operation. To emphasize just how important the savings from plant duplication are, a study of the chemical and refining industries indicated that the cost of technology transfer was lowered by 34 and 19 percent for the second and third start-ups, respectively.[36]

If the case for global standardization of production is so strong, why do differences among plants in the same company persist?

IMPEDIMENTS TO STANDARDIZATION OF GLOBAL OPERATIONS

Generally, it is easier for international companies to standardize concepts such as total quality management and synchronous manufacturing in their overseas affiliates than it is to standardize the actual manufacturing facilities. Units of an international multi-plant operation differ in size, machinery, and procedures because of the intervention of foreign environmental forces, especially the economic, cultural, and political forces.

Economic Forces The most important element of the economic forces that impede production standardization is the wide range of market sizes. To cope with the great variety of production requirements, the designer generally has the option of selecting either a capital-intensive process incorporating automated, high-output machinery or a labor-intensive process employing more people and general-purpose equipment with lower production capacity. Automated machinery is usually severely limited in flexibility in terms of the variety of products and range of sizes that can be produced, but once set up, it will turn out in a few days what may be a year's supply for some markets.[38] For many processes, this problem may be resolved by installing one machine of the type used by the hundreds in the larger home plant. However, sometimes this option is not available; some processes use only one or two large machines, even in manufacturing facilities with large output. Until recently, when the option was not available, plant designers had to choose between the high-output specialized machinery and the lower-output, general-purpose machines mentioned earlier. The major difference is that the general-purpose machine usually produces a product of lower quality, higher variability, and higher per-unit costs than does the special-purpose machine. As a result, general-purpose machines require their operators to have a broader range of skills than might be necessary for a special-purpose machine.

A third alternative is available: computer-integrated manufacturing (CIM), which many international companies are using. However, its cost and high technological content generally limit its application to industrialized nations and the more advanced developing nations. CIM systems enable a machine to make one part as easily as another in random order on an instruction from a bar code reader of the kind used in supermarkets. This reduces the economic batch quantity—the minimum number of a part that can be made economically by a factory—to one. As a result, it facilitates the potential for mass customization that we discussed earlier in this module. There is a limit, nevertheless, to the variety of shapes, sizes, and materials that can be accommodated.

Another economic factor that influences the designer's selection of processes is the cost of production. Automation tends to increase productivity per worker because it requires less labor and results in higher output per machine. But if the desired output requires that the machines be operated only a fraction of the time, the high capital costs of automated equipment may result in excessive production costs even though labor costs are low. In situations where production costs favor more general-purpose equipment with higher labor content, the designer may still be compelled to install high-capacity machines instead because of a lack of floor space.

Generally, the space occupied by a few high-capacity machines is less than that required for the greater number of general-purpose machines needed to produce the same output. However, because the correct type and quality of process materials are indispensable for specialized machinery, the engineers cannot recommend this equipment if such materials are

Workers in an Indian McDonald's Restaurant. ©Agence France Presse/Douglas E. Curran/ AFP/Getty Images.

backward vertical integration
An arrangement in which facilities are established to manufacture inputs used in the production of a firm's final products

CULTURE FACTS @internationalbiz

In the United States, a highly individualistic nation, making money is a primary driver in most business decisions and companies employ the fewest possible workers to get a task done. In some parts of the more collectivistic nation of China, including state-owned enterprise, a common goal is to keep as many workers employed as you can, even if they are not being fully utilized. #makingmoney #status #workersfirst

unobtainable either from local sources or through importation. Occasionally, management will bypass this obstacle by means of backward vertical integration, an arrangement in which facilities are established to manufacture inputs used in the production of a firm's final products. That is, manufacturing capacity to produce essential inputs will be included in the plant design even though it would be preferable from an economic standpoint to purchase those materials from outside vendors. For example, a textile factory might include a facility for producing nylon fibers.

The economic forces we have described are fundamental considerations in plant design, yet elements of the cultural and political forces may be sufficiently significant to override decisions based on purely economic reasoning.

Cultural Forces When a factory is to be built in an industrialized nation that has a sizable market and high labor costs, capital-intensive processes will undoubtedly be employed. However, such processes may also be employed in developing countries, which commonly lack skilled workers despite their abundant supply of labor. This situation favors the use of specialized machines. Although a few highly skilled persons are needed for maintenance and setup, the job of *attending* to these machines (starting, feeding stock) can often be performed by unskilled workers after a short training period. In contrast, general-purpose machinery typically requires many more skilled operators.

These operators could be trained in technical schools, but the low prestige of such employment, a cultural characteristic, affects both the demand for and the supply of vocational education. Students do not demand it, and the traditional attitude of educational administrators in many developing nations causes resources to be directed to professional education instead of the trades.

These economic and cultural variables, important as they are, are not the only considerations of management; the requirements of the host government must be met if the proposed plant is to become a reality.

Political Forces When planning a new manufacturing facility in a developing country, management is frequently confronted by an intriguing paradox. Although the country desperately needs new job creation, which favors labor-intensive processes, government officials often insist that the most modern equipment be installed if an international company wants to open a new plant. Local pride may be the cause, or it may be that these officials, wishing to see the new firm export, believe that only a factory with advanced technology can compete in world markets. They may not only be reluctant to take chances on "inferior" or untried alternatives, but they may also feel that low-productivity technology will keep the country dependent on the industrialized countries. In some developing countries, this fear has been formalized by laws prohibiting the importation of used machinery.

For example, global automakers have made investments of more than $200 billion in automobile and auto parts factories in China.[39] However, most of the large automakers' plants are not designed to exploit China's large pool of low-cost labor. Rather, the plants are about as capital-intensive as U.S. auto plants. Part of the reason for this is the Chinese government's desire to lure the latest technology, a goal it has promoted by a range of incentives. Agreeing to these demands of the government can also be simpler for the automakers. As Mustafa

Is Cognizant Leveraging Low-Cost Talent or Exploiting It?

India has become a global center for high-technology businesses in recent years, with nearly 4 million information technology (IT) workers in 2017. The IT services sector has been supported by strong educational systems established in India by the British during colonial times. "The difference between India's universities and a school like Harvard is that an Indian university is harder to get into," said Mukesh Mehta, vice president of corporate systems for Metropolitan Life Insurance Company.

Observing the thriving software industry in India, Cognizant Technology Solution's leaders recognized that their company could achieve a strong cost advantage over other U.S. companies by employing talented entry-level programmers in India for $6,000 to $9,000 per year, compared with an average salary in the United States of about $50,000. Providing software development and maintenance services, Cognizant competes on the basis of price, speed, and agility. Cognizant uses an innovative "offshore–onshore" business model in which about 25 percent of the company's nearly 275,000 computer science and engineering professionals work at customer sites in the United States or other Western nations. The remaining employees work at one of its more than 60 development centers, primarily in India.

Once a contract has been signed, a global "virtual project team" is set up. A small portion of the team is located at the client's site, mainly Indian nationals who are imported to the foreign location for a couple of years to handle project management activities and manage client relationships. The rest of the team is located in a low-cost location abroad, where software development, coding, maintenance, and other activities are completed. This approach allows Cognizant's project managers to interact intensely with its clients during working hours in the West, intimately understanding the clients' strategies and needs, while prototype development, coding, and system upgrading activities are conducted overnight in a "chasing the sun" model of customer support. Despite a fiercely competitive marketplace, Cognizant has achieved sustained success with its innovative business model. By 2018, 76 percent of Cognizant's $15 billion in revenue was from North America and 18 percent from Europe.

However, critics charge that the success of Cognizant and similar firms has been achieved at least in part by unfairly importing lower-cost foreign employees and undercutting salaries of U.S. workers. The H-1B visa program was established by the U.S. government to enable companies to hire, on a temporary basis, highly skilled workers from abroad if such workers were not

Chandra Sekaran, Executive Vice President and Managing Director, Cognizant Technology Solutions.
©G Krishnaswamy/The India Today Group/Getty Images.

available in the United States. The top 10 companies receiving the most H-1B visas to relocate immigrate workers to the United States were all companies involved with offshoring information technology work to countries such as India, and Cognizant was the biggest user of H-1B visas. "What these firms have done is exploit the loopholes in the H-1B program to bring on-site workers to learn the jobs [of] the Americans to then ship it back offshore," says Ron Hira, a professor of public policy at the Rochester Institute of Technology. "And also to bring in on-site workers who are cheaper on the H-1B and undercut American workers right here." The Center for Immigration Studies claimed that employees working in the U.S. information technology sector under the H-1B program earned an average of $13,000 less than their American peers, putting downward pressure on salaries of domestic workers. The U.S. Department of Labor investigated claims against Cognizant and found the company failed to pay "proper wages" to workers holding H-1B visas, in violation of federal labor laws, and "failed to offer all H-1B workers equal benefits or eligibility for equal benefits." Cognizant thus joined other companies such as Infosys and Patni Computer Systems, both of India, who have had to pay back wages, fines, or other penalties for their improper treatment of H-1B workers.

Critical Thinking Questions

1. Does the use of a multi-nation client management team approach create value for companies and workers in both a developing country like India and a developed country such as the United States? Why or why not?

2. Although many U.S. companies have argued that the H-1B temporary visa program is vital to their continued success because it allows them to import skilled workers who are difficult to find in the United States, critics charge that such programs are susceptible to abuse, harming both imported and domestic employees. What are the merits and limitations of each argument?

3. Is it better to allow foreign workers to come to the United States under a program such as the H-1B temporary visas, or to merely locate activities in a foreign site? Why? How might a program be designed to enable U.S. companies to bring in immigrant talent from abroad without harming the interests of employees in the United States?

Sources: "Helping Clients Win With Digital 2017 annual report," *Cognizant Technology Solutions*, 2018, www.cognizant.com; Patrick Thibodeau, "Cognizant Agrees to Pay H-1B Workers $500,000 in Back Wages," *Computerworld*, April 05, 2009, www.computerworld. com; Martin Kaste, "Who's Hiring H-1B Visa Workers? It's Not Who You Might Think," *National Public Radio*, April 03, 2013, www.npr.org; "Offshore Outsourcing Grows to Global Proportions," *Information Week*, February 02, 2002, www.informationweek.com; and Bala Shah, "Cognizant Guilty of Underpaying Techies," Techgoss.com, February 19, 2015.

Mohatarem, former senior economist at General Motors, stated, "Because of the way information travels these days, people in developing countries aren't any longer willing to buy cars that are one or two generations old. And if you're going to do the current-generation car, then keeping the process as similar as processes around the world makes sense."[40]

SOME DESIGN SOLUTIONS

More often than not, after consideration of environmental variables, the resultant plant design will be a scaled-down version of the parent company operation, a hybrid design, or a design using intermediate technology.

Scaled-Down Design for Local Manufacturing System Except for plants in large industrialized nations, the local manufacturing organization is commonly a scaled-down version of that found in the parent company. If the firm is organized by product companies or divisions (tires, industrial products, chemicals) in its home nation, the subsidiary will be divided into product departments. Manufacturing firms that use process organizations (departmentalized according to production processes) in the domestic operation will set up a similar structure in their foreign affiliates. In a paper-box factory, separate departments will cut the logs, produce the paper, and assemble the boxes. The only noticeable difference between the foreign and domestic operations is that in the foreign plant all these processes are more likely to be at one location because of the smaller size of each department.

The local manufacturing organization is rarely integrated either vertically or horizontally to the extent that the parent is. Some vertical integration is traditional, as in the case of the paper-box factory, and some will occur if it is necessary to ensure a supply of raw materials. In this situation, the subsidiary might be more vertically integrated than the parent, which depends on outside sources for many of its inputs. However, the additional investment is a deterrent to vertical integration, as are the extra profits gained by supplying inputs to these captive customers from the home plants. Some countries prohibit vertical integration for certain industries. In Mexico, for example, restrictions on private investment (Mexican or foreign) in the petroleum and petrochemical industry still exist and keep producers of products that use petrochemicals from achieving efficient levels of backward vertical integration. In contrast, some countries require a percentage of local content in finished products. When the subsidiary cannot meet the requirement by local sourcing, it may be forced to produce components that its parent does not.

Horizontal integration is much less prevalent in foreign subsidiaries, although restaurant chains, banks, food-processing plants, and other industries characterized by small production units will, of course, integrate horizontally in the manner of the domestic company. Overseas affiliates themselves become conglomerates when the parent company acquires a multinational firm.

DANIELLE DEMARIA: International Experience Can Bring Impactful Work and Lifelong Relationships

Danielle Demaria in Peru on an AIESEC internship.
Courtesy of Danielle Demaria.

Many people who study international business can pinpoint exactly what drew them in, whether that be growing up in a foreign country, learning a second language before they can even walk, and so on. For me, I can't even remember a time when I wasn't dreaming about traveling. My whole life I have been fascinated over what makes a culture unique, how people all over the world are so different from each other, yet so similar at the same time, and how exploring new parts of the world can shape someone into who they are today.

For that reason, it was somewhat obvious to me that I had to concentrate my studies in international business. I went on to obtain two undergraduate degrees in international business and finance, with a minor in Spanish. During my time as an undergraduate student, I quickly learned about the different international organizations my campus had to offer and decided to interview for the one in which I thought I'd make the best fit. That organization happened to be the largest student-run organization in the world, AIESEC. My time spent with this organization led me to hold a leadership position on campus, where I worked to promote AIESEC's opportunities abroad. Shortly thereafter, I ended up doing exactly what I was promoting, which was going abroad on an international internship for six weeks.

My internship entailed working for a non-government operated (NGO) organization in Lima, Peru, that promoted the growth and development of low-income towns by creating new libraries in areas with minimal resources. Not only did this internship fulfill my dream of working in a Spanish-speaking country to utilize my language skills, but also I was able to partake in really meaningful work that was positively impacting others. Typical responsibilities in my role as an intern included creating marketing content to send to universities, schools, and institutions to promote the libraries and ways to support the NGO, as well as going around on foot to universities in Lima and conversing with students interested in volunteering in the libraries. I was successful in hiring many new volunteers, as these students were eager to make an impact in their community and help others in need.

Beyond my rewarding experiences with the NGO, one of my favorite highlights of the whole opportunity was the bond I developed with my host family. I was fortunate to have been set up with the best host family I could have ever asked for, who truly made me feel like a member of the family. The relationships I developed with them are ones that will never cease to exist, but rather continue to grow as time goes on.

I conclude with a few pieces of advice for anyone interested in living, working, or traveling abroad, be it for one week or many years: Be as brave as you can. Don't be scared that your language skills aren't enough to get you through. Make meaningful connections whenever you can. And above all else, simply get out there and explore.

Source: Danielle Demaria.

Hybrid Design In designing plants for developing countries, engineers will commonly use a hybrid of capital-intensive processes when they are considered essential to ensure product quality and labor-intensive processes to take advantage of the abundance of unskilled labor. For example, they may stipulate machine welding rather than hand welding but then use semi-manual equipment for the painting, packaging, and materials handling activities.

Intermediate Technology In recent years, the press of a growing population and the rise in capital costs have forced the governments of developing nations to search for something less than highly automated processes. They are becoming convinced that there should be something midway between the capital- and labor-intensive processes that will create more jobs, require less capital, but still produce the desired product quality, especially in countries with lower levels of economic development and income. Governments are urging investors to consider an **intermediate technology**, or production methods between capital- and labor-intensive methods, which unfortunately are not readily available in the industrialized nations. This means that international companies cannot transfer the technology with which they are familiar but must develop new and different manufacturing methods. It is also possible that the savings in reduced capital costs of the intermediate technology may be nullified by higher start-up costs and the greater expense of its transfer.

intermediate technology
Production methods between capital- and labor-intensive methods

SUMMARY

LO C-1
Explain the concept of supply chain management.

Supply chain management is the process of coordinating and integrating the flow of materials, information, finances, and services within and among companies in the value chain, from suppliers to the ultimate consumer. Supply chain management is integral to the achievement of cost and quality objectives in companies and to international competitiveness.

LO C-2
Discuss the relationship between design and supply chain management.

The design of a company's products and services has a fundamental relationship with the types of inputs the company will require, including labor, materials, information, and financing. Compared to traditional sequential approaches to design, concurrent engineering approaches to design allow proposed designs to be subjected to earlier assessments on cost, quality, and manufacturability dimensions, enhancing the efficiency and effectiveness of subsequent supply chain management activities.

LO C-3
Describe the reasons for sourcing globally, the five global sourcing arrangements, and the benefits and challenges of global sourcing.

A firm may source globally for a variety of reasons, including obtaining inputs of lower cost, better quality or design, or

those unavailable locally. The alternatives for global sourcing include establishing a wholly owned subsidiary, an overseas joint venture, an in-bond plant contractor, an independent contractor overseas, or buying from an independent overseas manufacturer. Global sourcing can provide many benefits to a company, including streamlined operations, reduced costs, and improved quality and productivity. There can also be disadvantages from global sourcing, such as added costs associated with finding and importing from a supplier in another country, difficulty integrating purchasing with a company's overall business system, and security concerns.

LO C-4
Explain why manufacturing systems and logistical elements may vary, even within the same company.

Growing international competition requires firms to achieve efficiency and effectiveness in their international production activities, yet firms often have facilities in countries at various levels of development and which may vary considerably in cost and quality from one country to another. As a result, manufacturing systems and logistics practices within and across sites also vary considerably. Firms use a variety of approaches to manage costs and quality, including just-in-time production systems, total quality management, quality circles, synchronous manufacturing, mass customization, and Six Sigma. The design and implementation of these approaches within and across subsidiaries often require management to consider factors such as the relative pressure to achieve standardization as well as environmental forces that may hinder efforts at standardization, including economic, cultural, and political forces.

LO C-5
Explain the potential in, and challenges to, global standardization of production processes and procedures.

Standards help ensure that materials, products, processes, and services are appropriate for their purpose, helping companies meet market and competitive demands. Standardization of activities helps simplify organization and control at headquarters because replication enables the work to be accomplished with a smaller staff of support personnel and internal best practices can more readily be applied across a company's international operations. However, differences in the foreign environmental forces, especially the economic, cultural, and political forces, cause units of an international multi-plant operation to differ in size, machinery, and procedures, complicating efforts to achieve standardization of processes and procedures.

KEY TERMS

backward vertical integration 510
bottleneck 502
indirect procurement 497
intermediate technology 514
intrafirm trade 496
just-in-time (JIT) 499

logistics 504
manufacturing rationalization 507
mass customization 502
offshoring 495
outsourcing 492
quality circle 501

Six Sigma 503
standards 506
supply chain management 492
synchronous manufacturing 502
total quality management (TQM) 501

CRITICAL THINKING QUESTIONS

1. What recent developments have caused supply chain management to become increasingly important to international companies? Do you expect supply chain management to become less, or more, important as 3D printing technology becomes more commercially viable? Explain your rationale.

2. Is the reduction of inventory an appropriate goal of supply chain management systems? What benefits might result from reducing inventory? What problems might result from inventory reduction efforts?

3. What are the main differences between sequential and concurrent approaches to the design of products and services? What problems might a company encounter if it decided to use concurrent design?

4. Why would a company choose to source raw materials, components, or other products or services from a foreign supplier? What problems or concerns can arise from relying on foreign sources for a company's supplies, and how might these differ from the factors arising from outsourcing to a domestic firm?

5. What concerns arise as a firm purchases an increasing portion of its materials from outside firms, especially those located in foreign countries, rather than producing these materials itself? How

might this threaten the long-term competitiveness of a firm, and what might a firm do in order to lessen such risks?

6. In what ways may the emergence of global electronic procurement be a potential benefit for small- and mid-sized companies, and in what ways might global electronic procurement pose a threat to these companies?

7. What are the advantages to a worldwide firm of global standardization of its production facilities? Why might a firm not want to achieve such standardization across its network of facilities?

8. How might an international company's decision to adopt approaches such as just-in-time manufacturing systems or Six Sigma within its international network of subsidiaries result in a decline in its short- and longer-term performance?

9. How might global logistics practices be impacted by developments such as 3D printing technology or a sustained rise in the global price of oil?

10. What differences might you expect to see in the approach used for global manufacturing and supply chain management for a product that has stable demand and limited change in its basic design, versus a product that experiences substantial changes in demand and continued design changes?

globalEDGE RESEARCH TASK http://globalEDGE.msu.edu/

Use the globalEDGE website (http://globalEDGE.msu .edu) to complete the following exercises:

1. You are a researcher studying the supply chain efficiencies of countries and you've learned about the *International Logistics Performance Index* published by the World Bank that may help you. First, find the index on globalEDGE and view the heat map. Then, visit the external index page and find the answers to the following questions. What are the main indicators used to calculate this index? Which countries are ranked at the top? What are some emerging trends highlighted in the report card?

2. A nation's integration into the world economy is also as important as its international logistics performance. Locate "by Country" section in "Global Insights" and choose any country. In the "Indices" page, find the "DHL Global Connectedness Index" and review the heat map. What are the top and bottom five countries ranked by the index? Discuss similarities and differences of these countries. Review the key take-aways on the external index page and be ready to share the ones that you found interesting/important with your class.

MINICASE

MODERN MILLENNIALS APPAREL COMPANY OUTSOURCES DOMESTIC PRODUCTION

Modern Millennials Apparel Company Inc. is a major apparel manufacturer in the United States. It makes men's and women's casual wear, such as denim jeans, cotton slacks, skirts, and sweaters. Modern Millennials has taken the low-cost provider strategy and is constantly trying to find ways to cut costs and maintain its 4 percent profit margin while maintaining a competitive advantage over its major competitors. Because direct labor makes up approximately 65 percent of the total cost of an apparel item, Modern Millennials closed all of its domestic manufacturing facilities and outsourced the production to contractors in Vietnam. In the United States, Modern Millennials was paying an average hourly wage of $13.65 per hour. The Vietnamese labor rates average about $0.92 per hour, depending on the location of the factory. The company felt that relocating production to Vietnam was a viable change for the long-term success of the company. Not only could the company reduce labor costs by over 93 percent, but it would no longer have to deal with labor unions; plant maintenance; and government regulatory offices such as the Occupational Safety and Health Administration (OSHA), the Fair Labor Standards Act (FLSA), and the Equal Employment Opportunity Commission (EEOC).

It took Modern Millennials almost two years to complete the transition. After start-up costs in Vietnam, domestic plant closings, and the associated costs, Modern Millennials was ready to reap the benefits of its decisions. Modern Millennials slashed wholesale prices for the upcoming season to undercut the competition and planned for a 6 percent profit margin. It had increased sales by more than 20 percent, garnering a major portion of the business.

There were, however, a few discoveries that limited the company's cause to celebrate. It had relinquished almost all control over the manufacturing processes and product de-velopment after the initial designs were transmitted to the Vietnamese contractors. Production was set up to be delivered in four batches per season (eight batches per year) with orders transmitted approximately four months in advance. These contracted production amounts were firm and, later that year when business slowed, Modern Millennials could not lower the production rate nor refuse shipments. This resulted in large inventories of finished goods.

An additional and unexpected problem was caused by longer-than-expected transportation times from Vietnam to the Modern Millennials distribution center. Modern Millennials had originally planned for two-week in-transit inventory and customer delivery dates based on the import agents' estimated travel time across the Pacific but had not foreseen an additional two- to three-week delay caused by the backlog at the port of Los Angeles. This pushed back shipment dates to Modern Millennials' customers, resulting in a shorter retail selling period and nullifying Modern Millennials expected refill orders, further enhancing already high finished goods inventory levels. The holding costs associated with these high inventory levels negated a large amount of the forecasted savings Modern Millennials counted on for its profits.

In addition, customers were complaining that the fit and feel of the garments were different. The Vietnamese production facilities had altered the Modern Millennials product to fit their production processes. The Vietnamese had their own raw material suppliers and their products were slightly different than Modern Millennials domestic suppliers.

Another problem that became evident was the producer's lack of flexibility. Because of the high inventories, model changes became more expensive because more inventory had to be marked down to clear the way for the new product.

Modern Millennials began to see a decline in sales and became concerned for the future of the company.

The CEO called the top management team together and charged each one of them with finding ways to improve the situation. Joseph Dale, vice president of operations, felt that he had an answer to the company's problems. After investigation, he proposed that the company immediately buy or construct a wholly owned manufacturing subsidiary in Mexico in one of the industrial parks near the border, where low-cost labor could produce products and ship them tariff-free to the United States Finished goods could be transported from the Mexican plant to the Modern Millennials distribution center within 72 hours of completion. The plan would call for the Mexican plant to produce the rapid turnover product needed for quick replenishment. The Vietnamese contractors would be given the seasonal products that were not a part of the replenishment system and that could be produced and shipped in batches. The plan called for approximately 40 percent of the production to be moved to the Mexican facility while 60 percent would remain with Vietnam. Combined with an expected increased level of productivity by the production workers in Mexico, this change would yield an average labor cost of $1.42 per hour. Dale calculated that this change would decrease Modern Millennials on-hand and in-transit inventory dramatically, as well as reduce the level of end-of-season price markdowns necessary to eliminate outdated inventory, yielding a much higher profit for the company.

Critical Thinking Questions

1. Identify specific concepts in the case found in this module and discuss their relevance to the problems facing the company.

2. Considering all the problems incurred in Vietnam and the immense effort and capital needed to start up the Mexico operation, would it have been a better idea for Modern Millennials to keep its domestic operations? Why or why not?

Source: This case was contributed by Kevin Cruthirds of Nicholls State University and edited by J. Michael Geringer.

NOTES

1. Douglas M. Lambert, and Martha C. Cooper, "Issues in Supply Chain Management," *Industrial Marketing Management,* vol. 29, 2000, 65–83, http://www.hatfieldandassociates.com/pdf/issues_in_scm.pdf, accessed November 19, 2018.

2. Donald J. Bowersox, David J. Closs, and M. Bixby Cooper, *Supply Chain Logistics Management,* 4th ed., Burr Ridge, IL: McGraw-Hill Irwin, 2012, Chapter 1.

3. Knut Alicke, and Martin Losch, "Lean and Mean: How Does Your Supply Chain Shape Up?" https://www.mckinsey.com, accessed November 19, 2018; Robert D'Avanzo, "The Reward of Supply-Chain Excellence," *Optimize,* December 2003, 68; and Ashutosh Agrawal, "Turn Your Reverse Supply Chain into a Profit Center," *Supply Chain Quarterly,* Quarter 1, 2012, https://www.supplychainquarterly.com, accessed November 19, 2018.

4. Sunil Chopra, and ManMohan S. Sodhi, "Reducing the Risk of Supply Chain Disruptions," *Sloan Management Review,* Spring 2014, https://sloanreview.mit.edu; and Barry Cross, and Jason Bonin, "How to Manage Risk in a Global Supply Chain," *Ivey Business Journal,* November–December 2010, https://iveybusinessjournal.com.

5. Christopher Mims, "Inside the New Industrial Revolution," *The Wall Street Journal,* https://www.wsj.com, accessed November 19, 2018.

6. Yogesh Malik, Alex Niemeyer, and Brian Ruwadi, "Building the Supply Chain of the Future," *McKinsey Quarterly,* https://www.mckinsey.com, accessed November 19, 2018; Ernst & Young, *Driving Improved Supply Chain Results: Adapting to a Changing Global Marketplace,* https://www.ey.com, accessed November 19, 2018; Ben Benjabutr, "Supply Chain Case Study: The Executive's Guide," *SupplyChainOpz,* https://www.supplychainopz.com, accessed November 19, 2018; Joan Magretta, "The Power of Virtual Integration: An Interview with Dell Computer's Michael Dell," *Harvard Business Review,* March–April 1998, https://hbr.org; and Colby Ronald Chiles, and Marguarette Thi Dau, *An Analysis of Current Supply Chain Best Practices in the Retail Industry with Case Studies of Wal-Mart and Amazon.com,* Master's Thesis, Massachusetts Institute of Technology, June 2005, https://dspace.mit.edu/handle/1721.1/33314, accessed November 19, 2018.

7. Fung Group, "Supply Chain Management," https://www.funggroup.com, accessed November 19, 2018; Bisk, "Understanding Supply Chain Excellence," https://www.michiganstateuniversityonline.com, accessed November 19, 2018; and Joan Magretta, "Fast, Global, and Entrepreneurial: Supply Chain Management, Hong Kong Style—An Interview with Victor Fung," *Harvard Business Review,* September–October 1998, https://hbr.org; "Supply Chain Case Study: The Executive's Guide."

8. Yatish Desai, "Drive Supply Chain Excellence Through Performance Metrics," *Inside Supply Management,* December 2011/January 2012, 36–39; "Supply Chain Management," *Encyclopedia of Management,* https://www.referenceforbusiness.com, accessed November 19, 2018; and Ehap H. Sabri, "Creating High-Impact Supply Chain Metrics," *SupplyChain247,* https://www.supplychain247.com, accessed November 19, 2018.

9. Emma Tidey, "Starbucks Adopts Localization Strategy for Coffee Shops around the Globe," https://www.kwintessential.co.uk, accessed November 19, 2018; Rachel Tepper, "Starbucks Appeals to Regional Tastes with Tweaks to Décor and Offerings," *Huffington Post,* https://www.huffingtonpost.com, accessed November 19, 2018; Michael Zakkour, "Why Starbucks Succeeded in China: A Lesson for All Retailers," *Forbes,* https://www.forbes.com, accessed November 19, 2018; and Moinak Mitra, "How Starbucks Is Localizing

to Crack the Indian Coffee Chain Market," *The Economic Times*, https://economictimes.indiatimes.com, accessed November 19, 2018.

10. Fabian A. Geise, "Integration of Consumers into New Product Development by Social Media-Based Crowdsourcing—Findings from the Consumer Goods Industry in Germany," *Advances in Advertising Research* (Vol. VII), 2017, https://www.springer.com, accessed November 19, 2018; Rob Markey, and Fred Reichheld, "From Feedback to Action," *Bain & Company*, https://www.bain.com, accessed November 19, 2018; "My Starbucks Idea: Crowdsourcing for Customer Satisfaction and Innovation," https://digit.hbs.com, accessed November 19, 2018; and Accenture, *Effectively Incorporating Customer Feedback into the New Product Development Process*, http://i.nl02.net/beta0006/data/beta_white_roi.pdf, accessed November 19, 2018.

11. Andrew B. Bernard, J. Bradford Jensen, Stephen J. Redding, and Peter K. Schott, "Intra-Firm Trade and Product Contractibility," *American Economic Review Papers and Proceedings*, vol. 100, no. 2, May 2010, 444-48; Ashok Deo Bardhan, and Dwight Jaffee, 2005, "On Intra-Firm Trade and Multinationals: Foreign Outsourcing and Offshoring in Manufacturing," In Graham E.M. (ed,), *Multinationals and Foreign Investment in Economic Development*. International Economic Association Series. Palgrave Macmillan, London; and William J. Zeile, "U.S. Affiliates of Foreign Companies: Operations in 2000," *Survey of Current Business*, August 2002, 161.

12. Lee J. Krajewski, Manoj K. Malhotra, and Larry P. Ritzman, *Operations Management: Processes and Supply Chains*, 11th ed., Pearson, 2016; Jay Heizer, and Barry Render, *Principles of Operations Management*, 10th ed., Pearson, 2016; and Donald Bowersox, David Closs, and M. Bixby Cooper, *Supply Chain Logistics Management*, 4th ed., Burr Ridge, IL: McGraw-Hill/Irwin, 2012.

13. Merle Crawford, and Anthony Di Benedetto, *New Products Management*, 10th ed., Burr Ridge, IL: McGraw-Hill/Irwin, 2011, 8.

14. EY, *Indirect Procurement Optimisation: Unlocking Areas of Savings and Value Creation*, https://www.ey.com, accessed November 19, 2018; Rich Weissman, "Why Indirect Spend Is the Next Frontier for Supply Chain Cost Savings," *Supply Chain Dive*, https://www.supplychaindive.com, accessed November 19, 2018; Jeff Cooper, "Indirect Spend: The Next Generation of Savings for Manufacturers," https://www.manufacturing.net, accessed November 19, 2018; Godfrey Huguley, "4 Key Strategies for Wrangling Your Indirect Spend," *Take Supply Chain*, https://takesupplychain.com, accessed November 19, 2018; and UPS, *Indirect Procurement Outsourcing—Why, How and When*, https://www.ups-scs.com, accessed November 19, 2018.

15. David Hannon, "Owens Corning Plans to Go 80% Paperless by End-2004," *Purchasing*, January 15, 2004, 16-17.

16. Hedging is discussed in Module 15.

17. "The Pros and Cons: International and Domestic Sourcing," https://www.unleashedsoftware.com, accessed November 19, 2018; Andreas Pumpe and Franz Vallee, "A Typology for Selecting an Appropriate Total Landed Cost Method in International Supplier Selection Decisions," *Transportation Research Procedia*, vol. 25, 2017, 853-69; Teresa C. Fort, "Technology and Production Fragmentation: Domestic versus Foreign Sourcing," http://www.psurdc.psu.edu/sites/crdc/files/Fort.pdf, accessed November 19, 2018; and Marlin Steel, "The Real Cost of Outsourcing

Manufacturing Overseas," https://www.marlinwire.com, accessed November 19, 2018.

18. Thomas Pisello, "The ROI of RFID in the Supply Chain," *RFID Journal*, https://www.rfidjournal.com, accessed November 19, 2018; Avery Waits, "How Reducing Your Inventory Actually Helps You Make More Money," *SKU Vault*, https://www.skuvault.com, accessed November 19, 2018; and Ralph Cox, "25 Ways to Lower Inventory Costs," *Supply Chain Management Review*, https://www.scmr.com, accessed November 19, 2018.

19. Sang M. Lee, and Maling Ebrahimpour, "Just-in-Time Production System: Some Requirements for Implementation," *International Journal of Operations & Production Management*, vol. 4, no. 4, 1984, 3-15; A. A. Nurul Fateha, M. Y. Nafrizuan, and Y. Ahmad Razlan, "Review on Elements of JIT Implementation," *International Conference on Automotive, Mechanical and Materials Engineering (ICAMME 2012)*, Penang (Malaysia), May 19-20, 2012, 118-24, http://psrcentre.org, accessed November 19, 2018; and Akbar Javadian Kootanaee, K. Nagendra Babu, and Hamidreza Fooladi Talari, "Just-in-Time Manufacturing System: From Introduction to Implement," *International Journal of Economics, Business and Finance*, vol. 1, no. 2, March 2013, 7-25.

20. F. Robert Jacobs, and Richard Chase, *Operations and Supply Chain Management*, 13th ed, Burr Ridge, IL: McGraw-Hill, 2011, Chapter 13.

21. "Motivation Systems for Small-Group Quality Control Activities," *Japan Economic Journal*, June 28, 1988, 33-35.

22. Jorg Kempf, "Debottlenecking: Exploiting Opportunities to Boost Performance," *Process Worldwide*, https://www.process-worldwide.com, accessed November 19, 2018; Rick Johnston, "Approaches to Debottlenecking and Process Optimization," *BioProcess International*, https://bioprocessintl.com, accessed November 19, 2018; Demetri Petrides, Alexandros Koulouris, and Charles Siletti, "Throughput Analysis and Debottlenecking of Biomanufacturing Facilities," *BioPharm*, August 2002, 28-34, 64; and Musaed Muhammad M. Al Thubaiti, *A Novel Approach to Debottlenecking and Intensification: Integrated Techniques for Targeting and Design*, Ph.D. dissertation, Texas A&M University, December 2007.

23. Vicki Holt, "Five Expert Insights into Digital Manufacturing and Mass Customization," *Industry Week*, https://www.industryweek.com, accessed November 19, 2018; Erik Sherman, "Mass Customization: Let Your Customers Have It Their Way," *Inc.*, https://www.inc.com, accessed November 19, 2018; and Anshuk Gandhi, Carmen Magar, and Roger Roberts, "How Technology Can Drive the Next Wave of Mass Customization," *McKinsey on Business Technology*, no. 32, Winter 2013, https://www.mckinsey.com.

24. Gandhi et al., "How Technology Can Drive the Next Wave of Mass Customization"; and Arlene Weintraub, "Is Mass Customization the Future of Retail?" *Entrepreneur*, https://www.entrepreneur.com, accessed November 19, 2018.

25. Joseph M. Juran, and Joseph A. De Feo, *Juran's Quality Handbook: The Complete Guide to Performance Excellence*, 7th ed., Burr Ridge, IL: McGraw-Hill, 2016.

26. John Goodman, and Jon Theuerkauf, "What's Wrong with Six Sigma?" *Quality Progress*, January 2005, 37-42, http://asq.org, accessed November 19, 2018; Jiju Antony, and Bryan Rodgers, "Myth or Reality? Lean Six Sigma in Public Sector Organisations," https://www.quality.org, accessed November 19, 2018; and Maneesh Kumar, Jiju Antony, Christian N. Madu, Douglas C.

Montgomery, and Sung H. Park, "Common Myths of Six Sigma Demystified," *International Journal of Quality & Reliability Management*, vol. 25, no. 8, 2008, 878–95.

27. Jacobs, and Chase, *Operations and Supply Chain Management*, Chapter 12.

28. International Organization for Standardization, "About ISO," https://www.iso.org, accessed November 19, 2018.

29. J. Heizer, and B. Render, *Principles of Operations Management*, 4th ed., Upper Saddle River, NJ: Prentice Hall, 2001, 173.

30. Intel, "Delivering Quality Leadership," https://www.intel.com, accessed November 19, 2018; Chris J. McDonald, "The Evolution of Intel's Copy Exactly! Technology Transfer Method," *Intel Technology Journal*, Q4, 1998, 1–6, https://smtnet.com, accessed November 19, 2018; and Intel, "Manufacturing Process: Copy Exactly!" http://www.intel.com/content/www/us/en/quality/exact-copy.html, accessed February 19, 2015.

31. Intel, "Copy Exactly, Factory Strategy," http://www.intel.com/pressroom/kits/manufacturing/copy_exactly_bkgrnd.htm, accessed June 21, 2011; and Craig Barrett, "Copy Exactly: Establishing Competitive Manufacturing Capabilities," October 21, 2009, https://ecorner.stanford.edu.

32. Intel, "Copy Exactly, Factory Strategy," http://www.intel.com/pressroom/kits/manufacturing/copy_exactly_bkgrnd.htm, accessed June 21, 2011.

33. Brandon Hill, "Intel Tackles Voracious 14nm CPU Demand with New Vietnam Copy Exactly Fab," https://hothardware.com, accessed November 19, 2018.

34. David M. Anderson, "Product Line Rationalization," http://www.design4manufacturability.com, accessed November 19, 2018.

35. Based on information provided during a conversation with SKF executive. See also Martin Fritz, and Birgit Karlsson, *SKF—A Global Story: 1907–2007*, Stockholm: Informationsforlaget, 2006, http://investors.skf.com/skf-a-global-story.

36. David J. Teece, "Technology Transfer by Multinational Firms: The Resource Cost of Transferring Technological Know-how," *International Library of Critical Writings in Economics*, no. 139, Edward Elgar: 2002, 71–90.

37. Fran Townsend, as quoted in Dan Gilmore, "Supply Chain News: The 10 Best Quotes from CSCMP 2008," *Supply Chain Digest*, October 23, 2008, http://www.scdigest.com/assets/FirstThoughts/08-10-23.php.

38. A highly automated machine may make only one or two sizes or types of a product, whereas a general-purpose machine may be capable of producing not only all sizes of a product but other products as well. Its output, however, may be as little as 1 percent of that of a specialized machine.

39. Kelly Sims Gallagher, "Foreign Technology in China's Automobile Industry: Implications for Energy, Economic Development, and Environment," *China Environment Series*, no. 6, 1–17; and Wan-Wen Chu, "How the Chinese Government Promoted a Global Automobile Industry," *Industrial and Corporate Change* 20, no. 5, 2011, 1235–76.

40. David Wessel, "China Rewrites Rules for Building Wealth," *The Wall Street Journal*, January 29, 2004, A2.

GLOSSARY

A

absolute advantage   A nation's ability to produce more of a good or service than another country for the same or lower cost of inputs.

achievement vs. ascription   What a person does contrasted with who a person is.

ad valorem duty   An import duty levied as a percentage of the invoice value of imported goods.

advertising   Paid, nonpersonal presentation of ideas, goods, or services by an identified sponsor.

aesthetics   A culture's sense of beauty and good taste.

affiliates   Companies controlled by other companies, but less-than-majority owners may exercise control by a variety of means, both those involving stock ownership and those involving non-ownership mechanisms.

air waybill   A bill of landing issued by an air carrier.

allowances   Employee compensation payments added to base salaries of expatriates because of higher expenses encountered when living abroad.

American depository receipts (ADRs)   Foreign shares held by a custodian, usually a U.S. bank, in the issuer's home market and traded in dollars on the U.S. exchange.

antitrust laws   Laws that prevent inappropriately large concentrations of power and its abuse through price-fixing, market sharing, and monopolies.

arbitrage   The process of buying and selling instantaneously to make profit with no risk.

arbitration   A dispute resolution process agreed to by parties in lieu of going to court, in which one person or a body makes a binding decision.

ask price   Lowest-priced sell order currently in the market.

Association of Southeast Asian Nations (ASEAN)   Agreement among Southeast Asian nations that began as a security agreement, grew to a free trade agreement, and is continuing toward a common market, known as AFTA.

Atlas conversion factor   The arithmetic average of the current exchange rate and the exchange rates in the two preceding years, adjusted by the ratio of domestic inflation to the combined inflation rates of the euro zone, Japan, the United Kingdom, and the United States.

B

backward vertical integration   An arrangement in which facilities are established to manufacture inputs used in the production of a firm's final products.

balance of payments (BOP)   Record of a country's transactions with the rest of the world.

Bank for International Settlements (BIS)   Institution for central bankers; operates to build cooperation in order to foster monetary and financial stability.

banker's acceptance   A time draft with a maturity of less than 270 days that has been accepted by the bank on which the draft was drawn, thus becoming the accepting bank's obligation.

bid price   Highest-priced buy order currently in the market.

big data   The massive sets of data, both structured and unstructured, that businesses are collecting, which can be analyzed with advanced data analysis methods such as predictive analytics or user behavior analytics to provide valuable insights into consumer needs and trends.

biomass   A category of fuels whose energy source is photosynthesis, through which plants transform the sun's energy into chemical energy.

bonded warehouse   An area authorized by customs authorities for storage of goods on which payment of import duties is deferred until their removal.

bonuses   Expatriate employee compensation payments in addition to base salaries and allowances because of hardship, inconvenience, or danger.

bottleneck   Operation in a manufacturing system whose output sets the limit for the entire system's output.

bottom-up planning   Planning process that begins at the lowest level in the organization and continues upward.

brain drain   The loss by a country of its most intelligent and best-educated people.

branch   Legal extension of the parent company.

Bretton Woods   1944 conference at which allied nations' treasury and central bank representatives met to establish the International Monetary Fund and the World Bank.

Bretton Woods system   The international monetary system in place from 1945 to 1971, with par value based on gold and the U.S. dollar.

budget   An itemized projection of revenues and expenses for a future time period.

C

Carbon Disclosure Project (CDP)   Organization that provides reporting frameworks for greenhouse gas emissions and water use.

carbon footprint   A measure of the volume of greenhouse gas emissions caused by a product's manufacture and use.

climate   Meteorological conditions, including temperature, precipitation, and wind, that prevail in a region.

cluster analysis   Statistical technique that divides objects into groups based on similarity.

collective bargaining   The process in which a union represents the interests of workers bargaining in negotiations with management.

common market   Customs union that includes mobility of services, people, and capital within the union.

Common Market of the South (Mercosur or Mercosul) Currently a South American customs union of Argentina, Paraguay, Brazil, Uruguay, and Venezuela (suspended since 2016), with associate members Chile, Bolivia, Colombia, Ecuador, and Peru.

communitarianism Belief that the group is the beneficiary of actions.

comparative advantage When one nation is less efficient than another nation in the production of each of two goods, the less efficient nation has a comparative advantage in the production of that good for which its absolute disadvantage is less.

compensation packages For expatriate employees, packages that can incorporate many types of payments or reimbursements and must take into consideration exchange rates and inflation.

competition laws Another term for antitrust law, used by the European Union and other countries.

competitive advantage The ability of a company to achieve and maintain a unique and valuable competitive position both within a nation and globally, generating higher rates of profit than its competitors.

competitive strategies Action plans to enable organizations to reach their objectives.

compound duty A combination of specific and ad valorem duties.

concentrating solar thermal power (CSP) A system using mirrors or lenses to collect sunlight for heating water that powers an electrical generator.

confirmed L/C A confirmation made by a correspondent bank in the seller's country by which it agrees to honor the issuing bank's letter of credit.

Conformité Européene (CE) mark EU mark that indicates that merchandise conforms to European health, safety, and environmental requirements.

consolidation The process of translating subsidiary results and aggregating them into one financial report.

context The relevant environment.

contingency plans Plans for the best- or worst-case scenarios or for critical events that could have a severe impact on the firm.

contracted manufacturing An arrangement in which one firm contracts with another to produce products to its specifications.

controllable forces Internal forces that management administers to adapt to changes in the uncontrollable forces.

copyright Exclusive legal rights of authors, composers, creators of software, playwrights, artists, and publishers to publish and dispose of their work.

corporate visual identity (CVI) A firm's name, logo, slogan, graphics, color, and typeface that help identify the firm to consumers and other interested constituents.

Council of the European Union The EU's primary policy-setting institution.

countervailing duties Additional import taxes levied on imports that have benefited from export subsidies.

country risk assessment (CRA) An assessment of a country's economic situation and politics to determine how much risk to employees, property, and investment exists for the firm doing business there.

country screening A screening that uses countries as the basis for market selection.

cradle-to-cradle (C2C) design model A closed-loop design that recycles and reuses products.

cross-border acquisition The purchase of an existing business in another nation.

cultural paradox Contradictions in a culture's values.

culture shock The anxiety people often experience when they move from a culture that they are familiar with to one that is entirely different.

currency devaluation A reduction in the value of a country's currency relative to other currencies.

currency option hedge An option to buy or sell a specific amount of foreign currency at a specific time in order to protect against foreign currency risk.

current rate method An approach in foreign currency translation in which assets and liabilities are valued at current spot rates.

customhouse brokers Independent businesses that handle import shipments for compensation.

customs drawbacks Rebates on customs duties.

customs union Collaboration that adds common external tariffs to an FTA.

cybercrime Any illegal Internet-mediated activity that takes place in electronic networks.

D

developed economies A classification for high-income industrialized nations, which have high living standards and the most technically developed infrastructure.

developing economies A classification for the world's lower-income nations, which have less technically developed infrastructures and lower living standards.

direct investment The purchase of sufficient stock in a firm to obtain significant management control.

discretionary income The amount of income left after paying taxes and making essential purchases.

disintermediation The unraveling of traditional distribution structures, popularly called "cutting out the middlemen."

disposable income After-tax personal income.

Doha Development Agenda WTO extended conference on trade, also known as the Doha Round.

domestic environment All the uncontrollable forces originating in the home country that surround and influence the life and development of the firm.

dumping Selling a product abroad for less than the cost of production, less than the price in the home market, or less than the price to third-party countries.

dynamic capability theory Theory that for a firm to successfully invest overseas, it must have not only ownership of unique knowledge or resources, but also the ability to dynamically create, sustain, and exploit these capabilities over time.

E

eclectic theory of international production Theory proposing that for a firm to invest in facilities overseas, it must have three kinds of advantages: ownership specific, location specific, and internalization.

Economic and Monetary Union (EMU)   EU group that established use of the euro in the 18-country euro zone.

Economic and Social Council (ECOSOC)   UN body concerned with economic and social issues such as trade, development, education, and human rights.

economic exposure   The potential for the value of future cash flows to be affected by unanticipated exchange rate movements.

economic globalization   The tendency toward an international integration and interdependency of goods, technology, information, labor and capital, or the process of making this integration happen.

economic integration   Integration on economic and political levels.

economies of scale   The predictable decline in the average cost of producing each unit of output as a production facility gets larger and output increases.

efficient market approach   Assumption that current market prices fully reflect all available relevant information.

emerging market economies   Economies with per-capita incomes in the low to middle range that are in a transition toward developed status.

environment   All the forces influencing the life and development of the firm.

environmental scanning   A procedure in which the firm scans the world for changes in the environmental forces that might affect it.

environmental sustainability   State in which the demands placed upon the environment by people and commerce can be met without reducing the capacity of the environment to provide for future generations.

ethnocentric policy   A policy of hiring and promoting based on the parent company's home-country frame of reference.

ethnocentricity   The belief that your own culture is superior to other cultures.

European Commission   Body responsible for the European Union's day-to-day operations.

European Parliament   EU legislative body whose members are popularly elected from member-nations.

European Union (EU)   A body of 28 European countries committed to economic and political integration.

exchange rate   The price of one currency stated in terms of another.

expatriate   A person living outside his or her country of citizenship.

experience curve   The rising scale on which efficiency improves as a result of cumulative experience and learning.

explicit knowledge   Knowledge that is easy to communicate to others via words, pictures, formulas, or other means.

export bill of lading (B/L)   Document issued by the carrier that is a contract for the shipment, a receipt for the goods shipped, and a certificate of ownership.

export draft   An unconditional order drawn by the seller that instructs the buyer to pay the draft on presentation (sight draft) or at an agreed future date (time draft) and that must be paid before the buyer receives shipping documents.

exporting   The transportation of any domestic good or service to a destination outside a country or region.

extraterritorial application of laws   A country's attempt to apply its laws to nonresidents and foreigners, and to activities that take place beyond its borders.

F

factoring   The sale of an exporter's accounts receivable on ordinary goods, with the balance of the payment due upon delivery or soon after.

fiscal policies   Policies that address the collecting and spending of money by the government.

Fisher effect   The relationship between real and nominal interest rates: The real interest rate will be the nominal interest rate minus the expected rate of inflation.

fixed exchange rate   Exchange rate regime in which the currency's value is tied to the value of another currency or gold.

floating exchange rates   Exchange rates determined by supply and demand that allow currency values to float against one another.

foreign business   The operations of a company outside its home or domestic market.

Foreign Corrupt Practices Act (FCPA)   U.S. law that prohibits payments to foreign government officials in order to receive special treatment.

foreign direct investment (FDI)   Direct investments in equipment, structures, and organizations in a foreign country at a level sufficient to obtain significant management control; does not include mere foreign investment in stock markets.

foreign environment   All the uncontrollable forces originating outside the home country that surround and influence the firm.

foreign national pricing   Policy that sets local pricing based on market forces in another country.

forfaiting   The sale of an exporter's accounts receivable on capital goods, commodities, and other high-value goods, with the payment due at least 180 days out.

formal institutions   Institutions that influence behavior through laws and regulations.

forward currency market   Trading market for currency contracts deliverable 30, 60, 90, or 180 days in the future.

forward market hedge   Foreign currency contract sold or bought forward to protect against foreign currency movement.

forward rate   The exchange rate between two currencies for delivery in the future, usually 30, 60, 90, or 180 days.

franchising   A form of licensing in which one firm contracts with another to operate a business under an established name according to specific rules.

free trade area (FTA)   Area in which tariffs among members have been eliminated, but members keep their external tariffs.

free trade zone (FTZ)   An area designated by a government as outside its customs territory.

fronting loan   A loan made through an intermediary, usually a bank, from parent company to subsidiary.

functional currency   The primary currency of a business.

fundamental approach   Exchange rate prediction based on econometric models that attempt to capture the variables and their correct relationships.

G

General Assembly   Deliberative body of the United Nations made up of all member-nations, each with one vote regardless of size, wealth, or power.

geocentric policy   A policy of hiring and promoting based on ability and experience without considering race or citizenship.

geothermal power   Power from heat stored in the earth.

GINI index   A measure of the degree to which family income within a country is distributed equally.

global mind-set   A set of ideas and attitudes that combines an openness to and an awareness of diversity across markets and cultures with a propensity and ability to synthesize across this diversity.

Global Reporting Initiative (GRI)   Sustainability reporting framework developed among stakeholders.

global team   A team characterized by a high level of diversity, geographic dispersion, and virtual rather than face-to-face interaction.

gold standard   A monetary system that defines the value of its currency in terms of a fixed amount of gold.

greenfield investment   The establishment of new facilities from the ground up.

gross domestic product (GDP)   The total monetary value of all goods and services produced within a nation in a year.

gross national income (GNI)   The total value of all income generated by the residents of a nation, including both the domestic production of goods and services and income from abroad.

guest worker   Person who goes to a foreign country legally to perform certain types of jobs, on a temporary basis.

H

Harmonized Tariff Schedule of the United States (HTSA or HTSUS)   U.S. version of the Harmonized System, the global tariff code, used worldwide.

heavy oil   Oil that does not flow easily, presently sourced from oil sands and oil-bearing shale.

hedge   To hold assets (to take a position) in one market in order to offset exposure to price changes in an opposite position.

home-country national   Same as parent-country national.

horizontal corporation   A form of organization characterized by lateral decision processes, horizontal networks, and a strong corporate-wide business philosophy.

host-country national (HCN)   Employee who is a citizen of the nation in which the subsidiary is operating, which is different from the parent company's home nation.

hybrid organization   A structure organized by more than one dimension at the top level.

I

importing   The transportation of any good or service into a country or region, from a foreign origination point.

income distribution   A measure of how a nation's income is apportioned among its people.

income tax   Direct tax levied on earnings.

Incoterms   Predefined commercial terms established by the International Chamber of Commerce.

indirect procurement   The purchasing of goods and services that are not part of finished goods.

informal institutions   Institutions that influence behavior through norms, values, customs, and ideologies.

inland waterway   Waterway that provides access to interior regions.

instability   Characteristic of a government that cannot maintain itself in power or that makes sudden, unpredictable, or radical policy changes.

intellectual property (IP)   A creative work or invention that is protectable by patents, trademarks, trade names, copyrights, and trade secrets.

intermediate technology   Production methods between capital and labor-intensive methods.

internalization theory   Theory that to obtain a higher return on its investment, a firm will transfer its superior knowledge to a foreign subsidiary that it controls, rather than sell it in the open market.

international business   Business that is carried out across national borders.

international company (IC)   A company with operations in multiple nations.

International Court of Justice (ICJ)   UN body that makes legal decisions involving disputes between national governments.

international division   A division in the organization that is at the same level as the domestic division and is responsible for all non-home-country activities.

international environment   Interaction between domestic and foreign environmental forces, as well as interactions between the environmental forces of two countries.

international Fisher effect   Concept that the interest rate differentials for any two currencies will reflect the expected change in their exchange rates.

International Monetary Fund (IMF)   Institution that fosters global monetary cooperation, financial stability, international trade, high employment and sustainable economic growth, and reduction of poverty.

international pricing   Policy that sets prices of goods produced in one country and sold in another.

international product life cycle (IPLC)   A theory explaining why a product that begins as a nation's export eventually becomes its import.

international status   Entitles the expatriate employee to all the allowances and bonuses applicable to the place of residence and employment.

international strategy   A plan that guides the way firms make choices about developing and deploying scarce resources to achieve their international objectives.

intervention currency   A currency used by a country to intervene in the foreign currency exchange markets.

intrafirm trade   Trade that occurs between a parent company and its foreign affiliates.

irrevocable L/C   A stipulation that the L/C cannot be cancelled without the seller's consent.

iterative planning   Repetition of the bottom-up or top-down planning process until all differences have been reconciled.

J

Jamaica Agreement   The 1976 IMF agreement establishing flexible exchange rates among IMF members.

joint venture   A cooperative effort among two or more organizations that share a common interest in a business undertaking.

just-in-time (JIT)   A balanced system in which there is little or no delay time and idle in-process and finished goods inventory.

K

knowledge management   The practices that organizations and their managers use for identifying, creating, acquiring, developing, dispersing, and exploiting competitively valuable knowledge.

L

labor market   The pool of available potential employees with the necessary skills within commuting distance from an employer.

labor mobility   The movement of people from country to country or area to area seeking jobs.

labor union   An organization of workers, formed to advance the interest of its members.

law of one price   Concept that in an efficient market, like products will have like prices.

leadership   The behaviors and processes required for organizing a group of people in order to achieve a common purpose or goal.

leading and lagging   Timing payments early (lead) or late (lag), depending on anticipated currency movements, so that they have the most favorable impact for the company.

letter of credit (L/C)   Document issued by the buyer's bank in which the bank promises to pay the seller a specified amount under specified conditions.

licensing   A contractual arrangement in which one firm grants access to its patents, trade secrets, or technology to another for a fee.

life cycle assessment   An evaluation of the environmental aspects of a product or service throughout its life cycle.

litigation   Legal proceeding conducted to determine and enforce particular legal rights.

logistics   Managerial functions associated with the movement of materials such as raw materials, work in progress, or finished goods.

M

management contract   An arrangement by which one firm provides management to another firm.

manufacturing rationalization   Division of production among a number of production units, thus enabling each to produce only a limited number of components for all of a firm's assembly plants.

market factors   Economic data that correlate highly with market demand for a product.

market indicators   Economic data used to measure relative market strength of countries or geographic areas.

market screening   A modified version of environmental scanning in which the firm identifies desirable markets by eliminating the less desirable ones.

marketing mix   A set of strategy decisions made about the product and its promotion, pricing, and distribution in order to satisfy the needs and desires of customers in a target market.

mass customization   The use of flexible, usually computer-aided, manufacturing systems to produce and deliver customized products and services for different customers worldwide.

material culture or artifacts   All human-made objects.

matrix organization   An organizational structure composed of one or more superimposed organizational structures in an attempt to mesh product, regional, functional, and other expertise.

matrix overlay   An organization in which top-level divisions are required to heed input from a staff composed of experts of another organizational dimension in an attempt to avoid the double-reporting difficulty of a matrix organization but still mesh two or more dimensions.

mercantilism   An economic philosophy based on the belief that (1) a nation's wealth depends on accumulated treasure, usually precious metals such as gold and silver; and (2) to increase wealth, government policies should promote exports and discourage imports.

mission statement   A broad statement that defines the organization's purpose and scope.

monetary policies   Government policies that control the amount of money in circulation and its growth rate.

money market hedge   A method to hedge foreign currency exposure by borrowing and lending in the domestic and foreign money markets.

monochronic   Having to do with linear time, sequential activities.

monopolistic advantage theory   Theory that foreign direct investment is made by firms in industries with relatively few competitors, due to their possession of technical and other advantages over indigenous firms.

multilateral netting   Strategy in which subsidiaries transfer net intracompany cash flows through a centralized clearing center.

N

national competitiveness   A nation's relative ability to design, produce, distribute, or service products within an international trading context while earning increasing returns on its resources.

nationalization   The taking of private property by a government to make it public.

natural capital   Natural resources such as air, land, and water that provide us with the goods and services on which our survival depends.

natural resources   Anything supplied by nature on which people depend.

neutral vs. affective   The withholding of emotion contrasted with its expression.

new institutional theory   Understanding of institutions as social constructs, a collection of norms that structure the relations of individuals to one another.

nonrenewable energy   Energy that comes from sources that cannot be replenished, such as the fossil fuels—petroleum, coal, and natural gas—and nuclear power.

nontariff barriers (NTBs)   All forms of discrimination against imports other than import duties.

North American Free Trade Agreement (NAFTA)   Agreement creating a free trade area among Canada, Mexico, and the United States.

O

offshore financial center   Location that specializes in financing nonresidents, with low taxes and few banking regulations.

offshoring   Relocation of some or all of a business's activities or processes to a foreign location.

oligopolistic industry   An industry with a limited number of competing firms.

orderly marketing arrangements   Formal agreements between exporting and importing countries.

Organisation for Economic Co-operation and Development (OECD)   Group of developed countries dedicated to promoting their own and other nations' economic expansion.

organizational design   A process that determines how a company should be organized to ensure its worldwide business activities are integrated in an efficient and effective manner.

organizational structure   The way an organization formally arranges its domestic and international units and activities, and the relationships among these components.

outsourcing   Hiring others to perform some of the noncore activities and decision making in a company's value chain, rather than having the company and its employees continue to perform those activities.

overlapping demand   The existence of similar preferences and demand for products and services among nations with similar levels of per capita income.

Overseas Private Investment Corporation (OPIC)   A government corporation that offers U.S. investors in developing countries insurance against expropriation, currency inconvertibility, and damages from wars and revolutions.

P

par value   Stated value.

parent-country national (PCN)   Employee who is a citizen of the nation in which the parent company is headquartered; also called *home-country national*.

particularist   Condition in which context determines what concepts apply.

patent   A government grant giving the inventor of a product or process the exclusive right to manufacture, exploit, use, and sell that invention or process.

perfect competition   A market situation in which there is a sufficiently large number of well-informed buyers and sellers of a homogeneous product, such that no individual participant has enough power to determine the price of the product, resulting in a marketplace that is efficient in production and allocation of products.

policies   Broad guidelines issued by upper management to assist lower-level managers in handling recurring issues or problems.

polycentric policy   A policy of hiring and promoting based on the specific local context in which the subsidiary operates.

polychronic   Having to do with simultaneous activities, multitasking.

population density   A measure of the number of inhabitants per area unit (inhabitants per square kilometer or square mile).

population distribution   A measure of how the inhabitants are distributed over a nation's area.

portfolio investment   The purchase of stocks and bonds to obtain a return on the funds invested.

private international law   Law that governs relationships between individuals and companies that cross international borders.

privatization   The selling of government-owned property to the private sector.

pro forma invoice   Exporter's formal quotation, containing a description of the merchandise, price, delivery time, method of shipping, terms of sale, and points of exit and entry.

procedures   Guides that specify ways of carrying out a particular task or activity.

product differentiation   Unique differences producers build into their products with the intent of positively influencing demand.

product liability   A standard that holds a company and its officers and directors liable and possibly subject to fines or imprisonment when their product causes death, injury, or damage.

programmed-management approach   A middle-ground advertising strategy between globally standardized and entirely local programs.

promotion   Any form of communication between a firm and its publics, including advertising, public relations, sales promotions such as rebates and "buy one get one," and events and experiences, such as sponsoring events to both yield purchases in the short term and confidence in the firm in the long run.

public international law   Law that governs relationships between governments.

public relations   Various methods of communicating with the firm's publics to secure a favorable impression, rather than immediate sales.

purchasing power parity (PPP)   A means of adjusting the exchange rates for two currencies so the currencies have equivalent purchasing power.

Q

quality circle   Small work group that meets periodically to discuss ways to improve its functional areas and the quality of the product.

quota   Numerical limits placed on specific classes of imports.

R

random walk hypothesis   Assumption that the unpredictability of factors suggests that the best predictor of tomorrow's prices is today's prices.

rare earths   17 elements used in defense and technology applications.

reciprocal currency   In FX, using the dollar as the base currency, a currency that is quoted as dollars per unit of currency instead of in units of currency per dollar.

reengineering   Redesigning organizational structure, hierarchy, business systems, and processes in order to improve organizational efficiency.

regiocentric policy   A policy of hiring and promoting based on the specific regional context in which the subsidiary operates.

renewable energy   Energy that comes from sources that are naturally replenished, such as sunlight, wind, and water flow.

reserves   Assets held by a nation's central bank, used to back up government liabilities.

resource endowment   The land, labor, capital, and related production factors a nation possesses.

reverse brain drain   The return home of highly skilled immigrants who have made a contribution in their adopted country.

rural-to-urban shift   The movement of a nation's population from rural areas to cities.

S

sales forecast   A prediction of future sales performance.

sales promotion   Any of the various activities, such as preparation of point-of-purchase displays, contests, premiums, trade show exhibits, celebrity-embraced promotion, money-off offers, and coupons.

scenarios   Multiple, plausible stories about the future.

Secretariat   The staff of the United Nations, headed by the secretary-general.

Security Council   Main peacekeeping body of the United Nations, composed of 15 members including 5 permanent members.

segment screening   A screening that uses market segments, a within-country analysis of groups of consumers, as the basis for market selection.

self-reference criterion   Unconscious reference to your own cultural values when judging behaviors of others in a new and different environment.

shale   A fissile rock (capable of being split) composed of laminated layers of claylike, fine-grained sediment.

shipper's export declaration (SED)   U.S. Department of Commerce form used to control export shipments and record export statistics.

Six Sigma   Business management process for reducing defects and eliminating variation.

social desirability bias   The respondent's desire to please that leads to answers designed to please the interviewer rather than reflect the respondent's true beliefs or feelings.

social loafing   Tendency of some people to put forth less effort when they are members of a group.

solar photovoltaic power (PV)   Power based on the voltage created when certain materials are exposed to light.

special drawing rights (SDR)   An international reserve asset established by the IMF; the unit of account for the IMF and other international organizations.

specific duty   A fixed sum levied on a physical unit of an imported good.

specific vs. diffuse   Life divided into public and private spheres contrasted with life undifferentiated.

spot rate   The exchange rate between two currencies for delivery within two business days.

stability   Characteristic of a government that maintains itself in power and whose fiscal, monetary, and political policies are predictable and not subject to sudden, radical changes.

stakeholder theory   An understanding of how business operates that takes into account all identifiable interest holders.

standards   Documented agreements containing technical specifications or other precise criteria that will be used consistently as guidelines, rules, or definitions of the characteristics of a product, process, or service.

strategic alliance   Collaboration with competitors, customers, and/or suppliers that may take nonequity or equity form.

strategic behavior theory   Theory suggesting that strategic rivalry between firms in an oligopolistic industry will result in firms closely following and imitating each other's international investments in order to keep a competitor from gaining an advantage.

strategic business unit (SBU)   A self-contained business entity with a clearly defined market, specific competitors, the ability to carry out its business mission, and a size appropriate for control by a single manager.

strategic planning   The process by which an organization determines where it is going in the future, how it will get there, and how it will assess whether and to what extent it has achieved its goals.

strict liability   A standard that holds the designer or manufacturer liable for damages caused by a product without the need for a plaintiff to prove negligence in the product's design or manufacture.

subsidiaries   Companies controlled by other companies (known as parent companies) through ownership of enough voting stock to elect a majority of the voting members on the company's board of directors.

subsidies   Financial contributions, provided directly or indirectly by a government, that confer a benefit, including grants, preferential tax treatment, and government assumption of normal business expenses.

supply chain management   The process of coordinating and integrating the flow of materials, information, finances, and services within and among companies in the value chain from suppliers to the ultimate consumer.

swap contract   A spot sale/purchase of an asset against a future purchase/sale of an equal amount in order to hedge a financial position.

synchronous manufacturing   An entire manufacturing system with unbalanced operations that emphasizes total system performance.

T

tacit knowledge   Knowledge that an individual has but that is difficult to express clearly in words, pictures, or formulas and is therefore difficult to transmit to others.

tariffs   Taxes on imported goods for the purpose of raising their price to reduce competition for local producers or stimulate local production.

team norms   Legitimate, shared standards against which the appropriateness of behavior can be evaluated.

technical analysis   An approach that analyzes data for trends and then projects these trends forward.

temporal method   An approach in foreign currency translation in which monetary accounts are valued at the spot rate and accounts carried at historical cost are translated at their historic exchange rates.

terms of sale   Conditions of a sale that stipulate the point at which costs and risks are borne by the buyer.

terrorism   Unlawful acts of violence committed for a wide variety of reasons.

third-country national (TCN)   Employee who is a citizen of neither the parent company nation nor the host country.

top-down planning   Planning process that begins at the highest level in the organization and continues downward.

topography   The surface features of a region.

tort   An injury inflicted on another person, either intentionally or negligently.

total product   What the customer buys, including the physical product, brand name, accessories, after-sales service, warranty, instructions for use, company image, and package.

total quality management (TQM)   A companywide management approach in which the entire organization is managed so that it excels on all dimensions of product and services that are important to the customer.

trade deficit   The amount by which the value of imports into a nation exceeds the value of its exports.

trade fair   A large exhibition at which companies promote the sale of their products.

trade mission   A market visit by business people and/or government officials (state or federal) in search of business opportunities.

trade name   A name used by a merchant or manufacturer to designate and differentiate its products.

trade secret   Any information that a business wants to hold confidential.

trade surplus   The amount by which the value of a nation's exports exceeds the value of its imports.

trademark   A shape, color, design, phrase, abbreviation, or sound used by merchants or manufacturers to designate and differentiate their products.

trade-related intellectual property rights (TRIPS)   The WTO agreement that protects copyrights, trademarks, trade secrets, and other intellectual property matters.

transaction exposure   Change in the value of a financial position created by foreign currency changes between the establishment and the settlement of a contract.

transfer pricing   Pricing established for transactions between members of the enterprise.

translation exposure   Potential change in the value of a company's financial position due to exposure created during the consolidation process.

transnational corporation   An enterprise made up of entities in more than one nation, operating under a decision-making system that allows a common strategy and coherent policies.

treaty   Agreement between countries, also known as convention, compact, and protocol.

trend analysis   Statistical technique used to estimate future values by successive observations of a variable at regular time intervals that suggest patterns.

Triffin paradox   A problem in which a national currency that is also a reserve currency will eventually run a deficit, leading to lack of confidence in the reserve currency and a financial crisis.

triple-bottom-line accounting (3BL)   An approach to accounting that measures the firm's social and environmental performance in addition to its economic performance.

turnkey project   An export of technology, management expertise, and possibly capital equipment where a contractor agrees to design and erect a plant, supply the process technology, provide the production inputs, train the operating personnel, and, after a trial run, turn the facility over to the purchaser.

U

U.S. Export-Import Bank (Ex-Im Bank)   Government agency that provides loans, guarantees, and insurance programs to support American exporters.

uncontrollable forces   The external forces that management has no direct control over.

underground economy   The part of a nation's income that, because of unreporting or underreporting, is not measured by official statistics.

unit labor costs   Total direct labor costs divided by units produced.

United Nations (UN)   Organization of 193 countries dedicated to the promotion of peace and stability of the world.

United Nations Global Compact   A voluntary reporting scheme for businesses that covers critical areas affecting the conduct of international business—human rights, labor, the environment, and anti-corruption efforts.

universalist   Condition in which concepts apply to all.

V

value chain   A set of interlinked activities that adds value to the final product or service.

value chain analysis   An assessment conducted on the chain of interlinked activities of an organization or set of interconnected organizations, intended to determine where and to what extent value is added to the final product or service.

value-added tax (VAT)   Indirect tax collected from the parties as they add value to the product.

values statement   A clear, concise description of the fundamental values, beliefs, and priorities expected of the organization's members, reflecting how they are to behave with each other and with the company's customers, suppliers, and other members of the global community.

variable levy   An import duty set at the difference between world market prices and local government-supported prices.

vehicle currency   A currency used as a vehicle for international trade or investment.

vertical integration   The production by a firm of inputs for its own manufacturing processes.

virtual corporation   An organization that coordinates economic activity to deliver value to customers using resources outside the traditional boundaries of the organization.

vision statement   A description of the company's desired future position if it can acquire the necessary competencies and successfully implement its strategy.

voluntary export restraints (VERs)   Export quotas imposed by the exporting nation.

W

water footprint   A measure of the amount of water used in a product's manufacture and use.

withholding tax   Indirect tax paid by the payor, usually on passive income.

World Bank   Institution that lends money for development projects focused on reducing poverty.

World Trade Organization (WTO)   An international organization that establishes and helps implement rules of trade between nations.

COMPANY NAME INDEX

SUBJECT INDEX

ARCTIC OCEAN

80°N

160°W 140°W 120°W 100°W 80°W 60°W 40°W 20°

Greenland
(Denmark)

Alaska
(U.S.)

60°N

CANADA

NORTH
ATLANTIC
OCEAN

U
KIN

IRE

NORTH
PACIFIC
OCEAN

40°N

UNITED
STATES

POR

Tropic of Cancer

MEXICO

Western
Sahara
(Morocco)

20°N

Hawaii
(U.S.)

CAPE
VERDE

MAU

0 1000 Miles

0 1000 2000 Kilometers

Scale: 1 to 105,113,000

GUYANA

French Guiana

COLOMBIA

SURINAME

0° Equator

ECUADOR

KIRIBATI

PERU

Tokelau
(N.Z.)

Cook
Islands
(N.Z.)

BRAZIL

SAMOA American
Samoa

BOLIVIA

TONGA

Niue
(N.Z.)

20°S

French
Polynesia

Tropic of Capricorn

PARAGUAY

Pitcairn
(U.K.)

SOUTH
PACIFIC
OCEAN

ARGENTINA

URUGUAY

CHILE

40°S

G

SOUTH
ATLANTIC
OCEAN

G

20

UNITED
STATES

90°W 80°W 70°W Tropic of Cancer 60°W

BAHAMAS

20°N

60°S

10

DOMINICAN
REP.

CUBA

Puerto
Rico
(U.S.)

ANTIGUA AND
BARBUDA

MEXICO

ST. KITTS AND NEVIS
(Fr.) Guadeloupe

BELIZE

JAMAICA HAITI

DOMINICA

SOUTHERN OCEAN

GUATEMALA

Caribbean Sea

(Fr.) Martinique
ST. LUCIA

BARBADOS

Antarctic Circle

HONDURAS

ST. VINCENT AND THE GRENADINES

GRENADA

NICARAGUA

EL
SALVADOR

COSTA
RICA

10°N

0 200 Miles

TRINIDAD AND TOBAGO

0 200 400 Kilometers

PANAMA

VENEZUELA

0

Scale: 1 to 41,472,000

COLOMBIA

ANTARCTICA

0

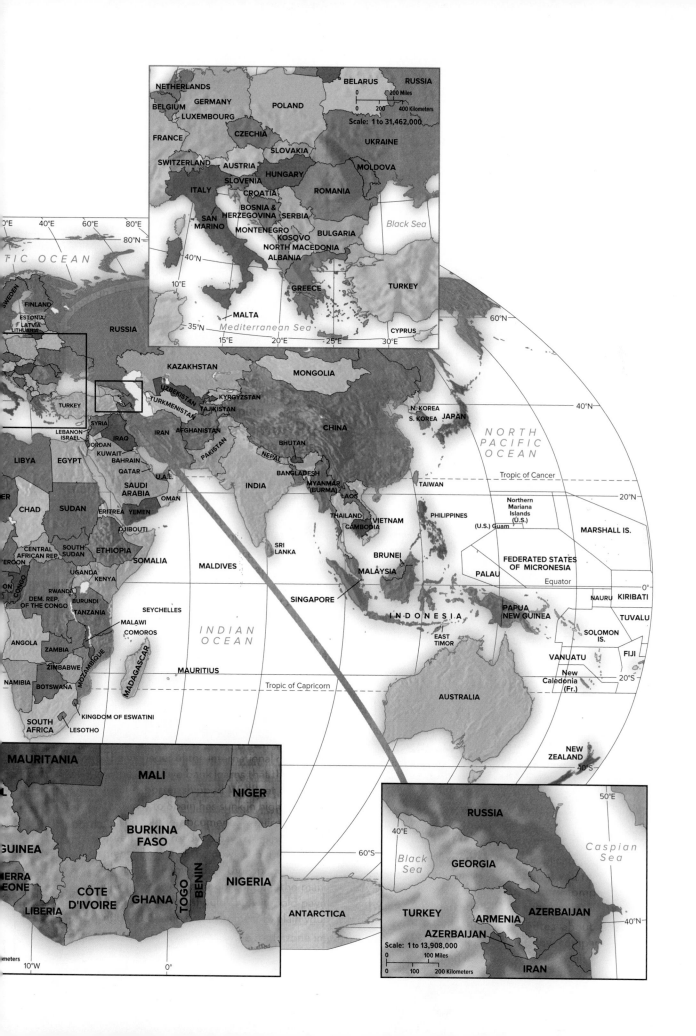